WILLIAM SHAKESPEARE was born in Stratford-upon-Avon in April, 1564, and his birth is traditionally celebrated on April 23. The facts of his life, known from surviving documents, are sparse. He was one of eight children born to John Shakespeare, a merchant of some standing in his community. William probably went to the King's New School in Stratford, but he had no university education. In November 1582, at the age of eighteen, he married Anne Hathaway, eight years his senior, who was pregnant with their first child, Susanna. She was born on May 26, 1583. Twins, a boy, Hamnet (who would die at age eleven), and a girl, Judith, were born in 1585. By 1592 Shakespeare had gone to London, working as an actor and already known as a playwright. A rival dramatist, Robert Greene, referred to him as "an upstart crow, beautified with our feathers." Shakespeare became a principal shareholder and playwright of the successful acting troupe the Lord Chamberlain's men (later, under James I, called the King's men). In 1599 the Lord Chamberlain's men built and occupied the Globe Theatre in Southwark near the Thames River. Here many of Shakespeare's plays were performed by the most famous actors of his time, including Richard Burbage, Will Kempe, and Robert Armin. In addition to his 37 plays, Shakespeare had a hand in others, including *Sir Thomas More* and *The Two Noble Kinsmen*, and he wrote poems, including *Venus and Adonis* and *The Rape of Lucrece*. His 154 sonnets were published, probably without his authorization, in 1609. In 1611 or 1612 he gave up his lodgings in London and devoted more and more of his time to retirement in Stratford, though he continued writing such plays as *The Tempest* and *Henry VIII* until about 1613. He died on April 23, 1616, and was buried in Holy Trinity Church, Stratford. No collected edition of his plays was published during his lifetime, but in 1623 two mem̶ John Heminges and Henry ec-tion now called the Fi

Bantam Shakespeare
The Complete Works—29 Volumes
Edited by David Bevington
With forewords by Joseph Papp on the plays

The Poems: Venus and Adonis, The Rape of Lucrece, The
Phoenix and Turtle, A Lover's Complaint,
the Sonnets

Antony and Cleopatra	*The Merchant of Venice*
As You Like It	*A Midsummer Night's Dream*
The Comedy of Errors	*Much Ado about Nothing*
Hamlet	*Othello*
Henry IV, Part One	*Richard II*
Henry IV, Part Two	*Richard III*
Henry V	*Romeo and Juliet*
Julius Caesar	*The Taming of the Shrew*
King Lear	*The Tempest*
Macbeth	*Twelfth Night*

Together in one volume:

Henry VI, Parts One, Two, and Three
King John and Henry VIII
Measure for Measure, All's Well that Ends Well, and
Troilus and Cressida
Three Early Comedies: Love's Labor's Lost, The Two
Gentlemen of Verona, The Merry
Wives of Windsor
Three Classical Tragedies: Titus Andronicus, Timon
of Athens, Coriolanus
The Late Romances: Pericles, Cymbeline, The Winter's
Tale, The Tempest

Two collections:

Four Comedies: The Taming of the Shrew, A Midsummer
Night's Dream, The Merchant of Venice,
Twelfth Night
Four Tragedies: Hamlet, Othello, King Lear, Macbeth

William Shakespeare

THE LATE ROMANCES

Pericles
Cymbeline
The Winter's Tale
The Tempest

Edited by
David Bevington

David Scott Kastan,
James Hammersmith,
and Robert Kean Turner,
Associate Editors

With a Foreword by
Joseph Papp

BANTAM BOOKS
TORONTO / NEW YORK / LONDON / SYDNEY / AUCKLAND

THE LATE ROMANCES

*A Bantam Book / published by arrangement
with Scott, Foresman and Company*

PUBLISHING HISTORY

*Scott, Foresman edition published / January 1980
Bantam edition, with newly edited text and substantially revised,
edited, and amplified notes, introductions, and other
materials, published / February 1988
Valuable advice on staging matters has been
provided by Richard Hosley.
Collations checked by Eric Rasmussen.
Additional editorial assistance by Claire McEachern.*

Library of Congress Cataloging-in-Publication Data

Shakespeare, William, 1564–1616.
    The late romances.

    (A Bantam classic)
    "Bantam edition, with newly edited text and substantially
revised, edited, and amplified notes, introductions, and other
materials"—T.p. verso.
    Bibliography: p.
    Contents: Pericles—Cymbeline—The winter's tale
—[etc.]
    I. Bevington, David M.   II. Title.
PR2759.B48   1988b   822.3'3   87-19543

ISBN 0-553-21288-5 (pbk.)

Published simultaneously in the United States and Canada

Bantam Books are published by Bantam Books, a division of Bantam
Doubleday Dell Publishing Group, Inc. Its trademark, consisting of the
words "Bantam Books" and the portrayal of a rooster, is Registered in U.S.
Patent and Trademark Office and in other countries. Marca Registrada.
Bantam Books, 1540 Broadway, New York, New York 10036.

PRINTED IN THE UNITED STATES OF AMERICA

O   0 9 8 7 6 5 4 3

Contents

Foreword

It's hard to imagine, but Shakespeare wrote all of his plays with a quill pen, a goose feather whose hard end had to be sharpened frequently. How many times did he scrape the dull end to a point with his knife, dip it into the inkwell, and bring up, dripping wet, those wonderful words and ideas that are known all over the world?

In the age of word processors, typewriters, and ballpoint pens, we have almost forgotten the meaning of the word "blot." Yet when I went to school, in the 1930s, my classmates and I knew all too well what an inkblot from the metal-tipped pens we used would do to a nice clean page of a test paper, and we groaned whenever a splotch fell across the sheet. Most of us finished the school day with ink-stained fingers; those who were less careful also went home with ink-stained shirts, which were almost impossible to get clean.

When I think about how long it took me to write the simplest composition with a metal-tipped pen and ink, I can only marvel at how many plays Shakespeare scratched out with his goose-feather quill pen, year after year. Imagine him walking down one of the narrow cobblestoned streets of London, or perhaps drinking a pint of beer in his local alehouse. Suddenly his mind catches fire with an idea, or a sentence, or a previously elusive phrase. He is burning with impatience to write it down—but because he doesn't have a ballpoint pen or even a pencil in his pocket, he has to keep the idea in his head until he can get to his quill and parchment.

He rushes back to his lodgings on Silver Street, ignoring the vendors hawking brooms, the coaches clattering by, the piteous wails of beggars and prisoners. Bounding up the stairs, he snatches his quill and starts to write furiously, not even bothering to light a candle against the dusk. "To be, or not to be," he scrawls, "that is the—." But the quill point has gone dull, the letters have fattened out illegibly, and in the middle of writing one of the most famous passages in the history of dramatic literature, Shakespeare has to stop to sharpen his pen.

Taking a deep breath, he lights a candle now that it's dark, sits down, and begins again. By the time the candle has burned out and the noisy apprentices of his French Huguenot landlord have quieted down, Shakespeare has finished Act 3 of *Hamlet* with scarcely a blot.

Early the next morning, he hurries through the fog of a London summer morning to the rooms of his colleague Richard Burbage, the actor for whom the role of Hamlet is being written. He finds Burbage asleep and snoring loudly, sprawled across his straw mattress. Not only had the actor performed in *Henry V* the previous afternoon, but he had then gone out carousing all night with some friends who had come to the performance.

Shakespeare shakes his friend awake, until, bleary-eyed, Burbage sits up in his bed. "Dammit, Will," he grumbles, "can't you let an honest man sleep?" But the playwright, his eyes shining and the words tumbling out of his mouth, says, "Shut up and listen—tell me what you think of *this*!"

He begins to read to the still half-asleep Burbage, pacing around the room as he speaks. ". . . Whether 'tis nobler in the mind to suffer the slings and arrows of outrageous fortune—"

Burbage interrupts, suddenly wide awake, "That's excellent, very good, 'the slings and arrows of outrageous fortune,' yes, I think it will work quite well. . . ." He takes the parchment from Shakespeare and murmurs the lines to himself, slowly at first but with growing excitement.

The sun is just coming up, and the words of one of Shakespeare's most famous soliloquies are being uttered for the first time by the first actor ever to bring Hamlet to life. It must have been an exhilarating moment.

Shakespeare wrote most of his plays to be performed live by the actor Richard Burbage and the rest of the Lord Chamberlain's men (later the King's men). Today, however, our first encounter with the plays is usually in the form of the printed word. And there is no question that reading Shakespeare for the first time isn't easy. His plays aren't comic books or magazines or the dime-store detective novels I read when I was young. A lot of his sentences are complex. Many of his words are no longer used in our everyday speech. His profound thoughts are often condensed into poetry, which is not as straightforward as prose.

Yet when you hear the words spoken aloud, a lot of the language may strike you as unexpectedly modern. For Shakespeare's plays, like any dramatic work, weren't really meant to be read; they were meant to be spoken, seen, and performed. It's amazing how lines that are so troublesome in print can flow so naturally and easily when spoken.

I think it was precisely this music that first fascinated me. When I was growing up, Shakespeare was a stranger to me. I had no particular interest in him, for I was from a different cultural tradition. It never occurred to me that his plays might be more than just something to "get through" in school, like science or math or the physical education requirement we had to fulfill. My passions then were movies, radio, and vaudeville—certainly not Elizabethan drama.

I was, however, fascinated by words and language. Because I grew up in a home where Yiddish was spoken, and English was only a second language, I was acutely sensitive to the musical sounds of different languages and had an ear for lilt and cadence and rhythm in the spoken word. And so I loved reciting poems and speeches even as a very young child. In first grade I learned lots of short nature verses—"Who has seen the wind?," one of them began. My first foray into drama was playing the role of Scrooge in Charles Dickens's *A Christmas Carol* when I was eight years old. I liked summoning all the scorn and coldness I possessed and putting them into the words, "Bah, humbug!"

From there I moved on to longer and more famous poems and other works by writers of the 1930s. Then, in junior high school, I made my first acquaintance with Shakespeare through his play *Julius Caesar*. Our teacher, Miss McKay, assigned the class a passage to memorize from the opening scene of the play, the one that begins "Wherefore rejoice? What conquest brings he home?" The passage seemed so wonderfully theatrical and alive to me, and the experience of memorizing and reciting it was so much fun, that I went on to memorize another speech from the play on my own.

I chose Mark Antony's address to the crowd in Act 3,

scene 2, which struck me then as incredibly high drama.
Even today, when I speak the words, I feel the same thrill I
did that first time. There is the strong and athletic Antony
descending from the raised pulpit where he has been speaking, right into the midst of a crowded Roman square. Holding the torn and bloody cloak of the murdered Julius
Caesar in his hand, he begins to speak to the people of
Rome:

> If you have tears, prepare to shed them now.
> You all do know this mantle. I remember
> The first time ever Caesar put it on;
> 'Twas on a summer's evening in his tent,
> That day he overcame the Nervii.
> Look, in this place ran Cassius' dagger through.
> See what a rent the envious Casca made.
> Through this the well-belovèd Brutus stabbed,
> And as he plucked his cursèd steel away,
> Mark how the blood of Caesar followed it,
> As rushing out of doors to be resolved
> If Brutus so unkindly knocked or no;
> For Brutus, as you know, was Caesar's angel.
> Judge, O you gods, how dearly Caesar loved him!
> This was the most unkindest cut of all . . .

I'm not sure now that I even knew Shakespeare had written a lot of other plays, or that he was considered "time-
less," "universal," or "classic"—but I knew a good speech
when I heard one, and I found the splendid rhythms of
Antony's rhetoric as exciting as anything I'd ever come
across.

Fifty years later, I still feel that way. Hearing good actors
speak Shakespeare gracefully and naturally is a wonderful
experience, unlike any other I know. There's a satisfying
fullness to the spoken word that the printed page just can't
convey. This is why seeing the plays of Shakespeare performed live in a theater is the best way to appreciate them.
If you can't do that, listening to sound recordings or watching film versions of the plays is the next best thing.

But if you do start with the printed word, use the play as a
script. Be an actor yourself and say the lines out loud. Don't
worry too much at first about words you don't immediately
understand. Look them up in the footnotes or a dictionary,

but don't spend too much time on this. It is more profitable (and fun) to get the sense of a passage and sing it out. Speak naturally, almost as if you were talking to a friend, but be sure to enunciate the words properly. You'll be surprised at how much you understand simply by speaking the speech "trippingly on the tongue," as Hamlet advises the Players.

You might start, as I once did, with a speech from *Julius Caesar*, in which the tribune (city official) Marullus scolds the commoners for transferring their loyalties so quickly from the defeated and murdered general Pompey to the newly victorious Julius Caesar:

> Wherefore rejoice? What conquest brings he home?
> What tributaries follow him to Rome
> To grace in captive bonds his chariot wheels?
> You blocks, you stones, you worse than senseless
>   things!
> O you hard hearts, you cruel men of Rome,
> Knew you not Pompey? Many a time and oft
> Have you climbed up to walls and battlements,
> To towers and windows, yea, to chimney tops,
> Your infants in your arms, and there have sat
> The livelong day, with patient expectation,
> To see great Pompey pass the streets of Rome.

With the exception of one or two words like "wherefore" (which means "why," not "where"), "tributaries" (which means "captives"), and "patient expectation" (which means patient waiting), the meaning and emotions of this speech can be easily understood.

From here you can go on to dialogues or other more challenging scenes. Although you may stumble over unaccustomed phrases or unfamiliar words at first, and even fall flat when you're crossing some particularly rocky passages, pick yourself up and stay with it. Remember that it takes time to feel at home with anything new. Soon you'll come to recognize Shakespeare's unique sense of humor and way of saying things as easily as you recognize a friend's laughter.

And then it will just be a matter of choosing which one of Shakespeare's plays you want to tackle next. As a true fan of his, you'll find that you're constantly learning from his plays. It's a journey of discovery that you can continue for the rest of your life. For no matter how many times you read or see a particular play, there will always be something new there that you won't have noticed before.

Why do so many thousands of people get hooked on Shakespeare and develop a habit that lasts a lifetime? What can he really say to us today, in a world filled with inventions and problems he never could have imagined? And how do you get past his special language and difficult sentence structure to understand him?

The best way to answer these questions is to go see a live production. You might not know much about Shakespeare, or much about the theater, but when you watch actors performing one of his plays on the stage, it will soon become clear to you why people get so excited about a playwright who lived hundreds of years ago.

For the story—what's happening in the play—is the most accessible part of Shakespeare. In *A Midsummer Night's Dream*, for example, you can immediately understand the situation: a girl is chasing a guy who's chasing a girl who's chasing another guy. No wonder *A Midsummer Night's Dream* is one of the most popular of Shakespeare's plays: it's about one of the world's most popular pastimes—falling in love.

But the course of true love never did run smooth, as the young suitor Lysander says. Often in Shakespeare's comedies the girl whom the guy loves doesn't love him back, or she loves him but he loves someone else. In *The Two Gentlemen of Verona*, Julia loves Proteus, Proteus loves Sylvia, and Sylvia loves Valentine, who is Proteus's best friend. In the end, of course, true love prevails, but not without lots of complications along the way.

For in all of his plays—comedies, histories, and tragedies—Shakespeare is showing you human nature. His characters act and react in the most extraordinary ways—and sometimes in the most incomprehensible ways. People are always trying to find motivations for what a character does. They ask, "Why does Iago want to destroy Othello?"

The answer, to me, is very simple—because that's the way Iago is. That's just his nature. Shakespeare doesn't explain his characters; he sets them in motion—and away they go. He doesn't worry about whether they're likable or not. He's interested in interesting people, and his most fascinating characters are those who are unpredictable. If you lean back in your chair early on in one of his plays, thinking you've figured out what Iago or Shylock (in *The Merchant of Venice*) is up to, don't be too sure—because that great judge of human nature, Shakespeare, will surprise you every time.

He is just as wily in the way he structures a play. In *Macbeth*, a comic scene is suddenly introduced just after the bloodiest and most treacherous slaughter imaginable, of a guest and king by his host and subject, when in comes a drunk porter who has to go to the bathroom. Shakespeare is tickling your emotions by bringing a stand-up comic on-stage right on the heels of a savage murder.

It has taken me thirty years to understand even some of these things, and so I'm not suggesting that Shakespeare is immediately understandable. I've gotten to know him not through theory but through practice, the practice of the *living* Shakespeare—the playwright of the theater.

Of course the plays are a great achievement of dramatic literature, and they should be studied and analyzed in schools and universities. But you must always remember, when reading all the words *about* the playwright and his plays, that *Shakespeare's* words came first and that in the end there is nothing greater than a single actor on the stage speaking the lines of Shakespeare.

Everything important that I know about Shakespeare comes from the practical business of producing and directing his plays in the theater. The task of classifying, criticizing, and editing Shakespeare's printed works I happily leave to others. For me, his plays really do live on the stage, not on the page. That is what he wrote them for and that is how they are best appreciated.

Although Shakespeare lived and wrote hundreds of years ago, his name rolls off my tongue as if he were my brother. As a producer and director, I feel that there is a professional relationship between us that spans the centuries. As a human being, I feel that Shakespeare has enriched my understanding of life immeasurably. I hope you'll let him do the same for you.

❖

Pericles, like *The Comedy of Errors* (an early play) and *The Winter's Tale* (a late play), is a fairy tale about a separated family's coming back together again. The story itself is wonderful, full of action and excitement—storms at sea, pirates, jousting knights, a young girl sold into prostitution (whose pure goodness protects her and touches everyone she meets), and all the other stuff of romance. And it carries you steadily forward to the great reconciliation scene (5.1), in which Pericles encounters his long-lost daughter, Marina.

This marvelous scene is a lot like the reconciliations in *The Comedy of Errors* and *Twelfth Night*, but here it's even more drawn out. Shakespeare keeps delaying the recognition: while Pericles realizes fairly early on in the scene that Marina is his daughter, it takes her a while longer to recognize him. Even though the whole story seems improbable when we read it, it never fails to move audiences when it is performed.

Another part of the play I've always liked is the scene with the three fishermen (2.1). Whenever I start reading a scene involving Shakespeare's ordinary people, I can't put it down. I especially like these guys; they remind me of the Gardener in *Richard II*, who makes comparisons between the state of his garden and the state of the commonwealth. For as these fishermen draw in their nets, they are also drawing conclusions about the society they live in. The Third Fisherman says, "Master, I marvel how the fishes live in the sea." And the First Fisherman replies, without missing a beat, "Why, as men do aland: the great ones eat up the little ones." As the hidden Pericles observes, "How from the finny subject of the sea / These fishers tell the infirmities of men." This is true of so many of Shakespeare's ordinary people; while they go about their daily lives, they scatter little bits of wisdom along the way for perceptive readers or attentive audiences to pick up.

✦

There is a lot for modern audiences in *Cymbeline*. The story itself isn't complex or inaccessible; one man bets another that his wife can be proved false. (Of course, if the man had known anything about how loyal Shakespeare's women always are, he wouldn't have bothered to bet!) Posthumus, the husband, is another one of those Shakespearean men, like Claudio in *Much Ado about Nothing*, Master Ford in *The Merry Wives of Windsor*, and Othello, who wrongly doubt their wives' integrity. There's the bettor, Iachimo, an Iago-like figure who preys on Posthumus's suspicions. And there is the strong, determined, faithful wife Imogen, who sets out to save her reputation and her husband, no matter what the obstacles. She is one of Shakespeare's strongest heroines, and a wonderful character; in fact, George Bernard Shaw, who didn't always have good things to say about Shakespeare, liked her best of all Shakespeare's women.

In addition to a good story and a good cast of characters, there's an appealing element of the supernatural in *Cymbeline*, with a family of ghosts and a god who descends on an eagle. Indeed, the whole play has a fairy-tale quality to it, the same marvelous aura of magical unreality that Shakespeare creates in several of his late romantic plays. The story is almost childlike in its simplicity, and the issues are straightforward; but as usual, Shakespeare works immeasurable richness of language, viewpoint, and character into this offbeat play.

❖

The Winter's Tale is something you tell to children at night in front of a fire—but not *just* to children, for adults are intrigued by it as well. It has a lot in common with *Pericles*, including a young girl separated from her family, a shipwreck, and a reconciliation. The great scene at the end of the play, where Hermione steps out of her statuelike frame and returns to her husband, Leontes, and her daughter, Perdita, works like a charm every time. Even though it seems so improbable, this moment stops short of melodrama because Shakespeare, as always, stays in touch with the humanity of his characters and his plays. That's what keeps him believable.

One thing in the play that many people do find unbelievable, however, is Leontes's sudden and irrational suspicion of Hermione and his best friend, Polixenes, in the first scene. It all happens so quickly that it doesn't seem to make sense. But you just have to accept Leontes for what he is. Shakespeare wasn't writing a psychological drama, he was writing a romantic play, and he isn't concerned with giving a plausible explanation for Leontes's anger. That's not the point he's making. Shakespeare needs to set the plot in motion right away, and so he achieves the buildup of Leontes's jealousy in a couple of lines.

But having said that, I do think there are quirks in people that make them suddenly react in certain ways; and I think Shakespeare knew this, too. Maybe that's what's behind Leontes's behavior. If I were directing the play, I think I would concentrate less on the *reasons* for Leontes's actions and try instead to find the mind that is capable of suddenly doubting his dearest friend and his trusted wife, seemingly without provocation.

The Winter's Tale has a lot in common with the other three plays in the collection. All are highly romantic plays, surrounded by a gentle aura of magic and fairy tale. All show the courage and spunk of women. And all four work and rework the themes of separation, doubt, and faithfulness.

♣

I prefer the human, personal elements in *The Tempest* to broad symbolic interpretations. One of my favorite parts of the play is the first meeting between the young girl Miranda and the young boy Ferdinand. I enjoy watching their relationship grow until she actually proposes to him, saying, "I am your wife, if you will marry me; / If not, I'll die your maid."

Then there's the wonderful scene where the jester-comedian Trinculo encounters the deformed slave Caliban—"What have we here, a man or a fish? Dead or alive?"—and creeps under Caliban's gaberdine (a kind of cloak) to stay out of the rain. Along comes Trinculo's companion Stephano, drunk and singing. When he sees a strange monster with two extra legs (Trinculo's) sticking out from under it, he exclaims, "Four legs and two voices— a most delicate monster!" and decides to save it by giving it a drink from his bottle of sack (sherry). When this is played onstage, it's a hilarious sight gag.

The most intriguing character in the play is unquestionably Prospero, the enigmatic, fascinating Prospero. We must understand his motivations, which are difficult to uncover at first. Here is a strange man who is always using his magic to keep the plot moving: he creates a storm, engineers his daughter's meeting with Ferdinand, keeps the other shipwreck survivors lost on the island, and commands his spirit Ariel to carry out his plans. His attitude toward Caliban is one of stern cruelty, and their relationship, too, cries out for greater exploration.

Never having directed the play, it is difficult for me to evaluate Prospero's role fully, but it's clear that through him Shakespeare creates the atmosphere of magic and fantasy in which *The Tempest* is bathed.

JOSEPH PAPP

JOSEPH PAPP GRATEFULLY ACKNOWLEDGES THE HELP OF
ELIZABETH KIRKLAND IN PREPARING THIS FOREWORD.

THE LATE
ROMANCES

The Late Romances

In the summer of 1608, as Shakespeare neared retirement, his acting company, the King's men, signed a twenty-one-year lease for the use of the Blackfriars playhouse—an indoor and rather intimate, artificially lighted theater inside the city of London, close to the site of St. Paul's Cathedral, which would serve as a winter playhouse for the company. A private theater had existed there since 1576, when the acting company known as the Children of the Chapel and then another juvenile company, Paul's boys, began acting their courtly plays for paying spectators in this building that had once belonged to the Dominicans, or Black Friars. The adult troupes of the late 1600s were well aware that they needed to cater more directly to courtly audiences. Their popular audiences were becoming increasingly disenchanted with the drama. Puritan fulminations against the stage had gained in effect, especially when many playwrights refused to disguise their satirical hostility toward Puritans and the London bourgeoisie. Several of Shakespeare's late plays may have been acted both at the Globe Theatre and at Blackfriars. The plays he wrote after 1608–1609, *Cymbeline*, *The Winter's Tale*, and *The Tempest*, all show the distinct influence of the dramaturgy of the private theaters. Also, we know that, while Shakespeare's plays certainly continued to be acted at the Globe to the very end of his career, an increasing number were acted at the court of King James.

Shakespeare's last plays, written with an eye to Blackfriars and the court as well as to the Globe, are usually called romances or tragicomedies or sometimes both. The term romance suggests a return to the kind of story the author and playwright Robert Greene (1558–1592) had derived from Greek romance: tales of adventure, long separation, and tearful reunion, involving shipwreck, capture by pirates, riddling prophecies, children set adrift in boats or abandoned on foreign shores, the illusion of death and subsequent restoration to life, the revelation of the identity of long-lost children by birthmarks, and the like. The term tragicomedy suggests a play in which the protagonist commits a seemingly fatal error or crime, or (as in *Pericles*) suffers an extraordinarily adverse fortune; in either case he must experience agonies of contrition and bereavement until he is providentially delivered from his tribulations. The overall tone is deeply melancholic and resigned, although suffused also with a sense of gratitude for the harmonies that are mysteriously restored.

Tragicomedy and pastoral romance were, in the period from 1606 to 1610, beginning to enjoy a fashionable courtly revival. The leading practitioners of the new genre were Francis Beaumont and John Fletcher, though Shakespeare made a highly significant contribution. The appropriateness of such plays to the elegant atmosphere of Blackfriars and the court is subtle but real. Their old-fashioned naiveté, which would seem to be out of place in a sophisticated milieu, is only superficial. Perhaps also sophisticated audiences responded to pastoral and romantic drama as a nostalgic evocation of an idealized past, a chivalric "golden world" fleetingly recovered through an artistic journey back to naiveté and innocence. The evocation of such a world demands the kind of studied but informal artifice we find in many tragicomic plays of the period: elaborate masques and allegorical shows, descents of enthroned gods from the heavens (as in *Cymbeline*), quaint chorus figures such as Old Gower or Time (in *Pericles* and *The Winter's Tale*), the quasi-operatic blend of music and spectacle. At their best, such plays compel belief in the artistic world created. The very improbability of the story becomes, paradoxically, part of the means by which an audience must "awake its faith" in a mysterious truth.

Shakespeare did not merely ape the new fashion in tragicomedy and romance. In fact, he may have done much to establish it. His *Pericles*, written seemingly in about 1606–1608 for the public stage before Shakespeare's company acquired Blackfriars, anticipated many important features not only of Shakespeare's own later romances but of Beaumont and Fletcher's *The Maid's Tragedy* and *Philaster* (c. 1608–1611). Still, Shakespeare was on the verge of retirement, and the future belonged to Beaumont and Fletcher. Shakespeare was gradually disengaging himself, spending more and more time in Stratford. His last known stint as an actor was in Ben Jonson's *Sejanus* in 1603. Some time in

1611 or 1612 he probably gave up his lodgings in London, though he still may have returned for such occasions as the opening performance of *Henry VIII* in 1613. He continued to be one of the proprietors of the newly rebuilt Globe, but his involvement in its day-to-day operations dwindled.

The themes that dominate Shakespeare's later romances suggest retirement—from the responsibilities of parenthood, from art, from the theater, from life itself. Fathers and their grown daughters are an omnipresent configuration in these plays. In the tender but complex relationship between the two, the father's business is to learn to accept his inevitable aging and the relocation of his daughter's interest in another man. (Shakespeare's own daughter Susanna was married to Dr. John Hall in Holy Trinity Church, Stratford, on June 5, 1607, and the couple's first child, Elizabeth, was christened on February 21, 1608.) This lesson must be learned, moreover, against a background like those of Shakespeare's great tragedies, with their relentless explorations of the possibilities of disaster in the father-daughter relationship. Brabantio refuses to recognize the right of Desdemona to marry Othello; King Lear is unwilling to see that he cannot expect his daughters, especially Cordelia, to love their father as the sole center of their lives. "Sure I shall never marry like my sisters, / To love my father all," says Cordelia (1.1.103–104).

The protagonists of Shakespeare's romances face similar dilemmas, though usually the outcomes are more benign. *Pericles* is filled with variations of the conflict, from the tragic and cautionary example of the incestuous King Antiochus to the pretended jealousy of King Simonides, whose possessiveness is only (or perhaps mainly) a ruse designed to make the young couple's eventual amorous reward all the sweeter. In this environment of fatherly possessiveness, Pericles must work out his own relationship to his daughter Marina. Cymbeline's resistance to his daughter Imogen's preference in love drives Posthumus Leonatus from the court and thereby sets in motion the potentially tragic events that are resolved only after years of separation, estrangement, and eventual reunion. Leontes in *The Winter's Tale*, having ordered that his daughter, Perdita, be exposed to the pitiless elements, is spared from being a murderer only by a strange providence that restores Perdita, the lost one, to him after many years of penance. As happens with Marina and Imogen, the reunion of this father and daughter is a rediscovery that coincides with the father's acknowledgment that his daughter is ready to marry and begin a family of her own. Prospero in *The Tempest*, like King Simonides, invents a jealous contretemps for Miranda and Ferdinand so that their love may seem all the more wondrous once it is earned by tribulation. We can see at the same time, though, that Prospero is partly acting out his own troubled feelings of possessiveness, trying to lay them to rest as best he can. He succeeds in freeing Miranda from her tie to him, whereas the fathers in the earlier romances, Pericles, Cymbeline, and Leontes, have had to struggle more painfully with their ties of affection. Even Prospero's success in freeing Miranda is all the more convincing because it is not easy.

Some of the fathers of the late romances are also husbands who rediscover their wives. Pericles's reunion with Perdita, as precious as it is, serves also as a prelude to his finding his wife, Thaisa, at the Temple of Diana. The daughter, so like her mother of many years before, is a manifestation of the eternal renewal of life; the mother, still lovely though now aged, displays the process of growing toward death that is common to all creatures. Pericles must learn to accept the aging of his wife and of himself, and must rediscover an affection for one whom he has cast aside. The story says that Thaisa was apparently dead when the sailors on board ship insisted on her being thrown overboard, but Pericles must grapple with his own responsibility for her long and arduous odyssey. During their separation, she devotes herself to the retired life of a priestess in the temple of the goddess of chastity, and it is her generosity that is needed to restore the wandering Pericles to marital happiness. (A similar motif of a wife lost at sea and found again after many years in a life of religious seclusion occurs in Shakespeare's early—or earliest—comedy, *The Comedy of Errors*.) In *The Winter's Tale*, Leontes's jealousy is directly to blame for his denunciation of his wife, Hermione, and in this instance it is clearly the husband's failure that is the cause of his wife's enforced seclusion. Like Thaisa and Emilia, Egeon's wife, Hermione adopts a life of chaste retirement. She too ages. Given a kind of spiritual authority by her innocence and suffering, Hermione bestows on her erring and contrite husband a forgiveness that he (rightly) believes himself not to deserve.

Through the grace of forgiving women and the ministrations of a benign comic providence, tragedy turns to poignant comedy in these plays. Essential to these transformations is that the men have not in fact done the dreadful things they have contemplated and even attempted. Thaisa, washed ashore by a storm of fortune that both afflicts and restores all mortals, is brought to life by Cerimon. Posthumus Leonatus orders the murder of his wife, but, unlike Othello, does not succeed, because a loyal servant puts human compassion ahead of obedience. Leontes wants to do away with his wife and daughter but is forestalled by his wife's apparent death and by beneficent happenings on the seacoast of Bohemia that include the participation of a bear. Later, an engaging thief and scoundrel named Autolycus is instrumental in ways, which no one could have predicted, to the restoration of happiness. Antonio and Sebastian attempt murder in *The Tempest* only to be thwarted by Ariel, whose invisible presence symbolizes the overseeing providence through which romance averts tragic circumstance. The gods or abstractly allegorical figures—the chorus figure Gower and the goddess Diana in *Pericles*, the spirits of the Leonati and the god Jupiter in *Cymbeline*, the chorus figure Time and the voice of Apollo through his oracle in *The Winter's Tale*, and Ariel, Iris, Ceres, Juno, and other spirits in *The Tempest*—repeatedly express their concern or intervene on the side of order and happiness. Forgiveness for erring men is possible in these plays (as, earlier, for Claudio in *Much Ado about Nothing* and Angelo in *Measure for Measure*, among others) because the men have been saved from their own worst instincts and have not committed their envisaged crimes.

Shakespeare's celebration of his art and his farewell to it are evident everywhere in these late plays. Cerimon, in *Pericles*, is an artist figure whose seemingly supernatural skill preserves the life of Thaisa and so makes possible the comic resolution. The gods manifest their will in Act 5 of *Cymbeline* in a way that stresses, through the very improbability and artifice of the event in the theater, the artist's role in contriving a providential restoration. Paulina, in *The*

Winter's Tale, fulfills a role essentially like that of Cerimon, bringing Hermione back to life and thus preserving the heroine for her climactic act of forgiveness. Paulina's reflections on her art as permissible rather than black magic (5.3.95–105), her insistence that Leontes and the others awake their faith in order to bring the miracle to fruition (ll. 89–95), and her reenactment of the miracle through which the dead are brought to life, all define the dramatist's art and justify the illusions through which theater works its magic. Prospero, aided by Ariel, is the most visibly theatrical and artistic of these miracle workers, as he leashes and unleashes storms, puts people to sleep and awakens them, and, in a moving peroration, boasts of his theatrical ability to wake sleepers from their graves.

The boast is, it turns out, only a preamble to his resolution to set aside the audacious power given him by art and to drown his books (5.1.33–57). In these late plays Shakespeare's farewell to his art is an integral part of his vision of setting aside everything that life holds dear. Yet the renunciation is also a celebration, a renewal, for life will go on and art will continue to cast its spells.

The Playhouse

This early copy of a drawing by Johannes de Witt of the Swan Theatre in London (c. 1596), made by his friend Arend van Buchell, is the only surviving contemporary sketch of the interior of a public theater in the 1590s.

From other contemporary evidence, including the stage directions and dialogue of Elizabethan plays, we can surmise that the various public theaters where Shakespeare's plays were produced (the Theatre, the Curtain, the Globe) resembled the Swan in many important particulars, though there must have been some variations as well. The public playhouses were essentially round, or polygonal, and open to the sky, forming an acting arena approximately 70 feet in diameter; they did not have a large curtain with which to open and close a scene, such as we see today in opera and some traditional theater. A platform measuring approximately 43 feet across and 27 feet deep, referred to in the de Witt drawing as the *proscaenium*, projected into the yard, *planities sive arena*. The roof, *tectum*, above the stage and supported by two pillars, could contain machinery for ascents and descents, as were required in several of Shakespeare's late plays. Above this roof was a hut, shown in the drawing with a flag flying atop it and a trumpeter at its door announcing the performance of a play. The underside of the stage roof, called the heavens, was usually richly decorated with symbolic figures of the sun, the moon, and the constellations. The platform stage stood at a height of 5½ feet or so above the yard, providing room under the stage for underworldly effects. A trapdoor, which is not visible in this drawing, gave access to the space below.

The structure at the back of the platform (labeled *mimorum aedes*), known as the tiring-house because it was the actors' attiring (dressing) space, featured at least two doors, as shown here. Some theaters seem to have also had a discovery space, or curtained recessed alcove, perhaps between the two doors—in which Falstaff could have hidden from the sheriff (*1 Henry IV*, 2.4) or Polonius could have eavesdropped on Hamlet and his mother (*Hamlet*, 3.4). This discovery space probably gave the actors a means of access to and from the tiring-house. Curtains may also have been hung in front of the stage doors on occasion. The de Witt drawing shows a gallery above the doors that extends across the back and evidently contains spectators. On occasions when action "above" demanded the use of this space, as when Juliet appears at her "window" (*Romeo and Juliet*, 2.2 and 3.5), the gallery seems to have been used by the actors, but large scenes there were impractical.

The three-tiered auditorium is perhaps best described by Thomas Platter, a visitor to London in 1599 who saw on that occasion Shakespeare's *Julius Caesar* performed at the Globe:

> The playhouses are so constructed that they play on a raised platform, so that everyone has a good view. There are different galleries and places [*orchestra, sedilia, porticus*], however, where the seating is better and more comfortable and therefore more expensive. For whoever cares to stand below only pays one English penny, but if he wishes to sit, he enters by another door [*ingressus*] and pays another penny, while if he desires to sit in the most comfortable seats, which are cushioned, where he not only sees everything well but can also be seen, then he pays yet another English penny at another door. And during the performance food and drink are carried round the audience, so that for what one cares to pay one may also have refreshment.

Scenery was not used, though the theater building itself was handsome enough to invoke a feeling of order and hierarchy that lent itself to the splendor and pageantry onstage. Portable properties, such as thrones, stools, tables, and beds, could be carried or thrust on as needed. In the scene pictured here by de Witt, a lady on a bench, attended perhaps by her waiting-gentlewoman, receives the address of a male figure. If Shakespeare had written *Twelfth Night* by 1596 for performance at the Swan, we could imagine Malvolio appearing like this as he bows before the Countess Olivia and her gentlewoman, Maria.

PERICLES

Introduction

Pericles is a deceptively simple play. Although it was popular in its own time and in recent years has proved to be successful and deeply moving onstage, the play may seem naive and trivial on the printed page. Its apparent lack of "depth" seems especially striking when we compare it with its contemporaries, *King Lear, Macbeth, Timon of Athens,* and *Antony and Cleopatra.* It purports to be the work of a medieval poet, John Gower, who as presenter, or chorus, apologizes to his sophisticated Jacobean audience ("born in these latter times / When wit's more ripe") for the "lame feet of my rhyme" and the quaintness of his ditty (1.0.11–12; 4.0.48). The narrative offers a series of sea voyages, separations, hairbreadth escapes, and reunions. Thrilling circumstances abound: Pericles fleeing the wrath of Antiochus; his wife, Thaisa, giving birth to their daughter, Marina, on board ship in the midst of a gigantic storm; and Marina later being rescued by pirates from a would-be murderer only to be sold by her new captors to a house of prostitution. Time leaps forward from Pericles's own youth to that of his daughter. The action takes place in remote lands, shifting constantly back and forth among six eastern Mediterranean localities: Antioch, Tyre, Tarsus, Pentapolis, Ephesus, and Mytilene. Conventional devices of plot include the expounding of riddles, the discovery of incest at court, the exposure of infants to the hostile elements, the miraculous restoration of life after seeming death, the appearance of the gods in a vision, and recognition of long-lost loved ones by means of signs or tokens.

These are the attributes of popular romance, a distinctly old-fashioned genre in 1606–1608 when *Pericles* was apparently written. Robert Greene had composed prose romances of this sort in the 1580s and early 1590s, including *Pandosto,* Shakespeare's source for *The Winter's Tale.* Sir Philip Sidney's *Arcadia* had endowed romance with noble eloquence and literary fashionableness, but that too was in the late 1580s. (The name Pericles may well owe something to the *Arcadia*'s Pyrocles, though Shakespeare may also have been attracted to the Pericles of fifth-century Athens and to the mellifluous quality of the name.) One source for

Pericles itself, a prose history of Apollonius of Tyre by Laurence Twine, was registered for publication in 1576, although no edition exists before that of 1594 or 1595. Earlier accounts of Apollonius (as the hero was originally named), going back to Greek romance, include a ninth-century *Historia Apollonii Regis Tyri*, Godfrey of Viterbo's *Pantheon* (c. 1186), John Gower's *Confessio Amantis* (c. 1383–1393), and the *Gesta Romanorum*. Why did Shakespeare's company refurbish such an outmoded romantic story in 1606–1608?

The puzzle is aggravated by questions of authorship and textual reliability. The editors of the First Folio did not include *Pericles* in the canon of Shakespeare's plays. Perhaps they experienced copyright difficulties or could not lay their hands on the promptbook, but it is also possible they either suspected or knew that Shakespeare was not the sole author. Printed editions were available to them: the first quarto of 1609 and the subsequent quartos of 1609, 1611, and 1619, each based on the preceding edition. The first quarto was, however, a bad text with occasional glaring contradictions. In Act 1, scene 2, for example, Pericles's lords wish him a safe journey when no one has yet spoken of his departure, and Helicanus rebukes these same lords for flattery even though they have not said anything remotely sycophantic. Other scenes present similar difficulties, especially in the first two acts. The characters do not always seem consistent: Cleon is condemned in Act 5 for having tried to murder Marina, even though our earlier impression of him is of a man who is genuinely horrified at his wife's villainy. He weakly bends to the will of Dionyza but is no murderer. Such inconsistencies and errors, and the naiveté of the whole, have generally led to three hypotheses: that Shakespeare worked with a collaborator such as Thomas Heywood or George Wilkins, that he revised an older play and left the first two acts pretty much as they were, or that he wrote the entire play, which was then "pirated" by two unemployed actors whose portions differed markedly in accuracy.

To complicate matters still further, a prose version of the story called *The Painful Adventures of Pericles* by George Wilkins appeared in 1608, purporting to be "the true History of the Play of Pericles"—that is, to be a prose account of a dramatic performance. This redaction is indeed close at times to the play we have, but at other times it departs widely. The departures of the later work are sometimes explained with the hypothesis that Wilkins based his account on an older play, one to which Wilkins might have contributed himself; another and more current opinion favors the notion that Wilkins took what he needed from the play we have, borrowing also from Twine's prose version or from his own imagination. Apparently, then, *Pericles* was such a popular stage success that it inspired Wilkins's *Painful Adventures* in 1608, a new reprint in 1607 of Twine's *Pattern of Painful Adventures* on which the play itself had been partly based, and a botched surreptitious quarto edition of the play in 1609. Shakespeare's sole authorship must remain in doubt, although the incongruities, especially in the first two acts, are sometimes explained as the result of faulty memorial reporting and compositorial error. Onstage, to be sure, even the first two acts make fine dramatic sense, establishing motifs and situations that are essential to the rest of the play, so that the overall impression in the theater is of cohesion.

The naiveté of *Pericles* is probably deliberate. Its romantic motifs continue on into that group of plays known generally as the late romances: *Cymbeline* (c. 1608–1610), *The Winter's Tale* (c. 1610–1611), and *The Tempest* (c. 1610–1611). Nor are these motifs entirely new in *Pericles:* the "problem" comedies *All's Well That Ends Well* and *Measure for Measure* use a tragicomic structure in which miraculous cures or providential interventions triumph over the semblance of death. *Pericles* occupies an integral place, then, in the development of Shakespearean comedy during the period of his great tragedies. To that development it offers a new emphasis on the simplicity of folk legend. Of the four late romances, *Pericles,* the earliest, is also the nearest in tone to romance of the 1580s. The play seems to have constituted a revival of that old genre and was so immensely popular that it did much to establish the vogue of tragicomedy exploited by Beaumont and Fletcher.

The Chorus, old Gower, gives to the episodic materials of the play a unified point of view. He speaks with the authority of one who has told the story before, even though his *Confessio Amantis* (c. 1383–1393) was probably not Shakespeare's immediate source. Gower adopts a kind of Chaucerian persona, appealing to "what mine authors say" (1.0.20) and apologizing for his rude simplicity. Like the Chorus of *Henry V,* he repeatedly urges his auditors to transcend the limitations of his naive art, using the power of imagination to bridge gaps in time and to suppose the stage a storm-tossed ship or the city of Antioch. His appearances divide the action into seven episodic segments, surely a more authentic structure than the five "acts" conventionally employed by later editions. He offers moral appraisals of his various characters, often before we have had a chance to see them, contrasting the good with the bad. Most important, he presides as a sort of benign deity over the changing fortunes of his characters, assuring us that as narrator he will not allow the virtuous to come to grief or the wicked to escape punishment. He thus paces our expectations and provides a comic reassurance appropriate to romance. He promises to "show you those in trouble's reign, / Losing a mite, a mountain gain." To the virtuous he will ultimately give his "benison." Under his direction, the vacillations of fortune take on a predictable rhythm, whereby the rewards of virtuous conduct may be delayed but cannot eventually fail. Pericles, he tells us, will suffer adversity "Till fortune, tired with doing bad, / Threw him ashore, to give him glad" (2.0.7–38). This pattern is repeated several times.

The characters often remind us of characters from a fairy story, outwardly stereotyped and one-dimensional, divided for the most part into contrasting types of villainy and virtue, and yet suggesting beneath their conventional surfaces the conflicts in family relationships that are essential to the fairy story. Incest is a recurrent motif, from its most blunt and evil manifestation in the court of Antiochus to more subtle inversions and variations in the relationships of Simonides and his daughter, Thaisa, and, most centrally, of Pericles and his daughter, Marina. The interest in fathers and daughters, and in the difficulties fathers have in coming to terms with their daughters' marrying other men, continues to fascinate Shakespeare from *Othello* and *King Lear* into all of his late romances. The mystery of incest is stated in terms of a riddle at the start of *Pericles,* and the moving dramatic conclusion in which the hero is reunited at last with his daughter seems to represent at some level a resolution of conflict between father and daughter. Pericles and Marina have "found" each other and themselves, literally in the narrative sense and also in some deeper psychic and spiritual way.

The characters expressing this and other conflicts are repeatedly paired opposite to one another as contrasting foils, illustrating a type of human depravity and its ideal opposite. One such contrast is that of tyranny and true monarchy. For example, both Antiochus and Simonides seem to welcome the various suitors who flock to their courts seeking the hand in marriage of the two kings' daughters. Antiochus does so deceitfully, however, since he is his daughter's incestuous lover. Pericles learns in Antioch the danger of perceiving too much about the private affairs of a suspicious and vengeful tyrant like Antiochus. Simonides is, on the other hand, a true prince, beloved by the simplest of his subjects, generous, lacking in envy, courteous to strangers, and more impressed with inner substance than with outward show. He approves of Pericles as a son-in-law, though (like Prospero in *The Tempest*) he imposes artificial restraints on the lovers to make their eventual triumph of love seem all the more sweet. Antiochus and his daughter are eventually shriveled up by a fire from heaven, whereas Simonides and Thaisa earn the just rewards of gracious hospitality. Another opposing pair of characters, Thaliard and Helicanus, are conventionally typed as false and true courtiers. Thaliard, ordered by Antiochus to murder Pericles, is evasive and self-serving; Helicanus, when offered the opportunity to supplant Pericles as ruler of Tyre, loyally awaits his master's return.

Pericles is apparently conceived in these same conventional terms as a prince of chivalry, young, brave, admirable both as a romantic wooer and as a resolute adventurer. His visit to the city of Tarsus, which has recently been toppled from wealth to poverty, shows him practicing the generosity that befits his lofty rank and innately noble qualities. Even when fortune strips him of his finery, his princely bearing is evident to discerning observers like King Simonides and Thaisa. Pericles thus differs outwardly from the flawed tragicomic protagonists more often found in the late romances, such as Posthumus in *Cymbeline* and Leontes in *The Winter's Tale*, who bring grief upon themselves and must suffer agonizing contrition before gaining an unexpected second chance. Pericles seems to be virtually without fault, a hero of romance rather than of tragedy. His soliloquies and eloquent speeches are not darkly introspective and psychological, like Leontes's. Although he grieves in sackcloth and ashes, he does so for undeserved misfortune rather than for his own follies. The play accordingly has little to say about humanity's perverse instinct for self-destruction. Yet critics have been unable to agree as to whether Pericles is simply a good man buffeted by misfortune or a man somehow perplexed by inner conflict. Are there unresolved wishes in his relationships to Thaisa and Marina that link him to the manifestly flawed protagonists of *Cymbeline* and *The Winter's Tale*, and, more explicitly, to Antiochus and his daughter in this play? What is it that causes his excessive despair in his grief and his withdrawal into absolute silence? Yet on the surface his story is one of undeserved misfortune leading at last to happy reunion and an end of his trials. He learns a more affirmative and patient response from his courageous daughter, Marina, whereupon his trials have run their necessary course. Even his learning such a lesson is of less importance than the sublime sense of mystery and joy that accompanies his reunion with Marina.

In several ways, Marina is a typical heroine of Shakespeare's late romances. Her name, like that of Perdita in *The Winter's Tale*, signifies loss and recovery. Marina is the gift of the sea, that mysterious power of fortune in *Pericles* that takes with one hand even while it gives with the other. Just as the sea tosses Pericles on the coast of Pentapolis and then returns to him the suit of armor in which he will joust for the love of fair Thaisa, so in another storm at sea Thaisa apparently dies giving birth to Marina. The child is a "fresh new seafarer" on the troubled voyage of life (3.1.41). The sea parts her from her mother and father and leads to the misunderstandings whereby Marina is supposed dead, but the sea also eventually deposits Pericles on the coast of Mytilene, where he finds his long-lost daughter. Like Perdita, Marina is associated with flowers and with Tellus, a divinity of the earth. The inscription on her monument, when she is thought dead, speaks of elemental strife between the sea and the shore caused by her death, in which the angry

sea gods "Make raging battery upon shores of flint"
(4.4.39–43). She is a princess from folk legend, like Snow
White or like Imogen in *Cymbeline*, who must flee the envious wrath of a witchlike stepmother and queen. Her true
mother, Thaisa, another princess in a folk tale, is washed
ashore in a treasure-filled chest, smelling sweetly and be-
tokening some miraculous change of fortune.

Most important, Marina is one who can preach conversion to the sinful and cure distempered souls. She recovers
her husband-to-be, Lysimachus, from the brothels of Mytilene, and even converts pimps and prostitutes by her innocent faith. As one with a strange power to bring new life to
dead hope, she resembles a number of mysterious artist-
figures and magicians in the late romances. One such is
Cerimon, who restores life to Thaisa. Like him, or like
Paulina in *The Winter's Tale*, whose devices are "lawful"
though seemingly magical, Marina offers cures that can be
rationally explained and yet appear to be miraculous. To
Pericles, her ministrations seem "the rarest dream that e'er
dull sleep / Did mock sad fools withal" (5.1.166–167). Yet
what she has taught him, by her own example, is simple patience; she has suffered even more than he, but nevertheless
knows how to endure, how to "look / Like Patience gazing on kings' graves and smiling / Extremity out of act"
(ll. 140–142).

Through her we understand finally why providence has
allowed so much misfortune to afflict the virtuous: only by
such testing can humanity learn to conquer time and death.
Time will always remain "the king of men; / He's both their
parent and he is their grave, / And gives them what he will,
not what they crave" (2.3.47–49). Nevertheless, providence
can turn the accidents of time and fortune to good purpose
for those who are Joblike in their patient faith. Even pirates unknowingly take part in a divine plan, rescuing
Marina from the clutches of the evil Dionyza. As Gower
puts it, those who are "assailed with fortune fierce and
keen" are also "Led on by heaven, and crowned with joy
at last" (5.3.90–92). To Pericles, such a delayed reward
is ample compensation for his sorrows, almost indeed an
unbearable joy. "No more, you gods!" he movingly pleads.
"Your present kindness / Makes my past miseries sports"
(ll. 41–42).

Pericles
in Performance

Pericles is one of a number of plays by Shakespeare that succeeded onstage in his own time but then had to wait until the twentieth century for a genuine revival of interest. Six quartos between 1609 and 1635, and several allusions to the play, attest to its popularity in the early seventeenth century. Ben Jonson deplored it as a "moldy tale," apparently rueful that it outdid some of his own efforts. Although Shakespeare's editors excluded it from the First Folio of 1623, and although it remains one of the least read of Shakespeare's plays (no doubt at least in part because textual difficulties and possibly composite authorship mar some early scenes), *Pericles* works in the theater. If John Downes is to be believed, *Pericles* was, remarkably, the first play by Shakespeare to be performed at the reopening of the theaters just prior to the Restoration of 1660 or very shortly thereafter, by Thomas Betterton and John Rhodes's actors at the old Cockpit Theatre. When Betterton and others of this group joined the Duke's company under William Davenant, the new company was assigned the rights to *Pericles* and probably acted it in the early 1660s.

Despite this promising start, *Pericles* was not the sort of play to be admired in its original form by Restoration and eighteenth-century audiences, and, after a period of complete neglect, was replaced in 1738 (at the Theatre Royal, Covent Garden) by George Lillo's adaptation called *Marina*. In order to unify Shakespeare's episodic and apparently disjointed plot, Lillo purged what he called the "humor mixed," while reducing the action to "a single tale." Since the play contained, in Lillo's view, too many episodes and too many locations, he got rid of Antiochus and his daughter, Simonides and the court of Pentapolis, and indeed everyone and everything not connected with Marina.

Lillo achieves unity of plot by beginning with the story of Philoten's jealousy of Marina. Philoten, mentioned in Shakespeare's play but not brought onstage, is the daughter of the now-dead Cleon and Dionyza, to whose care Pericles has entrusted his daughter. Philoten (rather than her mother, as in Shakespeare) hires Leonine to murder Marina—a task that he embraces as part of his ambition to occupy the throne of Tarsus with Philoten as his queen. Lillo amplifies the melodrama of Leonine's scene with Marina, Marina's seizure by pirates, and her life in a brothel (now in Ephesus, not Mitylene). When Lysimachus (the son of Cerimon in this version) comes to the brothel, bent on exposing its corruptions, he is inflamed at first by Marina's beauty but is soon won over by her goodness, whereupon he assists her to escape and escorts her to Ephesus. Here the Temple of Diana becomes the scene of final recognition and reunion of father, mother, and daughter. Philoten and Leonine, meantime, kill each other. Poetic justice triumphs; unity of action and melodrama give shape to the plot. The enlarged brothel scenes provide titillation along with the edifying spectacle of Lysimachus's conversion that presumably makes such entertainment wholesome, or at least permissible. Lillo, better known for *The London Merchant, or The History of George Barnwell* (1731), had in mind the middle-class tastes of his London audiences as well as neoclassical strictures on matters of time, place, and action.

After another long hiatus (almost broken in 1796, when the play was published "as intended to be performed at the Theatre Royal, Covent Garden"), *Pericles* was revived by Samuel Phelps at the Sadler's Wells Theatre, in 1854, in a version certainly closer than Lillo's to Shakespeare's play. Despite Phelps's wish to honor Shakespeare's original, however, this production fell prisoner to the tyranny of elaborate scenic design, then so much in vogue and the subject of emulation among theater managers. *Pericles* seemed to offer endless opportunities for scenic display and for archaeological reproduction of architecture, costume, and ceremony in several ancient countries along the Mediterranean; but its narrative discontinuities, bridged by the quaint choric figure of Gower in Shakespeare's play, demanded on the nineteenth-century stage something more in keeping with the audience's verisimilar expectations. Phelps's solution was to take Gower out and to rewrite some of the bridging material into the dialogue. He also ran scenes together, including scenes 2 and 3 of Act 1, 3 and 5 of Act 2, and 2 and 6 of Act 4. This last pairing yielded an ex-

tended brothel scene, albeit one that lacked the Pander
(who, like the incest riddle itself, had been expurgated from
the play) and had been retouched in such a way that, as
Henry Morley observed in his *Journal of a London Playgoer*
for October 21, "there remained not a syllable at which true
delicacy could have conceived offense."

Elaborate spectacle and scenery was Phelps's chief consideration. The running together of scenes 3 and 5 in Act 2
enabled him to stage the action at Pentapolis with the
sumptuous detail it presumably deserved (including a huge
banquet, a glittering dance, and a train of courtiers) rather
than having to veer off in midpoint for a scene located in
Tyre. Phelps omitted other scenes altogether, although,
with the exception of the Pander, he kept all of Shakespeare's characters. He paid particular attention to sea effects, especially a shipwreck in which Pericles was literally
thrown ashore, and scenes on deck made realistic by
machine-generated sensations of "the rolling of the billows
and the whistling of the winds" (as Morley described them).
The deck on which Pericles stood in Act 3, scene 1 ("*Enter
Pericles, a-shipboard*"), actually pitched and tossed. In the
final act, the scenes of recognition aboard Pericles's ship
and of reunion in the Temple of Diana at Ephesus were
linked visually by a sliding painted panorama. Rowers
manned their oars to transport Pericles from one location
to another in such a way that the theater itself seemed to
move in front of the panorama, while Diana made her appearance in a chariot amid the clouds. Phelps regarded
Pericles as one of his triumphs, and evidently lavished more
expenditure on this production than on anything else he
did. None of his Shakespearean revivals at Sadler's Wells
extended longer than *Pericles*'s fifty-five performances, and
at least one reviewer, the critic of *Lloyd's Weekly*, felt that
the production proved that "Mr. Phelps is the best commen-
tator of Shakespeare the people ever had."

As late as 1900, John Coleman staged a similarly restruc-
tured and expurgated adaptation at Stratford-upon-Avon,
leaving out Gower and most of Act 1. The play's performance history in the twentieth century, on the other hand,
has been characterized generally by at least four developments: the freeing of the play from verisimilar staging, the
reintroduction of Gower and other materials previously

omitted, the restoration of expurgated bawdy, and a very substantial increase in the number of successful productions. Obviously these factors are interrelated. The play has succeeded because directors and actors have learned to trust *Pericles*'s unusual kind of stage magic.

Productions by two disciples of William Poel, that tireless champion of a return to Elizabethan staging techniques, were influential in demonstrating that the play as originally conceived for the stage could succeed in the modern theater. The first, an energetic Old Vic performance directed by Robert Atkins in 1921, reintroduced Gower. The second, by Nugent Monck's Norwich Players at the Maddermarket Theatre in 1929, made use of that theater's Elizabethan apron stage, enabling the action to shift quickly from scene to scene. (Monck's earlier production at the Scala in 1926 did make some effort to adapt the speed and flexibility of Elizabethan staging to the theater's proscenium stage.) In 1939 Atkins again directed the play, this time at the Open Air Theatre in London's Regent's Park, with Robert Eddison's rueful Pericles and with ballets (including one of starving people at Tarsus) emphasizing the play's disjointed narrative. When Monck directed the play at Stratford-upon-Avon in 1947, with Paul Scofield as a swashbuckling Pericles and Daphne Slater as a tender Marina, the substantially cut and swiftly paced version played only a little longer than an hour and a half. Three years later, these same leading actors reappeared with John Harrison's Under Thirty Group in an essentially uncut version played without an interval at London's Rudolph Steiner Hall. Douglas Seale, directing Richard Pasco as Pericles at the Birmingham Repertory Theatre in 1954, employed a permanent set throughout, its raised platform and curving stairway emphasizing the storybook aspects of the play. In 1958, at Stratford-upon-Avon, Tony Richardson imaginatively directed a gorgeous *Pericles* with the West Indian actor Edric Conner as a seafaring, calypso-singing Gower.

More recent productions have often enriched and complicated the fairy-tale qualities of *Pericles* by insistently probing the self-conscious artifice of the play. In 1969 Terry Hands directed a cold, austere version of *Pericles* at Stratford-upon-Avon on a stage consisting of a three-walled white box. Four years later, first in Edinburgh and then at London's Roundhouse Theatre, Toby Robertson explored the play's contrast between innocence and corruption in a Brechtian modern-dress production, set in a male brothel and starring Derek Jacobi as Pericles. Less disturbingly, Edward Berkeley also examined the artificiality of Shakespeare's play by directing it for the New York Shakespeare Festival in 1974 as a traveling show; actors climbed down from wagons to entertain the audience with clowning before they began performing the play. A large map onstage was used to pinpoint the action and signboards were employed to announce the sudden scene shifts. The year 1983 saw the play energetically acted at the Theatre Royal Stratford East. One actor, Brian Protheroe, played all the rulers, while Felicity Dean played all of the daughters. David Ultz's direction employed an almost bare stage with large crates imaginatively used to invoke different settings.

Stratford, Ontario, has seen two successful productions, one in 1973, directed by Jean Gascon, with Edward Atienza's Gower passionately challenging the audience to accept the play's folktale quality, and one in 1986, directed by Richard Ouzounian, with Gower electrifyingly presented by a black female singer, Renee Rogers. The marked contrast of her gospel vocalizations with the style of the play itself called attention to the artifice of theater in a way that Shakespeare seems also to have intended (though he used a different idiom, that of an old-fashioned balladeer). Rogers's Gower moved the play from one setting to another through the medium of sung verse, while varied lighting effects, sounds, costuming, and visual decoration quickly gave the audience an array of impressions—shipwreck, tournament, courtship, storm at sea, seamy life in a bordello, a ship at anchor, a temple. Without attempting merely to copy the stagecraft that Shakespeare's original production must have used to generate its medley of visually impressive scenes, modern productions such as these have found equivalent ways in which costuming and the grouping of actors into varying stage pictures can work effectively to achieve the play's shifts of scene without the hindrance of realistic scenery.

PERICLES

LYSIMACHUS, *Governor of Mytilene*

PANDER,
BAWD, *his wife,* } *three bawds, or dealers*
BOLT, *their man,* } *in prostitution*

Two GENTLEMEN *of Mytilene*

SAILOR *of Tyre*
SAILOR *of Mytilene*
GENTLEMAN *of Tyre*
LORD *of Mytilene*

DIANA, *goddess of chastity*

Lords, Ladies, Gentlemen, Attendants, Servants, Messengers, young Ladies accompanying Marina, Vestal Virgins, inhabitants of Ephesus

SCENE: *In various eastern Mediterranean countries*]

1.0   *Enter Gower [before the palace of Antioch, on the walls of which can be seen a row of impaled heads].*

GOWER

To sing a song that old was sung,   1
From ashes ancient Gower is come,   2
Assuming man's infirmities   3
To glad your ear and please your eyes.
It hath been sung at festivals,
On ember eves and holy-ales;   6
And lords and ladies in their lives
Have read it for restoratives.   8
The purchase is to make men glorious,   9
Et bonum quo antiquius, eo melius.   10
If you, born in these latter times
When wit's more ripe, accept my rhymes,   12
And that to hear an old man sing   13
May to your wishes pleasure bring,
I life would wish, and that I might
Waste it for you, like taper light.   16
This Antioch, then. Antiochus the Great   17
Built up this city for his chiefest seat,
The fairest in all Syria—
I tell you what mine authors say.   20
This king unto him took a peer,   21
Who died and left a female heir,
So buxom, blithe, and full of face   23
As heaven had lent her all his grace;   24
With whom the father liking took   25

1.0. (Gower is seen to be standing before the palace of Antioch, where scene 1 will take place.)
1 old of old   **2 ancient Gower** the fourteenth-century poet John Gower, who related the adventures of Apollonius of Tyre (of which *Pericles* is a version) in his *Confessio Amantis*   **3 Assuming man's infirmities** taking on a mortal body   **6 ember eves** evenings before the ember days—the periodic fast days which coincide with the four changes of the seasons.   **holy-ales** i.e., church ales or festivals   **8 for restoratives** for its healing properties   **9 purchase** profit   **10 Et . . . melius** a good thing is better for being older. (Latin.)   **12 wit's more ripe** wisdom is more seasoned   **13 And that** i.e., and if   **16 Waste** spend   **17 This** i.e., this is   **20 authors** authorities   **21 peer** consort   **23 buxom** cheerful, lively.   **full of face** beautiful   **24 As** as if.   **his** its   **25 liking** a lustful desire

And her to incest did provoke.
Bad child, worse father, to entice his own
To evil should be done by none!   28
But custom what they did begin   29
Was with long use account'd no sin.
The beauty of this sinful dame
Made many princes thither frame   32
To seek her as a bedfellow,
In marriage pleasures playfellow;
Which to prevent he made a law,
To keep her still, and men in awe,   36
That whoso asked her for his wife,
His riddle told not, lost his life.   38
So for her many a wight did die,   39
As yon grim looks do testify.
            [*He points to the heads of the unsuccessful
                    suitors, displayed on the walls.*]
What now ensues, to the judgment of your eye
I give my cause, who best can justify.   *Exit.* 42

1.1   *Enter Antiochus, Prince Pericles, and followers.*

ANTIOCHUS
  Young Prince of Tyre, you have at large received
  The danger of the task you undertake.
PERICLES
  I have, Antiochus, and with a soul
  Emboldened with the glory of her praise
  Think death no hazard in this enterprise.
ANTIOCHUS   Music!
  Bring in our daughter, clothèd like a bride

---

28 **should** that should   29 **custom** continued practice (of)   32 **frame**
direct their steps   36 **still** always, forever.   **and men** and to keep men
38 **His riddle told not** if he left his (Antiochus's) riddle unsolved
39 **wight** person   42 **I . . . justify** i.e., I submit my case, my story, to
those who can best render a favorable verdict (the audience), or possibly
to the actors who can best justify the truth of it

1.1. Location: Antioch. The palace, as before.
1 **at large received** heard in detail

For th' embracements even of Jove himself,
At whose conception, till Lucina reigned, 9
Nature this dowry gave: to glad her presence, 10
The senate house of planets all did sit 11
To knit in her their best perfections. 12

[*Music.*] *Enter Antiochus' Daughter.*

PERICLES
See where she comes, appareled like the spring,
Graces her subjects, and her thoughts the king 14
Of every virtue gives renown to men! 15
Her face the book of praises where is read 16
Nothing but curious pleasures, as from thence 17
Sorrow were ever rased, and testy wrath 18
Could never be her mild companion. 19
You gods that made me man, and sway in love, 20
That have inflamed desire in my breast
To taste the fruit of yon celestial tree
Or die in the adventure, be my helps, 23
As I am son and servant to your will,
To compass such a boundless happiness! 25
ANTIOCHUS   Prince Pericles—
PERICLES
That would be son to great Antiochus.
ANTIOCHUS
Before thee stands this fair Hesperides, 28
With golden fruit, but dangerous to be touched,
For deathlike dragons here affright thee hard. 30

---

9 At . . . reigned i.e., from her conception until her birth. (Lucina was goddess of childbirth in her capacity as goddess of light.) **10–12 Nature . . . perfections** i.e., Nature bestowed on her, to make her presence gladsome, a favorable aspect of all the planets so that all perfect qualities would be combined in her **14 Graces her subjects** with graces for her subjects **15 gives** that gives **16 book of praises** collection of praiseworthy qualities **17 curious** exquisite. **as** as if **18 ever rased** forever erased **19 her mild companion** companion of her mildness **20 sway** rule **23 adventure** attempt **25 compass** encompass, achieve **28 Hesperides** (Correctly speaking, nymphs who guarded Juno's golden fruit. The name was frequently applied to the garden where these fruits grew. Here it applies to the Princess, beyond price but dangerous to seek.) **30 deathlike dragons** (Alludes to the dragon that guarded the garden of the Hesperides.)

Her face, like heaven, enticeth thee to view
Her countless glory, which desert must gain;   32
And which, without desert, because thine eye   33
Presumes to reach, all the whole heap must die.   34
Yon sometime famous princes, like thyself,   35
               [*Pointing to the heads on the walls*]
Drawn by report, adventurous by desire,   36
Tell thee with speechless tongues and semblance pale   37
That without covering, save yon field of stars,
Here they stand martyrs slain in Cupid's wars,
And with dead cheeks advise thee to desist
For going on death's net, whom none resist.   41

PERICLES
Antiochus, I thank thee, who hath taught
My frail mortality to know itself,
And by those fearful objects to prepare
This body, like to them, to what I must;   45
For death remembered should be like a mirror,   46
Who tells us life's but breath, to trust it error.
I'll make my will, then, and, as sick men do,
Who know the world, see heaven, but, feeling woe,   49
Grip not at earthly joys as erst they did,   50
So I bequeath a happy peace to you
And all good men, as every prince should do;
My riches to the earth from whence they came,
[*To the Princess*] But my unspotted fire of love to you.
Thus ready for the way of life or death,
I wait the sharpest blow, Antiochus.

ANTIOCHUS
Scorning advice, read the conclusion, then;   57
Which read and not expounded, 'tis decreed,
As these before thee, thou thyself shalt bleed.

32 countless glory innumerable beauties   **33–34 And . . . reach** i.e., and
if you presume to aspire to her without deserving   **34 heap** i.e., body of
Pericles   **35 sometime** once, formerly   **36 adventurous by desire** made
imprudently rash by passion   **37 semblance** appearance   **41 For going
on** from entering   **45 must** must someday be   **46 remembered** called to
mind   **49 Who . . . woe** i.e., who, weary of this world's miseries and
seeing the imminence of heavenly bliss   **50 Grip** clutch.   **erst** formerly   **57 conclusion** problem, riddle

DAUGHTER

   Of all 'sayed yet, mayst thou prove prosperous!   60
   Of all 'sayed yet, I wish thee happiness!   61

PERICLES

   Like a bold champion, I assume the lists,   62
   Nor ask advice of any other thought
   But faithfulness and courage.   *[He reads] the riddle.*

      I am no viper, yet I feed   65
      On mother's flesh which did me breed.   66
      I sought a husband, in which labor
      I found that kindness in a father.   68
      He's father, son, and husband mild;
      I mother, wife, and yet his child.
      How they may be, and yet in two,   71
      As you will live, resolve it you.

   [Aside.] Sharp physic is the last! But, O you powers   73
   That gives heaven countless eyes to view men's acts,   74
   Why cloud they not their sights perpetually
   If this be true which makes me pale to read it?
   Fair glass of light, I loved you, and could still,   77
   Were not this glorious casket stored with ill.
   But I must tell you now my thoughts revolt,
   For he's no man on whom perfections wait   80
   That, knowing sin within, will touch the gate.
   You are a fair viol, and your sense the strings   82
   Who, fingered to make man his lawful music,
   Would draw heaven down and all the gods to hearken,
   But, being played upon before your time,

60, 61 'sayed who have assayed, attempted   **62 champion** combatant.
assume the lists i.e., undertake the combat, enter the tournament
ground   **65–66 I am . . . breed** (Seager, *Shakespeare's Natural History*,
p. 331, quotes from Bartholomew, Trevisa's translation: "Viper is a
manner kind of serpents that is full venomous, and hath that name for
she bringeth forth brood by strength; for when her womb draweth to
the time of whelping, the whelps abideth not convenable time nor kind
passing, but gnaweth and fretteth the sides of their mother, and they
come so into this world with strength and with the death of the
mother.")   **68 kindness** (1) affection (2) kinship   **71 two** i.e., two people   **73 Sharp . . . last** i.e., this last condition—to stake my life on
solving this riddle—is bitter medicine   **74 eyes** i.e., the stars   **77 glass**
mirror or glass vessel (i.e., the Princess, fair in appearance only)   **80 on
. . . wait** with perfections as his attendants   **82 sense** senses

Hell only danceth at so harsh a chime.   86
Good sooth, I care not for you.   87

ANTIOCHUS
Prince Pericles, touch not, upon thy life,   88
For that's an article within our law
As dangerous as the rest. Your time's expired.
Either expound now or receive your sentence.

PERICLES   Great King,
Few love to hear the sins they love to act;
'Twould braid yourself too near for me to tell it.   94
Who has a book of all that monarchs do,   95
He's more secure to keep it shut than shown.
For vice repeated is like the wandering wind,   97
Blows dust in others' eyes to spread itself;   98
And yet the end of all is bought thus dear,   99
The breath is gone, and the sore eyes see clear   100
To stop the air would hurt them. The blind mole casts 101
Copped hills towards heaven, to tell the earth is
    thronged   102
By man's oppression, and the poor worm doth die for 't. 103
Kings are earth's gods; in vice their law's their will;
And if Jove stray, who dares say Jove doth ill?
It is enough you know; and it is fit,   106
What being more known grows worse, to smother it.   107
All love the womb that their first being bred;
Then give my tongue like leave to love my head.   109

ANTIOCHUS [*Aside*]
Heaven, that I had thy head! He has found the meaning.
But I will gloze with him.—Young Prince of Tyre,   111

86 only alone   **87 Good sooth** in truth   **88 touch not** (Antiochus evidently believes Pericles is about to touch the Princess's hand or some such forbidden thing.)   **94 braid . . . near** upbraid you too directly **95 Who** he who   **97 repeated** talked about   **98 Blows . . . itself** i.e., which in spreading itself blows dust in offenders' eyes   **99 thus dear** at this high price   **100–101 The breath . . . them** i.e., the speaker has lost his breath, whereas the offenders can see well enough, despite the irritating dust, to stop the breath of those who have attempted to indict them   **102 Copped** peaked.   **to tell** to tell that.   **thronged** beset **103 worm** i.e., creature. (The image is of a lowly creature like Pericles who dares to sound a warning against tyranny only at peril to himself.)   **106 you know** i.e., that you know that I know your riddle **107 What . . . it** to cover up a deed that is only worsened by revelation **109 like leave** similar permission   **111 gloze** talk smoothly and speciously

Though by the tenor of our strict edict,
Your exposition misinterpreting,   113
We might proceed to cancel of your days,   114
Yet hope, succeeding from so fair a tree   115
As your fair self, doth tune us otherwise.   116
Forty days longer we do respite you,
If by which time our secret be undone,   118
This mercy shows we'll joy in such a son.
And until then your entertain shall be   120
As doth befit our honor and your worth.   121

                    [*Exeunt.*] *Manet Pericles solus.*

PERICLES
How courtesy would seem to cover sin,   122
When what is done is like an hypocrite,
The which is good in nothing but in sight!   124
If it be true that I interpret false,
Then were it certain you were not so bad
As with foul incest to abuse your soul;
Where now you're both a father and a son
By your untimely claspings with your child,
Which pleasures fits a husband, not a father,
And she an eater of her mother's flesh
By the defiling of her parent's bed;
And both like serpents are, who, though they feed
On sweetest flowers, yet they poison breed.
Antioch, farewell, for wisdom sees those men   135
Blush not in actions blacker than the night
Will 'schew no course to keep them from the light.   137
One sin, I know, another doth provoke;
Murder's as near to lust as flame to smoke.
Poison and treason are the hands of sin,
Ay, and the targets, to put off the shame.   141
Then, lest my life be cropped to keep you clear,   142

113 Your . . . misinterpreting since your exposition interprets wrongly
114 to cancel of to cancellation of   **115 Yet . . . tree** yet hope (or fear) of
your answering correctly, issuing from so fair a royal stock   **116 tune
us** adjust or alter my intention. (*Us* is the royal "we.")   **118 undone**
unraveled, solved   **120 entertain** entertainment, reception   **121 s.d.
Manet** he remains onstage.   **solus** alone   **122 would seem** speciously
endeavors   **124 sight** appearance   **135 sees those men** sees that those
men who   **137 'schew** eschew, or possibly *shew*, shy away from.   **keep
. . . light** i.e., keep their guiltiness hidden   **141 targets** shields.   **put off**
deflect   **142 cropped** harvested, cut down.   **clear** free from blame

By flight I'll shun the danger which I fear.   *Exit.*

   Enter Antiochus.

ANTIOCHUS   He hath found the meaning,
For which we mean to have his head.
He must not live to trumpet forth my infamy,
Nor tell the world Antiochus doth sin
In such a loathèd manner;
And therefore instantly this prince must die,
For by his fall my honor must keep high.—
Who attends us there?

   Enter Thaliard.

THALIARD   Doth Your Highness call?
ANTIOCHUS
Thaliard, you are of our chamber, Thaliard,   153
And our mind partakes her private actions   154
To your secrecy; and for your faithfulness
We will advance you, Thaliard. Behold.
                    [*He gives poison and money.*]
Here's poison and here's gold. We hate the Prince
Of Tyre, and thou must kill him. It fits thee not
To ask the reason why, because we bid it.
Say, is it done?
THALIARD   My lord, 'tis done.
ANTIOCHUS   Enough.

   Enter a Messenger.

Let your breath cool yourself, telling your haste.   161
MESSENGER   My lord, Prince Pericles is fled.   [*Exit.*]
ANTIOCHUS [*To Thaliard*] As thou wilt live, fly after,
and like an arrow shot from a well-experienced archer
hits the mark his eye doth level at, so thou never re-   165
turn unless thou say Prince Pericles is dead.
THALIARD   My lord, if I can get him within my pistol's
length, I'll make him sure enough. So farewell to Your   168
Highness.

153 of our chamber my chamberlain   **154 partakes** imparts   **161 Let
. . . haste** i.e., cool your hot haste with the breath of your explanation
for it   **165 level** aim   **168 length** range.   **sure** harmless (i.e., dead)

ANTIOCHUS
  Thaliard, adieu! [*Exit Thaliard.*] Till Pericles be dead,
  My heart can lend no succor to my head.   [*Exit.*]

✤

1.2   *Enter Pericles with his Lords.*

PERICLES
  Let none disturb us. [*The Lords stay at the door.*] Why
    should this change of thoughts,   1
  The sad companion, dull-eyed melancholy,
  Be my so used a guest as not an hour   3
  In the day's glorious walk or peaceful night,   4
  The tomb where grief should sleep, can breed me quiet?
  Here pleasures court mine eyes, and mine eyes shun
    them,
  And danger, which I feared, is at Antioch,
  Whose arm seems far too short to hit me here.
  Yet neither pleasure's art can joy my spirits,
  Nor yet the other's distance comfort me.
  Then it is thus: the passions of the mind,
  That have their first conception by misdread,   12
  Have after-nourishment and life by care;   13
  And what was first but fear what might be done
  Grows elder now, and cares it be not done.   15
  And so with me: the great Antiochus,
  'Gainst whom I am too little to contend,
  Since he's so great can make his will his act,   18
  Will think me speaking though I swear to silence;
  Nor boots it me to say I honor him,   20
  If he suspect I may dishonor him.
  And what may make him blush in being known,   22
  He'll stop the course by which it might be known.
  With hostile forces he'll o'erspread the land,
  And with th' ostent of war will look so huge   25

1.2. Location: Tyre. The palace.
1 us i.e., me. **change of thoughts** altered disposition of mind **3 used**
familiar. **as that 4 walk** i.e., traversing of the sun **12 misdread**
fear **13 care** anxiety **15 cares** takes care, is anxious **18 so great can**
so powerful that he can **20 boots** avails **22 in being known** if it were
to become known **25 ostent** display

Amazement shall drive courage from the state,   26
Our men be vanquished ere they do resist,
And subjects punished that ne'er thought offense;
Which care of them, not pity of myself—
Who am no more but as the tops of trees
Which fence the roots they grow by and defend them— 31
Makes both my body pine and soul to languish,
And punish that before that he would punish.   33

    Enter [*Helicanus and*] *all the Lords to Pericles.*

FIRST LORD
  Joy and all comfort in your sacred breast!
SECOND LORD
  And keep your mind, till you return to us,   35
  Peaceful and comfortable!
HELICANUS
  Peace, peace, and give experience tongue.   37
  They do abuse the King that flatter him.
  For flattery is the bellows blows up sin;   39
  The thing the which is flattered, but a spark   40
  To which that blast gives heat and stronger glowing;   41
  Whereas reproof, obedient and in order,
  Fits kings as they are men, for they may err.
  When Signor Sooth here does proclaim peace,   44
  He flatters you, makes war upon your life.
  Prince, pardon me, or strike me, if you please;
  I cannot be much lower than my knees.   [*He kneels.*]
PERICLES
  All leave us else; but let your cares o'erlook   48

26 Amazement (that) dismay, consternation **31 fence** shield, shelter
33 punish . . . he punishes me beforehand (through fear) whom he
(Antiochus) **35 till you return to us** (Here the lords of Tyre appear to
know of Pericles's departure. In the next scene we find that he left
unlicensed of their loves, i.e., without their knowledge. The prose narratives that recount the same story state that his departure was accomplished secretly. This is one of the several inconsistencies of this rather
garbled text.) **37 give experience tongue** let the experienced speak
39 blows up that inflames, heats **40 the which** which **41 blast** i.e.,
flattering speech. (In Wilkins's *Painful Adventures,* this scene is more
clearly presented: Helicanus upbraids Pericles for his bad humor and
then justifies such plain talk as preferable to flattery.) **44 When**
while. **Signor Sooth** Sir Flattery, one who flatters. (Though, puzzlingly,
no one in this scene has in fact flattered Pericles; see note 41.) **48 else**
i.e., except Helicanus. **cares** watchfulness. **o'erlook** supervise

What shipping and what lading's in our haven,   49
And then return to us. [*Exeunt Lords.*] Helicanus,
Thou hast moved us. What seest thou in our looks?   51
HELICANUS   An angry brow, dread lord.
PERICLES
If there be such a dart in princes' frowns,
How durst thy tongue move anger to our face?
HELICANUS
How dares the plants look up to heaven,
From whence they have their nourishment?
PERICLES
Thou knowest I have power to take thy life from thee.
HELICANUS   I have ground the ax myself;
Do you but strike the blow.
PERICLES
Rise, prithee, rise. [*He rises.*] Sit down. Thou art no
    flatterer,
I thank thee for 't, and heaven forbid
That kings should let their ears hear their faults hid!   62
Fit counselor and servant for a prince,
Who by thy wisdom makes a prince thy servant,
What wouldst thou have me do?
HELICANUS
To bear with patience such griefs
As you yourself do lay upon yourself.
PERICLES
Thou speak'st like a physician, Helicanus,
That ministers a potion unto me
That thou wouldst tremble to receive thyself.
Attend me, then: I went to Antioch,
Where, as thou know'st, against the face of death
I sought the purchase of a glorious beauty   73
From whence an issue I might propagate,
Are arms to princes and bring joys to subjects.   75
Her face was to mine eye beyond all wonder;
The rest—hark in thine ear—as black as incest,
Which by my knowledge found, the sinful father
Seemed not to strike, but smooth. But thou know'st this,   79

49 **lading's** cargo is   51 **moved** angered   62 **hear . . . hid** hear words
that gloss over their faults   73 **purchase** acquisition   75 **Are** which are,
or such as are. (The antecedent is in the plural idea of *issue*, i.e.,
sons.)   **arms** weapons, defense   79 **smooth** gloss over, conciliate

'Tis time to fear when tyrants seem to kiss.
Which fear so grew in me, I hither fled
Under the covering of a careful night,   82
Who seemed my good protector, and, being here,
Bethought me what was past, what might succeed.   84
I knew him tyrannous, and tyrants' fears
Decrease not, but grow faster than the years;
And should he doubt—as doubt no doubt he doth—   87
That I should open to the listening air   88
How many worthy princes' bloods were shed
To keep his bed of blackness unlaid ope,   90
To lop that doubt he'll fill this land with arms
And make pretense of wrong that I have done him;
When all for mine—if I may call 't—offense   93
Must feel war's blow, who spares not innocence;   94
Which love to all, of which thyself art one,
Who now reprov'st me for 't—   96

HELICANUS Alas, sir!

PERICLES
Drew sleep out of mine eyes, blood from my cheeks,
Musings into my mind, with thousand doubts
How I might stop this tempest ere it came;
And finding little comfort to relieve them,
I thought it princely charity to grieve for them.

HELICANUS
Well, my lord, since you have given me leave to speak,
Freely will I speak. Antiochus you fear,
And justly too, I think, you fear the tyrant,
Who either by public war or private treason
Will take away your life.
Therefore, my lord, go travel for a while,
Till that his rage and anger be forgot,
Or till the Destinies do cut his thread of life.
Your rule direct to any; if to me,   111
Day serves not light more faithful than I'll be.

PERICLES I do not doubt thy faith;
But should he wrong my liberties in my absence?   114

---

82 careful protecting   **84 succeed** follow   **87 doubt** suspect   **88 open**
reveal   **90 unlaid ope** unrevealed   **93 all . . . offense** all (my subjects) for
my offense—if I may call it offense   **94 who** which, i.e., war   **96 now** just
now   **111 direct** delegate   **114 should he** what if he (Antiochus) should.
liberties royal rights and prerogatives, and those of my subjects

HELICANUS
  We'll mingle our bloods together in the earth,   115
  From whence we had our being and our birth.
PERICLES
  Tyre, I now look from thee, then, and to Tarsus
  Intend my travel, where I'll hear from thee,   118
  And by whose letters I'll dispose myself.
  The care I had and have of subjects' good
  On thee I lay, whose wisdom's strength can bear it.
  I'll take thy word for faith, not ask thine oath.
  Who shuns not to break one will sure crack both.   123
  But in our orbs we'll live so round and safe   124
  That time of both this truth shall ne'er convince: 125
  Thou showedst a subject's shine, I a true prince'.   126
                               Exeunt.

❖

1.3   *Enter Thaliard solus.*

THALIARD So, this is Tyre, and this the court. Here
must I kill King Pericles; and if I do it not, I am sure to
be hanged at home. 'Tis dangerous. Well, I perceive he 3
was a wise fellow and had good discretion that, being
bid to ask what he would of the King, desired he might
know none of his secrets. Now do I see he had some 6
reason for 't; for if a king bid a man be a villain, he's
bound by the indenture of his oath to be one. Husht! 8
Here comes the lords of Tyre.

    Enter Helicanus [*and*] *Escanes, with other lords*
    [*of Tyre*].

---

115 mingle . . . earth i.e., die fighting him **118 Intend** direct, purpose
123 Who he who **124 orbs** orbits, spheres. **round** with probity (but
punning on the idea of circularity in *round*. A line appears to be lost
here, rhyming with *safe*.) **125 time . . . convince** time will never confute
this truth regarding us two **126 shine** brightness, honor (as of true
gold). **prince'** prince's

1.3. Location: Tyre. The palace.
3–6 he . . . secrets (So the poet Philippides asked of Lysimachus; mentioned by Plutarch and Barnabe Riche.) **8 indenture** terms by which a
servant is bound to his master

HELICANUS
  You shall not need, my fellow peers of Tyre,
  Further to question me of your king's departure.
  His sealed commission, left in trust with me,   12
  Does speak sufficiently he's gone to travel.
THALIARD [*Aside*]   How? The King gone?
HELICANUS
  If further yet you will be satisfied
  Why, as it were, unlicensed of your loves   16
  He would depart, I'll give some light unto you.
  Being at Antioch—
THALIARD [*Aside*]   What from Antioch?
HELICANUS
  Royal Antiochus—on what cause I know not—
  Took some displeasure at him, at least he judged so;
  And doubting lest he had erred or sinned,   21
  To show his sorrow, he'd correct himself;   22
  So puts himself unto the shipman's toil,   23
  With whom each minute threatens life or death.
THALIARD [*Aside*]   Well, I perceive
  I shall not be hanged now, although I would;   26
  But since he's gone, the King's ears it must please
  He scaped the land, to perish at the seas.
  I'll present myself.—Peace to the lords of Tyre!
HELICANUS
  Lord Thaliard from Antiochus is welcome.
THALIARD   From him I come
  With message unto princely Pericles;
  But since my landing I have understood
  Your lord has betaken himself to unknown travels;
  Now message must return from whence it came.   35
HELICANUS
  We have no reason to desire it,   36
  Commended to our master, not to us.   37

---

12 sealed bearing the royal seal   **16 unlicensed . . . loves** without your
loving assent. (Cf. 1.2.35, note.)   **21 doubting lest** fearing that   **22 he'd
correct himself** he wished to impose a penalty on himself   **23 toil**
travail, hence dangers   **26 although I would** even though I wished to
be   **35 message** my message   **36 desire it** i.e., wish to know the message's contents. (Or *it* may refer to Thaliard's departure.)
37 Commended directed as it is

Yet ere you shall depart, this we desire,
As friends to Antioch, we may feast in Tyre.

Exeunt.

❖

1.4 *Enter Cleon, the Governor of Tarsus, with*
[Dionyza] his wife, and others.

CLEON
My Dionyza, shall we rest us here
And, by relating tales of others' griefs,
See if 'twill teach us to forget our own?
DIONYZA
That were to blow at fire in hope to quench it,
For who digs hills because they do aspire   5
Throws down one mountain to cast up a higher.
O my distressed lord, even such our griefs are;
Here they are but felt, and seen with mischief's eyes,   8
But like to groves, being topped, they higher rise.   9
CLEON O Dionyza,
Who wanteth food and will not say he wants it,   11
Or can conceal his hunger till he famish?   12
Our tongues and sorrows do sound deep our woes
Into the air; our eyes do weep till lungs
Fetch breath that may proclaim them louder, that, 15
If heaven slumber while their creatures want,   16
They may awake their helps to comfort them.   17
I'll then discourse our woes, felt several years,
And, wanting breath to speak, help me with tears.   19
DIONYZA I'll do my best, sir.
CLEON
This Tarsus, o'er which I have the government,

1.4. Location: Tarsus. The Governor's house.
5 who digs whoever digs up, removes. **aspire** mount up **8 Here
. . . eyes** i.e., our misfortunes seem bad enough in our present downcast
state. **mischief's** calamity's **9 topped** cut back. (If we inquire into our
present misfortunes they will only grow worse.) **11 wanteth** lacks
12 famish starve to death **15 them** i.e., *woes* (l. 13) **16 their creatures**
living beings, dependent on heaven's mercy **17 They . . . helps** i.e.,
mortals may awaken the assistance of the heavens **19 wanting** i.e.,
when I lack. **help me** i.e., you help me

A city on whom Plenty held full hand,   22
For Riches strewed herself even in her streets;   23
Whose towers bore heads so high they kissed the clouds,
And strangers ne'er beheld but wondered at;
Whose men and dames so jetted and adorned,   26
Like one another's glass to trim them by;   27
Their tables were stored full, to glad the sight,
And not so much to feed on as delight;
All poverty was scorned, and pride so great,
The name of help grew odious to repeat.   31
DIONYZA   O, 'tis too true.
CLEON
But see what heaven can do by this our change: 33
These mouths who but of late earth, sea, and air
Were all too little to content and please,
Although they gave their creatures in abundance,
As houses are defiled for want of use,   37
They are now starved for want of exercise.
Those palates who, not yet two summers younger,
Must have inventions to delight the taste,   40
Would now be glad of bread and beg for it.
Those mothers who, to nuzzle up their babes,   42
Thought naught too curious, are ready now   43
To eat those little darlings whom they loved.
So sharp are hunger's teeth that man and wife
Draw lots who first shall die to lengthen life.   46
Here stands a lord and there a lady weeping;
Here many sink, yet those which see them fall
Have scarce strength left to give them burial.
Is not this true?
DIONYZA
Our cheeks and hollow eyes do witness it.

22 on whom . . . hand over which Plenty poured her gifts generously
23 Riches (A singular concept, probably derived from the French *rich-
esse*, equivalent to "plenty"; the image is that of the cornucopia being
held aloft over the city.) her i.e., the city's   26 jetted strutted   27 glass
. . . by mirror by which to adorn themselves, or to mirror each other's
finery   31 The name . . . repeat i.e., that it became odious even to
mention the very possibility of asking for help   33 see . . . change see
by our change in fortune what heaven can do   37 for want through
lack   40 inventions novelties   42 nuzzle up nurture   43 naught too
curious nothing too choice (for their babes)   46 lengthen life i.e., provide food for the other to cannibalize

CLEON
O, let those cities that of Plenty's cup
And her prosperities so largely taste,
With their superfluous riots, hear these tears! 54
The misery of Tarsus may be theirs.

Enter a Lord.

LORD Where's the Lord Governor?
CLEON Here.
Speak out thy sorrows which thou bring'st in haste,
For comfort is too far for us to expect.
LORD
We have descried, upon our neighboring shore,
A portly sail of ships make hitherward. 61
CLEON I thought as much.
One sorrow never comes but brings an heir
That may succeed as his inheritor,
And so in ours. Some neighboring nation,
Taking advantage of our misery,
Hath stuffed these hollow vessels with their power
To beat us down, the which are down already,
And make a conquest of unhappy men,
Whereas no glory's got to overcome. 70
LORD
That's the least fear, for by the semblance 71
Of their white flags displayed they bring us peace,
And come to us as favorers, not as foes.
CLEON
Thou speak'st like him 's untutored to repeat: 74
Who makes the fairest show means most deceit. 75
But bring they what they will and what they can,
What need we fear?
Our ground's the lowest, and we are halfway there. 78
Go tell their general we attend him here,
To know for what he comes and whence he comes
And what he craves.

54 **superfluous riots** prodigal living.   **tears** i.e., sounds of weeping
51 **A portly . . . hitherward** a stately fleet of ships sails toward us
70 **Whereas . . . overcome** a conquest that brings no glory   71 **the least**
fear i.e., something not to be feared in the least   74 **him 's . . . repeat**
one who has never been taught to recite (the following maxim) and is
therefore unaware of its truth   75 **Who** he who   78 **Our . . . lowest** i.e.,
we can't be lower than the grave

LORD   I go, my lord.   [*Exit.*]
CLEON
  Welcome is peace, if he on peace consist;   83
  If wars, we are unable to resist.

    Enter Pericles with attendants.

PERICLES
  Lord Governor, for so we hear you are,
  Let not our ships and number of our men
  Be like a beacon fired t' amaze your eyes.   87
  We have heard your miseries as far as Tyre
  And seen the desolation of your streets;
  Nor come we to add sorrow to your tears,
  But to relieve them of their heavy load;
  And these our ships, you happily may think   92
  Are like the Trojan horse was stuffed within   93
  With bloody veins expecting overthrow,   94
  Are stored with corn to make your needy bread   95
  And give them life whom hunger starved half dead.
ALL [*Kneeling*]   The gods of Greece protect you!
  And we'll pray for you.
PERICLES   Arise, I pray you, rise.
  We do not look for reverence but for love,
  And harborage for ourself, our ships, and men.
CLEON [*Rising*]
  The which when any shall not gratify,   102
  Or pay you with unthankfulness in thought,
  Be it our wives, our children, or ourselves,
  The curse of heaven and men succeed their evils!   105
  Till when—the which I hope shall ne'er be seen—
  Your Grace is welcome to our town and us.
PERICLES
  Which welcome we'll accept, feast here awhile,
  Until our stars that frown lend us a smile.   *Exeunt.*

        ❖

83 on peace consist is resolved on peace   **87 amaze** terrify   **92 you
happily** which you perchance   **93 was** which was   **94 bloody veins** i.e.,
bloodthirsty Greek warriors.   **expecting overthrow** i.e., in anticipation
of the overthrow of Troy. (Or it perhaps modifies *you* in l. 92.)   **95 corn**
grain.   **your needy bread** desperately needed bread, or bread for your
needy people   **102 gratify** show gratitude for or toward   **105 succeed**
follow as a consequence of

2.0 *Enter Gower.*

GOWER

Here have you seen a mighty king
His child, iwis, to incest bring;   2
A better prince and benign lord,   3
That will prove awful both in deed and word.   4
Be quiet then as men should be,
Till he hath passed necessity.   6
I'll show you those in trouble's reign,   7
Losing a mite, a mountain gain.
The good in conversation,   9
To whom I give my benison,   10
Is still at Tarsus, where each man
Thinks all is writ he speken can;   12
And, to remember what he does,   13
Build his statue to make him glorious.
But tidings to the contrary   15
Are brought your eyes. What need speak I?

Dumb Show.

*Enter at one door Pericles talking with Cleon,
all the train with them. Enter at another door
a Gentleman, with a letter to Pericles; Pericles
shows the letter to Cleon; Pericles gives the
Messenger a reward, and knights him. Exit
Pericles at one door and Cleon at another.*

Good Helicane, that stayed at home—
Not to eat honey like a drone
From others' labors, for though he strive   19
To killen bad, keep good alive,
And to fulfill his prince' desire—

2.0.
2 iwis certainly   **3 A better prince** i.e., and you have also seen a better prince, Pericles   **4 awful** deserving of awe, respect   **6 necessity** those hardships imposed by fate   **7 those** i.e., those who   **9 The good in conversation** the good man (Pericles) in matters of conduct   **10 benison** blessing   **12 writ** holy writ.   **he speken can** that he (Pericles) speaks. (A deliberately medieval expression, as also in *killen, been, perishen,* and *Ne aught escapend,* lines 20, 28, 35, and 36.)   **13 remember** commemorate   **15 to the contrary** adverse   **19 for** (Difficult to explain as the text stands; some editors emend to "forth," others omit.)

Sends word of all that haps in Tyre:
How Thaliard came full bent with sin   23
And hid intent to murder him,   24
And that in Tarsus was not best
Longer for him to make his rest.
He, doing so, put forth to seas,   27
Where when men been there's seldom ease;   28
For now the wind begins to blow;
Thunder above and deeps below
Makes such unquiet that the ship
Should house him safe is wrecked and split,   32
And he, good prince, having all lost,
By waves from coast to coast is tossed.
All perishen of man, of pelf,   35
Ne aught escapend but himself;   36
Till fortune, tired with doing bad,
Threw him ashore, to give him glad.   38
And here he comes. What shall be next,
Pardon old Gower—this longs the text.   [*Exit.*] 40

2.1   *Enter Pericles, wet.*

PERICLES
Yet cease your ire, you angry stars of heaven!
Wind, rain, and thunder, remember earthly man   2
Is but a substance that must yield to you,
And I, as fits my nature, do obey you.
Alas, the seas hath cast me on the rocks,
Washed me from shore to shore, and left me breath
Nothing to think on but ensuing death.
Let it suffice the greatness of your powers
To have bereft a prince of all his fortunes,
And, having thrown him from your watery grave,
Here to have death in peace is all he'll crave.

23 **bent with** intent upon   24 **hid** hidden   27 **so** i.e., as advised
28 **been** are   32 **Should** that should   35 **pelf** goods, property   36 **Ne**
aught escapend nothing escaping   38 **glad** gladness   40 **longs the text**
belongs to the text of the play proper. (Or Gower may be saying that his
speech is now finished, being this long and no longer.)

2.1. Location: Pentapolis. The seaside.
2 **remember** remember that

Enter three Fishermen.

FIRST FISHERMAN   What, ho, Pilch!   12
SECOND FISHERMAN   Ha, come and bring away the nets!   13
FIRST FISHERMAN   What, Patchbreech, I say!   14
THIRD FISHERMAN   What say you, master?
FIRST FISHERMAN   Look how thou stirr'st now! Come   16
away, or I'll fetch th' with a wanion.   17
THIRD FISHERMAN   Faith, master, I am thinking of the
poor men that were cast away before us even now.   19
FIRST FISHERMAN   Alas, poor souls, it grieved my heart
to hear what pitiful cries they made to us to help them,
when, welladay, we could scarce help ourselves.   22
THIRD FISHERMAN   Nay, master, said not I as much
when I saw the porpoise how he bounced and tum-   24
bled? They say they're half fish, half flesh. A plague
on them, they ne'er come but I look to be washed.   26
Master, I marvel how the fishes live in the sea.
FIRST FISHERMAN   Why, as men do aland: the great   28
ones eat up the little ones. I can compare our rich mi-
sers to nothing so fitly as to a whale: 'a plays and tum-   30
bles, driving the poor fry before him, and at last devours them all at a mouthful. Such whales have I heard   32
on o' the land, who never leave gaping till they swal-   33
lowed the whole parish, church, steeple, bells, and all.
PERICLES [*Aside*]   A pretty moral.
THIRD FISHERMAN   But, master, if I had been the sexton,
I would have been that day in the belfry.
SECOND FISHERMAN   Why, man?
THIRD FISHERMAN   Because he should have swallowed
me too, and when I had been in his belly I would
have kept such a jangling of the bells that he should
never have left till he cast bells, steeple, church, and   42
parish up again. But if the good King Simonides were
of my mind—

12, 14 Pilch, Patchbreech (Names derived from the clothes they presumably wear; *Pilch*, a leather garment.)   13 bring away bring here, bring
along   16 Look . . . now i.e., get a move on   17 fetch th' deal you a
blow.   wanion vengeance   19 before us before our eyes   22 welladay
alas   24 porpoise (These actions of porpoises were recognized prognos-
tications of stormy weather.)   26 washed i.e., wetted by a storm
28 aland on the land   30 'a he   32–33 heard on heard of   42 cast
vomited

PERICLES [*Aside*] Simonides?

THIRD FISHERMAN We would purge the land of these
drones that rob the bee of her honey.

PERICLES [*Aside*]

How from the finny subject of the sea   48
These fishers tell the infirmities of men,
And from their watery empire recollect   50
All that may men approve or men detect!—   51
Peace be at your labor, honest fishermen.   52

SECOND FISHERMAN "Honest," good fellow? What's that? 53
If it be a day fits you, search out of the calendar, and 54
nobody look after it.   55

PERICLES

May see the sea hath cast upon your coast—   56

SECOND FISHERMAN What a drunken knave was the sea
to cast thee in our way!   58

PERICLES

A man whom both the waters and the wind,
In that vast tennis court, hath made the ball
For them to play upon, entreats you pity him.
He asks of you that never used to beg.   62

FIRST FISHERMAN No, friend, cannot you beg? Here's
them in our country of Greece gets more with begging
than we can do with working.

SECOND FISHERMAN Canst thou catch any fishes, then?

PERICLES I never practiced it.

SECOND FISHERMAN Nay then, thou wilt starve, sure,
for here's nothing to be got nowadays unless thou
canst fish for 't.   70

PERICLES

What I have been I have forgot to know,
But what I am, want teaches me to think on:
A man thronged up with cold. My veins are chill,   73
And have no more of life than may suffice

48 subject i.e., residents, citizens **50 recollect** gather up **51 may
. . . detect** may commend men or expose them **52–55 Peace . . . after it**
(Most commentators think something lost here, perhaps a line in which
Pericles bids the fishermen good day; if so, the Second Fisherman's
reply could mean, "if the day fits your wretched condition, scratch it
out of the calendar and let no one miss it.") **56 May** you may **58 cast**
(punning on *vomit*, as suggested by *drunken*; see l. 42) **62 used** made it
a practice **70 fish for 't** i.e., obtain it by sly means and insinuation
73 thronged up overwhelmed

To give my tongue that heat to ask your help—
Which if you shall refuse, when I am dead,
For that I am a man, pray you see me buried.   77

FIRST FISHERMAN   Die, quotha? Now gods forbid 't, an I   78
have a gown here! Come, put it on, keep thee warm.
[*He gives a garment; Pericles puts it on.*] Now, afore me,   80
a handsome fellow! Come, thou shalt go home, and
we'll have flesh for holidays, fish for fasting days, and
moreo'er puddings and flapjacks, and thou shalt be   83
welcome.

PERICLES   I thank you, sir.

SECOND FISHERMAN   Hark you, my friend. You said you
could not beg?

PERICLES   I did but crave.   88

SECOND FISHERMAN   But crave? Then I'll turn craver too,
and so I shall scape whipping.   90

PERICLES   Why, are your beggars whipped, then?

SECOND FISHERMAN   O, not all, my friend, not all; for if
all your beggars were whipped, I would wish no better
office than to be beadle. But, master, I'll go draw up   94
the net.   [*Exit with Third Fisherman.*]

PERICLES [*Aside*]
How well this honest mirth becomes their labor!   96

FIRST FISHERMAN   Hark you, sir, do you know where ye
are?

PERICLES   Not well.

FIRST FISHERMAN   Why, I'll tell you. This is called Pentapolis, and our king the good Simonides.

PERICLES   "The good Simonides" do you call him?

FIRST FISHERMAN   Ay, sir, and he deserves so to be called
for his peaceable reign and good government.

PERICLES   He is a happy king, since he gains from his
subjects the name of "good" by his government. How
far is his court distant from this shore?

---

77 For that because   **78 quotha** says he.   **an** if, so long as   **80 afore me**
(A mild oath.)   **83 puddings** sausages   **88 crave** request   **90 scape**
whipping i.e., escape the punishment for begging (as required by Elizabethan law. The Second Fisherman jokes that *crave* is only a polite term
for *beg*.)   **94 beadle** parish official responsible for administering corporal punishment (who would be busy and well paid if all those who beg
under the pretext of seeking favor at court were to be whipped)
96 becomes suits

FIRST FISHERMAN   Marry, sir, half a day's journey. And 108
I'll tell you, he hath a fair daughter, and tomorrow is
her birthday; and there are princes and knights come
from all parts of the world to joust and tourney for her 111
love.

PERICLES   Were my fortunes equal to my desires, I could
wish to make one there.   114

FIRST FISHERMAN   O, sir, things must be as they may;
and what a man cannot get, he may lawfully deal for
his wife's soul.   117

> *Enter the two [other] Fishermen, drawing
> up a net.*

SECOND FISHERMAN   Help, master, help! Here's a fish
hangs in the net like a poor man's right in the law;
'twill hardly come out. Ha! Bots on 't, 'tis come at last, 120
and 'tis turned to a rusty armor.

> *[He hauls in Pericles' armor.]*

PERICLES
An armor, friends? I pray you, let me see it.
Thanks, Fortune, yet that after all my crosses   123
Thou givest me somewhat to repair myself;
And though it was mine own, part of my heritage,   125
Which my dead father did bequeath to me
With this strict charge, even as he left his life:
"Keep it, my Pericles; it hath been a shield
Twixt me and death," and pointed to this brace;   129
"For that it saved me, keep it. In like necessity—   130
The which the gods protect thee from!—may 't
   defend thee."
It kept where I kept, I so dearly loved it,   132
Till the rough seas, that spares not any man,
Took it in rage, though calmed have given 't again.
I thank thee for 't. My shipwreck now's no ill,
Since I have here my father gave in his will.   136

---

108 Marry (A mild oath, originally "by the Virgin Mary.")   **111 tourney**
take part in a tournament   **114 make one** be among those   **117 his
wife's soul** (A difficult line; the text may be imperfect here.)   **120 Bots
on 't** i.e., plague take it. (*Bots* is a disease of horses.)   **123 crosses**
thwartings, misfortunes   **125 And though** even though   **129 brace**
mailed arm protector   **130 For that** because. **like** similar   **132 kept**
lodged   **136 my father** what my father

FIRST FISHERMAN   What mean you, sir?
PERICLES
  To beg of you, kind friends, this coat of worth,   138
  For it was sometime target to a king;   139
  I know it by this mark. He loved me dearly,
  And for his sake I wish the having of it,
  And that you'd guide me to your sovereign's court,
  Where with it I may appear a gentleman.
  And if that ever my low fortune's better,
  I'll pay your bounties; till then rest your debtor.   145
FIRST FISHERMAN   Why, wilt thou tourney for the lady?
PERICLES
  I'll show the virtue I have borne in arms.   147
FIRST FISHERMAN   Why, d' ye take it, and the gods give
  thee good on 't!   [Pericles puts it on.]   149
SECOND FISHERMAN   Ay, but hark you, my friend, 'twas
  we that made up this garment through the rough
  seams of the waters. There are certain condolements,   152
  certain vails. I hope, sir, if you thrive, you'll remember   153
  from whence you had them.   154
PERICLES   Believe 't, I will.
  By your furtherance I am clothed in steel,
  And spite of all the rapture of the sea   157
  This jewel holds his building on my arm.   158
  Unto thy value I will mount myself   159
  Upon a courser, whose delightful steps   160
  Shall make the gazer joy to see him tread.
  Only, my friend, I yet am unprovided
  Of a pair of bases.   163
SECOND FISHERMAN   We'll sure provide. Thou shalt have
  my best gown to make thee a pair; and I'll bring thee
  to the court myself.

---

138 coat i.e., armor, coat of mail   **139 target** shield, i.e., protector
145 pay repay.   **bounties** acts of generosity   **147 virtue** bravery,
knightly qualities   **149 on 't** of it, from it   **152 seams** (The metaphor is
from tailoring, as if the furrowed waves of the sea were seams.)
condolements (Probably confused with or derived from "dole.")
153 vails (1) perquisites, tips (2) tailors' remnants of cloth   **154 them**
i.e., the pieces of armor   **157 rapture** plundering   **158 holds his building** occupies its proper place (and will provide a means to buy a
courser)   **159 thy** i.e., the jewel's   **160 courser** spirited horse
163 bases pleated skirts attached to the doublet and reaching from the
waist to the knee, worn under the armor by a mounted knight

PERICLES

Then honor be but a goal to my will,   167
This day I'll rise, or else add ill to ill.   [*Exeunt.*]

✤

2.2   *Enter [King] Simonides, with attendance, and*
          Thaisa, [and take their places].

SIMONIDES

Are the knights ready to begin the triumph?   1
FIRST LORD   They are, my liege,
And stay your coming to present themselves.   3
SIMONIDES

Return them we are ready; and our daughter,   4
In honor of whose birth these triumphs are,
Sits here like Beauty's child, whom Nature gat   6
For men to see and, seeing, wonder at.   [*Exit one.*]
THAISA

It pleaseth you, my royal Father, to express
My commendations great, whose merit's less.
SIMONIDES

It's fit it should be so, for princes are   10
A model which heaven makes like to itself.
As jewels lose their glory if neglected,
So princes their renowns if not respected.
'Tis now your honor, daughter, to entertain   14
The labor of each knight in his device.   15
THAISA

Which, to preserve mine honor, I'll perform.

      The First Knight passes by [and his Squire
      presents his shield to the Princess].

SIMONIDES

Who is the first that doth prefer himself?   17

---

167 Then . . . will provided honor be the sole aim of my undertaking

**2.2. Location: Pentapolis. A public way leading to the lists. A pavilion
by the side of it for the reception of the King, Princess, Lords, etc.**
1 triumph tournament, festive spectacle   **3 stay** await   **4 Return** reply
to   **6 gat** begot   **10 princes** persons, both male and female, of royal
rank   **14 honor** i.e., honorable duty.   **entertain** receive, review
15 device emblem with motto on the knights' shields   **17 prefer** present

THAISA
  A knight of Sparta, my renownèd father,
  And the device he bears upon his shield
  Is a black Ethiop reaching at the sun;
  The word, *Lux tua vita mihi.*   21
SIMONIDES
  He loves you well that holds his life of you.
                                      The Second Knight [*passes by*].
  Who is the second that presents himself?
THAISA
  A prince of Macedon, my royal Father,
  And the device he bears upon his shield
  Is an armed knight that's conquered by a lady;
  The motto thus, in Spanish, *Piùe per dolcezza che per
    forza.*   *Third Knight* [*passes by*].   27
SIMONIDES
  And what's the third?
THAISA   The third of Antioch,
  And his device, a wreath of chivalry;   29
  The word, *Me pompae provexit apex.*   30
                                      Fourth Knight [*passes by*].
SIMONIDES   What is the fourth?
THAISA
  A burning torch that's turnèd upside down;
  The word, *Quod me alit, me extinguit.*   33
SIMONIDES
  Which shows that beauty hath his power and will,   34
  Which can as well inflame as it can kill.
                                      Fifth Knight [*passes by*].
THAISA
  The fifth, an hand environèd with clouds,
  Holding out gold that's by the touchstone tried;   37
  The motto thus, *Sic spectanda fides.*   38
                                 Sixth Knight, [*Pericles, passes by;*
                                 he himself presents his device to Thaisa].

---

21 word motto. **Lux . . . mihi** your light is my life. (Latin; also at ll. 30,
33, 38, 44.)   **27 Piùe . . . forza** more by gentleness than by force. (Italian,
not Spanish.)   **29 wreath of chivalry** twisted band joining the crest to
the knight's helmet   **30 Me . . . apex** the highest summit of honor has
led me on   **33 Quod . . . extinguit** who feeds my flame puts out my
light   **34 his** its   **37 touchstone** flint used to test gold for purity   **38 Sic
spectanda fides** thus is faith to be tried

SIMONIDES And what's
The sixth and last, the which the knight himself
With such a graceful courtesy delivered?

THAISA
He seems to be a stranger; but his present is   42
A withered branch, that's only green at top;
The motto, *In hac spe vivo*.   44

SIMONIDES A pretty moral;
From the dejected state wherein he is,
He hopes by you his fortunes yet may flourish.

FIRST LORD
He had need mean better than his outward show   48
Can any way speak in his just commend,   49
For by his rusty outside he appears
To have practiced more the whipstock than the lance.   51

SECOND LORD
He well may be a stranger, for he comes
To an honored triumph strangely furnished.   53

THIRD LORD
And on set purpose let his armor rust
Until this day, to scour it in the dust.   55

SIMONIDES
Opinion's but a fool, that makes us scan   56
The outward habit by the inward man.   57
But stay, the knights are coming.
We will withdraw into the gallery.   [*Exeunt.*] 59
                    Great shouts [within], and all cry
                              "The mean knight!"

❖

42 present presented device   **44 In . . . vivo** in this hope I live
48–49 He . . . commend i.e., he'd certainly better have some nobler
meaning, more than his present wretched outward appearance can in
any way speak to commend him.   **commend** commendation
51 whipstock handle of a whip (which he would use to drive work-
horses)   **53 strangely** (The witticism plays on *strangely*, oddly, and
stranger, a visitor from a foreign land.)   **55 scour** (The joke is that he
will polish his rusty armor by falling off his horse in the dust.)
56 Opinion judgment of a person's worth in terms of mere reputation
56–57 scan . . . man i.e., interpret the inner person by his mere exterior.
(The construction is inverted and probably corrupt.)   **59 s.d. mean**
humble, undistinguished in appearance

2.3   [*A banquet prepared.*] *Enter the King*
        [*Simonides, Thaisa, Marshal, Ladies, Lords,*
        attendants], *and Knights from tilting*, [*in*
        armor].

SIMONIDES   Knights,
  To say you're welcome were superfluous.
  To place upon the volume of your deeds,
  As in a title page, your worth in arms
  Were more than you expect or more than's fit,
  Since every worth in show commends itself.   6
  Prepare for mirth, for mirth becomes a feast.   7
  You are princes and my guests.
THAISA [*To Pericles*]   But you my knight and guest,   9
  To whom this wreath of victory I give
  And crown you king of this day's happiness.
                    [*She crowns Pericles with a wreath.*]
PERICLES
  'Tis more by fortune, lady, than by merit.
SIMONIDES
  Call it by what you will, the day is yours,
  And here, I hope, is none that envies it.
  In framing an artist, art hath thus decreed: 15
  To make some good but others to exceed;
  And you are her labored scholar.—Come, queen o'
      the feast—   17
  For, daughter, so you are—here take your place.
  [*To the Marshal.*] Marshal, the rest, as they deserve their
      grace.   19
KNIGHTS
  We are honored much by good Simonides.
                    [*They take their places.*]
SIMONIDES
  Your presence glads our days. Honor we love,
  For who hates honor hates the gods above.   22

2.3. Location: Pentapolis. The palace.
6 in show by being revealed through deeds   **7 becomes** suits   **9 you** you
are   **15 framing** making   **17 her labored scholar** the one on whom art
has bestowed the most pains   **19 the rest** i.e., place the rest of the
company.   **grace** favor   **22 who** he who

MARSHAL [*To Pericles*]   Sir, yonder is your place.
PERICLES   Some other is more fit.
FIRST KNIGHT
  Contend not, sir, for we are gentlemen
  Have neither in our hearts nor outward eyes   26
  Envied the great, nor shall the low despise.
PERICLES   You are right courteous knights.
SIMONIDES   Sit, sir, sit.   [*They sit.*]
  [*Aside.*] By Jove, I wonder, that is king of thoughts,   30
  These cates resist me, he not thought upon.   31
THAISA [*Aside*]
  By Juno, that is queen of marriage,
  All viands that I eat do seem unsavory,
  Wishing him my meat. [*To Simonides.*] Sure he's a
    gallant gentleman.
SIMONIDES [*To Thaisa*]
  He's but a country gentleman.
  He's done no more than other knights have done;
  He's broken a staff or so. So let it pass.
THAISA [*Aside*]
  To me he seems like diamond to glass.   38
PERICLES [*Aside*]
  Yon king's to me like to my father's picture,
  Which tells me in that glory once he was—   40
  Had princes sit like stars about his throne,
  And he the sun for them to reverence.
  None that beheld him but, like lesser lights,
  Did vail their crowns to his supremacy;   44
  Where now his son's like a glowworm in the night,   45
  The which hath fire in darkness, none in light.
  Whereby I see that Time's the king of men;
  He's both their parent and he is their grave,
  And gives them what he will, not what they crave.
SIMONIDES   What, are you merry, knights?

---

26 Have who have.   **outward eyes** i.e., eyes that see outward   **30-31 By Jove . . . upon** by Jove, who rules over human thoughts, I marvel that these delicacies do not seem appealing to me, since I would rather be thinking about him (Pericles)   **38 to** compared with   **40 that** similar, like   **44 vail** remove submissively   **45 glowworm in the night** i.e., a glowworm, best seen at night, but paled by the light of day (as the next line makes clear)

KNIGHTS
  Who can be other in this royal presence?
SIMONIDES
  Here, with a cup that's stored unto the brim—
  As you do love, fill to your mistress' lips—   53
  We drink this health to you.   [*He drinks a toast.*]
KNIGHTS   We thank Your Grace.
SIMONIDES   Yet pause awhile.
  Yon knight doth sit too melancholy,
  As if the entertainment in our court
  Had not a show might countervail his worth.   58
  Note it not you, Thaisa?
THAISA   What is 't to me, my Father?
SIMONIDES   O, attend, my daughter. Princes in this
  Should live like gods above, who freely give
  To everyone that come to honor them;
  And princes not doing so are like to gnats,
  Which make a sound but, killed, are wondered at.   65
  Therefore to make his entrance more sweet,
  Here, say we drink this standing-bowl of wine to him.   67
                              [*He drinks a toast.*]
THAISA
  Alas, my Father, it befits not me
  Unto a stranger knight to be so bold.
  He may my proffer take for an offense,
  Since men take women's gifts for impudence.
SIMONIDES   How?
  Do as I bid you, or you'll move me else.   73
THAISA [*Aside*]
  Now, by the gods, he could not please me better.
SIMONIDES
  And furthermore tell him we desire to know of him
  Of whence he is, his name and parentage.
THAISA [*Going to Pericles*]
  The King my father, sir, has drunk to you—
PERICLES   I thank him.

53 fill . . . lips i.e., each knight is to drink a full cup to his mistress
58 might countervail that could equal   **65 are wondered at** i.e., cause
amazement at the loud noise such small insects could make while
living   **67 standing-bowl** drinking vessel that stands on feet or on stem
and base   **73 move** anger

THAISA
　Wishing it so much blood unto your life.   79
PERICLES
　I thank both him and you, and pledge him freely.   80
THAISA
　And further, he desires to know of you
　Of whence you are, your name and parentage.
PERICLES
　A gentleman of Tyre, my name Pericles,
　My education been in arts and arms;   84
　Who, looking for adventures in the world,
　Was by the rough seas reft of ships and men,   86
　And after shipwreck driven upon this shore.
THAISA [*Returning to the King*]
　He thanks Your Grace; names himself Pericles,
　A gentleman of Tyre,
　Who only by misfortune of the seas,
　Bereft of ships and men, cast on this shore.   91
SIMONIDES
　Now, by the gods, I pity his misfortune
　And will awake him from his melancholy.—
　Come, gentlemen, we sit too long on trifles
　And waste the time which looks for other revels.
　Even in your armors, as you are addressed,   96
　Will well become a soldier's dance.   97
　I will not have excuse with saying this: 98
　Loud music is too harsh for ladies' heads,   99
　Since they love men in arms as well as beds.
　　　　　　　　　　　　　They dance.
　So this was well asked, 'twas so well performed.   101
　Come, sir,   [*Presenting Thaisa to Pericles*]
　Here's a lady that wants breathing too.   103
　And I have heard you knights of Tyre

---

79 Wishing . . . life (Wine was thought to replenish the blood.)
80 pledge him drink his health (in a return toast)　**84 been** has been.
arts and arms liberal education and military training　**86 reft** bereft
91 cast was cast　**96 addressed** accoutered　**97 Will** you will　**98 have
. . . this** allow any excuses to what I say　**99 Loud music** i.e., noise of
armor (?) (The next line punningly suggests a play on *men in arms* and
partners in bed.)　**101 So . . . asked** just as this was well worth suggesting　**103 breathing** exercise

Are excellent in making ladies trip,   105
And that their measures are as excellent.   106
PERICLES
In those that practice them they are, my lord.
SIMONIDES
O, that's as much as you would be denied   108
Of your fair courtesy.   *They dance.*
                    Unclasp, unclasp!   109
Thanks, gentlemen, to all; all have done well,
[*To Pericles*] But you the best.—Pages and lights, to
    conduct
These knights unto their several lodgings! [*To Pericles.*]
    Yours, sir,
We have given order to be next our own.
PERICLES   I am at Your Grace's pleasure.
SIMONIDES
Princes, it is too late to talk of love,
And that's the mark I know you level at.   116
Therefore each one betake him to his rest.
Tomorrow all for speeding do their best.   [*Exeunt.*] 118

❖

2.4   *Enter Helicanus and Escanes.*

HELICANUS   No, Escanes, know this of me,
Antiochus from incest lived not free;
For which, the most high gods not minding longer   3
To withhold the vengeance that they had in store
Due to this heinous capital offense,
Even in the height and pride of all his glory,
When he was seated in a chariot of
An inestimable value, and his daughter with him,
A fire from heaven came and shriveled up
Those bodies even to loathing; for they so stunk

---

105 trip dance lightly (with a suggestion of "go astray") **106 measures**
stately, formal dances (with sexual suggestion) **108–109 that's . . .**
courtesy that's the equivalent of your denial of your accomplishment
out of politeness **116 level** aim **118 speeding** succeeding (as wooers)

2.4. Location: Tyre. The Governor's house.
3 minding intending

That all those eyes adored them ere their fall   11
Scorn now their hand should give them burial.

ESCANES
  'Twas very strange.

HELICANUS   And yet but justice, for though
This king were great, his greatness was no guard
To bar heaven's shaft, but sin had his reward.   15

ESCANES 'Tis very true.

     Enter two or three Lords.

FIRST LORD
  See, not a man in private conference
Or council has respect with him but he.   18

SECOND LORD
  It shall no longer grieve without reproof.   19

THIRD LORD
  And cursed be he that will not second it.

FIRST LORD
  Follow me, then.—Lord Helicane, a word.

HELICANUS
  With me? And welcome. Happy day, my lords.

FIRST LORD
  Know that our griefs are risen to the top,   23
And now at length they overflow their banks.

HELICANUS
  Your griefs? For what? Wrong not your prince you love.

FIRST LORD
  Wrong not yourself, then, noble Helicane;
But if the Prince do live, let us salute him,
Or know what ground's made happy by his breath.
If in the world he live, we'll seek him out;
If in his grave he rest, we'll find him there,
And be resolved he lives to govern us,   31
Or dead, give 's cause to mourn his funeral
And leave us to our free election.

SECOND LORD
  Whose death's indeed the strongest in our censure;   34

---

11 adored that adored **15 his** its **18 respect** influence. **he** i.e., Escanes **19 grieve without reproof** cause grievance without (our) protest **23 griefs** grievances (also in line 25) **31 resolved** satisfied, assured **34 Whose . . . censure** and indeed his death is the likeliest probability in our judgment

And knowing this kingdom is without a head—
Like goodly buildings left without a roof   36
Soon fall to ruin—your noble self,
That best know how to rule and how to reign,
We thus submit unto, our sovereign.

ALL   Live, noble Helicane!

HELICANUS
Try honor's cause; forbear your suffrages.   41
If that you love Prince Pericles, forbear.   42
Take I your wish, I leap into the seas,   43
Where's hourly trouble for a minute's ease.
A twelvemonth longer let me entreat you
To forbear the absence of your king,   46
If in which time expired he not return,
I shall with agèd patience bear your yoke.
But if I cannot win you to this love,   49
Go search like nobles, like noble subjects,
And in your search spend your adventurous worth;   51
Whom if you find, and win unto return,   52
You shall like diamonds sit about his crown.

FIRST LORD
To wisdom he's a fool that will not yield;
And since Lord Helicane enjoineth us,
We with our travels will endeavor.   56

HELICANUS
Then you love us, we you, and we'll clasp hands.
When peers thus knit, a kingdom ever stands.

                                        [*Exeunt.*]

❖

2.5   *Enter the King* [*Simonides*], *reading of a letter,
         at one door; the Knights meet him.*

FIRST KNIGHT
Good morrow to the good Simonides.

36 **Like** as   41 **Try . . . suffrages** i.e., follow the honorable course;
refrain from choosing me in your *free election* (l. 33)   42 **If that** if
43 **Take . . . wish** if I should act on your wish   46 **forbear** put up with
49 **love** act of loyal devotion   51 **your adventurous worth** the wealth you
have to adventure   52 **win unto return** persuade him to return
56 **endeavor** i.e., try to find him

2.5. Location: Pentapolis. The palace.

SIMONIDES
　Knights, from my daughter this I let you know,
　That for this twelvemonth she'll not undertake
　A married life.
　Her reason to herself is only known,
　Which from her by no means can I get.
SECOND KNIGHT
　May we not get access to her, my lord?
SIMONIDES
　Faith, by no means. She hath so strictly tied
　Her to her chamber that 'tis impossible.
　One twelve moons more she'll wear Diana's livery.   10
　This by the eye of Cynthia hath she vowed,   11
　And on her virgin honor will not break it.
THIRD KNIGHT
　Loath to bid farewell, we take our leaves.

　　　　　　　　　　　　[*Exeunt Knights.*]

SIMONIDES So,
　They are well dispatched. Now to my daughter's letter.
　She tells me here she'll wed the stranger knight,
　Or nevermore to view nor day nor light.   17
　'Tis well, mistress. Your choice agrees with mine;
　I like that well. Nay, how absolute she's in 't,   19
　Not minding whether I dislike or no!
　Well, I do commend her choice
　And will no longer have it be delayed.
　Soft, here he comes. I must dissemble it.

　　　Enter Pericles.

PERICLES
　All fortune to the good Simonides!
SIMONIDES
　To you as much! Sir, I am beholding to you   25
　For your sweet music this last night. I do
　Protest my ears were never better fed
　With such delightful pleasing harmony.

---

10 wear Diana's livery continue to serve Diana, goddess of chastity
11 Cynthia the moon goddess, equated with Diana   **17 nor day nor**
either day or. (A double negative.)   **19 absolute** unconditional, positive
25 beholding beholden

PERICLES
It is Your Grace's pleasure to commend,
Not my desert.
SIMONIDES   Sir, you are music's master.
PERICLES
The worst of all her scholars, my good lord.
SIMONIDES   Let me ask you one thing:
What do you think of my daughter, sir?
PERICLES   A most virtuous princess.
SIMONIDES   And she is fair too, is she not?
PERICLES
As a fair day in summer, wondrous fair.
SIMONIDES
Sir, my daughter thinks very well of you,
Ay, so well that you must be her master
And she will be your scholar. Therefore look to it.
PERICLES
I am unworthy for her schoolmaster.
SIMONIDES
She thinks not so. Peruse this writing else.   41
                     [*He gives a letter.*]
PERICLES [*Aside*]   What's here?
A letter, that she loves the knight of Tyre!
'Tis the King's subtlety to have my life.—   44
O, seek not to entrap me, gracious lord,
A stranger and distressèd gentleman,
That never aimed so high to love your daughter,   47
But bent all offices to honor her.   48
SIMONIDES
Thou hast bewitched my daughter, and thou art
A villain.
PERICLES   By the gods, I have not!
Never did thought of mine levy offense,   52
Nor never did my actions yet commence
A deed might gain her love or your displeasure.   54
SIMONIDES
Traitor, thou liest!

---

41 else i.e., if you don't believe me   **44 subtlety** trick   **47 to** as to
48 bent all offices devoted all my service   **52 levy** raise, collect, receive;
or perhaps level, aim at (?)   **54 might** that might

PERICLES   Traitor?
SIMONIDES   Ay, traitor.
PERICLES
  Even in his throat—unless it be the King—
  That calls me traitor, I return the lie.
SIMONIDES [*Aside*]
  Now, by the gods, I do applaud his courage.
PERICLES
  My actions are as noble as my thoughts,
  That never relished of a base descent.   60
  I came unto your court for honor's cause,
  And not to be a rebel to her state;   62
  And he that otherwise accounts of me,
  This sword shall prove he's honor's enemy.
SIMONIDES No?
  Here comes my daughter. She can witness it.

        Enter Thaisa.

PERICLES
  Then, as you are as virtuous as fair,
  Resolve your angry father if my tongue   68
  Did e'er solicit, or my hand subscribe
  To any syllable that made love to you.
THAISA
  Why, sir, say if you had, who takes offense
  At that would make me glad?   72
SIMONIDES
  Yea, mistress, are you so peremptory?   73
  (*Aside.*) I am glad on 't with all my heart.—
  I'll tame you; I'll bring you in subjection!
  Will you, not having my consent,
  Bestow your love and your affections
  Upon a stranger? (*Aside.*) Who, for aught I know,
  May be, nor can I think the contrary,
  As great in blood as I myself.—
  Therefore hear you, mistress: either frame   81
  Your will to mine—and you, sir, hear you—

---

60 relished of showed any trace of   **62 her** i.e., honor's   **68 Resolve**
satisfy, explain to   **72 that** that which   **73 peremptory** willfully determined   **81 frame** accommodate, shape

Either be ruled by me, or I'll make you—
Man and wife.
Nay, come, your hands and lips must seal it too.
And being joined, I'll thus your hopes destroy;
And for further grief—God give you joy!
What, are you both pleased?

THAISA　Yes, if you love me, sir.

PERICLES
Even as my life my blood that fosters it.　　　　　90

SIMONIDES　What, are you both agreed?

BOTH　Yes, if 't please Your Majesty.

SIMONIDES
It pleaseth me so well that I will see you wed,
And then, with what haste you can, get you to bed.
　　　　　　　　　　　　　　　　　　Exeunt.

❖

90 my life i.e., my life loves

3.0   *Enter Gower.*

GOWER
Now sleep yslakèd hath the rout;   1
No din but snores the house about,
Made louder by the o'erfed breast
Of this most pompous marriage feast.   4
The cat, with eyne of burning coal,   5
Now couches 'fore the mouse's hole,
And crickets sing at the oven's mouth,
Are the blither for their drouth.   8
Hymen hath brought the bride to bed,   9
Where, by the loss of maidenhead,
A babe is molded. Be attent,   11
And time that is so briefly spent
With your fine fancies quaintly eche.   13
What's dumb in show I'll plain with speech.   14

[*Dumb Show.*]

*Enter Pericles and Simonides, at one door, with
attendants. A Messenger meets them, kneels, and
gives Pericles a letter. Pericles shows it
Simonides; the Lords kneel to him [Pericles].
Then enter Thaisa with child, with Lychorida, a
nurse. The King shows her the letter; she rejoices.
She and Pericles take leave of her father and
depart [with Lychorida and their attendants.
Then exeunt Simonides and the rest.]*

By many a dern and painful perch   15
Of Pericles the careful search,
By the four opposing coigns   17
Which the world together joins,
Is made with all due diligence
That horse and sail and high expense

3.0.
1 yslakèd laid to rest.   **rout** whole crowd, assembly   **4 pompous** ceremonial, splendid   **5 eyne** eyes   **8 Are . . . drouth** (and) are the happier for their dryness   **9 Hymen** god of marriage   **11 attent** attentive **13 quaintly eche** cleverly eke out   **14 plain** make plain   **15 dern** dark, drear.   **perch** measure of land   **17 coigns** corners, compass points

Can stead the quest. At last from Tyre,   21
Fame answering the most strange inquire,   22
To th' court of King Simonides
Are letters brought, the tenor these:
Antiochus and his daughter dead,
The men of Tyrus on the head
Of Helicanus would set on
The crown of Tyre, but he will none.
The mutiny he there hastes t' appease;
Says to 'em, if King Pericles
Come not home in twice six moons,
He, obedient to their dooms,   32
Will take the crown. The sum of this,
Brought hither to Pentapolis,
Yravishèd the regions round,   35
And everyone with claps can sound,   36
"Our heir apparent is a king!
Who dreamt, who thought of such a thing?"
Brief, he must hence depart to Tyre.   39
His queen, with child, makes her desire—
Which who shall cross?—along to go.
Omit we all their dole and woe.   42
Lychorida, her nurse, she takes,
And so to sea. Their vessel shakes
On Neptune's billow; half the flood   45
Hath their keel cut. But Fortune's mood   46
Varies again; the grizzled North   47
Disgorges such a tempest forth
That, as a duck for life that dives,
So up and down the poor ship drives.
The lady shrieks and, well anear,   51
Does fall in travail with her fear;   52
And what ensues in this fell storm   53
Shall for itself itself perform.
I nill relate; action may   55
Conveniently the rest convey,

21 stead assist **22 Fame . . . inquire** rumor answering inquiry into the
most remote areas **32 dooms** judgments **35 Yravishèd** delighted
36 can sound began to proclaim **39 Brief** in short **42 dole** sorrow (of
leavetaking) **45–46 half . . . cut** i.e., their vessel has completed half the
voyage **47 grizzled** gray, grizzly **51 well anear** alas **52 travail** labor
53 fell fierce **55 nill** will not

Which might not what by me is told.   57
In your imagination hold   58
This stage the ship, upon whose deck
The sea-tossed Pericles appears to speak.   [*Exit.*] 60

3.1   *Enter Pericles, a-shipboard.*

PERICLES
    Thou god of this great vast, rebuke these surges,   1
    Which wash both heaven and hell! And thou that hast   2
    Upon the winds command, bind them in brass,
    Having called them from the deep! O, still
    Thy deafening, dreadful thunders; gently quench   5
    Thy nimble, sulfurous flashes!—O, how, Lychorida,
    How does my queen?—Thou stormest venomously;
    Wilt thou spit all thyself? The seaman's whistle
    Is as a whisper in the ears of death,   9
    Unheard.—Lychorida!—Lucina, O   10
    Divinest patroness and midwife gentle
    To those that cry by night, convey thy deity
    Aboard our dancing boat; make swift the pangs
    Of my queen's travails!

      Enter Lychorida [with an infant].

              Now, Lychorida!
LYCHORIDA
    Here is a thing too young for such a place,
    Who, if it had conceit, would die, as I   16
    Am like to do. Take in your arms this piece   17
    Of your dead queen.
PERICLES   How? How, Lychorida?

57 Which . . . told which action could not dramatize easily the story I've just told   **58 hold** suppose   **60 appears to speak** appears and speaks

3.1. Location: A ship at sea.
1 Thou god i.e., Neptune.   **vast** expanse (of sea)   **2 thou** i.e., Aeolus, god of the winds   **5 Thy** i.e., Jupiter, god of thunder   **9–10 Is . . . Unheard** is no more audible than a whisper in the ears of a dead person   **10 Lucina** goddess of childbirth (as at 1.1.9)   **16 conceit** understanding (of its precarious position)   **17 like** likely

LYCHORIDA
   Patience, good sir. Do not assist the storm.   19
   Here's all that is left living of your queen,
   A little daughter. For the sake of it,
   Be manly and take comfort. [*She gives him the child.*]
PERICLES   O you gods!
   Why do you make us love your goodly gifts
   And snatch them straight away? We here below
   Recall not what we give, and therein may   25
   Use honor with you.
LYCHORIDA   Patience, good sir,   26
   Even for this charge.
PERICLES   Now, mild may be thy life!   27
   For a more blustrous birth had never babe.
   Quiet and gentle thy conditions! For   29
   Thou art the rudeliest welcome to this world   30
   That ever was prince's child. Happy what follows!
   Thou hast as chiding a nativity
   As fire, air, water, earth, and heaven can make
   To herald thee from the womb. Poor inch of nature!   34
   Even at the first thy loss is more than can   35
   Thy portage quit, with all thou canst find here.   36
   Now the good gods throw their best eyes upon 't!   37

Enter two Sailors, [one the ship's Master].

MASTER   What courage, sir? God save you!
PERICLES
   Courage enough. I do not fear the flaw;   39
   It hath done to me the worst. Yet for the love
   Of this poor infant, this fresh new seafarer,
   I would it would be quiet.
MASTER   Slack the bowlines there!—Thou wilt not, wilt
   thou? Blow, and split thyself.

---

19 assist i.e., with your sighs and tears   **25 Recall** take back. **therein**
in that respect   **26 Use honor** share, are entitled to, equal honor   **27 for
this charge** for the sake of this infant, this responsibility   **29 conditions**
circumstances   **30 the rudliest welcome** the most rudely welcomed
34 Poor inch of nature (This half-line is from Wilkins's *Painful Adventures.*)   **35–36 Even . . . here** your loss at birth (of your mother) exceeds
anything that your life can offer by way of compensation. (*Portage* is the
cargo one has aboard at the start of a voyage, i.e., one's natural endowments.) **quit** requite   **37 best eyes** most auspicious looks   **39 flaw**
gust, storm

SAILOR But sea room, an the brine and cloudy billow 45
kiss the moon, I care not.

MASTER Sir, your queen must overboard. The sea works
high, the wind is loud, and will not lie till the ship 48
be cleared of the dead.

PERICLES That's your superstition.

MASTER Pardon us, sir. With us at sea it hath been still 51
observed, and we are strong in custom. Therefore briefly 52
yield 'er, for she must overboard straight.   53

PERICLES As you think meet. Most wretched queen!

LYCHORIDA Here she lies, sir.   55

PERICLES
A terrible childbed hast thou had, my dear;
No light, no fire. Th' unfriendly elements
Forgot thee utterly, nor have I time
To give thee hallowed to thy grave, but straight
Must cast thee, scarcely coffined, in the ooze;
Where, for a monument upon thy bones,   61
And aye-remaining lamps, the belching whale   62
And humming water must o'erwhelm thy corpse,
Lying with simple shells. O Lychorida,
Bid Nestor bring me spices, ink and paper,
My casket and my jewels; and bid Nicander
Bring me the satin coffin. Lay the babe   67
Upon the pillow. Hie thee, whiles I say   68
A priestly farewell to her. Suddenly, woman.   69
                                    [*Exit Lychorida.*]

SAILOR Sir, we have a chest beneath the hatches,
caulked and bitumed ready.   71

PERICLES
I thank thee. Mariner, say what coast is this?

MASTER We are near Tarsus.

---

45 But sea room so long as we have room enough to maneuver without being driven on the rocks. **an** if **48 lie** subside **51 still** always
52 briefly quickly **53 straight** straightway (also in line 59) **55 Here
she lies** (Perhaps Lychorida reveals Thaisa's body by drawing the curtains of the "discovery space" rearstage, or possibly the sailors have
brought the Queen's body onstage, but it may be that Pericles apostrophizes her in her absence in ll. 56–64. Line 55 could mean, "Here is
what is left of the Queen, here is her daughter.") **61 for** in place of
62 aye-remaining ever-burning. **belching** blowing, spouting **67 coffin**
coffer **68 Hie thee** hasten **69 Suddenly** quickly **s.d. Exit Lychorida**
(Evidently she takes the babe with her.) **71 bitumed** caulked with pitch

PERICLES Thither, gentle mariner,
　Alter thy course for Tyre. When canst thou reach it?　75
MASTER By break of day, if the wind cease.
PERICLES O, make for Tarsus!
　There will I visit Cleon, for the babe
　Cannot hold out to Tyrus. There I'll leave it
　At careful nursing. Go thy ways, good mariner.　80
　I'll bring the body presently.　　　　　　*Exeunt.*　81

❖

3.2　　*Enter Lord Cerimon, with a Servant [and one
　　　or more other persons who have suffered from
　　　the storm].*

CERIMON Philemon, ho!

　　Enter Philemon.

PHILEMON Doth my lord call?
CERIMON
　Get fire and meat for these poor men.　　　　　3
　　　　　　　　　　　[Exit Philemon.]
　'T has been a turbulent and stormy night.
SERVANT
　I have been in many, but such a night as this
　Till now I ne'er endured.
CERIMON *[To Servant]*
　Your master will be dead ere you return;　　　7
　There's nothing can be ministered to nature
　That can recover him. *[To another.]* Give this to the
　　pothecary,　　　　　　　　　　　　　9
　And tell me how it works.　*[Exeunt all but Cerimon.]*

　　Enter two Gentlemen.

75 Alter . . . Tyre change your course, which has been for Tyre　**80 Go
thy ways** i.e., about it　**81 presently** immediately.　**s.d. Exeunt** (If
Thaisa's body was brought onstage before l. 55 it must presumably be
carried off now.)

3.2. Location: Ephesus. Cerimon's house.
3 meat food　**7 Your master** i.e., one of those who have suffered in
the storm and have been brought to Cerimon for help　**9 recover** restore.　**pothecary** druggist

FIRST GENTLEMAN Good morrow.
SECOND GENTLEMAN Good morrow to your lordship.
CERIMON
Gentlemen, why do you stir so early?
FIRST GENTLEMAN Sir,
Our lodgings, standing bleak upon the sea,   15
Shook as the earth did quake;   16
The very principals did seem to rend   17
And all to topple. Pure surprise and fear
Made me to quit the house.
SECOND GENTLEMAN
That is the cause we trouble you so early;
'Tis not our husbandry.   21
CERIMON O, you say well.
FIRST GENTLEMAN
But I much marvel that your lordship, having
Rich tire about you, should at these early hours   24
Shake off the golden slumber of repose.
'Tis most strange
Nature should be so conversant with pain,   27
Being thereto not compelled.
CERIMON   I hold it ever   28
Virtue and cunning were endowments greater   29
Than nobleness and riches. Careless heirs
May the two latter darken and expend,   31
But immortality attends the former,
Making a man a god. 'Tis known I ever
Have studied physic, through which secret art,   34
By turning o'er authorities, I have,   35
Together with my practice, made familiar
To me and to my aid the blest infusions   37
That dwells in vegetives, in metals, stones;   38
And can speak of the disturbances
That nature works, and of her cures; which doth give me

15 **bleak upon** exposed to   16 **as** as if   17 **principals** main timbers of
houses   21 **husbandry** thrifty management, zeal for rising early   24 **tire**
furnishings   27 **pain** toil   28 **hold it ever** have always believed that
29 **cunning** knowledge, skill   31 **expend** squander   34 **physic** medicine   35 **turning o'er authorities** turning the pages of learned texts
37 **my aid** i.e., the medical assistance I provide; or perhaps Philemon
and other assistants.   **infusions** medicinal properties, substances to be
administered   38 **vegetives** herbs, plants

A more content in course of true delight   41
Than to be thirsty after tottering honor,   42
Or tie my pleasure up in silken bags   43
To please the fool and death.   44

SECOND GENTLEMAN
  Your honor has through Ephesus poured forth
  Your charity, and hundreds call themselves
  Your creatures, who by you have been restored;   47
  And not your knowledge, your personal pain, but even 48
  Your purse, still open, hath built Lord Cerimon   49
  Such strong renown as time shall never—   50

      Enter two or three [Servants] with a chest.

FIRST SERVANT
  So, lift there.
CERIMON   What's that?
FIRST SERVANT   Sir, even now
  Did the sea toss up upon our shore this chest.
  'Tis of some wreck.
CERIMON   Set 't down. Let's look upon 't.
SECOND GENTLEMAN
  'Tis like a coffin, sir.
CERIMON   Whate'er it be,
  'Tis wondrous heavy. Wrench it open straight.
  If the sea's stomach be o'ercharged with gold,
  'Tis a good constraint of fortune it belches upon us.   57
SECOND GENTLEMAN
  'Tis so, my lord.
CERIMON   How close 'tis caulked and bitumed!
  Did the sea cast it up?
FIRST SERVANT
  I never saw so huge a billow, sir,
  As tossed it upon shore.
CERIMON   Wrench it open.
  Soft! It smells most sweetly in my sense.   62

---

41 more greater. **course** pursuit **42 tottering honor** wavering, unstable reputation **43 tie . . . bags** confine my pleasures to the hoarding of silken moneybags **44 the fool** anyone who is fool enough to trust in wealth. **death** (since all wealth ends in death) **47 Your creatures** i.e., people dependent for their very lives on your restoratives **48 not** not only **49 still** always **50 s.d. two or three** (One of these may well be Philemon, or at least the same actor; also at l. 88.) **57 constraint of** act controlled by, compulsion of **62 Soft** gently, wait a minute

SECOND GENTLEMAN   A delicate odor.
CERIMON
    As ever hit my nostril. So, up with it.
                              [*They open the chest.*]
    O you most potent gods! What's here? A corpse?
SECOND GENTLEMAN   Most strange!
CERIMON
    Shrouded in cloth of state, balmed and entreasured   67
    With full bags of spices! A passport too!   68
    Apollo, perfect me in the characters!   69
                              [*He reads from a scroll.*]
        "Here I give to understand,
            If e'er this coffin drives aland,
            I, King Pericles, have lost
            This queen, worth all our mundane cost.   73
            Who finds her, give her burying;   74
            She was the daughter of a king.
            Besides this treasure for a fee,
            The gods requite his charity!"
    If thou livest, Pericles, thou hast a heart
    That even cracks for woe! This chanced tonight.   79
SECOND GENTLEMAN
    Most likely, sir.
CERIMON   Nay, certainly tonight,
    For look how fresh she looks. They were too rough   81
    That threw her in the sea. Make a fire within.
    Fetch hither all my boxes in my closet.
                              [*Exit a Servant.*]
    Death may usurp on nature many hours,
    And yet the fire of life kindle again
    The o'erpressed spirits. I heard of an Egyptian
    That had nine hours lain dead,
    Who was by good appliance recovered.

        Enter one with [boxes,] napkins, and fire.

    Well said, well said! The fire and cloths.   89

---

67 cloth of state fabric fit for royalty; literally, a canopy for a chair of
state   **68 passport** document identifying the bearer   **69 Apollo** god of
eloquence and of medicine.   **perfect . . . characters** enable me to read
the writing   **73 mundane cost** worldly wealth   **74 Who** whoever
79 tonight last night   **81 rough** i.e., hasty   **89 Well said** well done

The rough and woeful music that we have,   90
Cause it to sound, beseech you.
The vial once more. How thou stirr'st, thou block!   92
The music there! [*Music*.] I pray you, give her air.
Gentlemen, this queen will live. Nature awakes;
A warmth breathes out of her. She hath not been
Entranced above five hours. See how she 'gins   96
To blow into life's flower again!

FIRST GENTLEMAN   The heavens,   97
Through you, increase our wonder and sets up
Your fame forever.

CERIMON   She is alive! Behold,
Her eyelids, cases to those heavenly jewels
Which Pericles hath lost, begin to part
Their fringes of bright gold. The diamonds
Of a most praisèd water doth appear,   103
To make the world twice rich.—Live, and make
Us weep to hear your fate, fair creature,
Rare as you seem to be.   *She moves.*

THAISA   O dear Diana,
Where am I? Where's my lord? What world is this?

SECOND GENTLEMAN   Is not this strange?

FIRST GENTLEMAN   Most rare.

CERIMON   Hush, my gentle neighbors!
Lend me your hands. To the next chamber bear her.
Get linen. Now this matter must be looked to,
For her relapse is mortal. Come, come!   113
And Aesculapius guide us!   114

                    They carry her away. Exeunt omnes.

                              ✤

3.3   *Enter Pericles at Tarsus, with Cleon and
          Dionyza [and Lychorida with Marina in her
          arms].*

---

90 rough discordant. (Cerimon may be apologizing for the only music he
can provide at short notice.)   **92 vial** (The quarto text reads *Violl*,
appropriate perhaps to the music just ordered, but could mean a vial of
medicine.)   **How thou stirr'st** i.e., how slow you are   **96 Entranced**
unconscious   **97 blow** bloom   **103 water** luster and clearness. (Used of
precious stones.)   **113 is mortal** would be fatal   **114 Aesculapius** god of
healing

3.3. Location: Tarsus. Cleon's (the Governor's) house.

PERICLES
Most honored Cleon, I must needs be gone.
My twelve months are expired, and Tyrus stands   2
In a litigious peace. You and your lady   3
Take from my heart all thankfulness! The gods   4
Make up the rest upon you!   5

CLEON
Your shakes of fortune, though they haunt you mortally,   6
Yet glance full wonderingly on us.   7

DIONYZA
O your sweet queen! That the strict fates had pleased
You had brought her hither, to have blessed mine eyes
   with her!

PERICLES
We cannot but obey the powers above us.
Could I rage and roar as doth the sea
She lies in, yet the end must be as 'tis.
My gentle babe Marina,
Whom, for she was born at sea, I have named so,   14
Here I charge your charity withal,   15
Leaving her the infant of your care,
Beseeching you to give her princely training,
That she may be mannered as she is born.   18

CLEON   Fear not, my lord, but think
Your Grace, that fed my country with your corn,
For which the people's prayers still fall upon you,
Must in your child be thought on. If neglection   22
Should therein make me vile, the common body,   23
By you relieved, would force me to my duty.
But if to that my nature need a spur,
The gods revenge it upon me and mine
To the end of generation!

PERICLES   I believe you.   27

2 twelve months (Pericles was given a year to return to Tyre; see
3.0.30–33.)   **3 litigious** disturbed by disputes (especially legal)   **4 Take**
receive   **4–5 The gods . . . you** may the gods requite your goodness as
fully as it deserves (of which my gratitude can supply only part)
5 upon to   **6–7 Your . . . on us** your violent shocks of fortune, though
they prey upon you with deadly intent, fill us too with amazement and
sorrow   **14 for** since   **15 withal** with   **18 mannered . . . born** taught
manners and graces to accord with her high birth   **22 neglection**
neglect   **23 common body** common people   **27 of generation** i.e., of my
descendants, or until all procreation ceases

Your honor and your goodness teach me to 't 28
Without your vows. Till she be married, madam,
By bright Diana, whom we honor, all
Unscissored shall this hair of mine remain,
Though I show ill in 't. So I take my leave. 32
Good madam, make me blessèd in your care 33
In bringing up my child.

DIONYZA   I have one myself,
Who shall not be more dear to my respect 35
Than yours, my lord.

PERICLES   Madam, my thanks and prayers.

CLEON
We'll bring Your Grace e'en to the edge o' the shore,
Then give you up to the masked Neptune and 38
The gentlest winds of heaven.

PERICLES
I will embrace your offer.—Come, dearest madam.—
O, no tears, Lychorida, no tears.
Look to your little mistress, on whose grace 42
You may depend hereafter.—Come, my lord.
                                    [*Exeunt.*]

✤

3.4   *Enter Cerimon and Thaisa.*

CERIMON
Madam, this letter and some certain jewels
Lay with you in your coffer, which are
At your command. Know you the character? 3
                    [*He shows her the letter.*]

THAISA
It is my lord's. That I was shipped at sea
I well remember, even on my eaning time; 5
But whether there delivered, by the holy gods,

28 **to 't** to do so   32 **show ill** look unattractive. (The quarto's *show will*
could mean "display willfulness.")   33 **blessèd in your care** fortunate in
having the care you provide   35 **to my respect** in my regard
38 **masked Neptune** i.e., the sea wearing a festive face, as though wearing a mask at a revel (?) or with its strength hidden (?)   42 **grace** favor

3.4. Location: Ephesus. Cerimon's house.
3 **character** handwriting   5 **eaning time** time of delivery

I cannot rightly say. But since King Pericles,
My wedded lord, I ne'er shall see again,
A vestal livery will I take me to,   9
And nevermore have joy.

CERIMON
Madam, if this you purpose as ye speak,
Diana's temple is not distant far,
Where you may abide till your date expire.   13
Moreover, if you please, a niece of mine
Shall there attend you.

THAISA
My recompense is thanks, that's all;
Yet my good will is great, though the gift small.
                                        Exeunt.

❖

9 A vestal livery garments of chastity, nun's habit   **13 date** term of life

4.0 *Enter Gower.*

GOWER
Imagine Pericles arrived at Tyre,
Welcomed and settled to his own desire.   2
His woeful queen we leave at Ephesus,
Unto Diana there 's a votaress.   4
Now to Marina bend your mind,
Whom our fast-growing scene must find
At Tarsus, and by Cleon trained
In music, letters, who hath gained
Of education all the grace,
Which makes her both the heart and place   10
Of general wonder. But, alack,   11
That monster Envy, oft the wrack   12
Of earnèd praise, Marina's life
Seeks to take off by treason's knife.   14
And in this kind hath our Cleon   15
One daughter, and a wench full grown,
Even ripe for marriage rite. This maid
Hight Philoten, and it is said   18
For certain in our story, she
Would ever with Marina be.
Be 't when she weaved the sleided silk   21
With fingers long, small, white as milk;   22
Or when she would with sharp needle wound
The cambric, which she made more sound
By hurting it; or when to the lute
She sung, and made the night bird mute,   26
That still records with moan; or when   27
She would with rich and constant pen   28
Vail to her mistress Dian; still   29
This Philoten contends in skill
With absolute Marina. So   31

4.0.
2 to in accordance with   **4 there 's** there as, or there (she) is
10–11 both . . . wonder the focal point of the admiration of all
12 wrack ruin, destruction   **14 treason's** treachery's   **15 kind** manner   **18 Hight** is called   **21 sleided** divided into filaments   **22 small** slender   **26 night bird** nightingale with its sad song (*moan,* l. 27)
27 still records with moan always sings plaintively   **28 constant** fixedly loyal   **29 Vail** do homage   **31 absolute** free from any imperfection

With the dove of Paphos might the crow   32
Vie feathers white. Marina gets   33
All praises, which are paid as debts,   34
And not as given. This so darks   35
In Philoten all graceful marks
That Cleon's wife, with envy rare,   37
A present murder does prepare   38
For good Marina, that her daughter
Might stand peerless by this slaughter.
The sooner her vile thoughts to stead,   41
Lychorida, our nurse, is dead;
And cursèd Dionyza hath
The pregnant instrument of wrath   44
Prest for this blow. The unborn event   45
I do commend to your content;   46
Only I carry wingèd Time
Post on the lame feet of my rhyme,   48
Which never could I so convey
Unless your thoughts went on my way.
Dionyza does appear,
With Leonine, a murderer.   *Exit.*

4.1   *Enter Dionyza with Leonine.*

DIONYZA
Thy oath remember. Thou hast sworn to do 't.
'Tis but a blow, which never shall be known.
Thou canst not do a thing in the world so soon
To yield thee so much profit. Let not conscience,   4
Which is but cold, inflaming love i' thy bosom,   5
Inflame too nicely; nor let pity, which   6

---

32 Paphos city sacred to Venus. (White doves pulled Venus' chariot.)
33 Vie feathers white challenge in whiteness of plumage   **34 as debts**
as owed to her   **35 given** i.e., gratuitous gifts, compliments.   **darks**
darkens, obscures   **37 rare** keen   **38 present** immediate   **41 stead**
assist   **44 pregnant** willing, ready   **45 Prest** prepared.   **event** outcome   **46 content** pleasure (in watching)   **48 Post** swiftly

4.1. Location: Tarsus. An open place near the seashore.
4–6 Let not . . . nicely do not let conscience, usually cold, inflame your
heart with love of goodness and scruples.   **too nicely** overscrupulously

Even women have cast off, melt thee, but be
A soldier to thy purpose.

LEONINE   I will do 't;
But yet she is a goodly creature.

DIONYZA
The fitter, then, the gods should have her.
Here she comes, weeping for her only nurse's death.   11
Thou art resolved?

LEONINE   I am resolved.

Enter Marina, with a basket of flowers.

MARINA
No, I will rob Tellus of her weed   14
To strew thy green with flowers. The yellows, blues,   15
The purple violets, and marigolds
Shall as a carpet hang upon thy grave
While summer days doth last. Ay me, poor maid,
Born in a tempest when my mother died,
This world to me is a lasting storm
Whirring me from my friends.   21

DIONYZA
How now, Marina? Why do you keep alone?   22
How chance my daughter is not with you?   23
Do not consume your blood with sorrowing;   24
Have you a nurse of me. Lord, how your favor's   25
Changed with this unprofitable woe!
Come, give me your flowers. On the sea margent   27
Walk with Leonine; the air is quick there,   28
And it pierces and sharpens the stomach.   29
Come, Leonine, take her by the arm, walk with her.

MARINA   No, I pray you,
I'll not bereave you of your servant.

DIONYZA   Come, come,
I love the King your father and yourself
With more than foreign heart. We every day   35

---

11 only nurse's i.e., Lychorida's. (*Only* means "one and only.")
14 Tellus goddess of the earth. **weed** garment (here, flowers) **15 green**
i.e., grass-covered grave **21 Whirring** whirling, blowing **22 keep**
remain **23 How chance** how does it happen that **24 with sorrowing**
i.e., with sighs, thought to cost the heart its blood **25 Have . . . me** i.e.,
take me as your nurse. **favor** face, appearance **27 margent** margin,
shore **28 quick** fresh, invigorating **29 stomach** appetite **35 more
. . . heart** i.e., as though we were related by blood

Expect him here. When he shall come and find
Our paragon to all reports thus blasted,   37
He will repent the breadth of his great voyage,
Blame both my lord and me that we have taken
No care to your best courses. Go, I pray you,   40
Walk, and be cheerful once again. Reserve   41
That excellent complexion which did steal
The eyes of young and old. Care not for me;   43
I can go home alone.
MARINA   Well, I will go,
  But yet I have no desire to it.
DIONYZA
  Come, come, I know 'tis good for you.
  Walk half an hour, Leonine, at the least.
  Remember what I have said.
LEONINE   I warrant you, madam.   48
DIONYZA
  I'll leave you, my sweet lady, for a while.
  Pray walk softly; do not heat your blood.   50
  What, I must have a care of you.
MARINA My thanks, sweet madam.   [*Exit Dionyza.*]
  Is this wind westerly that blows?
LEONINE   Southwest.
MARINA
  When I was born, the wind was north.
LEONINE   Was 't so?
MARINA
  My father, as Nurse says, did never fear,
  But cried "Good seamen!" to the sailors,
  Galling his kingly hands, haling ropes,   57
  And, clasping to the mast, endured a sea
  That almost burst the deck.
LEONINE When was this?
MARINA When I was born.
  Never was waves nor wind more violent;
  And from the ladder-tackle washes off   63

37 Our . . . blasted the person whom all regard as a paragon of beauty
thus withered **40 courses** interests **41 Reserve** preserve, show
once more **43 Care not for me** don't concern yourself about me
48 warrant promise **50 softly** gently, slowly **57 Galling** chafing,
blistering. **haling** hauling on **63 ladder-tackle** rope ladder in the
ship's rigging

A canvas-climber. "Ha!" says one, "wolt out?"   64
And with a dropping industry they skip   65
From stem to stern. The boatswain whistles, and
The master calls and trebles their confusion.

LEONINE   Come, say your prayers.

MARINA   What mean you?

LEONINE
  If you require a little space for prayer,
  I grant it. Pray, but be not tedious, for   71
  The gods are quick of ear, and I am sworn
  To do my work with haste.

MARINA   Why will you kill me?

LEONINE   To satisfy my lady.

MARINA   Why would she have me killed?
  Now, as I can remember, by my troth,   77
  I never did her hurt in all my life.
  I never spake bad word nor did ill turn
  To any living creature. Believe me, la,
  I never killed a mouse nor hurt a fly.
  I trod upon a worm against my will,
  But I wept for 't. How have I offended,
  Wherein my death might yield her any profit
  Or my life imply her any danger?

LEONINE   My commission
  Is not to reason of the deed, but do 't.

MARINA
  You will not do 't for all the world, I hope.
  You are well favored, and your looks foreshow   89
  You have a gentle heart. I saw you lately,
  When you caught hurt in parting two that fought;   91
  Good sooth, it showed well in you. Do so now.
  Your lady seeks my life; come you between
  And save poor me, the weaker.

LEONINE   I am sworn,
  And will dispatch.   [*He seizes her.*]

        Enter Pirates.

---

64 wolt out so you want to get out. (Addressed perhaps as a cruel jest to
the *canvas-climber* or sailor in the rigging who is washed overboard.)
65 with . . . industry dripping wet as they labor   **71 tedious** long-
winded   **77 as** as far as   **89 well favored** pleasant-looking.   **foreshow**
proclaim   **91 caught hurt** received an injury

FIRST PIRATE   Hold, villain!   [*Leonine runs away.*]
SECOND PIRATE   A prize, a prize!
THIRD PIRATE   Half-part, mates, half-part. Come, let's 98
   have her aboard suddenly.
                           Exeunt [*Pirates with Marina*].

      Enter Leonine.

LEONINE
   These roguing thieves serve the great pirate Valdes,
   And they have seized Marina. Let her go.
   There's no hope she will return. I'll swear she's dead
   And thrown into the sea. But I'll see further;
   Perhaps they will but please themselves upon her,
   Not carry her aboard. If she remain,
   Whom they have ravished must by me be slain.   *Exit.*

                           ✤

4.2   *Enter the three bawds* [*Pander, Bawd, and
           Bolt*].

PANDER   Bolt!
BOLT   Sir?
PANDER   Search the market narrowly. Mytilene is full of
   gallants. We lost too much money this mart by being 4
   too wenchless.
BAWD   We were never so much out of creatures. We
   have but poor three, and they can do no more than
   they can do; and they with continual action are even
   as good as rotten.
PANDER   Therefore let's have fresh ones, whate'er we
   pay for them. If there be not a conscience to be used in 11
   every trade, we shall never prosper.

---

98 Half-part shares

4.2. Location: Mytilene. A brothel.
s.d. bawds (Used for either sex to mean dealers in prostitution.)   **Bolt**
(The name phallically suggests a shaft, projectile, or arrow.)   **4 this
mart** at the last market time   **11 If . . . used** i.e., if one does not consci-
entiously offer good quality

BAWD   Thou sayst true. 'Tis not our bringing up of poor 13
bastards—as, I think, I have brought up some 14
eleven—

BOLT   Ay, to eleven, and brought them down again. 16
But shall I search the market?

BAWD   What else, man? The stuff we have, a strong 18
wind will blow it to pieces, they are so pitifully
sodden. 20

PANDER   Thou sayst true. There's two unwholesome, o' 21
conscience. The poor Transylvanian is dead that lay
with the little baggage. 23

BOLT   Ay, she quickly pooped him. She made him 24
roast meat for worms. But I'll go search the market.
                                                                      Exit.

PANDER   Three or four thousand chequins were as 26
pretty a proportion to live quietly, and so give over. 27

BAWD   Why to give over, I pray you? Is it a shame to get 28
when we are old?

PANDER   O, our credit comes not in like the commodity, 30
nor the commodity wages not with the danger. There- 31
fore, if in our youths we could pick up some pretty
estate, 'twere not amiss to keep our door hatched. Be- 33
sides, the sore terms we stand upon with the gods will
be strong with us for giving o'er. 35

BAWD   Come, other sorts offend as well as we. 36

13–14 'Tis . . . bastards i.e., raising bastard children doesn't bring us
enough wealth. (As Bolt points out, the children are raised only to be
introduced into prostitution.)   **16 to eleven** to the age of eleven.
brought . . . again i.e., lowered them into debauchery   **18 stuff** goods
20 sodden boiled (by being treated in the sweating tub for venereal
disease)   **21 unwholesome** who are diseased.   **o' on my   23 baggage**
whore   **24 pooped him** i.e., did for him, by infecting him with venereal
disease   **26 chequins** gold coins   **27 proportion to** portion or fortune
on which.   **give over** give up business   **28 get** earn money   **30 credit**
reputation.   **comes not in like** doesn't accumulate as readily as.
commodity profit   **31 wages not** does not keep pace   **33 keep
. . . hatched** keep the lower halfdoor (the hatch) closed, i.e., closed to
customers   **35 strong** strong inducement   **36 sorts** kinds of people.   **as
well as we** in addition to ourselves. (But the Pander, in reply, puns on
well as opposed to *worse*. Pandering is worse than other offenses because it is more carnal, and because, as an occupation, it is a profession
only in the sense of amorous avowals rather than of true vocation; it
trades in flesh but is not an honest *trade*.)

PANDER As well as we? Ay, and better too; we offend
worse. Neither is our profession any trade; it's no calling. But here comes Bolt.

Enter Bolt with the Pirates and Marina.

BOLT Come your ways, my masters. You say she's a 40
virgin?
FIRST PIRATE O, sir, we doubt it not.
BOLT Master, I have gone through for this piece you 43
see. If you like her, so; if not, I have lost my earnest. 44
BAWD Bolt, has she any qualities?
BOLT She has a good face, speaks well, and has excellent good clothes. There's no farther necessity of qual- 47
ities can make her be refused. 48
BAWD What's her price, Bolt?
BOLT I cannot be bated one doit of a thousand pieces. 50
PANDER Well, follow me, my masters; you shall have
your money presently. Wife, take her in. Instruct her 52
what she has to do, that she may not be raw in her 53
entertainment. [*Exeunt Pander and Pirates.*] 54
BAWD Bolt, take you the marks of her, the color of her
hair, complexion, height, her age, with warrant of her
virginity, and cry, "He that will give most shall have
her first." Such a maidenhead were no cheap thing, if
men were as they have been. Get this done as I com-
mand you.
BOLT Performance shall follow. *Exit.*
MARINA
Alack that Leonine was so slack, so slow!
He should have struck, not spoke; or that these pirates,
Not enough barbarous, had not o'erboard thrown me
For to seek my mother!
BAWD Why lament you, pretty one?
MARINA That I am pretty.
BAWD Come, the gods have done their part in you.

---

40 Come your ways come along.   **my masters** i.e., my good sirs, good
fellows   **43 gone through** made a deal.   **piece** piece of flesh, girl   **44 so**
well and good.   **earnest** earnest money, down payment   **47–48 necessity of qualities** requisite accomplishments   **48 can** i.e., the lack of
which can   **50 be bated** get the price lowered (? Or perhaps *I* should
read *It.*)   **doit** small coin.   **of** less than   **52 presently** immediately
53 raw inexperienced   **54 entertainment** reception of customers

MARINA   I accuse them not.

BAWD   You are light into my hands, where you are like 70
to live. 71

MARINA   The more my fault, 72
To scape his hands where I was like to die.

BAWD   Ay, and you shall live in pleasure.

MARINA   No.

BAWD   Yes, indeed shall you, and taste gentlemen of all
fashions. You shall fare well; you shall have the differ- 77
ence of all complexions. What do you stop your ears? 78

MARINA   Are you a woman?

BAWD   What would you have me be, an I be not a 80
woman?

MARINA   An honest woman, or not a woman. 82

BAWD   Marry, whip the gosling! I think I shall have 83
something to do with you. Come, you're a young fool- 84
ish sapling and must be bowed as I would have you.

MARINA   The gods defend me!

BAWD   If it please the gods to defend you by men, then 87
men must comfort you, men must feed you, men must
stir you up. Bolt's returned.

   [*Enter Bolt.*]

Now, sir, hast thou cried her through the market? 90

BOLT   I have cried her almost to the number of her 91
hairs; I have drawn her picture with my voice. 92

BAWD   And, I prithee, tell me how dost thou find the
inclination of the people, especially of the younger
sort?

BOLT   Faith, they listened to me as they would have
hearkened to their father's testament. There was a 97
Spaniard's mouth watered an he went to bed to her 98
very description.

BAWD   We shall have him here tomorrow with his best
ruff on.

---

70 are light have chanced to light.   **like** likely   **71 live** remain   **72 fault**
misfortune   **77–78 difference** variety   **78 complexions** appearances and
temperaments.   **What** why   **80 an** if   **82 honest** chaste   **83 whip the
gosling** i.e., the devil take this goose of a girl   **84 something to do** i.e.,
my hands full   **87 by men** by means of men   **90 cried** proclaimed,
advertised   **91–92 almost . . . hairs** almost to the point of numbering
the hairs of her head   **97 testament** will   **98 an** as if

BOLT Tonight, tonight. But, mistress, do you know
the French knight that cowers i' the hams?   103

BAWD Who, Monsieur Verolles?   104

BOLT Ay, he. He offered to cut a caper at the procla-   105
mation, but he made a groan at it and swore he would
see her tomorrow.

BAWD Well, well, as for him, he brought his disease   108
hither; here he does but repair it. I know he will come   109
in our shadow, to scatter his crowns in the sun.   110

BOLT Well, if we had of every nation a traveler, we
should lodge them with this sign.   112

BAWD [To Marina] Pray you, come hither awhile. You
have fortunes coming upon you. Mark me: you must
seem to do that fearfully which you commit willingly,
despise profit where you have most gain. To weep   116
that you live as ye do makes pity in your lovers; sel-
dom but that pity begets you a good opinion, and that
opinion a mere profit.   119

MARINA I understand you not.

BOLT O, take her home, mistress, take her home!   121
These blushes of hers must be quenched with some
present practice.

BAWD Thou sayest true, i' faith, so they must, for your   124
bride goes to that with shame which is her way to go   125
with warrant.   126

BOLT Faith, some do and some do not. But, mistress,
if I have bargained for the joint—   128

---

103 cowers i' the hams i.e., crouches, showing a weakness typical of
venereal disease   **104 Verolles** (From the French *vérole*, pox, syphilis.)
105 offered tried, made as if to.   **cut a caper** leap up and click his heels
together   **108–109 brought . . . hither** was already diseased when he
came. (Syphilis was popularly known in England as "the French disease.")   **109 repair** (1) return with (2) mend, renew   **110 in our shadow**
i.e., under our roof.   **crowns in the sun** i.e., gold coins, known as
"crowns of the sun," with perhaps the suggestion of squandering gold
on bright beauty. (A French crown also plays on the idea of a bald head
resulting from venereal disease.)   **112 lodge . . . sign** i.e., attract them to
lodge here by means of Marina's picture, metaphorically hung out as
though it were a shop sign   **116 despise** and must seem to despise
119 mere utter, absolute   **121 take her home** talk plainly, i.e., be direct
with her; or, take her inside   **124–125 your bride** even your ordinary
bride   **126 with warrant** with lawful sanction   **128 joint** roast of meat

BAWD   Thou mayst cut a morsel off the spit.   129
BOLT   I may so.
BAWD   Who should deny it?—Come, young one, I like
the manner of your garments well.
BOLT   Ay, by my faith, they shall not be changed   133
yet.   134
BAWD   Bolt, spend thou that in the town. [*She gives
money.*] Report what a sojourner we have; you'll lose
nothing by custom. When nature framed this piece,   137
she meant thee a good turn; therefore say what a par- 138
agon she is, and thou hast the harvest out of thine
own report.
BOLT   I warrant you, mistress, thunder shall not so
awake the beds of eels as my giving out her beauty   142
stirs up the lewdly inclined. I'll bring home some tonight.
BAWD   Come your ways. Follow me.
MARINA
If fires be hot, knives sharp, or waters deep,
Untied I still my virgin knot will keep.
Diana aid my purpose!
BAWD   What have we to do with Diana? Pray you, will
you go with us?   *Exeunt.*

❖

4.3   *Enter Cleon and Dionyza.*

DIONYZA
Why, are you foolish? Can it be undone?

129 off the spit while it is still roasting on the spit, before it is served
up to customers   **133–134 they shall . . . yet** (Marina's clothes proclaim
her to be a wellborn virgin; she does not wear a prostitute's distinctive
dress.)   **137 by custom** by increasing our trade (since you'll get a cut).
piece (1) masterpiece (2) piece of woman's flesh, as at l. 43   **138 a good
turn** (1) a favor (2) an occasion for sex, a *piece* in the sexual sense
142 beds of eels (Seager, *Natural History*, p. 98, quotes *Hortus Sanitatus*:
the eel "is disturbed by the sound of thunder." Used here with possible
bawdy connotation.)

4.3. Location: Tarsus. Cleon's (the Governor's) house.

CLEON
  O Dionyza, such a piece of slaughter
  The sun and moon ne'er looked upon!
DIONYZA
  I think you'll turn a child again.
CLEON
  Were I chief lord of all this spacious world,
  I'd give it to undo the deed. A lady   6
  Much less in blood than virtue, yet a princess
  To equal any single crown o' th' earth
  I' the justice of compare! O villain Leonine!   9
  Whom thou hast poisoned too.
  If thou hadst drunk to him, 't had been a kindness 11
  Becoming well thy fact. What canst thou say   12
  When noble Pericles shall demand his child?
DIONYZA
  That she is dead. Nurses are not the Fates;
  To foster is not ever to preserve.   15
  She died at night; I'll say so. Who can cross it, 16
  Unless you play the impious innocent   17
  And, for an honest attribute, cry out,   18
  "She died by foul play"?
CLEON   O, go to. Well, well, 19
  Of all the faults beneath the heavens, the gods
  Do like this worst.
DIONYZA   Be one of those that thinks
  The petty wrens of Tarsus will fly hence
  And open this to Pericles. I do shame   23
  To think of what a noble strain you are,
  And of how coward a spirit.
CLEON   To such proceeding
  Whoever but his approbation added,   26
  Though not his prime consent, he did not flow 27

---

6 lady i.e., Marina **9 I' . . . compare** if justly compared **11 drunk to him** i.e., drunk his health from the poisoned cup **12 fact** deed **15 To . . . preserve** i.e., one can foster life, but one cannot preserve it forever; that is in the hands of the Fates **16 cross** contradict **17 play . . . innocent** impiously play the innocent **18 attribute** reputation **19 go to** (A term of reproach or anger.) **23 open** reveal. (Birds were anciently thought to reveal murders.) **26 but** merely **27 prime** original, previous. **flow** i.e., proceed, come

   From honorable courses.
DIONYZA   Be it so, then.   28
  Yet none does know but you how she came dead,
  Nor none can know, Leonine being gone.
  She did distain my child and stood between   31
  Her and her fortunes. None would look on her,
  But cast their gazes on Marina's face,
  Whilst ours was blurted at and held a malkin   34
  Not worth the time of day. It pierced me through;
  And though you call my course unnatural,
  You not your child well loving, yet I find
  It greets me as an enterprise of kindness   38
  Performed to your sole daughter.
CLEON   Heavens forgive it!
DIONYZA   And as for Pericles,
  What should he say? We wept after her hearse,
  And yet we mourn. Her monument   43
  Is almost finished, and her epitaphs
  In glittering golden characters express
  A general praise to her and care in us
  At whose expense 'tis done.
CLEON   Thou art like the harpy,   47
  Which, to betray, dost, with thine angel's face,
  Seize with thine eagle's talons.
DIONYZA
  You're like one that superstitiously
  Do swear to the gods that winter kills the flies.   51
  But yet I know you'll do as I advise.   [*Exeunt.*]

❖

28 honorable courses noble family, tributary streambeds. (See *noble strain* in l. 24.) **31 distain** tarnish by comparison **34 blurted at** treated with scorn. **malkin** slut **38 greets** manifests itself favorably to. **kindness** natural affection **43 yet** still **47 harpy** monstrous bird with the face and torso of a woman **51 Do . . . flies** i.e., you blame the death of flies on winter, thus exculpating yourself before the gods; or, perhaps, you are one of those milktoasts who piously exclaim against death despite its being such a natural thing. (A line variously interpreted, but seemingly Dionyza accuses her husband of superstitiously and hypocritically washing his hands of the dirty business by which his own daughter has been helped; see ll. 36–39.)

4.4 [*Enter Gower, before the monument of Marina at Tarsus.*]

GOWER

Thus time we waste and long leagues make short,	1
Sail seas in cockles, have and wish but for 't,	2
Making to take your imagination	3
From bourn to bourn, region to region.	4
By you being pardoned, we commit no crime	
To use one language in each several clime	
Where our scenes seem to live. I do beseech you	
To learn of me, who stand i' the gaps to teach you,	8
The stages of our story. Pericles	
Is now again thwarting the wayward seas,	10
Attended on by many a lòrd and knight,	
To see his daughter, all his life's delight.	
Old Helicanus goes along. Behind	
Is left to govern, if you bear in mind,	
Old Escanes, whom Helicanus late	15
Advanced in time to great and high estate.	
Well-sailing ships and bounteous winds have brought	
This king to Tarsus—think his pilot thought;	18
So with his steerage shall your thoughts grow on—	19
To fetch his daughter home, who first is gone.	20
Like motes and shadows see them move awhile;	21
Your ears unto your eyes I'll reconcile.	22

[*Dumb Show.*]

Enter Pericles at one door with all his train,

4.4. Location: Tarsus.

s.d. the monument of Marina (Perhaps Gower reveals this monument by drawing a curtain hung before the "discovery space" here, or perhaps Cleon draws back the curtain at l. 22 s.d.) **1 waste** i.e., pass quickly over **2 cockles** scallop shells, or else small boats. (Supernatural creatures sometimes sail in this fashion. Gower is alluding to the imaginary crossing of the seas between scenes of the play.) **have . . . for 't** have something if we but wish it **3 Making . . . imagination** causing your imagination to be taken, by means of our fiction; or, proceeding by means of taking your imagination **4 bourn** frontier **8 stand i' the gaps** bridge the gaps (of time and space between scenes) **10 thwarting** crossing. **wayward** unruly, hostile **15 late** recently **18 think . . . thought** imagine that he is being piloted by our swift thoughts as we accompany him **19 his steerage** the steering of his ship. **grow on** proceed **20 first** already **21 motes** specks in a beam of light

Cleon and Dionyza at the other. Cleon shows
Pericles the tomb, whereat Pericles makes
lamentation, puts on sackcloth, and in a mighty
passion departs. [Then exeunt Cleon and
Dionyza.]

See how belief may suffer by foul show!   23
This borrowed passion stands for true-owed woe;   24
And Pericles, in sorrow all devoured,
With sighs shot through and biggest tears o'ershowered,
Leaves Tarsus and again embarks. He swears
Never to wash his face nor cut his hairs;
He puts on sackcloth, and to sea. He bears   29
A tempest, which his mortal vessel tears,   30
And yet he rides it out. Now please you wit   31
The epitaph is for Marina writ   32
By wicked Dionyza.
          [*He reads the inscription on Marina's monument.*]
"The fairest, sweetest, and best lies here,
   Who withered in her spring of year.
   She was of Tyrus the King's daughter,
   On whom foul death hath made this slaughter.
Marina was she called, and at her birth,
Thetis, being proud, swallowed some part o' th' earth.   39
Therefore the earth, fearing to be o'erflowed,
Hath Thetis' birth-child on the heavens bestowed;
Wherefore she does, and swears she'll never stint,   42
Make raging battery upon shores of flint."   43

No visor does become black villainy

---

22 s.d. passion grief   **23 foul show** foul dissembling   **24 This borrowed
. . . woe** i.e., this feigned lamentation of Dionyza and Cleon is substituted for genuine and deserved woe; or else, this grief simulated by the
actor of Pericles stands for genuine sorrow, as contrasted with the
feigning of Dionyza and Cleon   **29 He bears** i.e., he bears within him
30 mortal vessel human body, life (which suffers from mental anguish)   **31 wit** know   **32 is** that is   **39 Thetis** a sea nymph, often confused (as here) with Tethys, a Titaness and consort of Oceanus.
swallowed . . . earth (The fanciful image is that of the ocean rejoicing
over Marina's birth at sea with such destructive flood tides that the
earth resolves to be rid of Marina by sending her to heaven; it is in
angry reprisal that the sea continues to beat against the shore.)   **42 she**
i.e., Thetis.   **stint** cease   **43 Make . . . flint** continuously beats upon
rocky shores

So well as soft and tender flattery.
Let Pericles believe his daughter's dead
And bear his courses to be orderèd   47
By Lady Fortune, while our scene must play   48
His daughter's woe and heavy welladay   49
In her unholy service. Patience, then,   50
And think you now are all in Mytilene.   *Exit.*

❖

4.5 *Enter [from the brothel] two Gentlemen.*

FIRST GENTLEMAN Did you ever hear the like?

SECOND GENTLEMAN No, nor never shall do in such a
   place as this, she being once gone.

FIRST GENTLEMAN But to have divinity preached there!
   Did you ever dream of such a thing?

SECOND GENTLEMAN No, no. Come, I am for no more
   bawdy houses. Shall 's go hear the vestals sing?   7

FIRST GENTLEMAN I'll do anything now that is virtuous,
   but I am out of the road of rutting forever.   *Exeunt.* 9

4.6 *Enter three bawds [Pander, Bawd, and Bolt].*

PANDER Well, I had rather than twice the worth of her
   she had ne'er come here.

BAWD Fie, fie upon her! She's able to freeze the god
   Priapus and undo a whole generation. We must ei-   4
   ther get her ravished or be rid of her. When she
   should do for clients her fitment and do me the kind-   6
   ness of our profession, she has me her quirks, her rea-

47–48 bear . . . Fortune direct his passage as Fortune orders   **49 welladay**
wellaway, lamentation   **50 In her unholy service** i.e., in the brothel

4.5. Location: Mytilene. The brothel.
7 Shall 's shall we.   **vestals** vestal virgins   **9 rutting** sexual indulgence

4.6. Location: The brothel, as before.
4 Priapus god of fertility and lechery.   **undo . . . generation** (1) prevent
the engendering of the next generation (2) prevent the pleasures of the
present generation   **6 fitment** sexual duty.   **do me** do. (*Me* is an em-
phatic marker; see also *has me* in next line.)

sons, her master reasons, her prayers, her knees, that
she would make a puritan of the devil if he should
cheapen a kiss of her.   10

BOLT   Faith, I must ravish her, or she'll disfurnish us
of all our cavalleria and make our swearers priests.   12

PANDER   Now, the pox upon her greensickness for me!   13

BAWD   Faith, there's no way to be rid on 't but by the   14
way to the pox. Here comes the Lord Lysimachus dis-   15
guised.

BOLT   We should have both lord and loon if the pee-   17
vish baggage would but give way to customers.   18

     Enter Lysimachus.

LYSIMACHUS   How now? How a dozen of virginities?   19

BAWD   Now, the gods to-bless your honor!   20

BOLT   I am glad to see your honor in good health.

LYSIMACHUS   You may so; 'tis the better for you that
your resorters stand upon sound legs. How now?   23
Wholesome iniquity have you, that a man may deal   24
withal and defy the surgeon?   25

BAWD   We have here one, sir, if she would—but there
never came her like in Mytilene.

LYSIMACHUS   If she'd do the deeds of darkness, thou
wouldst say.

BAWD   Your honor knows what 'tis to say well enough.   30

LYSIMACHUS   Well, call forth, call forth.   [*Exit Pander.*]

BOLT   For flesh and blood, sir, white and red, you shall
see a rose; and she were a rose indeed, if she had
but—

LYSIMACHUS   What, prithee?

BOLT   O, sir, I can be modest.

---

10 cheapen bargain for   **12 cavalleria** cavaliers.   **our swearers** our
sworn (i.e., faithful) customers, or our profane customers (?)
13 greensickness i.e., moody obstinacy or squeamishness, like that
caused by anemia in young women.   **for me** as far as I'm concerned
14 on 't of it, of this difficulty   **15 pox** syphilis. (In l. 13, *pox* is used in
an oath, i.e., "the plague upon her.")   **17 loon** low fellow, person of low
birth   **17–18 peevish** perverse, stubborn   **19 How a** what price for
20 to-bless bless completely   **23 your resorters** those who resort to
your place, customers   **24 Wholesome iniquity** healthy prostitutes
25 withal with.   **surgeon** barber-surgeon (to treat syphilis)   **30 what 'tis
to say** what I'm trying to say

LYSIMACHUS   That dignifies the renown of a bawd no ₃₇
less than it gives a good report to a number to be ₃₈
chaste.   ₃₉

[*Enter Pander with Marina.*]

BAWD   Here comes that which grows to the stalk;
never plucked yet, I can assure you. Is she not a fair
creature?

LYSIMACHUS   Faith, she would serve after a long voyage ₄₃
at sea. Well, there's for you. [*He gives money.*] Leave us. ₄₄

BAWD   I beseech your honor, give me leave a word, and
I'll have done presently.

LYSIMACHUS   I beseech you, do.

BAWD [*Aside to Marina*]   First, I would have you note ₄₈
this is an honorable man.

MARINA   I desire to find him so, that I may worthily
note him.   ₅₁

BAWD   Next, he's the Governor of this country and a
man whom I am bound to.   ₅₃

MARINA   If he govern the country, you are bound to ₅₄
him indeed, but how honorable he is in that I know
not.

BAWD   Pray you, without any more virginal fencing,
will you use him kindly? He will line your apron with
gold.

MARINA   What he will do graciously I will thankfully
receive.

LYSIMACHUS   Ha' you done?

BAWD   My lord, she's not paced yet. You must take ₆₃
some pains to work her to your manage.—Come, we ₆₄
will leave his honor and her together. Go thy ways.

[*Exeunt Bawd, Pander, and Bolt.*]

LYSIMACHUS   Now, pretty one, how long have you been
at this trade?

MARINA   What trade, sir?

37–39 That . . . chaste i.e., modesty in speech gives good reputation to a
bawd, as well as attesting to the chastity of many women who deserve
no such reputation   **43–44 she . . . sea** i.e., she is just the thing for a
man who is sexually ravenous   **48, 51 note** (1) observe (2) set down as
having a certain character, in this case a good character   **53, 54 bound**
(1) obligated (2) subject   **63, 64 paced, manage** (Terms used in training
horses.)

LYSIMACHUS   Why, I cannot name 't but I shall offend.

MARINA   I cannot be offended with my trade. Please
you to name it.

LYSIMACHUS   How long have you been of this profession?

MARINA   E'er since I can remember.

LYSIMACHUS   Did you go to 't so young? Were you a
gamester at five, or at seven?   76

MARINA   Earlier too, sir, if now I be one.

LYSIMACHUS   Why, the house you dwell in proclaims
you to be a creature of sale.

MARINA   Do you know this house to be a place of such
resort, and will come into 't? I hear say you're of honorable parts and are the Governor of this place.   82

LYSIMACHUS   Why, hath your principal made known
unto you who I am?

MARINA   Who is my principal?

LYSIMACHUS   Why, your herbwoman, she that sets
seeds and roots of shame and iniquity. O, you have
heard something of my power, and so stand aloof for
more serious wooing. But I protest to thee, pretty one,
my authority shall not see thee, or else look friendly   90
upon thee. Come, bring me to some private place.
Come, come.

MARINA
If you were born to honor, show it now;
If put upon you, make the judgment good   94
That thought you worthy of it.

LYSIMACHUS
How's this? How's this? Some more. Be sage.

MARINA   For me,
That am a maid, though most ungentle fortune
Have placed me in this sty, where, since I came,
Diseases have been sold dearer than physic—
That the gods
Would set me free from this unhallowed place,
Though they did change me to the meanest bird   102
That flies i' the purer air!

76 gamester wanton woman   82 parts qualities   90 my authority
. . . thee i.e., I'll wink at your offenses, not enforce the laws against
prostitutes   94 If put upon you i.e., if your high position was conferred
after birth, not through inheritance   102 meanest lowest

LYSIMACHUS   I did not think
  Thou couldst have spoke so well, ne'er dreamt thou
    couldst.
  Had I brought hither a corrupted mind,
  Thy speech had altered it. Hold, here's gold for thee.   106
  Persevere in that clear way thou goest,   107
  And the gods strengthen thee!   [*He gives gold.*]
MARINA   The good gods preserve you!
LYSIMACHUS   For me, be you thoughten   110
  That I came with no ill intent, for to me
  The very doors and windows savor vilely.
  Fare thee well. Thou art a piece of virtue, and
  I doubt not but thy training hath been noble.
  Hold, here's more gold for thee.   [*He gives gold.*]
  A curse upon him, die he like a thief,
  That robs thee of thy goodness! If thou dost
  Hear from me, it shall be for thy good.

      [*Enter Bolt.*]

BOLT   I beseech your honor, one piece for me.
LYSIMACHUS   Avaunt, thou damnèd doorkeeper!
  Your house, but for this virgin that doth prop it,
  Would sink and overwhelm you. Away!   [*Exit.*]
BOLT   How's this? We must take another course with
  you. If your peevish chastity, which is not worth a
  breakfast in the cheapest country under the cope, shall   125
  undo a whole household, let me be gelded like a span-
  iel. Come your ways.
MARINA   Whither would you have me?
BOLT   I must have your maidenhead taken off, or the
  common hangman shall execute it. Come your ways.
  We'll have no more gentlemen driven away. Come
  your ways, I say.

    Enter Bawd [and Pander].

BAWD   How now, what's the matter?
BOLT   Worse and worse, mistress. She has here spoken
  holy words to the Lord Lysimachus.
BAWD   O, abominable!

106 had would have   **107 clear** virtuous   **110 be you thoughten** assure
yourself   **125 cope** firmament

BOLT She makes our profession as it were to stink
afore the face of the gods.

BAWD Marry, hang her up forever!

BOLT The nobleman would have dealt with her like a 140
nobleman, and she sent him away as cold as a snow- 141
ball, saying his prayers too.

BAWD Bolt, take her away. Use her at thy pleasure.
Crack the glass of her virginity and make the rest
malleable.

BOLT An if she were a thornier piece of ground than 146
she is, she shall be plowed.

MARINA Hark, hark, you gods!

BAWD She conjures. Away with her! Would she had
never come within my doors!—Marry, hang you!—She's
born to undo us.—Will you not go the way of women-
kind? Marry, come up, my dish of chastity with rose- 152
mary and bays!   [Exeunt Bawd and Pander.] 153

BOLT Come, mistress, come your ways with me.

MARINA Whither wilt thou have me?

BOLT To take from you the jewel you hold so dear.

MARINA Prithee, tell me one thing first.

BOLT Come now, your one thing. 158

MARINA

What canst thou wish thine enemy to be? 159

BOLT Why, I could wish him to be my master, or 160
rather, my mistress. 161

MARINA

Neither of these are so bad as thou art,
Since they do better thee in their command. 163
Thou hold'st a place for which the pained'st fiend 164
Of hell would not in reputation change.
Thou art the damnèd doorkeeper to every

140–141 **like a nobleman** i.e., as a nobleman would have done, using her
and rewarding her 146 **An if** even if 152 **Marry, come up** i.e., hoity-
toity 152–153 **rosemary and bays** (Customary garnishes for certain
foods; the Bawd means that Marina's chastity is beyond the ordinary;
she is a fancy dish.) 158 **thing** (Bolt plays on Marina's *one thing* (l. 157)
in a lewd sense, referring to her sexual anatomy.) 159 **What . . . to be**
i.e., what is the worst possible evil you could wish upon your enemy
160–161 **my master . . . mistress** i.e., like my master in wickedness, or
even more, like my mistress 163 **do . . . command** i.e., have the advantage of being over you and so can order you to do things they wouldn't
do themselves 164 **pained'st** most tormented

Coistrel that comes inquiring for his Tib.   167
To the choleric fisting of every rogue   168
Thy ear is liable; thy food is such
As hath been belched on by infected lungs.

BOLT What would you have me do? Go to the wars,
would you, where a man may serve seven years for   172
the loss of a leg and have not money enough in the
end to buy him a wooden one?

MARINA
Do anything but this thou doest. Empty
Old receptacles, or common shores, of filth;   176
Serve by indenture to the common hangman.   177
Any of these ways are yet better than this;
For what thou professest, a baboon, could he speak,
Would own a name too dear. That the gods   180
Would safely deliver me from this place!
Here, here's gold for thee.   [*She gives gold.*]
If that thy master would gain by me,
Proclaim that I can sing, weave, sew, and dance,
With other virtues, which I'll keep from boast,   185
And will undertake all these to teach.
I doubt not but this populous city will
Yield many scholars.   188

BOLT But can you teach all this you speak of?

MARINA
Prove that I cannot, take me home again   190
And prostitute me to the basest groom   191
That doth frequent your house.

BOLT Well, I will see what I can do for thee. If I can
place thee, I will.

MARINA But amongst honest women.

BOLT Faith, my acquaintance lies little amongst them.
But since my master and mistress hath bought you,
there's no going but by their consent. Therefore I will
make them acquainted with your purpose, and I

---

167 Coistrel knave. **Tib** common woman **168 choleric fisting** angry
blows **172 would you** would you have me. **for** i.e., to end up with
176 shores sewers, or garbage dumps at the water's edge **177 by
indenture** i.e., as an apprentice **180 own . . . dear** consider himself too
good for that **185 virtues** accomplishments **188 scholars** pupils
190 Prove if you find **191 groom** menial

doubt not but I shall find them tractable enough.
Come, I'll do for thee what I can. Come your ways.

Exeunt.

✤

5.0 *Enter Gower.*

GOWER

Marina thus the brothel scapes and chances
　Into an honest house, our story says.
She sings like one immortal, and she dances
　As goddesslike to her admirèd lays.　　　　　　　　4
Deep clerks she dumbs, and with her neele composes　5
　Nature's own shape, of bud, bird, branch, or berry,
That even her art sisters the natural roses;　　　　　7
　Her inkle, silk, twin with the rubied cherry,　　　8
That pupils lacks she none of noble race,
　Who pour their bounty on her, and her gain
She gives the cursèd bawd. Here we her place,
　And to her father turn our thoughts again,
Where we left him, on the sea. We there him lost,
　Where, driven before the winds, he is arrived
Here where his daughter dwells; and on this coast
　Suppose him now at anchor. The city strived　　　16
God Neptune's annual feast to keep, from whence
　Lysimachus our Tyrian ship espies,
His banners sable, trimmed with rich expense,　　　19
　And to him in his barge with fervor hies.　　　　20
In your supposing once more put your sight;　　　21
　Of heavy Pericles think this his bark,　　　　　22
Where what is done in action, more, if might,　　　23
　Shall be discovered. Please you, sit and hark.　*Exit.* 24

5.0.
4 lays songs　**5 Deep . . . dumbs** she silences profound scholars.　**neele** needle.　**7 That** so that.　**sisters** equals in appearance　**8 inkle** kind of tape; also linen or yarn from which it is made.　**twin with** resemble closely　**16 strived** outdid itself　**19, 20 His, him** its, it　**19 sable** black　**21 supposing** imagination　**22 heavy** sorrowful　**23 action** stage action.　**more, if might** i.e., and we would show more if it were possible　**24 discovered** revealed, shown

5.1   *Enter Helicanus. To him two Sailors, [one*
          belonging to the Tyrian vessel, the other to a
          barge of Mytilene that is evidently alongside,
          out of view].

TYRIAN SAILOR [*To the Sailor of Mytilene*]
  Where is Lord Helicanus? He can resolve you.   1
  O, here he is.
  Sir, there is a barge put off from Mytilene,
  And in it is Lysimachus the Governor,
  Who craves to come aboard. What is your will?
HELICANUS
  That he have his. Call up some gentlemen.
TYRIAN SAILOR   Ho, gentlemen! My lord calls.

          Enter two or three Gentlemen.

FIRST GENTLEMAN   Doth your lordship call?
HELICANUS   Gentlemen,
  There is some of worth would come aboard.   10
  I pray, greet him fairly.
                    [*The Gentlemen and the two Sailors*
                              go to meet Lysimachus.]

          Enter [as from the barge] Lysimachus, [escorted].

TYRIAN SAILOR [*To Lysimachus*]   Sir,
  This is the man that can, in aught you would,
  Resolve you.
LYSIMACHUS
  Hail, reverend sir! The gods preserve you!
HELICANUS   And you, to outlive the age I am,
  And die as I would do.
LYSIMACHUS   You wish me well.   17
  Being on shore, honoring of Neptune's triumphs,   18
  Seeing this goodly vessel ride before us,
  I made to it, to know of whence you are.

5.1. Location: On board Pericles' ship, off Mytilene. A pavilion for
Pericles is provided onstage, with a curtain before it, perhaps by means
of a "discovery space"; Pericles, reclining within, is "discovered" to
view at l. 37 by the drawing back of the curtain.
1 resolve answer, satisfy   **10 some of worth** some nobleman (who)
17 as I would do i.e., at the end of a long and honorable life
18 honoring . . . triumphs celebrating a festival in honor of Neptune

HELICANUS   First, what is your place?   21
LYSIMACHUS
  I am the Governor of this place you lie before.
HELICANUS   Sir,
  Our vessel is of Tyre, in it the King,
  A man who for this three months hath not spoken
  To anyone, nor taken sustenance
  But to prorogue his grief.   27
LYSIMACHUS
  Upon what ground is his distemperature?   28
HELICANUS
  'Twould be too tedious to repeat,
  But the main grief springs from the loss
  Of a belovèd daughter and a wife.
LYSIMACHUS   May we not see him?
HELICANUS   You may,
  But bootless is your sight. He will not speak   34
  To any.
LYSIMACHUS   Yet let me obtain my wish.
HELICANUS
  Behold him. [*Pericles is discovered to view.*] This was
    a goodly person,
  Till the disaster that, one mortal night,
  Drove him to this.
LYSIMACHUS
  Sir King, all hail! The gods preserve you!
  Hail, royal sir!
HELICANUS
  It is in vain. He will not speak to you.
FIRST LORD   Sir,
  We have a maid in Mytilene, I durst wager,
  Would win some words of him.
LYSIMACHUS   'Tis well bethought.
  She questionless, with her sweet harmony
  And other chosen attractions, would allure,   47
  And make a battery through his deafened ports,   48
  Which now are midway stopped.   49
  She is all happy as the fairest of all

21 **place** office   27 **prorogue** prolong   28 **distemperature** disturbance
of mind   34 **bootless** fruitless   47 **chosen** choice   48 **make . . . ports**
force an entrance through his deafened sense of hearing   49 **midway
stopped** shut so that communications get only halfway through

And, with her fellow maids, is now upon
The leafy shelter that abuts against
The island's side.   [*He signals to the Lord, who goes*
                                                        off to bring Marina.]

HELICANUS
    Sure, all effectless; yet nothing we'll omit   54
    That bears recovery's name. But since your kindness   55
    We have stretched thus far, let us beseech you
    That for our gold we may provision have,
    Wherein we are not destitute for want,
    But weary for the staleness.

LYSIMACHUS   O, sir, a courtesy   59
    Which if we should deny, the most just gods
    For every graft would send a caterpillar,   61
    And so inflict our province. Yet once more   62
    Let me entreat to know at large the cause   63
    Of your king's sorrow.

HELICANUS
    Sit, sir, I will recount it to you.—
    But see, I am prevented.   66

    [*Enter, as though from the barge, Lord, with*
    Marina, and a young lady.]

LYSIMACHUS
    O, here's the lady that I sent for.
    Welcome, fair one!—Is 't not a goodly presence?

HELICANUS   She's a gallant lady.

LYSIMACHUS
    She's such a one that, were I well assured
    Came of a gentle kind and noble stock,   71
    I'd wish no better choice, and think me rarely wed.—   72
    Fair one, all goodness that consists in bounty   73
    Expect even here, where is a kingly patient;
    If that thy prosperous and artificial feat   75
    Can draw him but to answer thee in aught,

54 effectless useless   **55 bears recovery's name** deserves the name of
cure   **59 for** because of   **61 graft** scion, shoot, grafted plant   **62 inflict**
afflict   **63 at large** in detail   **66 prevented** forestalled   **71 gentle kind**
noble kindred   **72 rarely** excellently   **73 all . . . bounty** (In the quarto,
which reads *beauty* for *bounty*, this phrase could mean: You, Marina,
possessed of all good that beauty can contain.)   **75 prosperous** producing favorable results.   **artificial** skillful

Thy sacred physic shall receive such pay
As thy desires can wish.

MARINA   Sir, I will use
My utmost skill in his recovery, provided
That none but I and my companion maid
Be suffered to come near him.

LYSIMACHUS   Come, let us leave her;
And the gods make her prosperous!
              [*They stand aside.*] *The song [by Marina].*

LYSIMACHUS [*Advancing*]
Marked he your music?

MARINA   No, nor looked on us.

LYSIMACHUS [*To Helicanus*]   See, she will speak to him.

MARINA [*To Pericles*]   Hail, sir! My lord, lend ear.

PERICLES   Hum, ha!   [*He pushes her away.*]

MARINA
I am a maid, my lord, that ne'er before
Invited eyes, but have been gazèd on   88
Like a comet. She speaks,
My lord, that maybe hath endured a grief
Might equal yours, if both were justly weighed.
Though wayward fortune did malign my state,   92
My derivation was from ancestors
Who stood equivalent with mighty kings;
But time hath rooted out my parentage,
And to the world and awkward casualties   96
Bound me in servitude. [*Aside.*] I will desist;
But there is something glows upon my cheek,
And whispers in mine ear, "Go not till he speak."

PERICLES
My fortunes—parentage—good parentage—
To equal mine!—Was it not thus? What say you?

MARINA
I said, my lord, if you did know my parentage,
You would not do me violence.

PERICLES
I do think so. Pray you, turn your eyes upon me.

---

88 Invited eyes asked to be looked at   **92 wayward** contrary.   **did
. . . state** has dealt malignantly with my condition   **96 awkward casualties** adverse misfortunes

You're like something that—What countrywoman?
Here of these shores?

MARINA   No, nor of any shores.
Yet I was mortally brought forth, and am   107
No other than I appear.

PERICLES
I am great with woe and shall deliver weeping.   109
My dearest wife was like this maid, and such a one
My daughter might have been. My queen's square
    brows;
Her stature to an inch; as wandlike straight;
As silver-voiced; her eyes as jewel-like
And cased as richly; in pace another Juno;   114
Who starves the ears she feeds, and makes them hungry
The more she gives them speech.—Where do you live?

MARINA
Where I am but a stranger. From the deck
You may discern the place.

PERICLES
Where were you bred? And how achieved you these
Endowments which you make more rich to owe?   120

MARINA
If I should tell my history, it would seem
Like lies disdained in the reporting.

PERICLES   Prithee, speak.   122
Falseness cannot come from thee, for thou lookest
Modest as Justice, and thou seemest a palace
For the crowned Truth to dwell in. I will believe thee
And make my senses credit thy relation   126
To points that seem impossible, for thou lookest
Like one I loved indeed. What were thy friends?   128
Didst thou not say, when I did push thee back—
Which was when I perceived thee—that thou cam'st
From good descending?

MARINA   So indeed I did.   131

---

107 mortally humanly   **109 great** (1) pregnant (2) heavy.   **deliver** (1) give
birth (2) speak   **114 cased** enclosed, framed.   **pace** gait, carriage
120 to owe by possessing   **122 in the reporting** even as I spoke them
126 credit believe.   **relation** account   **128 friends** relatives
131 descending descent

PERICLES
    Report thy parentage. I think thou saidst
    Thou hadst been tossed from wrong to injury,
    And that thou thought'st thy griefs might equal mine,
    If both were opened.
MARINA   Some such thing   135
    I said, and said no more but what my thoughts
    Did warrant me was likely.
PERICLES   Tell thy story.
    If thine, considered, prove the thousand part   138
    Of my endurance, thou art a man, and I   139
    Have suffered like a girl. Yet thou dost look
    Like Patience gazing on kings' graves and smiling   141
    Extremity out of act. What were thy friends?   142
    How lost thou them? Thy name, my most kind virgin?
    Recount, I do beseech thee. Come, sit by me.
MARINA   My name is Marina.
PERICLES   O, I am mocked,
    And thou by some incensèd god sent hither   147
    To make the world to laugh at me.
MARINA   Patience, good sir, or here I'll cease.
PERICLES
    Nay, I'll be patient. Thou little know'st how thou
    Dost startle me to call thyself Marina.
MARINA   The name
    Was given me by one that had some power,
    My father, and a king.
PERICLES   How, a king's daughter?
    And called Marina?
MARINA   You said you would believe me;
    But, not to be a troubler of your peace,
    I will end here.
PERICLES   But are you flesh and blood?
    Have you a working pulse, and are no fairy?   158
    Motion? Well, speak on. Where were you born?   159
    And wherefore called Marina?

135 opened revealed   **138 thousand** thousandth   **139 my endurance** what
I have endured   **141 gazing on kings' graves** i.e., viewing with equanimity
the evidence that all human greatness ends in death   **141–142 smiling . . .
act** disarming with a smile the worst that fortune can do   **147 sent** are
sent   **158 working** beating   **159 Motion** i.e., have you motion

MARINA   Called Marina
For I was born at sea.
PERICLES   At sea! What mother?   161
MARINA
My mother was the daughter of a king,
Who died the minute I was born,
As my good nurse Lychorida hath oft
Delivered weeping.
PERICLES   O, stop there a little!   165
This is the rarest dream that e'er dull sleep
Did mock sad fools withal. This cannot be   167
My daughter—buried!—Well, where were you bred?
I'll hear you more, to th' bottom of your story,
And never interrupt you.
MARINA
You scorn. Believe me, 'twere best I did give o'er.
PERICLES
I will believe you by the syllable   172
Of what you shall deliver. Yet give me leave:
How came you in these parts? Where were you bred?
MARINA
The King my father did in Tarsus leave me,
Till cruel Cleon, with his wicked wife,
Did seek to murder me; and having wooed
A villain to attempt it, who having drawn to do 't,   178
A crew of pirates came and rescued me,
Brought me to Mytilene. But, good sir,
Whither will you have me? Why do you weep? It may be 181
You think me an impostor. No, good faith,
I am the daughter to King Pericles,
If good King Pericles be.   184
PERICLES   Ho, Helicanus!
HELICANUS   Calls my lord?
PERICLES
Thou art a grave and noble counselor,
Most wise in general. Tell me, if thou canst,

---

161 For because   **165 Delivered** recited, told (also in l. 173)   **167 withal**
with   **172 by the syllable** i.e., to the letter   **178 drawn** drawn his
sword   **181 Whither . . . me** where are you leading me in this interrogation   **184 be** live

What this maid is, or what is like to be,
That thus hath made me weep?

HELICANUS   I know not,
But here's the regent, sir, of Mytilene
Speaks nobly of her.

LYSIMACHUS   She never would tell   192
Her parentage; being demanded that,
She would sit still and weep.

PERICLES
O Helicanus, strike me, honored sir,
Give me a gash, put me to present pain,
Lest this great sea of joys rushing upon me
O'erbear the shores of my mortality   198
And drown me with their sweetness.—O, come hither,
Thou that begett'st him that did thee beget,
Thou that wast born at sea, buried at Tarsus,
And found at sea again!—O Helicanus,
Down on thy knees! Thank the holy gods as loud
As thunder threatens us. This is Marina.—
What was thy mother's name? Tell me but that,
For truth can never be confirmed enough,
Though doubts did ever sleep.

MARINA
First, sir, I pray, what is your title?

PERICLES
I am Pericles of Tyre. But tell me now
My drowned queen's name, as in the rest you said
Thou hast been godlike perfect, the heir of kingdoms,   211
And another life to Pericles thy father.   212

MARINA
Is it no more to be your daughter than   213
To say my mother's name was Thaisa?
Thaisa was my mother, who did end
The minute I began.

PERICLES
Now, blessing on thee! Rise, thou'rt my child.—

___

192 Speaks who speaks   **198 O'erbear** overwhelm   **211 godlike perfect**
all-knowing like a god.   **the heir** i.e., if you can do this, you will show
yourself to be the heir   **212 another life** i.e., the bringer of a new life
213 Is it no more is nothing more required

Give me fresh garments.—Mine own Helicanus,   218
She is not dead at Tarsus, as she should have been,   219
By savage Cleon. She shall tell thee all,
When thou shalt kneel, and justify in knowledge   221
She is thy very princess.—Who is this?

HELICANUS
Sir, 'tis the Governor of Mytilene,
Who, hearing of your melancholy state,
Did come to see you.

PERICLES   I embrace you.
Give me my robes. I am wild in my beholding.   227
                        [*He is freshly attired.*]
O heavens bless my girl! But, hark, what music?
Tell Helicanus, my Marina, tell him
O'er, point by point, for yet he seems to doubt,   230
How sure you are my daughter. But, what music?   231

HELICANUS   My lord, I hear none.

PERICLES   None?
The music of the spheres! List, my Marina.   233

LYSIMACHUS
It is not good to cross him. Give him way.

PERICLES   Rarest sounds! Do ye not hear?

LYSIMACHUS
Music, my lord? I hear.

PERICLES   Most heavenly music!   236
It nips me unto listening, and thick slumber   237
Hangs upon mine eyes. Let me rest.   [*He sleeps.*]

LYSIMACHUS
A pillow for his head. So, leave him all.

---

218 Mine own Helicanus (Perhaps this should read "Mine own,
Helicanus!"—i.e., she is my own daughter.)   **219 should have been** was
thought to have been; or was intended to have been   **221 When** whereupon.   **justify in knowledge** assure yourself (that)   **227 wild . . . beholding** elated and delirious in everything I see, or, possibly, unkempt,
savage in appearance   **230 doubt** (or perhaps *dote*, be in a daze; the
quarto reads *doat*)   **231 sure** certainly   **233 music of the spheres**
celestial harmony supposedly produced by the ordered movements of
the heavenly bodies. (Whether the music is to be heard in the theater is
not clear.)   **236 I hear** (Lysimachus may hear music, or may say this to
humor Pericles and *give him way* [l. 234]. Editors sometimes regard the
word *music* in l. 236 as a stage direction, or assign *I hear* to Pericles.)
237 nips me arrests my attention

Well, my companion friends,
If this but answer to my just belief,   241
I'll well remember you.   [*Exeunt all but Pericles.*]   242

    Diana [appears to Pericles as in a vision].

DIANA
My temple stands in Ephesus. Hie thee thither
And do upon mine altar sacrifice.
There, when my maiden priests are met together
Before the people all,
Reveal how thou at sea didst lose thy wife.
To mourn thy crosses, with thy daughter's, call   248
And give them repetition to the life.   249
Or perform my bidding, or thou livest in woe;   250
Do 't, and happy, by my silver bow!
Awake, and tell thy dream.   [*She disappears.*]

PERICLES
Celestial Dian, goddess argentine,   253
I will obey thee. Helicanus!

    [*Enter Helicanus, Lysimachus, and Marina.*]

HELICANUS   Sir?

PERICLES
My purpose was for Tarsus, there to strike
The inhospitable Cleon, but I am
For other service first. Toward Ephesus
Turn our blown sails; eftsoons I'll tell thee why.   258
[*To Lysimachus.*] Shall we refresh us, sir, upon your
    shore
And give you gold for such provision
As our intents will need?

LYSIMACHUS   Sir,
With all my heart; and, when you come ashore,
I have another suit.

---

241 but . . . belief only turn out as I expect it to   **242 remember** reward   **s.d. Diana appears** (Perhaps she descends from the heavens, and
reascends at l. 252.)   **248 crosses** misfortunes.   **call** lift your voice
249 give . . . life repeat them point for point   **250 Or** either
253 argentine silvery in appearance (as appropriate to the moon goddess)   **258 blown** inflated by the wind and blown great distances.
eftsoons shortly, later on

PERICLES   You shall prevail,
  Were it to woo my daughter, for it seems
  You have been noble towards her.
LYSIMACHUS   Sir, lend me your arm.
PERICLES   Come, my Marina.   *Exeunt.*

                                ❧

5.2   [*Enter Gower, before the temple of Diana of
            Ephesus; Thaisa standing near the altar, as
            high priestess; a number of virgins on each
            side; Cerimon and other inhabitants of Ephesus
            attending.*]

GOWER
  Now our sands are almost run;
  More a little, and then dumb.
  This my last boon give me,
  For such kindness must relieve me:
  That you aptly will suppose   5
  What pageantry, what feats, what shows,
  What minstrelsy, and pretty din
  The regent made in Mytilin
  To greet the King. So he thrived   9
  That he is promised to be wived
  To fair Marina, but in no wise
  Till he had done his sacrifice   12
  As Dian bade; whereto being bound,   13
  The interim, pray you, all confound.   14
  In feathered briefness sails are filled,   15
  And wishes fall out as they're willed.
  At Ephesus the temple see,
  Our King and all his company.
  That he can hither come so soon
  Is by your fancies' thankful doom.   [*Exit.*] 20

5.2. Location: The temple of Diana at Ephesus.
s.d. before the temple (Perhaps Gower reveals this scene, by means of a
curtain, at l. 17.) **5 aptly** readily **9 So he thrived** he fared so well
12 he i.e., Pericles **13 bade** commanded **14 confound** do away with,
omit **15 feathered** winged **20 Is . . . doom** is thanks to the consent
(and willing participation) of your imaginations

5.3   [*Enter Pericles, with his train; Lysimachus,
          Helicanus, Marina, and a lady.*]

PERICLES
   Hail, Dian! To perform thy just command,   1
   I here confess myself the King of Tyre,
   Who, frighted from my country, did wed
   At Pentapolis the fair Thaisa.
   At sea in childbed died she, but brought forth
   A maid child called Marina, who, O goddess,
   Wears yet thy silver livery. She at Tarsus   7
   Was nursed with Cleon, who at fourteen years   8
   He sought to murder; but her better stars
   Brought her to Mytilene, 'gainst whose shore
   Riding, her fortunes brought the maid aboard us,   11
   Where, by her own most clear remembrance, she
   Made known herself my daughter.
THAISA   Voice and favor!   13
   You are, you are—O royal Pericles!   [*She faints.*]
PERICLES
   What means the nun? She dies! Help, gentlemen!
CERIMON   Noble sir,
   If you have told Diana's altar true,
   This is your wife.
PERICLES   Reverend appearer, no;   18
   I threw her overboard with these very arms.
CERIMON
   Upon this coast, I warrant you.
PERICLES   'Tis most certain.
CERIMON
   Look to the lady; O, she's but overjoyed.
   Early one blustering morn this lady was
   Thrown upon this shore. I oped the coffin,
   Found there rich jewels, recovered her, and placed her   24
   Here in Diana's temple.
PERICLES   May we see them?

5.3. **Location:** Scene continues; the temple, as before.
1 just exact   **7 Wears . . . livery** i.e., is still a virgin   **8 with Cleon** under
Cleon's care   **11 Riding** (we) riding at anchor   **13 favor** face, appearance   **18 Reverend appearer** you who appear reverend   **24 recovered**
revived

CERIMON
  Great sir, they shall be brought you to my house,
  Whither I invite you. Look, Thaisa is
  Recovered.
THAISA [*Rising*] O, let me look!
  If he be none of mine, my sanctity   30
  Will to my sense bend no licentious ear,   31
  But curb it, spite of seeing. O, my lord,   32
  Are you not Pericles? Like him you spake,
  Like him you are. Did you not name a tempest,
  A birth, and death?
PERICLES   The voice of dead Thaisa!
THAISA
  That Thaisa am I, supposèd dead
  And drowned.
PERICLES
  Immortal Dian!
THAISA   Now I know you better.
  When we with tears parted Pentapolis,   39
  The King my father gave you such a ring.   40
                        [*She points to his ring.*]
PERICLES
  This, this! No more, you gods! Your present kindness
  Makes my past miseries sports. You shall do well
  That on the touching of her lips I may   43
  Melt and no more be seen.—O, come, be buried
  A second time within these arms!   [*They embrace.*]
MARINA [*Kneeling*]   My heart
  Leaps to be gone into my mother's bosom.
PERICLES
  Look who kneels here! Flesh of thy flesh, Thaisa,
  Thy burden at the sea, and called Marina
  For she was yielded there.
THAISA   Blest, and mine own!   49
                        [*They embrace.*]

30–32 If . . . seeing if he is not my husband, my holy way of life will
lend no credence to my physical sense of sight and my sensual inclination, but will curb my longings (for marriage, my lost life of domestic
pleasure) despite what I see before me   **39 parted** departed from
40 s.d. She points to his ring (Possibly Pericles included this ring among
the jewels he laid in Thaisa's casket; or, more probably, she may recognize it on his finger now.)   **43 That** if   **49 For** because.   **yielded** born

HELICANUS
  Hail, madam, and my queen!
THAISA   I know you not.
PERICLES
  You have heard me say, when I did fly from Tyre
  I left behind an ancient substitute.
  Can you remember what I called the man?
  I have named him oft.
THAISA   'Twas Helicanus then.
PERICLES   Still confirmation!
  Embrace him, dear Thaisa, this is he. [*They embrace.*]
  Now do I long to hear how you were found,
  How possibly preserved, and who to thank,   59
  Besides the gods, for this great miracle.
THAISA
  Lord Cerimon, my lord; this man,
  Through whom the gods have shown their power, that
    can
  From first to last resolve you.
PERICLES   Reverend sir,   63
  The gods can have no mortal officer   64
  More like a god than you. Will you deliver   65
  How this dead queen re-lives?
CERIMON   I will, my lord.
  Beseech you, first go with me to my house,
  Where shall be shown you all was found with her,   68
  How she came placed here in the temple,
  No needful thing omitted.
PERICLES
  Pure Dian, I bless thee for thy vision, and
  Will offer night oblations to thee. Thaisa,   72
  This prince, the fair betrothèd of your daughter,
  Shall marry her at Pentapolis. And now
  This ornament   75
  Makes me look dismal will I clip to form;   76
  And what this fourteen years no razor touched,
  To grace thy marriage day, I'll beautify.

59 possibly by what possible means   **63 resolve you** satisfy your curios-
ity   **64 mortal officer** human agent   **65 deliver** recount   **68 all was**
all that was   **72 night oblations** nightly sacrifices, evening prayers
75 ornament i.e., hair and beard   **76 Makes** which makes.   **to form** to
proper shape

THAISA
  Lord Cerimon hath letters of good credit, sir,   79
  My father's dead.
PERICLES
  Heavens make a star of him! Yet there, my queen,   81
  We'll celebrate their nuptials, and ourselves
  Will in that kingdom spend our following days.
  Our son and daughter shall in Tyrus reign.
  Lord Cerimon, we do our longing stay   85
  To hear the rest untold. Sir, lead 's the way.

                          [Exeunt.]

    [Enter Gower.]

GOWER
  In Antiochus and his daughter you have heard
  Of monstrous lust the due and just reward.
  In Pericles, his queen, and daughter seen,
  Although assailed with fortune fierce and keen,
  Virtue preserved from fell destruction's blast,   91
  Led on by heaven, and crowned with joy at last.
  In Helicanus may you well descry
  A figure of truth, of faith, of loyalty.
  In reverend Cerimon there well appears
  The worth that learnèd charity aye wears.
  For wicked Cleon and his wife, when fame
  Had spread his cursèd deed to the honored name
  Of Pericles, to rage the city turn,   99
  That him and his they in his palace burn;
  The gods for murder seemèd so content
  To punish—although not done, but meant.   102
  So, on your patience evermore attending,
  New joy wait on you! Here our play has ending.

                          [Exit.]

---

79 of good credit trustworthy   **81 there** i.e., in Pentapolis   **85 do
. . . stay** merely postpone the completion of our desires   **91 fell** cruel
99 turn did turn   **102 although . . . meant** i.e., even though the crime
was only intended and not actually carried out

Date and Text

On May 20, 1608, Edward Blount entered in the Stationers' Register, the official record book of the London Company of Stationers (booksellers and printers), "A booke called. The booke of Pericles prynce of Tyre." He also entered *Antony and Cleopatra* at this time, possibly hoping to forestall illegal publishing of these two texts. If so, the plan succeeded with *Antony* but not with *Pericles*. A corrupt quarto of this play was printed in 1609 by William White:

THE LATE, And much admired Play, Called Pericles, Prince of Tyre. With the true Relation of the whole Historie, aduentures, and fortunes of the said Prince: As also, The no lesse strange, and worthy accidents, in the Birth and Life, of his Daughter MARIANA. As it hath been diuers and sundry times acted by his Maiesties Seruants, at the Globe on the Banck-side. By William Shakespeare. Imprinted at London for *Henry Gosson*, and are to be sold at the signe of the Sunne in Pater-noster row, &c. 1609.

Blount was a friend of the players, and the text he registered is likely to have been the prompt copy. (This would explain why it is referred to as "A booke called. The booke of Pericles" in the Stationers' Register, since prompt copies were known technically as "books.") White's text, on the other hand, is a memorially constructed text and at times unintelligible. Two reporters may have been at work, and the typesetting was done by at least three compositors. See the play's Introduction for some examples of inconsistency in the text. Unfortunately, this bad text is the best we have, though George Wilkins's *The Painful Adventures of Pericles* (see below) may have been influenced directly by the play and may well afford some clues as to the wording of the text; a recent and controversial hypothesis argues that *The Painful Adventures* is as much a "report" of the play as is the corrupt quarto. Subsequent quartos appeared in 1609, 1611, 1619, and 1630, but each was set up from the previous edition, and all attempts in them at improvement are editorial rather than authorial. *Pericles* did not appear at all in the First Folio of 1623, perhaps because the editors suspected it to be partly non-Shakespearean, or because they did not possess a reliable text. Arguments for multiple authorship, though based essentially on internal evidence of the play's manifest inconsistencies, are still taken seriously by scholars. George Wilkins especially has been proposed as collaborator in the first two acts. The defects of the first two acts are generally more extensive than those found even in such bad quartos as *Hamlet* or *Romeo and Juliet*. Philip Edwards has argued, on the other hand (*Shakespeare Survey 5*, 1952), that the differences between the first two acts and the last three can be accounted for by memorial reporting and compositorial error. This matter is still in dispute.

A play of *Pericles* (though probably differing textually from the one we have today) must have been in existence by the date of the Stationers' Register entry in May of 1608. A play of *Pericles* was seen by the Venetian Ambassador to England, Zorzi Giustinian, some time during his official stay from January 5, 1606, to November 23, 1608. George Wilkins's *The Painful Adventures of Pericles, Prince of Tyre*, published in 1608, was certainly derived in part from a play about Pericles: its title page offers the work "as it was lately presented by the worthy and ancient poet John Gower," and the final sentence of the Argument urges the reader "to receive this history in the same manner as it was under the habit of ancient Gower, the famous English poet, by the Kings Majesty's players excellently presented." The play to which Wilkins refers may have been Shakespeare's, or perhaps some earlier version—just how early, no one can say. As it stands, however, the play appears to represent the beginning of Shakespeare's fascination with the genre of romance. As such, its date is usually set between 1606 and 1608.

Textual Notes

These textual notes are not a historical collation, either of the early quartos and the early folios or of more recent editions; they are simply a record of departures in this edition from the copy text. The reading adopted in this edition appears in boldface, followed by the rejected reading from the copy text, i.e., the quarto of 1609. Only major alterations in punctuation are noted. Changes in lineation are not indicated, nor are some minor and obvious typographical errors.

Abbreviations used:
F the First Folio
Q the first quarto of 1609
s.d. stage direction
s.p. speech prefix

Copy text: the first quarto of 1609.

1.0. 1 s.p. Gower [not in Q; also in subsequent choruses throughout, except at 4.4, 5.2, and epilogue] **6 holy-ales** Holydayes **11 these** those **39 a** of

1.1. 8 For th' For **18 rased** racte **23 the** th' **25 boundless** bondlesse **57 s.p. Antiochus** [not in Q; also at l. 170] **63 advice** advise **100–101 clear . . . The** cleare: / To . . . them, the **106 know; . . . fit,** know, . . . fit; **112 our** your **114 cancel** counsell **128 you're** you **137 'schew** shew **160 s.d. Enter a Messenger** [after "done" in l. 160 in Q]

1.2. 3 Be my By me **5 quiet?** quiet, **16 me: the** me the **20 honor him** honour **25 th' ostent** the stint **30 am** once **41 blast** sparke **69–70 me . . . thyself.** me: . . . thy selfe, **72 Where, as** Whereas **80 seem** seemes **84 Bethought me** Bethought **85 fears** feare **87 doubt . . . he doth** doo't, as no doubt he doth **93 call 't** call **122 word for faith,** word, for faith **123 will sure** will **124 we'll** will **126 s.d. Exeunt** Exit

1.3. 1 s.p. Thaliard [not in Q] **27 ears it** seas **please** please: **28 seas** Sea **30 s.p. Helicanus** [not in Q] **34 betaken** betake **39 s.d. Exeunt** Exit

1.4. 5 aspire aspire? **13, 14 do** to **13 deep** deepe: **14 lungs** toungs **17 helps** helpers **36 they** thy **39 two summers** too sauers **44 loved.** lou'de, **58 thou** thee **67 Hath** That **these** the **69 men** mee **74 him 's** himnes **77 fear** leaue **78 lowest,** lowest? **97 s.p. All** Omnes **106 ne'er** neare

2.0. 11 Tarsus Tharstill **12 speken** spoken **22 Sends word** Sau'd one **24 intent** in Tent **murder** murdred [some corrected copies of Q have "had . . . murder"]

2.1. 6 left me left my **12 ho** to **Pilch** pelch **31–32 devours** deuowre **39 s.p. Third Fisherman** 1 **48 finny** fenny **53 that?** that, **55 it.** it? **78 quotha** ke-tha **82 holidays** all day **83 moreo'er** more; or **91 your** you **100 is** I **122 pray** pary **123 yet** yeat **130 it.** it **131 thee from** thee, Fame **may 't** may **148 d' ye** di'e [Q uncorr.] do'e [Q corr.] **157 rapture** rupture **160 delightful** delight

2.2. 1 s.p. [and elsewhere] Simonides King **4 daughter** daughter heere
27 Piùe . . . forza Pue Per doleera kee per forsa **28 what's** with **29 chivalry**
Chiually **30 pompae** Pompey **33 Quod** Qui

2.3. 3 To I **13 yours** your **27 Envied** Enuies **39 Yon** You **40 tells me** tels
45 son's sonne **52 stored** stur'd **53 you do** do you **109 s.d. They dance**
[after "unclasp" in Q] **113 to be** be **115 s.p. Simonides** [not in Q]

2.4. 22 welcome. Happy welcome happy **34 death's** death **40 s.d. All**
Omnes

2.5. 74 s.d. Aside [after l. 75 in Q] **76 you, not** you not, **78 s.d. Aside** [after
l. 79 in Q] **92 s.p. Both** Ambo

3.0. 2 the house about about the house **6 'fore** from **7 crickets** Cricket
13 eche each **17 coigns** Crignes **21 stead** steed **29 appease** oppresse
35 Yravishèd Iranyshed **46 Fortune's mood** fortune mou'd **57 not . . . told.**
not? . . . told, **58 hold** hold:

3.1. 1 Thou The **7 Thou stormest** then storme **8 spit** speat **11 midwife**
my wife **14 s.d. Enter Lychorida** [after "Lychorida" in Q] **34 Poor . . .**
nature [Wilkins; not in Q] **38 s.p. Master** 1. Sayl [also in ll. 43 and 47]
45 s.p. Sailor 2. Sayl **51 s.p. Master** 1 **52 custom** easterne **53 for . . .**
straight [printed in Q as part of the next line, after "As you think meet," the
line assigned to Pericles] **60 in the ooze** in oare **62 And aye-** The ayre
65 paper Taper **70 s.p. Sailor** 2 **73 s.p. Master** 2 [also in l. 76]
81 s.d. Exeunt Exit

3.2. 6 ne'er neare **19 quit** quite **51 s.p. [and elsewhere] First Servant** Seru
58 bitumed bottomed **61–62 open. / Soft!** open soft; **79 even** euer **87 lain**
lien **95 breathes** breath

3.3 s.d. at Tarsus Atharsus **6 haunt** hant **31 Unscissored** vnsisterd **hair**
heyre **32 ill** will **37 s.p. Cleon** Cler **41 [and elsewhere] Lychorida**
Lycherida

3.4. s.d. Thaisa Tharsa [also s.p. in l. 4] **5 eaning** learning **9 vestal** vastall
11 s.p. Cerimon Cler **17 s.d. Exeunt** Exit

4.0. 8 music, letters Musicks letters **10 her** hie **heart** art **14 Seeks** Seeke
15 hath our Cleon our Cleon hath **16 wench full grown** full growne wench
17 ripe right **rite** sight **21 she** they **25 to the** too'th **26 bird** bed
29 Dian; still Dian still, **32 With** [after "might" in Q] **35 given. This** giuen,
this **38 murder** murderer **47 carry** carried **48 on** one

4.1. 5 inflaming love i' thy in flaming, thy loue **11 nurse's** Mistresse
25 me. me? **27 On . . . margent** ere the sea marre it **36 here. When** here,
when **40 courses. Go** courses, go **66 stem** sterne **76–77 killed? / Now**
kild now? **99 s.d. Exeunt** Exit **105 aboard. If** aboard, if

4.2. 4 much much much **42 s.p. First Pirate** Sayler **73 was like** was
88 men must men **103 i' the** ethe **117–118 lovers; seldom but** Louers
seldome, but **124 s.p. Bawd** Mari **150 s.d. Exeunt** Exit

4.3. 1 are ere **6 A O** **12 fact** face **14–15 Fates; / To foster is** fates to foster
it, **27 prime** prince **33 Marina's** Mariana's **35 through** thorow

4.4. 3 your our   **7 seem** seemes   **8 i' the** with   **9 story.** storie   **10 the** thy
13 along. Behind along behind,   **14 mind,** mind.   **18 his** this   **19 grow on**
grone   **20 gone.** gone   **23 See** [Q adds an s.p. here: *Gowr.*]   **24 true-owed**
true olde   **26 o'ershowered,** ore-showr'd   **27 embarks. He** imbarques, hee
29 puts put   **to sea. He bears** to Sea he beares   **48 scene** Steare

4.5. 9 s.d. Exeunt Exit

4.6. s.d. three bawds Bawdes 3   **17 loon** Lowne   **22 may so;** may, so
37 dignifies dignities   **69 name 't** name   **88 aloof** aloft   **130 ways** way
132 s.d. Bawd Bawdes   **137 She** He   **154 ways** way   **167 Coistrel** custerell
195 women woman

5.0. 7 roses; Roses   **8 twin** Twine   **13 lost** left   **20 fervor** [Q corr.] former [Q
uncorr.]

5.1. 1 s.p. Tyrian Sailor 1. Say   **7 s.p. Tyrian Sailor** 2. Say   **12 s.p. Tyrian
Sailor** 1. Say [Q corr.] Hell [Q uncorr.]   **36 s.p. Lysimachus** [not in Q]   **37**
[assigned to Lysimachus in Q] [Q provides the s.p. *Hell.*]   **38 night** wight
43 s.p. First Lord Lord   **48 deafened ports** defend parts   **51 with her** her
is now now   **60 gods** God   **68 presence** present   **72 I'd** I do   **wed** to wed
73 one on   **bounty** beautie   **75 feat** fate   **83 Marked** Marke   **91 weighed.**
wayde,   **105 You're** your   **countrywoman** Countrey women   **106 Here** heare
shores . . . shores shewes . . . shewes   **114 cased** caste   **124 palace** Pallas
126 make my make   **129 say** stay   **134 thought'st** thoughts   **143 thou them**
thou   **166 dull** duld   **182 impostor** imposture   **185 s.p. Pericles** Hell
205 me but that, me, but that   **212 life** like   **228–229 music? / Tell** Musicke
tell,   **230 doubt** doat   **249 life** like   **264 suit** sleight

5.2. 8 Mytilin Metalin.   **9 King. So** King, so   **14 interim, pray you, all** Interim pray, you all   **15 filled** fild   **16 willed** wild

5.3. 6 who whom   **15 nun** mum   **22 one** in   **29–30 look! / If** looke if
38 Immortal I, mortall   **51 s.p. Pericles** Hell   **71 I bless** blesse   **79 credit,
sir,** credit. Sir,   **91 preserved** preferd   **92 Led** Lead   **98 deed to** deede,

Shakespeare's Sources

Shakespeare derived his *Pericles* from the ancient Greek romance of Apollonius of Tyre. He had used the story once before, in *The Comedy of Errors*. Medieval versions of this enduringly popular legend include the ninth-century Latin *Historia Apollonii Regis Tyri*, Godfrey of Viterbo's *Pantheon* (c. 1186), the *Gesta Romanorum* (a collection of ancient tales in Latin), John Gower's *Confessio Amantis* (c. 1383–1393), and an English chronicle of *Appolyn of Thyre* translated for the printer Wynkyn de Worde by Robert Copland from a French source (1510). Shakespeare, and possibly the author of a lost earlier dramatic version, were chiefly indebted to Gower's *Confessio* and to Laurence Twine's *The Pattern of Painful Adventures*, a prose version registered in 1576 but existing today only in two editions from about 1594–1595 and 1607.

The order of events in Twine is much the same as in Shakespeare: the hero Apollonius's difficulty with the incestuous King Antiochus, his relieving of the city of Tarsus, his shipwreck at Pentapolis and his falling in love with the King's daughter Lucina (Thaisa in the play), her childbearing and apparent death at sea, the discovery of her floating casket at Ephesus, her revival by the physician Cerimon and her retirement to the temple of Diana in Ephesus, her daughter Tharsia's (i.e., Marina's) capture by pirates and enslavement in a brothel, her conversion of Athanagoras (Lysimachus), the Governor of Machilenta (Mytilene), and Apollonius's eventual reunion with daughter and wife. Gower's account too is much the same, with slightly differing forms of the proper names: Appolinus's (Apollonius's) wife is referred to as the King's daughter, Appolinus's daughter is Thaise, the man she marries is Atenagoras (or Athenagoras) of Mytilene, and so on.

Other than changing some proper names, including that of the hero, Shakespeare did not introduce many significant alterations. To be sure, Shakespeare has given a more sordid impression of the brothel in which Marina must dwell, and has dignified the character of Lysimachus so as to render him worthy of marrying Marina. In Twine's prose account, Athanagoras actually tries to buy Tharsia from the pirates at an auction; when he is outbid by a bawd, he resolves to be the first to visit Tharsia in her new residence. Shakespeare has provided a more decorous action for Lysimachus, although traces of the older and more licentious character occasionally show through and create the impression of inconsistency. For the most part, however, Shakespeare's play stays unusually close to the episodic narrative structure of his sources.

The relationship of George Wilkins's *The Painful Adventures of Pericles, Prince of Tyre* (1608) to Shakespeare's play is complex and uncertain. Beyond doubt, Wilkins's prose account is based in part on a *Pericles* play; Wilkins acknowledges in his Argument that this same story has been recently presented "by the King's Majesty's Players." The play he used may, however, not have been the *Pericles* we know from the corrupt 1609 quarto. Parts of Wilkins's narrative are very close to the earlier *Pattern of Painful Adventures* by Twine. Kenneth Muir suggests (*Shakespeare's Sources*, 1957) that because Wilkins's novel is closer to the first two acts of Shakespeare's play than to the last three acts, Wilkins may have been using an older play that Shakespeare then revised, substantially rewriting the last three acts but changing little in the first two. Whether the presumed *Ur-Pericles* might have been Wilkins's own play is a matter of conjecture. The very existence of an *Ur-Pericles* is by no means universally accepted, but cannot be ruled out as a possibility.

Confessio Amantis
By John Gower
BOOK 8

[Gower, present in the account as narrator, gives much the same story as in the accompanying selection from Laurence Twine's *Painful Adventures* and in Shakespeare's play. The story picks up here as the hero, Appolinus (Apollonius) of Tyre, arrives by ship at Mytilene.]

Title: Confessio Amantis the confession of a lover

The lord which of the city was,
Whose name is Athenagoras,
Was there, and said he woulde see
What ship it is and who they be
That been therein. And after soon,
When that he sigh it was to doon,   1634
His barge was for him arrayed,
And he goeth forth and hath assayed.   1636
He found the ship of great array.   1637
But what thing it amounte may?   1638
He sigh they maden heavy cheer;   1639
But well him thinketh by the manner   1640
That they been worthy men of blood,   1641
And asketh of hem how it stood.   1642
And they him tellen all the caas: 1643
How that her lord fordrive was,   1644
And which a sorrow that he made,   1645
Of which there may no man him glad.   1646
He prayeth that he her lord may see,   1647
But they him told it may not be,
For he lieth in so dark a place
That there may no wight see his face.   1650
But for all that, though hem be loath,   1651
He found the ladder and down he goeth,
And to him spake, but none answer
Again of him ne might he hear,   1654
For aught that he can do or sayn;   1655
And thus he goeth him up again.
Tho was there spoke in many wise   1657
Amonges hem that weren wise   1658
Now this, now that, but at last

1634 he sigh . . . doon he saw what was to be done   **1636 hath assayed**
has examined   **1637 of great array** handsomely outfitted   **1638 what
. . . may** what does it all amount to, mean   **1639 He . . . cheer** he saw
they had gloomy countenances.   **maden** made   **1640 But . . . manner**
but it seems clear to him by their behavior   **1641 been . . . blood** are
men of worthy lineage and estate   **1642 hem** them   **1643 caas** case
1644 her their.   **fordrive was** had been driven about (by fortune)
1645 made suffered   **1646 him glad** offer him comfort   **1647 He . . . see**
i.e., Athenagoras asks that he be allowed to see Apollonius, their lord
1650 wight person   **1651 hem be loath** they are reluctant   **1654 ne
might he** he could not   **1655 sayn** say   **1657 Tho** then   **1658 hem** them.
weren were

The wisdom of the town thus cast   1660
That young Thaise was a-sent.
For if there be amendement   1662
To glad with this woeful king,   1663
She can so much of everything   1664
That she shall glad him anon.   1665
  A messager for her is gone,   1666
And she came with her harp in honde,   1667
And said hem that she woulde fonde   1668
By all the wayes that she can
To glad with this sorry man.
But what he was she wist nought,   1671
But all the ship her hath besought
That she her wit on him dispend,   1673
In aunter if he might amend,   1674
And sayn it shall be well acquit.   1675
  When she hath understonden it,
She goeth her down thereas he lay,   1677
Where that she harpeth many a lay,   1678
And like an angel song withal.   1679
But he no more than the wall
Took heed of anything he heard.
  And when she saw that he so fared,
She falleth with him unto wordes,
And telleth him of sundry bordes,   1684
And asketh him demandes strange,   1685
Whereof she made his herte change,   1686
And to her speech his ear he laide   1687
And hath marvel of that she saide.   1688
For in proverb and in problem   1689
She spake, and bade he shoulde deem   1690
In many a subtle question.

1660 cast determined **1662 amendement** remedy **1663 To glad with** with which to gladden **1664 can** understands **1665 glad** gladden **1666 messager** messenger **1667 honde** hand **1668 fonde** try **1671 what** who. **wist nought** knew not at all **1673 her wit ... dispend** expend her intelligence on him **1674 In aunter if** if peradventure **1675 sayn** say. **acquit** rewarded **1677 thereas** where **1678 Where that** where. **lay** song **1679 song withal** sung moreover **1684 bordes** jests, merry tales **1685 demandes** questions **1686 Whereof** whereby **1687 his ear he laide** he listened **1688 hath marvel of that** marvels at what **1689 problem** riddle **1690 deem** judge

But he for no suggestion
Which toward him she coulde steer
He woulde not one word answer;
But, as a madman, at last
His head weeping away he cast,   1696
And half in wrath he bade her go.
But yet she woulde not do so,
And in the darke forth she go'th
Till she him toucheth, and he wroth,   1700
And after her with his honde   1701
He smote. And thus, when she him fonde   1702
Diseasèd, courteously she said: 1703
"Avoy, my lord, I am a maid!   1704
An if ye wist what I am,   1705
And out of what lineage I cam,   1706
Ye woulde not be so savage."
With that he sobreth his courage   1708
And put away his heavy cheer.   1709
   But of hem two a man may lere   1710
What is to be so sib of blood.   1711
None wist of other how it stood,   1712
And yet the father at last
His herte upon this maide cast,
That he her loveth kindely,   1715
And yet he wist never why;
But all was knowe ere that they went.   1717
For God, which* wot her whole intent,   1718
Her hertes both anon discloseth.   1719
This king unto this maid opposeth,   1720
And asketh first what is her name,
And where she learnèd all this game,   1722
And of what kin she was come.

1696 cast turned   1700 wroth grew angry   1701 after thereupon
1702 fonde found   1703 Diseasèd vexed   1704 Avoy (An exclamation of
fear or surprise.)   1705 An if if.   wist knew   1706 cam came
1708 sobreth his courage calms his wrath   1709 heavy cheer sad countenance   1710 of hem two of these two (Appolinus or Apollonius and
Thaise).   lere learn   1711 is it is.   sib related   1712 None . . . other
i.e., neither knew concerning the other   1715 That so that.   kindely
according to natural feeling   1717 knowe known   1718 which wot her
who knew their   1719 Her their   1720 opposeth poses questions
1722 all this game i.e., all this

And she, that hath his wordes nome, 1724
Answereth and saith: "My name is Thaise,
That was sometime well at aise. 1726
In Tharse I was forthdrawe and fedde. 1727
There I learned, till I was spedde 1728
Of that I can. My father eke 1729
I not where that I should him seek; 1730
He was a king, men tolde me.
My mother dreint was* in the sea." 1732
Fro point to point all she him tolde 1733
That she hath long in herte holde, 1734
And never durst make her moan 1735
But only to this lord alone,
To whom her herte can naught hele, 1737
Turn it to woe, turn it to weal,
Turn it to good, turn it to harm.
   And he tho took her in his arm, 1740
But such a joy as he tho made
Was never seen; thus been they glad
That sorry hadden be toforn. 1743
Fro this day forth* Fortune hath sworn
To set him upward on the wheel.
So go'th the world, now woe, now weal.
   This king hath founde newe grace,
So that out of his darke place
He go'th him up into the light,
And with him came that sweete wight,
His daughter Thaise, and forth anon
They both into the cabin gon
Which was ordainèd for the King. 1753
And there he did off all his thing, 1754
And was arrayèd royally.
And out he came all openly,

1724 **nome** taken in   1726 **sometime** once upon a time.   **aise** ease
1727 **forthdrawe and fedde** brought up and nourished   1728 **was spedde** succeeded (in achieving)   1729 **Of that I can** that which I know. **eke** also   1730 **I not** I do not know   1732 **dreint** drowned   1733 **Fro** from   1734 **holde** held   1735 **moan** complaint   1737 **To whom . . . naught hele** from whom . . . hide nothing   1740 **tho** then. (Also in l. 1741.)   1743 **That . . . toforn** who had been sorrowful until now   1753 **ordainèd** appointed, readied   1754 **did** took.   **thing** things

Where Athenagoras he fond,   1757
Which was lord of all the lond.
He prayeth the King to come and see   1759
His castle both and his city.   1760
And thus they gone forth all in fere,   1761
This king, this lord, this maiden dear.
This lord tho made hem riche feste,   1763
With everything which was honest,   1764
To please with this worthy king.
There lacketh hem no manner thing.   1766
But yet, for all his noble array,
Wifeless he was unto that day,   1768
As he that yet was of young age.   1769
    So fell there into his courage   1770
The lusty woe, the glad pain   1771
Of love, which no man may* restrain
Yet never might as now tofore.   1773
This lord thinketh all this world lore   1774
But if the King will done him grace.   1775
He waiteth time, he waiteth place;
Him thought his herte would to-break   1777
Till he may to this maide speak
And to her father eke also
For marriage. And it fell so
That all was done right as he thought.
His purpose to an end he brought.
She wedded him as for her lord;   1783
Thus been they all of one accord.
    When all was done right as they wolde,   1785
The King unto his sonne tolde   1786
Of Tharse thilke traitery,   1787

1757 fond found   1759 He i.e., Athenagoras   1760 His castle both both
his castle   1761 all in fere all together   1763 tho then.   hem them.
feste feast   1764 honest honorable   1766 no manner thing nothing of
any kind   1768 unto that day at that time   1769 As he like one
1770 his courage i.e., Athenagoras's heart, mind   1771 lusty ardent,
pleasurable   1773 as now tofore before as now   1774 lore lost
1775 But if unless.   done him grace bestow favor on him   1777 Him
thought it seemed to him.   to-break break in pieces   1783 as for her
lord taking him to be her lord   1785 wolde would   1786 sonne i.e., son-
in-law   1787 Of . . . traitery of that treachery at Tharsus

And said how in his company
His daughter and himselven eke
Shall go vengeance for to seek.
   The shippes were ready soon,
And when they saw it was to doon,   1792
Without let of any went,   1793
With sail updrawe forth they went   1794
Towarde Tharse upon the tide.
But He that wot what shall betide,   1796
The highe God, which would him keep,   1797
When that this king was fast asleep   1798
By nightes time He hath him bid   1799
To sail unto another stead: 1800
To Ephesum he bade him drawe,   1801
And, as it was that time lawe,   1802
He shall do there his sacrifice.
And eke he bade in alle wise   1804
That in the temple, amongest all,
His fortune, as it is befall,   1806
Touching his daughter and his wife,
He shall beknowe, upon his life.   1808
   The King of this avision   1809
Hath great imagination   1810
What thing it signifye may;
And natheless, when it was day,   1812
He bade cast anchor and abode;   1813
And while that he on anchor rode,
The wind, that was tofore strange,   1815
Upon the point began to change,   1816
And turneth thither as it shoulde.

1792 it was to doon that things were in readiness   **1793 Without . . .
went** without hindrance in their path   **1794 updrawe** hoisted   **1796 wot
. . . betide** knows everything that will happen   **1797 keep** preserve,
protect   **1798 When that** when   **1799 He . . . bid** i.e., God commanded
Apollonius   **1800 stead** place   **1801 drawe** go   **1802 as . . . lawe** as the
custom stipulated at that time   **1804 in alle wise** at all events   **1806 is
befall** has fallen out, occurred   **1808 beknowe** reveal, make known.
upon his life as if his life depended on it   **1809 avision** vision
1810 Hath great imagination ponders much   **1812 natheless** nevertheless   **1813 He bade . . . abode** he bade the sailors drop anchor, and
waited   **1815 tofore strange** heretofore adverse   **1816 Upon the point** at
that point

Tho knew he well that God it woulde,   1818
And bade the Master make him yare,   1819
Tofore the wind for he would fare   1820
To Ephesum, and so he did.
And when he came into the stead
Whereas he shoulde lond, he londeth   1823
With all the haste he may, and fondeth   1824
To shapen him in such a wise   1825
That he may by the morrow arise
And done after the mandement   1827
Of Him which hath him thither sent.   1828
And, in the wise that he thought,   1829
Upon the morrow so he wrought.
His daughter and his son he nome   1831
And forth to the temple he come   1832
With a great rout in company,   1833
His giftes for to sacrify.   1834
    The citizens tho hearden say   1835
Of such a king that came to pray
Unto Diane, the goddesse,
And, left all other businesse,   1838
They comen thither for to see
The King and the solemnity.
    With worthy knightes environed,
The King himself hath abandoned   1842
To the temple in good intente.
The door is up, and in he wente,
Whereas, with great devotion   1845
Of holy contemplation
Within his herte, he made his shrifte.   1847
And, after that, a riche gifte
He offereth with great reverence;

1818 Tho then.   **it woulde** wished it so   **1819 make him yare** get the
ship in readiness   **1820 Tofore . . . fare** for he wished to sail before the
wind   **1823 Whereas** where.   **lond** land   **1824 fondeth** undertakes
1825 To shapen him to prepare himself   **1827 done** do.   **mandement**
commandment   **1828 Him which** i.e., God, who   **1829 in . . . thought**
just in the way he planned   **1831 nome** took   **1832 come** came
1833 rout crowd.   **in company** accompanying him   **1834 sacrify** offer
as a sacrifice   **1835 tho** then   **1838 left** having left   **1842 himself has
abandoned** has betaken or dedicated himself   **1845 Whereas** where
1847 shrifte confession

And there, in open audience   1850
Of hem that stooden all aboute,
He told hem, and declareth oute   1852
His hap, such as him is befalle;   1853
There was no thing forgot of alle.
His wife, as it was Goddes grace,   1855
Which was professèd in the place,   1856
As she that was abbesse there,   1857
Unto his tale hath laid her ear.   1858
She knew the voice and the visage.
For pure joy as in a rage
She straught to him all at ones,   1861
And fell a-swoon upon the stones
Whereof the temple floor was paved.
She was anon with water laved   1864
Till she came to herself againe,
And then she began to sayne:
"Ah, blessèd be the high sonde   1867
That I may see my husbonde,
Which whilom he and I were one!"   1869
    The King with that knew her anone,   1870
And took her in his arm and kissed;
And all the town this soon it wist.
Tho was there joye manifold,   1873
For every man this tale hath told
As for miracle, and weren glad.   1875
But never man such joye made
As doth the King, which hath his wife.

[Appolinus (Apollonius) and his queen invite Cerimon to return with them to Tyre and to accept their generous thanks.
As in Twine's narrative, Apollonius is venged on Stranulio
and his queen Dionyse. News comes of the death of King
Artestrates of Pentapolis, upon which Appolinus is crowned

1850 **audience** hearing   1852 **oute** aloud   1853 **hap** fortune
1855 **Goddes** God's   1856 **Which was professèd** i.e., who had taken the
vows of a religious order   1857 **As she that was** being as she was
1858 **laid** lent   1861 **straught** went. (Past tense of *stretch*, direct a
course.)   **ones** once   1864 **laved** sprinkled. (Literally, bathed.)
1867 **sonde** decree   1869 **whilom** once upon a time   1870 **anone** at once
1873 **Tho** then   1875 **As for** as being.   **weren** were

king of that country. Gower ends with a moralization on the instability of Fortune but with assurance that even Fortune will ultimately favor those who are true in love.]

———

Text based on *John Gower, De Confessio Amantis. Imprinted at London in Fleet Street by Thomas Berthelette, the 12th day of March, an. 1554.* Gower wrote the original in about 1383–1393. The text was first printed in 1483 by William Caxton and in 1532 by Thomas Berthelette.

In the following, departures from the original text appear in boldface; original readings are in roman.

1718 *which [1483; not in 1554] **1732** *was [1483; not in 1554] **1744** *forth [1483; not in 1554] **1772** *may [1483; not in 1554]

———

The Pattern of Painful Adventures
By Laurence Twine

[Chapters 1 through 3 relate the story of Antiochus's incest with his daughter, Apollonius's difficulty in knowing what to do about the riddle of incest, his escape from the murderous intent of Taliarchus, and his rescue of the city of Tharsus, or Tarsus.]

CHAPTER 4

How Apollonius, departing from Tharsus by the persuasion of Stranguilio and Dionisiades, his wife, committed shipwreck and was relieved by Altistrates, King of Pentapolis.

Thus had not Apollonius aboden[1] many days in the city of Tharsus but Stranguilio and Dionisiades, his wife, ear-

1 aboden abided, dwelt

nestly exhorted him, as seeming very careful and tender of
his welfare, rather to address himself unto Pentapolis or
among the Tirenians as a place most fit for his security,
where he might lie and hide himself in greatest assurance
and tranquillity. Wherefore hereunto he resolved himself
and with convenient expedition[2] prepared all things necessary for the journey. And when the day of his departure was
come, he was brought with great honor by the citizens unto
his ships, where, with a courteous farewell on each side
given, the marines weighed anchor, hoised[3] sails, and away
they go, committing themselves to the wind and water.

Thus sailed they forth along in their course three days
and three nights with prosperous wind and weather, until
suddenly the whole face of heaven and sea began to change;
for the sky looked black and the northern wind arose, and
the tempest increased more and more, insomuch that
Prince Apollonius and the Tyrians that were with him were
much appalled and began to doubt of[4] their lives. But lo,
immediately the wind blew fiercely from the southwest,
and the north came singing on the other side, the rain
poured down over their heads, and the sea yielded forth
waves as[5] it had been mountains of water, that the ships
could no longer wrestle with the tempest, and especially
the admiral,[6] wherein the good prince himself fared, but
needs must they yield unto the present calamity. There
might you have heard the winds whistling, the rain dashing,
the sea roaring, the cables cracking, the tacklings breaking,
the ship tearing,[7] the men miserable shouting out for their
lives. There might you have seen the sea searching[8] the ship,
the boards fleeting,[9] the goods swimming, the treasure
sinking, the men shifting to save themselves, where, partly
through violence of the tempest and partly through darkness of the night which then was come upon them, they
were all drowned, only Apollonius excepted, who, by the
grace of God and the help of a simple board, was driven
upon the shore of the Pentapolitans.

And when he had recovered to[10] land, weary as he was, he

---

2 **convenient expedition** due haste   3 **hoised** hoisted   4 **doubt of** fear
for   5 **as** as if   6 **admiral** flagship   7 **tearing** splitting apart
8 **searching** penetrating, reaching the weak places of   9 **fleeting** floating   10 **recovered to** reached

stood upon the shore and looked upon the calm sea, saying:
"O most false and untrusty sea! I will choose rather to fall
into the hands of the most cruel King Antiochus than venture to return again by thee into mine own country. Thou
hast showed thy spite upon me and devoured my trusty
friends and companions, by means whereof I am now left
alone, and it is the providence of almighty God that I have
escaped thy greedy jaws. Where shall I now find comfort?
Or who will succor him in a strange place that is not
known?"

And whilst he spake these words, he saw a man coming
towards him, and he was a rough fisherman with an hood
upon his head and a filthy leathern pelt upon his back, un-
seemly clad and homely to behold. When he drew near,
Apollonius, the present necessity constraining him thereto,
fell down prostrate at his feet and, pouring forth a flood of
tears, he said unto him: "Whosoever thou art, take pity
upon a poor sea-wrecked man, cast up now naked and in
simple state, yet born of no base degree but sprung forth of
noble parentage. And that thou mayest in helping me know
whom thou succorest, I am that Apollonius, Prince of
Tyrus, whom most part of the world knoweth, and I beseech
thee to preserve my life by showing me thy friendly relief."

When the fisherman beheld the comeliness and beauty of
the young gentleman, he was moved with compassion
towards him, and lifted him up from the ground and led him
into his house and feasted him with such fare as he presently had, and, the more amply to express his great affection towards him, he disrobed himself of his poor and
simple cloak and, dividing it into two parts, gave the one
half thereof unto Apollonius, saying: "Take here at my
hands such poor entertainment and furniture¹¹ as I have
and go into the city, where perhaps thou shalt find some of
better ability that will rue thine estate; and if thou do not,
return then again hither unto me and thou shalt not want
what may be performed by the poverty of a poor fisherman.
And in the meantime, of this one thing only I put thee in
mind: that when thou shalt be restored to thy former dignity, thou do not despise to think on the baseness of the
poor piece of garment." To which Apollonius answered: "If

11 entertainment and furniture provision and apparel

I remember not thee and it, I wish nothing else but that I may sustain the like shipwreck."

And when he had said so, he departed on the way which was taught him, and came unto the city gates, wherein he entered. And while he was thinking with himself which way to seek succor to sustain his life, he saw a boy running naked through the street, girded only with a towel about his middle and his head anointed with oil, crying aloud and saying: "Hearken all, as well citizens as[12] strangers and servants, hearken! Whosoever will be washed, let him come to the place of exercise." When Apollonius heard this, he followed the boy, and coming unto the place, cast off his cloak and stripped himself, and entered into the bain[13] and bathed himself with the liquor.[14]

And, looking about for some companion with whom he might exercise himself according unto the manner of the place and country, and finding none, suddenly unlooked-for entered Altistrates, king of the whole land, accompanied with a great troop of servitors. Anon he began to exercise himself at tennis with his men, which, when Apollonius espied, he intruded himself amongst them into the King's presence and struck back the ball to the King and served him in play with great swiftness. But when the King perceived the great nimbleness and cunning[15] which was in him, surpassing the residue,[16] "Stand aside," quoth he unto his men, "for methinks this young man is more cunning than I." When Apollonius heard himself commended, he stepped forth boldly into the mids[17] of the tennis court and, taking up a racket in his hand, he tossed[18] the ball skillfully and with wonderful agility. After play, he also washed the King very reverently in the bain. And, when all was done, he took his leave dutifully and so departed.

When Apollonius was gone, the King said unto them that were about him: "I swear unto you of truth, as I am a prince, I was never exercised nor washed better than this day, and that by the diligence of a young man I know not what[19] he is." And, turning back, "Go," said he unto one of his servants, "and know what that young man is that hath with such duty and diligence taken pains with me." The

---

12 as well . . . as both . . . and   **13 bain** public bath   **14 liquor** liquid used in the bath (i.e., water)   **15 cunning** skill   **16 residue** rest, others **17 mids** midst   **18 tossed** struck, hit back   **19 what** who

servant, going after Apollonius and seeing him clad in a filthy fisher's cloak, returned again to the King, saying: "If it like[20] Your Grace, the young man is a sea-wrecked man." "How knowest thou that?" said the King. The servant answered: "Though he told me not so himself, yet his apparel bewrayeth his state."[21] Then said the King to his servant: "Go apace[22] after him and say unto him that the King desireth to sup with him this night." Then the servant made haste after Apollonius and did the King's message to him, which, so soon as he heard, he granted thereto, much thanking the King's majesty, and came back with the servant.

When they were come to the gate, the servant went in first unto the King, saying: "The sea-wrecked man for whom Your Grace sent me is come, but is ashamed to come into your presence by reason of his base array." Whom the King commanded immediately to be clothed in seemly apparel and to be brought in to supper, and placed him at the table with him right over against[23] himself. Immediately the board was furnished with all kind of princely fare, the guests fed apace, every man on that which he liked. Only Apollonius sat still and ate nothing, but, earnestly beholding the gold, silver, and other kingly furniture whereof there was great plenty, he could not refrain from shedding tears. Then said one of the guests that sat at the table unto the King: "This young man, I suppose, envieth at Your Grace's prosperity." "No, not so," answered the King. "You suppose amiss. But he is sorry to remember that he hath lost more wealth than this is." And, looking upon Apollonius with a smiling countenance, "Be merry, young man," quoth he, "and eat thy meat[24] with us, and trust in God, who doubtless will send thee better fortune."

CHAPTER 5

How Lucina, King Altistrates's daughter, desirous to hear Apollonius's adventures, fell in love with him.

Now while they sat at meat,[1] discoursing of this and such-

20 **like** please   21 **bewrayeth his state** reveals his condition   22 **apace** quickly   23 **over against** opposite   24 **meat** food

1 **at meat** i.e., at the dinner table

like matters at the board, suddenly came in the King's daughter and only child, named Lucina, a singular beautiful lady and a maiden now of ripe years for marriage. And she approached nigh and kissed the King her father and all the guests that sat with him at the table.

And when she had done so, she returned unto her father and said: "Good Father, I pray you, what young man is this which sitteth in so honorable a place over against you, so sorrowful and heavy?"[2] "O sweet daughter," answered the King, "this young man is a sea-wrecked man, and hath done me great honor today at the bains and place of exercise, for which cause I sent for him to sup with me, but I know not neither what neither whence he is.[3] If you be desirous to know these things, demand of him, for you may[4] understand all things. And peradventure when you shall know you will be moved with compassion towards him."

Now, when the lady perceived her father's mind, she turned about unto Apollonius and said: "Gentleman, whose grace and comeliness sufficiently bewrayeth[5] the nobility of your birth, if it be not grievous unto you, show me your name, I beseech you, and your adventures." Then answered Apollonius: "Madam, if you ask my name, I have lost it in the sea. If you inquire of my nobility, I have left that at Tyrus." "Sir, I beseech you, then," said the Lady Lucina, "tell me this more plainly, that I may understand." Then Apollonius, craving license to speak, declared his name, his birth, and nobility, and unripped[6] the whole tragedy of his adventures in order as is before rehearsed; and when he had made an end of speaking, he burst forth into most plentiful tears.

Which when the King beheld he said unto Lucina: "Dear daughter, you have done evil in requiring to know the young man's name and his adventures, wherein you have renewed his forepassed griefs. But since now you have understood all the truth of him, it is meet, as it becometh the daughter of a king, you likewise extend your liberality towards him, and whatsoever you give him I will see it be performed." Then Lucina, having already in her heart professed to do

2 **heavy** sad   3 **neither what . . . he is** either who he is or where he is from   4 **may** are able to   5 **bewrayeth** reveals   6 **unripped** lay open, exposed to view

him good, and now perceiving very luckily her father's mind to be inclined to the desired purpose, she cast a friendly look upon him, saying: "Apollonius, now lay sorrow aside, for my father is determined to enrich you." And Apollonius, according to the courtesy that was in him, with sighs and sobs at remembrance of that whereof he had so lately spoken, yielded great thanks unto the fair lady Lucina.

Then said the King unto his daughter: "Madam, I pray you take your harp into your hands and play us some music to refresh our guest withal, for we have all too long hearkened unto sorrowful matters." And when she had called for her harp, she began to play so sweetly that all that were in company highly commended her, saying that in all their lives they never heard pleasanter harmony.

[When Apollonius plays in his turn, Lucina is "sharply surprised" with pangs of love for him. With her father's consent she bestows riches on him. Apollonius is prevailed on to stay at her father's court and become her schoolmaster. He and Lucina are married. Chapters 7–10 relate how he hears of Antiochus's death and sets sail with his wife toward Tyre, only to have her die of childbirth at sea. She is thrown into the water and carried ashore at Ephesus, where Cerimon, a physician, restores her to life and places her in the temple of Diana. Apollonius delivers his young daughter Tharsia into the care of Stanguilio and Dionisiades of Tharsus. From her dying nurse, Ligozides, Tharsia learns the identity of her parents.]

CHAPTER 11

How after the death of Ligozides, the nurse, Dionisiades, envying at the beauty of Tharsia, conspired her death, which should have been[1] *accomplished by a villain of the country.*

Tharsia much lamented the death of Ligozides, her nurse, and caused her body to be solemnly buried not far off in a field without[2] the walls of the city, and mourned for her a

1 should have been was intended to have been   **2 without** outside of

whole year following. But when the year was expired, she put off her mourning attire and put on her other apparel, and frequented the schools and the study of liberal sciences as before. And whensoever she returned from school, she would receive no meat before she had visited her nurse's sepulcher, which she did daily, entering thereinto and carrying a flagon of wine with her, where she used to abide a space[3] and to call upon her father and mother.

Now on a day it fortuned that, as she passed through the street with Dionisiades and her companion Philomacia, the people, beholding the beauty and comeliness of Tharsia, said: "Happy is that father that hath Tharsia to his daughter, but her companion that goeth with her is foul and evil favored." When Dionisiades heard Tharsia commended and her own daughter Philomacia so dispraised, she returned home wonderful wroth[4] and, withdrawing herself into a solitary place, began thus secretly to discourse of the matter: "It is now fourteen years since Apollonius, this foolish girl's father, departed from hence, and he never sendeth letters for her nor any remembrance unto her, whereby I conjecture that he is dead. Ligozides, her nurse, is departed,[5] and there is nobody now of whom I should stand in fear. And therefore I will now slay her and dress up mine own daughter in her apparel and jewels."

When she had thus resolved herself upon this wicked purpose, in the meanwhile there came home one of their country villains called Theophilus, whom she called and said thus unto him: "Theophilus, my trusty friend, if ever thou look for liberty,[6] or that I should do thee pleasure,[7] do so much for me as to slay Tharsia." Then said Theophilus: "Alas, mistress, wherein hath that innocent maiden offended, that she should be slain?" Dionisiades answered: "She innocent? Nay, she is a wicked wretch, and therefore thou shalt not deny to fulfill my request, but do as I command thee, or else I swear, by God, thou shalt dearly repent it." "But how shall I best do it, mistress?" said the villain.

---

3 a space for a time   **4 wonderful wroth** terribly angry   **5 departed** dead   **6 look for liberty** i.e., hope to be freed by my means. (Theophilus, called one of the *country villains* above, is both a lowborn rustic and a *villein*, a serf.)   **7 do thee pleasure** give you advancement

She answered: "She hath a custom, as soon as she re-turneth home from school, not to eat meat before that she have gone[8] into her nurse's sepulcher, where I would have thee stand ready with a dagger drawn in thine hand, and when she is come in, grip her by the hair of the head and so slay her. Then take her body and cast it into the sea, and when thou hast so done, I will make thee free,[9] and besides reward thee liberally."

Then took the villain a dagger and girded himself there-with, and with an heavy heart and weeping eyes went forth toward the grave, saying within himself: "Alas, poor wretch that I am, alas, poor Theophilus, that canst not deserve[10] thy liberty but by shedding of innocent blood!" And with that he went into the grave, and drew his dagger and made him ready for the deed.

Tharsia was now come from school, and made haste unto the grave with a flagon of wine as she was wont to do, and entered within the vault. Then the villain rushed violently upon her, and caught her by the hair of the head and threw her to the ground. And while he was now ready to stab her with the dagger, poor, silly[11] Tharsia, all amazed, casting up her eyes upon him, knew the villain, and holding up her hands said thus unto him: "O Theophilus, against whom have I so grievously offended that I must die therefor?" The villain answered: "Thou hast not offended, but thy father hath, which left thee behind him in Stranguilio's house with so great a treasure in money and princely ornaments." "O," said the maiden, "would to God he had not done so! But I pray thee, Theophilus, since there is no hope for me to escape with life, give me license to say my prayers before I die." "I give thee license," said the villain. "And I take God to record[12] that I am constrained to murder thee against my will."

---

8 eat meat . . . gone eat any food before going   **9 make thee free** i.e., free you from bondage. (See note 6 above.)   **10 deserve** earn   **11 silly** innocent   **12 to record** as my witness

Chapter 12

*How certain pirates rescued Tharsia when she should
have been[1] slain and carried her unto the city Machilenta to
be sold among other bondslaves.*

As fortune, or rather the providence of God, served, while
Tharsia was devoutly making her prayers, certain pirates,
which were come aland and stood under the side of an hill
watching for some prey, beholding an armed man offering
violence unto a maiden, cried unto him and said: "Thou
cruel tyrant, that maiden is our prey and not thy victory,
and therefore hold thine hands from her, as thou lovest thy
life!" When the villain heard that, he ran away as fast as he
could and hid himself behind the sepulcher. Then came the
pirates and rescued Tharsia and carried her away to their
ships, and hoised sails and departed.

And the villain returned home to his mistress and said
unto her: "That which you commanded me to do is dispatched, and therefore now I think it good that you put on a
mourning garment, and I also, and let us counterfeit great
sorrow and heaviness[2] in the sight of all the people, and say
that she died of some grievous disease."

But Stranguilio himself consented not to this treason,[3]
but so soon as he heard of the foul mischance, being as it
were amort* and mated[4] with heaviness and grief, he clad
himself in mourning array and lamented that woeful case,
saying: "Alas, in what mischief am I wrapped? What might
I do or say herein? The father of this maiden delivered this
city from the peril of death; for this city's sake he suffered
shipwreck, lost his goods, and endured penury. And now he
is requited with evil for good. His daughter, which he committed unto me to be brought up, is now devoured by a most
cruel lioness.[5] Thus I am deprived, as it were, of mine own
eyes[6] and forced to bewail the death of an innocent, and am
utterly spoiled[7] through the fierce biting of a most venom-

---

1 **should have been** was about to have been   2 **heaviness** sadness
3 **treason** treachery   4 **amort and mated** dejected and confounded
5 **lioness** i.e., Dionisiades. (She is also the *venomous serpent* of his next
sentence.)   6 **deprived . . . eyes** i.e., forced to weep   7 **spoiled** injured,
ruined

ous serpent." Then casting his eyes up towards heaven, "O God," said he, "thou knowest that I am innocent from the blood of silly[8] Tharsia, which thou hast to require[9] at Dionisiades's hands." And therewithal he looked towards his wife, saying: "Thou wicked woman, tell me, how hast thou made away Prince Apollonius's daughter, thou that livest both to the slander of God and man?"

Dionisiades answered in many words, evermore excusing herself, and, moderating the wrath of Stranguilio, she counterfeited a feigned sorrow by attiring herself and her daughter in mourning apparel, and in dissembling tears before the people of the city, to whom she said: "Dearly beloved friends and citizens of Tharsus, for this cause we do weep and mourn in your sight, because the joy of our eyes and staff of our old age, the maiden Tharsia, is dead, leaving unto us bitter tears and sorrowful hearts. Yet have we already taken order for her funerals[10] and buried her according to her degree."[11] These words were right grievous unto the people, and there was almost none that let not fall some tears for sorrow. And they went with one accord unto the marketplace, whereas[12] her father's image stood, made of brass, and erected also another unto her there, with this inscription: "Unto the virgin Tharsia, in lieu of[13] her father's benefits, the citizens of Tharsus have erected this monument."

CHAPTER 13

How the pirates which stole away Tharsia brought her to the city Machilenta and sold her to a common bawd, and how she preserved her virginity.

The meantime, while these troubles were at Tharsus, the pirates, being in their course[1] upon the sea, by benefit of a happy wind arrived at Machilenta and came into the city.

---

8 silly innocent   **9 which . . . require** i.e., which you must seek an accounting for.   **require** ask   **10 taken order . . . funerals** made arrangements for her funeral   **11 degree** rank   **12 whereas** where   **13 in lieu of** in payment for and recognition of

1 in their course on their way

Now had they taken many more men and women besides
Tharsia, whom all they brought ashore and set them to sell[2]
as slaves for money. Then came there sundry to buy such as
they lacked for their purposes, amongst whom a most vile
man-bawd, beholding the beauty and tender years of Tharsia, offered money largely for her. Howbeit Athanagoras,
who was prince of the same city, beholding likewise the noble countenance and regarding the great discretion of the
maiden in communication,[3] outbid the bawd and offered
for her ten sesterces[4] of gold. But the bawd, being loath to
lose so commodious[5] a prey, offered twenty. "And I will give
thirty," said Athanagoras. "Nay, I will give forty," said the
bawd. "And I fifty," quoth Athanagoras. And so they continued in outbidding one another until the bawd offered an
hundred sesterces of gold, to be payed ready down. "And
whosoever will give more," said he, "I will yet give ten sesterces more than he." Then Prince Athanagoras thus bethought him secretly in his mind: "If I should contend with
the bawd to buy her at so high a price, I must needs sell
other slaves to pay for her, which were both loss and shame
unto me. Wherefore I will suffer[6] him to buy her, and when
he setteth her to hire[7] I will be the first man that shall come
unto her, and I will gather the flower of her virginity, which
shall stand me in as great stead as if I had bought her."
Then the bawd paid the money, and took the maiden and
departed home.

And when he came into his house, he brought her into a
certain chapel where stood the idol of Priapus,[8] made of
gold and garnished with pearls and precious stones. This
idol was made after the shape of a man, with a mighty member, unproportionable to the body, always erected, whom
bawds and lechers do adore, making him their god and wor-
shipping him. Before this filthy idol he commanded Tharsia
with reverence to fall down. But she answered: "God forbid,
master, that I should worship such an idol. But sir," said
she, "are you a Lapsatenian?" "Why askest thou?" said the

---

2 **set them to sell** put them up for sale   3 **discretion . . . in communication** propriety of speech   4 **sesterces** Roman coins   5 **commodious**
profitable   6 **suffer** allow   7 **setteth her to hire** prostitutes her for
money   8 **Priapus** god of fertility (and hence of lechery)

bawd. "I ask," quoth she, "because the Lapsatenians do worship Priapus." This spake she of simplicity,[9] not knowing what he was. "Ah, wretch," answered he, "knowest thou not that thou art come into the house of a covetous bawd?" When Tharsia heard that, she fell down at his feet and wept, saying: "O master, take compassion upon my virginity and do not hire out my body for so vile a gain!" The bawd answered: "Knowest thou not that neither bawd nor hangman do regard tears or prayers?"

Then called he unto him a certain villain which was governor over his maids and said unto him: "Let this maiden be decked in virgin's apparel, precious and costly, and write this title upon her: 'whosoever deflowereth Tharsia shall pay ten pieces of gold, and afterward she shall be common unto the people for one piece at a time.'" The villain fulfilled his master's commandment, and the third day after that she was bought she was with great solemnity conducted through the street with music, the bawd himself with a great multitude going before, and so conveyed unto the brothel house.

When she was come thither, Athanagoras, the prince, disguising his head and face because he would not be known, came first in unto her. Whom when Tharsia saw, she threw herself down at his feet and said unto him: "For the love of God, gentleman, take pity on me, and by the name of God I adjure and charge you that you do no violence unto me, but bridle your lust, and hearken unto my unhappy estate and consider diligently from whence I am sprung. My father was poor Apollonius, Prince of Tyrus, whom force contrained to forsake his own country. My mother was daughter to Altistrates, King of Pentapolis, who died in the birth of me, poor wretch, upon the sea. My father also is dead, as was supposed, which caused Dionisiades, wife to Stranguilio of Tharsus—to whom my father committed me, of special trust, to be brought up, being but an infant— envying mine estate and thirsting after my wealth, to seek my death by the hands of a villain; which had been accomplished—and I would to God it had before I had seen

9 of simplicity in innocence

this day—but that I was suddenly taken away by the pirates, which sold me unto this filthy bawd." With these or such-like words declared she her heavy fortune, eftsoons[10] sobbing and bursting out into streams of tears, that for extreme grief she could scarcely speak. When she had in this manner uttered her sorrow, the good prince, being astonied and moved with compassion, said unto her: "Be of good cheer, Tharsia, for surely I rue thy case; and I myself have also a daughter at home, to whom I doubt[11] that the like chances may befall."

And when he had so said, he gave her twenty pieces of gold, saying: "Hold here a greater price or reward for thy virginity than thy master appointed.[12] And say as much unto others that come unto thee as thou hast done to me, and thou shalt withstand them." Then Tharsia fell on her knees and, weeping, said unto him: "Sir, I give you most hearty thanks for your great compassion and courtesy, and most heartily I beseech you upon my knees not to descry unto any that which I have said[13] unto you." "No, surely," answered Athanagoras, "unless I tell it unto my daughter, that she may take heed, when she cometh unto the like years, that she fall not into the like mishap." And when he had so said, he let fall a few tears and departed.

Now as he was going, he met with another pilgrim that with like devotion[14] came for to seek the same saint, who demanded[15] of him how he liked of the maiden's company. "Truly," answered Athanagoras, "never of any better." Then the young man, whose name was Aportatus, entered into the chamber, and the maiden, after the manner, shut the door to, and Athanagoras listened at the window. Then said Aportatus unto Tharsia: "How much did the Prince give unto thee?" She answered: "Forty pieces of gold." Then said he: "Receive here of me an whole pound weight of gold." The Prince, which heard this talk, thought then in his mind: "The more that you do give her, the more she will weep as thinking that you would look for recompense, the which she meaneth not to perform."

---

10 eftsoons immediately after, or repeatedly   **11 doubt** fear
12 appointed fixed as a fee   **13 descry . . . said** tell anyone what I have said (about my parentage and fortunes)   **14 like devotion** similar devotion (i.e., lust)   **15 demanded** asked

The maiden received the money, and fell down on her knees at his feet and declared unto him all her estate, with tears, as is before showed. When Aportatus heard that, he was moved with compassion and he took her up from the ground, saying: "Arise, Lady Tharsia, we are all men, and subject to the like chances." And therewithal he departed. And when he came forth, he found Prince Athanagoras before the door, laughing at him, to whom he said: "Is it well done, my liege, thus to delude a poor gentleman? Was there none to whom you might begin in tears[16] but unto me only?" Then communed[17] they further of the matter, and sware an oath between themselves that they would not bewray[18] these words unto any. And they withdrew themselves aside into a secret place, to see the going in and coming forth of other,[19] and they saw many which went in and gave their money and came forth again weeping. Thus Tharsia, through the grace of God and fair persuasions, preserved her body undefiled.

CHAPTER 14

How Tharsia withstood a second assault of her virginity, and by what means she was preserved.

When night was come, the master bawd used always[1] to receive the money which his women had gotten by the use of their bodies the day before. And when it was demanded of Tharsia, she brought him the money, as the price and hire of her virginity. Then said the bawd unto her: "It is well done, Tharsia. Use diligence henceforth, and see that you bring me thus much money every day." When the next day was passed also, and the bawd understood that she remained a virgin still, he was offended, and called unto him the villain that had charge over the maids and said unto him: "Sirrah, how chanceth it that Tharsia remaineth a vir-

---

16 to whom . . . tears i.e., whom you might distress and subject to the tears of Tharsia. (*Begin* may mean "entrap.") **17 communed** conversed **18 bewray** divulge **19 other** others

1 used always made it his custom

gin still? Take her unto thee and spoil her of her maidenhead, or be sure thou shalt be whipped."

Then said the villain unto Tharsia: "Tell me, art thou yet a
virgin?" She answered: "I am, and shall be as long as God
will suffer me." "How, then," said he, "hast thou gotten all
this money?" She answered, with tears, falling down upon
her knees: "I have declared mine estate, humbly requesting
all men to take compassion on my virginity." And now likewise, falling then down at his feet also, "Take pity on me,
good friend, which am a poor captive and the daughter of a
king, and do not defile me!" The villain answered: "Our
master the bawd is very covetous and greedy of money, and
therefore I see no means for thee to continue a virgin."
Whereunto Tharsia replied: "I am skillful in the liberal sciences and well exercised in all studies, and no man singeth
or playeth on instruments better than I. Wherefore, bring
me into the marketplace of the city, that men may hear my
cunning.[2] Or let the people propound any manner of questions and I will resolve them. And I doubt not but by this
practice I shall get store of money daily." When the villain
heard this device, and bewailed the maiden's mishap, he
willingly gave consent thereto, and brake with the bawd, his
master, touching that matter, who, hearing of her skill and
hoping for the gain, was easily persuaded.

Now, when she was brought into the marketplace, all the
people came thronging to see and hear so learned a virgin,
before whom she uttered her cunning in music and her eloquence in speaking, and answered manifestly unto all such
questions as were propounded unto her with such perspicu-
ity that all confessed themselves fully satisfied, and she
won great fame thereby and gained great sums of money.
But as for Prince Athanagoras, he had evermore a special
regard in the preservation of her virginity, none otherwise
than if she had been his own daughter, and rewarded the
villain very liberally for his diligent care over her.

CHAPTER 15

*How Apollonius, coming to Tharsus and not finding his
daughter, lamented her supposed death, and, taking ship*

2 **cunning** skill

again, was driven by a tempest to Machilenta, where Tharsia was.

Return we now again unto Prince Apollonius, who, whiles these things were doing at Machilenta, when the fourteenth year was expired, arrived at Tharsus and came into the city unto the house of Stranguilio and Dionisiades, with whom he had left his young daughter Tharsia. Whom when Stranguilio beheld and knew, he ran hastily unto his wife Dionisiades and said: "Thou reportedst that Prince Apollonius was dead, and lo now, where he is come to require his daughter! What shall we now do or say unto him?" Then cried she out: "Alas, wretched husband and wife that we are! Let us quickly put on our mourning attire and shed forth tears, and he will believe us that his daughter died a natural death." And when they had appareled themselves, they came forth unto Apollonius, who, seeing them in mourning attire, said unto them: "My trusty friends Stranguilio and Dionisiades, why weep ye thus at my coming? And tell me, I pray you—which I rather believe—whether these tears be not rather mine than yours."[1] "Not so, my lord Apollonius," answered the wicked woman. "And I would to God some other body and not mine husband or I were enforced to tell you these heavy tidings, that your dear daughter Tharsia is dead."

When Apollonius heard that word he was suddenly cut to the heart, and his flesh trembled that he could scarce stand on his legs. And long time he stood amazed, with his eyes intentively[2] fixed on the ground. But at length, recovering himself and taking fresh breath, he cast up his eyes upon her and said: "O woman, if my daughter be dead, as thou sayest she is, is the money also and apparel perished with her?" She answered: "Some is, and some yet remaineth. And as for your daughter, my lord, we were always in good hope that when you came you should have found her alive and merry. But to the intent you may the better believe us concerning her death, we have a sufficient witness. For our citizens, being mindful of your benefits bestowed upon them, have erected unto her a monument of brass by yours,

1 **whether . . . yours** i.e., whether it is not I who should be weeping
2 **intentively** intently

which you may go see if you please." And when she had so said, she brought forth such money, jewels, and apparel which it pleased her to say were remaining of Tharsia's store.

And Apollonius, believing indeed that she was dead, said unto his servants: "Take up this stuff and bear it away unto the ships, and I will go walk unto my daughter's monument." And when he came there, he read the superscription in manner as is above written, and he fell suddenly, as it were, into an outrageous affection,[3] and cursed his own eyes, saying: "O, most cruel eyes, why can you not yield forth sufficient tears and worthily bewail the death of my dear daughter?" And with that word, with grief and extreme sorrow, he fell into a swoon, from which, so soon as ever he was once revived, immediately he went unto the ships unto his servants, unto whom he said: "Cast me, I beseech you, into the very bottom of the sea. For I have no joy of my life, and my desire is to yield up my ghost in the water." But his servants used great persuasions with him to assuage his sorrow, wherein presently they somedeal[4] prevailed, as they might in so woeful a case. And partly the time, which is a curer of all cares, continually mitigated some part of the grief. And he, espying the wind to serve well for their departure, hoised up sail and bid the land adieu.

They had not thus sailed long in their course but the wind came about to a contrary quarter, and blew so stiffly that it troubled both sea and ships. The rain fell fiercely overhead, the sea wrought wondrously under the ships, and, to be short, the tempest was terrible for the time. It was then thought best in that extremity to strike sail and let the helm go, and to suffer the ship to drive with the tide, whither it should please God to direct it. But as joy evermore followeth heaviness, so was this sharp storm occasion of a sweet meeting of the father with the daughter, as in process[5] hereafter it shall appear. For while Apollonius's ship runneth thus at random, it striketh upon the shore of the city Machilenta, where at that present his daughter Tharsia remained.

---

3 outrageous affection extreme passion   **4 somedeal** to some extent
5 process the narrative

Now, it fortuned that this very day of their arrival was the birthday of Prince Apollonius, and, whenas the mariners saw themselves so happily come to the land, both for the gladness of the one and joy of the other[6] the Master of the ship and all the whole company gave a great shout.

When Apollonius, who lay solitarily under the hatches, heard such a sudden voice of mirth, he called unto the Master and demanded what it meant. The Master answered: "We rejoice, and be you glad also with us, my lord, for this day we do solemnize the feast of your birth." Then Apollonius sighed and said himself: "All keep holiday save I only, and let it suffice unto my servants that I only remain in sorrow and heaviness. Howbeit, I give unto them ten pieces of gold to buy what they will to keep holiday withal. But whosoever shall call me unto the feast or go about to provoke me unto mirth, I command that his thighs[7] shall be broken." So the cater[8] took the money and went aland, and provided necessaries and returned again unto the ship.

[The rest of *Painful Adventures* tells the tale narrated in the selection from Gower's *Confessio Amantis*, and in Shakespeare's play, of Apollonius's reunion with his daughter and his wife. Apollonius orders the bawd of Machilenta to be burnt, and exposes the villainy of Stranguilio and Dionisiades so that their subjects stone them to death. Apollonius and Lucina, with Tharsia, see King Altistrates in Pentapolis before he dies. Apollonius rewards the fisherman there, and pardons the pirates who stole Tharsia. Apollonius is given a son and heir by Lucina, named Altistrates after his grandfather, before Apollonius dies at a ripe old age as the beloved ruler of three kingdoms—Tyrus, Antiochia, and Pentapolis.]

---

6 the one and . . . the other i.e., Apollonius's birthday and reaching land   **7 his thighs** i.e., the bones in his thighs   **8 cater** buyer of "cates" or provisions; the caterer

Text based on *The Pattern of Painful Adventures: Containing the Most Excellent, Pleasant, and Variable History of the Strange Accidents that Befell unto Prince Apollonius, the Lady Lucina his Wife,* and *Tharsia His Daughter. Wherein the Uncertainty of This World and the Fickle State of Man's Life are Lively Described. Gathered into English by Laurence Twine, Gentleman.* Imprinted at London by Valentine Simmes for the Widow Newman, n.d. (1594?).

In the following, the departure from the original text appears in boldface; the original reading is in roman.

p. 134 *amort a mopte

Further Reading

Barber, C. L. " 'Thou that Beget'st Him that Did Thee Beget'. Transformation in *Pericles* and *The Winter's Tale*." *Shakespeare Survey* 22 (1969): 59–67. Barber differentiates *Pericles* and *The Winter's Tale* from Shakespeare's festive comedies by observing that whereas the comedies move to the creation of new families, the romances trace a movement toward the reunion of families who have been separated. The comedies free innocent sexuality from the inhibitions of the family, while in these two romances the families must be freed from the threat of sexual degradation. The romances thus portray the transformation of love rather than merely its liberation.

Berry, Francis. "Word and Picture in the Final Plays." In *Later Shakespeare*, ed. John Russell Brown and Bernard Harris. Stratford-upon-Avon Studies 8. London: Edward Arnold; New York: St. Martin's Press, 1966. Berry sees in *Pericles* a play of daring shifts of focus. Its temporal, spatial, and stylistic dislocations suit Shakespeare's thematic exploration of the effect of parents' past actions on the present lives of their children, and point toward the fuller integration of striking verbal and visual elements in the plays that follow *Pericles*.

Brockbank, J. Philip. "*Pericles* and the Dream of Immortality." *Shakespeare Survey* 24 (1971): 105–116. For Brockbank, *Pericles* demonstrates the workings of a miraculous providence permitting the renewal of life. The play, however, is art, not allegory: we are allowed an artistically satisfying dream of immortality, but one in which the insistence upon its own art reveals the reassuring moral order to be a triumph of human creativity rather than divine.

Dunbar, Mary Judith. " 'To the Judgement of Your Eye': Iconography and the Theatrical Art of *Pericles*." In *Shakespeare, Man of the Theatre*, ed. Kenneth Muir, Jay L. Halio, and D. J. Palmer. Newark, Del.: Univ. of Delaware Press, 1983. Dunbar argues that Shakespeare's use in *Pericles* of traditional iconography—such as the skulls at Antiochus's court, the various emblems of Fortune, and the tableaux of grief and patience—is central to both the play's intellectual design and its theatrical coherence.

Eliot, T. S. "Marina." *The Complete Poems and Plays, 1909–1950*. New York: Harcourt Brace and World, 1952. Eliot considered *Pericles* a "very great play," and its recognition scene "the finest of all": a "perfect example of the 'ultra-dramatic,' a dramatic action of beings who are more than human, or rather, seen in a light more than that of day." His poem "Marina" (1930) interpretively reimagines the transformative power of the moment of recognition and must stand as one of the most important and perceptive readings of Shakespeare's play.

Ewbank, Inga-Stina. " 'My name is Marina': The Language of Recognition." In *Shakespeare's Styles: Essays in Honour of Kenneth Muir*, ed. Philip Edwards, Inga-Stina Ewbank, and G. K. Hunter. Cambridge and New York: Cambridge Univ. Press, 1980. Ewbank examines Shakespeare's rhetorical control of the scene of recognition between Pericles and Marina, where Shakespeare gets as close as he ever does to "expressing the inexpressible." Ewbank compares the scene with similar ones in the tragedies and comedies, isolating those features in *Pericles* that can be considered peculiar to romance.

Felperin, Howard. "The Great Miracle: *Pericles*." *Shakespearean Romance*. Princeton, N.J.: Princeton Univ. Press, 1972. The presence of Gower and the self-conscious archaism of the early scenes are for Felperin signals to an audience that *Pericles* is not naturalistic drama. He argues that in *Pericles* Shakespeare self-consciously turns to an archaic dramatic tradition: the miracle play of the late medieval drama. In the miracle play Shakespeare found formal and thematic elements that serve his renewed interest in patterns of fall and redemption and his focus on scenes of recognition.

Frye, Northrop. *A Natural Perspective: The Development of Shakespearean Comedy and Romance*, esp. pp. 27–33. New York: Columbia Univ. Press, 1965. Frye argues that *Pericles* is a "radical experiment in processional narrative," spectacular and virtually operatic "with its narrative *recitativo* and its dramatized *arias*." Nonetheless the play's appeal is "childlike and concrete," evoking primitive responses from an audience to its archetypal action.

Hoeniger, F. David. "Gower and Shakespeare in *Pericles*." *Shakespeare Quarterly* 33 (1982): 461–479. To Hoeniger, those aspects of the play's first two acts that seem "so obviously defective and crude" are evidence not of divided authorship but of the play's "highly unusual character and technique." The play daringly exploits the interplay between Gower's archaic aesthetic notions and Shakespeare's more sophisticated dramaturgy.

Kermode, Frank. *"Pericles." William Shakespeare: The Final Plays.* London: Longmans, Green, 1963. Though Kermode believes the play to be neither completely successful nor entirely by Shakespeare, he finds the play significant as it serves as the prototype of Shakespeare's movement beyond tragedy. The play's focus on reunion and on the restoration of harmony after suffering and loss provides the pattern of romance that Shakespeare developed out of a renewed interest in the laws of comic form and the dramatic and moral possibilities of that form.

Knight, G. Wilson. "The Writing of *Pericles*." *The Crown of Life: Essays in Interpretation of Shakespeare's Final Plays.* London: Oxford Univ. Press, 1947. Knight argues that *Pericles* is a thoroughly organic play in which Shakespeare takes familiar themes and carries them to a new and higher level of intensity: "It is Shakespeare's total poetry on the brink of self-knowledge," a parable that moves past loss in a "miraculous reversal" that "makes tragedy in its short illusion a game."

Muir, Kenneth. "Shakespeare's Hand in *Pericles*." *Shakespeare as Collaborator.* London: Methuen; New York, Barnes and Noble, 1960. Muir considers the critical debate on whether *Pericles* is entirely Shakespeare's own work or a collaborative effort, and concludes that the text we have is Shakespeare's reworking of an earlier, lost version of the play (which he has modified lightly in the first two acts, extensively in the final three).

Peterson, Douglas L. *"Pericles:* The World as 'A Lasting Storm.'" *Time, Tide, and Tempest: A Study of Shakespeare's Romances.* San Marino, Calif.: Huntington Library, 1973. The "sudden and unexpected tempests (real and metaphorical)" of the play represent for Peterson the adversity that tests human faith and constancy. As Peri-

cles learns that the world is purposeful and benign, the
play becomes "a complex emblem" celebrating the restorative power of love.

Pitcher, John. "The Poet and Taboo: The Riddle of Shakespeare's *Pericles*." *Essays and Studies* 35 (1982): 14–29.
Examining a series of structural symmetries in *Pericles*,
Pitcher argues that the theme of incest unifies the play,
organizing its episodic narrative. In Mytilene, however,
Marina's virtue prevents "the crime of the past threading
its symmetry into the future," and the play reaffirms
sanctioned marriages and the social order.

CYMBELINE

Introduction

The genre of *Cymbeline* can be suggested by such critical terms as romance, tragicomedy, and the comedy of forgiveness. As in *Pericles*, *The Winter's Tale*, and other late plays, Shakespeare turns to the improbable fictions of romance: a stepmother-queen skilled in poisons and envious of her fair and virtuous stepdaughter (as in *Snow White*), lost sons recognized by the inevitable birthmark, the reunion of many persons long separated by exile and wandering, the intervention of the gods by means of a riddling and inane prophecy. These are the distinguishing features of English romance in the 1580s, a titillating vogue exploited by Robert Greene and other professional writers of the period. From two romantic plays of the 1580s—*Sir Clyomon and Sir Clamydes* and *The Rare Triumphs of Love and Fortune*— Shakespeare may in fact have drawn source material. Why did he turn to such old-fashioned models in 1608–1610? The choice has puzzled many critics, and has prompted them to speak condescendingly of Shakespeare's dotage or to assign parts of the play (notably the descent of Jupiter) to some other dramatist.

Shakespeare nevertheless courted the improbabilities, even the deliberate absurdities, of romance with a serious artistic purpose. In part he was responding to a new literary fashion, evident especially in the private theaters, for a tragicomedy of refined sensibility—a literary fashion that produced Francis Beaumont and John Fletcher's *Philaster*. This play of about 1609 features, like *Cymbeline*, a rapidly moving and ingeniously woven plot of separation and reunion, a king's daughter betrothed by her father to a churl and then wrongly accused of infidelity, a young maiden in male disguise, and other comparable details. Whether *Cymbeline* preceded or followed *Philaster* is a matter difficult to determine, since *Cymbeline* can be dated only approximately in 1608–1610 on grounds of style; but in any case Shakespeare's fascination with romance goes back at least to *All's Well That Ends Well* (c. 1601–1604) and *Pericles* (c. 1606–1608). His experiments in the genre must be viewed as innovative and unique. Despite the affinities to Fletcher-ian tragicomedy, Shakespeare never indulges in the cloying sensationalism, the exaggerated heightening of exotic emotion, and (except in *The Winter's Tale*) the trickery of concealing essential information from the audience, such as we find in works of Beaumont and Fletcher. Shakespeare's interest in romantic improbability is related to the serious motif of redemption, of an unexpected and undeserved second chance for erring humanity.

The tragic possibilities are manifold. Cymbeline, like Lear (another king from British legendary history in Raphael Holinshed's *Chronicles*, 1587,) tyrannically repulses a virtuous daughter and rewards the vicious members of his family with predictably unhappy consequences. Posthumus Leonatus, like Othello, commands the death of his beloved mistress because he believes a groundless but cunningly presented accusation of her infidelity; finally, concluding that he has destroyed the only person capable of giving order to his life, he despairingly longs for death. Whereas in a similar situation Lear and Othello suffer the tragic consequences of their choice, Cymbeline and Posthumus are spared. Some benign force, integral to the world of this play, prevents fallible mortals from pursuing their misguided intentions to the point of irreversible injury. Posthumus relies for his vengeance on the virtuous Pisanio, who cannot bring himself to slay Imogen. The Queen's box of "poison," given ultimately to Imogen by the well-meaning but duped Pisanio, is only a sleeping potion concocted by that kindly manipulator behind the scenes, Doctor Cornelius. These fortunate avoidances of disaster recall other such narrow escapes in *Much Ado about Nothing*, *All's Well That Ends Well*, and *Measure for Measure*. They also anticipate similar events in *The Winter's Tale*.

Because *Cymbeline* begins with dilemmas like those of *King Lear* and *Othello*, the prevailing tone is at first serious. (The editors of the 1623 First Folio printed the play among the tragedies.) The King's behavior toward Imogen and her virtuous but nonaristocratic husband, Posthumus, is tyrannical. Disinterested observers condemn the wicked Queen's dominance over Cymbeline, and laugh privately at the Queen's cowardly and ridiculous son Cloten. A good man like Belarius suffers lifelong banishment from the envious court and spends his exile dwelling in caves. Many conventional features of romantic narrative—wandering and return, loss and rediscovery, apparent death and rebirth—are set in motion by the need to escape from a court dominated by the wicked Queen. One by one, honest persons of the play—Posthumus, Imogen, Pisanio—leave society in disfavor to be reunited in the wild landscape of Belarius and his foster sons. Italy is no better a place than the English court. Its evil genius is Iachimo, apostle of animal appetite, duplicity, and a cynical indifference to human values.

Despite the prevailing tragic mood at first, there are promises of brighter prospects. Posthumus's birth is attended by wondrous circumstances that would appear to single him out for an extraordinary career. In the first scene, moreover, we learn that the King's only two sons were stolen from their nursery in their infancy—an obvious hint that they will turn up sooner or later. Cloten, too, strikes us as a ludicrous suitor for Imogen, the type of buffoonish rival appropriate to a love comedy. Because he is witless, superficial, and preoccupied with clothes, he deserves to be exposed and ridiculed. Even his death is grostesquely comic. He acts as a foil or caricature to Posthumus, in whose clothes he is erroneously taken by Imogen to be her dead husband; the outward resemblance of the two men suggests to us that Posthumus has not been unlike Cloten when he has suspected Imogen of betraying him and has vowed revenge. Cloten's death signals an end to Posthumus's disposition to be fooled by appearances.

The initial somber mood, with its threat of tragic outcome, is further lightened by the juxtaposition of sorrow and hope. When Arviragus and Guiderius mourn the "death" of Imogen with an exquisite song on the vanity of human striving, we respond to the appropriateness of the sentiment and yet qualify our sorrow with our consoling knowledge that she has really taken a sleeping potion. Similarly, when Posthumus jests eloquently about death with his jailer and prepares to find his only freedom in surcease, we cannot ignore Jupiter's assurance of eventual redress in the action immediately preceding. As in *Measure for Measure*, suffering and regret are framed in the benign context of a providential design that the audience alone can fully appreciate.

Tragicomedy threatens and consoles at the same time. The chief source of anxiety is Posthumus's renunciation of Imogen. The sensationalism of the plot derives in part from the use of the "wager" motif found in several Italianate *novelle*, such as the ninth tale of the second day in Giovanni Boccaccio's *Decameron*. The psychological portrait of Posthumus's wavering and fall, like that of Othello or Leontes, is intense and ugly, fraught with grotesque images of sexual coupling. As with Othello and Leontes, Posthumus is threatened by his wife's sexuality and is unable to respond securely to her offered love that is appropriately sensual and spiritual. He is comfortable only when he thinks of her as sexually restrained even in her marriage bed, praying forbearance of her husband with "A pudency so rosy the sweet view on 't / Might well have warmed old Saturn" (2.5.11–12). He is aroused by virginal unresponsiveness, repelled by too great a responsiveness. Such unbalanced expectations leave him prone to insinuations that women practice deception. Once Imogen has been made to appear carnal to him, she becomes monstrous and insatiable in his imagination. He conjures up the imagined sexual triumph of Iachimo in animalistic terms: "Perchance he spoke not, but, / Like a full-acorned boar, a German one, / Cried 'O!' and mounted" (ll. 15–17). Like Othello, he insists on being proved a cuckold; once he has experienced jealousy, he can expect only one conclusion. He longs "to tear her limbmeal," and like Lear he would violently destroy "The woman's part in me" (2.4.150; 2.5.20). Such perversity in a man who is in most respects noble threatens disaster and demands either a tragic ending or the unexpected second chance of tragicomedy. Posthumus receives that second chance, but meantime he has raised a familiarly Shakespearean question about his responsibility for his fall. How could he have avoided accusing Imogen falsely?

Powerful forces militate against Posthumus. Iachimo is a plausible villain, in the vein of Don John (*Much Ado about Nothing*), Iago (*Othello*), and Edmund (*King Lear*). Like them he plots to arouse envy and dissension in others, by means of appearance falsely presented to the senses. We can readily understand him in human terms as a quarrelsome and lecherous man, and yet his sinister delight in mischief also suggests a more all-encompassing and diabolical evil. His contention is that every woman has her price (and every man too). When he discovers in Imogen a wholesomeness that will not yield to his insinuations, he seeks to destroy her as a dangerous refutation of his low premise about human nature. He states the confrontation between them in cosmic terms: "Though this a heavenly angel, hell is here" (2.2.50). He does not, to be sure, boast gleefully to the audience or dominate the play as Iago does; moreover, he himself experiences the beneficent change brought about by the play's happy ending, and speaks in praise of Imogen's virtue. As befits a tragicomedy, he is more sinister than potent, almost at times a travesty of a tragic villain. Nevertheless, in his scenes of villainy his function is that of a diabolical tempter working through humanity's frail senses. His use of the ring as evidence recalls the handkerchief in *Othello*. Iachimo creates a minutely circumstantial inference of Imogen's transgression and lets Posthumus's inclination to believe the worst do the rest.

Like Othello, then, Posthumus must bear the blame for his loss of faith. The tempter can prevail upon our senses, but humanity's own wavering heart chooses evil. Trustworthy observers perceive Posthumus's fallacy and indicate the correct response; as Philario says, "This is not strong enough to be believed / Of one persuaded well of" (2.4.134–135). True faith urges that, being what she is, Imogen could not do the thing alleged. She is, like Helena and Desdemona before her, a virtuous woman who responds to her undeserved tribulations with forbearance (though even her patience has a limit, and she too is capable of overreacting and misjudging). She overbalances faithlessness with her forgiveness. Her perseverance in virtue confounds Iachimo's thesis and rescues Posthumus from his worst self. Iachimo and she are spiritual contestants for the allegiance of Posthumus's faith. She triumphs not through Posthumus's choice (which is for evil) but through her own unassailable goodness. Belatedly, too, Posthumus makes the amends that are necessary if we are to accept him as the restored hero. He forgives Imogen even before he knows of her innocence, seeks death as an atonement, and moves by degrees through sin to regret, confession of guilt, and penance. His peasant costume in Act 5 signals the resignation of worldly desire he must achieve to be worthy of an almost miraculous second chance. As a fallen human being he can never truly deserve that mercy, but he can strive at least to atone for what he has done.

The story of King Cymbeline's long-lost sons is similarly tragicomic, and is even more explicitly indebted to the conventions of romance with its motifs of banishment, wandering, and eventual recognition and reunion. The sylvan setting of this romantic narrative lends to the second half of the play a primal vigor and mystery (as also in *The Winter's Tale*). Arviragus and Guiderius remind us of medieval legends about Parzival: that is, like Parzival they are young princes raised in a wilderness, lacking courtly training and yet possessing an "invisible instinct" (4.2.179) that prompts them to assert their royal blood. Ignoring their foster father's warning about the ingratitude and decadence of the courtly society he has abandoned, the princes long to prove themselves in deeds of chivalry. They are a rejuvenating force in this play, bringing together the ideals of medieval knighthood and the unsullied strength of their sylvan world. Cloten, that effete semblance of a courtier and their foil in every respect, is appropriately killed by these agents of "divine Nature" (l. 172). They cherish Imogen as one of their own, and grieve for her seeming death with the vivid immediacy of those who have lived with nature. Her seeming death and reawakening is for them something like the restorative cycle of the seasons, bringing a renewal of natural vigor that nicely complements the spiritual grace she embodies for Posthumus. Her name to them is appropriately "Fidele." Old Belarius's reconciliation with Cymbeline signals an end to political injustice, still another consequence of humanity's fallen condition for which grace must be provided.

The story of the war between Britain and Rome, derived in part from Holinshed's *Chronicles*, contributes also to the process of spiritual rebirth. The war sets in motion a series of apparently unrelated events, including the return to Britain of Posthumus and Iachimo, without which the play's happy conclusion would be impossible. Although the war itself is destructive and is supported chiefly by Cloten and the Queen (whose patriotic speeches show us just how hollow a thing patriotism can be), the war does lead ultimately to new life for Britain as well as for the romantic lovers.

Sudden turns in the battle, especially when an old man and two boys defend a narrow lane against an army, are seen as marvels directed by some higher power. In the benign aftermath of war, the King, no longer misled by evil counselors, finds reconciliation with his daughter and her husband as well as with Rome. The final scene, in which the seeming accidents of fortune are unraveled, is a structural tour de force of comic discovery.

The three main plots of *Cymbeline*—of Posthumus and Imogen, of the King's lost sons, and of the war between Britain and Rome—may seem outwardly unconnected with one another. Certainly the play ranges over a wide geographical space and introduces a host of characters, many of whom never meet until the final scene. Yet the three plots are unified by being structurally like one another. In each, we perceive a pattern of fall from innocence, followed by conflict and eventual redemption. Posthumus is tempted into a loss of faith and attempted murder from which he recovers through penance. The saga of the King's sons provides a secular equivalent in its story of estrangement, mistaken identity, and eventual recovery of loss. Politically, Britain is alienated from Rome through the machinations of the Queen only to rediscover after many years a new harmony. The plots impinge on one another in ways that seem contrived (as, for example, when the accidents of war finally bring together Imogen, Posthumus, and Iachimo in the presence of Cymbeline), and yet we understand at last that the contrivance is providential and benign, intended to test humanity and then reward those who have persevered or at least found true contrition.

Shakespeare thus creates a world of the play in which seeming accident is benign. His spokesman as deus ex machina (literally illustrating that term, for Jupiter "descends" from the stage roof by means of some mechanical device) is Jupiter. The scene of this divine intervention (5.4) is so blatantly unrealistic that, as we have seen, many critics have wished to exonerate Shakespeare of having written it; but this very unreality is the keynote of the play's ending. Jupiter places the suffering we have witnessed in a larger perspective: "Whom best I love I cross, to make my gift, / The more delayed, delighted. Be content" (5.4.101–102). In the tragicomic view, suffering is merely a manifestation of a design, engineered and supervised by a loving deity, to test and strengthen us. The test affirms Imogen's strength, shows Posthumus a reason to cherish what he would otherwise destroy, and even reclaims the evil agent by whom the test had been administered. As Caius Lucius insists to the long-suffering Fidele, "Some falls are means the happier to arise" (4.2.406).

Cymbeline
in Performance

Like several other of Shakespeare's late plays, including
The Winter's Tale, Cymbeline is too romantic and irregular
to have satisfied most theater managers in the late seventeenth and the eighteenth centuries. Its stage history until
the nineteenth century is largely that of repeated adaptation. Only two references to performances of the play before 1642 have survived: Simon Forman saw *Cymbeline* at
the Globe Theatre sometime before September 1611, recalling in his *Book of Plays* the plot and all the major characters' names except that of Imogen; and King Charles I is
reported to have "well liked" the play when it was performed before him on January 1, 1634, by the King's players. After 1642 *Cymbeline*'s first reappearance was in the
form of *The Injured Princess, or The Fatal Wager* by
Thomas D'Urfey at the Theatre Royal, Drury Lane, in 1682.
This adaptation entirely replaced Shakespeare's play in the
ensuing decades, at the theater in Lincoln's Inn Fields and
then at the Theatre Royal, Covent Garden, until its last performance in 1738.

D'Urfey's alterations are not unlike those made by John
Dryden and William Davenant in their version of *The Tempest:* the addition of a counterplot to provide antithetical
balance, an added interest in the delicious agonies of lovers
in distress, and a cutting away of much Shakespearean material to make room for the new symmetries. D'Urfey's
added plot dramatizes the fortunes of Clarinna, daughter of
Pisanio and an attendant of Eugenia (D'Urfey's renamed
Imogen). Clarinna is kidnapped by the villains, Cloten and
Shatillion (i.e., Iachimo), with the help of Eugenia's wicked
stepmother, the Queen. Her captors threaten Clarinna with
a fate worse than death and oblige her to suffer other terrors of imprisonment until she manages to elude them and
find eventual happiness. These tribulations are consider-
ably augmented by her father's loss of faith in her innocence and his desertion of her, but in time Pisanio rallies to
the cause and saves Clarinna from ravishment, being

blinded by Cloten as he does so. The wager between Ur-
saces (Posthumus) and Shatillion has taken place in France,
as in the source story in Boccaccio's *Decameron*.

Other names are changed besides those of Imogen, Iachimo, and Posthumus: Philario becomes Beaupré and
Guiderius becomes Palladour. D'Urfey's names sound like
those of Restoration heroic drama, and for good reason.
The mixture of tragedy and comedy in Shakespeare's play,
although hardly sanctioned by classical precept, was evidently acceptable to Restoration audiences; to the extent
that *Cymbeline* belongs to the tragicomic tradition of
Guarini, Beaumont, and Fletcher, all that D'Urfey needed to
do was unify the action through added symmetries (arrang-
ing matters, for example, so that the villains, Cloten and
Shatillion-Iachimo, work in concert rather than in separate
plots) and do everything possible to augment sensationalism and titillation.

Theophilus Cibber's *Cymbeline* at the Haymarket Theatre in 1744 was evidently close to Shakespeare's original,
and two years later at Covent Garden, Hannah Pritchard
starred as Imogen in a production that used a restored
Shakespearean text. David Garrick revived an essentially
Shakespearean version (albeit in a substantially shortened
text, cutting 569 lines from Act 5 alone) in 1761 at Drury
Lane, and found the role of Posthumus well enough suited
to his talents that he played it a number of times in succeeding years. Still, the response of the late eighteenth century
to *Cymbeline* was ambivalent. On the one hand, the play's
ancient British setting and passionate story of jealousy ap-
pealed to pre-Romantic sensibilities. On the other hand, the
play appeared to contain gross absurdities and a virtual an-
nihilation of the dramatic unities. Readers and spectators
of a neoclassical persuasion felt that *Cymbeline* had to be
pruned of its manifest improbabilities if its beauties were
to be at all discernible.

The Covent Garden revival of 1759 sought to remedy the
presumed defects. The reviser on this occasion was William
Hawkins, previously a fellow of Pembroke College and Professor of Poetry at Oxford, who, acknowledging that he
found something pleasingly romantic and British about
Shakespeare's story, saw a compelling need also to "reduce" *Cymbeline* "as much as possible to the regular stan-

dard of the drama." Hawkins provided the play with the dramatic unities "almost upon the plan of Aristotle himself" by limiting the action to two locales, Cymbeline's royal castle and the vicinity of Belarius's cave in mountainous Wales.

As Hawkins restructures the order of events, Lucius and his Roman legions are present from the start. Cloten and Iachimo (renamed Pisanio) are villainously in league, as in D'Urfey's adaptation, working to make Posthumus jealous of his wife so that Cloten can satisfy his own nefarious craving for her. Time and place are unified to an important extent by commencing the play well after the banishment of Posthumus from court and by excising his travels in Italy, including the wager; instead, he is in Wales, and has written to his servant Philario (i.e., Shakespeare's Pisanio) commanding him to kill Imogen, who, having been disinherited by her father and thrown into prison, has managed to escape disguised as a boy. Philario grows suspicious of Imogen, as in D'Urfey's play (though not in Shakespeare's), adding thereby to Imogen's melodramatic plight. Testing Imogen at the cave in Wales by telling her she has drunk poison, Philario is persuaded of her innocence by her virtuous response in the face of a presumably imminent death. In the ensuing action Palador (Guiderius) kills not only Cloten but Pisanio (Iachimo), who confesses his villainy before he dies and gives Palador a letter written by Cloten that implicates this villain in the false slandering of Imogen. The ending thus clears Posthumus of all wrong and makes him a rather uninteresting beleaguered hero (who, among his other deeds, has saved the life of Cymbeline during the battle), while reducing Pisanio-Iachimo to the flat dimensions of a stereotypical villain. No doubt the most lasting achievement of this production was the dirge composed by Thomas Arne to be sung at Imogen's mistaken funeral.

Nineteenth-century productions of *Cymbeline* were drawn to its potential for scenic beauty, at court, in Italy, and in the Welsh hills. John Philip Kemble (who had first acted the play at Drury Lane in 1785) revived it in 1801 with some renaming of characters and with considerable expenditure on the sets, properties, and costumes, especially in the dance sequence that Kemble devised for Cloten's unsuccessful serenading of Imogen and in the scene of Iachimo's concealment in Imogen's bedchamber. The latter featured a bed for Imogen so imposing, according to a contemporary account, that the actor of Iachimo (William Barrymore), though tall of stature, "stood almost in need of a ladder to take a view of Imogen's person." Kemble's sister, Sarah Siddons, played the part of Imogen, and their brother Charles that of Guiderius. A production at Covent Garden in 1825 took an operatic turn, with some thirteen songs including "Hark, hark, the lark" (2.3.20–28). Charles Kemble, at Covent Garden in 1827, strove for authentic detail, modeling the scenery and costuming on "the habits, weapons, and buildings of the Gaulish and Belgic colonists of the southern counties of Britain before their subjugation by the Romans." Kemble examined ancient coins, literary accounts by Julius Caesar, Pliny, and Suetonius, as well as the ancient arms and armor in the collection of Samuel Meyrick. William Charles Macready exercised similar care in the devising of stage picture during revivals at Covent Garden in 1838 and on other subsequent occasions until 1847, usually playing Posthumus to Helen Faucit's Imogen. (He had first played Posthumus in 1811 in Newcastle and in London in 1818.) The year 1847 also saw Samuel Phelps's first *Cymbeline* at the Sadler's Wells Theatre, a production that gave Charles Dickens "extraordinary gratification"; Phelps revived the play in 1850, 1854, 1857, and 1860. The Theatre Royal in Marylebone handsomely produced *Cymbeline* in 1849, and the reborn Drury Lane under the management of Edmund Falconer and F. B. Chatterton successfully revived the play in 1864 with Helen Faucit as Imogen and Phelps as Posthumus. At the Queen's Theatre in 1872, in a production starring George Rignold as Posthumus, an attempt was made to present Cymbeline's palace in Anglo-Saxon architecture and with Posthumus in a sort of Viking costume.

Possibly the most splendid production in this opulent vein was that of Henry Irving at the Lyceum Theatre in 1896, with Ellen Terry as Imogen and Irving as Iachimo. Undeterred by the mix of visual styles called for in a play that is obviously more romantic than historical, Irving positively embraced the opportunity for showing Celtic Britain in one scene and ancient Rome in another. Although the expensive sets required a good deal of cutting and rearranging of scenes, as in most of his big productions, Irving did not flinch from including Italy along with the court of Cymbeline and the Welsh mountainside; on the contrary, he took the occasion of Posthumus's being in Rome to stage a dance in Philario's house with all the trappings of Roman luxury. In fact Irving went to the unnecessary trouble of showing two Roman interiors, the triclinium or dining room with three couches in Philario's house, and the atrium, or central court. The scenic splendors in Britain were of the first century, showing the garden of Cymbeline's palace, rooms in the palace, Imogen's bedchamber, the terrain before the cave of Belarius, the country near Milford Haven, and the field of battle. The Britons were picturesque in their kilts. "Hark, hark, the lark" was sung to a new setting. Among the things that were omitted to make room for the spectacle was Posthumus's dream vision (5.4). Irving seems to have been responding to judgments like that expressed in the *Athenaeum* of September 26, 1896: "To produce the play in its integrity would have been impossible. Apart from the fact that the mere question of time would prohibit such a plan, there are large hunks of *Cymbeline* wholly unsuited to stage exposition as at present understood" (quoted in George Odell's *Shakespeare from Betterton to Irving*, vol. 2, p. 396).

Nevertheless, a desire for change could be sensed. *The Times*, in its review of Irving's production, wondered if, in place of the spectacular realistic illusion and its effect of textual mutilation, "it would not be well to adopt on the stage a more or less fantastic setting, with something of that indefiniteness of place, period, and costume, which the modern stage-manager for some reason will only allow to comic opera." Certainly twentieth-century productions of *Cymbeline*, though not as numerous as revivals of the better-known plays, have answered *The Times*'s call, freeing the stage from the scenic literalism that jarringly and anachronistically brings together such contrasting worlds as Italy, the English court, and Wales, and that in any case was invoked on Shakespeare's original stage not by painted sets but by the actors' costumes, gestures, and words.

The movement away from Victorian spectacle was clearly

signaled when Ben Greet directed Sybil Thorndike as Imogen at the Old Vic in 1918, in a production marked by its rapid pace and simplified staging. Nugent Monck, who like Greet had worked with William Poel, the champion of Elizabethan staging techniques, similarly directed the play in 1923 at Norwich on the intimate stage of the Maddermarket Theatre, and again twenty years later. When in 1946 Monck was invited to direct *Cymbeline* at Stratford-upon-Avon, the production, with Paul Scofield as Cloten, continued the commitment to what *The Times* approvingly called "Elizabethan simplicity." Barry Jackson, with H. K. Ayliff, directed a modern-dress *Cymbeline* at the Birmingham Repertory in 1923 that "bewildered" the critics. Indeed it "eventually created," as Jackson happily reported, "a national and worldwide controversy." An even more radical treatment of the play took place at the Cambridge Festival Theatre in 1934 when Terence Gray produced his highly stylized *Cymbeline* on a giant checkerboard. In 1937 Ben Iden Payne, at Stratford-upon-Avon, directed the play as a Jacobean court masque, featuring a permanent setting with acting spaces among the pillars and arches for the play's different locales. In 1950, at the Open Air Playhouse in Montreal, the innovative Theodore Komisarjevsky directed *Cymbeline* as his final production of Shakespeare. Komisarjevsky's bright, good-natured version of the play starred Christopher Plummer as Posthumus. In modern dress, the play opened at a cocktail party with "Sophisticated Lady" playing in the background, and at one point two characters exited, singing, "We're off to see the Wizard, the wonderful Wizard of Oz."

Komisarjevsky's inventive theatrical wizardry marked the end of a half century of theatrical experimentation that allowed *Cymbeline* to be freed from the Victorian pictorial tradition that, whatever virtues it might otherwise possess, certainly slowed down the play. Twentieth-century attempts to recover the tradition have been few, although a romantic production at Stratford-upon-Avon in 1957, with Peter Hall as director and Peggy Ashcroft as Imogen, employed a cluttered Gothic set (by Lila de Nobili) in which the rhythms of the production tended to be lost. More attuned to the temper of recent years, A. J. Antoon directed the play at New

York's Delacorte Theater, in 1971, as a grotesque fairy tale. Cloten's severed head became a bouncing ball; Cymbeline was an ancient clown given to sudden rages; and the battle between Britain and Rome was staged between papier-mâché animals and birds. John Barton, Barry Kyle, and Clifford Williams directed the play at Stratford-upon-Avon in 1974, with Tim Piggott-Smith as Posthumus, Susan Fleetwood as Imogen, and Ian Richardson as a comic Iachimo. Barton emphasized a coherent narrative line by using Cornelius as a presenter of the action, "an intermediary," as *The Times* reported, "between the modern spectator and the fabulous events." David Jones's *Cymbeline* at Stratford-upon-Avon in 1979, with Judi Dench as Imogen, playfully drew attention to the play's incongruities, as did the modern-dress version directed by Robin Phillips in 1986 at Stratford, Ontario. Phillips used three separate period styles and settings for the play's three plots: Belarius's cave was located in prehistoric Wales, the war scenes were set during World War I, and the scenes in the court were placed in the decadently fashionable Europe of the late 1920s. Jupiter was a World War I ace in goggles, appearing from above in a burst of light. Wales was the primitive land of Tarzan, as far visually from the dolce vita of European high society as one could imagine. The stage in the final scene was cluttered as events sped toward the incredible resolution, and the entire company called attention to the artifice of the production as they exited singing up the aisles.

George Bernard Shaw's notorious alteration of the last act, *Cymbeline Refinished*, replaced Shakespeare's final act in a production at the Embassy Theatre in London in 1937. It challenged the play's improbable romantic conclusion with typical Shavian iconoclasm by cutting out Posthumus's vision of descending Jupiter, by eliminating virtually all the heroic feats of arms of Belarius's royal stepsons, and by recreating Shakespeare's characters in the mode of Ibsen. Yet for all the diverting quality of this revision, *Cymbeline* is precisely what Shaw resisted. It offers not Ibsen's naturalistic world but a self-consciously theatrical universe in which descents of the gods are somehow expected and a part of the playworld.

The play's mix of genres, its seeming naïveté and simplicity, the deliberate courting of the improbable, all declare the play's delight in its artificiality—an artificiality that directors have learned to embrace, rather than overcome, with techniques of staging that call attention to their very theatricality.

CYMBELINE

[*Dramatis Personae*

CYMBELINE, *King of Britain*
QUEEN, *wife of Cymbeline*
CLOTEN, *her son by a former husband*
IMOGEN, *daughter of Cymbeline by a former queen*
POSTHUMUS LEONATUS, *a gentleman, Imogen's husband*
BELARIUS, *a banished lord, disguised as Morgan*
GUIDERIUS, ⎰*sons of Cymbeline, disguised*
ARVIRAGUS, ⎱*as Polydore and Cadwal,*
 ⎱*supposed sons of Morgan*

PISANIO, *servant of Posthumus*
CORNELIUS, *a physician*
Two LORDS *attending Cloten*
Two GENTLEMEN *of Cymbeline's court*
HELEN, *a lady attending Imogen*
Another LADY *attending Imogen, or possibly the same*
A LADY *attending the Queen*
A British LORD
Two British CAPTAINS
Two JAILERS
Two MESSENGERS

PHILARIO, *friend of Posthumus,*⎱ *Italians*
IACHIMO, *friend of Philario,* ⎰
A FRENCHMAN, *friend of Philario*

CAIUS LUCIUS, *general of the Roman forces*
Two Roman SENATORS
A TRIBUNE
A Roman CAPTAIN
Philharmonus, a SOOTHSAYER

JUPITER
The Ghost of SICILIUS *Leonatus, father of Posthumus*
The Ghost of Leonatus' MOTHER
The Ghosts of Leonatus' two BROTHERS

*Lords, Ladies, Attendants, Musicians attending Cloten, a
 Dutchman, a Spaniard, Senators, Tribunes, Captains, and
 Soldiers*

SCENE: *Britain; Italy*]

1.1 *Enter two Gentlemen.*

FIRST GENTLEMAN
  You do not meet a man but frowns. Our bloods   1
  No more obey the heavens than our courtiers'   2
  Still seem as does the King's.
SECOND GENTLEMAN   But what's the matter?   3
FIRST GENTLEMAN
  His daughter, and the heir of 's kingdom, whom
  He purposed to his wife's sole son—a widow   5
  That late he married—hath referred herself   6
  Unto a poor but worthy gentleman. She's wedded,
  Her husband banished, she imprisoned. All
  Is outward sorrow, though I think the King   9
  Be touched at very heart.
SECOND GENTLEMAN   None but the King?
FIRST GENTLEMAN
  He that hath lost her, too. So is the Queen,   11
  That most desired the match. But not a courtier,
  Although they wear their faces to the bent   13
  Of the King's looks, hath a heart that is not
  Glad at the thing they scowl at.
SECOND GENTLEMAN   And why so?
FIRST GENTLEMAN
  He that hath missed the Princess is a thing
  Too bad for bad report, and he that hath her—
  I mean, that married her, alack, good man!
  And therefore banished—is a creature such
  As, to seek through the regions of the earth
  For one his like, there would be something failing 21
  In him that should compare. I do not think   22
  So fair an outward and such stuff within   23
  Endows a man but he.

1.1. Location: Britain. At the court of King Cymbeline.
1–3 Our . . . King's i.e., the constitutions and dispositions of us mortals
are not more obedient to the influence of the heavenly bodies than our
courtiers' demeanors and looks follow those of the King   **5 purposed to**
intended for   **6 late** lately.   **referred** given (in marriage)   **9 outward**
mere pretense of (as explained in ll. 9–22)   **11 He . . . her** i.e., Cloten,
the Queen's son, Imogen's unsuccessful wooer (also in l. 16)   **13 bent**
inclination   **21 his like** like him   **22 him . . . compare** anyone chosen
for comparison   **23 stuff** (1) substance (2) fabric (as the imagery of
ll. 26–27 further suggests)

SECOND GENTLEMAN   You speak him far.   24
FIRST GENTLEMAN
   I do extend him, sir, within himself,   25
   Crush him together rather than unfold   26
   His measure duly.
SECOND GENTLEMAN What's his name and birth?   27
FIRST GENTLEMAN
   I cannot delve him to the root. His father   28
   Was called Sicilius, who did join his honor   29
   Against the Romans with Cassibelan,   30
   But had his titles by Tenantius, whom   31
   He served with glory and admired success,
   So gained the sur-addition Leonatus;   33
   And had, besides this gentleman in question,
   Two other sons, who in the wars o' the time
   Died with their swords in hand; for which their father,
   Then old and fond of issue, took such sorrow   37
   That he quit being, and his gentle lady,   38
   Big of this gentleman our theme, deceased   39
   As he was born. The King he takes the babe   40
   To his protection, calls him Posthumus Leonatus,
   Breeds him and makes him of his bedchamber,   42
   Puts to him all the learnings that his time   43
   Could make him the receiver of, which he took,
   As we do air, fast as 'twas ministered,
   And in 's spring became a harvest, lived in court—   46
   Which rare it is to do—most praised, most loved,
   A sample to the youngest, to th' more mature   48

24 speak him far go far in praising him   **25 I . . . himself** I stretch his
virtues within the limits of what he actually is   **26 unfold** expand,
disclose, unwrap   **27 measure** i.e., dimensions, worth.   **duly** to the
degree that he merits   **28 delve . . . root** i.e., account fully for his lineage   **29 join his honor** give his honorable assistance in arms
30 Cassibelan Cymbeline's uncle; see 3.1.5. (According to Holinshed,
Cassibelan was Cymbeline's great-uncle, being younger brother and
successor to King Lud.)   **31 Tenantius** Cymbeline's father, son of King
Lud. (In Holinshed, Tenantius is Cassibelan's nephew.)   **33 sur-addition**
additional title, surname.   **Leonatus** lion-born   **37 fond of issue** devoted to his children   **38 quit being** left existence, died.   **gentle** noble
39 Big . . . theme i.e., pregnant with Posthumus   **40 King he** i.e., King
42 of his bedchamber one of his intimate retinue   **43 Puts to** sets
before.   **time** time of life, age   **46 a harvest** i.e., ripe in learning
48 sample example

A glass that feated them, and to the graver   49
A child that guided dotards. To his mistress,   50
For whom he now is banished, her own price   51
Proclaims how she esteemed him; and his virtue
By her election may be truly read   53
What kind of man he is.

SECOND GENTLEMAN   I honor him
Even out of your report. But pray you, tell me,
Is she sole child to the King?

FIRST GENTLEMAN   His only child.
He had two sons; if this be worth your hearing,
Mark it: The eldest of them at three years old,
I' the swaddling-clothes the other, from their nursery
Were stol'n, and to this hour no guess in knowledge   60
Which way they went.

SECOND GENTLEMAN   How long is this ago?

FIRST GENTLEMAN   Some twenty years.

SECOND GENTLEMAN
That a king's children should be so conveyed,   64
So slackly guarded, and the search so slow
That could not trace them!

FIRST GENTLEMAN   Howsoe'er 'tis strange,
Or that the negligence may well be laughed at,
Yet is it true, sir.

SECOND GENTLEMAN   I do well believe you.

FIRST GENTLEMAN
We must forbear. Here comes the gentleman,   69
The Queen, and Princess.   *Exeunt.*

   Enter the Queen, Posthumus, and Imogen.

QUEEN
No, be assured you shall not find me, daughter,
After the slander of most stepmothers,   72
Evil-eyed unto you. You're my prisoner, but

---

49 A glass . . . them a mirror that reflected their best features, one that offered him as a model for their best selves   **49–50 to . . . dotards** i.e., to older courtiers he offered wise example as if a child were to instruct doddering old men   **50 To** as for   **51 her own price** the price she willingly paid (of her father's hostility)   **53 election** choice   **60 guess in knowledge** credible conjecture   **64 conveyed** carried off   **69 forbear** stop talking and withdraw   **72 After the slander** according to what is slanderously told

Your jailer shall deliver you the keys
That lock up your restraint. For you, Posthumus,   75
So soon as I can win th' offended King
I will be known your advocate. Marry, yet   77
The fire of rage is in him, and 'twere good
You leaned unto his sentence with what patience   79
Your wisdom may inform you.

POSTHUMUS   Please Your Highness,   80
I will from hence today.

QUEEN   You know the peril.
I'll fetch a turn about the garden, pitying
The pangs of barred affections, though the King
Hath charged you should not speak together.   *Exit.*

IMOGEN   O
Dissembling courtesy! How fine this tyrant
Can tickle where she wounds! My dearest husband,
I something fear my father's wrath, but nothing—   87
Always reserved my holy duty—what   88
His rage can do on me. You must be gone,
And I shall here abide the hourly shot
Of angry eyes, not comforted to live   91
But that there is this jewel in the world
That I may see again.

POSTHUMUS   My queen, my mistress!
O lady, weep no more, lest I give cause   94
To be suspected of more tenderness   95
Than doth become a man. I will remain   96
The loyal'st husband that did e'er plight troth.
My residence in Rome at one Philario's,   98
Who to my father was a friend, to me
Known but by letter; thither write, my queen,
And with mine eyes I'll drink the words you send,
Though ink be made of gall.

75 lock . . . restraint i.e., lock you up and confine you   **77 Marry** i.e.,
indeed. (Originally, "by the Virgin Mary.")   **79 leaned unto** deferred to
80 inform instill in   **87 something** somewhat.   **nothing** not in the least
88 reserved excepted.   **duty** i.e., duty of a wife. (She does not fear for
herself except insofar as her father could annul her marriage. Or she
means "duty of a daughter," in that her father's rage can never drive
her to desert her duty to him.)   **91 comforted to live** finding comfort in
life   **94–96 lest . . . man** i.e., lest I too shed tears, which would be
unmanly in me   **98 Rome** i.e., Rome is

Enter Queen.

QUEEN   Be brief, I pray you.
If the King come, I shall incur I know not
How much of his displeasure. [*Aside.*] Yet I'll move him
To walk this way. I never do him wrong   105
But he does buy my injuries, to be friends,   106
Pays dear for my offenses.   [*Exit.*]   107
POSTHUMUS [*To Imogen*]   Should we be taking leave
As long a term as yet we have to live,
The loathness to depart would grow. Adieu!
IMOGEN   Nay, stay a little!
Were you but riding forth to air yourself,   112
Such parting were too petty. Look here, love:
This diamond was my mother's. Take it, heart,
But keep it till you woo another wife   115
When Imogen is dead.
              [*She gives a ring, or puts it on his finger.*]
POSTHUMUS   How, how? Another?
You gentle gods, give me but this I have,
And cere up my embracements from a next   118
With bonds of death! Remain, remain thou here   119
While sense can keep it on. And, sweetest, fairest,   120
As I my poor self did exchange for you
To your so infinite loss, so in our trifles   122
I still win of you. For my sake wear this.   123
It is a manacle of love; I'll place it
Upon this fairest prisoner.
              [*He puts a bracelet upon her arm.*]
IMOGEN   O the gods!
When shall we see again?

       Enter Cymbeline and lords.

POSTHUMUS   Alack, the King!   126

105-107 I . . . offenses whenever I wrong him, he mistakes those injuries for kindnesses and, as it were, pays handsomely for those injuries
in order to remain friends   **112 air yourself** take some fresh air
115 But only   **118 cere up** wrap in cerecloth, or waxed cloth used for
wrapping a dead body; perhaps with a play on sealing a document with
wax (see *bonds* in the next line)   **119 Remain** (The ring will remind him
of Imogen always.)   **120 sense** sensory feeling.   **it** (Said of the ring.)
122 trifles i.e., love tokens   **123 still** always   **126 see** see each other

CYMBELINE [*To Posthumus*]
  Thou basest thing, avoid hence, from my sight!   127
  If after this command thou freight the court   128
  With thy unworthiness, thou diest. Away!
  Thou'rt poison to my blood.

POSTHUMUS   The gods protect you,
  And bless the good remainders of the court!   131
  I am gone.   *Exit.*

IMOGEN   There cannot be a pinch in death   132
  More sharp than this is.

CYMBELINE   O disloyal thing
  That shouldst repair my youth, thou heap'st   134
  A year's age on me.

IMOGEN   I beseech you, sir,   135
  Harm not yourself with your vexation.
  I am senseless of your wrath; a touch more rare   137
  Subdues all pangs, all fears.

CYMBELINE   Past grace? Obedience?

IMOGEN
  Past hope and in despair; that way past grace.   139

CYMBELINE
  That mightst have had the sole son of my queen!

IMOGEN
  O blessèd, that I might not! I chose an eagle   141
  And did avoid a puttock.   142

CYMBELINE
  Thou took'st a beggar, wouldst have made my throne
  A seat for baseness.

IMOGEN   No, I rather added
  A luster to it.

CYMBELINE   O thou vile one!

IMOGEN   Sir,
  It is your fault that I have loved Posthumus.

127 avoid hence begone   **128 freight** burden   **131 remainders of** those
who remain at   **132 pinch** pang   **134 repair** restore   **135 A year's age**
an age of years (?) or perhaps the King makes a grim jest of understate-
ment   **137 senseless of** insensible to. **a touch** a feeling (of love for
Posthumus and pain at his banishment)   **139 despair . . . grace** (Imogen
puns bitterly on *grace*, by which the King meant "gracious dutifulness";
in her religious metaphor, to despair is to be beyond God's grace.)
141 might not was not able to (responding antithetically to the King's
mightst, just as *blessèd* is antithetical to *past grace* in l. 139)   **142 puttock** kite, bird of prey

You bred him as my playfellow, and he is
A man worth any woman, overbuys me   148
Almost the sum he pays.

CYMBELINE   What, art thou mad?   149

IMOGEN
Almost, sir. Heaven restore me! Would I were
A neatherd's daughter, and my Leonatus   151
Our neighbor shepherd's son!

       Enter Queen.

CYMBELINE   Thou foolish thing!—
[*To the Queen.*] They were again together. You have done
Not after our command. Away with her
And pen her up.

QUEEN   Beseech your patience.—Peace,   155
Dear lady daughter, peace!—Sweet sovereign,
Leave us to ourselves, and make yourself some comfort
Out of your best advice.

CYMBELINE   Nay, let her languish   158
A drop of blood a day and, being agèd,   159
Die of this folly!   *Exit* [*with lords*].

QUEEN   Fie, you must give way.   160

       Enter Pisanio.

Here is your servant.—How now, sir? What news?

PISANIO
My lord your son drew on my master.

QUEEN   Ha?   162
No harm, I trust, is done?

PISANIO   There might have been,
But that my master rather played than fought
And had no help of anger. They were parted   165
By gentlemen at hand.

148–149 overbuys . . . pays pays more for me than I am worth by almost
as much as the price he pays (which is himself)   **149 mad** insane. (But
Imogen uses the word to mean "mad with grief"; cf. her pun on *grace* in
l. 139.)   **151 neatherd's** cowherd's   **155 Beseech** I beseech   **158 best
advice** most mature reflection.   **languish** pine away   **159 drop of blood**
(Sighs were supposed to deprive the heart of a drop of blood.)
160 Fie . . . way (Said to the departing King as a way of pretending, for
Imogen's benefit, the Queen's concern for her.)   **162 My . . . master** i.e.,
Cloten drew his sword on Posthumus   **165 had . . . anger** was not
whetted on by anger

QUEEN   I am very glad on 't.   166
IMOGEN
  Your son's my father's friend; he takes his part   167
  To draw upon an exile. O, brave sir!   168
  I would they were in Afric both together,   169
  Myself by with a needle, that I might prick
  The goer-back.—Why came you from your master?
PISANIO
  On his command. He would not suffer me
  To bring him to the haven, left these notes
  Of what commands I should be subject to
  When 't pleased you to employ me.
QUEEN   This hath been
  Your faithful servant. I dare lay mine honor   176
  He will remain so.
PISANIO   I humbly thank Your Highness.
QUEEN [To Imogen]
  Pray, walk awhile.
IMOGEN [To Pisanio] About some half hour hence,   179
  Pray you, speak with me. You shall at least
  Go see my lord aboard. For this time leave me.
                                        Exeunt.

                        ❖

1.2   Enter Cloten and two Lords.

FIRST LORD   Sir, I would advise you to shift a shirt. The   1
  violence of action hath made you reek as a sacrifice.
  Where air comes out, air comes in; there's none
  abroad so wholesome as that you vent.   4
CLOTEN   If my shirt were bloody, then to shift it. Have   5
  I hurt him?

166 on 't of it   **167 takes his part** sides with the King; or, plays the role
one would expect of him   **168 To draw** in drawing   **169 in Afric** i.e., in
some deserted spot   **176 lay** wager   **179 walk awhile** i.e., walk with me
awhile

1.2. Location: Britain. At the court of Cymbeline, as before. The time is
virtually continuous; Cloten still sweats from his duel (1.1.162).
1 shift change   **4 abroad** outside you. (The First Lord flatteringly suggests that the outside air is not as wholesome as that of Cloten's own
sweet body, as though the outside air were the cause of the odor of
perspiration, but the effect of *reek* and *vent* is to inform us at any rate
that the odor is rank.)   **5 then to shift it** in that case I would change it

SECOND LORD [*Aside*] No, faith, not so much as his pa- 7
tience.   8
FIRST LORD Hurt him? His body's a passable carcass if 9
he be not hurt. It is a thoroughfare for steel if it be not 10
hurt.
SECOND LORD [*Aside*] His steel was in debt; it went o' 12
the backside the town.   13
CLOTEN The villain would not stand me.   14
SECOND LORD [*Aside*] No, but he fled forward still, to- 15
ward your face.
FIRST LORD Stand you? You have land enough of your
own, but he added to your having, gave you some 18
ground.   19
SECOND LORD [*Aside*] As many inches as you have 20
oceans. Puppies!   21
CLOTEN I would they had not come between us.
SECOND LORD [*Aside*] So would I, till you had measured
how long a fool you were upon the ground.
CLOTEN And that she should love this fellow and
refuse me!
SECOND LORD [*Aside*] If it be a sin to make a true elec- 27
tion, she is damned.   28
FIRST LORD Sir, as I told you always, her beauty and her
brain go not together. She's a good sign, but I have 30
seen small reflection of her wit.   31
SECOND LORD [*Aside*] She shines not upon fools, lest
the reflection should hurt her.   33
CLOTEN Come, I'll to my chamber. Would there had
been some hurt done!

7–8 his patience (Posthumus' patience has been sorely tried by this
encounter, but little else.) **9 passable** (1) penetrable (2) tolerably good
9–10 if . . . hurt i.e., I don't know what you mean by "hurt" otherwise
12–13 His . . . town i.e., Cloten's rapier avoided the fight in a cowardly
fashion, as a debtor hides in back streets (with an antithetical play in
backside / thoroughfare) **14 stand me** stand up to me **15 still** continually **18–19 gave . . . ground** fell back before your advance (with pun
on literal meaning) **20–21 As . . . oceans** i.e., none **21 Puppies** arrogant, vain cubs **27–28 election** choice. (With a pun on the theological
meaning.) **30 go not together** do not match. **sign** semblance, appearance **31 wit** intelligence **33 reflection** (The Second Lord plays on
reflection, "shining," in l. 31, suggesting here that if Imogen were
to show favor to fools, it would *reflect* or bring reproach on
her character.)

SECOND LORD [*Aside*] I wish not so, unless it had been
  the fall of an ass, which is no great hurt.
CLOTEN You'll go with us?   38
FIRST LORD I'll attend your lordship.
CLOTEN Nay, come, let's go together.
SECOND LORD Well, my lord.   *Exeunt.*

❖

1.3   *Enter Imogen and Pisanio.*

IMOGEN
  I would thou grew'st unto the shores o' the haven
  And questionedst every sail. If he should write
  And I not have it, 'twere a paper lost   3
  As offered mercy is. What was the last   4
  That he spake to thee?
PISANIO   It was his queen, his queen!
IMOGEN
  Then waved his handkerchief?
PISANIO   And kissed it, madam.
IMOGEN
  Senseless linen, happier therein than I!   7
  And that was all?
PISANIO   No, madam; for so long
  As he could make me with this eye or ear
  Distinguish him from others, he did keep
  The deck, with glove, or hat, or handkerchief
  Still waving, as the fits and stirs of 's mind
  Could best express how slow his soul sailed on,
  How swift his ship.
IMOGEN   Thou shouldst have made him
  As little as a crow, or less, ere left   15
  To after-eye him.
PISANIO   Madam, so I did.   16

---

38 You'll . . . us (Addressed to the Second Lord, or to both.)

1.3. Location: Britain. At the court of Cymbeline.
3–4 'twere . . . is i.e., the loss of such a letter would be as unfortunate
as a pardon offered but failing to arrive before the execution, or as
God's mercy similarly having no effect   **7 Senseless** without feeling
15–16 ere . . . him before you left off following him with your gaze

IMOGEN

I would have broke mine eyestrings, cracked them, but 17
To look upon him till the diminution
Of space had pointed him sharp as my needle—
Nay, followed him till he had melted from
The smallness of a gnat to air, and then
Have turned mine eye and wept. But, good Pisanio,
When shall we hear from him?

PISANIO   Be assured, madam,
With his next vantage.   24

IMOGEN

I did not take my leave of him, but had
Most pretty things to say. Ere I could tell him
How I would think on him at certain hours
Such thoughts and such; or I could make him swear
The shes of Italy should not betray
Mine interest and his honor; or have charged him
At the sixth hour of morn, at noon, at midnight
T' encounter me with orisons, for then   32
I am in heaven for him; or ere I could   33
Give him that parting kiss which I had set
Betwixt two charming words, comes in my father, 35
And like the tyrannous breathing of the north   36
Shakes all our buds from growing.

        Enter a Lady.

LADY   The Queen, madam,
Desires Your Highness' company.

IMOGEN

Those things I bid you do, get them dispatched.   39
I will attend the Queen.

PISANIO   Madam, I shall.   *Exeunt.*

❧

17 eyestrings the muscles, nerves, or tendons of the eye, thought to
break or crack at loss of sight.   **but** merely   **24 next vantage** first
opportunity   **32 encounter** join.   **orisons** prayers   **33 in heaven** i.e.,
praying   **35 charming** having magical potency   **36 north** north wind
39 bid bade, ordered

1.4   *Enter Philario, Iachimo, a Frenchman, a*
         Dutchman, and a Spaniard.

IACHIMO   Believe it, sir, I have seen him in Britain. He
was then of a crescent note, expected to prove so wor-   2
thy as since he hath been allowed the name of. But I   3
could then have looked on him without the help of
admiration, though the catalogue of his endowments   5
had been tabled by his side and I to peruse him by   6
items.

PHILARIO   You speak of him when he was less furnished
than now he is with that which makes him both with-   9
out and within.   10

FRENCHMAN   I have seen him in France. We had very
many there could behold the sun with as firm eyes   12
as he.

IACHIMO   This matter of marrying his king's daughter,
wherein he must be weighed rather by her value than
his own, words him, I doubt not, a great deal from the   16
matter.   17

FRENCHMAN   And then his banishment.

IACHIMO   Ay, and the approbation of those that weep   19
this lamentable divorce under her colors are wonder-   20
fully to extend him, be it but to fortify her judgment, 21
which else an easy battery might lay flat for taking a   22
beggar without less quality. But how comes it he is to   23
sojourn with you? How creeps acquaintance?   24

PHILARIO   His father and I were soldiers together, to

**1.4. Rome. Philario's house. Perhaps a feast is in progress; see 5.5.157.
2 crescent note** growing reputation of importance   **3 allowed the name
of** granted to have the reputation for   **5 admiration** wonder. (Iachimo
insists he was not dazzled by Posthumus.)   **6 tabled** set down in a list
9–10 makes . . . within establishes him as regards both his fortune and
his character   **12 behold the sun** i.e., like an eagle, a royal bird supposedly able to stare at the sun unblinkingly   **16–17 words . . . matter**
causes him to be described in accounts that go beyond the truth
19 weep weep for   **20 divorce** i.e., separation through banishment.
under her colors i.e., in Imogen's party, carrying her banner   **20–21 are
. . . extend him** seek by all means possible to praise him beyond his
merit   **22–23 which . . . quality** i.e., which judgment of hers would
otherwise be vulnerable to attack for having chosen a beggar lacking
the qualities they ascribe to him   **24 How creeps acquaintance** how has
he crept into your favor

whom I have been often bound for no less than my
life.

 Enter Posthumus.

Here comes the Briton. Let him be so entertained
amongst you as suits, with gentlemen of your know- 29
ing, to a stranger of his quality.—I beseech you all, be 30
better known to this gentleman, whom I commend to
you as a noble friend of mine. How worthy he is I will
leave to appear hereafter rather than story him in his 33
own hearing.

FRENCHMAN Sir, we have known together in Orleans. 35

POSTHUMUS Since when I have been debtor to you for
courtesies which I will be ever to pay and yet pay still. 37

FRENCHMAN Sir, you o'errate my poor kindness. I was
glad I did atone my countryman and you. It had been 39
pity you should have been put together with so mortal 40
a purpose as then each bore, upon importance of so 41
slight and trivial a nature.

POSTHUMUS By your pardon, sir, I was then a young
traveler; rather shunned to go even with what I heard 44
than in my every action to be guided by others' experiences. But upon my mended judgment—if I offend 46
not to say it is mended—my quarrel was not altogether slight.

FRENCHMAN Faith, yes, to be put to the arbitrament of 49
swords, and by such two that would by all likelihood
have confounded one the other or have fallen both. 51

IACHIMO Can we, with manners, ask what was the dif- 52
ference? 53

FRENCHMAN Safely, I think; 'twas a contention in public, which may without contradiction suffer the re- 55
port. It was much like an argument that fell out last 56

29–30 knowing knowledge of affairs, *savoir faire* **30 stranger** foreigner.
quality rank **33 story** give an account of **35 known together** been
acquainted **37 which . . . still** which I will always be indebted to you
for, even if I go on paying forever **39 atone** set at one, reconcile
40 put together set opposite one another in a duel. **mortal** deadly
41 importance matter, occasion **44 shunned to go even** declined to
agree **46 upon** even upon. **mended** improved **49 arbitrament** arbitra-
tion **51 confounded** destroyed **52–53 difference** quarrel **55–56 without . . . report** without objection be reported or told. **suffer** permit,
tolerate

night, where each of us fell in praise of our country 57
mistresses, this gentleman at that time vouching—and 58
upon warrant of bloody affirmation—his to be more 59
fair, virtuous, wise, chaste, constant, qualified, and less 60
attemptable than any the rarest of our ladies in France. 61

IACHIMO That lady is not now living, or this gentleman's opinion by this worn out.   63

POSTHUMUS She holds her virtue still, and I my mind.   64

IACHIMO You must not so far prefer her 'fore ours of 65
Italy.

POSTHUMUS Being so far provoked as I was in France, I
would abate her nothing, though I profess myself her 68
adorer, not her friend.   69

IACHIMO As fair and as good—a kind of hand-in-hand 70
comparison—had been something too fair and too 71
good for any lady in Britain. If she went before others 72
I have seen, as that diamond of yours outlusters many 73
I have beheld, I could not but believe she excelled
many. But I have not seen the most precious diamond
that is, nor you the lady.

POSTHUMUS I praised her as I rated her. So do I my
stone.

IACHIMO What do you esteem it at?

POSTHUMUS More than the world enjoys.

IACHIMO Either your unparagoned mistress is dead, or
she's outprized by a trifle.

POSTHUMUS You are mistaken. The one may be sold or
given, or if there were wealth enough for the pur- 84
chase or merit for the gift. The other is not a thing for
sale, and only the gift of the gods.   86

57–58 our country mistresses the lady each of us loves in his native
land   **59 bloody affirmation** affirming the truth with his blood
60 qualified having fine qualities   **61 attemptable** open to attempts on
her virtue.   **any the rarest** any of the finest   **63 by this** by now
64 mind opinion   **65 prefer her** advance her claims   **68 would abate
her nothing** would not lower my estimate of her in the slightest
68–69 though . . . friend even though I should (as at that time, in France)
profess myself to be her adorer or worshiper in the "courtly" sense,
not her accepted lover   **70–71 hand-in-hand comparison** comparison
claiming equality only, not superiority   **71 had** would have   **72 went
before** were superior to   **73 diamond** i.e., the ring Imogen gave
Posthumus   **84 or if** if either   **86 only . . . gods** the gift of the
gods alone

IACHIMO Which the gods have given you?

POSTHUMUS Which, by their graces, I will keep.

IACHIMO You may wear her in title yours; but you 89
know strange fowl light upon neighboring ponds. 90
Your ring may be stolen too. So your brace of unpriz- 91
able estimations, the one is but frail and the other ca- 92
sual. A cunning thief or a that-way-accomplished cour- 93
tier would hazard the winning both of first and last.

POSTHUMUS Your Italy contains none so accomplished a
courtier to convince the honor of my mistress, if, in 96
the holding or loss of that, you term her frail. I do
nothing doubt you have store of thieves; notwith- 98
standing, I fear not my ring. 99

PHILARIO Let us leave here, gentlemen. 100

POSTHUMUS Sir, with all my heart. This worthy signor,
I thank him, makes no stranger of me; we are familiar 102
at first. 103

IACHIMO With five times so much conversation I
should get ground of your fair mistress, make her go 105
back even to the yielding, had I admittance and op- 106
portunity to friend. 107

POSTHUMUS No, no.

IACHIMO I dare thereupon pawn the moiety of my estate 109
to your ring, which in my opinion o'ervalues it some- 110
thing. But I make my wager rather against your confi- 111
dence than her reputation, and, to bar your offense
herein too, I durst attempt it against any lady in the
world.

POSTHUMUS You are a great deal abused in too bold a 115
persuasion, and I doubt not you sustain what you're 116
worthy of by your attempt.

---

89 wear . . . yours possess her in name, claim title to her   **90–91 ponds, ring** (with bawdy suggestion)   **91–92 your . . . estimations** of the pair of objects (ring and lady) that you esteem beyond value   **92–93 casual** susceptible to accident (such as theft)   **93 that-way-accomplished** i.e., accomplished in seducing women   **96 to convince** as to overcome **98 nothing** not at all.   **store** plenty   **99 fear not** fear not for   **100 leave** leave off, cease   **102–103 familiar at first** on familiar terms right from the start   **105 get ground** gain the advantage   **105–106 go back** succumb, give way. (The metaphor is from fencing, with sexual suggestion.)   **107 to friend** to assist me   **109 moiety** half   **110–111 something** somewhat   **115–116 abused . . . persuasion** deceived by too bold an opinion   **116 sustain** will sustain, receive

IACHIMO What's that?

POSTHUMUS A repulse—though your attempt, as you call it, deserve more: a punishment too.

PHILARIO Gentlemen, enough of this. It came in too suddenly; let it die as it was born, and, I pray you, be better acquainted.

IACHIMO Would I had put my estate and my neighbor's 124
on th' approbation of what I have spoke! 125

POSTHUMUS What lady would you choose to assail?

IACHIMO Yours, whom in constancy you think stands so safe. I will lay you ten thousand ducats to your ring 128
that, commend me to the court where your lady is, 129
with no more advantage than the opportunity of a second conference, and I will bring from thence that honor of hers which you imagine so reserved. 132

POSTHUMUS I will wage against your gold, gold to it. 133
My ring I hold dear as my finger; 'tis part of it.

IACHIMO You are a friend, and therein the wiser. If you 135
buy ladies' flesh at a million a dram, you cannot preserve it from tainting. But I see you have some religion in you, that you fear. 138

POSTHUMUS This is but a custom in your tongue. You bear a graver purpose, I hope.

IACHIMO I am the master of my speeches and would undergo what's spoken, I swear. 142

POSTHUMUS Will you? I shall but lend my diamond till your return. Let there be covenants drawn between 's. My mistress exceeds in goodness the hugeness of your unworthy thinking. I dare you to this match; here's my ring.   [*He wagers his ring.*] 147

PHILARIO I will have it no lay. 148

IACHIMO By the gods, it is one. If I bring you no suffi-

---

124 put wagered   **125 approbation** attestation, confirmation   **128 lay** wager   **129 commend me** if you provide me a letter of introduction   **132 reserved** kept safe   **133 wage** lay as a wager.   **to it** in equal amount   **135 You . . . wiser** i.e., you know her too well, being her lover, to bet your ring on her   **138 that** since.   **fear** (1) experience "the fear of the Lord" that is the beginning of true wisdom (2) are fearful   **142 undergo** undertake   **147 s.d. wagers his ring** (Possibly Posthumus hands the ring to Iachimo or to Philario as official of the wager, or perhaps he still keeps it himself; see 2.4.108.)   **148 I . . . lay** I will not let it be a wager

cient testimony that I have enjoyed the dearest bodily
part of your mistress, my ten thousand ducats are
yours; so is your diamond too. If I come off and leave
her in such honor as you have trust in, she your jewel,
this your jewel, and my gold are yours—provided I
have your commendation for my more free entertain-   155
ment.   156

POSTHUMUS   I embrace these conditions. Let us have articles betwixt us. Only, thus far you shall answer: if
you make your voyage upon her and give me directly   159
to understand you have prevailed, I am no further your 160
enemy; she is not worth our debate. If she remain un-
seduced, you not making it appear otherwise, for your
ill opinion and th' assault you have made to her chastity you shall answer me with your sword.

IACHIMO   Your hand; a covenant. [*They shake hands.*]
We will have these things set down by lawful counsel,
and straight away for Britain, lest the bargain should
catch cold and starve. I will fetch my gold and have   168
our two wagers recorded.

POSTHUMUS   Agreed. [*Exeunt Posthumus and Iachimo.*]

FRENCHMAN   Will this hold, think you?

PHILARIO   Signor Iachimo will not from it. Pray let us 172
follow 'em.   *Exeunt.*

❖

1.5   *Enter Queen, Ladies, and Cornelius.*

QUEEN
Whiles yet the dew's on ground, gather those flowers.
Make haste. Who has the note of them?

A LADY   I, madam.   2

QUEEN   Dispatch.   *Exeunt Ladies.*
Now, Master Doctor, have you brought those drugs?

---

155 commendation introduction (to Imogen)   **155–156 free entertainment** ready welcome   **159 directly** straightforwardly, unequivocally
160 you that you   **168 starve** die   **172 from it** depart from it

1.5. Location: Britain. At the court of Cymbeline.
2 note list

CORNELIUS
Pleaseth Your Highness, ay. Here they are, madam.   5
                    [*He presents a small box.*]
But I beseech Your Grace, without offense—
My conscience bids me ask—wherefore you have   7
Commanded of me these most poisonous compounds,
Which are the movers of a languishing death,
But though slow, deadly?
QUEEN   I wonder, Doctor,
Thou ask'st me such a question. Have I not been
Thy pupil long? Hast thou not learned me how   12
To make perfumes? Distill? Preserve? Yea, so
That our great king himself doth woo me oft
For my confections? Having thus far proceeded—   15
Unless thou think'st me devilish—is 't not meet
That I did amplify my judgment in   17
Other conclusions? I will try the forces   18
Of these thy compounds on such creatures as
We count not worth the hanging—but none human—
To try the vigor of them and apply
Allayments to their act, and by them gather   22
Their several virtues and effects.
CORNELIUS   Your Highness   23
Shall from this practice but make hard your heart.   24
Besides, the seeing these effects will be
Both noisome and infectious.
QUEEN   O, content thee.   26

    Enter Pisanio.

[*Aside.*] Here comes a flattering rascal; upon him
Will I first work. He's for his master,   28
And enemy to my son.—How now, Pisanio?—
Doctor, your service for this time is ended;

5 Pleaseth may it please. **s.d. He presents a small box** (Perhaps Cornelius hesitates before actually giving it to her; she may snatch it from
him.) **7 wherefore** why **12 learned** taught **15 confections** compounds
(of drugs) **17 did** i.e., should **18 conclusions** experiments. **try** test
22 Allayments antidotes. **act** action. **them** i.e., the experiments.
gather collect a record of **23 several** various **24 but** only **26 noisome**
noxious, foul-smelling. **content thee** do not trouble yourself **28 He's
for** i.e., he's an agent for

Take your own way.

CORNELIUS [*Aside*]   I do suspect you, madam,   31
   But you shall do no harm.

QUEEN [*To Pisanio*]   Hark thee, a word.

CORNELIUS [*Aside*]
   I do not like her. She doth think she has
   Strange lingering poisons. I do know her spirit
   And will not trust one of her malice with
   A drug of such damned nature. Those she has
   Will stupefy and dull the sense awhile,
   Which first, perchance, she'll prove on cats and dogs,   38
   Then afterward up higher; but there is
   No danger in what show of death it makes
   More than the locking-up the spirits a time,
   To be more fresh, reviving. She is fooled
   With a most false effect, and I the truer   43
   So to be false with her.

QUEEN   No further service, Doctor,
   Until I send for thee.

CORNELIUS   I humbly take my leave.   *Exit.*

QUEEN [*To Pisanio*]
   Weeps she still, sayst thou? Dost thou think in time
   She will not quench, and let instructions enter   49
   Where folly now possesses? Do thou work.
   When thou shalt bring me word she loves my son,
   I'll tell thee on the instant thou art then
   As great as is thy master; greater, for
   His fortunes all lie speechless, and his name
   Is at last gasp. Return he cannot, nor
   Continue where he is. To shift his being   56
   Is to exchange one misery with another,
   And every day that comes comes to decay   58
   A day's work in him. What shalt thou expect   59
   To be depender on a thing that leans,   60
   Who cannot be new built, nor has no friends,
   So much as but to prop him? [*The Queen drops the box;*

---

31 Take your own way be off, go about your business   **38 prove** test
43 truer more honest   **49 quench** become cool.   **instructions** good
counsel   **56 shift his being** change his abode   **58–59 And . . . him** i.e.,
and every new day that arrives means the undoing of a day's fruitful
endeavor as far as he's concerned   **59 What . . . expect** what can you
expect for yourself   **60 leans** is about to fall

Pisanio takes it up.] Thou tak'st up
Thou know'st not what; but take it for thy labor.
It is a thing I made, which hath the King
Five times redeemed from death. I do not know
What is more cordial. Nay, I prithee, take it;   66
It is an earnest of a farther good   67
That I mean to thee. Tell thy mistress how
The case stands with her; do 't as from thyself.   69
Think what a chance thou changest on, but think   70
Thou hast thy mistress still—to boot, my son,   71
Who shall take notice of thee. I'll move the King   72
To any shape of thy preferment such   73
As thou'lt desire; and then myself, I chiefly,
That set thee on to this desert, am bound   75
To load thy merit richly. Call my women.
Think on my words.   *Exit Pisanio.*
                    A sly and constant knave,
Not to be shaked; the agent for his master,   78
And the remembrancer of her to hold   79
The handfast to her lord. I have given him that   80
Which, if he take, shall quite unpeople her   81
Of liegers for her sweet, and which she after,   82
Except she bend her humor, shall be assured   83
To taste of too.

Enter Pisanio, and Ladies [with flowers].

                    So, so. Well done, well done.
The violets, cowslips, and the primroses
Bear to my closet. Fare thee well, Pisanio;   86
Think on my words.   *Exeunt Queen and Ladies.*

---

66 cordial restorative (literally, to the heart)   **67 earnest** first payment
69 as from thyself as if from your own advice   **70 Think . . . on** think
what an improvement in your fortunes you come upon in this change of
service   **71 Thou . . . still** i.e., you will have Imogen as your patroness
still, as the wife of Cloten, your new lord.   **to boot** and besides her (you
will have)   **72 take notice of thee** look out for you, offer advancement to
you   **73 preferment** advancement   **75 That . . . desert** who urged you to
take this action for which you will be rewarded   **78 shaked** shaken (in
his loyalty)   **79 remembrancer of her** one who reminds her   **80 handfast** marriage contract   **81 unpeople her** deprive her of the services
82 liegers ambassadors.   **her sweet** i.e., Posthumus   **83 Except . . .
humor** unless she change her mind (about not accepting Cloten)
86 closet private chamber

PISANIO   And shall do.
  But when to my good lord I prove untrue,
  I'll choke myself. There's all I'll do for you.   *Exit.*

❖

1.6   *Enter Imogen alone.*

IMOGEN
  A father cruel and a stepdame false,
  A foolish suitor to a wedded lady
  That hath her husband banished. O, that husband!   3
  My supreme crown of grief, and those repeated   4
  Vexations of it! Had I been thief-stol'n,
  As my two brothers, happy! But most miserable
  Is the desire that's glorious. Blest be those,   7
  How mean soe'er, that have their honest wills,   8
  Which seasons comfort.—Who may this be? Fie!   9

       Enter Pisanio and Iachimo.

PISANIO
  Madam, a noble gentleman of Rome
  Comes from my lord with letters.
IACHIMO   Change you, madam;   11
  The worthy Leonatus is in safety
  And greets Your Highness dearly.
                          [*He presents a letter.*]
IMOGEN   Thanks, good sir.
  You're kindly welcome.   [*She reads.*]
IACHIMO [*Aside*]
  All of her that is out of door most rich!   15
  If she be furnished with a mind so rare,
  She is alone th' Arabian bird, and I   17
  Have lost the wager. Boldness be my friend!

1.6. Location: Britain. At the court.
3 That . . . banished whose husband is banished **4 repeated** already
enumerated **7 the desire that's glorious** i.e., the ungratified yearning of
a person in high station **8 mean** lowly. **honest wills** simple desires
9 seasons adds relish to **11 Comes** who comes. **letters** i.e., (probably)
a letter. **Change you** i.e., cheer up, don't be sad; or, *Change you,
madam?* i.e., does your expression change at news of letters from Rome
15 out of door external **17 Arabian bird** i.e., phoenix, therefore unique

Arm me, audacity, from head to foot!
Or, like the Parthian, I shall flying fight—   20
Rather, directly fly.
IMOGEN (*Reads*) "He is one of the noblest note, to   22
whose kindnesses I am most infinitely tied. Reflect   23
upon him accordingly, as you value your trust—
                              Leonatus."
So far I read aloud.
But even the very middle of my heart
Is warmed by th' rest and takes it thankfully.
You are as welcome, worthy sir, as I
Have words to bid you, and shall find it so
In all that I can do.
IACHIMO   Thanks, fairest lady.
What, are men mad? Hath nature given them eyes
To see this vaulted arch and the rich crop   33
Of sea and land, which can distinguish twixt
The fiery orbs above and the twinned stones   35
Upon th' unnumbered beach, and can we not   36
Partition make with spectacles so precious   37
Twixt fair and foul?
IMOGEN   What makes your admiration?   38
IACHIMO
It cannot be i' th' eye, for apes and monkeys
Twixt two such shes would chatter this way and   40
Contemn with mows the other; nor i' the judgment,   41
For idiots in this case of favor would   42
Be wisely definite; nor i' th' appetite: 43
Sluttery, to such neat excellence opposed,   44
Should make desire vomit emptiness,   45
Not so allured to feed.   46

20 Parthian (The Parthians were proverbial in ancient times for discharging a flight of arrows as they fled.)   **22 note** reputation
23 Reflect bestow attention   **33 vaulted arch** sky.   **crop** harvest, produce   **35 twinned** exactly alike   **36 unnumbered** numberless   **37 Partition** distinction.   **with . . . precious** i.e., with organs of vision so acutely
sensitive   **38 admiration** wonder   **40 chatter this way** i.e., indicate
approval of Imogen   **41 Contemn** show scorn toward.   **mows** grimaces,
wry faces   **42 in . . . favor** in question concerning a face of such grace
and beauty   **43 Be wisely definite** choose wisely   **44–46 Sluttery . . .
feed** i.e., sluttishness itself, confronted with such pure excellence,
would void its own empty desire, not being tempted to feed its lust
on Imogen

IMOGEN
  What is the matter, trow?
IACHIMO   The cloyèd will—   47
  That satiate yet unsatisfied desire, that tub   48
  Both filled and running—ravening first the lamb,   49
  Longs after for the garbage.
IMOGEN   What, dear sir,
  Thus raps you? Are you well?   51
IACHIMO
  Thanks, madam, well. [To Pisanio.] Beseech you, sir,
  Desire my man's abode where I did leave him.   53
  He's strange and peevish.
PISANIO   I was going, sir,   54
  To give him welcome.   Exit.
IMOGEN
  Continues well my lord? His health, beseech you?
IACHIMO Well, madam.
IMOGEN
  Is he disposed to mirth? I hope he is.
IACHIMO
  Exceeding pleasant; none a stranger there   59
  So merry and so gamesome. He is called
  The Briton reveler.
IMOGEN   When he was here
  He did incline to sadness, and ofttimes   62
  Not knowing why.
IACHIMO   I never saw him sad.
  There is a Frenchman his companion, one
  An eminent monsieur that, it seems, much loves
  A Gallian girl at home. He furnaces   66
  The thick sighs from him, whiles the jolly Briton—   67
  Your lord, I mean—laughs from 's free lungs, cries, "O,   68
  Can my sides hold, to think that man, who knows
  By history, report, or his own proof   70

---

47 trow do you think. **will** lustful appetite **48 satiate** glutted, *cloyèd*,
as in l. 47. (The perverted sexual appetite is at once glutted and insatiable.) **49 running** emptying itself. **ravening** devouring greedily
51 raps transports, makes rapt **53 Desire . . . abode** bid my servant
remain **54 strange and peevish** a stranger and easily upset **59 none a
stranger** no other foreigner **62 sadness** seriousness **66 Gallian** Gallic,
French. **furnaces** gives forth like a furnace **67 thick** rapid **68 from 's
free lungs** i.e., without restraint, heartily **70 proof** experience

What woman is, yea, what she cannot choose
But must be, will 's free hours languish   72
For assurèd bondage?''
IMOGEN   Will my lord say so?   73
IACHIMO
Ay, madam, with his eyes in flood with laughter.
It is a recreation to be by
And hear him mock the Frenchman. But heavens know
Some men are much to blame.
IMOGEN   Not he, I hope.
IACHIMO
Not he; but yet heaven's bounty towards him might   78
Be used more thankfully. In himself, 'tis much;   79
In you, which I account his, beyond all talents.   80
Whilst I am bound to wonder, I am bound
To pity too.
IMOGEN   What do you pity, sir?
IACHIMO
Two creatures heartily.
IMOGEN   Am I one, sir?
You look on me. What wrack discern you in me   84
Deserves your pity?
IACHIMO   Lamentable! What,   85
To hide me from the radiant sun, and solace   86
I' the dungeon by a snuff?
IMOGEN   I pray you, sir,   87
Deliver with more openness your answers
To my demands. Why do you pity me?   89
IACHIMO   That others do—
I was about to say—enjoy your—But
It is an office of the gods to venge it,   92
Not mine to speak on 't.
IMOGEN   You do seem to know   93

72 will 's will his. free (1) independent (2) licentious. (Sexual insinuation occurs throughout Iachimo's speech, in *merry, gamesome, reveler,
jolly*, etc.) languish give up to languishing   73 assurèd (1) certain
(2) betrothed   78 bounty generosity (in bestowing on him his own
qualities, and Imogen)   79 In . . . much i.e., as for his own qualities,
heaven has been generous   80 In you i.e., as for heaven's generosity in
giving him you. beyond all talents i.e., that goes far beyond his own
heaven-given endowments   84 wrack ruin   85 Deserves that deserves
86 hide me i.e., hide. solace take delight   87 snuff smoking candle-
wick   89 demands inquiries   92 office function   93 on 't of it

Something of me, or what concerns me. Pray you—
Since doubting things go ill often hurts more   95
Than to be sure they do; for certainties
Either are past remedies, or, timely knowing,   97
The remedy then born—discover to me   98
What both you spur and stop.

IACHIMO   Had I this cheek   99
To bathe my lips upon; this hand, whose touch,
Whose every touch, would force the feeler's soul
To th' oath of loyalty; this object, which
Takes prisoner the wild motion of mine eye,
Fixing it only here; should I, damned then,
Slaver with lips as common as the stairs
That mount the Capitol; join grips with hands   106
Made hard with hourly falsehood—falsehood as   107
With labor; then by-peeping in an eye   108
Base and illustrous as the smoky light   109
That's fed with stinking tallow; it were fit
That all the plagues of hell should at one time
Encounter such revolt.

IMOGEN   My lord, I fear,   112
Has forgot Britain.

IACHIMO   And himself. Not I,   113
Inclined to this intelligence, pronounce   114
The beggary of his change, but 'tis your graces   115
That from my mutest conscience to my tongue   116
Charms this report out.

IMOGEN   Let me hear no more.

IACHIMO
O dearest soul, your cause doth strike my heart
With pity that doth make me sick. A lady
So fair, and fastened to an empery   120

95 **doubting** fearing that   97 **timely knowing** if one knows in time
98 **then born** i.e., is then born.   **discover** reveal   99 **What . . . stop** i.e.,
what you simultaneously urge toward disclosure and then conceal, as if
spurring and then reining in a horse   106 **grips** claspings   107–108 **as
With labor** as much as if they had been made hard by actual labor
108 **by-peeping** giving sidelong glances   109 **illustrous** not lustrous
112 **Encounter** meet (with punishment).   **revolt** inconstancy
113–114 **Not . . . pronounce** not through any inclination to disclose this
information do I report   115 **The beggary of his change** his change to
baseness   116 **mutest conscience** most silent inner knowledge
120 **empery** empire (i.e., her graces and possessions)

Would make the great'st king double—to be partnered   121
With tomboys hired with that self exhibition   122
Which your own coffers yield; with diseased ventures   123
That play with all infirmities for gold   124
Which rottenness can lend nature; such boiled stuff   125
As well might poison poison! Be revenged,
Or she that bore you was no queen, and you
Recoil from your great stock.   128

IMOGEN   Revenged?
How should I be revenged? If this be true—
As I have such a heart that both mine ears   131
Must not in haste abuse—if it be true,   132
How should I be revenged?

IACHIMO   Should he make me
Live like Diana's priest betwixt cold sheets   134
Whiles he is vaulting variable ramps,   135
In your despite, upon your purse? Revenge it.   136
I dedicate myself to your sweet pleasure,
More noble than that runagate to your bed,   138
And will continue fast to your affection,   139
Still close as sure.

IMOGEN [Calling]   What ho, Pisanio!   140

IACHIMO
Let me my service tender on your lips.

IMOGEN
Away! I do condemn mine ears that have
So long attended thee. If thou wert honorable,   143
Thou wouldst have told this tale for virtue, not
For such an end thou seek'st—as base as strange.

---

121 **Would** that would. **double** as having twice the majesty and power
121–122 partnered With put on a level with, made to share rights with
122 tomboys wantons. **self exhibition** very allowance (of money)
123 ventures commercial women, things risked in the way of commercial profit **124–125 That . . . nature** who for money chance all the
infirmities of mind and body that rottenness (venereal disease) can lend
to human nature. (*Lend*, because we can be said only to "borrow"
infirmities until we die.) **125 boiled stuff** i.e., women treated by
"sweating" for venereal disease **128 Recoil** fall away, degenerate
131 As i.e., I say "if," since **132 Must . . . abuse** must not overhastily
wrong (by being too credulous) **134 priest** i.e., priestess **135 vaulting . . . ramps** mounting various prostitutes **136 In your despite** in
contempt of you. **upon your purse** spending your money **138 runagate** renegade **139 fast** firm **140 Still close** always secret
143 attended listened to

Thou wrong'st a gentleman who is as far
From thy report as thou from honor, and
Solicits here a lady that disdains   148
Thee and the devil alike.—What ho, Pisanio!—
The King my father shall be made acquainted
Of thy assault. If he shall think it fit   151
A saucy stranger in his court to mart   152
As in a Romish stew and to expound   153
His beastly mind to us, he hath a court
He little cares for and a daughter who
He not respects at all.—What ho, Pisanio!

IACHIMO
O happy Leonatus! I may say
The credit that thy lady hath of thee   158
Deserves thy trust, and thy most perfect goodness
Her assured credit. Blessèd live you long,
A lady to the worthiest sir that ever
Country called his, and you his mistress, only   162
For the most worthiest fit! Give me your pardon.
I have spoke this to know if your affiance   164
Were deeply rooted, and shall make your lord
That which he is new o'er; and he is one   166
The truest mannered, such a holy witch   167
That he enchants societies into him.   168
Half all men's hearts are his.

IMOGEN   You make amends.   169

IACHIMO
He sits 'mongst men like a descended god.
He hath a kind of honor sets him off   171
More than a mortal seeming. Be not angry,   172
Most mighty Princess, that I have adventured
To try your taking of a false report, which hath
Honored with confirmation your great judgment

---

148 Solicits solicitest   **151 fit** fit that   **152 to mart** should bargain
153 stew house of prostitution   **158 credit . . . of** faith . . . in
162 called his called its own   **164 affiance** fidelity   **166 new o'er** refreshed and renewed, made over again   **166–167 one . . . mannered**
uniquely, above all others honorably disposed   **167 witch** charmer,
fascinating person   **168 societies into him** whole groups of people to
his circle (with a play on the idea of a magic circle)   **169 Half . . . his** all
men give him half their hearts   **171 sets** that sets   **172 More . . . seeming** beyond the appearance of ordinary mortals, or, as if seeming to be
more than mortal

In the election of a sir so rare,   176
Which you know cannot err. The love I bear him   177
Made me to fan you thus, but the gods made you,   178
Unlike all others, chaffless. Pray, your pardon.   179

IMOGEN
All's well, sir. Take my power i' the court for yours.

IACHIMO
My humble thanks. I had almost forgot
T' entreat Your Grace but in a small request,
And yet of moment too, for it concerns   183
Your lord, myself, and other noble friends
Are partners in the business.

IMOGEN   Pray, what is 't?   185

IACHIMO
Some dozen Romans of us and your lord—
The best feather of our wing—have mingled sums   187
To buy a present for the Emperor;
Which I, the factor for the rest, have done   189
In France. 'Tis plate of rare device, and jewels   190
Of rich and exquisite form, their values great,
And I am something curious, being strange,   192
To have them in safe stowage. May it please you
To take them in protection?

IMOGEN   Willingly;
And pawn mine honor for their safety. Since
My lord hath interest in them, I will keep them   196
In my bedchamber.

IACHIMO   They are in a trunk,
Attended by my men. I will make bold
To send them to you, only for this night;
I must aboard tomorrow.

IMOGEN   O, no, no.

IACHIMO
Yes, I beseech, or I shall short my word   201

---

176 election choice   **177 Which** who   **178 fan** test. (A metaphor from
winnowing of grain.)   **179 chaffless** without chaff, i.e., perfect
183 moment importance   **185 Are** who are   **187 The best . . . wing** i.e.,
the choicest spirit of our company   **189 factor** agent   **190 plate** ware
plated with precious metal.   **jewels** pieces of jewelry   **192 something
curious** somewhat anxious.   **strange** a foreigner   **196 interest** share
201 short fall short of

By lengthening my return. From Gallia   202
I crossed the seas on purpose and on promise   203
To see Your Grace.
IMOGEN   I thank you for your pains.
But not away tomorrow!
IACHIMO   O, I must, madam.
Therefore I shall beseech you, if you please
To greet your lord with writing, do 't tonight.
I have outstood my time, which is material   208
To th' tender of our present.
IMOGEN   I will write.   209
Send your trunk to me; it shall safe be kept
And truly yielded you. You're very welcome. *Exeunt.* 211

❖

202 Gallia Gaul, France **203 on promise** i.e., because I promised
Posthumus **208 outstood** outstayed **209 tender of our present** offering
of our gift **211 truly yielded you** duly returned to you

2.1 *Enter Cloten and the two Lords.*

CLOTEN Was there ever man had such luck? When I
kissed the jack upon an upcast, to be hit away! I had 2
a hundred pound on 't. And then a whoreson jacka- 3
napes must take me up for swearing, as if I borrowed 4
mine oaths of him and might not spend them at my
pleasure.

FIRST LORD What got he by that? You have broke his 7
pate with your bowl. 8

SECOND LORD [*Aside*] If his wit had been like him that
broke it, it would have run all out. 10

CLOTEN What a gentleman is disposed to swear, it is
not for any standers-by to curtail his oaths, ha? 12

SECOND LORD No, my lord; [*Aside*] nor crop the ears of
them.

CLOTEN Whoreson dog! I gave him satisfaction? Would 15
he had been one of my rank! 16

SECOND LORD [*Aside*] To have smelled like a fool.

CLOTEN I am not vexed more at anything in the earth. A 18
pox on 't! I had rather not be so noble as I am. They 19
dare not fight with me because of the Queen my
mother. Every jack-slave hath his bellyful of fighting, 21
and I must go up and down like a cock that nobody 22
can match. 23

2.1. Location: Britain. At the court.
2 kissed the jack touched and lay near the small bowl used as target in
the game of bowls. **upcast** i.e., crucial throw in the game of bowls
3–4 whoreson jackanapes wretched ape, coxcomb **4 take me up** take
me to task **7–8 broke his pate** i.e., ruptured the skin with a superficial
head wound. (But the Second Lord jokes as though a *broken* head
would allow brains to run out.) **10 run all out** i.e., because Cloten's
brains are watery. (The image is also suggestive of running away.)
12 curtail shorten, as one might bob the tail (and sometimes the ears) of
a curtal dog; hence, *crop the ears* (of the *oaths*) in the next speech
15 gave was to give. (To *give satisfaction* is to accept a challenge to a
duel from one who feels himself insulted—something that Cloten professes himself unwilling to do because the opponent is of lower social
rank, though Cloten's real motive appears to have been cowardice.)
16 rank social class. (But the Second Lord takes it in the sense of
"rankness of smell.") **18–19 A pox on 't** i.e., a plague on it **21 jack-
slave** lowborn fellow **22–23 cock . . . match** (Like the champion cock in
cockfighting, complains Cloten, I am unchallenged because all are
socially unequal to me.)

SECOND LORD [*Aside*] You are cock and capon too, and 24
you crow, cock, with your comb on. 25

CLOTEN Sayest thou? 26

SECOND LORD It is not fit your lordship should under- 27
take every companion that you give offense to. 28

CLOTEN No, I know that, but it is fit I should commit 29
offense to my inferiors. 30

SECOND LORD Ay, it is fit for your lordship only.

CLOTEN Why, so I say.

FIRST LORD Did you hear of a stranger that's come to
court tonight? 34

CLOTEN A stranger, and I not know on 't?

SECOND LORD [*Aside*] He's a strange fellow himself, and
knows it not.

FIRST LORD There's an Italian come, and, 'tis thought,
one of Leonatus' friends.

CLOTEN Leonatus? A banished rascal; and he's another,
whatsoever he be. Who told you of this stranger?

FIRST LORD One of your lordship's pages.

CLOTEN Is it fit I went to look upon him? Is there no
derogation in 't? 44

SECOND LORD You cannot derogate, my lord. 45

CLOTEN Not easily, I think.

SECOND LORD [*Aside*] You are a fool granted; therefore 47
your issues, being foolish, do not derogate. 48

CLOTEN Come, I'll go see this Italian. What I have lost
today at bowls I'll win tonight of him. Come, go.

SECOND LORD I'll attend your lordship.
          Exeunt [*Cloten and First Lord*].

---

24 capon castrated rooster (used quibblingly for *cap-on,* i.e., with fool's cap or coxcomb) **25 with your comb on** (There is a play here on "coxcomb" and "cock's comb.") **26 Sayest thou** what do you say **27–28 undertake** engage with, give satisfaction to **28 companion** fellow. **give offense to** attack or insult in the code of duelling. (But the speaker also suggests that Cloten gives offense to virtually everyone by being who he is. The insinuation is present in l. 31 as well: no one but your lordship is so adept at giving offense.) **29–30 commit offense to** attack, initiate action against (with unintended sense of "defecate upon") **34 tonight** last night **44 derogation** action unbecoming my position **45 cannot derogate** (1) cannot do anything undignified (2) have no dignity to lose **47 a fool granted** (1) admitted by everyone to be a fool (2) given the formal title of fool **48 issues** offspring, i.e., deeds, actions

That such a crafty devil as is his mother
Should yield the world this ass! A woman that
Bears all down with her brain, and this her son   54
Cannot take two from twenty, for his heart,   55
And leave eighteen. Alas, poor Princess,
Thou divine Imogen, what thou endur'st,
Betwixt a father by thy stepdame governed,
A mother hourly coining plots, a wooer
More hateful than the foul expulsion is
Of thy dear husband, than that horrid act
Of the divorce he'd make! The heavens hold firm
The walls of thy dear honor, keep unshaked
That temple, thy fair mind, that thou mayst stand
T' enjoy thy banished lord and this great land!   *Exit.*

❖

2.2   *Enter Imogen in her bed, and a lady, [Helen,
attending].*

IMOGEN
Who's there? My woman Helen?
HELEN   Please you, madam.
IMOGEN
What hour is it?
HELEN   Almost midnight, madam.
IMOGEN
I have read three hours then. Mine eyes are weak.
                              [*She gives her the book.*]
Fold down the leaf where I have left. To bed.
Take not away the taper; leave it burning.
And if thou canst awake by four o' the clock,
I prithee, call me. Sleep hath seized me wholly.
        [*Exit lady, Helen, leaving the book beside the bed.*]
To your protection I commend me, gods.

54 Bears all down carries all before her, triumphs over everyone   **55 for his heart** for the life of him

2.2. Location: Britain. Imogen's bedchamber in Cymbeline's palace.
s.d. in her bed (On the Elizabethan stage a bed presumably would be
"thrust out" at this point, and the trunk carried on containing
Iachimo—unless he uses the trapdoor or other such device. Imogen has
a book; a lighted candle is provided.)

From fairies and the tempters of the night   9
Guard me, beseech ye.
            Sleeps. Iachimo [comes] from the trunk.

IACHIMO
    The crickets sing, and man's o'erlabored sense
    Repairs itself by rest. Our Tarquin thus   12
    Did softly press the rushes ere he wakened   13
    The chastity he wounded. Cytherea,   14
    How bravely thou becom'st thy bed, fresh lily,   15
    And whiter than the sheets! That I might touch!
    But kiss, one kiss! Rubies unparagoned,
    How dearly they do 't! 'Tis her breathing that   18
    Perfumes the chamber thus. The flame o' the taper
    Bows toward her and would underpeep her lids
    To see th' enclosèd lights, now canopied
    Under these windows, white and azure-laced   22
    With blue of heaven's own tinct. But my design—   23
    To note the chamber. I will write all down: [*Writing*]
    Such and such pictures; there the window; such
    Th' adornment of her bed; the arras, figures,   26
    Why, such and such; and the contents o' the story. 27
    Ah, but some natural notes about her body,   28
    Above ten thousand meaner movables   29
    Would testify t' enrich mine inventory.
    O sleep, thou ape of death, lie dull upon her,   31
    And be her sense but as a monument   32
    Thus in a chapel lying! Come off, come off;
                        [*Taking off her bracelet*]
    As slippery as the Gordian knot was hard!   34
    'Tis mine; and this will witness outwardly,

---

9 fairies i.e., evil spirits   **12 Our Tarquin** the Roman Sextus Tarquinius,
who raped Lucrece   **13 press the rushes** (Elizabethan floors were strewn
with rushes or reeds.)   **14 Cytherea** Venus   **15 bravely** handsomely
18 do 't i.e., kiss each other   **22 windows** i.e., eyelids   **23 tinct** color, hue
26 arras hangings of tapestry.   **figures** carvings   **27 story** room (?), or
subject set forth in embroidery on the tapestry (?)   **28 notes** marks
29 meaner movables less important furnishings   **31 ape** i.e., imitator.
dull heavy   **32 be . . . monument** let her be as insensible as a horizontal
effigy on a tomb   **34 slippery** easy to slip off.   **Gordian knot** (According
to prophecy, whoever untied the knot binding the yoke to the pole of the
chariot of Gordius, peasant King of Phrygia, should be king of all Asia.
Alexander severed the knot with his sword.)

As strongly as the conscience does within,   36
To th' madding of her lord. On her left breast   37
A mole cinque-spotted, like the crimson drops   38
I' the bottom of a cowslip. Here's a voucher
Stronger than ever law could make. This secret
Will force him think I have picked the lock and ta'en
The treasure of her honor. No more. To what end?
Why should I write this down that's riveted,
Screwed to my memory? She hath been reading late
The tale of Tereus; here the leaf's turned down   45
Where Philomel gave up. I have enough.
To th' trunk again, and shut the spring of it.
Swift, swift, you dragons of the night, that dawning
May bare the raven's eye! I lodge in fear;   49
Though this a heavenly angel, hell is here.

                                        Clock strikes.

One, two, three. Time, time!   51
                    [*He goes into the trunk.*] *Exeunt.*

                                ✳

2.3   *Enter Cloten and Lords.*

FIRST LORD   Your lordship is the most patient man in
   loss, the most coldest that ever turned up ace.   2
CLOTEN   It would make any man cold to lose.   3
FIRST LORD   But not every man patient after the noble
   temper of your lordship. You are most hot and furious
   when you win.
CLOTEN   Winning will put any man into courage. If I

---

36 **conscience** consciousness, internal conviction   37 **madding** madden-
ing   38 **cinque-spotted** with five spots   45 **Tereus** mythical king of
Thrace, who raped Philomela, sister of his wife, Procne. (He had Philomela's tongue cut out so that she could not tell the story, but she wove it
into a tapestry.)   49 **raven's eye** (The raven was supposed to wake at early
dawn.)   51 **s.d. Exeunt** (Presumably the bed, and trunk with Iachimo
inside, are carried offstage, unless Iachimo exits by trapdoor or other
means as a way of reentering the "trunk.")

2.3. Location: Britain. Adjoining Imogen's apartments. The sense of
time is nearly continuous, since it is early morn.
2 **most coldest** coolest, most deliberate.   **turned up ace** made the losing
throw of one at dice (with a pun on *ass*)   3 **cold** gloomy, dispirited

could get this foolish Imogen, I should have gold
enough. It's almost morning, is 't not?

FIRST LORD　Day, my lord.

CLOTEN　I would this music would come. I am advised
to give her music o' mornings; they say it will pene- 12
trate. 13

Enter Musicians.

Come on, tune. If you can penetrate her with your
fingering, so; we'll try with tongue too. If none will 15
do, let her remain, but I'll never give o'er. First, a very
excellent good-conceited thing; after, a wonderful 17
sweet air, with admirable rich words to it—and then 18
let her consider. *[Music plays.]*

Song.

MUSICIAN *[Sings]*
　　Hark, hark, the lark at heaven's gate sings,
　　　And Phoebus 'gins arise, 21
　　His steeds to water at those springs
　　　On chaliced flowers that lies;
　　And winking marybuds begin 24
　　　To ope their golden eyes.
　　With everything that pretty is,
　　　My lady sweet, arise,
　　　　Arise, arise!

CLOTEN　So, get you gone. If this penetrate, I will con- 29
sider your music the better; if it do not, it is a vice in 30
her ears, which horsehairs and calves' guts, nor the 31
voice of unpaved eunuch to boot, can never amend. 32
　　　　　　　　　　　　　　　　[Exeunt Musicians.]

Enter Cymbeline and Queen.

SECOND LORD　Here comes the King.

12–13 penetrate (1) affect the feelings (2) penetrate her sexually; continued in *fingering* and *tongue*, l. 15. (See also ll. 72, 77, and notes.) **15 so**
it is well **17 good-conceited** imaginatively invented **18 air** accompanied song for single voice **21 Phoebus** i.e., the sun god with his chariot
and horses **24 winking marybuds** closed buds of marigolds, as though
with closed eyes **29–30 consider** reward (?) value (?) **31 horsehairs
and calves' guts** i.e., bowstrings and fiddlestrings **32 unpaved** un-
stoned, castrated

CLOTEN   I am glad I was up so late, for that's the reason
I was up so early. He cannot choose but take this ser-
vice I have done fatherly.—Good morrow to Your   36
Majesty, and to my gracious mother.

CYMBELINE
Attend you here the door of our stern daughter?
Will she not forth?

CLOTEN   I have assailed her with musics, but she vouch-
safes no notice.

CYMBELINE
The exile of her minion is too new;   42
She hath not yet forgot him. Some more time   43
Must wear the print of his remembrance on 't,   44
And then she's yours.

QUEEN   You are most bound to the King,
Who lets go by no vantages that may   46
Prefer you to his daughter. Frame yourself   47
To orderly solicits, and be friended   48
With aptness of the season; make denials   49
Increase your services; so seem as if
You were inspired to do those duties which
You tender to her; that you in all obey her,
Save when command to your dismission tends,   53
And therein you are senseless.   54

CLOTEN   Senseless? Not so.

        [*Enter a Messenger.*]

MESSENGER
So like you, sir, ambassadors from Rome;   56
The one is Caius Lucius.

CYMBELINE   A worthy fellow,   57
Albeit he comes on angry purpose now;
But that's no fault of his. We must receive him

---

36 fatherly as a father would receive it, graciously and thankfully
42 minion darling   **43–44 more . . . on 't** more time must elapse, erasing the image of him on the memory   **46 vantages** favorable occasions
47 Prefer recommend.   **Frame** conform, prepare   **48 solicits** solicitings,
importunings   **48–49 be . . . season** make timely use of your best opportunity   **49 denials** i.e., Imogen's refusals   **53 dismission** dismissal,
rejection   **54 senseless** insensible (to her commands; but Cloten understands the word as meaning "stupid")   **56 So like you** if you please
57 The one one of them, the chief

According to the honor of his sender;
And towards himself, his goodness forespent on us,   61
We must extend our notice. Our dear son,
When you have given good morning to your mistress,
Attend the Queen and us. We shall have need
T' employ you towards this Roman. Come, our queen.
                              Exeunt [all but Cloten].

CLOTEN
If she be up, I'll speak with her; if not,
Let her lie still and dream.—By your leave, ho!—
I know her women are about her. What
If I do line one of their hands? 'Tis gold   69
Which buys admittance—oft it doth—yea, and makes
Diana's rangers false themselves, yield up   71
Their deer to th' stand o' th' stealer; and 'tis gold 72
Which makes the true man killed and saves the thief,
Nay, sometimes hangs both thief and true man. What
Can it not do and undo? I will make
One of her women lawyer to me, for   76
I yet not understand the case myself.—   77
By your leave.   *Knocks.*

    Enter a Lady.

LADY
Who's there that knocks?
CLOTEN   A gentleman.
LADY   No more?
CLOTEN
Yes, and a gentlewoman's son.
LADY [*Aside*]   That's more
Than some, whose tailors are as dear as yours,   81
Can justly boast of.—What's your lordship's pleasure?

---

61 his goodness forespent (because of) his goodness previously bestowed   **69 line** i.e., with gold   **71 rangers** gamekeepers, i.e., nymphs
(vowed to chastity).   **false** turn false   **72 stand** (1) station of huntsman
waiting for game (2) erection   **76 lawyer to** advocate for   **77 understand the case** know how to conduct my suit (with pun on *stand* again,
l. 72, and on *case* meaning "vagina" as well as a legal *case* requiring a
lawyer)   **81 dear** costly. (The Lady jests that expensive clothes are no
guarantee of gentility.)

CLOTEN
　Your lady's person. Is she ready?
LADY   Ay,   83
　[*Aside*] To keep her chamber.
CLOTEN   There is gold for you;
　Sell me your good report.   [*He offers money.*] 85
LADY
　How? My good name? Or to report of you
　What I shall think is good?—The Princess!   87
                                        [*Exit Lady.*]

　　　　Enter Imogen.

CLOTEN
　Good morrow, fairest sister. Your sweet hand.
IMOGEN
　Good morrow, sir. You lay out too much pains
　For purchasing but trouble. The thanks I give
　Is telling you that I am poor of thanks
　And scarce can spare them.
CLOTEN   Still, I swear I love you.
IMOGEN
　If you but said so, 'twere as deep with me.   93
　If you swear still, your recompense is still
　That I regard it not.
CLOTEN   This is no answer.
IMOGEN
　But that you shall not say I yield being silent,   96
　I would not speak. I pray you, spare me. Faith,
　I shall unfold equal discourtesy   98
　To your best kindness. One of your great knowing   99
　Should learn, being taught, forbearance.
CLOTEN
　To leave you in your madness, 'twere my sin.
　I will not.

83 ready dressed. (But the Lady quibbles in another sense of "prepared, inclined.") **85 good report** favorable speech. (But the Lady quibbles on the sense of "reputation, good name.") **87 What . . . good** what seems good to me to report (favorable or unfavorable) **93 deep** binding, efficacious. (Imogen replies that Cloten's oath adds nothing to his unwelcome protestation of love.) **96 But . . . silent** if it were not for the fact that you might interpret my silence as giving consent **98 unfold equal discourtesy** display discourtesy equal **99 knowing** knowledge, discernment. (Said with tactful irony.)

IMOGEN
  Fools are not mad folks.
CLOTEN   Do you call me fool?   103
IMOGEN   As I am mad, I do.   104
  If you'll be patient, I'll no more be mad;
  That cures us both. I am much sorry, sir,
  You put me to forget a lady's manners
  By being so verbal; and learn now for all   108
  That I, which know my heart, do here pronounce,   109
  By th' very truth of it, I care not for you,
  And am so near the lack of charity   111
  To accuse myself I hate you—which I had rather   112
  You felt than make 't my boast.
CLOTEN   You sin against   113
  Obedience, which you owe your father. For   114
  The contract you pretend with that base wretch,   115
  One bred of alms and fostered with cold dishes,
  With scraps o' the court, it is no contract, none.
  And though it be allowed in meaner parties—   118
  Yet who than he more mean?—to knit their souls,
  On whom there is no more dependency   120
  But brats and beggary, in self-figured knot,   121
  Yet you are curbed from that enlargement by   122
  The consequence o' the crown, and must not foil   123
  The precious note of it with a base slave,   124
  A hilding for a livery, a squire's cloth,   125
  A pantler—not so eminent.
IMOGEN   Profane fellow!   126

103 Fools . . . folks i.e., I may be a fool to refuse you or to waste time
talking with you, but that doesn't make me mad (?); or, if I'm mad, as
you say, at least I'm not a fool like you (?)   **104 As I am mad** insofar
as I am mad (and you, after all, were the one who said I was mad)
108 By . . . verbal (If the phrase refers to Cloten, the meaning of *verbal*
is "verbose"; if to Imogen, "plainspoken.")   **for all** once and for all
109 which who   **111 the lack of charity** to lacking Christian charity
112 To accuse . . . you as to be obliged to accuse myself of hating you
113 felt i.e., perceived without my having to say it   **114 For** as for
115 pretend allege falsely as your pretext   **118 meaner parties** persons
of lower social rank   **120 On whom** from whose marriage.   **dependency** consequence   **121 But** i.e., than.   **self-figured** self-contracted
122 enlargement liberty, freedom of action   **123 consequence** succession, all that follows as a result of your being heir to the throne.   **foil**
defile, foul   **124 note** distinction   **125 hilding for a livery** good-for-
nothing fellow fit only for wearing a servant's uniform.   **cloth** dress,
livery   **126 pantler** pantry-servant.   **not** not even

Wert thou the son of Jupiter and no more
But what thou art besides, thou wert too base
To be his groom. Thou wert dignified enough,   129
Even to the point of envy, if 'twere made   130
Comparative for your virtues, to be styled   131
The underhangman of his kingdom, and hated
For being preferred so well.

CLOTEN   The south fog rot him!   133

IMOGEN
He never can meet more mischance than come
To be but named of thee. His meanest garment   135
That ever hath but clipped his body is dearer   136
In my respect than all the hairs above thee,   137
Were they all made such men.—How now, Pisanio!

    Enter Pisanio.

CLOTEN   "His garment!" Now the devil—

IMOGEN
To Dorothy my woman hie thee presently.   140

CLOTEN
"His garment!"

IMOGEN   I am sprited with a fool,   141
Frighted, and angered worse. Go bid my woman
Search for a jewel that too casually
Hath left mine arm. It was thy master's. 'Shrew me   144
If I would lose it for a revenue
Of any king's in Europe. I do think
I saw 't this morning; confident I am
Last night 'twas on mine arm; I kissed it.
I hope it be not gone to tell my lord
That I kiss aught but he.

PISANIO   'Twill not be lost.

IMOGEN
I hope so. Go and search.   [*Exit Pisanio.*]

CLOTEN   You have abused me.

129 **his** i.e., Posthumus'.   **wert dignified** would be elevated in dignity
130-131 **if . . . virtues** i.e., if you both were given positions corresponding to your innate qualities   133 **preferred** advanced.   **south fog** (The
south wind was supposed to be laden with poisonous vapors and diseases.)   135 **of** by   136 **clipped** embraced   137 **respect** regard.   **above
thee** on your head   140 **hie thee presently** go at once   141 **sprited with**
haunted by   144 **'Shrew me** beshrew me. (A mild oath.)

"His meanest garment!"

IMOGEN   Ay, I said so, sir.
If you will make 't an action, call witness to 't.   153

CLOTEN
I will inform your father.

IMOGEN   Your mother too.
She's my good lady and will conceive, I hope,   155
But the worst of me. So I leave you, sir,
To th' worst of discontent.   *Exit.*

CLOTEN   I'll be revenged.
"His meanest garment!" Well.   *Exit.*

❧

2.4   *Enter Posthumus and Philario.*

POSTHUMUS
Fear it not, sir. I would I were so sure
To win the King as I am bold her honor   2
Will remain hers.

PHILARIO   What means do you make to him?   3

POSTHUMUS
Not any, but abide the change of time,
Quake in the present winter's state, and wish
That warmer days would come. In these feared hopes   6
I barely gratify your love; they failing,   7
I must die much your debtor.

PHILARIO
Your very goodness and your company
O'erpays all I can do. By this, your king   10
Hath heard of great Augustus; Caius Lucius   11
Will do 's commission throughly. And I think   12
He'll grant the tribute, send th' arrearages,   13
Or look upon our Romans, whose remembrance   14

---

153 **action** action at law   155 **good lady** i.e., patroness. (Said ironically.)
conceive believe, think.   **hope** (Continues the irony, though it can also
mean "expect.")

2.4. Location: Rome. Philario's house.
2 **bold** confident   3 **means** overtures.   **him** i.e., the King   6 **feared**
mixed with fear   7 **gratify** repay   10 **this** this time   11 **of** from   12 **do**
's do his.   **throughly** thoroughly   13 **He'll** i.e., Cymbeline will.   **arrear-**
ages arrears, parts of the tribute due but unpaid   14 **Or** before (he
will).   **look upon** face

Is yet fresh in their grief.
POSTHUMUS   I do believe,   15
Statist though I am none, nor like to be,   16
That this will prove a war; and you shall hear
The legions now in Gallia sooner landed
In our not-fearing Britain than have tidings
Of any penny tribute paid. Our countrymen
Are men more ordered than when Julius Caesar   21
Smiled at their lack of skill but found their courage
Worthy his frowning at. Their discipline,
Now mingled with their courages, will make known
To their approvers they are people such   25
That mend upon the world.

> *Enter Iachimo.*

PHILARIO   See! Iachimo!   26
POSTHUMUS
The swiftest harts have posted you by land,   27
And winds of all the corners kissed your sails   28
To make your vessel nimble.
PHILARIO   Welcome, sir.
POSTHUMUS
I hope the briefness of your answer made   30
The speediness of your return.
IACHIMO   Your lady
Is one of the fairest that I have looked upon.
POSTHUMUS
And therewithal the best, or let her beauty
Look through a casement to allure false hearts   34
And be false with them.
IACHIMO   Here are letters for you.
                            [*He gives a letter or letters.*]
POSTHUMUS
Their tenor good, I trust.

---

15 their i.e., the Britons', or, caused by the Romans   **16 Statist** statesman   **21 more ordered** better disciplined and governed   **25 their
approvers** those who test their courage   **25–26 such . . . world** whose
reputation is improving   **27 harts** i.e., horses as swift as deer. (Proverbially swift runners.)   **posted** sped   **28 of all the corners** from every
corner   **30 your answer** the answer you were given   **34 Look through a
casement** (As a whore might do to attract customers. The *casement* here
is her body, or perhaps her laced bodice.)

IACHIMO   'Tis very like.   36
PHILARIO
  Was Caius Lucius in the Briton court
  When you were there?
IACHIMO   He was expected then,
  But not approached.
POSTHUMUS   All is well yet.   40
  Sparkles this stone as it was wont, or is 't not
  Too dull for your good wearing? [*Indicating the ring.*]
IACHIMO   If I have lost it,   42
  I should have lost the worth of it in gold.
  I'll make a journey twice as far t' enjoy
  A second night of such sweet shortness which
  Was mine in Britain, for the ring is won.
POSTHUMUS
  The stone's too hard to come by.
IACHIMO   Not a whit,
  Your lady being so easy.
POSTHUMUS   Make not, sir,
  Your loss your sport. I hope you know that we
  Must not continue friends.
IACHIMO   Good sir, we must,
  If you keep covenant. Had I not brought
  The knowledge of your mistress home, I grant   52
  We were to question farther; but I now   53
  Profess myself the winner of her honor,
  Together with your ring, and not the wronger
  Of her or you, having proceeded but
  By both your wills.
POSTHUMUS   If you can make 't apparent
  That you have tasted her in bed, my hand
  And ring is yours; if not, the foul opinion
  You had of her pure honor gains or loses   60
  Your sword or mine, or masterless leaves both   61

36 like likely   **40 All is well yet** (Posthumus is evidently reassured by
what he has read of the letter.)   **42 s.d. Indicating the ring** (The ring
possibly is in the custody of Philario as official of the wager; although
Posthumus appears to have it himself at l. 108, he may then take it from
Philario and give it to Iachimo.)   **52 knowledge** i.e., carnal knowledge
53 question dispute, i.e., settle matters by a duel   **60–61 gains . . . mine**
i.e., gains one of us the other's sword

To who shall find them.

IACHIMO   Sir, my circumstances,   62
Being so near the truth as I will make them,
Must first induce you to believe; whose strength
I will confirm with oath, which I doubt not
You'll give me leave to spare when you shall find   66
You need it not.

POSTHUMUS   Proceed.

IACHIMO   First, her bedchamber—
Where, I confess, I slept not, but profess
Had that was well worth watching—it was hanged   69
With tapestry of silk and silver; the story
Proud Cleopatra when she met her Roman,
And Cydnus swelled above the banks, or for   72
The press of boats or pride. A piece of work
So bravely done, so rich, that it did strive   74
In workmanship and value, which I wondered   75
Could be so rarely and exactly wrought,
Since the true life on 't was—

POSTHUMUS   This is true;   77
And this you might have heard of here, by me
Or by some other.

IACHIMO   More particulars
Must justify my knowledge.

POSTHUMUS   So they must,   80
Or do your honor injury.

IACHIMO   The chimney
Is south the chamber, and the chimneypiece   82
Chaste Dian bathing. Never saw I figures
So likely to report themselves. The cutter   84
Was as another nature, dumb; outwent her,   85
Motion and breath left out.

POSTHUMUS   This is a thing   86

62 **who** whoever. **circumstances** detailed observations **66 spare** leave
out **69 that** that which. **watching** remaining awake (for) **72 Cydnus** a
river in Cilicia, or modern-day southern Turkey, the scene of the meeting of Antony and Cleopatra. (See *Antony and Cleopatra*, 2.2.196–236.)
or for either because of **74 bravely** handsomely **74–75 it did . . . value**
it was a question whether the workmanship or the intrinsic value
contained in the material was the greater **77 on 't** of it **80 justify**
confirm **82 chimneypiece** sculptured mantelpiece **84 So . . . themselves** so like what they purported to represent **84–85 cutter . . . dumb**
sculptor rivaled nature in creative power, though creating works unable
to speak. **her** i.e., nature **86 left out** excepted

Which you might from relation likewise reap,   87
Being, as it is, much spoke of.

IACHIMO   The roof o' the chamber
With golden cherubins is fretted. Her andirons—   89
I had forgot them—were two winking Cupids   90
Of silver, each on one foot standing, nicely
Depending on their brands.

POSTHUMUS   This is her honor!   92
Let it be granted you have seen all this—and praise
Be given to your remembrance—the description   94
Of what is in her chamber nothing saves   95
The wager you have laid.

IACHIMO   Then, if you can
Be pale, I beg but leave to air this jewel. See!
                              [*He shows the bracelet.*]
And now 'tis up again. It must be married   98
To that your diamond; I'll keep them.

POSTHUMUS   Jove!
Once more let me behold it. Is it that
Which I left with her?

IACHIMO   Sir—I thank her—that.
She stripped it from her arm; I see her yet;
Her pretty action did outsell her gift,   103
And yet enriched it too. She gave it me
And said she prized it once.

POSTHUMUS   Maybe she plucked it off
To send it me.

IACHIMO   She writes so to you, doth she?

POSTHUMUS
O, no, no, no! 'Tis true. Here, take this too.
                              [*He gives the ring.*]
It is a basilisk unto mine eye,   109
Kills me to look on 't. Let there be no honor
Where there is beauty, truth where semblance, love
Where there's another man. The vows of women   112
Of no more bondage be to where they are made   113

87 **relation** hearsay, second hand   89 **fretted** adorned with carved or
embossed work in decorative patterns   90 **winking** i.e., blind   92 **Depending** leaning. **brands** torches   94 **remembrance** ability to remember   95 **nothing** not at all   98 **up** put up, pocketed   103 **outsell** exceed
in value   109 **basilisk** fabulous serpent or dragon whose look was fatal
112 **The vows** i.e., let the vows   113 **bondage** obligation. **where** i.e., the
men to whom

Than they are to their virtues, which is nothing.
O, above measure false!
PHILARIO   Have patience, sir,
  And take your ring again; 'tis not yet won.
  It may be probable she lost it; or   117
  Who knows if one her women, being corrupted,   118
  Hath stolen it from her?
POSTHUMUS   Very true,
  And so, I hope, he came by 't. Back my ring!
                      [*He takes back the ring.*]
  Render to me some corporal sign about her
  More evident than this; for this was stolen.
IACHIMO
  By Jupiter, I had it from her arm.
POSTHUMUS
  Hark you, he swears; by Jupiter he swears.
  'Tis true—nay, keep the ring—'tis true. I am sure
  She would not lose it. Her attendants are
  All sworn and honorable. They induced to steal it?
  And by a stranger? No, he hath enjoyed her.
  The cognizance of her incontinency   130
  Is this. She hath bought the name of whore thus dearly.
  There, take thy hire, and all the fiends of hell   132
  Divide themselves between you!
                   [*He gives the ring again.*]
PHILARIO   Sir, be patient.   133
  This is not strong enough to be believed
  Of one persuaded well of.
POSTHUMUS   Never talk on 't.   135
  She hath been colted by him.
IACHIMO   If you seek   136
  For further satisfying, under her breast—
  Worthy the pressing—lies a mole, right proud
  Of that most delicate lodging. By my life,
  I kissed it, and it gave me present hunger
  To feed again, though full. You do remember
  This stain upon her?

---

117 probable provable   **118 one her** one of her   **130 cognizance** mark
or token by which a thing is recognized, as a servant is identified by his
livery and identifying mark   **132–133 all . . . you** i.e., may you and
Imogen suffer equal torments in hell   **135 persuaded well of** well
thought of.   **on 't** of it   **136 colted** enjoyed sexually

POSTHUMUS   Ay, and it doth confirm
　Another stain, as big as hell can hold,
　Were there no more but it.
IACHIMO   Will you hear more?
POSTHUMUS
　Spare your arithmetic! Never count the turns.   145
　Once, and a million!
IACHIMO   I'll be sworn—
POSTHUMUS   No swearing.   146
　If you will swear you have not done 't, you lie,
　And I will kill thee if thou dost deny
　Thou'st made me cuckold.
IACHIMO   I'll deny nothing.
POSTHUMUS
　O, that I had her here, to tear her limbmeal!   150
　I will go there and do 't, i' the court, before
　Her father. I'll do something—   *Exit.*
PHILARIO   Quite beside   152
　The government of patience! You have won.
　Let's follow him and pervert the present wrath   154
　He hath against himself.
IACHIMO   With all my heart.   *Exeunt.*

2.5   *Enter Posthumus.*

POSTHUMUS
　Is there no way for men to be, but women   1
　Must be half-workers? We are all bastards,
　And that most venerable man which I
　Did call my father was I know not where
　When I was stamped. Some coiner with his tools   5

---

145 turns (with a bitter suggestion of "tricks," sexual encounters with a customer)   **146 Once, and a million** i.e., what does it matter if once or a million times; it's all the same   **150 limbmeal** limb from limb
152 beside beyond   **154 pervert** divert

2.5. Location: Philario's house, as before. The scene may be virtually continuous.
1 be exist   **5 stamped** (The image of procreation as an act of coinage by the father occurs often in Shakespeare.)   **tools** (with bitter suggestion of the male sexual organ)

Made me a counterfeit; yet my mother seemed
The Dian of that time. So doth my wife   7
The nonpareil of this. O, vengeance, vengeance!   8
Me of my lawful pleasure she restrained
And prayed me oft forbearance; did it with
A pudency so rosy the sweet view on 't   11
Might well have warmed old Saturn, that I thought her   12
As chaste as unsunned snow. O, all the devils!
This yellow Iachimo, in an hour, was 't not?   14
Or less? At first? Perchance he spoke not, but,   15
Like a full-acorned boar, a German one,   16
Cried "O!" and mounted; found no opposition
But what he looked for should oppose and she   18
Should from encounter guard. Could I find out
The woman's part in me! For there's no motion   20
That tends to vice in man but I affirm
It is the woman's part. Be it lying, note it,
The woman's; flattering, hers; deceiving, hers;
Lust and rank thoughts, hers, hers; revenges, hers;
Ambitions, covetings, change of prides, disdain,   25
Nice longing, slanders, mutability,   26
All faults that have a name, nay, that hell knows,
Why, hers, in part or all, but rather all.
For even to vice
They are not constant, but are changing still   30
One vice but of a minute old for one
Not half so old as that. I'll write against them,   32
Detest them, curse them. Yet 'tis greater skill   33
In a true hate to pray they have their will;
The very devils cannot plague them better.   *Exit.*

7 **Dian** Diana, goddess of chastity   8 **nonpareil** one that has no equal.
this this time   11 **pudency** modesty.   **rosy** blushing (that).   **on 't** of it
12 **Saturn** father of Jupiter, associated with old age   14 **yellow** sallow
15 **At first** right at first   16 **full-acorned** full of acorns, favorite food of
boars. (In German, *eichel*, acorn, also means "penis" because of its
glanslike shape.)   18 **But . . . oppose** i.e., except for the pleasant physical friction or barrier (the hymen) he expected in entering. (Imogen is
no longer a virgin, being married, but the hymen still symbolizes what
she should *guard* from *encounter*, l. 19.)   20 **part** (with bitter sexual
suggestion).   **motion** impulse   25 **change of prides** varying vanities (in
dress, etc.)   26 **Nice** fastidious, wanton.   **mutability** inconstancy
30 **still** continuously   32 **write against** denounce   33 **skill** reason

3.1   *Enter in state, Cymbeline, Queen, Cloten, and
lords at one door, and at another, Caius Lucius
and attendants.*

CYMBELINE
  Now say, what would Augustus Caesar with us?
LUCIUS
  When Julius Caesar, whose remembrance yet
  Lives in men's eyes, and will to ears and tongues
  Be theme and hearing ever, was in this Britain
  And conquered it, Cassibelan, thine uncle—
  Famous in Caesar's praises no whit less
  Than in his feats deserving it—for him
  And his succession granted Rome a tribute,
  Yearly three thousand pounds, which by thee lately
  Is left untendered.
QUEEN   And, to kill the marvel,   10
  Shall be so ever.
CLOTEN   There be many Caesars
  Ere such another Julius. Britain's a world
  By itself, and we will nothing pay
  For wearing our own noses.
QUEEN   That opportunity   14
  Which then they had to take from 's, to resume   15
  We have again. Remember, sir, my liege,   16
  The kings your ancestors, together with
  The natural bravery of your isle, which stands
  As Neptune's park, ribbed and palèd in   19
  With rocks unscalable and roaring waters,
  With sands that will not bear your enemies' boats,
  But suck them up to the topmast. A kind of conquest
  Caesar made here, but made not here his brag
  Of "Came and saw and overcame." With shame—
  The first that ever touched him—he was carried
  From off our coast, twice beaten; and his shipping,

3.1. Location: Britain. At the court of Cymbeline.
10 kill the marvel end the surprise (by making nonpayment a regular
practice)   **14 our own noses** i.e., British, not Roman, noses. (See Cloten's jibe at the Romans' *crooked noses* in l. 37.)   **15–16 to resume . . .
again** we now have the opportunity to take it back   **19 ribbed** enclosed.
palèd fenced

Poor ignorant baubles on our terrible seas,   27
Like eggshells moved upon their surges, cracked   28
As easily 'gainst our rocks. For joy whereof
The famed Cassibelan, who was once at point—   30
O giglot fortune!—to master Caesar's sword,   31
Made Lud's Town with rejoicing fires bright   32
And Britons strut with courage.

CLOTEN   Come, there's no more tribute to be paid. Our
kingdom is stronger than it was at that time; and, as I
said, there is no more such Caesars. Other of them may
have crooked noses, but to owe such straight arms,   37
none.

CYMBELINE   Son, let your mother end.   39

CLOTEN   We have yet many among us can grip as hard   40
as Cassibelan. I do not say I am one; but I have a hand.
Why tribute? Why should we pay tribute? If Caesar
can hide the sun from us with a blanket, or put the
moon in his pocket, we will pay him tribute for light;
else, sir, no more tribute, pray you now.

CYMBELINE [*To Lucius*]   You must know,
Till the injurious Romans did extort   47
This tribute from us, we were free. Caesar's ambition,
Which swelled so much that it did almost stretch
The sides o' the world, against all color here   50
Did put the yoke upon 's, which to shake off
Becomes a warlike people, whom we reckon
Ourselves to be. We do say then to Caesar,
Our ancestor was that Mulmutius which
Ordained our laws, whose use the sword of Caesar
Hath too much mangled, whose repair and franchise   56
Shall, by the power we hold, be our good deed,
Though Rome be therefore angry. Mulmutius made our
    laws,

---

27 ignorant silly, unskilled.   **baubles** trifles   **28 their surges** the waves
of the sea   **30 Cassibelan** (The incident referred to is recorded of
Nennius, brother of Cassibelan, in Holinshed.)   **30–31 at point . . . to
master** on the point . . . of mastering   **31 giglot** lewd, wanton   **32 Lud's
Town** London (supposedly named after King Lud, Cymbeline's grandfather)   **37 owe** own   **39 end** finish speaking   **40 can grip** who can
grasp (a sword)   **47 injurious** insolent   **50 against all color** in defiance
of all rightful claim. (*Color*, arguable ground or claim, may also pun on
yoke, "collar," in the next line.)   **56 whose . . . franchise** the repair and
free exercise of which laws

Who was the first of Britain which did put
His brows within a golden crown and called
Himself a king.
LUCIUS   I am sorry, Cymbeline,
That I am to pronounce Augustus Caesar—
Caesar, that hath more kings his servants than
Thyself domestic officers—thine enemy.
Receive it from me, then: war and confusion   65
In Caesar's name pronounce I 'gainst thee. Look
For fury not to be resisted. Thus defied,   67
I thank thee for myself.
CYMBELINE   Thou art welcome, Caius.
Thy Caesar knighted me; my youth I spent
Much under him. Of him I gathered honor,
Which he to seek of me again perforce   71
Behooves me keep at utterance. I am perfect   72
That the Pannonians and Dalmatians for   73
Their liberties are now in arms, a precedent
Which not to read would show the Britons cold.   75
So Caesar shall not find them.
LUCIUS   Let proof speak.   76
CLOTEN   His Majesty bids you welcome. Make pastime
with us a day or two, or longer. If you seek us after-
wards in other terms, you shall find us in our saltwater
girdle. If you beat us out of it, it is yours; if you fall in
the adventure, our crows shall fare the better for you,
and there's an end.
LUCIUS   So, sir.
CYMBELINE
I know your master's pleasure and he mine.
All the remain is "Welcome!"   *Exeunt.* 85

❖

65 confusion discomfiture, destruction   67 Thus defied you having
been thus defied   71 he to seek since he seeks it   72 keep at utterance
defend to the last extremity. (From the French *à outrance*.)   perfect well
aware   73 for to defend   75 cold lacking spirit   76 proof experiment,
trial (by way of combat)   85 All the remain all that remains (to be said)

3.2   *Enter Pisanio, reading of a letter.*

PISANIO
How? Of adultery? Wherefore write you not
What monster's her accuser? Leonatus,
O master, what a strange infection
Is fall'n into thy ear! What false Italian,
As poisonous-tongued as handed, hath prevailed   5
On thy too ready hearing? Disloyal? No.
She's punished for her truth and undergoes,   7
More goddesslike than wifelike, such assaults
As would take in some virtue. O my master,   9
Thy mind to her is now as low as were   10
Thy fortunes. How? That I should murder her,
Upon the love and truth and vows which I   12
Have made to thy command? I, her? Her blood?
If it be so to do good service, never
Let me be counted serviceable. How look I,
That I should seem to lack humanity
So much as this fact comes to? [*He reads.*] "Do 't. The
   letter   17
That I have sent her, by her own command
Shall give thee opportunity." O damned paper,
Black as the ink that's on thee! Senseless bauble,   20
Art thou a fedarie for this act, and look'st   21
So virginlike without? Lo, here she comes.

    Enter Imogen.

I am ignorant in what I am commanded.   23
IMOGEN   How now, Pisanio?
PISANIO
Madam, here is a letter from my lord.
IMOGEN [*Taking the letter*]
Who, thy lord that is my lord, Leonatus?

3.2. Location: Britain. At the court of Cymbeline.
s.d. reading of reading   **5 As . . . handed** as skilled in slander as in the
art of secret poisoning (for which the Italians were notorious)   **7 truth**
fidelity.   **undergoes** i.e., withstands   **9 take in** cause to yield   **10 to her**
compared to hers   **12 Upon** i.e., on top of   **17 fact** deed   **20 Senseless**
bauble trifle incapable of feeling   **21 fedarie** accomplice   **23 am igno-**
rant will pretend not to know

O, learned indeed were that astronomer   27
That knew the stars as I his characters;   28
He'd lay the future open. You good gods,
Let what is here contained relish of love,   30
Of my lord's health, of his content—yet not   31
That we two are asunder; let that grieve him.
Some griefs are med'cinable; that is one of them, 33
For it doth physic love—of his content   34
All but in that! Good wax, thy leave. [*She breaks the seal.*]
   Blest be
You bees that make these locks of counsel! Lovers 36
And men in dangerous bonds pray not alike;   37
Though forfeiters you cast in prison,   38
You clasp young Cupid's tables. Good news, gods!   39
   [*She reads.*] "Justice and your father's wrath, should
he take me in his dominion, could not be so cruel 41
to me as you, O the dearest of creatures, would even 42
renew me with your eyes. Take notice that I am in
Cambria, at Milford Haven. What your own love will out 44
of this advise you, follow. So he wishes you all hap-
piness that remains loyal to his vow, and your increas- 46
ing in love.   Leonatus Posthumus." 47
O, for a horse with wings! Hear'st thou, Pisanio?
He is at Milford Haven. Read, and tell me
How far 'tis thither. If one of mean affairs   50
May plod it in a week, why may not I
Glide thither in a day? Then, true Pisanio,
Who long'st like me to see thy lord, who long'st—
O, let me bate—but not like me, yet long'st,   54
But in a fainter kind—O, not like me,

---

27 astronomer astrologer   **28 characters** handwriting   **30 relish** taste
31 not i.e., not content   **33 med'cinable** curative, health-giving
34 physic make healthy, strong   **36 locks of counsel** waxen seals enclos-
ing confidential matters   **37 in dangerous bonds** under contracts
risking penalties (which are similarly sealed with wax)   **38 forfeiters**
those who forfeit their bonds.   **you** (Addressed to the bees as makers of
wax.)   **39 clasp** seal (with wax).   **tables** writing tablets, used here for
love letters   **41 take** apprehend   **42 as** but that. (The letter, however, is
studiously ambiguous, and suggests also that no one can be so cruel as
she.)   **44 Cambria** Wales   **46–47 your increasing in love** (he wishes)
your advancement and prosperity in love   **50 mean affairs** ordinary
business   **54 bate** reduce in amount, modify

For mine's beyond beyond; say, and speak thick—   56
Love's counselor should fill the bores of hearing,   57
To th' smothering of the sense—how far it is   58
To this same blessèd Milford. And by th' way   59
Tell me how Wales was made so happy as
T' inherit such a haven. But first of all,
How we may steal from hence, and for the gap
That we shall make in time from our hence-going
And our return, to excuse. But first, how get hence?
Why should excuse be born or ere begot?   65
We'll talk of that hereafter. Prithee, speak,
How many score of miles may we well ride
Twixt hour and hour?

PISANIO   One score twixt sun and sun,   68
Madam, 's enough for you—and too much too.

IMOGEN
Why, one that rode to 's execution, man,
Could never go so slow. I have heard of riding wagers   71
Where horses have been nimbler than the sands
That run i' the clock's behalf. But this is fool'ry.   73
Go bid my woman feign a sickness, say
She'll home to her father; and provide me presently
A riding suit no costlier than would fit
A franklin's huswife.

PISANIO   Madam, you're best consider.   77

IMOGEN
I see before me, man. Nor here, nor here,   78
Nor what ensues, but have a fog in them   79
That I cannot look through. Away, I prithee!
Do as I bid thee. There's no more to say.
Accessible is none but Milford way.

                              Exeunt [*separately*].

❖

56 beyond beyond i.e., even greater than something already great.
thick many words quickly   **57 the bores of hearing** the ears   **58 To . . .
sense** i.e., to the point of overwhelming the sense of hearing   **59 by th'
way** as we go   **65 excuse** i.e., excuse for our absence.   **or ere begot** i.e.,
even before the need for it arises   **68 Twixt hour and hour** i.e., in an
hour.   **One . . . and sun** twenty miles a day   **71 riding** racing   **73 i' . . .
behalf** i.e., doing the service of a clock, in an hourglass   **77 franklin's**
yeoman's. (A franklin was a farmer who owned his own land but was
not of noble birth.)   **you're best** you had better   **78 before me** immediately in front of me.   **Nor . . . here** (She gestures: not to this side, not to
that.)   **79 ensues** happens later. (Imogen can only look directly ahead to
Milford Haven, nowhere else and not beyond.)

3.3   *Enter [from the cave] Belarius; Guiderius and*
           Arviragus [following].

BELARIUS
  A goodly day not to keep house with such   1
  Whose roof's as low as ours. Stoop, boys; this gate
  Instructs you how t' adore the heavens and bows you   3
  To a morning's holy office. The gates of monarchs   4
  Are arched so high that giants may jet through   5
  And keep their impious turbans on, without
  Good morrow to the sun.—Hail, thou fair heaven!
  We house i' the rock, yet use thee not so hardly   8
  As prouder livers do.
GUIDERIUS   Hail, heaven!
ARVIRAGUS   Hail, heaven!   9
BELARIUS
  Now for our mountain sport. Up to yond hill;
  Your legs are young. I'll tread these flats. Consider,
  When you above perceive me like a crow,   12
  That it is place which lessens and sets off,   13
  And you may then revolve what tales I have told you   14
  Of courts, of princes, of the tricks in war.
  This service is not service, so being done,   16
  But being so allowed. To apprehend thus   17
  Draws us a profit from all things we see;
  And often, to our comfort, shall we find
  The sharded beetle in a safer hold   20
  Than is the full-winged eagle. O, this life
  Is nobler than attending for a check,   22
  Richer than doing nothing for a bauble,   23

3.3. Location: Wales. Before the cave of Belarius.
1 keep house stay at home   **3 bows you** makes you bow   **4 holy office**
i.e., morning prayer   **5 jet** walk pompously, strut   **8 use . . . hardly**
treat you not so badly, do not offend heaven as much (with a play on the
idea of *rock* and *hard*)   **9 prouder livers** those who live more proudly
and magnificently   **12 like a crow** appearing through distance as small
as a crow   **13 place** position.   **sets off** enhances   **14 revolve** ponder
16–17 This . . . allowed i.e., any act of service at court is valued not for
itself, but is valued by the lord as proof of his greatness in acknowledging or accepting such tokens of submission   **20 sharded** living in dung,
or, covered with the sheaths of insects' wings.   **hold** stronghold   **22 attending . . . check** doing service (at court) only to be rewarded with a
rebuke   **23 bauble** trifle

Prouder than rustling in unpaid-for silk;   24
Such gain the cap of him that makes him fine,   25
Yet keeps his book uncrossed. No life to ours.   26

GUIDERIUS

Out of your proof you speak. We poor unfledged   27
Have never winged from view o' the nest, nor know not
What air's from home. Haply this life is best,   29
If quiet life be best, sweeter to you
That have a sharper known, well corresponding
With your stiff age; but unto us it is
A cell of ignorance, traveling abed,   33
A prison for a debtor that not dares
To stride a limit.

ARVIRAGUS   What should we speak of   35
When we are old as you? When we shall hear
The rain and wind beat dark December, how,   37
In this our pinching cave, shall we discourse   38
The freezing hours away? We have seen nothing.
We are beastly: subtle as the fox for prey,
Like warlike as the wolf for what we eat.   41
Our valor is to chase what flies. Our cage   42
We make a choir, as doth the prisoned bird,
And sing our bondage freely.

BELARIUS   How you speak!   44
Did you but know the city's usuries
And felt them knowingly; the art o' the court,
As hard to leave as keep, whose top to climb
Is certain falling, or so slippery that
The fear's as bad as falling; the toil o' the war,
A pain that only seems to seek out danger   50
I' the name of fame and honor, which dies i' the search
And hath as oft a slanderous epitaph

---

24 unpaid-for for which the wearer is in debt to his tailor   **25 gain . . . fine** win the respectful greeting of him who dresses elegantly, or of his tailor   **26 keeps . . . uncrossed** does nothing to cancel his record of debts.   **to** compared to   **27 proof** experience   **29 What . . . home** what the air is like away from home.   **Haply** perhaps   **33 abed** i.e., in imagination only, in dreams   **35 stride a limit** overpass a bound (where he will be liable for arrest)   **37 beat dark December** i.e., beat down, as befitting dark December   **38 pinching** nippingly cold, or confining   **41 Like** alike, equally   **42 flies** flees   **44 freely** (Said ironically: their only freedom is to sing of their bondage.)   **50 pain** labor

As record of fair act; nay, many times
Doth ill deserve by doing well; what's worse,   54
Must curtsy at the censure. O boys, this story
The world may read in me. My body's marked
With Roman swords, and my report was once   57
First with the best of note. Cymbeline loved me,   58
And when a soldier was the theme, my name
Was not far off. Then was I as a tree
Whose boughs did bend with fruit. But in one night
A storm, or robbery, call it what you will,
Shook down my mellow hangings, nay, my leaves   61
And left me bare to weather.

GUIDERIUS   Uncertain favor!
BELARIUS
My fault being nothing—as I have told you oft—
But that two villains, whose false oaths prevailed
Before my perfect honor, swore to Cymbeline
I was confederate with the Romans. So
Followed my banishment, and this twenty years
This rock and these demesnes have been my world,   70
Where I have lived at honest freedom, paid   71
More pious debts to heaven than in all
The fore-end of my time. But up to th' mountains!   73
This is not hunters' language. He that strikes
The venison first shall be the lord o' the feast;
To him the other two shall minister,
And we will fear no poison, which attends
In place of greater state. I'll meet you in the valleys.
                    Exeunt [Guiderius and Arviragus].
How hard it is to hide the sparks of nature!
These boys know little they are sons to the King,
Nor Cymbeline dreams that they are alive.
They think they are mine; and though trained up thus
    meanly
I' the cave wherein they bow, their thoughts do hit
The roofs of palaces, and nature prompts them
In simple and low things to prince it much   85

---

54 deserve earn   **57 report** reputation   **58 note** distinction, importance
63 hangings hanging fruit   **70 demesnes** domains, regions   **71 at
honest freedom** (Compare the phrases "at peace," "at liberty.")
73 fore-end earlier part   **85 prince it** play the prince

Beyond the trick of others. This Polydore,   86
The heir of Cymbeline and Britain, who
The King his father called Guiderius—Jove!
When on my three-foot stool I sit and tell
The warlike feats I have done, his spirits fly out
Into my story; say, "Thus mine enemy fell,
And thus I set my foot on 's neck," even then
The princely blood flows in his cheek, he sweats,
Strains his young nerves, and puts himself in posture   94
That acts my words. The younger brother, Cadwal,
Once Arviragus, in as like a figure   96
Strikes life into my speech and shows much more   97
His own conceiving. [*Sounds of hunting are heard.*]—
   Hark, the game is roused!—   98
O Cymbeline, heaven and my conscience knows
Thou didst unjustly banish me; whereon,
At three and two years old, I stole these babes,
Thinking to bar thee of succession as
Thou refts me of my lands. Euriphile,   103
Thou wast their nurse; they took thee for their mother,
And every day do honor to her grave.
Myself, Belarius, that am Morgan called,
They take for natural father.—The game is up.   107

                                                Exit.

                          ❖

3.4   *Enter Pisanio and Imogen.*

IMOGEN
   Thou toldst me, when we came from horse, the place   1
   Was near at hand. Ne'er longed my mother so
   To see me first as I have now. Pisanio, man,   3
   Where is Posthumus? What is in thy mind
   That makes thee stare thus? Wherefore breaks that sigh

---

86 **trick** manner 94 **nerves** sinews 96 **in . . . figure** acting his part
equally well 97–98 **shows . . . conceiving** i.e., adds to my story his own
conception 103 **Thou refts** you have bereft, deprived 107 **up** roused

3.4. Location: Wales. Country near Milford Haven.
1 **came from horse** dismounted 3 **have** i.e., have longing to see
Posthumus

From th' inward of thee? One but painted thus
Would be interpreted a thing perplexed   7
Beyond self-explication. Put thyself   8
Into a havior of less fear, ere wildness   9
Vanquish my staider senses. What's the matter?   10
                    [*He offers her a letter.*]
Why tender'st thou that paper to me with
A look untender? If 't be summer news,
Smile to 't before; if winterly, thou need'st
But keep that countenance still. My husband's hand?
That drug-damned Italy hath outcrafted him,   15
And he's at some hard point. Speak, man. Thy tongue   16
May take off some extremity, which to read   17
Would be even mortal to me.
PISANIO   Please you, read,
And you shall find me, wretched man, a thing
The most disdained of fortune.
IMOGEN (*Reads*) "Thy mistress, Pisanio, hath played the
   strumpet in my bed, the testimonies whereof lies
   bleeding in me. I speak not out of weak surmises but
   from proof as strong as my grief and as certain as I
   expect my revenge. That part thou, Pisanio, must act
   for me, if thy faith be not tainted with the breach of
   hers. Let thine own hands take away her life. I shall
   give thee opportunity at Milford Haven—she hath
   my letter for the purpose—where, if thou fear to strike
   and to make me certain it is done, thou art the pander
   to her dishonor and equally to me disloyal."
PISANIO
What shall I need to draw my sword? The paper
Hath cut her throat already. No, 'tis slander,
Whose edge is sharper than the sword, whose tongue
Outvenoms all the worms of Nile, whose breath   35
Rides on the posting winds and doth belie   36

---

7 perplexed distressed   **8 Beyond self-explication** beyond the ability to
express this condition   **9 havior of less fear** less fearsome behavior
9–10 ere . . . senses before frenzy and panic overcome my calm
15 drug-damned condemned for its drugs and poisons.   **outcrafted him**
outwitted him, overcome him by craft   **16 hard point** dangerous crisis
17 take . . . extremity reduce somewhat the shock   **35 worms** serpents
36 posting hastening.   **belie** spread lies throughout

All corners of the world. Kings, queens, and states,   37
Maids, matrons, nay, the secrets of the grave
This viperous slander enters.—What cheer, madam?

IMOGEN
False to his bed? What is it to be false?
To lie in watch there and to think on him?   41
To weep twixt clock and clock? If sleep charge nature, 42
To break it with a fearful dream of him   43
And cry myself awake? That's false to 's bed, is it?

PISANIO   Alas, good lady!

IMOGEN
I false? Thy conscience witness! Iachimo,   46
Thou didst accuse him of incontinency.
Thou then lookedst like a villain; now methinks
Thy favor's good enough. Some jay of Italy,   49
Whose mother was her painting, hath betrayed him.   50
Poor I am stale, a garment out of fashion,
And, for I am richer than to hang by the walls,   52
I must be ripped. To pieces with me! O,
Men's vows are women's traitors! All good seeming,
By thy revolt, O husband, shall be thought   55
Put on for villainy; not born where 't grows,   56
But worn a bait for ladies.

PISANIO   Good madam, hear me.

IMOGEN
True honest men being heard like false Aeneas   58
Were in his time thought false, and Sinon's weeping   59

37 states statesmen   41 in watch awake   42 twixt . . . clock from hour
to hour.   charge nature i.e., overcome wakefulness   43 fearful dream
of him dream fearful about his safety   46 Thy conscience witness let
your conscience bear me witness. (She apostrophizes Posthumus.)
49 favor's countenance is.   jay i.e., flashy or light woman
50 Whose . . . painting i.e., who owed her beauty to cosmetics
52 for . . . than because I am too fine.   to hang by the walls i.e., like
discarded clothing or armor   55 revolt inconstancy   56 born i.e., innate
58 being heard like when they were heard to speak like.   Aeneas
(Thought of as the pattern of faithless love because of his desertion of
Dido.)   59 Were . . . false i.e., were mistrusted because of Aeneas'
deceptive speech, which was indeed false; his smooth falsehood cast
doubt even on perfectly honest professions of love.   Sinon Greek who
by his guile persuaded the Trojans to introduce within the walls of Troy
the wooden horse filled with armed men

Did scandal many a holy tear, took pity   60
From most true wretchedness. So thou, Posthumus,   61
Wilt lay the leaven on all proper men;   62
Goodly and gallant shall be false and perjured   63
From thy great fail.—Come, fellow, be thou honest;   64
Do thou thy master's bidding. When thou seest him,
A little witness my obedience. Look,   66
       [*Drawing her sword and offering it to him*]
I draw the sword myself. Take it, and hit
The innocent mansion of my love, my heart.
Fear not; 'tis empty of all things but grief.
Thy master is not there, who was indeed
The riches of it. Do his bidding; strike.
Thou mayst be valiant in a better cause,   72
But now thou seem'st a coward.
PISANIO [*Rejecting the sword*]   Hence, vile instrument!
Thou shalt not damn my hand.
IMOGEN   Why, I must die;
And if I do not by thy hand, thou art
No servant of thy master's. Against self-slaughter
There is a prohibition so divine
That cravens my weak hand. Come, here's my heart.   78
Something's afore 't. Soft, soft! We'll no defense;   79
Obedient as the scabbard. What is here? [*She takes
    letters from her bodice.*]   80
The scriptures of the loyal Leonatus,   81
All turned to heresy? Away, away,
Corrupters of my faith! [*She throws away the letters.*]
  You shall no more
Be stomachers to my heart. Thus may poor fools   84
Believe false teachers. Though those that are betrayed

---

60 scandal bring scandal to, discredit   **60–61 took pity From** prevented
the bestowing of well-deserved pity upon   **62 lay . . . men** take credit
away from all well-deserving and honorable men (just as sour *leaven* or
fermenting dough causes more dough to ferment and spoil).   **proper**
honest   **63 be** i.e., be thought   **64 fail** fault, offense   **66 A little witness**
testify somewhat to   **72 Thou mayst be** maybe you are   **78 cravens**
makes cowardly   **79 Something's** i.e., Posthumus' letter is.   **Soft** i.e.,
wait a minute   **80 Obedient** i.e., as willing to receive the sword
81 scriptures writings, letters (with a play on "Holy Scriptures")
84 stomachers ornamental coverings for the breast

Do feel the treason sharply, yet the traitor
Stands in worse case of woe. And thou, Posthumus,   87
That didst set up   88
My disobedience 'gainst the King my father
And make me put into contempt the suits
Of princely fellows, shalt hereafter find
It is no act of common passage, but   92
A strain of rareness; and I grieve myself   93
To think, when thou shalt be disedged by her   94
That now thou tirest on, how thy memory   95
Will then be panged by me.—Prithee, dispatch.   96
The lamb entreats the butcher. Where's thy knife?
Thou art too slow to do thy master's bidding
When I desire it too.

PISANIO   O gracious lady,
Since I received command to do this business
I have not slept one wink.

IMOGEN   Do 't, and to bed then.

PISANIO
I'll wake mine eyeballs blind first.

IMOGEN   Wherefore then   102
Didst undertake it? Why hast thou abused
So many miles with a pretense? This place?
Mine action and thine own? Our horses' labor?
The time inviting thee? The perturbed court,
For my being absent, whereunto I never
Purpose return? Why hast thou gone so far,
To be unbent when thou hast ta'en thy stand,   109
Th' elected deer before thee?

PISANIO   But to win time   110
To lose so bad employment, in the which   111
I have considered of a course. Good lady,
Hear me with patience.

IMOGEN   Talk thy tongue weary. Speak.

---

87 Stands . . . woe i.e., risks the penalty of damnation   **88 set up** incite,
encourage   **92–93 It . . . rareness** that my choice (of you) was no act of a
common sort but a rare trait   **94 disedged** surfeited, having the edge of
appetite taken off   **95 thou tirest on** you tear or devour ravenously (as a
bird of prey)   **96 panged** pained, tortured   **102 wake . . . blind** remain
awake until I can no longer see   **109 To be unbent** to unbend your bow
again (and thus refuse to shoot)   **110 elected** chosen   **111 which** i.e.,
which time

I have heard I am a strumpet, and mine ear,
Therein false struck, can take no greater wound,   115
Nor tent to bottom that. But speak.

PISANIO   Then, madam,   116
I thought you would not back again.

IMOGEN   Most like,   117
Bringing me here to kill me.

PISANIO   Not so, neither.
But if I were as wise as honest, then
My purpose would prove well. It cannot be
But that my master is abused. Some villain,   121
Ay, and singular in his art, hath done   122
You both this cursèd injury.

IMOGEN
Some Roman courtesan.

PISANIO   No, on my life.
I'll give but notice you are dead, and send him
Some bloody sign of it, for 'tis commanded
I should do so. You shall be missed at court,
And that will well confirm it.

IMOGEN   Why, good fellow,
What shall I do the while? Where bide? How live?
Or in my life what comfort, when I am
Dead to my husband?

PISANIO   If you'll back to the court—

IMOGEN
No court, no father, nor no more ado
With that harsh, noble, simple nothing,
That Cloten, whose love suit hath been to me
As fearful as a siege.

PISANIO   If not at court,
Then not in Britain must you bide.

IMOGEN   Where then?
Hath Britain all the sun that shines? Day, night,
Are they not but in Britain? I' the world's volume   138
Our Britain seems as of it but not in 't,   139

115 take receive **116 tent . . . that** probe that wound to the bottom
117 back go back (to court). **like** likely **121 abused** deceived **122 sin-gular** unexcelled **138 but** except **139 as . . . in 't** i.e., as part of it but a small and relatively insignificant part, on the periphery, like a page torn out of a volume

In a great pool a swan's nest. Prithee, think
There's livers out of Britain.
PISANIO   I am most glad   141
You think of other place. Th' ambassador,
Lucius the Roman, comes to Milford Haven
Tomorrow. Now, if you could wear a mind
Dark as your fortune is, and but disguise   145
That which, t' appear itself, must not yet be   146
But by self-danger, you should tread a course
Pretty and full of view; yea, haply near   148
The residence of Posthumus, so nigh at least
That, though his actions were not visible, yet
Report should render him hourly to your ear
As truly as he moves.
IMOGEN   O, for such means!
Though peril to my modesty, not death on 't,   153
I would adventure.
PISANIO   Well, then, here's the point.
You must forget to be a woman; change
Command into obedience; fear and niceness—   156
The handmaids of all women, or, more truly,
Woman its pretty self—into a waggish courage;   158
Ready in gibes, quick-answered, saucy, and
As quarrelous as the weasel. Nay, you must   160
Forget that rarest treasure of your cheek,
Exposing it—but O, the harder heart!   162
Alack, no remedy—to the greedy touch
Of common-kissing Titan, and forget   164

141 **livers** persons living   145 **Dark** obscure, mean   146 **That** i.e., the
fact that you are a woman.   **appear itself** reveal itself for what it truly
is   148 **Pretty . . . view** advantageous and promising, affording a fair
prospect.   **haply** perhaps (with a suggestion also of "happily, fortunately")   153 **Though . . . on 't** as long as the risk to my modesty would
not be fatal to it   156 **Command** i.e., as befitting one of royal birth.
(Imogen will be disguising her royal birth and assuming the guise of
one who must obey orders.)   **niceness** fastidiousness, reserve
158 **waggish** roguish, masculine   160 **quarrelous** quarrelsome
162 **harder** too hard. (Pisanio is either reproaching his own cruelty in
speaking so, or that of Posthumus, or possibly suggesting that Imogen
must harden her heart.)   164 **common-kissing** kissing everybody and
everything.   **Titan** god of the sun

> Your laborsome and dainty trims, wherein   155
> You made great Juno angry.

IMOGEN   Nay, be brief.   166
I see into thy end and am almost
A man already.

PISANIO   First, make yourself but like one.
Forethinking this, I have already fit—   169
'Tis in my cloak bag—doublet, hat, hose, all
That answer to them. Would you in their serving,   171
And with what imitation you can borrow
From youth of such a season, 'fore noble Lucius   173
Present yourself, desire his service, tell him   174
Wherein you're happy—which will make him know,   175
If that his head have ear in music—doubtless   176
With joy he will embrace you, for he's honorable   177
And, doubling that, most holy. Your means abroad,   178
You have me, rich, and I will never fail   179
Beginning nor supplyment. [*He gives her a cloak bag.*]

IMOGEN   Thou art all the comfort   180
The gods will diet me with. Prithee, away.
There's more to be considered, but we'll even   182
All that good time will give us. This attempt
I am soldier to, and will abide it with   184
A prince's courage. Away, I prithee.

PISANIO
Well, madam, we must take a short farewell,
Lest, being missed, I be suspected of
Your carriage from the court. My noble mistress,   188
Here is a box; I had it from the Queen. [*He gives a box.*]

---

165 laborsome . . . trims elaborate and dainty apparel   **166 angry** i.e., jealous   **169 Forethinking** foreseeing, anticipating.   **fit** ready   **171 answer to** go along with.   **Would you** if you would.   **in their serving** assisted by them   **173 of . . . season** i.e., of such an age as you will represent   **174 his service** employment in his service   **175 happy** gifted, skillful.   **make him know** convince him   **176 If . . . music** i.e., if he has an ear for music, since he then cannot fail to appreciate your voice   **177 embrace** take you in (to his service)   **178 Your means abroad** as for your financial means while you are abroad   **179 rich** adequately supplied with funds   **180 supplyment** continuation of supply   **182 even** keep pace with, profit by   **184 soldier to** enlisted in, devoted to.   **abide it** sustain it, stick with it   **188 Your carriage** having removed you

What's in 't is precious. If you are sick at sea
Or stomach-qualmed at land, a dram of this
Will drive away distemper. To some shade,   192
And fit you to your manhood. May the gods
Direct you to the best!
IMOGEN   Amen. I thank thee.
                                  Exeunt [separately].

❖

3.5   *Enter Cymbeline, Queen, Cloten, Lucius,*
           [Attendants,] and Lords.

CYMBELINE
  Thus far, and so farewell.
LUCIUS   Thanks, royal sir.   1
  My emperor hath wrote I must from hence;   2
  And am right sorry that I must report ye
  My master's enemy.
CYMBELINE   Our subjects, sir,
  Will not endure his yoke, and for ourself
  To show less sovereignty than they must needs
  Appear unkinglike.
LUCIUS   So, sir. I desire of you   7
  A conduct overland to Milford Haven.   8
  Madam, all joy befall Your Grace, and you!   9
CYMBELINE
  My lords, you are appointed for that office;   10
  The due of honor in no point omit.
  So farewell, noble Lucius.
LUCIUS [*To Cloten*]   Your hand, my lord.
CLOTEN
  Receive it friendly; but from this time forth
  I wear it as your enemy.

---

192 **distemper** illness.   **shade** secluded and protected spot

3.5. Location: At the court of Cymbeline.
1 **Thus far** thus far we can escort you   2 **wrote** written (also in l. 21)
7 **So** i.e., very good. (A polite way of closing the discussion.)   8 **conduct**
safe-conduct, escort   9 **and you** (Possibly addressed to Cloten, or, more
probably, to the King. Lucius bids farewell to Cloten at l. 12.)   10 **office**
duty (as escorts of Lucius)

LUCIUS   Sir, the event   14
  Is yet to name the winner. Fare you well.
CYMBELINE
  Leave not the worthy Lucius, good my lords,
  Till he have crossed the Severn. Happiness!
                                        Exeunt Lucius, etc.

QUEEN
  He goes hence frowning, but it honors us
  That we have given him cause.
CLOTEN   'Tis all the better;
  Your valiant Britons have their wishes in it.
CYMBELINE
  Lucius hath wrote already to the Emperor
  How it goes here. It fits us therefore ripely   22
  Our chariots and our horsemen be in readiness.
  The powers that he already hath in Gallia   24
  Will soon be drawn to head, from whence he moves   25
  His war for Britain.
QUEEN   'Tis not sleepy business,
  But must be looked to speedily and strongly.
CYMBELINE
  Our expectation that it would be thus
  Hath made us forward. But, my gentle queen,   29
  Where is our daughter? She hath not appeared
  Before the Roman, nor to us hath tendered
  The duty of the day. She looks us like   32
  A thing more made of malice than of duty.
  We have noted it.—Call her before us, for
  We have been too slight in sufferance.
                                    [*Exit an Attendant.*]
QUEEN   Royal sir,   35
  Since the exile of Posthumus, most retired
  Hath her life been; the cure whereof, my lord,
  'Tis time must do. Beseech Your Majesty,
  Forbear sharp speeches to her. She's a lady
  So tender of rebukes that words are strokes
  And strokes death to her.

14 event outcome **22 fits** befits. **ripely** speedily **24 powers** armed
forces **25 drawn to head** brought together, assembled **29 forward** well
prepared **32 looks us** seems to us (?) looks at us (?) **35 slight in
sufferance** permissive

Enter [Attendant as] a messenger.

CYMBELINE   Where is she, sir? How
  Can her contempt be answered?
ATTENDANT   Please you, sir,   42
  Her chambers are all locked, and there's no answer
  That will be given to th' loudest of noise we make.
QUEEN
  My lord, when last I went to visit her,
  She prayed me to excuse her keeping close,   46
  Whereto constrained by her infirmity
  She should that duty leave unpaid to you   48
  Which daily she was bound to proffer. This
  She wished me to make known, but our great court   50
  Made me to blame in memory.
CYMBELINE   Her doors locked?
  Not seen of late? Grant, heavens, that which I fear
  Prove false!   *Exit.*
QUEEN   Son, I say, follow the King.
CLOTEN
  That man of hers, Pisanio, her old servant,
  I have not seen these two days.
QUEEN   Go, look after.
                                    Exit [Cloten].
  Pisanio, thou that stand'st so for Posthumus!   56
  He hath a drug of mine; I pray his absence
  Proceed by swallowing that, for he believes   58
  It is a thing most precious. But for her,
  Where is she gone? Haply despair hath seized her,
  Or, winged with fervor of her love, she's flown
  To her desired Posthumus. Gone she is
  To death or to dishonor, and my end
  Can make good use of either. She being down,
  I have the placing of the British crown.

      Enter Cloten.

  How now, my son?
CLOTEN   'Tis certain she is fled.

42 answered accounted for   **46 close** in private   **48 She . . . leave** she
found herself obliged to leave that duty   **50 great court** important
courtly business   **56 thou that stand'st** you who stand up so for, look
out for the interests of   **58 by** from

Go in and cheer the King. He rages; none
Dare come about him.

QUEEN   All the better. May
This night forestall him of the coming day!   69

                         Exit Queen.

CLOTEN
I love and hate her. For she's fair and royal,   70
And that she hath all courtly parts more exquisite   71
Than lady, ladies, woman—from every one   72
The best she hath, and she, of all compounded,   73
Outsells them all—I love her therefore. But   74
Disdaining me and throwing favors on   75
The low Posthumus slanders so her judgment   76
That what's else rare is choked; and in that point   77
I will conclude to hate her, nay, indeed,
To be revenged upon her. For when fools
Shall—

     Enter Pisanio. [He attempts to avoid Cloten.]

         Who is here? What, are you packing, sirrah?   80
Come hither. Ah, you precious pander! Villain,
Where is thy lady? In a word, or else
Thou art straightway with the fiends.

               [He threatens him with his sword.]
PISANIO   O, good my lord!

CLOTEN
Where is thy lady? Or, by Jupiter,
I will not ask again. Close villain,   85
I'll have this secret from thy heart or rip
Thy heart to find it. Is she with Posthumus,
From whose so many weights of baseness cannot
A dram of worth be drawn?

PISANIO   Alas, my lord,
How can she be with him? When was she missed?
He is in Rome.

---

69 forestall deprive (i.e., bring about his death)   **70 For** because
71 that because.   **parts** endowments, graces   **72 Than lady, ladies,
woman** than any lady, or all ladies, or indeed womankind   **72–73 from
. . . she hath** she has the best qualities of each   **74 Outsells** outvalues,
excels   **75 Disdaining** her disdaining   **76 slanders** discredits   **77 rare**
excellent   **80 packing** plotting.   **sirrah** (Form of address to a social
inferior; also at ll. 106 and 108.)   **85 Close** secretive

CLOTEN   Where is she, sir? Come nearer.   91
No farther halting. Satisfy me home   92
What is become of her.
PISANIO
O, my all-worthy lord!
CLOTEN   All-worthy villain!
Discover where thy mistress is at once,   95
At the next word. No more of "worthy lord"!
Speak, or thy silence on the instant is
Thy condemnation and thy death.
PISANIO   Then, sir,
This paper is the history of my knowledge
Touching her flight.   [*He presents a letter.*]
CLOTEN   Let's see 't. I will pursue her
Even to Augustus' throne.
PISANIO [*Aside*]   Or this or perish.   101
She's far enough, and what he learns by this
May prove his travel, not her danger.
CLOTEN [*Reading*]   Hum!
PISANIO [*Aside*]
I'll write to my lord she's dead. O Imogen,
Safe mayst thou wander, safe return again!
CLOTEN   Sirrah, is this letter true?
PISANIO   Sir, as I think.
CLOTEN   It is Posthumus' hand, I know 't. Sirrah, if thou
wouldst not be a villain, but do me true service, un-
dergo those employments wherein I should have
cause to use thee with a serious industry—that is,   111
what villainy soe'er I bid thee do, to perform it directly
and truly—I would think thee an honest man. Thou
shouldst neither want my means for thy relief nor my
voice for thy preferment.   115
PISANIO   Well, my good lord.
CLOTEN   Wilt thou serve me? For since patiently and
constantly thou hast stuck to the bare fortune of that
beggar Posthumus, thou canst not, in the course of
gratitude, but be a diligent follower of mine. Wilt thou
serve me?

91 Come nearer answer more to the point   **92 home** completely
95 Discover disclose   **101 Or** either   **111 industry** assiduity   **115 preferment** advancement

PISANIO   Sir, I will.

CLOTEN   Give me thy hand; here's my purse. [*He gives* 123
money.] Hast any of thy late master's garments in thy 124
possession?

PISANIO   I have, my lord, at my lodging the same suit
he wore when he took leave of my lady and mistress.

CLOTEN   The first service thou dost me, fetch that suit
hither. Let it be thy first service. Go.

PISANIO   I shall, my lord.   *Exit.*

CLOTEN   Meet thee at Milford Haven!—I forgot to ask
him one thing; I'll remember 't anon.—Even there,
thou villain Posthumus, will I kill thee. I would these
garments were come. She said upon a time—the bit-
terness of it I now belch from my heart—that she held
the very garment of Posthumus in more respect than 136
my noble and natural person, together with the adorn-
ment of my qualities. With that suit upon my back
will I ravish her; first kill him, and in her eyes. There
shall she see my valor, which will then be a torment to
her contempt. He on the ground, my speech of insult- 141
ment ended on his dead body, and when my lust hath 142
dined—which, as I say, to vex her I will execute in the
clothes that she so praised—to the court I'll knock her
back, foot her home again. She hath despised me re- 145
joicingly, and I'll be merry in my revenge.

Enter Pisanio [with the clothes].

Be those the garments?

PISANIO   Ay, my noble lord.

CLOTEN   How long is 't since she went to Milford
Haven?

PISANIO   She can scarce be there yet.

CLOTEN   Bring this apparel to my chamber; that is the
second thing that I have commanded thee. The third
is that thou wilt be a voluntary mute to my design. Be 154
but duteous and true, preferment shall tender itself to

123 purse (Cloten is not giving Pisanio salary but making him his
pursebearer.)   **124 late** recent. (Not "dead.")   **136 more respect** higher
regard   **141–142 insultment** contemptuous triumph   **145 foot** kick
154 Be if you be

thee. My revenge is now at Milford. Would I had
wings to follow it! Come, and be true.   *Exit.*

PISANIO
  Thou bidd'st me to my loss; for true to thee
  Were to prove false, which I will never be,
  To him that is most true. To Milford go,
  And find not her whom thou pursuest. Flow, flow,
  You heavenly blessings, on her! This fool's speed   162
  Be crossed with slowness; labor be his meed!   *Exit.* 163

❧

3.6   *Enter Imogen alone [in boy's clothes].*

IMOGEN
  I see a man's life is a tedious one.
  I have tired myself, and for two nights together
  Have made the ground my bed. I should be sick
  But that my resolution helps me. Milford,
  When from the mountain top Pisanio showed thee,
  Thou wast within a ken. O Jove, I think   6
  Foundations fly the wretched—such, I mean,   7
  Where they should be relieved. Two beggars told me
  I could not miss my way. Will poor folks lie,
  That have afflictions on them, knowing 'tis
  A punishment or trial? Yes; no wonder,   11
  When rich ones scarce tell true. To lapse in fullness   12
  Is sorer than to lie for need, and falsehood   13
  Is worse in kings than beggars. My dear lord!
  Thou art one o' the false ones. Now I think on thee,
  My hunger's gone; but even before I was   16
  At point to sink for food. [*She sees the cave.*] But what is
    this?   17

---

162 This fool's may this fool's   **163 crossed** thwarted.   **meed** reward

3.6. Location: Wales. Before the cave of Belarius.
6 within a ken within sight   **7 Foundations** (1) fixed places (2) charitable
institutions.   **fly the wretched** i.e., are never there when most needed
11 trial test of virtue. (Poverty may be a Job-like affliction visited on
those God wishes to test, in which case lying is dangerously wrong.)
12 lapse in fullness lie and commit other sins in a state of prosperity
13 sorer worse, more wicked   **16 but even before** just now   **17 for** for
lack of

Here is a path to 't. 'Tis some savage hold.   18
I were best not call; I dare not call. Yet famine,
Ere clean it o'erthrow nature, makes it valiant.   20
Plenty and peace breeds cowards; hardness ever   21
Of hardiness is mother.—Ho! Who's here?   22
If anything that's civil, speak; if savage,   23
Take or lend. Ho!—No answer? Then I'll enter.   24
Best draw my sword; an if mine enemy   25
But fear the sword like me, he'll scarcely look on 't.
Such a foe, good heavens!   27

                    [*She draws her sword, and*]
                              exit [*into the cave*].

            Enter Belarius, Guiderius, and Arviragus.

BELARIUS
You, Polydore, have proved best woodman and   28
Are master of the feast. Cadwal and I
Will play the cook and servant; 'tis our match.   30
The sweat of industry would dry and die   31
But for the end it works to. Come, our stomachs   32
Will make what's homely savory; weariness   33
Can snore upon the flint, when resty sloth   34
Finds the down pillow hard. Now peace be here,
Poor house, that keep'st thyself!
GUIDERIUS   I am throughly weary.   36
ARVIRAGUS
I am weak with toil, yet strong in appetite.
GUIDERIUS
There is cold meat i' the cave. We'll browse on that   38
Whilst what we have killed be cooked.
BELARIUS [*Looking into the cave*]   Stay, come not in.
But that it eats our victuals, I should think
Here were a fairy.

---

18 hold stronghold, fastness   **20 clean** altogether   **21 hardness** hardship   **22 Of hardiness is mother** breeds courage   **23 civil** civilized   **24 Take or lend** rob me (or something worse), or give me food   **25 Best** it were best to.   **an if** if   **27 Such . . . heavens** i.e., may the heavens grant me a foe as timid as myself   **28 woodman** woodsman, huntsman   **30 match** agreement, bargain   **31–32 The sweat . . . works to** human labor would dry up and cease if it were not for the desired end   **33 homely** plain   **34 resty** sluggish, indolent   **36 keep'st thyself** i.e., is untended, empty.   **throughly** thoroughly   **38 browse** nibble

GUIDERIUS   What's the matter, sir?
BELARIUS
  By Jupiter, an angel! Or, if not,
  An earthly paragon! Behold divineness
  No elder than a boy!

      Enter Imogen.

IMOGEN   Good masters, harm me not.   45
  Before I entered here, I called, and thought
  To have begged or bought what I have took. Good troth, 47
  I have stol'n naught, nor would not, though I had found
  Gold strewed i' the floor. Here's money for my meat.
                              [*She offers money.*]
  I would have left it on the board so soon
  As I had made my meal, and parted
  With prayers for the provider.
GUIDERIUS   Money, youth?
ARVIRAGUS
  All gold and silver rather turn to dirt,   53
  As 'tis no better reckoned but of those   54
  Who worship dirty gods.
IMOGEN   I see you're angry.
  Know, if you kill me for my fault, I should
  Have died had I not made it.
BELARIUS   Whither bound?   57
IMOGEN   To Milford Haven.
BELARIUS   What's your name?
IMOGEN
  Fidele, sir. I have a kinsman who
  Is bound for Italy. He embarked at Milford,   61
  To whom being going, almost spent with hunger,
  I am fall'n in this offense.
BELARIUS   Prithee, fair youth,   63
  Think us no churls, nor measure our good minds
  By this rude place we live in. Well encountered!
  'Tis almost night. You shall have better cheer
  Ere you depart, and thanks to stay and eat it.
  Boys, bid him welcome.

45 masters i.e., sirs. (Addressed to ordinary folk.) **47 Good troth** in
truth **53 All gold** i.e., let all gold **54 but of** except by **57 made**
committed **61 embarked** was to have embarked **63 in** into

GUIDERIUS   Were you a woman, youth,
I should woo hard but be your groom in honesty,   69
Ay, bid for you as I do buy.   70
ARVIRAGUS [*To Guiderius*] I'll make 't my comfort
He is a man; I'll love him as my brother.
[*To Imogen.*] And such a welcome as I'd give to him   73
After long absence, such is yours. Most welcome!
Be sprightly, for you fall 'mongst friends.
IMOGEN   'Mongst friends, 75
If brothers. [*Aside.*] Would it had been so that they   76
Had been my father's sons! Then had my prize   77
Been less, and so more equal ballasting   78
To thee, Posthumus.
BELARIUS   He wrings at some distress.   79
GUIDERIUS
Would I could free 't!
ARVIRAGUS   Or I; whate'er it be,
What pain it cost, what danger! Gods!
BELARIUS   Hark, boys. 81
                              [*He whispers to them.*]
IMOGEN [*To herself*]   Great men
That had a court no bigger than this cave,
That did attend themselves and had the virtue   84
Which their own conscience sealed them, laying by   85
That nothing-gift of differing multitudes,   86
Could not outpeer these twain. Pardon me, gods!   87
I'd change my sex to be companion with them,
Since Leonatus's false.
BELARIUS   It shall be so.   89
Boys, we'll go dress our hunt. Fair youth, come in.   90

---

69 but be i.e., but I'd be, before I should fail to be   **70 Ay, bid . . . buy**
i.e., yes, I would bid for you as one who would seek to buy you   **73 him**
i.e., such a brother   **75–76 'Mongst . . . brothers** i.e., certainly I am
among friends, if the three of us are to be like brothers   **77 prize**
(1) value, since I would not then be heir to the throne (2) *prize* in the
nautical sense of a captured sea vessel   **78 ballasting** cargo of a sea
vessel giving it stability   **79 wrings** writhes   **81 What pain it cost**
whatever pain it would cost me; or, what pain it must have cost (to
Imogen)   **84 attend** wait on   **85 conscience sealed** self-knowledge
assured   **85–86 laying . . . multitudes** disregarding the valueless gift of
adulation from the fickle populace   **87 outpeer** excel   **89 It shall be so**
(Belarius finishes his conversation apart with Arviragus and Guiderius.)
90 hunt game taken in the hunt

Discourse is heavy, fasting; when we have supped,
We'll mannerly demand thee of thy story,
So far as thou wilt speak it.
GUIDERIUS   Pray draw near.
ARVIRAGUS
  The night to th' owl and morn to th' lark less welcome.
IMOGEN   Thanks, sir.
ARVIRAGUS   I pray, draw near.   *Exeunt.*

❖

3.7   *Enter two Roman Senators and Tribunes.*

FIRST SENATOR
  This is the tenor of the Emperor's writ:
  That since the common men are now in action
  'Gainst the Pannonians and Dalmatians,
  And that the legions now in Gallia are
  Full weak to undertake our wars against
  The fall'n-off Britons, that we do incite   6
  The gentry to this business. He creates
  Lucius proconsul, and to you the tribunes,
  For this immediate levy, he commends   9
  His absolute commission. Long live Caesar!   10
A TRIBUNE
  Is Lucius general of the forces?
SECOND SENATOR   Ay.
A TRIBUNE
  Remaining now in Gallia?
FIRST SENATOR   With those legions
  Which I have spoke of, whereunto your levy
  Must be supplyant. The words of your commission   14
  Will tie you to the numbers and the time   15
  Of their dispatch.
A TRIBUNE   We will discharge our duty.
                                          Exeunt.

❖

3.7. Location: Rome. A public place, perhaps the Senate House.
6 fall'n-off revolted   9 commends entrusts   10 absolute commission
unlimited authority   14 supplyant reinforcing, auxiliary   15 tie you to
specify for you

4.1　　*Enter Cloten alone, [dressed in Posthumus'*
　　　　　garments].

CLOTEN　I am near to the place where they should meet,
　if Pisanio have mapped it truly. How fit his garments　2
　serve me! Why should his mistress, who was made
　by him that made the tailor, not be fit too? The
　rather—saving reverence of the word—for 'tis said a　5
　woman's fitness comes by fits. Therein I must play the　6
　workman. I dare speak it to myself, for it is not vain-
　glory for a man and his glass to confer in his own
　chamber—I mean, the lines of my body are as well
　drawn as his; no less young, more strong, not beneath
　him in fortunes, beyond him in the advantage of the　11
　time, above him in birth, alike conversant in general　12
　services, and more remarkable in single oppositions.　13
　Yet this imperceiverant thing loves him in my despite.　14
　What mortality is! Posthumus, thy head, which now　15
　is growing upon thy shoulders, shall within this hour
　be off, thy mistress enforced, thy garments cut to
　pieces before her face; and all this done, spurn her
　home to her father, who may haply be a little angry　19
　for my so rough usage; but my mother, having power　20
　of his testiness, shall turn all into my commendations.　21
　My horse is tied up safe. Out, sword, and to a sore　22
　purpose! [*He draws.*] Fortune put them into my hand!
　This is the very description of their meeting place, and
　the fellow dares not deceive me.　　　　　　　　　[*Exit.*]

4.2　　*Enter Belarius, Guiderius, Arviragus, and*
　　　　　Imogen from the cave.

BELARIUS [*To Imogen*]
　You are not well. Remain here in the cave;

4.1. Location: Wales. Near the cave of Belarius.
2 his Posthumus'　**5 saving reverence** asking pardon (i.e., for the inde-
cent punning on *fitness* and *fit.*)　**for** because　**6 fitness** i.e., sexual
inclination.　**fits** i.e., fits and starts　**11–12 the advantage of the time**
superiority in social opportunity　**12–13 alike . . . services** equally
versed in military matters　**13 single oppositions** single combat　**14 imperceiverant** dull of perception　**15 What mortality is** what a thing life
is　**19 haply** perchance　**20–21 power of** control over　**22 sore** grievous

**4.2. Location: Before the cave of Belarius. The scene may be virtually
continuous.**

We'll come to you after hunting.
ARVIRAGUS [*To Imogen*]   Brother, stay here.
   Are we not brothers?
IMOGEN   So man and man should be,   3
   But clay and clay differs in dignity,   4
   Whose dust is both alike. I am very sick.   5
GUIDERIUS [*To Arviragus and Belarius*]
   Go you to hunting. I'll abide with him.
IMOGEN
   So sick I am not, yet I am not well;   7
   But not so citizen a wanton as   8
   To seem to die ere sick. So please you, leave me;   9
   Stick to your journal course. The breach of custom   10
   Is breach of all. I am ill, but your being by me
   Cannot amend me; society is no comfort
   To one not sociable. I am not very sick,
   Since I can reason of it. Pray you, trust me here—   14
   I'll rob none but myself—and let me die,   15
   Stealing so poorly.
GUIDERIUS   I love thee—I have spoke it—   16
   How much the quantity, the weight as much,   17
   As I do love my father.
BELARIUS   What? How? How?
ARVIRAGUS
   If it be sin to say so, sir, I yoke me   19
   In my good brother's fault. I know not why
   I love this youth; and I have heard you say
   Love's reason's without reason. The bier at door,
   And a demand who is 't shall die, I'd say
   "My father, not this youth."
BELARIUS [*Aside*]   O noble strain!   24

3–5 **So . . . alike** i.e., we are brothers, as all humans should be, being
made out of the same dust, though social distinctions impose their
artificial differences.   **clay and clay** different persons.   **dignity** social
position, rank.   **dust** (of which we are made and to which we return)
7 **So sick I am not** I am not that sick   8 **citizen** effeminate, city-bred.
wanton spoiled or pampered person   9 **To seem to die ere sick** i.e., to
suffer imaginary agonies without really being sick at all   10 **journal**
daily   14 **reason of** talk sensibly about   15 **I'll . . . myself** i.e., I'll do
nothing worse than deprive myself of your company, or steal out of
your company (?)   16 **Stealing so poorly** i.e., making no greater theft
than that   17 **How . . . as much** just as much in quantity and weight
19 **yoke me** join company   24 **strain** inherited disposition

O worthiness of nature! Breed of greatness!
Cowards father cowards and base things sire base;
Nature hath meal and bran, contempt and grace.
I'm not their father; yet who this should be   28
Doth miracle itself, loved before me.   29
[*Aloud.*] 'Tis the ninth hour o' the morn.
ARVIRAGUS   Brother, farewell.
IMOGEN
I wish ye sport.
ARVIRAGUS   You health. [*To Belarius.*] So please you, sir. 31
IMOGEN [*Aside*]
These are kind creatures. Gods, what lies I have heard!
Our courtiers say all's savage but at court.
Experience, O, thou disprov'st report!
Th' imperious seas breeds monsters; for the dish,   35
Poor tributary rivers as sweet fish.   36
I am sick still, heartsick. Pisanio,
I'll now taste of thy drug.   [*She swallows some.*]
GUIDERIUS   I could not stir him.   38
He said he was gentle, but unfortunate;   39
Dishonestly afflicted, but yet honest.   40
ARVIRAGUS
Thus did he answer me, yet said hereafter
I might know more.
BELARIUS   To the field, to the field!—
We'll leave you for this time. Go in and rest.
ARVIRAGUS
We'll not be long away.
BELARIUS   Pray be not sick,
For you must be our huswife.
IMOGEN   Well or ill,
I am bound to you.   *Exit* [*to the cave*].
BELARIUS   And shalt be ever.   47

28–29 who . . . before me it is miraculous that this youth, whoever he is,
should be loved in preference to me   **31 You** i.e., I wish you.   **So please
you** at your service   **35 imperious** imperial   **36 as sweet fish** i.e., breed
as sweet fish (for eating) as can be found anywhere. (In other words,
goodness can be found in unpretentious surroundings, not only at
court.)   **38 stir him** persuade him to tell about himself   **39 gentle**
wellborn   **40 Dishonestly afflicted** afflicted by adverse and ignominious
fortune   **47 bound** obligated. (But Belarius answers in the sense of
"bound by affection.")

This youth, howe'er distressed, appears he hath had   48
Good ancestors.
ARVIRAGUS   How angel-like he sings!
GUIDERIUS
But his neat cookery! He cut our roots in characters   50
And sauced our broths as Juno had been sick   51
And he her dieter.
ARVIRAGUS   Nobly he yokes
A smiling with a sigh, as if the sigh
Was that it was for not being such a smile;   54
The smile mocking the sigh, that it would fly
From so divine a temple to commix
With winds that sailors rail at.
GUIDERIUS   I do note   57
That grief and patience, rooted in him both,
Mingle their spurs together.
ARVIRAGUS   Grow, patience,   59
And let the stinking elder, grief, untwine   60
His perishing root with the increasing vine!   61
BELARIUS
It is great morning. Come, away!—Who's there?   62

Enter Cloten, [not seeing them at first].

CLOTEN
I cannot find those runagates. That villain   63
Hath mocked me. I am faint.
BELARIUS   "Those runagates"?
Means he not us? I partly know him. 'Tis   65
Cloten, the son o' the Queen. I fear some ambush.
I saw him not these many years, and yet   67
I know 'tis he. We are held as outlaws. Hence!   68
GUIDERIUS
He is but one. You and my brother search

48 he hath had i.e., to have had   **50 characters** letters, designs   **51 as** as
if   **54 that** what   **57 winds . . . at** i.e., the rude wind, so infinitely
rougher than the sigh   **59 spurs** roots   **60 elder** elder tree (on which
Judas is supposed to have hanged himself).   **untwine** cease to twine
61 perishing baleful.   **with . . . vine** (1) i.e., with patience (2) i.e., as
patience increases. (Arviragus expresses a wish that patience may
increase in Fidele and thereby cure his grief.)   **62 great morning** broad
day   **63 runagates** renegades, runaways   **65 partly** slightly   **67 saw**
have seen   **68 held** regarded

What companies are near. Pray you, away.   70
Let me alone with him.
                    [*Exeunt Belarius and Arviragus.*]
CLOTEN   Soft, what are you   71
That fly me thus? Some villain mountaineers?
I have heard of such. What slave art thou?
GUIDERIUS   A thing
More slavish did I ne'er than answering
A slave without a knock.
CLOTEN   Thou art a robber,   75
A lawbreaker, a villain. Yield thee, thief.
GUIDERIUS
To who? To thee? What art thou? Have not I
An arm as big as thine? A heart as big?
Thy words, I grant, are bigger, for I wear not
My dagger in my mouth. Say what thou art,
Why I should yield to thee.
CLOTEN   Thou villain base,
Know'st me not by my clothes?   82
GUIDERIUS   No, nor thy tailor, rascal,
Who is thy grandfather. He made those clothes,   84
Which, as it seems, make thee.
CLOTEN   Thou precious varlet,   85
My tailor made them not.
GUIDERIUS   Hence, then, and thank
The man that gave them thee. Thou art some fool;
I am loath to beat thee.
CLOTEN   Thou injurious thief,   88
Hear but my name, and tremble.
GUIDERIUS   What's thy name?
CLOTEN   Cloten, thou villain.
GUIDERIUS
Cloten, thou double villain, be thy name,
I cannot tremble at it. Were it Toad, or Adder, Spider,
'Twould move me sooner.
CLOTEN   To thy further fear,

70 companies companions   **71 Let . . . him** leave me alone to deal with
him.   **Soft** i.e., wait a minute   **75 without a knock** without giving him a
blow   **82 Know'st . . . clothes** (Cloten is dressed as one from the
court.)   **84–85 grandfather . . . thee** (A jest on the proverbial idea that
the tailor, or several tailors, make the man.)   **85 precious varlet** arrant
rascal   **88 injurious** insulting, malicious

Nay, to thy mere confusion, thou shalt know   94
I am son to the Queen.
GUIDERIUS   I am sorry for 't; not seeming
So worthy as thy birth.
CLOTEN   Art not afeard?
GUIDERIUS
Those that I reverence, those I fear—the wise.   97
At fools I laugh, not fear them.
CLOTEN   Die the death!   98
When I have slain thee with my proper hand,   99
I'll follow those that even now fled hence
And on the gates of Lud's Town set your heads.
Yield, rustic mountaineer!   *Fight, and exeunt.*

          Enter Belarius and Arviragus.

BELARIUS   No company's abroad?
ARVIRAGUS
None in the world. You did mistake him, sure.
BELARIUS
I cannot tell. Long is it since I saw him,
But time hath nothing blurred those lines of favor   106
Which then he wore. The snatches in his voice   107
And burst of speaking were as his. I am absolute   108
'Twas very Cloten.
ARVIRAGUS   In this place we left them.   109
I wish my brother make good time with him,   110
You say he is so fell.
BELARIUS   Being scarce made up,   111
I mean to man, he had not apprehension   112
Of roaring terrors; for defect of judgment   113
Is oft the cause of fear.

          Enter Guiderius [with Cloten's head].

                    But see, thy brother.   114

94 mere confusion utter ruin   **97 fear** regard with awe   **98 Die the
death** (A solemn pronouncement of the sentence of death.)   **99 proper**
own   **106 nothing** not at all.   **lines of favor** facial lines   **107 snatches**
hesitations   **108 absolute** positive   **109 very Cloten** Cloten himself   **110
make good time** acquit himself well   **111 fell** fierce   **111–114 Being . . .
fear** i.e., even in his youth, when he was scarcely a man and hence
might have experienced the fear that comes of imperfect judgment,
Cloten rashly had no conception of what a reasonable man would
regard as roaring terrors (?) (Editors sometimes emend *defect* to *th'
effect* or *cause* to *cease*.)

GUIDERIUS
  This Cloten was a fool, an empty purse;
  There was no money in 't. Not Hercules
  Could have knocked out his brains, for he had none.
  Yet I not doing this, the fool had borne   118
  My head as I do his.
BELARIUS   What hast thou done?
GUIDERIUS
  I am perfect what: cut off one Cloten's head,   120
  Son to the Queen, after his own report,   121
  Who called me traitor, mountaineer, and swore
  With his own single hand he'd take us in,   123
  Displace our heads where—thanks, ye gods!—they grow,   124
  And set them on Lud's Town.
BELARIUS   We are all undone.
GUIDERIUS
  Why, worthy Father, what have we to lose
  But that he swore to take, our lives? The law   127
  Protects not us. Then why should we be tender   128
  To let an arrogant piece of flesh threat us,
  Play judge and executioner all himself,
  For we do fear the law? What company   131
  Discover you abroad?
BELARIUS   No single soul
  Can we set eye on; but in all safe reason
  He must have some attendants. Though his humor   134
  Was nothing but mutation—ay, and that   135
  From one bad thing to worse—not frenzy,
  Not absolute madness could so far have raved
  To bring him here alone. Although perhaps
  It may be heard at court that such as we
  Cave here, hunt here, are outlaws, and in time
  May make some stronger head, the which he hearing—   141
  As it is like him—might break out and swear   142
  He'd fetch us in, yet is 't not probable   143

118 Yet . . . this yet if I had not done this. **had** would have **120 perfect** well aware **121 after** according to **123 take us in** overcome us **124 where** from where **127 that** that which **128 tender** quick, keen **131 For** because **134 humor** disposition **135 mutation** changeability **141 head** armed force **142 break out** burst out (in speech) **143 fetch us in** capture us

To come alone, either he so undertaking   144
Or they so suffering. Then on good ground we fear, 145
If we do fear this body hath a tail
More perilous than the head.

ARVIRAGUS   Let ordinance   147
Come as the gods foresay it. Howsoe'er,
My brother hath done well.

BELARIUS   I had no mind   149
To hunt this day. The boy Fidele's sickness
Did make my way long forth.

GUIDERIUS   With his own sword,   151
Which he did wave against my throat, I have ta'en
His head from him. I'll throw 't into the creek
Behind our rock, and let it to the sea
And tell the fishes he's the Queen's son, Cloten.
That's all I reck.   *Exit.*

BELARIUS   I fear 'twill be revenged.   156
Would, Polydore, thou hadst not done 't, though valor
Becomes thee well enough.

ARVIRAGUS   Would I had done 't,
So the revenge alone pursued me! Polydore,   159
I love thee brotherly, but envy much
Thou hast robbed me of this deed. I would revenges 161
That possible strength might meet would seek us
    through   162
And put us to our answer.

BELARIUS   Well, 'tis done.   163
We'll hunt no more today, nor seek for danger
Where there's no profit. I prithee, to our rock.
You and Fidele play the cooks. I'll stay
Till hasty Polydore return, and bring him   167
To dinner presently.

ARVIRAGUS   Poor sick Fidele!
I'll willingly to him. To gain his color   169

---

144 To come that he would come **145 suffering** permitting **147 ordinance** what is ordained **149 mind** inclination **151 make . . . forth** make my wanderings (from the cave) seem long. **his** i.e., Cloten's **156 reck** care **159 So** so that. **pursued** would have pursued **161 Thou** that thou **161–163 I would . . . answer** I wish that such revenges as it were possible for human strength to take on would seek us thoroughly and put us to the test, force us to respond **167 hasty** rash **169 gain his color** restore the color (to his cheeks)

I'd let a parish of such Clotens blood,   170
And praise myself for charity.   *Exit [into the cave].*
BELARIUS   O thou goddess,
Thou divine Nature, how thyself thou blazon'st   172
In these two princely boys! They are as gentle
As zephyrs blowing below the violet,
Not wagging his sweet head; and yet as rough,
Their royal blood enchafed, as the rud'st wind   176
That by the top doth take the mountain pine
And make him stoop to the vale. 'Tis wonder
That an invisible instinct should frame them   179
To royalty unlearned, honor untaught,
Civility not seen from other, valor   181
That wildly grows in them but yields a crop   182
As if it had been sowed. Yet still it's strange
What Cloten's being here to us portends,
Or what his death will bring us.

    Enter Guiderius.

GUIDERIUS   Where's my brother?
I have sent Cloten's clodpoll down the stream   186
In embassy to his mother. His body's hostage   187
For his return.   *Solemn music.*
BELARIUS   My ingenious instrument!   188
Hark, Polydore, it sounds. But what occasion
Hath Cadwal now to give it motion? Hark!
GUIDERIUS
Is he at home?
BELARIUS   He went hence even now.
GUIDERIUS
What does he mean? Since death of my dear'st mother
It did not speak before. All solemn things   193

---

170 **let . . . blood** i.e., drain the blood from a parish full of such Clotens   172 **how . . . blazon'st** how you proudly display yourself   176 **enchafed** being heated (with anger).   **rud'st** roughest   179 **frame** shape, direct   181 **not seen from other** i.e., not learned by observing it in some other person   182 **wildly grows** grows wild   186 **clodpoll** blockhead, head (with a play on Cloten's name)   187 **body's** body is. **hostage** (Guiderius' grim joke is that, since the head has been sent as ambassador in a parley between warring sides, the body will be held as hostage to ensure the safe return of the "ambassador.")   188 **ingenious** skillfully made (?)   193 **did not speak** has not spoken

Should answer solemn accidents. The matter?   194
Triumphs for nothing and lamenting toys   195
Is jollity for apes and grief for boys.
Is Cadwal mad?

> *Enter Arviragus, with Imogen, [as] dead, bearing*
> *her in his arms.*

BELARIUS   Look, here he comes,
And brings the dire occasion in his arms
Of what we blame him for.

ARVIRAGUS   The bird is dead
That we have made so much on. I had rather   200
Have skipped from sixteen years of age to sixty,
To have turned my leaping-time into a crutch,   202
Than have seen this.

GUIDERIUS   O sweetest, fairest lily!
My brother wears thee not the one half so well   204
As when thou grew'st thyself.

BELARIUS   O Melancholy,   205
Who ever yet could sound thy bottom, find   206
The ooze to show what coast thy sluggish crare   207
Might eas'liest harbor in?—Thou blessèd thing,   208
Jove knows what man thou mightst have made; but I,   209
Thou diedst, a most rare boy, of melancholy.
How found you him?

ARVIRAGUS   Stark, as you see,   211
Thus smiling, as some fly had tickled slumber,   212
Not as death's dart being laughed at; his right cheek 213
Reposing on a cushion.

GUIDERIUS   Where?

ARVIRAGUS   O' the floor,

194 answer correspond to.   **accidents** events   **195 lamenting toys** grief
over trifles (such as Cloten's death)   **200 on** of   **202 leaping-time** time
of energetic youth   **204–205 My . . . thyself** i.e., it is not even half so
beautiful a sight to see you carried by my brother, as though he were
wearing a lily, as when you lived and grew   **206 sound thy bottom**
measure your depth   **207 what coast** what kind of coast. (Who can ever
know where Melancholy will lodge, says Belarius, when she afflicts
even so fair a youth as this? They all conclude that "Fidele" died of
melancholy.)   **crare** skiff, small boat   **208 thing** i.e., Fidele   **209 but I**
i.e., but I know that   **211 Stark** stiff   **212 as** as if   **213 Not as . . .**
laughed at not as though laughing at death's dart (which Belarius
believes Fidele to be doing)

His arms thus leagued. I thought he slept, and put   215
My clouted brogues from off my feet, whose rudeness   216
Answered my steps too loud.
GUIDERIUS   Why, he but sleeps.
  If he be gone, he'll make his grave a bed;
  With female fairies will his tomb be haunted,
  And worms will not come to thee.
ARVIRAGUS   With fairest flowers   220
  Whilst summer lasts and I live here, Fidele,
  I'll sweeten thy sad grave. Thou shalt not lack
  The flower that's like thy face, pale primrose, nor
  The azured harebell, like thy veins, no, nor   224
  The leaf of eglantine, whom, not to slander,   225
  Outsweetened not thy breath. The ruddock would   226
  With charitable bill—O bill sore shaming
  Those rich-left heirs that let their fathers lie
  Without a monument!—bring thee all this,
  Yea, and furred moss besides, when flowers are none,
  To winter-ground thy corpse.
GUIDERIUS   Prithee, have done,   231
  And do not play in wenchlike words with that   232
  Which is so serious. Let us bury him
  And not protract with admiration what   234
  Is now due debt. To the grave!
ARVIRAGUS   Say, where shall 's lay him?   235
GUIDERIUS
  By good Euriphile, our mother.
ARVIRAGUS   Be 't so.
  And let us, Polydore, though now our voices
  Have got the mannish crack, sing him to th' ground,
  As once to our mother; use like note and words,   239
  Save that "Euriphile" must be "Fidele."

---

215 **leagued** folded   216 **clouted brogues** hobnailed boots   220 **to thee**
(Addressed to Imogen.)   224 **like thy veins** i.e., blue   225 **eglantine**
i.e., the sweetbrier rose   225–226 **whom . . . breath** i.e., it is no slander
to the eglantine to say that its fragrance was not sweeter than your
breath   226 **ruddock** robin redbreast. (According to fable, the robin
would cover graves with flowers and moss, thus showing more tenderness and reverence than forgetful humans.)   231 **winter-ground** cover so
as to protect from frost.   **have done** stop   232 **wenchlike** womanish
234 **admiration** wonder   235 **due debt** i.e., a ceremonial obligation (of
burial) that must be paid now.   **shall 's** shall we   239 **like** similar

GUIDERIUS Cadwal,
  I cannot sing. I'll weep, and word it with thee;
  For notes of sorrow out of tune are worse
  Than priests and fanes that lie.
ARVIRAGUS   We'll speak it, then.   244
BELARIUS
  Great griefs, I see, med'cine the less, for Cloten
  Is quite forgot. He was a queen's son, boys,
  And, though he came our enemy, remember
  He was paid for that. Though mean and mighty, rotting   248
  Together, have one dust, yet reverence,   249
  That angel of the world, doth make distinction   250
  Of place 'tween high and low. Our foe was princely,
  And though you took his life as being our foe,
  Yet bury him as a prince.
GUIDERIUS Pray you, fetch him hither.
  Thersites' body is as good as Ajax'   255
  When neither are alive.
ARVIRAGUS   If you'll go fetch him,
  We'll say our song the whilst. Brother, begin.
                         [*Exit Belarius.*]
GUIDERIUS
  Nay, Cadwal, we must lay his head to th' east.   258
  My father hath a reason for 't.
ARVIRAGUS   'Tis true.
GUIDERIUS
  Come on then and remove him.
                         [*They lay out Imogen with her
                           head to the east.*]
ARVIRAGUS   So. Begin.

                         Song
GUIDERIUS
      Fear no more the heat o' the sun,
        Nor the furious winter's rages;

244 fanes temples **248 mean** those lowly born **249-250 reverence . . .
world** (Reverence, or ceremonial respect for rank, presides over the
world like an *angel* or attendant spirit.) **255 Thersites' . . . Ajax'** (Thersites was the base scoffer in the *Iliad;* Ajax, a Greek hero.) **258 lay . . .
east** (Opposite to the Christian custom, and hence suggestive here of
pre-Christian worship.)

Thou thy worldly task hast done,
   Home art gone, and ta'en thy wages.
Golden lads and girls all must,
As chimney sweepers, come to dust.

ARVIRAGUS
   Fear no more the frown o' the great;
      Thou art past the tyrant's stroke.
   Care no more to clothe and eat;
      To thee the reed is as the oak.   270
   The scepter, learning, physic, must   271
   All follow this and come to dust.

GUIDERIUS
   Fear no more the lightning flash,
ARVIRAGUS
      Nor th' all-dreaded thunderstone.   274
GUIDERIUS
   Fear not slander, censure rash;
ARVIRAGUS
      Thou hast finished joy and moan.
BOTH
   All lovers young, all lovers must
   Consign to thee and come to dust.   278
GUIDERIUS
   No exorciser harm thee!   279
ARVIRAGUS
   Nor no witchcraft charm thee!
GUIDERIUS
   Ghost unlaid forbear thee!   281
ARVIRAGUS
   Nothing ill come near thee!
BOTH
   Quiet consummation have,   283
   And renownèd be thy grave!

---

270 reed, oak (Contrasting symbols of a fragility that survives by being flexible and a mightiness often overthrown. Fidele is past caring for the lesson contained in this contrast.)   **271 physic** medical learning **274 thunderstone** (The supposed solid body accompanying a stroke of lightning.)   **278 Consign to** cosign with, share a similar fate with, submit to the same terms with   **279 exorciser** conjurer   **281 unlaid** not laid to rest   **283 consummation** end, death

Enter Belarius, with the [headless] body of Cloten.

GUIDERIUS
We have done our obsequies. Come, lay him down.
                  [Cloten is laid next to Imogen.]

BELARIUS
Here's a few flowers, but 'bout midnight, more.
                  [They strew flowers.]
The herbs that have on them cold dew o' the night
Are strewings fitt'st for graves. Upon their faces.   288
You were as flowers, now withered; even so
These herblets shall, which we upon you strew.
Come on, away; apart upon our knees.
The ground that gave them first has them again.
Their pleasures here are past, so is their pain.
        Exeunt [Belarius, Guiderius, and Arviragus].

IMOGEN *(Awakes)*
Yes, sir, to Milford Haven. Which is the way?
I thank you. By yond bush? Pray, how far thither?
Ods pittikins! Can it be six mile yet?   296
I have gone all night. Faith, I'll lie down and sleep.   297
But soft, no bedfellow? *[She sees or touches Cloten's
   body.]* O gods and goddesses!
These flowers are like the pleasures of the world,
This bloody man the care on 't. I hope I dream,   300
For so I thought I was a cave keeper   301
And cook to honest creatures. But 'tis not so.
'Twas but a bolt of nothing, shot at nothing,   303
Which the brain makes of fumes. Our very eyes   304
Are sometimes like our judgments, blind. Good faith,
I tremble still with fear; but if there be
Yet left in heaven as small a drop of pity

---

288 Upon their faces i.e., strew flowers on the dead persons' faces, or
perhaps on the front of their bodies. (Since Cloten is headless. The line
may be corrupt.)   **296 Ods pittikins** God's pity. (A diminutive oath.)
297 gone walked   **300 the care on 't** i.e., is like the troubles of this
world   **301 For so** for in just the same way. (Since my thought of dwelling in a cave has proved to be a dream, may this awful sight prove one
too.)   **cave keeper** one who dwells in a cave   **303 bolt** arrow
304 fumes vapors engendered of humors which, according to current
theory, rose up into the brain and, by affecting imagination in the
forechamber of the brain, caused dreams

As a wren's eye, feared gods, a part of it!   308
The dream's here still. Even when I wake, it is
Without me, as within me; not imagined, felt.   310
A headless man? The garments of Posthumus?
I know the shape of 's leg; this is his hand,
His foot Mercurial, his Martial thigh,   313
The brawns of Hercules; but his Jovial face—   314
Murder in heaven? How? 'Tis gone. Pisanio,
All curses madded Hecuba gave the Greeks,   316
And mine to boot, be darted on thee! Thou,
Conspired with that irregulous devil, Cloten,   318
Hath here cut off my lord. To write and read   319
Be henceforth treacherous! Damned Pisanio
Hath with his forgèd letters—damned Pisanio—
From this most bravest vessel of the world
Struck the maintop! O Posthumus! Alas,   323
Where is thy head? Where's that? Ay me! Where's that?
Pisanio might have killed thee at the heart
And left this head on. How should this be? Pisanio?
'Tis he and Cloten. Malice and lucre in them   327
Have laid this woe here. O, 'tis pregnant, pregnant!   328
The drug he gave me, which he said was precious
And cordial to me, have I not found it   330
Murd'rous to th' senses? That confirms it home.   331
This is Pisanio's deed, and Cloten.—O!   332
Give color to my pale cheek with thy blood,   333
That we the horrider may seem to those
Which chance to find us. O, my lord, my lord!
                        [*She falls on the body.*]

     Enter Lucius, Captains, and a Soothsayer.

CAPTAIN
To them the legions garrisoned in Gallia,   336

308 wren's eye i.e., a very small eye, rendering a small teardrop. **a part** i.e., give me a part **310 Without** outside of **313 Mercurial** nimble and swift like the foot of Mercury. **Martial** powerful for war like that of Mars **314 brawns** muscles. **Jovial** Jove-like **316 madded** maddened. **Hecuba** wife of Priam, King of Troy **318 Conspired** conspiring. **irregulous** lawless **319 Hath** hast **323 maintop** top of mainmast, i.e., head **327 lucre** greed **328 pregnant** i.e., evident **330 cordial** restorative to the heart **331 home** utterly **332 Cloten** i.e., Cloten's **333 Give . . . blood** (Imogen may daub her cheeks with what she supposes to be Posthumus' blood, or may simply fall on the body.) **336 To them** i.e., in addition to the forces we've already mentioned

After your will, have crossed the sea, attending   337
You here at Milford Haven with your ships.
They are in readiness.

LUCIUS   But what from Rome?

CAPTAIN
The Senate hath stirred up the confiners   340
And gentlemen of Italy, most willing spirits,
That promise noble service, and they come
Under the conduct of bold Iachimo,
Sienna's brother.

LUCIUS   When expect you them?   344

CAPTAIN
With the next benefit o' the wind.

LUCIUS   This forwardness
Makes our hopes fair. Command our present numbers
Be mustered; bid the captains look to 't.—Now, sir,
What have you dreamed of late of this war's purpose?

SOOTHSAYER
Last night the very gods showed me a vision—
I fast and prayed for their intelligence—thus: 350
I saw Jove's bird, the Roman eagle, winged
From the spongy south to this part of the west,   352
There vanished in the sunbeams, which portends—
Unless my sins abuse my divination—   354
Success to th' Roman host.

LUCIUS   Dream often so,
And never false. [*He sees Cloten and Imogen.*] Soft, ho,
     what trunk is here
Without his top? The ruin speaks that sometime
It was a worthy building. How? A page?
Or dead or sleeping on him? But dead rather;   359
For nature doth abhor to make his bed
With the defunct, or sleep upon the dead.
Let's see the boy's face.

CAPTAIN   He's alive, my lord.

LUCIUS
He'll then instruct us of this body.—Young one,
Inform us of thy fortunes, for it seems

337 After according to   **340 confiners** inhabitants   **344 Sienna's** the
Duke of Sienna's   **350 fast** fasted   **352 spongy** damp   **354 abuse**
falsify   **359 Or** either

They crave to be demanded. Who is this
Thou mak'st thy bloody pillow? Or who was he
That, otherwise than noble nature did,   367
Hath altered that good picture? What's thy interest
In this sad wrack? How came 't? Who is 't?   369
What art thou?

IMOGEN   I am nothing; or if not,
Nothing to be were better. This was my master,
A very valiant Briton and a good,
That here by mountaineers lies slain. Alas,
There is no more such masters. I may wander
From east to occident, cry out for service,
Try many, all good, serve truly, never
Find such another master.

LUCIUS   'Lack, good youth!
Thou mov'st no less with thy complaining than   378
Thy master in bleeding. Say his name, good friend.

IMOGEN
Richard du Champ. [*Aside.*] If I do lie and do
No harm by it, though the gods hear, I hope
They'll pardon it.—Say you, sir?

LUCIUS   Thy name?

IMOGEN   Fidele, sir.

LUCIUS
Thou dost approve thyself the very same;   383
Thy name well fits thy faith, thy faith thy name.
Wilt take thy chance with me? I will not say
Thou shalt be so well mastered, but be sure
No less beloved. The Roman Emperor's letters
Sent by a consul to me should not sooner
Than thine own worth prefer thee. Go with me.   389

IMOGEN
I'll follow, sir. But first, an 't please the gods,   390
I'll hide my master from the flies as deep
As these poor pickaxes can dig; and when   392
With wild wood-leaves and weeds I ha' strewed his grave
And on it said a century of prayers,   394

---

367 otherwise . . . did i.e., unlike the noble way that nature portrayed
him **369 wrack** ruin **378 mov'st** i.e., to pity **383 approve** prove. **the
very same** (*Fidele* means "faithful.") **389 prefer** recommend **390 an 't**
if it **392 pickaxes** i.e., fingers **394 century of** hundred

Such as I can, twice o'er, I'll weep and sigh,
And leaving so his service, follow you,
So please you entertain me.

LUCIUS   Ay, good youth,   397
And rather father thee than master thee.
My friends,
The boy hath taught us manly duties. Let us
Find out the prettiest daisied plot we can
And make him with our pikes and partisans   402
A grave. Come, arm him. Boy, he's preferred   403
By thee to us, and he shall be interred
As soldiers can. Be cheerful; wipe thine eyes.
Some falls are means the happier to arise.
                          Exeunt, [bearing Cloten's body].

*

4.3   *Enter Cymbeline, Lords, [Attendants,] and
           Pisanio.*

CYMBELINE
Again, and bring me word how 'tis with her.
                          [*Exit an Attendant.*]
A fever with the absence of her son,   2
A madness, of which her life's in danger. Heavens,
How deeply you at once do touch me! Imogen,   4
The great part of my comfort, gone; my queen
Upon a desperate bed, and in a time
When fearful wars point at me; her son gone,
So needful for this present! It strikes me past
The hope of comfort.—But for thee, fellow,
Who needs must know of her departure and
Dost seem so ignorant, we'll enforce it from thee   11
By a sharp torture.

PISANIO   Sir, my life is yours;
I humbly set it at your will. But for my mistress,   13
I nothing know where she remains, why gone,

---

397 entertain employ   **402 partisans** long-handled weapons, halberds
403 arm him lift him up

4.3. Location: Britain. At the court of Cymbeline.
2 with brought on by   **4 touch** wound, afflict   **11 seem** pretend to be
13 for as for (also in l. 19)

Nor when she purposes return. Beseech Your Highness,
Hold me your loyal servant.

A LORD   Good my liege,   16
The day that she was missing he was here.
I dare be bound he's true and shall perform
All parts of his subjection loyally. For Cloten,   19
There wants no diligence in seeking him,   20
And will no doubt be found.

CYMBELINE   The time is troublesome.   21
[*To Pisanio.*] We'll slip you for a season, but our jealousy 22
Does yet depend.

A LORD   So please Your Majesty,   23
The Roman legions, all from Gallia drawn,
Are landed on your coast with a supply
Of Roman gentlemen by the Senate sent.

CYMBELINE
Now for the counsel of my son and queen!
I am amazed with matter.

A LORD   Good my liege,   28
Your preparation can affront no less   29
Than what you hear of. Come more, for more you're
  ready.   30
The want is but to put those powers in motion   31
That long to move.

CYMBELINE   I thank you. Let's withdraw,
And meet the time as it seeks us. We fear not
What can from Italy annoy us, but   34
We grieve at chances here. Away!   35

                              Exeunt [*all but Pisanio*].

PISANIO
I heard no letter from my master since
I wrote him Imogen was slain. 'Tis strange.
Nor hear I from my mistress, who did promise
To yield me often tidings. Neither know I

---

16 Hold regard   **19 subjection** duty as a subject   **20 wants** is lacking
21 will he will.   **troublesome** filled with deep troubles   **22 slip you** let
you go.   **jealousy** suspicion   **23 depend** impend, threaten   **28 amazed
with matter** confused and overwhelmed by the pressure of affairs
29 preparation military force already mustered   **29–30 affront ... Than**
confront in combat as large (an army) as   **30 Come more** if more (enemy) come   **31 want is but** sole thing needed is.   **powers** armed
forces   **34 annoy** injure   **35 chances** accidents (the Queen's illness, etc.)

What is betid to Cloten, but remain   40
Perplexed in all. The heavens still must work.
Wherein I am false I am honest; not true, to be true.
These present wars shall find I love my country,
Even to the note o' the King, or I'll fall in them.   44
All other doubts, by time let them be cleared;   45
Fortune brings in some boats that are not steered.

                                                    Exit.

                        ❖

4.4   *Enter Belarius, Guiderius, and Arviragus.*

GUIDERIUS
  The noise is round about us.
BELARIUS   Let us from it.
ARVIRAGUS
  What pleasure, sir, find we in life, to lock it
  From action and adventure?
GUIDERIUS   Nay, what hope
  Have we in hiding us? This way the Romans   4
  Must or for Britons slay us or receive us   5
  For barbarous and unnatural revolts   6
  During their use, and slay us after.
BELARIUS   Sons,   7
  We'll higher to the mountains, there secure us.
  To the King's party there's no going. Newness
  Of Cloten's death—we being not known, not mustered
  Among the bands—may drive us to a render   11
  Where we have lived, and so extort from 's that
  Which we have done, whose answer would be death   13
  Drawn on with torture.
GUIDERIUS   This is, sir, a doubt   14
  In such a time nothing becoming you   15

---

40 is betid has happened   **44 Even . . . King** to the extent of attracting
the favorable notice of the King (for my bravery)   **45 let them** i.e., let us
pray that they

4.4. Location: Wales. Before the cave of Belarius.
4 This way i.e., by such a course of conduct   **5 Must or** must either
6 revolts deserters, rebels   **7 During their use** as long as they find us
useful   **11 bands** army rolls.   **render** rendering of an account, relation   **13 answer** consequence   **14 Drawn on with** brought about and
lengthened by   **15 nothing** not at all

Nor satisfying us.
ARVIRAGUS   It is not likely
That when they hear the Roman horses neigh,
Behold their quartered fires, have both their eyes   18
And ears so cloyed importantly as now,   19
That they will waste their time upon our note,   20
To know from whence we are.
BELARIUS   O, I am known
Of many in the army. Many years,
Though Cloten then but young, you see, not wore him
From my remembrance. And besides, the King
Hath not deserved my service nor your loves,
Who find in my exile the want of breeding,   26
The certainty of this hard life, aye hopeless   27
To have the courtesy your cradle promised,   28
But to be still hot summer's tanlings and   29
The shrinking slaves of winter.
GUIDERIUS   Than be so
Better to cease to be. Pray, sir, to th' army.
I and my brother are not known; yourself
So out of thought, and thereto so o'ergrown,   33
Cannot be questioned.
ARVIRAGUS   By this sun that shines,
I'll thither. What thing is 't that I never   35
Did see man die, scarce ever looked on blood
But that of coward hares, hot goats, and venison!   37
Never bestrid a horse save one that had
A rider like myself, who ne'er wore rowel   39
Nor iron on his heel! I am ashamed
To look upon the holy sun, to have
The benefit of his blest beams, remaining
So long a poor unknown.
GUIDERIUS   By heavens, I'll go.

---

18 quartered fires campfires   **19 cloyed importantly** filled with urgent
business   **20 upon our note** in observing us   **26–28 Who . . . promised**
you who find in exile with me a lack of proper education and hardship
from which there is no escape, without hope of ever achieving the
cultivated existence promised you by your high birth   **29 But** i.e., but
destined instead.   **tanlings** those tanned by the sun   **33 thereto** in
addition.   **o'ergrown** i.e., with hair and beard   **35 What thing** i.e., what
a disgraceful thing   **37 hot** lecherous   **39 rowel** wheel of a spur

If you will bless me, sir, and give me leave,
I'll take the better care, but if you will not,   45
The hazard therefore due fall on me by   46
The hands of Romans!
ARVIRAGUS   So say I. Amen.
BELARIUS
No reason I, since of your lives you set
So slight a valuation, should reserve
My cracked one to more care. Have with you, boys!   50
If in your country wars you chance to die,   51
That is my bed too, lads, and there I'll lie.
Lead, lead. [*Aside.*] The time seems long; their blood
   thinks scorn
Till it fly out and show them princes born.   *Exeunt.*

❖

45 take the better care i.e., proceed with better prospects of success
46 hazard therefore due i.e., danger resulting from disobedience and
lack of parental blessing   **50 cracked** i.e., with age.   **Have with you** i.e.,
come on, then   **51 country** country's

5.1 *Enter Posthumus alone [in Italian dress, with a bloody handkerchief].*

POSTHUMUS
Yea, bloody cloth, I'll keep thee, for I wished
Thou shouldst be colored thus. You married ones,
If each of you should take this course, how many
Must murder wives much better than themselves
For wrying but a little! O Pisanio!   5
Every good servant does not all commands;
No bond but to do just ones. Gods, if you   7
Should have ta'en vengeance on my faults, I never
Had lived to put on this; so had you saved   9
The noble Imogen to repent, and struck
Me, wretch, more worth your vengeance. But alack,
You snatch some hence for little faults; that's love,   12
To have them fall no more; you some permit   13
To second ills with ills, each elder worse,   14
And make them dread it, to the doers' thrift.   15
But Imogen is your own. Do your best wills,
And make me blest to obey! I am brought hither
Among th' Italian gentry, and to fight
Against my lady's kingdom. 'Tis enough
That, Britain, I have killed thy mistress; peace,
I'll give no wound to thee. Therefore, good heavens,
Hear patiently my purpose: I'll disrobe me
Of these Italian weeds and suit myself   23
As does a Briton peasant; so I'll fight
Against the part I come with; so I'll die   25
For thee, O Imogen, even for whom my life
Is every breath a death; and thus, unknown,
Pitied nor hated, to the face of peril   28
Myself I'll dedicate. Let me make men know
More valor in me than my habits show.   30

5.1. Location: Britain. An open place.
5 wrying swerving from the right course **7 bond but** obligation except
9 put on incite, encourage (?) burden myself with (?) **12–13 that's . . .
more** that is a loving act, since it makes them sin no more **14 second**
follow up. **elder** subsequent (sin) **15 make . . . thrift** i.e., make those
evil-doers repent their deeds, to their ultimate spiritual profit **23 suit**
clothe **25 part** party, side **28 Pitied** neither pitied **30 habits** clothes

Gods, put the strength o' the Leonati in me!
To shame the guise o' the world, I will begin   32
The fashion: less without and more within.   *Exit.* 33

5.2 *Enter Lucius, Iachimo, and the Roman army at
one door, and the Briton army at another,
Leonatus Posthumus following, like a poor
soldier. They march over and go out. Then
enter again, in skirmish, Iachimo and
Posthumus; he vanquisheth and disarmeth
Iachimo, and then leaves him.*

IACHIMO
The heaviness and guilt within my bosom
Takes off my manhood. I have belied a lady,
The princess of this country, and the air on 't   3
Revengingly enfeebles me; or could this carl,   4
A very drudge of nature's, have subdued me
In my profession? Knighthoods and honors borne
As I wear mine are titles but of scorn.
If that thy gentry, Britain, go before   8
This lout as he exceeds our lords, the odds
Is that we scarce are men and you are gods.   *Exit.*

*The battle continues; the Britons fly; Cymbeline
is taken. Then enter, to his rescue, Belarius,
Guiderius, and Arviragus.*

BELARIUS
Stand, stand! We have th' advantage of the ground;
The lane is guarded. Nothing routs us but
The villainy of our fears.
GUIDERIUS, ARVIRAGUS   Stand, stand, and fight!

---

32 **guise** custom   33 **fashion: less without** the fashion of relying less on
outward show

**5.2. Location: Britain. Field of battle. The scene is probably continuous
with the previous.**
s.d. poor of low rank and poorly outfitted   3 **on 't** of it   4 **or** otherwise.
carl churl, peasant   8 **go before** excel

Enter Posthumus and seconds the Britons. They
rescue Cymbeline and exeunt. Then enter Lucius,
Iachimo, and Imogen.

LUCIUS
Away, boy, from the troops, and save thyself!
For friends kill friends, and the disorder's such
As war were hoodwinked.

IACHIMO   'Tis their fresh supplies.   16

LUCIUS
It is a day turned strangely. Or betimes   17
Let's reinforce, or fly.   *Exeunt.*

5.3   *Enter Posthumus [dressed as a British peasant*
still], and a Briton Lord.

LORD
Cam'st thou from where they made the stand?

POSTHUMUS   I did,
Though you, it seems, come from the fliers?

LORD   I did.

POSTHUMUS
No blame be to you, sir, for all was lost,
But that the heavens fought. The King himself   4
Of his wings destitute, the army broken,   5
And but the backs of Britons seen, all flying
Through a strait lane; the enemy fullhearted,   7
Lolling the tongue with slaughtering, having work   8
More plentiful than tools to do 't, struck down
Some mortally, some slightly touched, some falling   10
Merely through fear, that the strait pass was dammed
With dead men hurt behind and cowards living   12
To die with lengthened shame.   13

---

16 As as if. **hoodwinked** blindfolded. (War swings his weapons blindly, without looking to see who is struck.) **17 Or betimes** either swiftly

5.3. Location: The field of battle, as before.
4 But that if it had not been for the fact that **5 wings** flanks of the army **7 strait** narrow. **fullhearted** full of courage and confidence **8 Lolling** letting hang out **10 touched** wounded **12 behind** from the rear (while running away) **13 lengthened** lingering (for the rest of their lives)

LORD   Where was this lane?
POSTHUMUS
  Close by the battle, ditched, and walled with turf;
  Which gave advantage to an ancient soldier,
  An honest one, I warrant, who deserved   16
  So long a breeding as his white beard came to,   17
  In doing this for 's country. Athwart the lane,
  He, with two striplings—lads more like to run   19
  The country base than to commit such slaughter,   20
  With faces fit for masks, or rather fairer   21
  Than those for preservation cased, or shame—   22
  Made good the passage, cried to those that fled,   23
  "Our Britain's harts die flying, not our men.
  To darkness fleet souls that fly backwards. Stand!   25
  Or we are Romans and will give you that   26
  Like beasts which you shun beastly, and may save   27
  But to look back in frown. Stand, stand!" These three, 28
  Three thousand confident, in act as many—
  For three performers are the file when all   30
  The rest do nothing—with this word "Stand, stand,"
  Accommodated by the place, more charming   32
  With their own nobleness, which could have turned   33
  A distaff to a lance, gilded pale looks,   34
  Part shame, part spirit renewed, that some, turned
    coward   35
  But by example—O, a sin in war,   36

16 **honest** worthy   17 **breeding** life, support. (His long white beard
betokens the length of years that he deserves to be honored.)   19 **like**
likely   20 **base** prisoner's base, a game in which rapid running is the
means to victory   21 **fit for masks** delicate enough to deserve sheltering
from the elements   22 **those . . . shame** i.e., ladies' faces masked (*cased*)
either for protection against the elements or for modesty   23 **Made
good** secured   25 **darkness** i.e., ignominy, hell. **fleet** hasten   26 **are
Romans** i.e., will act like Romans. **that** i.e., death blows   27 **beastly**
like cowards. **save** prevent   28 **But . . . frown** only by looking back in
defiance, only if you turn and defy the enemy   30 **file** i.e., entire force
(as in "rank and file")   32 **Accommodated** provided with advantage.
more charming and more importantly working their spell on others as
if by magic (thus persuading them to turn and fight)   33 **With** by the
example of. **turned** transformed   34 **A distaff to a lance** i.e., a house-
wife into a soldier. **gilded** imparted a flush of color to   35 **Part . . .
renewed** (moved them so that) shame revived some, courage others
35–36 **turned . . . example** converted into cowards only by imitation

Damned in the first beginners!—'gan to look   37
The way that they did and to grin like lions   38
Upon the pikes o' the hunters. Then began   39
A stop i' the chaser, a retire, anon   40
A rout, confusion thick. Forthwith they fly   41
Chickens, the way which they stooped eagles; slaves, 42
The strides they victors made. And now our cowards, 43
Like fragments in hard voyages, became   44
The life o' the need. Having found the back door open 45
Of the unguarded hearts, heavens, how they wound!
Some slain before, some dying, some their friends   47
O'erborne i' the former wave, ten chased by one,   48
Are now each one the slaughterman of twenty.
Those that would die or ere resist are grown   50
The mortal bugs o' the field.
LORD   This was strange chance: 51
A narrow lane, an old man, and two boys!
POSTHUMUS
Nay, do not wonder at it. You are made
Rather to wonder at the things you hear
Than to work any. Will you rhyme upon 't   55
And vent it for a mockery? Here is one: 56
"Two boys, an old man twice a boy, a lane,   57
Preserved the Britons, was the Romans' bane."

---

37 first beginners i.e., those who first set an example of cowardice.
'gan began   **38 they** i.e., Belarius and his two "sons."   **grin** bare the
teeth   **39 Upon** directly against, face to face with   **40 stop i' the chaser**
stopping of those who had been the pursuers, i.e., the Romans.   **retire**
retreat   **41 Forthwith** immediately.   **fly** flee   **42 Chickens** i.e., like
chickens.   **the way . . . eagles** along the very path that just before they
had swooped over like eagles   **42–43 slaves . . . made** retracing, like
slaves, the steps they took as victors   **44 fragments** scraps, fragments of
food, something to fall back on as a last resort   **45 The life o' the need**
vital support in time of necessity.   **back door** i.e., vulnerable soft spot
of the Romans   **47–48 Some . . . by one** i.e., some who were given up for
dead or dying, and some comrades overwhelmed in the previous Roman
assault who had yielded by the tens to each Roman soldier   **50 would
die** previously were ready to die.   **or ere** rather than   **51 mortal bugs**
deadly bugbears, terrors   **55 work any** perform any such wonders
yourself. (Said reproachfully.)   **55–56 Will . . . one** i.e., would you like to
be-rhyme this event in ballad fashion and thus make a mockery of it
with your cheap exploitation? Here is a sample.   **vent** air, circulate
57 twice a boy in his second childhood

LORD
  Nay, be not angry, sir.
POSTHUMUS   'Lack, to what end?   59
  Who dares not stand his foe, I'll be his friend;   60
  For if he'll do as he is made to do,   61
  I know he'll quickly fly my friendship too.   62
  You have put me into rhyme.
LORD   Farewell. You're angry.
                                             Exit.

POSTHUMUS
  Still going? This is a lord! O noble misery,   64
  To be i' the field, and ask "What news?" of me!
  Today how many would have given their honors
  To have saved their carcasses! Took heel to do 't,
  And yet died too! I, in mine own woe charmed,   68
  Could not find Death where I did hear him groan,
  Nor feel him where he struck. Being an ugly monster,
  'Tis strange he hides him in fresh cups, soft beds,
  Sweet words, or hath more ministers than we
  That draw his knives i' the war. Well, I will find him;
  For being now a favorer to the Briton,   74
                    [*Removing his British garb*]
  No more a Briton, I have resumed again   75
  The part I came in. Fight I will no more,   76
  But yield me to the veriest hind that shall   77
  Once touch my shoulder. Great the slaughter is   78
  Here made by the Roman; great the answer be   79
  Britons must take. For me, my ransom's death.
  On either side I come to spend my breath,   81
  Which neither here I'll keep nor bear again,
  But end it by some means for Imogen.

59 'Lack alack. to what end why should I be angry 60–62 Who . . .
too i.e., I can put up with the friendship of any coward (like yourself),
for, if he is true to his colors he'll run away and thus rid me of his
company. Who whoever. stand stand against. made inclined
64 going fleeing. noble misery miserable specimen of the nobility
68 charmed i.e., made invulnerable as if by a spell 74 being . . . favorer
to i.e., since Death now favors 75 No . . . Briton I remaining no longer
a Briton 76 The part . . . in i.e., my Roman guise (in which my capture
and execution seem assured) 77 hind peasant 78 touch my shoulder
i.e., place me under arrest 79 answer retaliation. be is that 81 spend
my breath give up my life

    Enter two [British] Captains and soldiers.

FIRST CAPTAIN
  Great Jupiter be praised! Lucius is taken.
  'Tis thought the old man and his sons were angels.
SECOND CAPTAIN
  There was a fourth man, in a silly habit,   86
  That gave th' affront with them.
FIRST CAPTAIN   So 'tis reported,   87
  But none of 'em can be found.—Stand! Who's there?
POSTHUMUS A Roman,
  Who had not now been drooping here if seconds   90
  Had answered him.
SECOND CAPTAIN   Lay hands on him; a dog!   91
  A leg of Rome shall not return to tell   92
  What crows have pecked them here. He brags his service
  As if he were of note. Bring him to th' King.

    Enter Cymbeline, Belarius, Guiderius, Arviragus,
    Pisanio, [soldiers, attendants,] and Roman
    captives. The Captains present Posthumus to
    Cymbeline, who delivers him over to a Jailer.
                            [Then exeunt.]

                        ❖

5.4   *Enter Posthumus [in chains] and [two]*
        Jailer[s].

FIRST JAILER
  You shall not now be stol'n; you have locks upon you.

---

86 silly simple, rustic   **87 affront** attack   **90 drooping** languishing.
seconds supporters   **91 answered him** followed his lead   **92 leg** i.e., one
of the lower extremities, one who does the walking (and the running
away)

**5.4. Location: A British prison or stockade. Possibly the scene is contin-
uous; see the next note.**
s.d. Enter (The scene may be continuous, with Posthumus and the
jailers remaining onstage, though the Folio does mark an entrance for
Posthumus and one jailer, and the scene does appear to call for manacles [ll. 9, 191]. On the unlocalized Elizabethan stage the change of
scene is achieved chiefly by the actors and their dialogue.)

So graze as you find pasture.
SECOND JAILER   Ay, or a stomach.   2
                                    [*Exeunt Jailers.*]
POSTHUMUS
Most welcome, bondage! For thou art a way,
I think, to liberty. Yet am I better
Than one that's sick o' the gout, since he had rather
Groan so in perpetuity than be cured
By th' sure physician, Death, who is the key
T' unbar these locks. My conscience, thou art fettered
More than my shanks and wrists. You good gods, give
    me
The penitent instrument to pick that bolt,   10
Then, free forever! Is 't enough I am sorry?
So children temporal fathers do appease;
Gods are more full of mercy. Must I repent,   13
I cannot do it better than in gyves,   14
Desired more than constrained. To satisfy,   15
If of my freedom 'tis the main part, take   16
No stricter render of me than my all.   17
I know you are more clement than vile men,
Who of their broken debtors take a third,   19
A sixth, a tenth, letting them thrive again
On their abatement. That's not my desire.   21
For Imogen's dear life take mine; and though
'Tis not so dear, yet 'tis a life; you coined it.   23
'Tween man and man they weigh not every stamp;   24
Though light, take pieces for the figure's sake;   25
You rather mine, being yours. And so, great powers,   26

2 graze . . . pasture i.e., like a horse, fettered by one leg   10 penitent . . .
bolt i.e., penitence to unlock the fetters encumbering my conscience and
to find the death I seek   13 Must I repent if I must repent   14 gyves
fetters   15 constrained forced (upon me).   satisfy make atonement
16 If . . . part i.e., if such atonement is essential to freeing my conscience   17 stricter render sterner repayment   19 broken bankrupt
21 abatement diminished principal   23 so dear as valuable as hers
24 'Tween . . . stamp in commercial transactions men don't weigh every
coin exactly   25 Though . . . sake even if some coins may be under the
exact weight, men accept them for the sake of the image stamped
thereon, i.e., the image of the king   26 You . . . yours i.e., you should all
the more readily take my life, even though I am a light (worthless) coin,
since I am stamped in your image

If you will take this audit, take this life   27
And cancel these cold bonds. O Imogen!   28
I'll speak to thee in silence.   [*He sleeps.*]

> *Solemn music. Enter, as in an apparition, Sicilius*
> *Leonatus, father to Posthumus, an old man,*
> *attired like a warrior; leading in his hand an*
> *ancient matron, his wife, and mother to*
> *Posthumus, with music before them. Then, after*
> *other music, follows the two young Leonati,*
> *brothers to Posthumus, with wounds as they died*
> *in the wars. They circle Posthumus round as he*
> *lies sleeping.*

SICILIUS

No more, thou Thunder-master, show   30
  Thy spite on mortal flies.   31
With Mars fall out, with Juno chide,
  That thy adulteries   33
    Rates and revenges.   34
Hath my poor boy done aught but well,
  Whose face I never saw?
I died whilst in the womb he stayed
  Attending nature's law;   38
Whose father then—as men report   39
  Thou orphans' father art—   40
Thou shouldst have been, and shielded him
  From this earth-vexing smart.   42

MOTHER

Lucina lent not me her aid,   43
  But took me in my throes,
That from me was Posthumus ripped,
  Came crying 'mongst his foes,
    A thing of pity!

---

27 take this audit accept this accounting   **28 bonds** (1) fetters, both
literal and figurative (2) legal contracts   **30 Thunder-master** i.e., Jupiter   **31 mortal flies** i.e., petty creatures, mere humans   **33 That** who
(i.e., Juno)   **34 Rates** scolds   **38 Attending nature's law** i.e., awaiting
the completion of his term in the womb   **39–40 Whose father . . . art**
(Psalm 68:5 praises God as "A father of the fatherless.")   **42 earth-**
vexing smart suffering to which all life is prone   **43 Lucina** goddess of
childbirth

SICILIUS
> Great nature, like his ancestry,   48
>> Molded the stuff so fair   49
> That he deserved the praise o' the world
>> As great Sicilius' heir.

FIRST BROTHER
> When once he was mature for man,   52
>> In Britain where was he   53
> That could stand up his parallel,
>> Or fruitful object be
> In eye of Imogen, that best
>> Could deem his dignity?   57

MOTHER
> With marriage wherefore was he mocked,
>> To be exiled and thrown
> From Leonati seat, and cast
>> From her his dearest one,
>>> Sweet Imogen?

SICILIUS
> Why did you suffer Iachimo,
>> Slight thing of Italy,   64
> To taint his nobler heart and brain
>> With needless jealousy,
> And to become the geck and scorn   67
>> O' th' other's villainy?

SECOND BROTHER
> For this from stiller seats we came,   69
>> Our parents and us twain,
> That striking in our country's cause   71
>> Fell bravely and were slain,
> Our fealty and Tenantius' right   73
>> With honor to maintain.

FIRST BROTHER
> Like hardiment Posthumus hath   75
>> To Cymbeline performed.
> Then, Jupiter, thou king of gods,

---

48 like acting in concert with, or taking the part of   **49 stuff** substance   **52 mature for man** grown to manhood   **53 he** any man   **57 deem** judge   **64 Slight** worthless   **67 geck** dupe   **69 stiller seats** quieter abodes (i.e., the Elysian Fields)   **71 That** who   **73 Tenantius'** Cymbeline's father's   **75 Like hardiment** similar bold exploits

    Why hast thou thus adjourned   78
    The graces for his merits due,
      Being all to dolors turned?

SICILIUS
    Thy crystal window ope; look out.
      No longer exercise
    Upon a valiant race thy harsh
      And potent injuries.

MOTHER
    Since, Jupiter, our son is good,
      Take off his miseries.

SICILIUS
    Peep through thy marble mansion. Help,
      Or we poor ghosts will cry
    To th' shining synod of the rest   89
      Against thy deity.

BROTHERS
    Help, Jupiter, or we appeal,
      And from thy justice fly.

Jupiter descends in thunder and lightning, sitting
upon an eagle. He throws a thunderbolt. The
ghosts fall on their knees.

JUPITER
No more, you petty spirits of region low,
  Offend our hearing. Hush! How dare you ghosts
Accuse the Thunderer, whose bolt, you know,
  Sky-planted, batters all rebelling coasts?   96
Poor shadows of Elysium, hence, and rest
  Upon your never-withering banks of flowers.
Be not with mortal accidents oppressed.   99
  No care of yours it is; you know 'tis ours.
Whom best I love I cross, to make my gift,
  The more delayed, delighted. Be content.   102
Your low-laid son our godhead will uplift.
  His comforts thrive, his trials well are spent.   104
Our Jovial star reigned at his birth, and in   105

---

78 adjourned deferred   **89 synod of the rest** assembly of the gods
96 Sky-planted growing out of the sky   **99 accidents** events   **102 de-**
lighted (the more) delighted in   **104 spent** ended   **105 Jovial star** the
planet Jupiter, the happiest of all planets to be born under

Our temple was he married. Rise, and fade.   106
He shall be lord of Lady Imogen,
    And happier much by his affliction made.
This tablet lay upon his breast, wherein
    Our pleasure his full fortune doth confine.   110
                            [*He delivers a tablet.*]
And so away! No farther with your din
    Express impatience, lest you stir up mine.
    Mount, eagle, to my palace crystalline.   *Ascends.*

SICILIUS
    He came in thunder; his celestial breath
    Was sulfurous to smell. The holy eagle
    Stooped, as to foot us. His ascension is   116
    More sweet than our blest fields. His royal bird   117
    Prunes the immortal wing and cloys his beak,   118
    As when his god is pleased.

ALL   Thanks, Jupiter!

SICILIUS
    The marble pavement closes; he is entered   120
    His radiant roof. Away! And, to be blest,
    Let us with care perform his great behest.
                    [*The ghosts place the tablet on
                    Posthumus' breast, and*] *vanish.*

POSTHUMUS [*Waking*]
    Sleep, thou hast been a grandsire and begot
    A father to me; and thou hast created
    A mother and two brothers. But, O scorn,   125
    Gone! They went hence so soon as they were born.
    And so I am awake. Poor wretches that depend
    On greatness' favor dream as I have done,
    Wake and find nothing. But, alas, I swerve!   129
                            [*He sees the tablet.*]
    Many dream not to find, neither deserve,   130
    And yet are steeped in favors; so am I,

---

106 fade vanish   **110 confine** precisely state   **116 Stooped** swooped
down.   **as** as if.   **foot** seize (in his talons)   **116–117 His . . . fields** his
ascent gives off a sweet odor surpassing that of the Elysian Fields
118 Prunes preens.   **cloys** claws, strokes with the claw   **120 marble
pavement** heavens (above the Elizabethan stage; cf. *marble mansion* in
l. 87)   **125 scorn** mockery   **129 swerve** mistake, go astray   **130 to find**
of finding

That have this golden chance and know not why.
What fairies haunt this ground? A book? O rare one!   133
Be not, as is our fangled world, a garment   134
Nobler than that it covers! Let thy effects
So follow, to be most unlike our courtiers,   136
As good as promise.

    (*Reads*.) "Whenas a lion's whelp shall, to himself 138
unknown, without seeking find and be embraced by
a piece of tender air; and when from a stately cedar
shall be lopped branches which, being dead many
years, shall after revive, be jointed to the old stock, and
freshly grow; then shall Posthumus end his miseries,
Britain be fortunate and flourish in peace and plenty."
'Tis still a dream, or else such stuff as madmen
Tongue and brain not; either both or nothing,   146
Or senseless speaking or a speaking such   147
As sense cannot untie. Be what it is,   148
The action of my life is like it, which
I'll keep, if but for sympathy.   150

     Enter [*First*] *Jailer.*

FIRST JAILER   Come, sir, are you ready for death?
POSTHUMUS   Overroasted rather; ready long ago.
FIRST JAILER   Hanging is the word, sir. If you be ready 153
   for that, you are well cooked.
POSTHUMUS   So, if I prove a good repast to the spectators, the dish pays the shot.   156
FIRST JAILER   A heavy reckoning for you, sir. But the
   comfort is, you shall be called to no more payments,
   fear no more tavern bills, which are often the sadness 159
   of parting as the procuring of mirth. You come in
   faint for want of meat, depart reeling with too much

---

133 book i.e., the tablet or scroll. **rare** excellent **134 fangled** characterized by fripperies or gaudiness **136 to** so as to **138 Whenas**
when **146 Tongue** speak. **brain** understand. **either both** either of the
two (a dream, or madness) (?) **147 Or** either. **senseless speaking** (as in
madness) **147–148 speaking . . . cannot untie** (as in a dream).
sense reason **150 sympathy** i.e., resemblance (between my life and
this mystery) **153 Hanging** (1) hanging up like cooking meat (2) being
hanged as a criminal **156 the dish . . . shot** (1) the food is worth the
tavern reckoning (2) my death settles my account **159 often** as often

drink; sorry that you have paid too much, and sorry
that you are paid too much; purse and brain both 163
empty; the brain the heavier for being too light, the 164
purse too light, being drawn of heaviness. Of this 165
contradiction you shall now be quit. O, the charity of 166
a penny cord! It sums up thousands in a trice. You 167
have no true debitor and creditor but it; of what's past, 168
is, and to come, the discharge. Your neck, sir, is pen, 169
book, and counters; so the acquittance follows. 170

POSTHUMUS I am merrier to die than thou art to live.

FIRST JAILER Indeed, sir, he that sleeps feels not the
toothache. But a man that were to sleep your sleep, 173
and a hangman to help him to bed, I think he would
change places with his officer; for, look you, sir, you 175
know not which way you shall go.

POSTHUMUS Yes, indeed do I, fellow.

FIRST JAILER Your death has eyes in 's head then; I have
not seen him so pictured. You must either be directed 179
by some that take upon them to know, or to take upon 180
yourself that which I am sure you do not know, or
jump the after-inquiry on your own peril. And how 182
you shall speed in your journey's end, I think you'll 183
never return to tell one.

POSTHUMUS I tell thee, fellow, there are none want eyes 185
to direct them the way I am going but such as wink 186
and will not use them.

FIRST JAILER What an infinite mock is this, that a man
should have the best use of eyes to see the way of
blindness! I am sure hanging's the way of winking. 190

---

163 are paid are subdued (by excessive drink) **164 heavier** heavier with
sleep **165 drawn** tapped, emptied **166 charity** benevolent action, one
that settles all debts **167 sums up** (1) totals up a reckoning (2) collects,
summarizes. **trice** (1) instant (2) tricing up, hauling up by a rope
168 debitor and creditor account book **169 discharge** (1) payment of
debt (2) disburdening, release, as in death **170 counters** metal disks
used for calculating. **acquittance** (1) discharge of an account (2) deliverance **173 a man that were to** if there were a man who was destined
to **175 officer** i.e., the hangman **179 so pictured** i.e., in the traditional
death's-head, an eyeless skull **180 take upon them** undertake, profess **182 jump** gamble on **183 speed** succeed **185 none want** none
who lack **186 wink** close the eyes **190 hanging's . . . winking** hanging
will close up the eyes

Enter a Messenger.

MESSENGER Knock off his manacles. Bring your prisoner to the King.

POSTHUMUS Thou bring'st good news. I am called to be
made free.   [*He is freed from his irons.*] 194
FIRST JAILER I'll be hanged then.   195
POSTHUMUS Thou shalt be then freer than a jailer; no
bolts for the dead.   *Exeunt [all but the First Jailer].*
FIRST JAILER Unless a man would marry a gallows and
beget young gibbets, I never saw one so prone. Yet, 199
on my conscience, there are verier knaves desire to 200
live, for all he be a Roman; and there be some of them 201
too that die against their wills. So should I, if I were 202
one. I would we were all of one mind, and one mind 203
good. O, there were desolation of jailers and gal- 204
lowses! I speak against my present profit, but my wish 205
hath a preferment in 't.   [*Exit.*] 206

❖

5.5   *Enter Cymbeline, Belarius, Guiderius,*
Arviragus, Pisanio, [officers, attendants,]
and lords.

CYMBELINE
Stand by my side, you whom the gods have made
Preservers of my throne. Woe is my heart
That the poor soldier that so richly fought,

---

194 made free i.e., executed and thereby freed from existence **195 I'll
be hanged then** (The jailer is using a conventional expression, like "I'll
be damned if that's so," but Posthumus replies that he means *free* in a
spiritual sense.) **199 prone** ready, eager **200–203 there . . . were one**
i.e., he's not such a bad fellow, even if he is a Roman; worse men than
he desire to live when they're to be executed, as I would in such a
plight. (Romans were supposed to be stoical in the face of death.)
204–205 there . . . gallowses i.e., if all men were good, there would be no
work left for jailers and gallows **206 a preferment** i.e., a preference for
us all to live in a better world (with a hope that this pious wish may
stand me in good stead at my day of reckoning, and thus "prefer" me to
bliss). Possibly the jailer thinks of more worldly promotion to a better
office.

5.5. Location: Britain. The camp of King Cymbeline.

Whose rags shamed gilded arms, whose naked breast
Stepped before targes of proof, cannot be found.   5
He shall be happy that can find him, if
Our grace can make him so.
BELARIUS   I never saw   7
  Such noble fury in so poor a thing,
  Such precious deeds in one that promised naught
  But beggary and poor looks.
CYMBELINE   No tidings of him?
PISANIO
  He hath been searched among the dead and living,
  But no trace of him.
CYMBELINE   To my grief, I am
  The heir of his reward, [*To Belarius, Guiderius, and
      Arviragus*] which I will add
  To you, the liver, heart, and brain of Britain,   14
  By whom I grant she lives. 'Tis now the time
  To ask of whence you are. Report it.
BELARIUS   Sir,
  In Cambria are we born, and gentlemen.
  Further to boast were neither true nor modest,
  Unless I add we are honest.
CYMBELINE   Bow your knees.
                                   [*They kneel.*]
  Arise my knights o' the battle. I create you   20
  Companions to our person and will fit you
  With dignities becoming your estates.   [*They rise.*] 22

      Enter Cornelius and Ladies.

  There's business in these faces. Why so sadly
  Greet you our victory? You look like Romans,
  And not o' the court of Britain.
CORNELIUS   Hail, great King!
  To sour your happiness, I must report
  The Queen is dead.
CYMBELINE   Who worse than a physician   27
  Would this report become? But I consider   28

5 **targes of proof** shields hardened to withstand tests   7 **grace** favor
14 **liver, heart, and brain** i.e., heart and soul   20 **knights o' the battle**
knights created on the battlefield   22 **estates** i.e., new status   27-28
Who . . . become i.e., a report of death does not speak well for the
doctor, of all people

By med'cine life may be prolonged, yet death
Will seize the doctor too. How ended she?
CORNELIUS
With horror, madly dying, like her life,
Which, being cruel to the world, concluded
Most cruel to herself. What she confessed
I will report, so please you. These her women
Can trip me if I err, who with wet cheeks   35
Were present when she finished.
CYMBELINE   Prithee, say.
CORNELIUS
First, she confessed she never loved you, only
Affected greatness got by you, not you;   38
Married your royalty, was wife to your place,
Abhorred your person.
CYMBELINE   She alone knew this;
And, but she spoke it dying, I would not   41
Believe her lips in opening it. Proceed.   42
CORNELIUS
Your daughter, whom she bore in hand to love   43
With such integrity, she did confess
Was as a scorpion to her sight, whose life,
But that her flight prevented it, she had   46
Ta'en off by poison.
CYMBELINE   O most delicate fiend!   47
Who is 't can read a woman? Is there more?
CORNELIUS
More, sir, and worse. She did confess she had
For you a mortal mineral which, being took,   50
Should by the minute feed on life and, ling'ring,   51
By inches waste you. In which time she purposed,
By watching, weeping, tendance, kissing, to   53
O'ercome you with her show and, in fine,   54
When she had fitted you with her craft, to work   55
Her son into th' adoption of the crown;   56
But, failing of her end by his strange absence,

35 **trip** refute, contradict   **38 Affected** desired   **41 but** were it not
that   **42 opening** revealing   **43 bore in hand** pretended   **46 had** would
have   **47 Ta'en off** ended.   **delicate** subtle   **50 mortal mineral** deadly
poison   **51 by the minute** minute by minute   **53 tendance** attentiveness   **54 in fine** in conclusion   **55 fitted you** shaped you to her wish
56 adoption right of an adopted heir

Grew shameless desperate; opened, in despite   58
Of heaven and men, her purposes; repented   59
The evils she hatched were not effected; so
Despairing died.

CYMBELINE   Heard you all this, her women?

LADIES   We did, so please Your Highness.

CYMBELINE   Mine eyes
Were not in fault, for she was beautiful;
Mine ears, that heard her flattery; nor my heart,   65
That thought her like her seeming. It had been vicious 66
To have mistrusted her. Yet, O my daughter,
That it was folly in me thou mayst say,
And prove it in thy feeling. Heaven mend all!   69

> *Enter Lucius, Iachimo, [the Soothsayer,] and*
> *other Roman prisoners, [guarded; Posthumus]*
> *Leonatus behind, and Imogen.*

Thou com'st not, Caius, now for tribute. That
The Britons have rased out, though with the loss   71
Of many a bold one, whose kinsmen have made suit
That their good souls may be appeased with slaughter
Of you their captives, which ourself have granted.
So think of your estate.   75

LUCIUS
Consider, sir, the chance of war. The day
Was yours by accident. Had it gone with us,
We should not, when the blood was cool, have
    threatened
Our prisoners with the sword. But since the gods
Will have it thus, that nothing but our lives
May be called ransom, let it come. Sufficeth
A Roman with a Roman's heart can suffer.
Augustus lives to think on 't; and so much   83
For my peculiar care. This one thing only   84

---

58 opened revealed   **59 repented** regretted   **65 Mine . . . flattery** i.e., my
ears were not at fault, that heard her fine speeches (which we now
know to have been flattery)   **66 had been vicious** would have been
wrong   **69 in thy feeling** by feeling it, by what you have suffered
71 rased out erased   **75 estate** spiritual estate (in preparation for your
death)   **83 think on 't** i.e., consider what revenge to take   **84 my peculiar care** my concern for myself

I will entreat: my boy, a Briton born,
Let him be ransomed. Never master had
A page so kind, so duteous, diligent,
So tender over his occasions, true,   88
So feat, so nurselike. Let his virtue join   89
With my request, which I'll make bold Your Highness   90
Cannot deny. He hath done no Briton harm,
Though he have served a Roman. Save him, sir,
And spare no blood besides.

CYMBELINE   I have surely seen him;   93
His favor is familiar to me. Boy,   94
Thou hast looked thyself into my grace   95
And art mine own. I know not why, wherefore,
To say "Live, boy." Ne'er thank thy master. Live,   97
And ask of Cymbeline what boon thou wilt,   98
Fitting my bounty and thy state, I'll give it,
Yea, though thou do demand a prisoner,
The noblest ta'en.

IMOGEN   I humbly thank Your Highness.

LUCIUS
I do not bid thee beg my life, good lad,
And yet I know thou wilt.

IMOGEN   No, no, alack,
There's other work in hand. I see a thing   104
Bitter to me as death. Your life, good master,
Must shuffle for itself.

LUCIUS   The boy disdains me,
He leaves me, scorns me. Briefly die their joys   107
That place them on the truth of girls and boys.   108
Why stands he so perplexed?   [She studies Iachimo.]

CYMBELINE   What wouldst thou, boy?   109
I love thee more and more. Think more and more
What's best to ask. Know'st him thou look'st on? Speak,
Wilt have him live? Is he thy kin? Thy friend?

---

88 tender over his occasions solicitous of his master's needs   **89 feat**
adroit, neat   **90 make bold** venture   **93 And** even if (you)   **94 favor**
face   **95 looked . . . grace** won my favor by your appearance   **97 Ne'er**
thank thy master i.e., don't attribute your being saved to his request
98 ask if you ask   **104 thing** i.e., the ring on Iachimo's finger   **107–108**
Briefly . . . That swiftly die the joys of those who   **108 truth** fidelity
109 perplexed distressed

IMOGEN
    He is a Roman, no more kin to me
    Than I to Your Highness; who, being born your vassal, 114
    Am something nearer.
CYMBELINE   Wherefore ey'st him so?   115
IMOGEN
    I'll tell you, sir, in private, if you please
    To give me hearing.
CYMBELINE   Ay, with all my heart,
    And lend my best attention. What's thy name?
IMOGEN
    Fidele, sir.
CYMBELINE Thou'rt my good youth, my page;
    I'll be thy master. Walk with me; speak freely.
                    [*Cymbeline and Imogen converse apart.*]
BELARIUS [*To Arviragus and Guiderius*]
    Is not this boy revived from death?
ARVIRAGUS   One sand another   122
    Not more resembles that sweet rosy lad   123
    Who died, and was Fidele. What think you?   124
GUIDERIUS   The same dead thing alive.
BELARIUS
    Peace, peace! See further. He eyes us not; forbear.
    Creatures may be alike. Were 't he, I am sure
    He would have spoke to us.
GUIDERIUS   But we saw him dead.
BELARIUS
    Be silent; let's see further.
PISANIO [*Aside*]   It is my mistress.
    Since she is living, let the time run on   130
    To good or bad.
                    [*Cymbeline and Imogen come forward.*]
CYMBELINE   Come, stand thou by our side.   131
    Make thy demand aloud. [*To Iachimo.*] Sir, step you forth;
    Give answer to this boy, and do it freely,   133
    Or, by our greatness and the grace of it,   134

114 **who** i.e., I, Fidele   115 **something** somewhat   122–124 **One . . . died**
i.e., one grain of sand does not resemble another more than this youth
resembles the sweet rose-cheeked lad who died   130–131 **let . . . bad**
i.e., let come what must come   133 **freely** without reserve   134 **the
grace of** that which adorns

Which is our honor, bitter torture shall
Winnow the truth from falsehood.—On, speak to him.

IMOGEN
My boon is that this gentleman may render   137
Of whom he had this ring.
                    [*She points to the ring Iachimo wears.*]

POSTHUMUS [*Aside*]   What's that to him?

CYMBELINE
That diamond upon your finger, say
How came it yours?

IACHIMO
Thou'lt torture me to leave unspoken that   141
Which, to be spoke, would torture thee.

CYMBELINE   How? Me?

IACHIMO
I am glad to be constrained to utter that
Which torments me to conceal. By villainy
I got this ring. 'Twas Leonatus' jewel,
Whom thou didst banish; and—which more may grieve
    thee,
As it doth me—a nobler sir ne'er lived
Twixt sky and ground. Wilt thou hear more, my lord?

CYMBELINE
All that belongs to this.

IACHIMO   That paragon, thy daughter,
For whom my heart drops blood and my false spirits   150
Quail to remember—Give me leave; I faint.

CYMBELINE
My daughter? What of her? Renew thy strength.
I had rather thou shouldst live while nature will   153
Than die ere I hear more. Strive, man, and speak.

IACHIMO
Upon a time—unhappy was the clock
That struck the hour!—it was in Rome—accurst
The mansion where!—'twas at a feast—O, would
Our viands had been poisoned, or at least

---

137 render state   **141 to leave** for leaving, if I leave. (You'll torture me
to force me to talk, says Iachimo, when what I have to say will torture
you.)   **150 and** and whom   **153 live . . . will** continue to live as long as
nature permits (with your death sentence forgiven)

Those which I heaved to head!—the good Posthumus— 159
What should I say? He was too good to be
Where ill men were, and was the best of all
Amongst the rar'st of good ones—sitting sadly,
Hearing us praise our loves of Italy   163
For beauty that made barren the swelled boast   164
Of him that best could speak; for feature, laming   165
The shrine of Venus or straight-pight Minerva,   166
Postures beyond brief nature; for condition,   167
A shop of all the qualities that man   168
Loves woman for, besides that hook of wiving,   169
Fairness which strikes the eye—

CYMBELINE   I stand on fire.
Come to the matter.

IACHIMO   All too soon I shall,
Unless thou wouldst grieve quickly. This Posthumus,
Most like a noble lord in love and one
That had a royal lover, took his hint,   174
And not dispraising whom we praised—therein
He was as calm as virtue—he began
His mistress' picture; which by his tongue being made,
And then a mind put in 't, either our brags   178
Were cracked of kitchen trulls, or his description   179
Proved us unspeaking sots.

CYMBELINE   Nay, nay, to th' purpose. 180
IACHIMO
Your daughter's chastity—there it begins.
He spake of her as Dian had hot dreams   182
And she alone were cold; whereat I, wretch,
Made scruple of his praise and wagered with him   184

---

159 heaved to head raised to my lips   **163–168 Hearing . . . shop** hearing us offer high-flown praise of our Italian mistresses for beauty that made impotent even the exaggerated boast of our most eloquent speaker, for figures that made even the image of Venus in her temple or stately, straight-backed Minerva seem crippled by comparison—so beyond the hasty workmanship of nature were the carriages we ascribed to our mistresses—and for qualities of mind and character that constituted a virtual storehouse   **169 hook of wiving** bait for marriage   **174 hint** occasion   **178 put in 't** inserted into the picture   **179 cracked of** boastfully offered in praise of.   **kitchen trulls** kitchen maids   **180 unspeaking sots** inarticulate blockheads unable to describe our mistresses adequately   **182 as** as if   **184 Made scruple** expressed doubts

Pieces of gold 'gainst this which then he wore
Upon his honored finger, to attain
In suit the place of 's bed and win this ring   187
By hers and mine adultery. He, true knight,
No lesser of her honor confident
Than I did truly find her, stakes this ring;
And would so, had it been a carbuncle   191
Of Phoebus' wheel, and might so safely, had it   192
Been all the worth of 's car. Away to Britain   193
Post I in this design. Well may you, sir,   194
Remember me at court, where I was taught
Of your chaste daughter the wide difference   196
Twixt amorous and villainous. Being thus quenched
Of hope, not longing, mine Italian brain   198
'Gan in your duller Britain operate   199
Most vilely; for my vantage, excellent.   200
And, to be brief, my practice so prevailed   201
That I returned with simular proof enough   202
To make the noble Leonatus mad
By wounding his belief in her renown   204
With tokens thus and thus; averring notes   205
Of chamber hanging, pictures, this her bracelet—   206
          [*Showing the bracelet*]
Oh cunning, how I got it!—nay, some marks
Of secret on her person, that he could not
But think her bond of chastity quite cracked,
I having ta'en the forfeit. Whereupon—   210
Methinks I see him now—
POSTHUMUS [*Advancing*]   Ay, so thou dost,
Italian fiend! Ay me, most credulous fool,
Egregious murderer, thief, anything
That's due to all the villains past, in being,
To come! O, give me cord, or knife, or poison,
Some upright justicer! Thou, King, send out

---

187 In suit by urging my suit   **191 would so** would have done so
192 Phoebus' wheel i.e., the wheel of the sun-god's chariot   **193 's car**
his chariot   **194 Post** hasten   **196 Of** by   **198 not longing** though not of
my desire   **199 duller** i.e., slower-minded (supposedly caused by the
northern climate)   **200 vantage** profit   **201 practice** scheming
202 simular simulated, or pretended, plausible   **204 renown** good
name   **205 averring** avouching, citing   **206 hanging** hangings   **210 the
forfeit** i.e., what was forfeited by the breaking of her bond of chaste
loyalty

For torturers ingenious! It is I
That all th' abhorred things o' th' earth amend   218
By being worse than they. I am Posthumus,
That killed thy daughter—villain-like, I lie—
That caused a lesser villain than myself,
A sacrilegious thief, to do 't. The temple
Of virtue was she, yea, and she herself.   223
Spit, and throw stones, cast mire upon me, set
The dogs o' the street to bay me! Every villain
Be called Posthumus Leonatus, and
Be "villainy" less than 'twas! O Imogen!   227
My queen, my life, my wife! O Imogen,
Imogen, Imogen!
IMOGEN   Peace, my lord. Hear, hear—
POSTHUMUS
Shall 's have a play of this? Thou scornful page,   230
There lie thy part.   [*He strikes her; she falls.*]
PISANIO   O, gentlemen, help!   231
                              [*He goes to her assistance.*]
Mine and your mistress! O my lord Posthumus,
You ne'er killed Imogen till now. Help, help!
Mine honored lady!
CYMBELINE   Does the world go round?   234
POSTHUMUS
How comes these staggers on me?
PISANIO   Wake, my mistress!   235
CYMBELINE
If this be so, the gods do mean to strike me
To death with mortal joy.
PISANIO   How fares my mistress?
IMOGEN   O, get thee from my sight!
Thou gav'st me poison. Dangerous fellow, hence!
Breathe not where princes are.
CYMBELINE   . The tune of Imogen!   241

---

218 That . . . amend who make all loathsome things seem better in
comparison   **223 she herself** i.e., virtue herself   **227 Be . . . 'twas** let
the name "villainy" signify something less heinous than it used to
230 Shall 's shall we   **231 There lie thy part** your part is to lie there on
the ground   **234 Does . . . round** i.e., is the ground turning under my
feet. (An expression of dizziness.)   **235 staggers** dizziness, bewilderment   **241 tune** accent, voice

PISANIO Lady,
  The gods throw stones of sulfur on me if   243
  That box I gave you was not thought by me
  A precious thing. I had it from the Queen.
CYMBELINE
  New matter still?
IMOGEN   It poisoned me.
CORNELIUS   O gods!
  I left out one thing which the Queen confessed,
  [*To Pisanio*] Which must approve thee honest. "If
    Pisanio   248
  Have," she said, "given his mistress that confection   249
  Which I gave him for cordial, she is served
  As I would serve a rat."
CYMBELINE   What's this, Cornelius?
CORNELIUS
  The Queen, sir, very oft importuned me
  To temper poisons for her, still pretending   253
  The satisfaction of her knowledge only
  In killing creatures vile, as cats and dogs,
  Of no esteem. I, dreading that her purpose
  Was of more danger, did compound for her
  A certain stuff which, being ta'en, would cease   258
  The present power of life, but in short time
  All offices of nature should again
  Do their due functions.—Have you ta'en of it?
IMOGEN
  Most like I did, for I was dead.
BELARIUS   My boys,   262
  There was our error.
GUIDERIUS   This is, sure, Fidele.
IMOGEN [*To Posthumus*]
  Why did you throw your wedded lady from you?
  Think that you are upon a rock, and now   265
  Throw me again.   [*They embrace.*]
POSTHUMUS   Hang there like fruit, my soul,
  Till the tree die!

---

243 stones of sulfur thunderbolts **248 approve** prove **249 confection**
composition of drugs **253 temper** mix **258 cease** cause to cease
262 like likely **265 a rock** i.e., solid ground (?) (Some editors conjecture
lock, a wrestling embrace.)

CYMBELINE   How now, my flesh, my child?
　What, mak'st thou me a dullard in this act?   268
　Wilt thou not speak to me?
IMOGEN [*Kneeling*]   Your blessing, sir.
BELARIUS [*To Guiderius and Arviragus*]
　Though you did love this youth, I blame ye not,
　You had a motive for 't.
CYMBELINE   My tears that fall   271
　Prove holy water on thee! Imogen,
　Thy mother's dead.
IMOGEN [*Rising*]   I am sorry for 't, my lord.
CYMBELINE
　O, she was naught; and long of her it was   274
　That we meet here so strangely. But her son
　Is gone, we know not how nor where.
PISANIO   My lord,
　Now fear is from me, I'll speak truth. Lord Cloten,
　Upon my lady's missing, came to me
　With his sword drawn, foamed at the mouth, and swore
　If I discovered not which way she was gone   280
　It was my instant death. By accident
　I had a feignèd letter of my master's   282
　Then in my pocket, which directed him
　To seek her on the mountains near to Milford;
　Where, in a frenzy, in my master's garments,
　Which he enforced from me, away he posts
　With unchaste purpose and with oath to violate
　My lady's honor. What became of him
　I further know not.
GUIDERIUS   Let me end the story:
　I slew him there.
CYMBELINE   Marry, the gods forfend!   290
　I would not thy good deeds should from my lips   291
　Pluck a hard sentence. Prithee, valiant youth,
　Deny 't again.   293

---

268 mak'st . . . dullard do you treat me like a dolt (by leaving me out)
271 motive cause　**274 naught** wicked.　**long of** on account of　**280 discovered** disclosed　**282 feignèd** (Pisanio would not have wished to show Cloten the real letter, since it ordered Pisanio to kill Imogen.)　**290 forfend** forbid　**291 thy good deeds** i.e., you, who fought so valiantly against the Romans　**293 again** i.e., in speaking again and denying what you've just said

GUIDERIUS   I have spoke it, and I did it.
CYMBELINE   He was a prince.
GUIDERIUS
  A most incivil one. The wrongs he did me
  Were nothing princelike, for he did provoke me
  With language that would make me spurn the sea
  If it could so roar to me. I cut off 's head,
  And am right glad he is not standing here
  To tell this tale of mine.
CYMBELINE   I am sorrow for thee.   301
  By thine own tongue thou art condemned and must
  Endure our law. Thou'rt dead.
IMOGEN   That headless man
  I thought had been my lord.
CYMBELINE   Bind the offender
  And take him from our presence.
                    [*Guards start to bind Guiderius.*]
BELARIUS   Stay, sir King.
  This man is better than the man he slew,
  As well descended as thyself, and hath
  More of thee merited than a band of Clotens
  Had ever scar for. [*To the Guard.*] Let his arms alone;   309
  They were not born for bondage.
CYMBELINE   Why, old soldier,
  Wilt thou undo the worth thou art unpaid for
  By tasting of our wrath? How of descent
  As good as we?
ARVIRAGUS   In that he spake too far.
CYMBELINE [*To Belarius*]
  And thou shalt die for 't.
BELARIUS   We will die all three
  But I will prove that two on 's are as good   315
  As I have given out him. My sons, I must   316
  For mine own part unfold a dangerous speech,   317
  Though, haply, well for you.
ARVIRAGUS   Your danger's ours.

---

301 tell . . . mine i.e., tell of cutting off my head   **309 Had ever scar for**
ever merited by their battle scars   **315 But I will** if I do not.   **on 's** of
us   **316 given out** reported   **317 For . . . speech** unfold a speech that is
dangerous for me

GUIDERIUS
  And our good his.
BELARIUS   Have at it then, by leave.   319
  Thou hadst, great King, a subject who
  Was called Belarius.
CYMBELINE   What of him? He is
  A banished traitor.
BELARIUS   He it is that hath
  Assumed this age; indeed a banished man,   323
  I know not how a traitor.
CYMBELINE   Take him hence!
  The whole world shall not save him.
BELARIUS   Not too hot.
  First pay me for the nursing of thy sons,
  And let it be confiscate all so soon
  As I have received it.
CYMBELINE   Nursing of my sons?
BELARIUS
  I am too blunt and saucy. Here's my knee. [*He kneels.*]
  Ere I arise, I will prefer my sons;   330
  Then spare not the old father. Mighty sir,
  These two young gentlemen, that call me father
  And think they are my sons, are none of mine;
  They are the issue of your loins, my liege,
  And blood of your begetting.
CYMBELINE   How? My issue?
BELARIUS
  So sure as you your father's. I, old Morgan,
  Am that Belarius whom you sometime banished.
  Your pleasure was my mere offense, my punishment 338
  Itself, and all my treason; that I suffered   339
  Was all the harm I did. These gentle princes—   340
  For such and so they are—these twenty years   341
  Have I trained up; those arts they have as I

---

319 And our good his i.e., and whatever fortune comes to us we share
with him, Belarius. (Said perhaps to the King.) **Have at it** i.e., here
goes. **by leave** with your permission **323 Assumed** reached, at-
tained **330 prefer** promote **338–340 Your . . . did** i.e., what it pleased
you to denounce me for was all the offense I committed; so too my
punishment and my supposed treason were the creation of your royal
whim; what I suffered was the extent of my wrongdoing **340 gentle**
nobly born **341 such and so** i.e., both princes and gentle

Could put into them. My breeding was, sir, as
Your Highness knows. Their nurse, Euriphile,
Whom for the theft I wedded, stole these children
Upon my banishment. I moved her to 't,
Having received the punishment before
For that which I did then. Beaten for loyalty   348
Excited me to treason. Their dear loss,
The more of you 'twas felt, the more it shaped   350
Unto my end of stealing them. But, gracious sir,   351
Here are your sons again, and I must lose
Two of the sweet'st companions in the world.
The benediction of these covering heavens
Fall on their heads like dew! For they are worthy
To inlay heaven with stars.
CYMBELINE   Thou weep'st and speak'st.   356
The service that you three have done is more   357
Unlike than this thou tell'st. I lost my children;   358
If these be they, I know not how to wish
A pair of worthier sons.
BELARIUS [*Rising*]   Be pleased awhile.   360
This gentleman, whom I call Polydore,
Most worthy prince, as yours, is true Guiderius;
This gentleman, my Cadwal, Arviragus,
Your younger princely son. He, sir, was lapped   364
In a most curious mantle, wrought by th' hand   365
Of his queen mother, which for more probation   366
I can with ease produce.
CYMBELINE   Guiderius had
Upon his neck a mole, a sanguine star;   368
It was a mark of wonder.
BELARIUS   This is he,   369
Who hath upon him still that natural stamp.
It was wise nature's end in the donation   371

---

348 Beaten being beaten   **350 of** by   **350–351 shaped . . . of** fitted my
purpose in   **356 To . . . stars** to be inlaid in heaven, like stars
356–358 Thou . . . tell'st i.e., your weeping seems a testimony of the
truth of what you speak, and your story is in any event more credible—
strange though it seems—than the brave service you three did in battle. **Unlike** incredible   **360 Be pleased awhile** i.e., be so kind as to
listen a while longer   **364 lapped** enfolded   **365 curious** exquisitely
made   **366 probation** proof   **368 sanguine** blood-red   **369 of wonder**
wonderful   **371 end** aim, purpose. **in the donation** in giving it to him

To be his evidence now.

CYMBELINE   O, what, am I   372
A mother to the birth of three? Ne'er mother   373
Rejoiced deliverance more. Blest pray you be,   374
That, after this strange starting from your orbs,   375
You may reign in them now! O Imogen,   376
Thou hast lost by this a kingdom.

IMOGEN   No, my lord,
I have got two worlds by 't. O my gentle brothers,
Have we thus met? O, never say hereafter
But I am truest speaker. You called me brother,
When I was but your sister; I you brothers,
When ye were so indeed.

CYMBELINE   Did you e'er meet?

ARVIRAGUS
Ay, my good lord.

GUIDERIUS   And at first meeting loved;
Continued so until we thought he died.

CORNELIUS
By the Queen's dram she swallowed.

CYMBELINE   O rare instinct!
When shall I hear all through? This fierce abridgment   386
Hath to it circumstantial branches, which   387
Distinction should be rich in. Where, how lived you?   388
And when came you to serve our Roman captive?
How parted with your brothers? How first met them?
Why fled you from the court? And whither? These,
And your three motives to the battle, with   392
I know not how much more, should be demanded,
And all the other by-dependencies   394
From chance to chance; but nor the time nor place   395
Will serve our long interrogatories. See,
Posthumus anchors upon Imogen,
And she, like harmless lightning, throws her eye

---

372 his evidence evidence of his identity   **373–374 Ne'er . . . more** never
did deliverance (in childbed) more rejoice a mother   **375 starting . . .
orbs** shooting from your orbits, i.e., leaving your places at court
376 reign i.e., both as royal persons and as planets with influence
386 fierce abridgment drastically compressed account   **387–388 circumstantial . . . in** i.e., details and ramifications to be distinguished in
all their abundance   **392 your three motives** the motives of you three
394 by-dependencies attendant circumstances   **395 chance to chance**
event to event

On him, her brothers, me, her master, hitting
Each object with a joy; the counterchange 400
Is severally in all. Let's quit this ground 401
And smoke the temple with our sacrifices. 402
[*To Belarius*.] Thou art my brother; so we'll hold thee
　　ever.
IMOGEN [*To Belarius*]
　You are my father too, and did relieve me 404
　To see this gracious season.
CYMBELINE　　　　　　　All o'erjoyed, 405
Save these in bonds. Let them be joyful too,
For they shall taste our comfort.
IMOGEN [*To Lucius*]　　　　　My good master,
　I will yet do you service.
LUCIUS　　　　　　　Happy be you!
CYMBELINE
　The forlorn soldier, that so nobly fought, 409
　He would have well becomed this place and graced 410
　The thankings of a king.
POSTHUMUS　　　　　I am, sir,
The soldier that did company these three
In poor beseeming; 'twas a fitment for 413
The purpose I then followed. That I was he,
Speak, Iachimo. I had you down and might
Have made you finish.
IACHIMO [*Kneeling*]　　I am down again; 416
But now my heavy conscience sinks my knee, 417
As then your force did. Take that life, beseech you,
Which I so often owe; but your ring first; 419
And here the bracelet of the truest princess
That ever swore her faith. [*He gives ring and bracelet*.]
POSTHUMUS　　　　Kneel not to me.
The power that I have on you is to spare you;
The malice towards you to forgive you. Live,
And deal with others better.　　[*Iachimo rises*.]

400–401 the counterchange . . . all the exchange (of happy glances)
involves each of us to everyone else　**402 smoke** fill with incense
404 relieve bring rescue and deliverance to, as to a besieged town
405 To see so that I might see　**409 forlorn** lost, missing　**410 graced**
adorned　**413 beseeming** appearance.　**fitment** makeshift disguise　**416
made you finish** put an end to you　**417 sinks** causes to sink　**419 often**
many times over

CYMBELINE   Nobly doomed!   424
  We'll learn our freeness of a son-in-law;   425
  Pardon's the word to all.
ARVIRAGUS [*To Posthumus*]   You holp us, sir,   426
  As you did mean indeed to be our brother;   427
  Joyed are we that you are.
POSTHUMUS
  Your servant, princes. [*To Lucius.*] Good my lord of
    Rome,
  Call forth your soothsayer. As I slept, methought
  Great Jupiter, upon his eagle backed,
  Appeared to me, with other spritely shows   432
  Of mine own kindred. When I waked, I found
  This label on my bosom [*Showing tablet*], whose
    containing   434
  Is so from sense in hardness that I can   435
  Make no collection of it. Let him show   436
  His skill in the construction.
LUCIUS   Philarmonus!   437
SOOTHSAYER
  Here, my good lord.
LUCIUS   Read, and declare the meaning.
SOOTHSAYER (*Reads*) "Whenas a lion's whelp shall, to
  himself unknown, without seeking find and be em-
  braced by a piece of tender air; and when from a stately
  cedar shall be lopped branches which, being dead
  many years, shall after revive, be jointed to the old
  stock, and freshly grow; then shall Posthumus end his
  miseries, Britain be fortunate and flourish in peace
  and plenty."
  Thou, Leonatus, art the lion's whelp;
  The fit and apt construction of thy name,
  Being Leo-natus, doth import so much.   449
  [*To Cymbeline.*] The piece of tender air, thy virtuous
    daughter,

---

424 doomed decreed, judged   **425 freeness** liberality, generosity
426 holp helped   **427 As** as if   **432 spritely** ghostly, in the form of
spirits.   **shows** appearances   **434 label** tablet, paper   **434–435 whose
. . . hardness** whose meaning is so remote from sense in its difficulty
436 collection of inference or deduction from   **437 construction** con-
struing of it   **449 Leo-natus** one born of the lion

Which we call *"mollis aer,"* and *"mollis aer"*   451
We term it *"mulier";* which *"mulier"* I divine
Is this most constant wife; who, even now,   453
Answering the letter of the oracle,   [*To Posthumus*] 454
Unknown to you, unsought, were clipped about   455
With this most tender air.

CYMBELINE   This hath some seeming.   456

SOOTHSAYER
The lofty cedar, royal Cymbeline,
Personates thee, and thy lopped branches point
Thy two sons forth; who, by Belarius stolen,
For many years thought dead, are now revived,
To the majestic cedar joined, whose issue
Promises Britain peace and plenty.

CYMBELINE   Well,
My peace we will begin. And, Caius Lucius,
Although the victor, we submit to Caesar
And to the Roman empire, promising
To pay our wonted tribute, from the which
We were dissuaded by our wicked queen,
Whom heavens in justice both on her and hers   468
Have laid most heavy hand.

SOOTHSAYER
The fingers of the powers above do tune
The harmony of this peace. The vision
Which I made known to Lucius ere the stroke
Of this yet scarce-cold battle at this instant
Is full accomplished; for the Roman eagle,
From south to west on wing soaring aloft,
Lessened herself, and in the beams o' the sun   476
So vanished; which foreshowed our princely eagle,   477
Th' imperial Caesar, should again unite
His favor with the radiant Cymbeline,
Which shines here in the west.

CYMBELINE   Laud we the gods,   480

451 mollis aer tender air. (A fanciful derivation of Latin *mulier,*
woman.)   **453 who** (Perhaps referring to Posthumus, but the grammar
is loose and the point of reference may shift after l. 454.)   **454 Answering** corresponding with   **455 were clipped about** i.e., you were embraced   **456 seeming** plausibility   **468 Whom** on whom.   **hers** i.e.,
Cloten   **476 Lessened herself** i.e., grew smaller to sight   **477 foreshowed** foreshowed that   **480 Laud** praise

And let our crooked smokes climb to their nostrils   481
From our blest altars. Publish we this peace
To all our subjects. Set we forward. Let
A Roman and a British ensign wave
Friendly together. So through Lud's Town march,
And in the temple of great Jupiter
Our peace we'll ratify, seal it with feasts.
Set on there! Never was a war did cease,   488
Ere bloody hands were washed, with such a peace.   489

Exeunt.

---

481 **crooked** curling, twining   488 **Set on there** forward march.   **was a war** was there a war that   489 **Ere . . . washed** before hands were washed in blood or free of blood

Date and Text

Cymbeline was first printed in the First Folio of 1623, where it was included among the tragedies. The text, a good one, was evidently set from a careful transcript (perhaps by the scrivener Ralph Crane) of an earlier transcript, derived either from Shakespeare's own papers or from a theatrical promptbook that had incorporated many authorial stage directions. The first recorded performance was in 1611. Dr. Simon Forman, a quack astrologer, jotted down a description of *Cymbeline* in his commonplace book for that year; and, although he did not record the actual date he saw the play, he must have done so some time between April and his sudden death on September 8 of that year. Stylistically the play appears to follow *Pericles* (c. 1606–1608) and to precede *The Winter's Tale* (c. 1610–1611). Dating must be considered approximate.

Textual Notes

These textual notes are not a historical collation, either of the early folios or of more recent editions; they are simply a record of departures in this edition from the copy text. The reading adopted in this edition appears in boldface, followed by the rejected reading from the copy text, i.e., the First Folio. Only major alterations in punctuation are noted. Changes in lineation are not indicated, nor are some minor and obvious typographical errors.

Abbreviations used:
F the First Folio
s.d. stage direction
s.p. speech prefix

Copy text: the First Folio.

1.1. 59 swaddling-clothes the other, swathing cloathes, the other   **70** [F begins "Scena Secunda" here]   **98 Philario's** Filorio's   **118 cere** seare   **160 s.d. Enter Pisanio** [after *Exit*, l. 160 in F]

1.2 [F labels "Scena Tertia"]

1.3 [F labels "Scena Quarta"]   **9 this** his

1.4 [F labels "Scena Quinta"]   **28 Briton** Britaine   **46–47 offend not** offend   **72 Britain** Britanie   **others** others.   **74 but believe** beleeue   **84–85 purchase** purchases   **128 thousand** thousands   **136–137 preserve** preseure

1.5 [F labels "Scena Sexta"]   **3 s.d. Exeunt** Exit   **77 s.d. Exit Pisanio** [after l. 76 in F]   **87 s.d. Exeunt** Exit

1.6 [F labels "Scena Septima"]   **7 desire** desires   **28 takes** take   **36 th' unnumbered** the number'd   **67 Briton** Britaine [and so elsewhere for nominative form]   **104 Fixing** Fiering   **109 illustrous** illustrious   **169 men's** men   **170 descended** defended

2.1. 27 your you   **34 tonight** night   **51 s.d. Exeunt** Exit   **62 divorce he'd make!** diuorce, heel'd make   **65 s.d. Exit** Exeunt

2.2. 1 s.p. Helen La [also at l. 2]   **49 bare** beare   **51 s.d. Exeunt** Exit

2.3. 20 s.p. Musician [not in F]   **29 s.p. Cloten** [not in F]   **30 vice** voyce   **32 amend** amed   **48 solicits** solicity   **130 envy, if** Enuie. If   **139 garment** Garments   **156 you** your

2.4. 6 hopes hope   **18 legions** Legion   **24 mingled** wing-led   **34 through** thorough   **37 s.p. Philario** Post   **48 not** note   **58 you** yon   **60 loses** looses   **63 near** nere   **127 lose** loose   **138 the** her

2.5. 16 German one Iarmen on   **27 have a name** name

3.1. 20 rocks Oakes   **53 be. We do say** be, we do. Say

3.2. 2 monster's her accuser Monsters her accuse   **67 score** store   **ride** rid   **78 here, nor** heere, not

3.3. 2 Stoop Sleepe   **23 bauble** Babe   **28 know** knowes   **31 known, well** knowne. Well   **34 for** or   **83 wherein they** whereon the   **86 Polydore** Pala-dour   **106 Morgan** Mergan

3.4. 79 afore 't a-foot   **90 make** makes   **102 blind first** first

3.5. 17 s.d. Exeunt Exit   **32 looks** looke   **40 strokes** stroke;,   **42 s.p. Attendant** Mes   **55 s.d. Exit** [after "days" in F]   **141–142 insultment** insulment

3.6. 27 [F begins "Scena Septima" here]

3.7 [F labels "Scena Octaua"]   **9 commends** commands

4.1. 18 her face thy face

4.2. 50–52 He . . . dieter [assigned in F to Arviragus]   **58 him** them   **59 Grow, patience** Grow patient   **124 thanks, ye** thanks the   **134 humor** Honor   **188 ingenious** ingenuous   **207 crare** care   **208 Might** Might'st   **226 ruddock** Raddocke   **293 is** are   **294 s.p. Imogen** [not in F]   **339 are** are heere

4.3. 40 betid betide

4.4. 2 find we we finde   **17 the** their   **27 hard** heard

5.1. 1 wished am wisht

5.3. 24 harts hearts   **42 stooped** stopt   **43 they** the   **47 before, some** before some

5.4. 1 s.p. [and throughout scene] First Jailer Gao   **50 deserved** d seru'd   **81 look** looke, looke   **165 Of** Oh, of   **169 sir** Sis   **197 s.d. Exeunt** [at l. 206 in F]

5.5. 54 fine time   **62 s.p. Ladies** La   **65 heard** heare   **128 saw** see   **136 On** one   **207 got it** got   **264 from** fro   **315 on 's** one's   **319 leave.** leaue   **338 mere** neere   **339 treason;** Treason   **382 ye** we   **390 brothers** Brother   **391 whither? These,** whether these?   **392 battle,** Battaile?   **395 chance;** chance?   **409 so** no   **439 s.d. Soothsayer** [not in F]   **473 this yet** yet this

Shakespeare's Sources

Cymbeline deals with legendary and romantic history in which traces of historical events can still be dimly perceived. A Cunobelinus, or Cymbeline, was in fact leader of the Celtic chieftains in southeast England during the period of Roman hegemony there, following Julius Caesar's invasion of the island in 54 B.C. Cunobelinus ruled from about 5 to 40 A.D., with his capital at Camulodunum (Colchester). He was a friend and ally of Augustus Caesar and enjoyed a peaceful reign. When the kingdom had passed to his sons (one of whom apparently was Caractacus), the Romans under Claudius pursued once again their conquest of England and subdued much of the southeast, though Caractacus escaped to Wales and became a leader of the resistance.

Beginning with Geoffrey of Monmouth's *Historia Regum Britanniae* (c. 1136), King Kymbelinus becomes a quasi-legendary figure. Geoffrey adds him to the genealogy of kings (along with Leir, Locrine, et al.) descended from Aeneas' great-grandson Brut, the mythical founder of Britain. Kymbelinus' reign was peaceful, according to Geoffrey, since the King, having been raised in Augustus Caesar's household, willingly paid tribute to Rome without being asked. When Kymbelinus' elder son Guiderius succeeded to the throne, however, said Geoffrey, he defied the Emperor Claudius over the tribute. Guiderius fell in battle and was succeeded by his brother Arviragus, who more than held his own against Claudius, eventually settling matters by negotiation.

By the time of Raphael Holinshed's *Chronicles* (1587 edition), the facts are badly confused. As can be seen in the selection that follows, Holinshed admits he cannot be sure whether Kymbeline or some other British leader fought against Augustus Caesar, or whether Kymbeline paid tribute; he does report that Guiderius fought Augustus Caesar (rather than Claudius), but is uncertain as to whether the Romans lost or won. Edmund Spenser's *The Faerie Queene* (2.10.50–51) affirms that Kimbeline fought the Romans over tribute and was slain in battle, whereupon his brother Aviragus took his place and compelled the Roman Claudius to a peace. (In other words, Spenser has conflated Cymbeline and Guiderius.) Shakespeare, like Spenser, imagines the great struggle with Rome and subsequent peace settlement to have taken place during Cymbeline's reign; following Holinshed, he assumes that Rome was then governed by Augustus Caesar. Shakespeare also seems to have consulted a vivid account of the battle in Thomas Blenerhasset's contribution to the *Second Part of the Mirror for Magistrates* (1578) and another account of Cymbeline's reign by John Higgins in the 1587 *Mirror for Magistrates*. Finally, Shakespeare turned for his background material to quite a different story in Holinshed, concerning a Scottish farmer named Hay who with his two sons helped defend Scotland against the Danes in 976. Shakespeare presumably found this story when reading for *Macbeth*, since it stands between the two accounts—Donwald's murder of Duff and Macbeth's murder of Duncan—that Shakespeare used in writing *Macbeth*. The exploits of Hay and his two sons resemble those of Belarius and the two princes in the final battle of *Cymbeline*.

The quasi-historical setting accounts for only a small part of *Cymbeline*, and Shakespeare had no special reason to set the facts straight. Most of his material is, after all, romantic. The central plot of a wager over a wife's virtue may have come from Giovanni Boccaccio's *Decameron*, ninth tale of the second day, although as a type this ancient story was widespread and presumably available to Shakespeare in many forms. Earlier versions include the thirteenth-century French *Roi Flore et la belle Jeanne*, the *Roman de la Violette* by Gerbert de Montreuil, a miracle play by Gautier de Coincy, and others. Boccaccio was available to Shakespeare in French translation but not in English. (It is provided here in an anonymous English translation of 1620.)

A summary of Boccaccio's story suggests a number of particulars to which Shakespeare was indebted. Boccaccio tells of an Italian merchant, Bernabò of Genoa, who, at a gathering in Paris of fellow merchants discussing the wantonness of their wives, dares to affirm the absolute chastity of his own wife, Zinevra. A young merchant, Ambrogiuolo, makes a wager that he can seduce Zinevra and return with proof in three months. Going at once to Genoa, Ambrogiuolo discovers that Zinevra is indeed incorruptible. He therefore bribes an elderly lady, whom Zinevra has befriended, to convey him hidden in a chest to the lady's bedroom. When the lady is asleep he steals forth from hiding, memorizes details of her room, notes particularly a mole upon her left breast, and takes with him a purse, gown, ring, and sash. Returning to Paris, he convinces his fellow merchants and Bernabò that he has succeeded. Bernabò hereupon travels to within a few miles of Genoa, summons his wife, and secretly orders his servant to kill her on the way. The servant is reluctant to do so, however, and gladly takes only her cloak as evidence of having finished the job. Zinevra now makes her way disguised as a man to Alexandria and enters the service of the Sultan. One day she happens to recognize her own purse and sash in a Venetian clothes shop in Palestine, inquires as to their owner, meets Ambrogiuolo in this way (who has journeyed to Palestine selling merchandise), and hears from Ambrogiuolo's own boastful lips the story of his treachery. She cannily manages to bring Ambrogiuolo and Bernabò before the Sultan, throws off her male disguise, and reveals the whole story. She pardons Bernabò and is reunited with him, but Ambrogiuolo is sentenced by the Sultan to be tied to a stake, smeared with honey, and left to be devoured by insects.

Shakespeare has altered the setting and has surrounded the story with other matters such as King Cymbeline's lost sons, his quarrel with Rome, his difficulties with his queen and her son, Cloten, and the like. Shakespeare's ending is much more forgiving toward Iachimo than in the narrative source. The circumstances of the denouement are changed. Still, the plot of Posthumus, Imogen, and Iachimo is extensively indebted to Boccaccio.

Shakespeare seems also to have known an English version, *Frederyke of Jennen* (Antwerp, 1518; London, 1520 and 1560), translated from the Dutch. In some details it is closer to Shakespeare's play than is Boccaccio's story. For example, the merchants who witness the wager include a Spaniard, a Frenchman, a Florentine, and a Genoese (cf. 1.4). Three of these merchants are not present when the villain returns to prove his victory, just as in Act 2, scene 4, of Shakespeare's play. Also, the husband repents even before learning of his wife's innocence, as does Posthumus. Shakespeare greatly accentuates this motif of penance and forgiveness. Another source is a romantic play called *The Rare Triumphs of Love and Fortune*, acted before Elizabeth in 1582, in which the princess Fidelia is banished by her father for loving Hermione, is betrayed and pursued by her boorish brother, Armenio (cf. Cloten), and is hospitably received by a banished courtier named Bomelio who lives hermitlike in a cave. "Fidele" is the name used by Shakespeare's Imogen to disguise her identity. Folk motifs are apparent throughout *Cymbeline*; the cruel Queen inevitably reminds us of Snow White's stepmother. Although Shakespeare may not have been acquainted with that particular story, he clearly was interested in folk legend when he wrote *Cymbeline*. One other anonymous romantic play, *Sir Clyomon and Sir Clamydes* (c. 1570–1583), may have given Shakespeare some suggestions for his Welsh scenes.

Francis Beaumont and John Fletcher's *Philaster* was written about the same time as *Cymbeline* and is sometimes thought to resemble Shakespeare's play. Philaster is, like Posthumus, in love with a princess whose father intends her for another suitor. Still, most of the similarities can be attributed to the conventions of the romance genre just then coming into vogue. In any case, no one can be sure whether Shakespeare's play came after or before *Philaster*. It may well be that Shakespeare was the innovator.

The First and Second Volumes
of Chronicles (1587 edition)
Compiled by Raphael Holinshed

VOLUME 1, THE HISTORY OF ENGLAND
THE THIRD BOOK, THE EIGHTEENTH CHAPTER

Kymbeline, or Cymbeline, the son of Theomantius, was of the Britons made king after the decease of his father in the year of the world 3944,[1] after the building of Rome 728, and before the birth of our Savior 33. This man, as some write, was brought up at Rome and there made knight by Augus-

---

1 3944 (This date is from the assumed date of the creation of the world by God as recorded in Genesis 1.)

tus Caesar, under whom he served in the wars, and was in
such favor with him that he was at liberty to pay his tribute
or not. Little other mention is made of his doings except
that during his reign the Savior of the world, our Lord Jesus
Christ, the only son of God, was born of a virgin about the
twenty-third year of the reign of this Kymbeline.... Touching the continuance of the years of Kymbeline's reign some
writers do vary, but the best-approved affirm that
he reigned thirty-five years and then died and was buried
at London, leaving behind him two sons, Guiderius and
Arviragus.

But here is to be noted that, although our histories do
affirm that as well this Kymbeline as also[2] his father
Theomantius lived in quiet with the Romans and continually to them paid the tributes which the Britons had cove-
nanted with Julius Caesar to pay, yet we find in the Roman
writers that after Julius Caesar's death, when Augustus had
taken upon him the rule of the Empire, the Britons refused
to pay that tribute. Whereat, as Cornelius Tacitus[3] report-
eth, Augustus, being otherwise occupied, was contented to
wink. Howbeit, through earnest calling upon to recover his
right by such as were desirous to see the uttermost of the
British kingdom,[4] at length, to wit in the tenth year after the
death of Julius Caesar, which was about the thirteenth year
of the said Theomantius, Augustus made provision to pass
with an army over into Britain and was come forward upon
his journey into Gallia Celtica or, as we may say, into these
hither parts of France.

But here receiving advertisements[5] that the Pannonians,
which inhabited the country now called Hungary, and the
Dalmatians, whom now we call Slavonians, had rebelled, he
thought it best first to subdue those rebels near home
rather than to seek new countries and leave such in hazard
whereof he had present possession. And so, turning his
power against the Pannonians and Dalmatians, he left off
for a time the wars of Britain.... By our writers it is re-

2 as well . . . as also both this Kymbeline and   3 Cornelius Tacitus
(c. A.D. 55–117), author of histories and annals of Rome during his
lifetime and shortly before   4 through earnest . . . kingdom i.e., as a
result of his (Augustus') being earnestly urged by those who wished to
see the British kingdom brought low to claim once again his rights in
Britain.   uttermost end   5 advertisements notice, information

ported that Kymbeline, being brought up in Rome and
knighted in the court of Augustus, ever showed himself a
friend to the Romans and chiefly was loath to break with
them because[6] the youth of the Briton nation should not be
deprived of the benefit to be trained and brought up among
the Romans, whereby they might learn both to behave themselves like civil[7] men and to attain to the knowledge of feats
of war.

But whether for this respect or for that it pleased the almighty God so to dispose the minds of men at that present,
not only the Britons but in manner all other nations were
contented to be obedient to the Roman Empire. That this
was true in the Britons, it is evident enough by Strabo's[8]
words, which are in effect as followeth. "At this present,"
saith he, "certain princes of Britain, procuring by ambassadors and dutiful demeanors the amity of the Emperor Augustus, have offered in the Capitol unto the gods presents or
gifts, and have ordained[9] the whole isle in a manner to be
appertinent, proper, and familiar to the Romans. They are
burdened with sore customs which they pay for wares, either to be sent forth into Gallia or brought from thence,
which are commonly ivory vessels, shears, ouches[10] or ear-
rings, and other conceits[11] made of amber and glasses, and
suchlike manner of merchandise. So that now there is no
need of any army or garrison of men-of-war to keep the isle,
for there needeth not past one legion of footmen, or some
wing of horsemen, to gather up and receive the tribute. . . ."
Thus far Strabo.

THE NINETEENTH CHAPTER

Guiderius, the first son of Kymbeline (of whom Harrison[12] saith nothing), began his reign in the seventeenth year
after the incarnation of Christ. This Guiderius, being a man

---

6 because in order that   **7 civil** civilized, well-bred   **8 Strabo** a Stoic
and a traveler, c. 64 B.C.–A.D. 19, who described the geography of the
important countries of the Roman Empire; an authority on Britain like
the historian Tacitus mentioned two paragraphs previously   **9 ordained**
governed   **10 ouches** brooches   **11 conceits** trifles, fancy articles
12 Harrison William Harrison, author of *The Description of England*,
printed in Holinshed's *Chronicles*

of stout[13] courage, gave occasion of breach of peace betwixt
the Britons and Romans, denying to pay them tribute and
procuring the people to new insurrections which by one
means or other made open rebellion, as Gildas[14] saith.

. . . . .

VOLUME 2, THE HISTORY OF SCOTLAND

[The following account from the reign of Kenneth, son of
Malcolm, in 976, is historically unconnected with Cymbeline but does provide an account of Hay and his sons in battle that resembles the deeds of Belarius, Arviragus, and
Guiderius in Shakespeare's play. King Kenneth's army is
defending Scotland against a Danish invasion.]

The Danes, being backed with the mountain, were constrained to leave the same and with all speed to come forward upon their enemies, that by joining they might avoid
the danger of the Scottishmen's arrows and darts. By this
means therefore they came to hand strokes, in manner before the sign was given on either part to the battle. The fight
was cruel on both sides, and nothing hindered the Scots so
much as going about to cut off the heads of the Danes ever
as they might overcome them.[15] Which manner being noted
of the Danes, and perceiving that there was no hope of life
but in victory, they rushed forth with such violence upon
their adversaries that first the right and then after the left
wing[16] of the Scots was constrained to retire and flee back,
the middleward[17] stoutly yet keeping their ground; but the
same[18] stood in such danger, being now left naked[19] on the
sides, that the victory must needs have remained with the
Danes had not a renewer of the battle come in time by
the appointment, as is to be thought, of almighty God.

For as it chanced, there was in the next field at the same
time an husbandman,[20] with two of his sons busy about his
work, named Hay, a man strong and stiff in making and
shape of body but endued with a valiant courage. This Hay,
beholding the King with the most part of the nobles fight-

13 stout brave   14 Gildas early British historian, c. 516–570   15 ever
as . . . them whenever they overcame any in battle   16 wing flank
17 middleward main body of soldiers   18 the same i.e., the main body
of troops   19 naked exposed   20 husbandman farmer

ing with great valiancy in the middleward, now destitute of
the wings and in great danger to be oppressed by the great
violence of his enemies, caught a plow beam in his hand
and, with the same exhorting his sons to do the like, hasted
towards the battle, there to die rather amongst other[21] in
defense of his country than to remain alive after the
discomfiture, in miserable thralldom and bondage, of the
cruel and most unmerciful enemies. There was near to the
place of the battle a long lane fenced on the sides with
ditches and walls made of turf, through the which the Scots
which fled were beaten down by the enemies on heaps.

Here Hay with his sons, supposing they might best stay[22]
the flight, placed themselves overthwart the lane, beat them
back whom they met fleeing, and spared neither friend nor
foe; but down they went, all such as came within their
reach, wherewith divers hardy personages cried unto their
fellows to return back unto the battle, for there was a new
power of Scottishmen come to their succors by whose aid
the victory might be easily obtained of their most cruel adversaries the Danes. Therefore might they choose whether
they would be slain of their own fellows coming to their aid,
or to return again to fight with the enemies. The Danes, being here stayed in the lane by the great valiancy of the
father and the sons, thought verily there had been some
great succors of Scots come to the aid of their king, and
thereupon ceasing from further pursuit fled back in great
disorder unto the other of their fellows fighting with the
middleward of the Scots.

The Scots also that before was chased, being encouraged
herewith, pursued the Danes unto the place of the battle
right fiercely. Whereupon Kenneth, perceiving his people
to be thus recomforted and his enemies partly abashed,[23]
called upon his men to remember their duties; and now,
sith[24] their adversaries' hearts began, as they might perceive, to faint, he willed them to follow upon them manfully, which if they did he assured them that the victory
undoubtedly should be theirs. The Scots, encouraged with
the King's words, laid about them so earnestly that in the
end the Danes were constrained to forsake the field, and the

21 other others   22 stay halt   23 abashed discomfited, confounded
24 sith since

Scots, eagerly pursuing in the chase, made great slaughter of them as they fled. This victory turned highly to the praise of the Scottish nobility, the which, fighting in the middle-ward, bare[25] still the brunt of the battle, continuing manfully therein even to the end. But Hay, who in such wise as is before mentioned stayed them that fled, causing them to return again to the field, deserved immortal fame and commendation, for by his means chiefly was the victory achieved. And therefore, on the morrow after, when the spoil of the field and of the enemies' camp (which they had left void) should be divided, the chiefest part was bestowed on him and his two sons by consent of all the multitude, the residue being divided amongst the soldiers and men-of-war according to the ancient custom used amongst this nation.

The second edition of Raphael Holinshed's *Chronicles* was published in 1587. This selection is based on that edition, Volume 1, *The History of England*, folios 32–33, and Volume 2, *The History of Scotland*, folio 155.

from The Decameron
By Giovanni Boccaccio

THE SECOND DAY, NINTH NOVEL
THE STORY OF BERNABÒ AND ZINEVRA

Bernabò, a merchant of Genoa, being deceived by another merchant named Ambrogiuolo, lost a great part of his goods; and commanding his innocent wife to be murdered, she escaped and in the habit of a man became servant to the Sultan. The deceiver being found at last, she compassed such means that her husband Bernabò came into Alexandria; and there, after due punishment inflicted on the false deceiver, she resumed the garments again of a woman and returned home with her husband to Genoa. Wherein is declared that, by overliberal commending the chastity of women, it falleth out oftentimes to be very dangerous, especially by the means of treacherers,[1] who yet in the end are justly punished for their treachery.

25 bare bore

1 treacherers deceivers

There was a fair and good inn in Paris, much frequented by many great Italian merchants, according to such variety of occasions and business as urged their often resorting thither. One night among many other, having had a merry supper together, they began to discourse on divers matters; and falling from one relation[2] to another, they communed[3] in very friendly manner concerning their wives left at home in their houses. Quoth the first: "I cannot well imagine what my wife is now doing. But I am able to say for myself that if a pretty female should fall into my company, I could easily forget my love to my wife and make use of such an advantage offered."

A second replied: "And, trust me, I should do no less, because I am persuaded that, if my wife be willing to wander, the law is in her own hand, and I am far enough from home. Dumb walls blab no tales, and offenses unknown are seldom or never called in question."

A third man jumped* in censure with[4] his former fellows of the jury. And it plainly appeared that all the rest were of the same opinion, condemning their wives overrashly and alleging that, when husbands strayed so far from home, their wives had wit enough to make use of their time.

Only one man among them all, named Bernabò Lomellino and dwelling in Genoa, maintained the contrary, boldly avouching that by the especial favor of Fortune he had a wife so perfectly complete in all graces and virtues as any lady in the world possibly could be and that Italy scarcely contained her equal. For she was goodly of person[5] and yet very young, quick, quaint,[6] mild, and courteous; and not anything appertaining to the office of a wife, either for domestic affairs or any other employment whatsoever, but in womanhood she went beyond all other. No lord, knight, esquire, or gentleman could be better served at his table than himself daily was, with more wisdom, modesty, and discretion. After all this he praised her for riding, hawking, hunting, fishing, fowling, reading, writing, inditing,[7] and most absolute[8] keeping his books of accounts, that neither himself or any other merchant could therein excel her. After in-

2 relation account, conversation **3 communed** conversed **4 jumped in censure with** readily joined in the judgment of **5 goodly of person** physically attractive **6 quaint** wise, clever **7 inditing** writing down, composing **8 absolute** consummate, accurate and complete

finite other commendations he came to the former point of
their argument, concerning the easy falling of women into
wantonness, maintaining with a solemn oath that no
woman possibly could be more chaste and honest[9] than she;
in which respect he was verily persuaded that if he stayed
from her ten years' space—yea, all his lifetime—out of his
house, yet never would she falsify her faith to him or be
lewdly allured[10] by any other man.

Among these merchants thus communing together there
was a young proper[11] man named Ambrogiuolo of Piacenza,
who began to laugh at the last praises which Bernabò had
used of his wife and, seeming to make a mockery thereat,
demanded if the Emperor had given him this privilege
above all other married men. Bernabò, being somewhat offended, answered: "No emperor hath done it, but the especial blessing of heaven, exceeding all the emperors on the
earth in grace, and thereby have I* received this favor."

Whereto Ambrogiuolo presently[12] thus replied: "Bernabò, without all question to the contrary I believe that
what thou hast said is true. But for aught I can perceive,
thou hast slender judgment in the nature of things, because
if thou didst observe them well, thou couldst not be of so
gross understanding. For by comprehending matters in
their true kind and nature, thou wouldst speak of them
more correctly than thou dost. And to the end thou mayst
not imagine that we who have spoken of our wives do think
any otherwise of them than as well and honestly as thou
canst of thine, nor that anything else did urge these
speeches of them, or falling into this kind of discourse, but
only by a natural instinct and admonition, I will proceed
familiarly a little further with thee upon the matter already
propounded.

"I have evermore understood that man was the most noble creature formed by God to live in this world, and woman
in the next degree to him. But man, as generally is believed
and as is discerned by apparent effects,[13] is the most perfect
of both. Having then the most perfection in him, without all
doubt he must be so much the more firm and constant. So
in like manner it hath been and is universally granted that

9 **honest** chaste, faithful   10 **allured** tempted   11 **proper** handsome
12 **presently** at once   13 **apparent effects** obvious and visible signs

woman is more various and mutable, and the reason thereof may be approved[14] by many natural circumstances, which were needless now to make any mention of. If a man then be possessed of the greater stability and yet cannot contain himself from condescending,[15] I say not to one that entreats him,[16] but to desire any other that may please him, and, besides, to covet the enjoying of his own pleasing contentment (a thing not chancing to him once in a month but infinite times in a day's space), what can you then conceive of a frail woman, subject by nature to entreaties, flatteries, gifts, persuasions, and a thousand other enticing means which a man that is affected[17] to her can use? Dost thou think then that she hath any power to contain?[18]

"Assuredly, though thou shouldst rest so resolved,[19] yet cannot I be of the same opinion. For I am sure thou believest, and must needs confess it, that thy wife is a woman made of flesh and blood as other women are. If it be so, she cannot be without the same desires and the weakness or strength as other women have to resist such natural appetites as her own are. In regard whereof, it is merely[20] impossible, although she be most honest, but[21] she must needs do that which other women do. For there is nothing else possible, either to be denied or affirmed to the contrary, as thou most unadvisedly hast done."

Bernabò answered in this manner: "I am a merchant and no philosopher, and like a merchant I mean to answer thee. I am not to learn[22] that these accidents by thee related may happen to fools who are void of understanding or shame. But such as are wise and endued with virtue have always such a precious esteem of their honor that they will contain those principles of constancy which men are merely[23] careless of; and I justify[24] my wife to be one of them."

"Believe me, Bernabò," replied Ambrogiuolo, "if so often as thy wife's mind is addicted to wanton folly a badge of

---

14 **approved** proven, demonstrated   15 **contain . . . condescending** prevent himself from stooping   16 **I say . . . entreats him** i.e., not even to mention being able to resist a woman who openly approaches him   17 **affected** attracted   18 **contain** be continent, chaste   19 **rest so resolved** remain of that opinion   20 **merely** utterly   21 **honest, but** chaste, but that   22 **I . . . learn** I do not need to be told   23 **men are merely** ordinary men are   24 **justify** maintain, affirm

scorn[25] should arise on thy forehead to render testimony of
her female frailty, I believe the number of them would be
more than willingly you would wish them to be. And among
all married men in every degree the notes[26] are so secret of
their wives' imperfections that the sharpest sight is not
able to discern them. And the wiser sort of men are willing
not to know them,[27] because shame and loss of honor is
never imposed but in cases evident and apparent.

"Persuade thyself then, Bernabò, that what women may
accomplish in secret they will rarely fail to do. Or if they
abstain, it is through fear and folly. Wherefore, hold it for a
certain rule that that woman is only chaste that never was
solicited personally, or if she endured any such suit, either
she answered yea or no.[28] And albeit I know this to be true
by many infallible and natural reasons, yet could I not
speak so exactly as I do if I had not tried experimentally the
humors and affections of divers women. Yea, and let me tell
thee more, Bernabò: were I in private company with thy
wife, howsoever pure and precise[29] thou presumest her to
be, I should account it a matter of no impossibility to find in
her the selfsame frailty."

Bernabò's blood began now to boil, and patience being a
little put down by choler,[30] thus he replied: "A combat of
words requires overlong continuance. For I maintain the
matter which thou deniest, and all this sorts[31] to nothing in
the end. But seeing thou presumest that all women are so
apt and tractable and thyself so confident of thine own
power, I willingly yield, for the better assurance of my
wife's constant loyalty, to have my head smitten off if thou
canst win her to any such dishonest[32] act by any means
whatsoever thou canst use unto her; which if thou canst not
do, thou shalt only lose a thousand ducats of gold."

Now began Ambrogiuolo to be heated with these words,
answering thus: "Bernabò, if I had won[33] the wager, I know
not what I should do with thy head. But if thou be willing to
stand upon the proof,[34] pawn down[35] five thousand ducats
of gold—a matter of much less value than thy head—

25 a badge of scorn i.e., cuckold's horns   26 notes signs, tokens   27 not to
know them i.e., to look the other way   28 either . . . no i.e., her answer
was equivocal   29 precise strict, scrupulous   30 choler wrath   31 sorts
comes   32 dishonest unchaste   33 had won should win   34 stand . . .
proof put matters to the test   35 pawn down deposit as security

against a thousand ducats of mine, granting me a lawful[36]
limited time, which I require to be no more than the space
of three months after the day of my departing hence. I will
stand bound[37] to go for[38] Genoa and there win such kind
consent of thy wife as shall be to mine own content.* In witness whereof I will bring back with me such private and
especial tokens as thou thyself shalt confess that I have not
failed—provided that thou do first promise upon thy faith
to absent thyself thence during my limited time and be no
hindrance to me by thy letters concerning the attempt by
me undertaken.''

Bernabò said: "Be it a bargain. I am the man that will
make good my five thousand ducats." And albeit the other
merchants then present earnestly labored to break the wager, knowing great harm must needs ensue thereon, yet
both the parties were so hot and fiery as all the other men
spake to no effect. But writings were made, sealed,[39] and
delivered[40] under either[41] of their hands, Bernabò remaining at Paris and Ambrogiuolo departing for Genoa.

There he remained some few days, to learn the street's
name where Bernabò dwelt, as also the conditions and
qualities of his wife, which scarcely pleased him when he
heard them, because they were far beyond her husband's
relation and she reputed to be the only wonder of women;
whereby he plainly perceived that he had undertaken a very
idle[42] enterprise. Yet would he not give it over so, but proceeded therein a little further.

He wrought such means that he came acquainted with a
poor woman who often frequented Bernabò's house and
was greatly in favor with his wife, upon whose poverty he so
prevailed by earnest persuasions, but much more by large
gifts of money, that he won her to further him in this manner following. A fair and artificial[43] chest he caused to be
purposely made wherein himself might be aptly contained
and so conveyed into the house of Bernabò's wife under
color of a formal excuse[44]—that the poor woman should be

36 **lawful** specified by contract 37 **bound** obligated by contract 38 **for**
to 39 **sealed** validated with waxen seals 40 **delivered** handed over
formally to a third party (as in "signed, sealed, and delivered")
41 **either** both 42 **idle** fruitless 43 **artificial** artfully designed
44 **under . . . excuse** under pretext of an excuse that is merely one of
outward form or appearance

absent from the city two or three days, and she[45] must keep
it safe till she* return. The gentlewoman, suspecting no
guile, but that the chest was the receptacle of all the woman's wealth, would trust it in no other room than her own
bedchamber, which was the place where Ambrogiuolo most
desired to be.

Being thus conveyed into the chamber—the night going
on apace, and the gentlewoman fast asleep in her bed, a
lighted taper stood burning on the table by her, as in her
husband's absence she ever used[46] to have—Ambrogiuolo
softly opened the chest according as cunningly he had contrived it and, stepping forth in his socks made of cloth, observed the situation of the chamber, the paintings, pictures,
and beautiful hangings, with all things else that were remarkable; which perfectly he committed to his memory.
Going near to the bed, he saw her lie there sweetly sleeping
and her young daughter in like manner by her, she seeming
then as complete and pleasing a creature as when she was
attired in her best bravery.[47] No especial note or mark could
he descry whereof he might make credible report but only a
small wart upon her left pap with some few hairs growing
thereon appearing to be as yellow as gold.

Sufficient had he seen and durst presume no further. But
taking one of her rings which lay upon the table, a purse of
hers hanging by on the wall, a light wearing-robe of silk,
and her girdle,[48] all which he put into the chest and, being in
himself, closed it fast as it was before, so continuing there
in the chamber two several[49] nights, the gentlewoman neither mistrusting or missing anything. The third day being
come, the poor woman, according as formerly was concluded, came to have home her chest again and brought it
safely into her own house, where Ambrogiuolo, coming
forth of it, satisfied the poor woman to her own liking, returning with all the forenamed things so fast as conveniently he could to Paris.

Being arrived there long before his limited time, he called
the merchants together who were present at the passed
words and wager, avouching before Bernabò that he had
won his five thousand ducats and performed the task he un-

dertook. To make good his protestation, first he described
the form of the chamber, the curious[50] pictures hanging
about it, in what manner the bed stood, and every circumstance else besides. Next he showed the several things
which he brought away thence with him, affirming that he
had received them of herself. Bernabò confessed that his
description of the chamber was true and acknowledged
moreover that these other things did belong to his wife.

"But," quoth he, "this may be gotten by corrupting some
servant of mine, both for intelligence of the chamber as also
of the ring, purse, and what else is besides, all which suffice
not to win the wager without some other more apparent
and pregnant token."

"In troth," answered Ambrogiuolo, "methinks these
should serve for sufficient proofs. But, seeing thou art so
desirous to know more, I plainly tell thee that fair Zinevra
thy wife hath a small round wart upon her left pap and
some few little golden hairs growing thereon."

When Bernabò heard these words, they were as so many
stabs to his heart, yea, beyond all compass of patient sufferance; and by the changing of his color it was noted manifestly, being unable to utter one word, that Ambrogiuolo
had spoken nothing but the truth. Within a while after, he
said: "Gentlemen, that which Ambrogiuolo hath said is
very true. Wherefore let him come when he will, and he
shall be paid"—which accordingly he performed on the
very next day even to the utmost penny, departing then from
Paris towards Genoa with a most malicious intention to his
wife.

Being come near to the city, he would not enter it, but
rode to a country house of his standing about ten miles distant thence. Being there arrived, he called a servant in
whom he reposed especial trust, sending him to Genoa with
two horses, writing to his wife that he was returned and she
should come thither to see him. But secretly he charged his
servant that, so soon as he had brought her to a convenient
place, he should there kill her without any pity or compassion and then return to him again.

When the servant was come to Genoa and had delivered
his letter and message, Zinevra gave him most joyful wel-

50 curious skillfully wrought

come, and on the morrow morning, mounting on horseback
with the servant, rode merrily towards the country house.
Divers things she discoursed on by the way, till they
descended into a deep solitary valley, very thickly beset
with high and huge spreading trees, which the servant supposed to be a meet place for the execution of his master's
command. Suddenly drawing forth his sword and holding
Zinevra fast by the arm, he said: "Mistress, quickly commend your soul to God, for you must die before you pass
any further."

Zinevra, seeing the naked sword and hearing the words so
peremptorily delivered, fearfully answered: "Alas, dear
friend, mercy for God's sake! And before thou kill me, tell
me wherein I have offended thee and why thou must kill
me?"

"Alas, good mistress," replied the servant, "you have not
any way offended me. But in what occasion you have displeased your husband, it is utterly unknown to me. For he
hath strictly commanded me, without respect of pity or
compassion, to kill you by the way as I bring you, and if I do
it not he hath sworn to hang me by the neck. You know,
good mistress, how much I stand obliged to him and how
impossible it is for me to contradict anything that he com-
mandeth. God is my witness that I am truly compassionate
of you, and yet by no means may I let you live."

Zinevra, kneeling before him weeping, wringing her
hands, thus replied: "Wilt thou turn monster and be a murderer of her that never wronged thee, to please another
man, and on a bare command? God, who truly knoweth all
things, is my faithful witness that I never committed any
offense whereby to deserve the dislike of my husband,
much less so harsh a recompense as this is. But flying from
mine own justification and appealing to thy manly[51] mercy,
thou mayst, wert thou but so well pleased,[52] in a moment
satisfy both thy master and me in such manner as I will
make plain and apparent to thee. Take thou my garments.
Spare me only thy doublet[53] and such a bonnet as is fitting
for a man. So return with my habit to thy master, assuring
him that the deed is done. And here I swear to thee by that

---

51 manly human and chivalrous   **52 but so well pleased** only willing to
do so   **53 doublet** close-fitting upper garment, like a jacket

life which I enjoy but[54] by thy mercy, I will so strangely[55] disguise myself and wander so far off from these countries[56] as neither he or thou nor any person belonging to these parts shall ever hear any tidings of me.''

The servant, who had no great good will to kill her, very easily grew pitiful, took off her upper[57] garments, and gave her a poor ragged doublet, a silly chaperon,[58] and such small store of money as he had, desiring her to forsake that country, and so left her to walk on foot out of the valley. When he came to his master and had delivered him her garments, he assured him that he had not only accomplished his command but also was most secure from any discovery, because he had no sooner done the deed but four or five very ravenous wolves came presently running to the dead body and gave it burial in their bellies. Bernabò, soon after returning to Genoa, was much blamed for such unkind[59] cruelty to his wife. But his constant avouching of her treason[60] to him, according then to the country's custom, did clear him from all pursuit of law.

Poor Zinevra was left thus alone and disconsolate; and night stealing fast upon her, she went to a silly[61] village near adjoining where, by the means of a good old woman, she got such provision as the place afforded, making the doublet fit to her body and converting her petticoat to a pair of breeches according to the mariners' fashion. Then, cutting her hair and quaintly[62] disguised like to a sailor, she went to the seacoast. By good fortune she met there with a gentleman of Catalonia whose name was Signor Encararch, who came on land from his ship, which lay hulling[63] there about Alba, to refresh himself at a pleasant spring. Encararch taking her to be a man, as she appeared no otherwise by her habit, upon some conference[64] passing between them she was entertained[65] into his service, and being brought aboard the ship, she went under the name of Sicurano da Finale. There she had better apparel bestown on her by the gentleman, and her service proved so pleasing and accept-

<hr>

54 but only   55 strangely greatly, beyond recognition   56 these countries this region   57 upper outer   58 silly chaperon simple hood or cap
59 unkind unnatural   60 treason i.e., disloyalty   61 silly rustic, humble
62 quaintly ingeniously   63 hulling with sails furled, not under way
64 conference conversation   65 entertained received, hired

able to him that he liked her care and diligence beyond all comparison.

It came to pass within a short while after that this gentleman of Catalonia sailed with some charge[66] of his into Alexandria, carrying thither certain peregrine falcons which he presented to the Sultan, who oftentimes welcomed this gentleman to his table, where he observed the behavior of Sicurano, attending on his master's trencher,[67] and therewith was so highly pleased that he requested to have him from the gentleman, who, for his more advancement, willingly parted with his so lately entertained servant. Sicurano was so ready and discreet in his daily services that he grew in as great grace with the Sultan as before he had done with Encararch.

At a certain season in the year, as customary order (there observed) had formerly been, in the city of Acre,[68] which was under the Sultan's subjection, there yearly met a great assembly of merchants, as Christians, Moors, Jews, Saracens, and many other nations[69] besides, as at a common mart or fair. And to the end that the merchants, for the better sale of their goods, might be there in the safer assurance, the Sultan used to send thither some of his ordinary[70] officers, and a strong guard of soldiers besides, to defend them from all injuries and molestation, because he reaped thereby no mean[71] benefit. And who should be now sent about this business but his new-elected favorite, Sicurano, because she was skillful and perfect[72] in the languages?

Sicurano being come to Acre as lord and captain of the guard for the merchants and for the safety of their merchandises, she discharged her office most commendably, walking with her train through every part of the fair, where she observed a worthy company of merchants—Sicilians, Pisans, Genoese, Venetians, and other Italians—whom the more willingly she noted in remembrance of her native country. At one especial time among other, chancing into a shop or booth belonging to the Venetians, she espied hanging up with other costly wares a purse and a girdle which

---

66 **charge** cargo   67 **trencher** wooden platter and the food on it, i.e., supply of food for the table   68 **Acre** St. Jean d'Acre, on the Mediterranean coast of Jerusalem   69 **nations** peoples, races, and nationalities   70 **ordinary** regular   71 **mean** small   72 **perfect** well versed

suddenly she remembered to be sometime[73] her own.
Whereat she was not a little abashed in her mind. But without making any such outward show, courteously she requested to know whose they were and whether they should
be sold[74] or no.

Ambrogiuolo of Piacenza was likewise come thither, and
great store of merchandises he had brought with him in a
carrack appertaining[75] to the Venetians. And he, hearing the
Captain of the Guard demand whose they were, stepped
forth before him and smiling answered that they were his,
but not to be sold; yet if he liked them, gladly he would bestow them on him. Sicurano, seeing him smile, suspected
lest himself had by some unfitting behavior been the occasion thereof, and therefore with a more settled countenance
he said: "Perhaps thou smilest because I that am a man,
professing arms, should question after such womanish
toys."[76]

Ambrogiuolo replied: "My lord, pardon me, I smile not at
you or your demand[77] but at the manner how I came by
these things."

Sicurano, upon this answer, was ten times more desirous
than before, and said: "If Fortune favored thee in friendly
manner by the obtaining of these things, if it may be spoken
tell me how thou hadst them."

"My lord," answered Ambrogiuolo, "these things with
many more besides were given me by a gentlewoman of
Genoa named Madam Zinevra, the wife to one Bernabò Lomellino, in recompense of one night's lodging with her, and
she desired me to keep them for her sake. Now the main
reason of my smiling was the remembrance of her husband's folly in waging five thousand ducats of gold against
one thousand of mine that I should not obtain my will of his
wife, which I did and thereby won the wager. But he, who
better deserved to be punished for his folly than she who
was but sick of all women's disease,[78] returning from Paris
to Genoa caused her to be slain, as afterward it was reported by himself."

When Sicurano heard this horrible lie, immediately she

---

73 sometime formerly   **74 should be sold** were for sale   **75 carrack
appertaining** large merchant ship belonging   **76 toys** trifles
77 demand request   **78 disease** failing, i.e., inconstancy

conceived[79] that this was the occasion of her husband's ha
tred to her and all the hard haps[80] which she had since suf
fered. Whereupon she reputed it for more than a mortal sin
if such a villain should pass without due punishment. Si
curano seemed[81] to like well this report and grew into such
familiarity with Ambrogiuolo that, by her persuasions
when the fair was ended, she took him higher[82] with her
into Alexandria and all his wares along with him, furnish
ing him with a fit and convenient shop, where he made great
benefit of his merchandises, trusting all his monies in the
Captain's custody because it was the safest course for him
and so he continued there with no mean[83] contentment.

Much did she pity her husband's perplexity, devising by
what good and warrantable means she might make known
her innocency to him. Wherein her place and authority did
greatly stead her. And she wrought with[84] divers gallant
merchants of Genoa that then remained in Alexandria, and
by virtue of the Sultan's friendly letters besides, to bring
him thither upon an especial occasion. Come he did, albeit
in poor and mean order,[85] which soon was better altered by
her appointment, and he very honorably, though in private,
entertained[86] by divers of her worthy friends till time did
favor what she further intended.

In the expectation of Bernabò's arrival, she had so prevailed with Ambrogiuolo that the same tale which he formerly told to her he delivered again in presence of the
Sultan, who seemed to be well pleased with it. But after she
had once seen her husband, she thought upon her more serious business, providing herself of an apt opportunity
when she entreated such favor of the Sultan that both the
men might be brought before him, where, if Ambrogiuolo
would not confess without constraint that which he had
made his vaunt of concerning Bernabò's wife, he might be
compelled thereto perforce.

Sicurano's word was a law with the Sultan, so that, Ambrogiuolo and Bernabò being brought face-to-face, the Sultan, with a stern and angry countenance, in the presence of

79 conceived understood   80 haps occurrences   81 seemed pretended
82 higher further, to a better place (?)   83 mean small   84 wrought
with made arrangements with, brought it about by means of   85 mean
order shabby state or condition   86 entertained received, welcomed

a most princely assembly, commanded Ambrogiuolo to declare the truth, yea, upon peril of his life, by what means he won the wager of the five thousand golden ducats he received of Bernabò. Ambrogiuolo, seeing Sicurano there present, upon whose favor he wholly relied, yet perceiving her looks likewise to be as dreadful as the Sultan's and hearing her threaten him with most grievous torments except he revealed the truth indeed, you may easily guess, fair company, in what condition he stood at that instant.

Frowns and fury he beheld on either side, and Bernabò standing before him, with a world of famous witnesses, to hear his lie confounded by his own confession and his tongue to deny what it had before so constantly avouched. Yet dreaming on no other pain or penalty but restoring back the five thousand ducats of gold and the other things by him purloined, truly he revealed the whole form of his falsehood. Then Sicurano, according as the Sultan had formerly commanded him,[87] turning to Bernabò, said: "And thou, upon the suggestion of this foul lie, what didst thou to thy wife?"

"Being," quoth Bernabò, "overcome with rage for the loss of my money and the dishonor I supposed to receive by my wife, I caused a servant of mine to kill her; and as he credibly avouched, her body was devoured by ravenous wolves in a moment after."

These things being thus spoken and heard in the presence of the Sultan, and no reason as yet made known why the case was so seriously urged and to what end it would succeed, Sicurano spake in this manner to the Sultan: "My gracious lord, you may plainly perceive in what degree that poor gentlewoman might make her vaunt, being so well provided both of a loving friend and a husband. Such was the friend's love that in an instant and by a wicked lie he robbed her both of her renown and honor and bereft her also of her husband. And her husband, rather crediting another's falsehood than the invincible truth whereof he had faithful knowledge by long and very honorable experience, caused her to be slain and made food for devouring wolves. Besides all this, such was the good will and affection borne to that

87 **him** i.e., Sicurano, really *her*, Zinevra. (The male pronoun recurs occasionally elsewhere in the story.)

woman both by friend and husband that the longest continuer of them in her company makes them alike in knowledge of her. But, because your great wisdom knoweth perfectly what each of them have worthily deserved, if you please, in your ever-known gracious benignity, to permit the punishment of the deceiver and pardon the party so deceived, I will procure such means that she shall appear here in your presence and theirs."

The Sultan, being desirous to give Sicurano all manner of satisfaction, having followed the course[88] so industriously, bade him[89] to produce the woman, and he was well contented. Whereat Bernabò stood much amazed, because he verily believed that she was dead. And Ambrogiuolo, foreseeing already a preparation for punishment, feared that the repayment of the money would not now serve his turn, not knowing also what he should further hope or suspect if the woman herself did personally appear, which he imagined would be a miracle. Sicurano having thus obtained the Sultan's permission, in tears humbling herself at his feet, in a moment she lost her manly voice and demeanor, as knowing that she was now no longer to use them but must truly witness what she was indeed, and therefore thus spake: "Great Sultan, I am the miserable and unfortunate Zinevra, that for the space of six whole years have wandered through the world in the habit of a man, falsely and most maliciously slandered by this villainous traitor Ambrogiuolo, and by this unkind cruel husband betrayed to his servant to be slain and left to be devoured by savage beasts."

Afterward, desiring such garments as better fitted for her, and showing her breasts, she made it apparent before the Sultan and his assistants that she was the very same woman indeed. Then turning herself to Ambrogiuolo, with more than manly courage she demanded of him when and where it was that he lay with her, as villainously he was not ashamed to make his vaunt. But he, having already acknowledged the contrary, being stricken dumb with shameful disgrace, was not able to utter one word.

---

88 course i.e., course of events or of the argument   **89 him** i.e., her, Zinevra disguised as Sicurano

The Sultan, who had always reputed Sicurano to be a man, having heard and seen so admirable an accident,[90] was so amazed in his mind that many times he was very doubtful whether this was a dream or an absolute relation of truth. But after he had more seriously considered thereon and found it to be real and infallible, with extraordinary gracious praises he commended the life, constancy, conditions, and virtues of Zinevra, whom till that time he had always called Sicurano. So committing her to the company of honorable ladies to be changed from her manly habit, he pardoned Bernabò her husband, according to her request formerly made, although he had more justly deserved death; which likewise himself confessed, and falling at the feet of Zinevra desired her in tears to forgive his rash transgression, which most lovingly she did, kissing and embracing him a thousand times.

Then the Sultan strictly commanded that on some high and eminent place of the city Ambrogiuolo should be bound and impaled on a stake, having his naked body anointed all over with honey, and never to be taken off until of itself it fell in pieces, which according to the sentence was presently[91] performed. Next, he gave express charge[92] that all his[93] money and goods should be given to Zinevra, which valued above ten thousand double ducats. Forthwith* a solemn feast was prepared, wherein much honor was done to Bernabò, being the husband of Zinevra. And to her, as to a most worthy woman and matchless wife, he gave in costly jewels, as also vessels of gold and silver plate, so much as amounted to above ten thousand double ducats more.

When the feasting was finished he caused a ship to be furnished for them, granting them license to depart for Genoa when they pleased, whither they returned most rich and joyfully, being welcomed home with great honor; especially Madam Zinevra, whom everyone supposed to be dead. And always after, so long as she lived, she was most famous for her manifold virtues.

But as for Ambrogiuolo, the very same day that he was impaled on the stake, anointed with honey, and fixed in the

90 **admirable an accident** astonishing an event   91 **presently** at once
92 **charge** command   93 **his** i.e., Ambrogiuolo's

place appointed, to his no mean[94] torment, he not only died but likewise was devoured to the bare bones by flies, wasps, and hornets, whereof the country notoriously aboundeth. And his bones in full form and fashion remained strangely black for a long while after, knit together by the sinews, as a witness to many thousands of people which afterward beheld his carcass of his wickedness against so good and virtuous a woman that had not so much as a thought of any evil towards him. And thus was the proverb truly verified, that shame succeedeth after ugly sin, and the deceiver is trampled and trod by such as himself hath deceived.

Text is based on an anonymous English translation of *The Decameron, Containing an Hundred Pleasant Novels*. London: Isaac Jaggard, 1620, folios 68–73ᵛ. Proper names are regularized or modernized as follows: *Bernabò* for *Bernardo*, *Ambrogiuolo* for *Ambroginolo* or *Ambrosio*, *Zinevra* for *Geneura*, *Encararch* for *Enchararcho*, *Genoa* for *Geneway*, *Piacenza* for *Placentia*, *Alba* for *Albagia*, *Catalonia* for *Cathalogna*, *Acre* for *Acres*, and *Sultan* for *Soldan*.

In the following, departures from the original text appear in boldface; original readings are in roman.

p. 313 *jumped vnapt   p. 314 *have I haue   p. 317 *content consent   p. 318 *she he
p. 327 *Forthwith Forth-with with

---

94 no mean not inconsiderable

Further Reading

Brockbank, J. Philip. "History and Histrionics in *Cymbeline.*" *Shakespeare Survey* 11 (1958): 42–49. Rpt. in *Shakespeare's Later Comedies: An Anthology of Modern Criticism,* ed. D. J. Palmer. Harmondsworth, Eng.: Penguin, 1971. Brockbank examines the integration of historical source material and theatrical convention in *Cymbeline.* Shakespeare creates a mythic vision of Britain's history by fusing historical materials and self-conscious artifice, confirming the play's thematic emphasis on reconciliation and its providential restoration of a golden world.

Felperin, Howard. "Tragical-Comical-Historical-Pastoral: *Cymbeline* and *Henry VIII.*" *Shakespearean Romance.* Princeton, N.J.: Princeton Univ. Press, 1972. Felperin locates the unity of the play's design in its synthesis of chivalric romance, the Tudor myth of the British past, and the patterns of Christian history, and traces the pattern of restoration and renewal that occurs in all three plots. Felperin finds, however, that finally *Cymbeline* is a victim of its romantic achievement; its idealized version of history "seals off the play from the world we know."

Freer, Coburn. *"Cymbeline." The Poetics of Jacobean Drama.* Baltimore: Johns Hopkins Univ. Press, 1981. Exploring the relationship between poetic effects and dramatic experience, Freer sensitively analyzes the subtle alterations in tone, rhythm, and diction that determine the structure of *Cymbeline.* He shows how stylistic variation reveals changes in Imogen's and Cymbeline's understanding of themselves and their situation and how style also reveals Iachimo's lack of moral growth.

Frye, Northrop. *A Natural Perspective: The Development of Shakespearean Comedy and Romance,* esp. pp. 65–71. New York: Columbia Univ. Press, 1965. *Cymbeline* contains so many obstacles to the happy resolution it achieves that Frye sees it as the "apotheosis of the problem comedies." The play, however, departs from the pattern of the earlier comedies in its self-conscious ordering of its comic design: Shakespeare himself emerges as the tuner of the play's harmonies, revealing his primary interest in the techniques and conventions of romance.

Hartwig, Joan. "*Cymbeline:* 'A Speaking Such as Sense Cannot Untie.'" *Shakespeare's Tragicomic Vision.* Baton Rouge, La.: Louisiana State Univ. Press, 1972. Through its complex plotting, *Cymbeline* gradually distances its characters and its audience "from the values that they had held to be significant," Hartwig writes, allowing fresh and more generous perceptions to replace those based on limited and narrow purchases on reality.

Hunter, Robert Grams. "*Cymbeline.*" *Shakespeare and the Comedy of Forgiveness.* New York: Columbia Univ. Press, 1965. The play, Hunter argues, presents a secularized version of the moral pattern of medieval miracle plays, in which erring sinners are redeemed by love. *Cymbeline's* enactment of this conventional pattern of sin, repentance, and regeneration gives the play its unity and permits its reunions and final harmony.

Jones, Emrys. "Stuart *Cymbeline.*" *Essays in Criticism* 11 (1961): 84–99. Rpt. in *Shakespeare's Later Comedies: An Anthology of Modern Criticism,* ed. D. J. Palmer. Harmondsworth, Eng.: Penguin, 1971. Jones argues that the play's incongruities and absurdities disappear when the play is understood as a topical commentary upon the reign and political vision of King James I. The peace and harmony of the play's extraordinary ending are intended as an elaborate compliment to the King and his aspirations of unifying Britain and restoring peace to Europe.

Kastan, David Scott. "*Cymbeline:* 'A Strain of Rareness.'" *Shakespeare and the Shapes of Time.* Hanover, N.H.: Univ. Press of New England, 1982. Kastan finds the unity of the play in the common redemptive structure of its three plots. Each enacts a version of the fortunate fall, and each, from the individual rejuvenation of Posthumus to the reunion of the royal family to the international peace of the political action, defines an increasingly more inclusive pattern of harmony, guaranteed by the gods but generated by human acts of love.

Kermode, Frank. "*Cymbeline.*" *William Shakespeare: The Final Plays.* London: Longmans, Green, 1963. Kermode considers *Cymbeline* a dense but "superb" play, in which Shakespeare's interest lies less in personalities and probabilities than in a theatrical ordering that serves to reveal a principle of harmony often obscured by the turbulence of life. Shakespeare's dramatic energies are focused on creating a powerful recognition scene, one that almost incredibly unites the play's complex plots and themes.

Kirsch, Arthur C. "*Cymbeline* and Coterie Dramaturgy." *ELH* 34 (1967): 285–306. Rpt. in *Shakespeare's Later Comedies: An Anthology of Modern Criticism*, ed. D. J. Palmer. Harmondsworth, Eng.: Penguin, 1971. Arguing that the purchase of the Blackfriars Theatre in 1608 by the King's men was a source of dramatic stimulus for Shakespeare, Kirsch finds in *Cymbeline* evidence of the influence of the dramaturgy of the private, indoor theaters. The play's self-conscious artifice, its tragicomic structure, its use of and the conspicuous operations of providence can be traced to the dramatic techniques and concerns of the coterie theaters.

Miola, Robert. "*Cymbeline:* Beyond Rome." *Shakespeare's Rome*. Cambridge: Cambridge Univ. Press, 1983. Miola holds that *Cymbeline* is Shakespeare's last Roman play, one that concludes that his dramatic scrutiny of Rome and Roman values. In the play, British virtue triumphs over Roman might and British humility overcomes Roman honor, yet with the reconciliation of the nations at the end, the extended Trojan family is at last united.

Moffet, Robin. "*Cymbeline* and the Nativity." *Shakespeare Quarterly* 13 (1962): 207–218. Moffet sees the nativity of Christ, which purportedly took place during the reign of Cymbeline, as the moral center of a play that shows a world of sin and error redeemed by divine intervention. Moffet discusses how Shakespeare's alterations of his source material and structuring of the action reveal the centrality of Christ's nativity to a play that neither stages nor mentions the event.

Peterson, Douglas L. "*Cymbeline:* Legendary History and Arcadian Romance." *Time, Tide, and Tempest: A Study of Shakespeare's Romances*. San Marino, Calif.: Huntington Library, 1973. Peterson finds both a destructive and a renewing action in *Cymbeline*, each of which is articulated in a distinct dramatic mode. The tragic action resembles the pseudo-historical realism of *King Lear*, while the restorative pattern is rendered in the emblematic techniques of *Pericles*. The shift of representational modes permits "the extravagant possibilities of romance" to renew the world of the play.

Shaw, George Bernard. *"Cymbeline." Shaw on Shakespeare*, ed. Edwin Wilson. New York: E. P. Dutton, 1961. Wilson's selections reveal Shaw's continued fascination and exasperation with the play. In 1896 Shaw described it as "stagey trash of the most melodramatic order," yet a half century later he returned to it, rewriting its final act in "Cymbeline Refinished" (1945), which now seems less a telling critique of Shakespeare's art than a revealing indication of the problems his nonnaturalistic drama posed for Shaw and as well as for the Victorians.

Skura, Meredith. "Interpreting Posthumus' Dream from Above and Below: Families, Psychoanalysts, and Literary Critics." In *Representing Shakespeare: New Psychoanalytic Essays*, ed. Murray M. Schwartz and Coppélia Kahn. Baltimore: Johns Hopkins Univ. Press, 1980. Skura's essay is a psychoanalytic examination of Shakespeare's treatment of family relations in Cymbeline. Her analysis focuses on Posthumus, whose dream at the climax of the play is a "family recognition scene" that underscores the centrality of family in the achievement of selfhood and in the fully realized structure of comedy.

Wickham, Glynne. "Riddle and Emblem: A Study in the Dramatic Structure of *Cymbeline*." In *English Renaissance Studies Presented to Dame Helen Gardner in Honour of Her Seventieth Birthday*, ed. John Carey. Oxford: Clarendon Press, 1980. Like Jones (see above), Wickham considers the topicality of the play. He finds in the play's imagery reference to the ruling images of the reign of King James and proposes that the play was presented at court in 1609. The play's riddles and emblems comment indirectly upon the King's "hopes for Britain's future."

THE
WINTER'S
TALE

Introduction

The Winter's Tale (c. 1610–1611), with its almost symmetrical division into two halves of bleak tragedy and comic romance, illustrates perhaps more clearly than any other Shakespearean play the genre of tragicomedy. To be sure, all the late romances feature journeys of separation, apparent deaths, and tearful reconciliations. Marina and Thaisa in *Pericles*, Imogen in *Cymbeline*, and Ferdinand in *The Tempest*, all supposed irrecoverably lost, are brought back to life by apparently miraculous devices. Of the four late romances, however, *The Winter's Tale* uses the most formal structure to evoke the antithesis of tragedy and romance. It is sharply divided into contrasting halves by a gap of sixteen years. The tragic first half takes place almost entirely in Sicilia, whereas the action of the second half is limited for the most part to Bohemia. At the court of Sicilia we see tyrannical jealousy producing a spiritual climate of "winter / In storm perpetual"; in Bohemia we witness a pastoral landscape and a sheepshearing evoking "the sweet o' the year," "When daffodils begin to peer" (3.2.212–213; 4.3.1–3). Paradoxically, the contrast between the two halves is intensified by parallels between the two: both begin with Camillo onstage and proceed to scenes of confrontation and jealousy in which, ironically, the innocent cause of jealousy in the first half, Polixenes, becomes the jealous tyrant of the second half. This mirroring reminds us of the cyclical nature of time and the hope it brings of renewal as we move from tragedy to romantic comedy.

Although this motif of a renewing journey from jaded court to idealized countryside reminds us of *As You Like It* and other early comedies, we sense in the late romances and especially in *The Winter's Tale* a new preoccupation with humanity's tragic folly. The vision of human depravity is world-weary and pessimistic, as though infected by the gloomy spirit of the great tragedies. And because humanity is so bent on destroying itself, the restoration is at once more urgently needed and more miraculous than in the "festive" world of early comedy. Renewal is mythically associated with the seasonal cycle from winter to summer.

King Leontes's tragedy seems at first irreversible and terrifying, like that of Shakespeare's greatest tragic protagonists. He suffers from irrational jealousy, as does Othello, and attempts to destroy the person on whom all his happiness depends. Unlike Othello, however, Leontes needs no diabolical tempter such as Iago to poison his mind against Queen Hermione. Leontes is undone by his own fantasies. No differences in race or age can explain Leontes's fears of estrangement from Hermione. She is not imprudent in her conduct, like her counterpart in Robert Greene's *Pandosto* (1588), the prose romance from which Shakespeare drew his narrative. Although Hermione is graciously fond of Leontes's dear friend Polixenes and urges him to stay longer in Sicilia, she does so only with a hospitable warmth demanded by the occasion and encouraged by her husband. In every way, then, Shakespeare strips away from Leontes the motive and the occasion for plausible doubting of his wife. All observers in the Sicilian court are incredulous and shocked at the King's accusations. Even so, Leontes is neither an unsympathetic nor an unbelievable character. Like Othello, Leontes cherishes his wife and perceives with a horrifying intensity what a fearful cost he must pay for his suspicions. Not only his marriage, but his lifelong friendship with Polixenes, his sense of pride in his children, and his enjoyment of his subjects' warm regard, all must be sacrificed to a single overwhelming compulsion.

Whatever may be the psychological cause of this obsession, it manifests itself as a revulsion against all sexual behavior. Like mad Lear, Leontes imagines lechery to be the unavoidable fact of the cosmos and of the human condition, the lowest common denominator to which all persons (including Hermione) must stoop. He is persuaded that "It is a bawdy planet," in which cuckolded man has "his pond fished by his next neighbor, by / Sir Smile, his neighbor" (1.2.195–201). Leontes's tortured soliloquies are laden with sexual images, of unattended "gates" letting in and out the enemy "With bag and baggage," and of a "dagger" that must be "muzzled / Lest it should bite its master" (ll. 197, 206, 156–157). As in *King Lear*, order is inverted to disorder, sanity to madness, legitimacy to illegitimacy. Sexual misconduct is emblematic of a universal malaise: "Why, then the world and all that's in 't is nothing, / The covering sky is nothing, Bohemia nothing, / My wife is nothing" (ll. 292–294). Other characters too see the trial of Hermione as a testing of humanity's worth: if Hermione proves false, Antigonus promises, he will treat his own wife as a stable horse and will "geld" his three daughters (2.1.148). Prevailing images are of spiders, venom, infection, sterility, and the "dungy earth" (l. 158).

Cosmic order is never really challenged, however. Leontes's fantasies of universal disorder are chimerical. His wife is in fact chaste, Polixenes true, and the King's courtiers loyal. Camillo refuses to carry out Leontes's order to murder Polixenes, not only because he knows murder to be wrong but because history offers not one example of a man "that had struck anointed kings / And flourished after" (1.2.357–358). The cosmos of this play is one in which crimes are invariably and swiftly punished. The Delphic oracle vindicates Hermione and gives Leontes stern warning. When Leontes persists in his madness, his son Mamillius's death follows as an immediate consequence. As Leontes at once perceives, "Apollo's angry, and the heavens themselves / Do strike at my injustice" (3.2.146–147). Leontes paradoxically welcomes the lengthy contrition he must undergo, for it confirms a pattern in the universe of just cause and effect. Although as tragic protagonist he has discovered the truth about Hermione moments too late, and so must pay richly for his error, Leontes has at least recovered faith in Hermione's transcendent goodness. His nightmare now over, he accepts and embraces suffering as a necessary atonement.

The transition to romance is therefore anticipated to an extent by the play's first half, even though the tone of the last two acts is strikingly different. The old Shepherd signals a momentous change when he speaks to his son of a cataclysmic storm and a ravenous bear set in opposition to the miraculous discovery of a child: "Now bless thyself. Thou mett'st with things dying, I with things newborn" (3.3.110–111). Time comes onstage as Chorus, like Gower in *Pericles*, to remind us of the conscious artifice of the dramatist. He can "o'erthrow law" and carry us over sixteen years as if we had merely dreamed out the interim (4.1). Shakespeare flaunts the improbability of his story by giving Bohemia a seacoast (much to the distress of Ben Jonson), and by employing animals onstage in a fanciful way ("*Exit, pursued by a bear*"; 3.3.57 s.d.). The narrative uses many typical devices of romance: a babe abandoned to the elements, a princess brought up by shepherds, a prince disguised as a swain, a sea voyage, and a recognition scene. Love is threatened not by the internal psychic obstacle of jealousy, but by the external obstacles of parental opposition and a seeming disparity of social rank between the lovers. Comedy easily finds solutions for such difficulties by the unraveling of illusion. This comic world also properly includes clownish shepherds, coy shepherdesses, and Autolycus, the roguish peddler, whose songs help set the mood of jollity and whose machinations contribute in an unforeseen manner to the working out of the love plot. Autolycus is in many ways the presiding genius of the play's second half, as dominant a character as Leontes in the first half and one whose delightful function is to do good "against my will" (5.2.125). In this paradox of knavery converted surprisingly to benign ends, we see how the comic providence of Shakespeare's tragicomic world makes use of the most implausible and outrageous happenings in pursuit of its own inscrutable design.

The conventional romantic ending is infused, however, with a sadness and a mystery that take the play well beyond what is usual in comedy. Mamillius and Antigonus are really dead, and that irredeemable fact is not forgotten in the play's final happy moments. Conversely, in Shakespeare's most notable departure from his source, Greene's *Pandosto*, Hermione is brought back to life. All observers regard this event, and the rediscovery of Perdita, as grossly implausible, "so like an old tale that the verity of it is in strong suspicion" (5.2.29–30). The play's very title, *The Winter's Tale*, reinforces this sense of naive improbability. Why does Shakespeare stress this riddling paradox of an unbelievable reality, and why does he deliberately mislead his audience into believing that Hermione has in fact died (3.3.15–45), using a kind of theatrical trickery found in no other Shakespearean play? The answer may well be that, in Paulina's words, we must awake our faith, accepting a narrative of death and return to life that cannot ultimately be comprehended by reason. On the rational level we are told that Hermione has been kept in hiding for sixteen years, in order to bring Leontes's contrition to fulfillment. Such an explanation seems psychologically incomprehensible, however, for it casts both Hermione and her keeper Paulina in the role of sadistic punishers of the King. Instead we are drawn toward an emblematic interpretation, bearing in mind that it is more an evocative hint than a complete truth. Throughout the play, Hermione has been repeatedly associated with "Grace" and with the goddess Proserpina, whose return from the underworld, after "Three crabbèd months had soured themselves to death" (1.2.102), signals the coming of spring. Perdita, also associated with Proserpina (4.4.116), is welcomed by her father "As is the spring to th' earth" (5.1.152). The emphasis on the bond of father and daughter (rather than father and son), so characteristic of Shakespeare's late plays and especially his romances, goes importantly beyond the patriarchalism of Shakespeare's earlier plays in its exploration of family relationships. Paulina has a similarly emblematic role, that of Conscience, patiently guiding the King to a divinely appointed renewal of his joy. Paulina speaks of herself as an artist figure, like Prospero in *The Tempest*, performing wonders of illusion, though she rejects the assistance of wicked powers. These emblematic hints do not rob the story of its human drama, but they do lend a transcendent significance to Leontes's bittersweet story of sinful error, affliction, and an unexpected second happiness.

The Winter's Tale
in Performance

A play that spans sixteen years, locates its action in two such widely separated places as Sicilia and Bohemia, provides landlocked Bohemia with a seacoast, divides itself more or less equally between tragedy and comedy, and brings on an allegorical figure such as Time had no hope of surviving in the Restoration and eighteenth century even if written by the immortal Shakespeare. *The Winter's Tale*, after enjoying great popularity in public and at court from 1611 (when diarist Dr. Simon Forman saw it at the Globe Theatre) until 1634 (when the King's men performed it at the palace at Whitehall for at least the fifth time), fell into neglect. It was allotted to His Majesty's servants under Thomas Killigrew in the 1660s but not acted by them. After a belated revival by Henry Giffard at the theater in Goodman's Fields, London, in 1741, in which the play was performed as an extended interval in "a concert of vocal and instrumental music," and a run at the Theatre Royal, Covent Garden, the next season, the play suffered the fate of adaption at the hands of redactors seeking to remedy its presumed manifest defects.

Mcnamara Morgan's solution, in his *The Sheep-Shearing, or Florizel and Perdita* produced, at Covent Garden in 1754, was to address systematically the problem of the violated unities of time, place, and action. He cut the first half entirely and focused instead on the romance of the two lovers, leading up to the revelation of Perdita's noble birth. The tragicomic story of Leontes and Hermione was entirely absent. Bithynia, substituted for Bohemia at the suggestion of the Shakespeare scholar Thomas Hanmer, was safely allotted a seacoast; Perdita's shepherd stepfather turned out to be Antigonus in disguise. Morgan augmented the role of Autolycus, but had the good sense to keep the sheepshearing scene reasonably intact. Dr. Thomas Arne provided music and the set.

David Garrick's *Florizel and Perdita* (Theatre Royal, Drury Lane, 1756) followed Morgan's example by beginning after the "wide gap of time" that divides Shakespeare's play in two and locating the action in one place (called Bithynia at first, Bohemia in later printed versions). Garrick was not content, however, to leave aside the story of Leontes and Hermione. To include it without seriously impairing the dramatic unities required some ingenuity. Garrick's text solves this difficulty by recalling through dialogue what took place in Sicily sixteen years before, by shipwrecking Leontes and Cleomenes on the coast of Polixenes's country (where Leontes has come in hopes of atoning for his mad jealousy), and by bringing the shipwrecked visitors to the sheepshearing. Paulina also lives now in Polixenes's kingdom, and Hermione dwells in concealment with her. Garrick's only concession to Shakespeare's first three acts, other than expository recall, is to retain the scene of Perdita's discovery on the coast with its irresistible chase by a bear. Garrick explains his modifications in a prologue that captures both eighteenth-century veneration for Shakespeare and the conviction that his genius needed to be rescued from the inanities and barbarism of his own theater:

> The five long acts, from which our three are taken,
> Stretched out to sixteen years, lay by, forsaken.
> Lest then this precious liquor run to waste,
> 'Tis now confined and bottled for your taste.
> 'Tis my chief wish, my joy, my only plan
> To lose no drop of this immortal man.

Garrick played Leontes to the memorable Hermione of Hannah Pritchard and the no less remarkable Perdita of Susannah Cibber, who sang one of the songs added (perhaps from Morgan's version) for the occasion. Autolycus, played by Richard Yates, spoke new comic material as in Morgan's version.

The Winter's Tale did well in the late eighteenth and early nineteenth centuries, though often, especially at first, in the altered guises provided for it by Garrick and Morgan. Hannah Pritchard continued to play Hermione until 1785. A succession of actresses followed Susannah Cibber as Perdita, among them Maria Macklin, Hannah Mary Pritchard, George Anne Bellamy, and Elizabeth Younge. Autolycus's augmented role attracted the comic talents of, after Yates,

Ned Shuter, E. L. Blanchard, and John Bannister, Jr. John Philip Kemble, at Drury Lane in 1802 and afterward at Covent Garden, did restore the text to something more approaching Shakespeare's, thereby delighting William Hazlitt and compensating to some degree for that critic's disappointments with staged versions of *King Lear* and other Shakespeare plays. Sarah Siddons acted Hermione in Kemble's production of 1802 and continued in the part until 1811. William Charles Macready acted Leontes at Bath in 1815, at Drury Lane in 1823, at Covent Garden in 1837 (in fact he opened his management at that theater with *The Winter's Tale*, casting Helen Faucit as Hermione), and at Drury Lane in 1843. Macready's text, like Kemble's, was no longer heavily indebted to Garrick and Morgan.

The adapted play seems to have done well in the United States. An operatic version made its appearance in 1761, and Morgan's text was performed at New York's John Street Theatre in 1795. Shakespeare's text came into its own in America with William Burton's productions at his intimate theater on Chambers Street in New York in 1851 and 1856, and then, more lavishly, in 1857 at the Broadway Theatre. Burton restored much of Shakespeare's text (including the Chorus of Time), although he also retained twenty lines that Garrick added at the end of Act 5, scene 2, and provided much stage business, especially for his role as Autolycus. Reviewers were enthusiastic about the productions even if they generally remarked more upon the scenic effects than the acting. A cutout of Mount Etna located Act 1 clearly in Sicily, and later in the act the volcano could be seen to erupt as the background to Leontes's fearful jealousy. The innocent pastoral world of Bohemia was invoked by a cottage enveloped in flowers and vines and set in a landscape of streams, meadows, and distant mountains "suffused with a roseate atmosphere of sunlight." The whole scene, according to one reviewer, was "full of that Heaven that lies about us in our infancy."

Like Burton, nineteenth-century English actor-managers were drawn to the pictorial capabilities of *The Winter's Tale*, with both good and bad results: the play's powerful stage images of discovery and reunion lent themselves to fine theatrical effects, but an overemphasis on scenic splendor hampered the movement of the play and required cutting or rearrangement. Samuel Phelps, at the Sadler's Wells Theatre in 1845 and afterward, paid particular attention to the mise-en-scène, especially in the final act. Amid classic interiors in a polychromatic style of decoration, lighting and drapery were so artfully displayed on the impressive figure of Amelia Warner as Hermione that the audience burst into applause on the removal of the curtain.

Charles Kean, at the Princess's Theatre in 1856, hit on the scheme of contrasting the Greek dress of Syracuse in the early scenes with Asiatic costuming in Bithynia (i.e., Bohemia). Convinced that ancient Syracuse had rivaled Athens in architectural splendor, Kean undertook to bring before his spectators "*tableaux vivants* of the private and public life of the ancient Greeks, at a time when the arts flourished to . . . perfection." His Syracuse of about 300 B.C. showed the fountains of Arethusa and the Temple of Minerva, a banqueting hall in the royal palace with couches for the reclining guests, musicians playing a hymn to Apollo, slaves handing out wine and garlands, and a Pyrrhic dance performed by thirty-six handsome young women in warlike garb. Hermione's dungeon in Act 2 resembled the infamous "Ear of Dionysius" where Syracusan tyrants are reputed to have abused their prisoners. The Queen faced trial in a reconstruction of the great public theater of Syracuse. A Chorus, bridging the interval between the play's two halves, was accompanied by an allegorical pageant of Time in which clouds dispersed, the Moon in her chariot sank into the ocean, and Phoebus Apollo arose in his chariot in a blaze of light. In the play's second half, a distant view of Nicaea, capital of Bithynia, could be seen beyond the rural beauties of the sheepshearing scene, and a graceful dance of shepherds and shepherdesses gave way to a celebration of Bacchus by three hundred or more writhing satyrs in wild disguise. The statue scene culminated in a torchlight procession. A young Ellen Terry played Mamillius, and she long remembered the triumphant spectacle.

Despite some outcries that Shakespeare was disappearing under the weight of so much scenery, theater managers vied with one another for new effects. F. B. Chatterton, manager at Drury Lane, produced *The Winter's Tale* in 1878 without the allegorical pageant of Time and without the bear that had so vigorously chased after Antigonus at the Princess's

Theatre, but with a Pyrrhic dance in Act 1, a frenzied Dionysiac festival in Act 4, and a trial of Hermione in the theater at Syracuse. Architectural details were painstakingly researched to produce the effect of the ancient Mediterranean world, and several newly painted scenes of Syracuse and of other classical vistas added to the verisimilar effect. Mary Anderson wowed audiences at the Lyceum Theatre in 1887 with her doubling of the matronly Hermione and the girlish Perdita, but cut the text in a way that betrayed a somewhat cavalier attitude. "No audience of these days," she said, "would desire to have *The Winter's Tale* produced in its entirety." She was especially severe in her excisions of the roguery practiced by Autolycus on the old Shepherd and his son, evidently regarding the material as overly scurrilous, and she ended the play with a couplet from *All's Well That Ends Well*. Johnston Forbes-Robertson played Leontes. The scenic splendor began in the palace of Leontes, replete with Grecian pillars and a distant landscape. An upper terrace, with marble benches and velvet drapes, accommodated much of the action. Hermione's trial took place in a Grecian hall of solid masonry; the rustic festival occurred amidst flowery banks and overarching trees. Hermione's appearance as a statue was set at the top of a flight of marble steps, enabling the magnificent Miss Anderson to descend in picturesque dignity and grace. Naturally the number of scenes had to be reduced, though Anderson expedited shifts by the use of "drops." To all this Herbert Beerbohm Tree could hardly add a great deal, though he certainly tried, at His Majesty's Theatre in 1906, rearranging the play into three acts (Sicily-Bohemia-Sicily) to facilitate his elaborate scenic ambitions.

In 1881 the company of the Royal Theatre of Saxe-Meinigen acted the play at Drury Lane in a German translation by Ludwig Tieck and August Wilhelm von Schlegel. The production was remarkable for its emphasis upon ensemble playing and its meticulous attention to textual detail. Although the Saxe-Meinigen production was enormously successful, it remained for Harley Granville-Barker, the first modern director to assert the advantages of a more flexible stage, to free the play from the static, pictorial traditions of the Victorian theater. His revolutionary production at the Savoy Theatre in 1912 employed a huge apron stage that extended halfway into the parquet, giving the impression of an Elizabethan playhouse and making possible nearly continuous action. The costumes were deliberately antiromantic and nonrealistic, and indeed the production strove to discern what is discordant and alienating in Shakespeare's play. Granville-Barker's staging, both execrated as a travesty and hailed as a major achievement, certainly anticipated the idiom of more recent years.

At London's Phoenix Theatre in 1951, Peter Brook, like Granville-Barker, used a permanent set to ensure the swift flow of the action. Eschewing the picturesque for the psychological, Brook's *The Winter's Tale* emphasized the insane world created by Leontes (John Gielgud) and the efforts of Paulina (Flora Robson) to break through the darkness of his diseased mind. The production successfully combined the symbolic and the realistic. The storm scene took place upon a cold and desolate coast: "for once," theater critic J. C. Trewin wrote, "I had no desire to laugh while Antigonus . . . fled terrified along the angry shore." After Antigonus's exit, snow began to fall heavily, and Time shivered forth to speak his chorus. As he spoke, the storm gradually diminished and the stage was slowly suffused with light; when he finished, the sun shone brightly upon the sheepshearing scene. Peter Wood, directing the play at Stratford-upon-Avon in 1960, followed Brook in his search for psychological credibility. The elegance of the court did not obscure the nightmare of sexual jealousy. Wood brilliantly used subtle physical gestures to reveal psychological states. The reviewer for *The Times* noted Leontes's "infatuated fondling of his Queen's shoulders," and in Act 1, scene 2, Mamillius suddenly clasped his father around the thighs, obviously startling Leontes (Eric Porter).

If Brook and Wood successfully probed the play's psychological substratum, recent productions have responded more directly to the theatrical possibilities suggested by Granville-Barker. In 1969 Trevor Nunn directed the play at Stratford-upon-Avon in a style that was aggressively nonrealistic. According to Christopher Morley, who designed the set (a three-sided white box forming the playing area with various small white boxes serving as furniture), the production emerged from a desire "to develop a house style in which nothing is ever literally represented." And virtually nothing was. The play began with Leontes in a rectangular box, visible through flashes of lightning, while the beginning of Time's speech was heard in the dark theater. Judi Dench doubled in the parts of Hermione and Perdita. In 1976 Nunn again directed the play, working this time with John Barton. Again, roles were revealingly doubled: most interestingly, Time and the bear were played by John Nettles. The destructive forces of nature were made an aspect of Time itself, as Nettles, wearing Time's flowing robes and carrying an abstract bear mask, stalked Antigonus, holding the mask before his face and pounding his staff once on the stage before he carried Antigonus away. Bears indeed were ubiquitous, present as a design motif on wall hangings and carpets, and in a bearskin lying on a couch. The audience was reminded that Time the implacable destroyer could not be avoided. Even in the pastoral scenes of Bohemia, a leafless tree remained onstage to qualify the play's promise of renewal. In its powerful visual images the production directly engaged the play's unreality. The shocking jealousy of Ian McKellen's Leontes seemed natural, if appalling, in this world rich in the symbolic resonances of "an old tale."

No longer wary of the play's artificiality, modern productions are prompt to call attention to the theatricality embodied in Time's bland assurance that he can leap over sixteen years, or in the self-conscious device of bringing a statue to life. A Stratford-upon-Avon production of 1986, directed by Terry Hands and starring Jeremy Irons as Leontes, concentrated visually at first on cool whites and blues for Leontes's Regency court, and then shifted into red, yellow, and orange for the scenes of rustic banqueting in the second half. A great bearskin rug on the polished floor of Leontes's palace, constantly visible with its shining eyes, became the bear that devoured Antigonus at the beginning of part two. In David Williams's production at Stratford, Canada, in the same year, a pageant of Time led off the entire performance, so that the play was seen as part of a never-ending process of aging and renewal. The statue scene (with Goldie Semple as Hermione) succeeded because the spectators were made aware that they were in the theater, with an actress practicing her craft, miming the process of bringing life to her role as any actor or actress must do with any role. Paulina's function as artist figure and as stand-in for the dramatist called attention to the way in which theater works its magic. This crucial point is easily lost when realistic scenery attempts to substitute illusion for theatrical event. The seacoast of Bohemia and its inimitable bear are phenomena of the stage, paradoxically all the more persuasive when spectators actively enlist their imaginations and become partners in the theatrical moment.

THE
WINTER'S
TALE

The Names of the Actors

LEONTES, *King of Sicilia*
MAMILLIUS, *young prince of Sicilia*
CAMILLO,
ANTIGONUS,
CLEOMENES, } *four Lords of Sicilia*
DION,

HERMIONE, *Queen to Leontes*
PERDITA, *daughter to Leontes and Hermione*
PAULINA, *wife to Antigonus*
EMILIA, *a lady [attending Hermione]*

POLIXENES, *King of Bohemia*
FLORIZEL, *Prince of Bohemia*
ARCHIDAMUS, *a lord of Bohemia*
Old SHEPHERD, *reputed father of Perdita*
CLOWN, *his son*
AUTOLYCUS, *a rogue*

[MOPSA,
[DORCAS, } *Shepherdesses.*]

[A MARINER
A JAILER
Two LADIES *attending Hermione*
Two SERVANTS *attending Leontes*
One or more LORDS *attending Leontes*
An OFFICER *of the court*
A GENTLEMAN *attending Leontes*
Three GENTLEMEN *of the court of Sicilia*
A SERVANT *of the Old Shepherd*

TIME, *as Chorus*]

Other Lords and Gentlemen, [Ladies, Officers,] and Servants;
Shepherds and Shepherdesses; [Twelve Countrymen
disguised as Satyrs]

[SCENE: *Sicilia, and Bohemia.*]

1.1 *Enter Camillo and Archidamus.*

ARCHIDAMUS If you shall chance, Camillo, to visit Bohemia on the like occasion whereon my services are
now on foot, you shall see, as I have said, great difference betwixt our Bohemia and your Sicilia.

CAMILLO I think this coming summer the King of Sicilia means to pay Bohemia the visitation which he ⁶
justly owes him.

ARCHIDAMUS Wherein our entertainment shall shame ⁸
us, we will be justified in our loves; for indeed—   ⁹

CAMILLO Beseech you—

ARCHIDAMUS Verily, I speak it in the freedom of my ¹¹
knowledge. We cannot with such magnificence—in ¹²
so rare—I know not what to say. We will give you
sleepy drinks, that your senses, unintelligent of our ¹⁴
insufficiency, may, though they cannot praise us, as
little accuse us.

CAMILLO You pay a great deal too dear for what's given
freely.

ARCHIDAMUS Believe me, I speak as my understanding
instructs me and as mine honesty puts it to utterance.

CAMILLO Sicilia cannot show himself overkind to Bo- ²¹
hemia. They were trained together in their childhoods,
and there rooted betwixt them then such an affection
which cannot choose but branch now. Since their ²⁴
more mature dignities and royal necessities made separation of their society, their encounters, though not ²⁶
personal, hath been royally attorneyed with inter- ²⁷
change of gifts, letters, loving embassies, that they
have seemed to be together though absent, shook
hands as over a vast, and embraced as it were from the ³⁰

1.1. Location: Sicilia. The court of Leontes.
6 Bohemia i.e., the King of Bohemia (also at ll. 21–22)   **8–9 Wherein . . .
loves** i.e., in whatever way our attempts to entertain you will shame us
by falling short of your entertainment of us, we will make up for by our
affection.   **justified** absolved, as of spiritual sin, by faith or love
11–12 in . . . knowledge as my knowledge entitles me to speak
14 sleepy sleep-inducing.   **unintelligent** unaware   **21 Sicilia** the King of
Sicilia   **24 branch** put forth new growth, flourish (also perhaps with
opposite and unconscious suggestion of "divide")   **26 their society** their
being together   **27 personal** in person.   **attorneyed** carried out by
deputy   **30 vast** boundless space

ends of opposed winds. The heavens continue their ³¹
loves!

ARCHIDAMUS I think there is not in the world either
malice or matter to alter it. You have an unspeakable
comfort of your young prince Mamillius. It is a gentle- ³⁵
man of the greatest promise that ever came into my
note.   ³⁷

CAMILLO I very well agree with you in the hopes of
him. It is a gallant child, one that indeed physics the ³⁹
subject, makes old hearts fresh. They that went on ⁴⁰
crutches ere he was born desire yet their life to see him
a man.

ARCHIDAMUS Would they else be content to die?

CAMILLO Yes, if there were no other excuse why they
should desire to live.

ARCHIDAMUS If the King had no son, they would desire to
live on crutches till he had one.   *Exeunt.*

❖

1.2   *Enter Leontes, Hermione, Mamillius, Polixenes,*
       Camillo.

POLIXENES
Nine changes of the watery star hath been   ¹
The shepherd's note since we have left our throne   ²
Without a burden. Time as long again   ³
Would be filled up, my brother, with our thanks,
And yet we should for perpetuity   ⁵
Go hence in debt. And therefore, like a cipher,   ⁶
Yet standing in rich place, I multiply   ⁷
With one "We thank you" many thousands more
That go before it.

LEONTES   Stay your thanks awhile
And pay them when you part.

POLIXENES   Sir, that's tomorrow.

31 ends . . . winds i.e., opposite ends of the earth. **The heavens** may the
heavens **35 of** in the person of **37 note** observation **39–40 physics
the subject** acts as a medicine to the people

1.2. Location: The same.
1 watery star moon **2 note** observation. **we** i.e., I. (The royal "we.")
3 burden i.e., occupant **5 for perpetuity** forever **6–7 like . . . place** like
a zero at the end of a number, multiplying its quantity

I am questioned by my fears of what may chance   11
Or breed upon our absence, that may blow   12
No sneaping winds at home to make us say   13
"This is put forth too truly." Besides, I have stayed   14
To tire your royalty.

LEONTES   We are tougher, brother,
Than you can put us to 't.

POLIXENES   No longer stay.   16

LEONTES
One sennight longer.

POLIXENES   Very sooth, tomorrow.   17

LEONTES
We'll part the time between 's, then, and in that   18
I'll no gainsaying.

POLIXENES   Press me not, beseech you, so.   19
There is no tongue that moves, none, none i' the world
So soon as yours could win me. So it should now,
Were there necessity in your request, although
'Twere needful I denied it. My affairs
Do even drag me homeward, which to hinder
Were in your love a whip to me, my stay   25
To you a charge and trouble. To save both,   26
Farewell, our brother.

LEONTES   Tongue-tied, our Queen? Speak you.

HERMIONE
I had thought, sir, to have held my peace until
You had drawn oaths from him not to stay. You, sir,
Charge him too coldly. Tell him you are sure
All in Bohemia's well; this satisfaction   31
The bygone day proclaimed. Say this to him,   32
He's beat from his best ward.

LEONTES   Well said, Hermione.   33

11–14 I am . . . truly i.e., I am anxious what may happen in Bohemia, either by chance or bred directly out of my absence; I am anxious lest biting or envious winds may be abroad that will cause me to say my fears were all too plausible   **16 Than . . . to 't** than anything you can do to try me   **17 sennight** sevennight, week.   **Very sooth** truly   **18 part the time** split the difference, i.e., divide a week in two   **19 I'll no gainsaying** I will take no refusal   **25 Were . . . whip** would be to make your fondness for me a punishment   **26 charge** expense, burden   **31–32 this . . . proclaimed** yesterday brought news to satisfy on that score (that all is well in Bohemia)   **32 Say** if you say   **33 ward** defensive posture. (A fencing term.)

HERMIONE

To tell he longs to see his son were strong.   34
But let him say so, then, and let him go;
But let him swear so and he shall not stay,   36
We'll thwack him hence with distaffs.
[*To Polixenes.*] Yet of your royal presence I'll adventure   38
The borrow of a week. When at Bohemia   39
You take my lord, I'll give him my commission   40
To let him there a month behind the gest   41
Prefixed for 's parting.—Yet, good deed, Leontes,   42
I love thee not a jar o' the clock behind   43
What lady she her lord.—You'll stay?

POLIXENES   No, madam.   44

HERMIONE

Nay, but you will?

POLIXENES   I may not, verily.

HERMIONE   Verily?

You put me off with limber vows; but I,   47
Though you would seek t' unsphere the stars with oaths,
Should yet say, "Sir, no going." Verily,
You shall not go. A lady's "verily" is
As potent as a lord's. Will you go yet?
Force me to keep you as a prisoner,
Not like a guest: so you shall pay your fees   53
When you depart, and save your thanks. How say you?
My prisoner or my guest? By your dread "verily,"
One of them you shall be.

POLIXENES   Your guest, then, madam.

To be your prisoner should import offending,   57
Which is for me less easy to commit
Than you to punish.

HERMIONE   Not your jailer, then,
But your kind hostess. Come, I'll question you

34 **tell** tell us that.   **strong** a strong argument   36 **he shall not stay** i.e.,
we wouldn't let him stay even if he wanted to   38 **adventure** risk (because, as she explains, she'll undertake to repay each week with a
month)   39 **borrow** borrowing   40 **take** capture; receive   41 **let him** let
him stay.   **gest** time allotted for a halt in a royal progress or journey
42 **good deed** i.e., in truth   43 **jar** tick   44 **What lady she** any lady
47 **limber** limp   53 **fees** payments often demanded by jailers of prisoners at the time of their release   57 **import offending** imply my having
offended

Of my lord's tricks and yours when you were boys.
You were pretty lordings then?

POLIXENES   We were, fair Queen,
Two lads that thought there was no more behind   63
But such a day tomorrow as today,
And to be boy eternal.

HERMIONE   Was not my lord
The verier wag o' the two?   66

POLIXENES
We were as twinned lambs that did frisk i' the sun
And bleat the one at th' other. What we changed   68
Was innocence for innocence; we knew not
The doctrine of ill-doing, nor dreamed
That any did. Had we pursued that life,
And our weak spirits ne'er been higher reared
With stronger blood, we should have answered heaven   73
Boldly "Not guilty," the imposition cleared   74
Hereditary ours.

HERMIONE   By this we gather   75
You have tripped since.

POLIXENES   O my most sacred lady,
Temptations have since then been born to 's, for
In those unfledged days was my wife a girl;   78
Your precious self had then not crossed the eyes
Of my young playfellow.

HERMIONE   Grace to boot!   80
Of this make no conclusion, lest you say   81
Your queen and I are devils. Yet go on.
Th' offenses we have made you do we'll answer,
If you first sinned with us, and that with us   84
You did continue fault, and that you slipped not   85
With any but with us.

LEONTES   Is he won yet?   86

63 behind to come **66 The verier wag** truly the more mischievous
68 changed exchanged **73 stronger blood** i.e., mature sexual passions
74–75 the imposition . . . ours i.e., excepting of course the original sin
that is the condition of all mortals; or, perhaps, being freed from original sin itself (if we had continued in that pure state) **78 unfledged** not
yet feathered, i.e., immature **80 Grace to boot** i.e., Heaven help me
81 Of . . . conclusion don't follow your implied line of reasoning to its
logical conclusion **84 that** if (also in l. 85) **85 fault** offense **86 Is
he won yet** (Leontes has been standing aside for much of their
conversation.)

HERMIONE
He'll stay, my lord.
LEONTES   At my request he would not.
Hermione, my dearest, thou never spok'st
To better purpose.
HERMIONE   Never?
LEONTES   Never but once.
HERMIONE
What? Have I twice said well? When was 't before?
I prithee, tell me. Cram 's with praise and make 's
As fat as tame things. One good deed dying tongueless   92
Slaughters a thousand waiting upon that.   93
Our praises are our wages. You may ride 's
With one soft kiss a thousand furlongs ere
With spur we heat an acre. But to the goal: 96
My last good deed was to entreat his stay.
What was my first? It has an elder sister,
Or I mistake you. O, would her name were Grace!
But once before I spoke to the purpose. When?
Nay, let me have 't; I long.
LEONTES   Why, that was when
Three crabbèd months had soured themselves to death
Ere I could make thee open thy white hand
And clap thyself my love. Then didst thou utter,   104
"I am yours forever."
HERMIONE   'Tis grace indeed.
Why, lo you now, I have spoke to the purpose twice:
The one forever earned a royal husband,
Th' other for some while a friend.
                    [*She gives her hand to Polixenes.*]
LEONTES [*Aside*]   Too hot, too hot!
To mingle friendship far is mingling bloods.   109
I have *tremor cordis* on me. My heart dances,   110
But not for joy, not joy. This entertainment   111
May a free face put on, derive a liberty   112

92 **tongueless** unpraised, unsung   93 **Slaughters ... that** i.e., will
inhibit many other good deeds, since they are encouraged by praise
96 **heat** traverse as in a race.   **to the goal** to come to the point
104 **clap** clasp hands, plight troth   109 **mingling bloods** (Sexual inter-
course was thought to produce a mingling of bloods.)   110 **tremor
cordis** fluttering of the heart   111 **entertainment** i.e., of Polixenes by
Hermione   112 **free face** innocent appearance

From heartiness, from bounty, fertile bosom, 113
And well become the agent. 'T may, I grant. 114
But to be paddling palms and pinching fingers,
As now they are, and making practiced smiles
As in a looking glass, and then to sigh, as 'twere
The mort o' the deer; O, that is entertainment 118
My bosom likes not, nor my brows.—Mamillius, 119
Art thou my boy?

MAMILLIUS   Ay, my good lord.

LEONTES   I' fecks, 120
Why, that's my bawcock. What, hast smutched thy nose? 121
They say it is a copy out of mine. Come, captain,
We must be neat; not neat, but cleanly, captain. 123
And yet the steer, the heifer, and the calf
Are all called neat.—Still virginaling 125
Upon his palm?—How now, you wanton calf? 126
Art thou my calf?

MAMILLIUS   Yes, if you will, my lord.

LEONTES
Thou want'st a rough pash and the shoots that I have 128
To be full like me. Yet they say we are 129
Almost as like as eggs. Women say so,
That will say anything. But were they false
As o'erdyed blacks, as wind, as waters, false 132
As dice are to be wished by one that fixes 133
No bourn twixt his and mine, yet were it true 134
To say this boy were like me. Come, sir page,
Look on me with your welkin eye. Sweet villain! 136

---

113 fertile bosom i.e., generous affection **114 well . . . agent** look well in her (Hermione) who does these things **118 mort** note sounded on a horn at the death of the hunted deer **119 brows** (Alludes to cuckolds' horns, the supposed badge of men whose wives are unfaithful.) **120 I' fecks** in faith **121 bawcock** i.e., fine fellow. (French *beau coq*.) **123 not . . . cleanly** (Leontes changes the word because *neat* also means "cattle" and hence reminds him of cuckolds' horns.) **125 virginaling** touching hands, as in playing on the virginals, a keyed instrument **126 wanton** frisky **128 Thou want'st** you lack. **rough pash** shaggy head. **shoots** horns. (Another allusion to cuckolds' horns.) **129 full** fully **132 o'erdyed blacks** black garments that have been weakened by too much dye, or dyed in another color (thereby betraying a forgetfulness in the erstwhile mourner) **133–134 one . . . mine** i.e., one who intends to cheat me at dice. **bourn** boundary **136 welkin** sky-blue

Most dear'st! My collop! Can thy dam?—may 't be?—   137
Affection, thy intention stabs the center.   138
Thou dost make possible things not so held,   139
Communicat'st with dreams—how can this be?—   140
With what's unreal thou coactive art,   141
And fellow'st nothing. Then 'tis very credent   142
Thou mayst cojoin with something; and thou dost,   143
And that beyond commission, and I find it,   144
And that to the infection of my brains
And hardening of my brows.

POLIXENES   What means Sicilia?   146

HERMIONE
He something seems unsettled.   147

POLIXENES   How, my lord?   147
What cheer? How is 't with you, best brother?

HERMIONE   You look
As if you held a brow of much distraction.
Are you moved, my lord?

LEONTES   No, in good earnest.   150
How sometimes nature will betray its folly,
Its tenderness, and make itself a pastime   152
To harder bosoms! Looking on the lines   153
Of my boy's face, methought I did recoil   154
Twenty-three years, and saw myself unbreeched,   155
In my green velvet coat, my dagger muzzled
Lest it should bite its master and so prove,
As ornaments oft do, too dangerous.
How like, methought, I then was to this kernel,
This squash, this gentleman.—Mine honest friend,   160
Will you take eggs for money?   161

---

137 collop small piece of meat; i.e., of my own flesh. **dam** mother
138–143 Affection . . . something Strong passion, your intense power
pierces to the very center, the soul of man. You deal in matters normally considered fantastic; you partake of the nature of dreams. How
can this be? You collaborate with unreality, and create imagined fantasies. It's all the likelier, then, that such imaginings may also become
real. **144 commission** what is lawful **146 What means Sicilia** i.e., why
is the King of Sicilia looking so distracted **147 something** somewhat
150 moved angry **152 pastime** occasion for amusement **153 To harder
bosoms** for persons who are less tenderhearted **154 methought** it
seemed to me. **recoil** i.e., go back in memory **155 unbreeched** not yet
wearing breeches **160 squash** unripe peascod or pea pod. **honest**
worthy **161 take eggs for money** i.e., be imposed upon, taken advantage of, cheated. (Proverbial.)

MAMILLIUS   No, my lord, I'll fight.

LEONTES
You will? Why, happy man be 's dole!—My brother,   163
Are you so fond of your young prince as we
Do seem to be of ours?

POLIXENES   If at home, sir,
He's all my exercise, my mirth, my matter,   166
Now my sworn friend and then mine enemy,
My parasite, my soldier, statesman, all.
He makes a July's day short as December,
And with his varying childness cures in me   170
Thoughts that would thick my blood.

LEONTES   So stands this squire   171
Officed with me. We two will walk, my lord,   172
And leave you to your graver steps. Hermione,
How thou lov'st us, show in our brother's welcome.   174
Let what is dear in Sicily be cheap.   175
Next to thyself and my young rover, he's
Apparent to my heart.

HERMIONE   If you would seek us,   177
We are yours i' the garden. Shall 's attend you there?   178

LEONTES
To your own bents dispose you. You'll be found,   179
Be you beneath the sky. [Aside.] I am angling now,
Though you perceive me not how I give line.   181
Go to, go to!   182
How she holds up the neb, the bill to him,   183
And arms her with the boldness of a wife   184
To her allowing husband!

         [Exeunt Polixenes and Hermione.]
         Gone already!   185

163 happy . . . dole may good fortune be his lot. (Proverbial.)
166 matter concern   **170 childness** childlike ways   **171 thick my blood** (Melancholy thoughts were supposed to thicken the blood.)   **172 Officed** placed in particular function   **174–175 How . . . cheap** (A hidden second meaning in these lines may be intentional: show just how much you love me by the way you encourage Polixenes's attentions, and thereby cheapen the most precious thing in Sicily.)   **177 Apparent** heir apparent (perhaps with a suggestion too of "evident, revealed")   **178 Shall 's** shall we   **179 To . . . dispose you** act according to your inclinations (with more bitter double meaning, continued in *You'll be found*, i.e., found out)   **181 give line** pay out line (to let the fish hook himself well)   **182 Go to** (An expression of remonstrance.)   **183 neb** beak, i.e., nose, mouth   **184 arms her with** assumes   **185 allowing** approving

Inch thick, knee-deep, o'er head and ears a forked one!—   186
Go, play, boy, play. Thy mother plays, and I   187
Play too, but so disgraced a part, whose issue   188
Will hiss me to my grave. Contempt and clamor
Will be my knell. Go, play, boy, play. There have been,
Or I am much deceived, cuckolds ere now;
And many a man there is, even at this present,
Now while I speak this, holds his wife by th' arm,
That little thinks she has been sluiced in 's absence   194
And his pond fished by his next neighbor, by
Sir Smile, his neighbor. Nay, there's comfort in 't
Whiles other men have gates and those gates opened,   197
As mine, against their will. Should all despair
That have revolted wives, the tenth of mankind   199
Would hang themselves. Physic for 't there's none.   200
It is a bawdy planet, that will strike   201
Where 'tis predominant; and 'tis powerful, think it,   202
From east, west, north, and south. Be it concluded,
No barricado for a belly. Know 't,   204
It will let in and out the enemy
With bag and baggage. Many thousand on 's   206
Have the disease and feel 't not.—How now, boy?

MAMILLIUS
I am like you, they say.

LEONTES   Why, that's some comfort.
What, Camillo there?

CAMILLO [*Coming forward*] Ay, my good lord.

LEONTES
Go play, Mamillius; thou'rt an honest man.

                        [*Exit Mamillius.*]
Camillo, this great sir will yet stay longer.

---

186 forked horned   **187 play** play games.   **plays** i.e., in a sexual liai-
son   **188 Play** play a role.   **issue** outcome (with a pun on the sense of
"offspring" and "exit," i.e., death)   **194 has been sluiced** (The water in
his pond, so to speak, has been drained off by a cheating neighbor.)
197 gates sluice gates, suggestive of the wife's chastity that has been
opened and robbed   **199 revolted** unfaithful   **200 Physic** medicine
201 It i.e., the cause of unchastity, the planet Venus.   **strike** blast,
destroy by a malign influence   **202 predominant** in the ascendant. (Said
of a planet.)   **think it** be assured of this   **204 barricado** barricade
206 bag and baggage (with sexual suggestion, as earlier in *dagger*
[l. 156], *sluiced, gates, let in and out,* etc.)   **on 's** of us

CAMILLO
You had much ado to make his anchor hold.
When you cast out, it still came home.

LEONTES   Didst note it?   213

CAMILLO
He would not stay at your petitions, made
His business more material.

LEONTES   Didst perceive it?   215

[*Aside.*] They're here with me already, whispering,
    rounding,   216
"Sicilia is a so-forth." 'Tis far gone   217
When I shall gust it last.—How came 't, Camillo,   218
That he did stay?

CAMILLO   At the good Queen's entreaty.

LEONTES
"At the Queen's" be 't. "Good" should be pertinent,   220
But so it is, it is not. Was this taken   221
By any understanding pate but thine?
For thy conceit is soaking, will draw in   223
More than the common blocks. Not noted, is 't,   224
But of the finer natures? By some severals   225
Of headpiece extraordinary? Lower messes   226
Perchance are to this business purblind? Say.   227

CAMILLO
Business, my lord? I think most understand
Bohemia stays here longer.

LEONTES
Ha?

CAMILLO Stays here longer.

LEONTES   Ay, but why?

CAMILLO
To satisfy Your Highness and the entreaties
Of our most gracious mistress.

---

213 still continually. **came home** came back to the ship, failed to
hold **215 material** important **216 They're ... already** people are
already onto my secret. **rounding** whispering, gossiping **217 a so-
forth** a so-and-so, a you-know-what **218 gust** taste, i.e., hear of
220 pertinent i.e., appropriately applied **221 so it is** as things stand.
taken perceived **223 conceit** understanding. **soaking** i.e., very receptive **224 blocks** blockheads **225 But ... natures** except by those of
rarefied intellect. **severals** individuals **226 Lower messes** those who
sit lower at table, i.e., inferior men **227 purblind** totally blind

LEONTES   Satisfy?   232
Th' entreaties of your mistress? Satisfy?
Let that suffice. I have trusted thee, Camillo,
With all the nearest things to my heart, as well   235
My chamber councils, wherein, priestlike, thou   236
Hast cleansed my bosom. I from thee departed
Thy penitent reformed. But we have been
Deceived in thy integrity, deceived
In that which seems so.
CAMILLO   Be it forbid, my lord!   240
LEONTES
To bide upon 't, thou art not honest; or,   241
If thou inclin'st that way, thou art a coward,   242
Which hoxes honesty behind, restraining   243
From course required; or else thou must be counted   244
A servant grafted in my serious trust   245
And therein negligent; or else a fool
That seest a game played home, the rich stake drawn, 247
And tak'st it all for jest.
CAMILLO   My gracious lord,
I may be negligent, foolish, and fearful;
In every one of these no man is free,
But that his negligence, his folly, fear,
Among the infinite doings of the world
Sometimes puts forth. In your affairs, my lord,   253
If ever I were willful-negligent,
It was my folly; if industriously   255
I played the fool, it was my negligence,   256
Not weighing well the end; if ever fearful
To do a thing where I the issue doubted,   258

---

232 Satisfy (Leontes takes the word in a sexual sense.) **235 as well** as
well as with   **236 chamber councils** private affairs   **240 Be it forbid**
i.e., God forbid I should do such a thing   **241 To bide upon 't**
(1) to dwell on this matter still further, or (2) for you to insist thus on
your integrity.   **or** either   **242 inclin'st that way** i.e., prefer being
honest under ordinary circumstances   **243 Which** i.e., which cowardice.   **hoxes** hamstrings   **244 From course required** i.e., from the direction honest inquiry must take to find the truth   **245 grafted . . . trust**
taken into my complete confidence. (*Grafted* means "deeply embedded,"
like a graft.)   **247 home** i.e., for keeps, in earnest. (With perhaps a
sexual double meaning, continued in *rich stake drawn*.)   **drawn** won
253 puts forth shows itself   **255 industriously** willfully   **256 played the
fool** i.e., took some matter lightly   **258 issue** outcome.   **doubted** feared

Whereof the execution did cry out   259
Against the nonperformance, 'twas a fear   260
Which oft infects the wisest. These, my lord,
Are such allowed infirmities that honesty   262
Is never free of. But, beseech Your Grace,
Be plainer with me. Let me know my trespass
By its own visage. If I then deny it,   265
'Tis none of mine.
LEONTES   Ha' not you seen, Camillo—
But that's past doubt; you have, or your eyeglass   267
Is thicker than a cuckold's horn—or heard—   268
For to a vision so apparent, rumor   269
Cannot be mute—or thought—for cogitation
Resides not in that man that does not think—   271
My wife is slippery? If thou wilt confess,
Or else be impudently negative   273
To have nor eyes nor ears nor thought, then say   274
My wife's a hobbyhorse, deserves a name   275
As rank as any flax-wench that puts to   276
Before her trothplight. Say 't and justify 't.   277
CAMILLO
I would not be a stander-by to hear
My sovereign mistress clouded so without
My present vengeance taken. Shrew my heart,   280
You never spoke what did become you less
Than this, which to reiterate were sin   282
As deep as that, though true.
LEONTES   Is whispering nothing?   283
Is leaning cheek to cheek? Is meeting noses?

259–260 Whereof . . . nonperformance in which the completion of the
task showed how wrong I was in being unwilling to undertake it
262 allowed acknowledged. **that** as **265 visage** face, i.e., plain appearance **267 eyeglass** lens of the eye **268 cuckold's horn** (A thin sheet of
horn can be seen through like a lens, though a cuckold's horn is another matter.) **269 a vision so apparent** something so plainly visible
271 think i.e., think so **273 Or else** the only possible alternative to
which is to **273–274 be . . . have** impudently deny that you have
274 nor eyes neither eyes **275 hobbyhorse** wanton woman **276 flax-
wench** common slut. **puts to** engages in sex **277 justify** affirm
280 present immediate. **Shrew** beshrew, curse **282–283 which . . .
true** i.e., to repeat which accusation would be to sin as deeply as her
supposed adultery or your sinfulness in thus accusing her, even if it
were true (which it isn't)

Kissing with inside lip? Stopping the career   285
Of laughter with a sigh—a note infallible
Of breaking honesty? Horsing foot on foot?   287
Skulking in corners? Wishing clocks more swift,
Hours minutes, noon midnight? And all eyes   289
Blind with the pin and web but theirs, theirs only,   290
That would unseen be wicked? Is this nothing?
Why, then the world and all that's in 't is nothing,
The covering sky is nothing, Bohemia nothing,
My wife is nothing, nor nothing have these nothings,
If this be nothing.

CAMILLO   Good my lord, be cured
Of this diseased opinion, and betimes,   296
For 'tis most dangerous.

LEONTES   Say it be, 'tis true.   297

CAMILLO
No, no, my lord.

LEONTES   It is. You lie, you lie!
I say thou liest, Camillo, and I hate thee,
Pronounce thee a gross lout, a mindless slave,
Or else a hovering temporizer, that   301
Canst with thine eyes at once see good and evil,
Inclining to them both. Were my wife's liver
Infected as her life, she would not live   304
The running of one glass.

CAMILLO   Who does infect her?   305

LEONTES
Why, he that wears her like her medal, hanging   306
About his neck, Bohemia—who, if I
Had servants true about me, that bare eyes   308
To see alike mine honor as their profits,
Their own particular thrifts, they would do that   310
Which should undo more doing. Ay, and thou,   311

---

285 career full gallop   **287 honesty** chastity.   **Horsing foot on foot**
placing one's foot on that of another person and then moving the feet
up and down together   **289 Hours minutes** wishing hours were minutes   **290 pin and web** cataract of the eye. (The lovers wish to think
themselves unobserved.)   **296 betimes** quickly   **297 Say it be** i.e., even
if it is dangerous   **301 hovering** wavering   **304 Infected as her life** as
full of disease as is her moral conduct   **305 glass** hourglass   **306 like
her medal** like a miniature portrait of her, worn in a locket   **308 bare**
bore   **310 thrifts** gains   **311 undo** prevent

His cupbearer—whom I from meaner form   312
Have benched and reared to worship, who mayst see   313
Plainly as heaven sees earth and earth sees heaven
How I am galled—mightst bespice a cup   315
To give mine enemy a lasting wink,   316
Which draft to me were cordial.

CAMILLO   Sir, my lord,   317
I could do this, and that with no rash potion,   318
But with a lingering dram that should not work
Maliciously like poison. But I cannot   320
Believe this crack to be in my dread mistress,   321
So sovereignly being honorable.   322
I have loved thee—

LEONTES   Make that thy question, and go rot!   323
Dost think I am so muddy, so unsettled,   324
To appoint myself in this vexation, sully   325
The purity and whiteness of my sheets—
Which to preserve is sleep, which being spotted
Is goads, thorns, nettles, tails of wasps—
Give scandal to the blood o' the Prince my son,
Who I do think is mine and love as mine,
Without ripe moving to 't? Would I do this?   331
Could man so blench?

CAMILLO   I must believe you, sir.   332
I do, and will fetch off Bohemia for 't;   333
Provided that, when he's removed, Your Highness
Will take again your queen as yours at first,
Even for your son's sake, and thereby for sealing   336
The injury of tongues in courts and kingdoms
Known and allied to yours.

LEONTES   Thou dost advise me

312 **meaner form** humbler station   313 **benched** placed on the bench of
authority. **worship** dignity, honor   315 **galled** rubbed, chafed
316 **lasting wink** everlasting closing of the eyes (in death)   317 **were
cordial** would be restorative   318 **rash** quick-acting   320 **Maliciously**
virulently   321 **crack** flaw. **dread** worthy of awe   322 **sovereignly**
supremely   323 **Make . . . rot** i.e., if you're going to raise questions like
that, may you rot in hell   324 **muddy** muddle-headed   325 **To . . .
vexation** to ordain that I should suffer this affliction   331 **ripe** ample,
urgent   332 **blench** swerve (from sensible conduct)   333 **fetch off** do
away with; or, with deliberate ambiguity, rescue (as also in *removed* in
the next line)   336 **sealing** silencing

Even so as I mine own course have set down.
I'll give no blemish to her honor, none.

CAMILLO   My lord,
Go then, and with a countenance as clear
As friendship wears at feasts, keep with Bohemia   343
And with your queen. I am his cupbearer.
If from me he have wholesome beverage,
Account me not your servant.

LEONTES   This is all.
Do 't and thou hast the one half of my heart;
Do 't not, thou splitt'st thine own.

CAMILLO   I'll do 't, my lord.

LEONTES
I will seem friendly, as thou hast advised me.   *Exit.*

CAMILLO
O miserable lady! But, for me,
What case stand I in? I must be the poisoner
Of good Polixenes, and my ground to do 't
Is the obedience to a master, one
Who in rebellion with himself will have
All that are his so too. To do this deed,   355
Promotion follows. If I could find example   356
Of thousands that had struck anointed kings
And flourished after, I'd not do 't; but since   358
Nor brass, nor stone, nor parchment bears not one,   359
Let villainy itself forswear 't. I must
Forsake the court. To do 't or no is certain   361
To me a breakneck. Happy star reign now!   362
Here comes Bohemia.

        Enter Polixenes.

POLIXENES   This is strange. Methinks
My favor here begins to warp. Not speak?—   364
Good day, Camillo.

343 keep remain in company   **355 All . . . too** i.e., all who follow him
similarly in rebellion against his best self and obedience to his worst
self.   **To do** if I do   **356 If** even if   **358–359 but . . . one** i.e., but since
recorded history shows no instances of men who have killed a king and
prospered afterwards   **361 To do 't or no** i.e., either to kill Polixenes or
not to kill him   **362 breakneck** destruction, ruin.   **Happy** propitious,
favorable   **364 warp** change, shrivel, grow askew (as wood warps).   **Not
speak** (Leontes has just passed by Polixenes without speaking.)

CAMILLO   Hail, most royal sir!
POLIXENES
   What is the news i' the court?
CAMILLO   None rare, my lord.   366
POLIXENES
   The King hath on him such a countenance
   As he had lost some province and a region   368
   Loved as he loves himself. Even now I met him
   With customary compliment, when he,
   Wafting his eyes to th' contrary and falling   371
   A lip of much contempt, speeds from me, and
   So leaves me to consider what is breeding   373
   That changeth thus his manners.
CAMILLO   I dare not know, my lord.
POLIXENES
   How, dare not? Do not? Do you know, and dare not?   376
   Be intelligent to me. 'Tis thereabouts,   377
   For to yourself what you do know you must,   378
   And cannot say you dare not. Good Camillo,   379
   Your changed complexions are to me a mirror
   Which shows me mine changed too; for I must be   381
   A party in this alteration, finding   382
   Myself thus altered with 't.
CAMILLO   There is a sickness
   Which puts some of us in distemper, but
   I cannot name the disease; and it is caught
   Of you that yet are well.
POLIXENES   How? Caught of me?   386
   Make me not sighted like the basilisk.   387
   I have looked on thousands who have sped the better   388
   By my regard, but killed none so. Camillo,   389
   As you are certainly a gentleman, thereto   390

---

366 rare noteworthy   **368 As** as if   **371 Wafting . . . contrary** averting
his eyes.   **falling** letting fall   **373 breeding** hatching   **376 Do not** i.e., or
do you mean you don't know   **377 intelligent** intelligible.   **'Tis thereabouts** it must be something of this sort, i.e., that you know and dare
not tell   **378–379 For . . . dare not** i.e., for in your heart, whatever it is
you know, you must in fact know, and can't claim it's a matter of not
daring to know   **381–382 for . . . alteration** i.e., for my looks must
have changed too, reflecting this change in my position   **386 Of** by
387 sighted provided with a gaze.   **basilisk** a fabled serpent whose gaze
was fatal   **388 sped** prospered   **389 regard** look   **390 thereto** in addition to which

Clerklike experienced, which no less adorns   391
Our gentry than our parents' noble names,   392
In whose success we are gentle, I beseech you,   393
If you know aught which does behoove my knowledge
Thereof to be informed, imprison 't not
In ignorant concealment.

CAMILLO   I may not answer.   396

POLIXENES
A sickness caught of me, and yet I well?
I must be answered. Dost thou hear, Camillo?
I conjure thee, by all the parts of man   399
Which honor does acknowledge, whereof the least
Is not this suit of mine, that thou declare
What incidency thou dost guess of harm   402
Is creeping toward me; how far off, how near;
Which way to be prevented, if to be;   404
If not, how best to bear it.

CAMILLO   Sir, I will tell you,
Since I am charged in honor and by him
That I think honorable. Therefore mark my counsel,
Which must be even as swiftly followed as
I mean to utter it, or both yourself and me
Cry lost, and so good night!

POLIXENES   On, good Camillo.   410

CAMILLO
I am appointed him to murder you.   411

POLIXENES
By whom, Camillo?

CAMILLO   By the King.

POLIXENES   For what?

CAMILLO
He thinks, nay, with all confidence he swears,
As he had seen 't or been an instrument

391 **Clerklike** like an educated man   392 **gentry** gentlemanlike condition   393 **whose success** succession from whom.   **gentle** wellborn
396 **ignorant concealment** concealment that would keep me ignorant, or that would proceed from pretended ignorance on your part   399 **parts** obligations   402 **incidency** likelihood   404 **if to be** if it can be (prevented)   410 **good night** i.e., this is the end   411 **him** by him (Leontes); or, the one

To vice you to 't, that you have touched his queen   415
Forbiddenly.
POLIXENES   O, then my best blood turn
To an infected jelly, and my name
Be yoked with his that did betray the Best!   418
Turn then my freshest reputation to
A savor that may strike the dullest nostril   420
Where I arrive, and my approach be shunned,
Nay, hated too, worse than the great'st infection
That e'er was heard or read!
CAMILLO   Swear his thought over   423
By each particular star in heaven and
By all their influences, you may as well
Forbid the sea for to obey the moon   426
As or by oath remove or counsel shake   427
The fabric of his folly, whose foundation   428
Is piled upon his faith and will continue   429
The standing of his body.
POLIXENES   How should this grow?   430
CAMILLO
I know not. But I am sure 'tis safer to
Avoid what's grown than question how 'tis born.
If therefore you dare trust my honesty,
That lies enclosèd in this trunk which you   434
Shall bear along impawned, away tonight!   435
Your followers I will whisper to the business,   436
And will by twos and threes at several posterns   437
Clear them o' the city. For myself, I'll put
My fortunes to your service, which are here
By this discovery lost. Be not uncertain,   440

---

415 vice force, as with a carpenter's tool; or, impel, tempt. (The *Vice* was a tempter in the morality play.) **418 his . . . Best** the name of him (Judas) who betrayed Christ **420 savor** stench **423 Swear . . . over** i.e., even if you should deny his suspicion with oaths **426 for to** to **427 or . . . or** either . . . or **428 fabric** edifice **428–430 whose . . . body** the foundation of which is built upon an unshaken conviction, and which will last as long as the body exists **430 standing** life, existence. **How . . . grow** i.e., how could this suspicion have arisen **434 trunk** body (with a suggestion too of a traveling trunk) **435 impawned** i.e., as a pledge of good faith **436 whisper to** secretly inform of and urge **437 posterns** rear gates **440 discovery** revelation, disclosure

For, by the honor of my parents, I
Have uttered truth, which if you seek to prove,   442
I dare not stand by; nor shall you be safer   443
Than one condemned by the King's own mouth, thereon
His execution sworn.

POLIXENES   I do believe thee;
I saw his heart in 's face. Give me thy hand.
Be pilot to me, and thy places shall   447
Still neighbor mine. My ships are ready, and   448
My people did expect my hence departure
Two days ago. This jealousy
Is for a precious creature. As she's rare,
Must it be great; and as his person's mighty,
Must it be violent; and as he does conceive
He is dishonored by a man which ever
Professed to him, why, his revenges must   455
In that be made more bitter. Fear o'ershades me.
Good expedition be my friend, and comfort   457
The gracious Queen, part of his theme, but nothing   458
Of his ill-ta'en suspicion! Come, Camillo,   459
I will respect thee as a father if
Thou bear'st my life off. Hence! Let us avoid.   461

CAMILLO
It is in mine authority to command
The keys of all the posterns. Please Your Highness
To take the urgent hour. Come, sir, away.   *Exeunt.*

❖

442 **prove** test   443 **stand by** affirm publicly; stay   447–448 **thy . . .
mine** your official position will always be near to me   455 **Professed**
openly professed friendship   457–459 **Good . . . suspicion** may good
speed befriend me, and may my quick departure ease the predicament
of the gracious Queen, who is the object of the King's suspicions but
who is guiltless of them   461 **avoid** depart

2.1 *Enter Hermione, Mamillius, [and] Ladies.*

HERMIONE
  Take the boy to you. He so troubles me
  'Tis past enduring.
FIRST LADY [*Taking Mamillius from the Queen*]
                    Come, my gracious lord,
  Shall I be your playfellow?
MAMILLIUS
  No, I'll none of you.
FIRST LADY   Why, my sweet lord?   4
MAMILLIUS
  You'll kiss me hard and speak to me as if
  I were a baby still.—I love you better.
SECOND LADY
  And why so, my lord?
MAMILLIUS   Not for because   7
  Your brows are blacker; yet black brows, they say,
  Become some women best, so that there be not   9
  Too much hair there, but in a semicircle,
  Or a half-moon made with a pen.
SECOND LADY   Who taught' this? 11
MAMILLIUS
  I learned it out of women's faces. Pray now,
  What color are your eyebrows?
FIRST LADY   Blue, my lord.
MAMILLIUS
  Nay, that's a mock. I have seen a lady's nose
  That has been blue, but not her eyebrows.
FIRST LADY   Hark ye,
  The Queen your mother rounds apace. We shall
  Present our services to a fine new prince
  One of these days, and then you'd wanton with us,   18
  If we would have you.
SECOND LADY   She is spread of late
  Into a goodly bulk. Good time encounter her!   20

2.1. Location: Sicilia. The royal court.
4 none of you have nothing to do with you **7 for because** because **9 so**
provided **11 taught'** taught you **18 wanton** sport, play **20 Good . . .**
her may she have a happy issue

HERMIONE [*Calling to her women*]
  What wisdom stirs amongst you?—Come, sir, now
  I am for you again. Pray you, sit by us
  And tell 's a tale.
MAMILLIUS   Merry or sad shall 't be?
HERMIONE   As merry as you will.
MAMILLIUS
  A sad tale's best for winter. I have one
  Of sprites and goblins.
HERMIONE   Let's have that, good sir.
  Come on, sit down. Come on, and do your best
  To fright me with your sprites. You're powerful at it.
MAMILLIUS
  There was a man—
HERMIONE   Nay, come sit down, then on.
                            [*Mamillius sits.*]
MAMILLIUS
  Dwelt by a churchyard. I will tell it softly;
  Yond crickets shall not hear it.   31
HERMIONE
  Come on, then, and give 't me in mine ear.
                        [*They converse privately.*]

  [*Enter*] *Leontes, Antigonus, Lords,* [*and others*].

LEONTES
  Was he met there? His train? Camillo with him?
A LORD
  Behind the tuft of pines I met them. Never
  Saw I men scour so on their way. I eyed them   35
  Even to their ships.
LEONTES   How blest am I
  In my just censure, in my true opinion!   37
  Alack, for lesser knowledge! How accurst   38
  In being so blest! There may be in the cup   39
  A spider steeped, and one may drink, depart,   40
  And yet partake no venom, for his knowledge

31 **crickets** i.e., the court ladies, tittering and laughing   **35 scour**
scurry   **37 censure** judgment   **38 Alack . . . knowledge** would that I
knew less   **39 blest** i.e., with knowledge (that causes unhappiness)
40 A spider (The superstition referred to here is that the drinker is not
poisoned by the spider in the cup unless he knows the spider to be
there.)

Is not infected; but if one present
Th' abhorred ingredient to his eye, make known
How he hath drunk, he cracks his gorge, his sides,   44
With violent hefts. I have drunk, and seen the spider.   45
Camillo was his help in this, his pander.
There is a plot against my life, my crown.
All's true that is mistrusted. That false villain   48
Whom I employed was pre-employed by him.
He has discovered my design, and I   50
Remain a pinched thing, yea, a very trick   51
For them to play at will. How came the posterns   52
So easily open?

A LORD   By his great authority,
Which often hath no less prevailed than so
On your command.

LEONTES   I know 't too well.
[*To Hermione.*] Give me the boy. I am glad you did
    not nurse him.
Though he does bear some signs of me, yet you
Have too much blood in him.

HERMIONE   What is this? Sport?   59

LEONTES
Bear the boy hence; he shall not come about her.
Away with him! And let her sport herself
With that she's big with, for 'tis Polixenes
Has made thee swell thus.   [*Mamillius is led out.*]

HERMIONE   But I'd say he had not,   63
And I'll be sworn you would believe my saying,
Howe'er you lean to the nayward.

LEONTES   You, my lords,   65
Look on her, mark her well. Be but about
To say "She is a goodly lady," and   67
The justice of your hearts will thereto add
"'Tis pity she's not honest, honorable."   69
Praise her but for this her without-door form,   70
Which on my faith deserves high speech, and straight   71

44 gorge throat   **45 hefts** heavings, retchings   **48 mistrusted** suspected   **50 discovered** disclosed   **51 pinched** tortured, ridiculous.
trick plaything   **52 play** play with   **59 Sport** a joke   **63 I'd** I need only   **65 nayward** negative, opposite   **67 goodly** attractive   **69 honest** chaste   **70 without-door** outward, external   **71 straight** straightway, at once

The shrug, the hum or ha, these petty brands   72
That calumny doth use—O, I am out,   73
That mercy does, for calumny will sear   74
Virtue itself—these shrugs, these hums and ha's,
When you have said she's goodly, come between   76
Ere you can say she's honest. But be 't known,
From him that has most cause to grieve it should be,
She's an adulteress.

HERMIONE   Should a villain say so,
The most replenished villain in the world,   80
He were as much more villain. You, my lord,   81
Do but mistake.

LEONTES   You have mistook, my lady,
Polixenes for Leontes. O thou thing!
Which I'll not call a creature of thy place,   84
Lest barbarism, making me the precedent,
Should a like language use to all degrees   86
And mannerly distinguishment leave out   87
Betwixt the prince and beggar. I have said
She's an adulteress; I have said with whom.
More, she's a traitor, and Camillo is
A fedarie with her, and one that knows   91
What she should shame to know herself
But with her most vile principal, that she's   93
A bed-swerver, even as bad as those   94
That vulgars give bold'st titles, ay, and privy   95
To this their late escape.

HERMIONE   No, by my life,
Privy to none of this. How will this grieve you,
When you shall come to clearer knowledge, that
You thus have published me! Gentle my lord,   99

---

72 brands i.e., signs, stigmas   **73 out** wrong, in error   **74 does** uses.
(Leontes's point is that no one commits calumny by suggesting with a
shrug that Hermione is unchaste; calumny attacks *virtue itself*, whereas
Hermione has only the false appearance of virtue.)   **76 come between**
interrupt   **80 replenished** full, complete   **81 He . . . villain** his saying so
would double his villainy   **84 Which . . . place** (The King will not
desecrate Hermione's exalted rank by calling her what she really is.)
86 degrees social ranks   **87 mannerly distinguishment** polite distinctions   **91 fedarie** confederate, accomplice   **93 principal** partner
94 bed-swerver adulteress   **95 vulgars . . . titles** common people call by
the rudest names.   **privy** in on the secret   **99 published** proclaimed.
Gentle my my noble

You scarce can right me throughly then to say   100
You did mistake.

LEONTES   No. If I mistake
In those foundations which I build upon,
The center is not big enough to bear   103
A schoolboy's top. Away with her to prison!
He who shall speak for her is afar off guilty   105
But that he speaks.

HERMIONE   There's some ill planet reigns.   106
I must be patient till the heavens look
With an aspect more favorable. Good my lords,
I am not prone to weeping, as our sex
Commonly are, the want of which vain dew
Perchance shall dry your pities; but I have
That honorable grief lodged here which burns
Worse than tears drown. Beseech you all, my lords,
With thoughts so qualified as your charities   114
Shall best instruct you, measure me; and so   115
The King's will be performed!

LEONTES   Shall I be heard?   116

HERMIONE
Who is 't that goes with me? Beseech Your Highness
My women may be with me, for you see
My plight requires it.—Do not weep, good fools;   119
There is no cause. When you shall know your mistress
Has deserved prison, then abound in tears
As I come out. This action I now go on   122
Is for my better grace. Adieu, my lord.   123
I never wished to see you sorry; now
I trust I shall. My women, come, you have leave.

LEONTES   Go, do our bidding. Hence!
          [*Exit Queen, guarded, with Ladies.*]

A LORD
Beseech Your Highness, call the Queen again.

ANTIGONUS
Be certain what you do, sir, lest your justice

100 throughly thoroughly.   **to say** by saying   **103 center** earth
105 afar off indirectly   **106 But . . . speaks** merely by speaking
114 qualified tempered   **115 measure** judge   **116 heard** i.e., obeyed
119 fools (Here, a term of endearment.)   **122 come out** am released
from prison   **123 my better grace** my greater honor (when my name is
cleared; perhaps also with a suggestion of being ennobled by suffering)

Prove violence, in the which three great ones suffer:
Yourself, your queen, your son.

A LORD   For her, my lord,
I dare my life lay down and will do 't, sir,
Please you t' accept it, that the Queen is spotless
I' th' eyes of heaven and to you—I mean
In this which you accuse her.

ANTIGONUS   If it prove
She's otherwise, I'll keep my stables where   135
I lodge my wife. I'll go in couples with her;   136
Than when I feel and see her no farther trust her.   137
For every inch of woman in the world,
Ay, every dram of woman's flesh is false,
If she be.

LEONTES   Hold your peaces.

A LORD   Good my lord—   140

ANTIGONUS
It is for you we speak, not for ourselves.
You are abused, and by some putter-on   142
That will be damned for 't. Would I knew the villain,
I would land-damn him. Be she honor-flawed,   144
I have three daughters—the eldest is eleven,
The second and the third, nine and some five—   146
If this prove true, they'll pay for 't. By mine honor,
I'll geld 'em all! Fourteen they shall not see
To bring false generations. They are co-heirs,   149
And I had rather glib myself than they   150
Should not produce fair issue.

LEONTES   Cease, no more!   151
You smell this business with a sense as cold
As is a dead man's nose; but I do see 't and feel 't
As you feel doing thus, and see withal   154

135–136 I'll . . . wife (If Hermione is an adulteress, says Antigonus, then
all women are no better than animals, to be penned up and guarded
suspiciously.)   136 in couples i.e., like two hounds leashed together and
hence inseparable   137 Than . . . her trust her no further than I can
feel her next to me and actually see her   140 she i.e., Hermione
142 abused deceived. putter-on instigator   144 land-damn (Meaning
uncertain.)   146 some about   149 false generations illegitimate children.   They are co-heirs i.e., they will share my inheritance (since I
have no son to inherit all)   150 glib castrate, geld   151 fair legitimate
154 thus (Leontes presumably grasps Antigonus by the arm or pinches
him or tweaks his nose.) withal in addition

The instruments that feel.

ANTIGONUS   If it be so,   155
We need no grave to bury honesty;
There's not a grain of it the face to sweeten
Of the whole dungy earth.

LEONTES   What? Lack I credit?   158

A LORD
I had rather you did lack than I, my lord,
Upon this ground; and more it would content me   160
To have her honor true than your suspicion,
Be blamed for 't how you might.

LEONTES   Why, what need we   162
Commune with you of this, but rather follow
Our forceful instigation? Our prerogative   164
Calls not your counsels, but our natural goodness 165
Imparts this; which if you—or stupefied   166
Or seeming so in skill—cannot or will not   167
Relish a truth like us, inform yourselves   168
We need no more of your advice. The matter,
The loss, the gain, the ordering on 't, is all   170
Properly ours.

ANTIGONUS   And I wish, my liege,
You had only in your silent judgment tried it,
Without more overture.

LEONTES   How could that be?   173
Either thou art most ignorant by age,   174
Or thou wert born a fool. Camillo's flight,
Added to their familiarity—
Which was as gross as ever touched conjecture,   177
That lacked sight only, naught for approbation   178
But only seeing, all other circumstances
Made up to th' deed—doth push on this proceeding. 180
Yet, for a greater confirmation—

---

155 instruments i.e., Leontes's fingers   **158 credit** credibility
160 Upon this ground in this matter   **162 we** I. (The royal "we.")
164 instigation incentive   **164–166 Our prerogative . . . this** my royal
prerogative is under no obligation to consult you, but rather out of
natural generosity I inform you of the matter   **166 or** either   **167 Or
. . . skill** or pretending to be stupefied out of cunning   **168 Relish** savor,
appreciate   **170 on 't** of it   **173 overture** public disclosure   **174 by
age** through the folly of old age   **177 as gross . . . conjecture** as pal-
pably evident as any conjecture ever touched upon and verified
178 approbation proof   **180 Made up** added up.   **push on** urge onward

For in an act of this importance 'twere
Most piteous to be wild—I have dispatched in post   183
To sacred Delphos, to Apollo's temple,   184
Cleomenes and Dion, whom you know
Of stuffed sufficiency. Now from the oracle   186
They will bring all, whose spiritual counsel had   187
Shall stop or spur me. Have I done well?

A LORD   Well done, my lord.

LEONTES
Though I am satisfied, and need no more
Than what I know, yet shall the oracle
Give rest to the minds of others, such as he   192
Whose ignorant credulity will not
Come up to th' truth. So have we thought it good   194
From our free person she should be confined,   195
Lest that the treachery of the two fled hence   196
Be left her to perform. Come, follow us.
We are to speak in public, for this business
Will raise us all.

ANTIGONUS [Aside] To laughter, as I take it,   199
If the good truth were known.   *Exeunt.*

❧

2.2   *Enter Paulina, a Gentleman, [and attendants].*

PAULINA
The keeper of the prison, call to him.
Let him have knowledge who I am. [*Gentleman goes to
    the door.*] Good lady,   2
No court in Europe is too good for thee;
What dost thou then in prison?

    [*Enter*] *Jailer.*

                              Now, good sir,
You know me, do you not?

183 **wild** rash.   **post** haste   184 **Delphos** (See note at 3.1.2.)   186 **Of
stuffed sufficiency** abundantly qualified   187 **had** having been obtained   192 **he** any person (such as Antigonus)   194 **Come up to** face
195 **From** away from.   **free** accessible   196 **treachery** i.e., suspected
plot to murder Leontes (see l. 47)   199 **raise** rouse

2.2. Location: Sicilia. A prison.
2 **Good lady** (Addressed to the absent Hermione.)

JAILER   For a worthy lady
And one who much I honor.

PAULINA   Pray you, then,
Conduct me to the Queen.

JAILER   I may not, madam.
To the contrary I have express commandment.

PAULINA
Here's ado, to lock up honesty and honor from
Th' access of gentle visitors! Is 't lawful, pray you,
To see her women? Any of them? Emilia?

JAILER   So please you, madam,
To put apart these your attendants, I   13
Shall bring Emilia forth.

PAULINA   I pray now, call her.—
Withdraw yourselves.
                    [*Gentleman and attendants withdraw.*]

JAILER   And, madam,
I must be present at your conference.

PAULINA   Well, be 't so, prithee.   [*Exit Jailer.*]
Here's such ado, to make no stain a stain
As passes coloring.

       [*Enter Jailer, with*] Emilia.

                    Dear gentlewoman,   20
How fares our gracious lady?

EMILIA
As well as one so great and so forlorn
May hold together. On her frights and griefs—   23
Which never tender lady hath borne greater—   24
She is something before her time delivered.   25

PAULINA
A boy?

EMILIA   A daughter, and a goodly babe,
Lusty and like to live. The Queen receives   27
Much comfort in 't, says, "My poor prisoner,
I am innocent as you."

PAULINA   I dare be sworn.

---

13 put apart dismiss   **20 passes coloring** surpasses any justification,
passes all excuse (with a pun on *coloring* in the sense of *stain* in the
previous line)   **23 On** in consequence of   **24 Which** than which
25 something somewhat (also in l. 55)   **27 Lusty** vigorous.   **like** likely

These dangerous unsafe lunes i' the King, beshrew
  them!   30
He must be told on 't, and he shall. The office   31
Becomes a woman best; I'll take 't upon me.   32
If I prove honeymouthed, let my tongue blister   33
And never to my red-looked anger be   34
The trumpet any more. Pray you, Emilia,
Commend my best obedience to the Queen.   36
If she dares trust me with her little babe,
I'll show 't the King and undertake to be
Her advocate to th' loud'st. We do not know   39
How he may soften at the sight o' the child.
The silence often of pure innocence
Persuades when speaking fails.

EMILIA   Most worthy madam,
Your honor and your goodness is so evident
That your free undertaking cannot miss   44
A thriving issue. There is no lady living   45
So meet for this great errand. Please your ladyship   46
To visit the next room, I'll presently   47
Acquaint the Queen of your most noble offer,
Who but today hammered of this design,   49
But durst not tempt a minister of honor   50
Lest she should be denied.

PAULINA   Tell her, Emilia,
I'll use that tongue I have. If wit flow from 't   52
As boldness from my bosom, let 't not be doubted
I shall do good.

EMILIA   Now be you blest for it!
I'll to the Queen.—Please you, come something nearer.

JAILER
Madam, if 't please the Queen to send the babe,
I know not what I shall incur to pass it,   57
Having no warrant.

---

30 lunes fits of lunacy   **31 on 't** of it   **32 Becomes** suits   **33 blister** (It
was popularly supposed that lying blistered the tongue.)   **34 red-looked**
red-faced   **36 Commend** deliver   **39 to th' loud'st** as loudly as I can
44 free generous   **45 thriving issue** successful outcome   **46 meet**
suited.   **Please** if it please   **47 presently** at once   **49 hammered of**
formulated, conceived   **50 tempt** solicit (to serve as ambassador in such
a case)   **52 wit** wisdom, common sense   **57 to pass it** if I let it pass

PAULINA   You need not fear it, sir.
  This child was prisoner to the womb and is
  By law and process of great Nature thence
  Freed and enfranchised, not a party to
  The anger of the King nor guilty of,
  If any be, the trespass of the Queen.

JAILER   I do believe it.

PAULINA
  Do not you fear. Upon mine honor, I
  Will stand betwixt you and danger.   *Exeunt.*

                         ✤

2.3   *Enter Leontes.*

LEONTES
  Nor night nor day, no rest! It is but weakness
  To bear the matter thus, mere weakness. If
  The cause were not in being—part o' the cause,
  She th' adulteress, for the harlot King   4
  Is quite beyond mine arm, out of the blank   5
  And level of my brain, plot-proof, but she   6
  I can hook to me—say that she were gone,   7
  Given to the fire, a moiety of my rest   8
  Might come to me again.—Who's there?

      [*Enter a*] *Servant.*

SERVANT   My lord?

LEONTES   How does the boy?

SERVANT
  He took good rest tonight; 'tis hoped   11
  His sickness is discharged.

LEONTES   To see his nobleness!
  Conceiving the dishonor of his mother,   13

2.3. Location: Sicilia. The royal court.
4 harlot lewd. (Originally applied to either sex.)   **5–6 out . . . level**
beyond the range. (Archery terms: *blank* is the center of the target or
the close range needed for a direct shot at it, as in "point-blank"; *level*
is the action of aiming.)   **7 hook** (as with grappling hooks)   **8 Given to
the fire** burned at the stake (as a traitor conspiring against the King).
moiety portion   **11 tonight** last night   **13 Conceiving** grasping the
enormity of

He straight declined, drooped, took it deeply,
Fastened and fixed the shame on 't in himself,   15
Threw off his spirit, his appetite, his sleep,
And downright languished.—Leave me solely. Go,   17
See how he fares. [*Exit Servant.*] Fie, fie! No thought
    of him.   18
The very thought of my revenges that way
Recoil upon me—in himself too mighty,
And in his parties, his alliance. Let him be,
Until a time may serve. For present vengeance,
Take it on her. Camillo and Polixenes
Laugh at me, make their pastime at my sorrow.
They should not laugh if I could reach them, nor
Shall she, within my power.

> *Enter Paulina [with a baby]; Antigonus and Lords
> [and a Servant, trying to hold her back].*

A LORD   You must not enter.
PAULINA
Nay, rather, good my lords, be second to me.   27
Fear you his tyrannous passion more, alas,
Than the Queen's life? A gracious innocent soul,
More free than he is jealous.
ANTIGONUS   That's enough.   30
SERVANT
Madam, he hath not slept tonight, commanded
None should come at him.
PAULINA   Not so hot, good sir.
I come to bring him sleep. 'Tis such as you,
That creep like shadows by him and do sigh
At each his needless heavings, such as you   35
Nourish the cause of his awaking. I   36
Do come with words as medicinal as true,
Honest as either, to purge him of that humor   38
That presses him from sleep.
LEONTES   What noise there, ho?

---

15 on 't of it   **17 solely** alone   **18 him** i.e., Polixenes   **27 be second to**
aid, second   **30 free** innocent   **35 heavings** sighs or groans
36 awaking inability to sleep   **38 humor** distemper

PAULINA
No noise, my lord, but needful conference
About some gossips for Your Highness.

LEONTES   How?   41
Away with that audacious lady! Antigonus,
I charged thee that she should not come about me.
I knew she would.

ANTIGONUS   I told her so, my lord,
On your displeasure's peril and on mine,
She should not visit you.

LEONTES   What, canst not rule her?

PAULINA
From all dishonesty he can. In this,
Unless he take the course that you have done—
Commit me for committing honor—trust it,   49
He shall not rule me.

ANTIGONUS   La you now, you hear!   50
When she will take the rein I let her run,
But she'll not stumble.

PAULINA   Good my liege, I come—
And I beseech you hear me, who professes
Myself your loyal servant, your physician,
Your most obedient counselor, yet that dares
Less appear so in comforting your evils   56
Than such as most seem yours—I say, I come   57
From your good queen.

LEONTES   Good queen?

PAULINA
Good queen, my lord, good queen, I say good queen,
And would by combat make her good, so were I   61
A man, the worst about you.

LEONTES   Force her hence.   62

PAULINA
Let him that makes but trifles of his eyes
First hand me. On mine own accord I'll off,

41 **gossips** godparents for the baby at its baptism   **49 Commit** i.e., to
prison   **50 La . . . hear** i.e., there now, you hear how she will go on
talking   **56–57 in comforting . . . yours** when it comes to encouraging
your evil courses than those flatterers who seem to be your most loyal
servants   **61 by combat** by trial by combat.   **make** prove   **62 worst**
least manly, or lowest in rank

But first I'll do my errand. The good Queen,
For she is good, hath brought you forth a daughter—
Here 'tis—commends it to your blessing.

                         [She lays down the baby.]

LEONTES   Out!
A mankind witch! Hence with her, out o' door!   68
A most intelligencing bawd!

PAULINA   Not so.   69
I am as ignorant in that as you
In so entitling me, and no less honest
Than you are mad; which is enough, I'll warrant,
As this world goes, to pass for honest.

LEONTES   Traitors!
Will you not push her out? *[To Antigonus.]* Give her
    the bastard.
Thou dotard, thou art woman-tired, unroosted   75
By thy Dame Partlet here. Take up the bastard!   76
Take 't up, I say. Give 't to thy crone.

PAULINA   Forever
Unvenerable be thy hands if thou
Tak'st up the Princess by that forcèd baseness   79
Which he has put upon 't!

LEONTES   He dreads his wife.

PAULINA
So I would you did. Then 'twere past all doubt
You'd call your children yours.

LEONTES   A nest of traitors!

ANTIGONUS
I am none, by this good light.

PAULINA   Nor I, nor any   83
But one that's here, and that's himself; for he
The sacred honor of himself, his queen's,
His hopeful son's, his babe's, betrays to slander,
Whose sting is sharper than the sword's; and will not—

---

68 mankind masculine, behaving like a man   **69 intelligencing bawd**
acting as go-between and spy (for the Queen and Polixenes)   **75 woman-
tired** henpecked. (From *tire* in falconry, meaning "tear with the
beak.")   **unroosted** driven from perch   **76 Partlet** or Pertilote, a common name for a hen (as in *Reynard the Fox* and in Chaucer's "Nun's
Priest's Tale")   **79 by that forcèd baseness** under that wrongfully
imposed name of bastard   **83 by this good light** by my eyesight. (A
common oath.)

For, as the case now stands, it is a curse
He cannot be compelled to 't—once remove
The root of his opinion, which is rotten
As ever oak or stone was sound.

LEONTES   A callet   91
Of boundless tongue, who late hath beat her husband
And now baits me! This brat is none of mine;
It is the issue of Polixenes.
Hence with it, and together with the dam
Commit them to the fire!

PAULINA   It is yours;
And, might we lay th' old proverb to your charge,
So like you, 'tis the worse. Behold, my lords,
Although the print be little, the whole matter
And copy of the father—eye, nose, lip,
The trick of 's frown, his forehead, nay, the valley,   101
The pretty dimples of his chin and cheek, his smiles,
The very mold and frame of hand, nail, finger.
And thou, good goddess Nature, which hast made it
So like to him that got it, if thou hast   105
The ordering of the mind too, 'mongst all colors
No yellow in 't, lest she suspect, as he does,   107
Her children not her husband's!

LEONTES   A gross hag!
And, lozel, thou art worthy to be hanged,   109
That wilt not stay her tongue.

ANTIGONUS   Hang all the husbands   110
That cannot do that feat, you'll leave yourself
Hardly one subject.

LEONTES   Once more, take her hence.

PAULINA
A most unworthy and unnatural lord
Can do no more.

LEONTES   I'll ha' thee burnt.

PAULINA   I care not.

---

91 callet scold   **101 trick** characteristic expression.   **valley** cleft of the
chin (?)   **105 got** begot   **107 No yellow** let there be no yellow, i.e., the
color of jealousy. (A chaste woman could hardly expect that her own
children are illegitimate, but Paulina may be speaking hyperbolically.)
109 lozel worthless person, scoundrel. (Addressed to Antigonus.)
110 stay restrain

It is an heretic that makes the fire,   115
Not she which burns in 't. I'll not call you tyrant;   116
But this most cruel usage of your queen,
Not able to produce more accusation   118
Than your own weak-hinged fancy, something savors
Of tyranny and will ignoble make you,
Yea, scandalous to the world.

LEONTES   On your allegiance,
Out of the chamber with her! Were I a tyrant,
Where were her life? She durst not call me so   123
If she did know me one. Away with her!

PAULINA
I pray you, do not push me; I'll be gone.
Look to your babe, my lord; 'tis yours. Jove send her
A better guiding spirit!—What needs these hands?   127
You that are thus so tender o'er his follies
Will never do him good, not one of you.
So, so. Farewell, we are gone.   *Exit.*

LEONTES
Thou, traitor, hast set on thy wife to this.
My child? Away with 't! Even thou, that hast
A heart so tender o'er it, take it hence
And see it instantly consumed with fire;
Even thou and none but thou. Take it up straight.
Within this hour bring me word 'tis done,
And by good testimony, or I'll seize thy life,
With what thou else call'st thine. If thou refuse
And wilt encounter with my wrath, say so;
The bastard brains with these my proper hands   140
Shall I dash out. Go, take it to the fire,
For thou sett'st on thy wife.

ANTIGONUS   I did not, sir.
These lords, my noble fellows, if they please,
Can clear me in 't.

LORDS   We can. My royal liege,
He is not guilty of her coming hither.

LEONTES   You're liars all.

115–116 It is . . . in 't i.e., only a heretic can be burned guiltily; an
innocent person may be burned, but in that case the one who does the
burning is the guilty party, having committed the heresy of loss of
faith   **118 Not able** you not being able   **123 Where . . . life** i.e., how
could she escape execution at my command   **127 What . . . hands** i.e.,
what need is there to push me   **140 proper** own

A LORD

  Beseech Your Highness, give us better credit.   147
  We have always truly served you, and beseech'   148
  So to esteem of us; and on our knees we beg,
  As recompense of our dear services   150
  Past and to come, that you do change this purpose,
  Which being so horrible, so bloody, must
  Lead on to some foul issue. We all kneel.

LEONTES

  I am a feather for each wind that blows.
  Shall I live on to see this bastard kneel
  And call me father? Better burn it now
  Than curse it then. But be it; let it live.
  It shall not neither. [*To Antigonus.*] You, sir, come
    you hither,
  You that have been so tenderly officious
  With Lady Margery, your midwife there,   160
  To save this bastard's life—for 'tis a bastard,
  So sure as this beard's gray. What will you adventure 162
  To save this brat's life?

ANTIGONUS   Anything, my lord,

  That my ability may undergo
  And nobleness impose. At least thus much:
  I'll pawn the little blood which I have left
  To save the innocent—anything possible.

LEONTES [*Holding his sword*]

  It shall be possible. Swear by this sword
  Thou wilt perform my bidding.

ANTIGONUS [*His hand on the hilt*] I will, my lord.

LEONTES

  Mark and perform it, seest thou; for the fail   170
  Of any point in 't shall not only be
  Death to thyself but to thy lewd-tongued wife,
  Whom for this time we pardon. We enjoin thee,
  As thou art liege man to us, that thou carry
  This female bastard hence, and that thou bear it
  To some remote and desert place quite out
  Of our dominions, and that there thou leave it,
  Without more mercy, to its own protection

147 credit belief   **148 beseech'** beseech you   **150 dear** loyal, heartfelt
160 Margery (A derisive term, evidently equivalent to *Partlet* in l. 76.)
162 this beard's (Probably Antigonus's.)   **170 seest thou** i.e., do you
hear. **fail** failure

And favor of the climate. As by strange fortune
It came to us, I do in justice charge thee,
On thy soul's peril and thy body's torture,
That thou commend it strangely to some place   182
Where chance may nurse or end it. Take it up.
ANTIGONUS [*Taking up the baby*]
I swear to do this, though a present death
Had been more merciful. Come on, poor babe.
Some powerful spirit instruct the kites and ravens
To be thy nurses! Wolves and bears, they say,
Casting their savageness aside, have done
Like offices of pity. Sir, be prosperous
In more than this deed does require!—And blessing   190
Against this cruelty fight on thy side,
Poor thing, condemned to loss!   *Exit* [*with the baby*].
LEONTES   No, I'll not rear   192
Another's issue.

          Enter a Servant.

SERVANT   Please Your Highness, posts   193
From those you sent to th' oracle are come
An hour since. Cleomenes and Dion,
Being well arrived from Delphos, are both landed,
Hasting to th' court.
A LORD   So please you, sir, their speed
Hath been beyond account.
LEONTES   Twenty-three days   198
They have been absent. 'Tis good speed, foretells
The great Apollo suddenly will have   200
The truth of this appear. Prepare you, lords.
Summon a session, that we may arraign   202
Our most disloyal lady; for, as she hath
Been publicly accused, so shall she have
A just and open trial. While she lives
My heart will be a burden to me. Leave me,
And think upon my bidding.   *Exeunt* [*separately*].

          ✤

182 **commend . . . place** commit it to some foreign place, or as a
stranger   190 **more** i.e., more ways, more extent (?)   **require** deserve
192 **loss** destruction   193 **posts** messengers   198 **beyond account** i.e.,
unprecedented, or beyond explanation   200 **suddenly** at once
202 **session** trial

3.1 *Enter Cleomenes and Dion.*

CLEOMENES
  The climate's delicate, the air most sweet,
  Fertile the isle, the temple much surpassing   2
  The common praise it bears.
DION   I shall report,
  For most it caught me, the celestial habits—   4
  Methinks I so should term them—and the reverence
  Of the grave wearers. O, the sacrifice!
  How ceremonious, solemn, and unearthly
  It was i' th' offering!
CLEOMENES   But of all, the burst
  And the ear-deafening voice o' th' oracle,
  Kin to Jove's thunder, so surprised my sense   10
  That I was nothing.
DION   If th' event o' the journey   11
  Prove as successful to the Queen—O, be 't so!—
  As it hath been to us rare, pleasant, speedy,
  The time is worth the use on 't.
CLEOMENES   Great Apollo   14
  Turn all to th' best! These proclamations,
  So forcing faults upon Hermione,
  I little like.
DION   The violent carriage of it   17
  Will clear or end the business. When the oracle,
  Thus by Apollo's great divine sealed up,   19
  Shall the contents discover, something rare   20
  Even then will rush to knowledge. Go. Fresh horses!
  And gracious be the issue!   *Exeunt.*

✤

3.1. Location: Sicilia. On the way to Leontes's court.
2 isle (Shakespeare follows Greene's *Pandosto* in fictitiously placing
Delphi on an island. Delphi, sometimes known as Delphos [see 2.1.184,
2.3.196, and 3.2.126], was often confused with Delos, the island birth-
place of Apollo and location also of an oracle.) **4 habits** vestments
10 surprised overwhelmed **11 event** outcome **14 is worth . . . on 't** has
been well employed **17 carriage** execution, management **19 great
divine** chief priest **20 discover** reveal

3.2   *Enter Leontes, Lords, [and] Officers.*

LEONTES
This sessions, to our great grief we pronounce,
Even pushes 'gainst our heart: the party tried
The daughter of a king, our wife, and one
Of us too much beloved. Let us be cleared   4
Of being tyrannous, since we so openly
Proceed in justice, which shall have due course
Even to the guilt or the purgation.   7
Produce the prisoner.

OFFICER
It is His Highness' pleasure that the Queen
Appear in person here in court. Silence!

  *[Enter] Hermione, as to her trial, [Paulina, and]
  Ladies.*

LEONTES   Read the indictment.
OFFICER   [*Reads*] "Hermione, Queen to the worthy
Leontes, King of Sicilia, thou art here accused and ar-
raigned of high treason, in committing adultery with
Polixenes, King of Bohemia, and conspiring with
Camillo to take away the life of our sovereign lord the
King, thy royal husband; the pretense whereof being   17
by circumstances partly laid open, thou, Hermione,
contrary to the faith and allegiance of a true subject,
didst counsel and aid them, for their better safety, to
fly away by night."

HERMIONE
Since what I am to say must be but that
Which contradicts my accusation, and
The testimony on my part no other
But what comes from myself, it shall scarce boot me 25
To say "not guilty." Mine integrity,
Being counted falsehood, shall, as I express it,
Be so received. But thus: if powers divine
Behold our human actions, as they do,

3.2. Location: Sicilia. A place of justice, probably at court.
4 Of by   7 purgation clearing from the accusation   17 pretense purpose, design   25 boot avail

I doubt not then but innocence shall make
False accusation blush and tyranny
Tremble at patience. You, my lord, best know,
Who least will seem to do so, my past life
Hath been as continent, as chaste, as true,
As I am now unhappy; which is more
Than history can pattern, though devised   36
And played to take spectators. For behold me—   37
A fellow of the royal bed, which owe   38
A moiety of the throne, a great king's daughter,   39
The mother to a hopeful prince—here standing
To prate and talk for life and honor 'fore
Who please to come and hear. For life, I prize it   42
As I weigh grief, which I would spare. For honor,   43
'Tis a derivative from me to mine,   44
And only that I stand for. I appeal   45
To your own conscience, sir, before Polixenes   46
Came to your court, how I was in your grace,
How merited to be so; since he came,
With what encounter so uncurrent I   49
Have strained t' appear thus; if one jot beyond   50
The bound of honor, or in act or will
That way inclining, hardened be the hearts
Of all that hear me, and my near'st of kin
Cry fie upon my grave!
LEONTES   I ne'er heard yet
That any of these bolder vices wanted   55
Less impudence to gainsay what they did   56
Than to perform it first.
HERMIONE   That's true enough,
Though 'tis a saying, sir, not due to me.   58
LEONTES
You will not own it.

---

36 history story, here presented in the theater. **pattern** show a similar example for **37 take** please, charm **38 which owe** who own **39 moiety** share **42 Who please** whoever chooses **42–45 For . . stand for** as for life, I value it as I value grief, and would as willingly do without; as for honor, it is transmitted from me to my descendants, and that only I make a stand for **46 conscience** consideration, inward knowledge **49–50 With . . . thus** (I ask) by what behavior so improper I have transgressed so that I appear thus (in disgrace and on trial) **55–56 wanted Less** were more lacking in **58 due** applicable

HERMIONE   More than mistress of   59
 Which comes to me in name of fault, I must not 60
 At all acknowledge. For Polixenes,   61
 With whom I am accused, I do confess
 I loved him as in honor he required;   63
 With such a kind of love as might become
 A lady like me; with a love even such,
 So, and no other, as yourself commanded;
 Which not to have done I think had been in me
 Both disobedience and ingratitude
 To you and toward your friend, whose love had spoke, 69
 Even since it could speak, from an infant, freely
 That it was yours. Now, for conspiracy,   71
 I know not how it tastes, though it be dished 72
 For me to try how. All I know of it
 Is that Camillo was an honest man;
 And why he left your court, the gods themselves,
 Wotting no more than I, are ignorant.   76
LEONTES
 You knew of his departure, as you know
 What you have underta'en to do in 's absence.
HERMIONE Sir,
 You speak a language that I understand not.
 My life stands in the level of your dreams,   81
 Which I'll lay down.
LEONTES   Your actions are my dreams. 82
 You had a bastard by Polixenes,
 And I but dreamed it. As you were past all shame—
 Those of your fact are so—so past all truth,   85
 Which to deny concerns more than avails; for as 86
 Thy brat hath been cast out, like to itself,   87

59–61 More . . . acknowledge I will not acknowledge that I am answerable for more than what may be called ordinary human faults. (Hermione insists she is not guilty of the *bolder vices* of l. 55.) **61 For** as for **63 required** deserved **69 whose love** i.e., the mutual love between Leontes and Polixenes **71 That it was yours** that this mutual love was a part of your soul. **for** as for **72 dished** served up **76 Wotting** i.e., supposing they know **81 level** aim, range **82 Your . . . dreams** i.e., you have performed what I have fantasized, and what you have done preys on my mind **85 Those of your fact** all those who do what you did **86 concerns . . . avails** may seem an understandable concern on your part but will not help **87 like to itself** as it ought to be (since it has no father)

No father owning it—which is indeed
More criminal in thee than it—so thou
Shalt feel our justice, in whose easiest passage   90
Look for no less than death.

HERMIONE   Sir, spare your threats.   91
The bug which you would fright me with I seek.   92
To me can life be no commodity.   93
The crown and comfort of my life, your favor,
I do give lost, for I do feel it gone,   95
But know not how it went. My second joy
And firstfruits of my body, from his presence
I am barred, like one infectious. My third comfort,
Starred most unluckily, is from my breast,   99
The innocent milk in its most innocent mouth,
Haled out to murder; myself on every post   101
Proclaimed a strumpet; with immodest hatred   102
The childbed privilege denied, which longs   103
To women of all fashion; lastly, hurried   104
Here to this place, i' th' open air, before
I have got strength of limit. Now, my liege,   106
Tell me what blessings I have here alive
That I should fear to die? Therefore proceed.
But yet hear this; mistake me not. No life,   109
I prize it not a straw. But for mine honor,
Which I would free, if I shall be condemned
Upon surmises, all proofs sleeping else
But what your jealousies awake, I tell you
'Tis rigor and not law. Your honors all,   114
I do refer me to the oracle.
Apollo be my judge!

A LORD   This your request
Is altogether just. Therefore bring forth,
And in Apollo's name, his oracle.

                            [*Exeunt certain Officers.*]

90–91 in whose . . . death i.e., which will impose the death sentence at
least, perhaps torture also   **92 bug** bugbear, bogey, imaginary object of
terror   **93 commodity** asset   **95 give** reckon as, or give up as
99 Starred most unluckily born under a most unlucky star   **101 post**
posting place for public notices   **102 immodest** immoderate   **103 longs**
belongs, i.e., is fitting   **104 all fashion** every rank   **106 got . . . limit** i.e.,
regained my strength after having borne a child   **109 No life** i.e., I do
not ask for life   **114 rigor** tyranny

HERMIONE
The Emperor of Russia was my father.
O, that he were alive and here beholding
His daughter's trial! That he did but see
The flatness of my misery, yet with eyes   122
Of pity, not revenge!

[*Enter Officers, with*] *Cleomenes* [*and*] *Dion.*

OFFICER [*Holding a sword*]
You here shall swear upon this sword of justice,
That you, Cleomenes and Dion, have
Been both at Delphos, and from thence have brought
This sealed-up oracle, by the hand delivered
Of great Apollo's priest, and that since then
You have not dared to break the holy seal
Nor read the secrets in 't.
CLEOMENES, DION   All this we swear.
LEONTES
Break up the seals and read.   131
OFFICER [*Reads*]   "Hermione is chaste, Polixenes blame-
less, Camillo a true subject, Leontes a jealous tyrant,
his innocent babe truly begotten, and the King shall
live without an heir if that which is lost be not
found."
LORDS
Now blessèd be the great Apollo!
HERMIONE   Praised!
LEONTES
Hast thou read truth?
OFFICER   Ay, my lord, even so
As it is here set down.
LEONTES
There is no truth at all i' th' oracle.
The sessions shall proceed. This is mere falsehood.

[*Enter a Servant.*]

SERVANT
My lord the King, the King!
LEONTES   What is the business?

122 flatness absoluteness   **131 up** open

SERVANT
  O sir, I shall be hated to report it!   143
  The Prince your son, with mere conceit and fear   144
  Of the Queen's speed, is gone.
LEONTES   How? Gone?
SERVANT   Is dead.   145
LEONTES
  Apollo's angry, and the heavens themselves
  Do strike at my injustice. [*Hermione swoons.*] How
      now there?
PAULINA
  This news is mortal to the Queen. Look down
  And see what death is doing.
LEONTES   Take her hence.
  Her heart is but o'ercharged; she will recover.
  I have too much believed mine own suspicion.
  Beseech you, tenderly apply to her
  Some remedies for life.
      [*Exeunt Paulina and Ladies, with Hermione.*]
                          Apollo, pardon
  My great profaneness 'gainst thine oracle!
  I'll reconcile me to Polixenes,
  New woo my queen, recall the good Camillo,
  Whom I proclaim a man of truth, of mercy;
  For, being transported by my jealousies
  To bloody thoughts and to revenge, I chose
  Camillo for the minister to poison
  My friend Polixenes; which had been done
  But that the good mind of Camillo tardied   162
  My swift command, though I with death and with
  Reward did threaten and encourage him,
  Not doing it and being done. He, most humane   165
  And filled with honor, to my kingly guest
  Unclasped my practice, quit his fortunes here, 167
  Which you knew great, and to the hazard
  Of all incertainties himself commended,   169

143 to report for reporting   **144 conceit and fear** i.e., anxious concern
145 speed fate, fortune   **162 tardied** delayed   **165 Not . . . done** i.e.,
death if he did not do it, and reward if he did   **167 Unclasped my**
practice disclosed my plot   **169 himself commended** entrusted himself

No richer than his honor. How he glisters   170
Through my rust! And how his piety
Does my deeds make the blacker!

    [*Enter Paulina.*]

PAULINA   Woe the while!
  O, cut my lace, lest my heart, cracking it,
  Break too!
A LORD   What fit is this, good lady?
PAULINA
  What studied torments, tyrant, hast for me?
  What wheels, racks, fires? What flaying, boiling
  In leads or oils? What old or newer torture
  Must I receive, whose every word deserves
  To taste of thy most worst? Thy tyranny,
  Together working with thy jealousies—
  Fancies too weak for boys, too green and idle   181
  For girls of nine—O, think what they have done,
  And then run mad indeed, stark mad! For all
  Thy bygone fooleries were but spices of it.   184
  That thou betrayedst Polixenes, 'twas nothing;
  That did but show thee, of a fool, inconstant   186
  And damnable ingrateful. Nor was 't much
  Thou wouldst have poisoned good Camillo's honor,
  To have him kill a king—poor trespasses,   189
  More monstrous standing by; whereof I reckon   190
  The casting forth to crows thy baby daughter
  To be or none or little, though a devil   192
  Would have shed water out of fire ere done 't.   193
  Nor is 't directly laid to thee, the death
  Of the young Prince, whose honorable thoughts,
  Thoughts high for one so tender, cleft the heart   196
  That could conceive a gross and foolish sire   197
  Blemished his gracious dam. This is not, no,
  Laid to thy answer. But the last—O lords,

170 No richer than with no riches except. **glisters** shines   **181 idle**
foolish   **184 spices** foretastes, samples   **186 of a fool, inconstant** i.e.,
being a fool naturally and then inconstant into the bargain   **189 To**
have by having. **poor** slight   **190 More . . . by** when more monstrous
sins are at hand for comparison   **192 or none** either none   **193 shed . . .**
fire wept from his fiery eyes, or while surrounded by hellfire
196 tender young   **197 conceive** apprehend that

When I have said, cry woe! The Queen, the Queen,   200
The sweet'st, dear'st creature's dead, and vengeance
    for 't
Not dropped down yet.

A LORD   The higher powers forbid!

PAULINA
I say she's dead. I'll swear 't. If word nor oath
Prevail not, go and see. If you can bring
Tincture or luster in her lip, her eye,
Heat outwardly or breath within, I'll serve you
As I would do the gods. But, O thou tyrant!
Do not repent these things, for they are heavier
Than all thy woes can stir. Therefore betake thee   209
To nothing but despair. A thousand knees
Ten thousand years together, naked, fasting,
Upon a barren mountain, and still winter   212
In storm perpetual, could not move the gods
To look that way thou wert.

LEONTES   Go on, go on.   214
Thou canst not speak too much. I have deserved
All tongues to talk their bitt'rest.

A LORD [*To Paulina*]   Say no more.
Howe'er the business goes, you have made fault
I' the boldness of your speech.

PAULINA   I am sorry for 't.
All faults I make, when I shall come to know them,   219
I do repent. Alas, I have showed too much
The rashness of a woman! He is touched
To th' noble heart. What's gone and what's past help
Should be past grief.—Do not receive affliction   223
At my petition. I beseech you, rather   224
Let me be punished, that have minded you   225
Of what you should forget. Now, good my liege,
Sir, royal sir, forgive a foolish woman.
The love I bore your queen—lo, fool again!—
I'll speak of her no more, nor of your children;
I'll not remember you of my own lord,   230

200 said finished speaking   **209 woes can stir** penance can remove
212 still always   **214 To look . . . wert** to regard you   **219 I make** that I
make   **223–224 Do . . . petition** do not afflict yourself with remorse at
my urging   **225 minded you** put you in mind   **230 remember** remind

Who is lost too. Take your patience to you,   231
And I'll say nothing.

LEONTES   Thou didst speak but well
When most the truth, which I receive much better
Than to be pitied of thee. Prithee, bring me
To the dead bodies of my queen and son.
One grave shall be for both. Upon them shall
The causes of their death appear, unto
Our shame perpetual. Once a day I'll visit
The chapel where they lie, and tears shed there
Shall be my recreation. So long as nature
Will bear up with this exercise, so long
I daily vow to use it. Come and lead me
To these sorrows.   *Exeunt.*

❖

3.3   *Enter Antigonus [and] a Mariner, [with a] babe.*

ANTIGONUS
    Thou art perfect then, our ship hath touched upon   1
    The deserts of Bohemia?

MARINER   Ay, my lord, and fear   2
    We have landed in ill time. The skies look grimly
    And threaten present blusters. In my conscience,   4
    The heavens with that we have in hand are angry
    And frown upon 's.

ANTIGONUS
    Their sacred wills be done! Go, get aboard;
    Look to thy bark. I'll not be long before
    I call upon thee.

MARINER   Make your best haste, and go not
    Too far i' the land. 'Tis like to be loud weather.   10
    Besides, this place is famous for the creatures
    Of prey that keep upon 't.

ANTIGONUS   Go thou away.   12

---

231 **Take . . . you** be patient

3.3. Location: Bohemia. The seacoast.
1 **perfect** certain   2 **deserts of Bohemia** i.e., deserted region on the coast.
(Shakespeare follows Greene's *Pandosto* in giving Bohemia a sea-
coast.)   4 **present** immediate.   **conscience** opinion   10 **like** likely.   **loud**
stormy   12 **keep upon 't** inhabit it

I'll follow instantly.

MARINER   I am glad at heart
To be so rid o' the business.   *Exit.*

ANTIGONUS   Come, poor babe.
I have heard, but not believed, the spirits o' the dead
May walk again. If such thing be, thy mother
Appeared to me last night, for ne'er was dream
So like a waking. To me comes a creature,
Sometimes her head on one side, some another;
I never saw a vessel of like sorrow,
So filled and so becoming. In pure white robes,   21
Like very sanctity, she did approach
My cabin where I lay, thrice bowed before me,
And, gasping to begin some speech, her eyes
Became two spouts. The fury spent, anon
Did this break from her: "Good Antigonus,
Since fate, against thy better disposition,
Hath made thy person for the thrower-out
Of my poor babe, according to thine oath,
Places remote enough are in Bohemia;
There weep and leave it crying. And, for the babe   31
Is counted lost forever, Perdita,   32
I prithee, call 't. For this ungentle business   33
Put on thee by my lord, thou ne'er shalt see
Thy wife Paulina more." And so, with shrieks,
She melted into air. Affrighted much,
I did in time collect myself and thought
This was so and no slumber. Dreams are toys;   38
Yet for this once, yea, superstitiously,
I will be squared by this. I do believe   40
Hermione hath suffered death, and that
Apollo would, this being indeed the issue
Of King Polixenes, it should here be laid,
Either for life or death, upon the earth
Of its right father. Blossom, speed thee well!
                    [*He lays down the baby.*]

21 **So . . . becoming** i.e., so filled with sorrow and so attractive thus
31 **for** because   32 **Perdita** i.e., the lost one   33 **ungentle** ignoble
38 **toys** trifles   40 **squared** directed in my course

There lie, and there thy character; there these,   46
    [*He places a box and a fardel beside the baby*]
Which may, if fortune please, both breed thee, pretty,   47
And still rest thine. [*Thunder.*] The storm begins.
    Poor wretch,   48
That for thy mother's fault art thus exposed
To loss and what may follow! Weep I cannot,   50
But my heart bleeds; and most accurst am I
To be by oath enjoined to this. Farewell!
The day frowns more and more. Thou'rt like to have
A lullaby too rough. I never saw
The heavens so dim by day. A savage clamor!
Well may I get aboard! This is the chase.
I am gone forever.   *Exit, pursued by a bear.*

    [*Enter a*] *Shepherd.*

SHEPHERD I would there were no age between ten and
three-and-twenty, or that youth would sleep out the
rest, for there is nothing in the between but getting
wenches with child, wronging the anciency, stealing,   61
fighting—Hark you now, would any but these boiled   62
brains of nineteen and two-and-twenty hunt this   63
weather? They have scared away two of my best sheep,
which I fear the wolf will sooner find than the master.
If anywhere I have them, 'tis by the seaside, browsing
of ivy. Good luck, an 't be thy will! [*Seeing the child.*]   67
What have we here? Mercy on 's, a bairn, a very pretty   68
bairn! A boy or a child, I wonder? A pretty one, a very   69
pretty one. Sure some scape. Though I am not bookish,   70
yet I can read waiting-gentlewoman in the scape.

46 character writing, written account (i.e., the same as that which
subsequently will serve to identify Perdita). **these** i.e., the gold and
jewels found by the Shepherd, also later used to identify her **s.d. box,
fardel** (The box, containing gold and jewels, is later produced by the old
Shepherd and the Clown; see 4.4.758–759. They also have a *fardel*, or
bundle, consisting evidently of the bearing cloth [3.3.112] and/or mantle
[5.2.34] in which the babe is found.) **47 breed thee** keep you, pay for
your support. **pretty** pretty one **48 And still rest thine** i.e., and still
provide a heritage with what is unspent **50 To loss** to being lost.
Weep I cannot i.e., I cannot weep as the Queen instructed me (l. 31)
61 anciency old people **62–63 boiled brains** addlepated youths
67 Good . . . will i.e., may God grant me good luck in finding my
sheep **68 bairn** child **69 child** i.e., female infant **70 scape** sexual
escapade

This has been some stair-work, some trunk-work, 72
some behind-door-work. They were warmer that got 73
this than the poor thing is here. I'll take it up for pity.
Yet I'll tarry till my son come; he hallooed but even
now.—Whoa, ho, hoa!   76

    Enter Clown.

CLOWN   Hilloa, loa!
SHEPHERD   What, art so near? If thou'lt see a thing to
talk on when thou art dead and rotten, come hither.
What ail'st thou, man?
CLOWN   I have seen two such sights, by sea and by
land! But I am not to say it is a sea, for it is now the
sky; betwixt the firmament and it you cannot thrust a
bodkin's point.   84
SHEPHERD   Why, boy, how is it?
CLOWN   I would you did but see how it chafes, how it
rages, how it takes up the shore! But that's not to the 87
point. O, the most piteous cry of the poor souls! Sometimes to see 'em, and not to see 'em; now the ship
boring the moon with her mainmast, and anon swallowed with yeast and froth, as you'd thrust a cork into 91
a hogshead. And then for the land service, to see how 92
the bear tore out his shoulder bone; how he cried to
me for help and said his name was Antigonus, a nobleman. But to make an end of the ship: to see how
the sea flapdragoned it! But first, how the poor souls 96
roared and the sea mocked them, and how the poor
gentleman roared and the bear mocked him, both roaring louder than the sea or weather.
SHEPHERD   Name of mercy, when was this, boy?
CLOWN   Now, now. I have not winked since I saw these 101

72–73 stair-work . . . behind-door-work i.e., sexual liaisons under or
behind the stairs or using a trunk for concealment   **73 got** begot
76 s.d. Clown country fellow, rustic   **84 bodkin's** needle's. (A *bodkin*
can also be a dagger, awl, etc.)   **87 takes up** (1) contends with, rebukes
(2) swallows   **91 yeast** foam   **92 hogshead** large barrel. (The image is of
a cork swimming in a turbulent expanse of frothing liquid.)   **land
service** (1) dish of food served on land (2) military service on land (as
distinguished from naval service); here, the doings on land
96 flapdragoned swallowed as one would a flapdragon, i.e., a raisin or
the like swallowed out of burning brandy in the game of snapdragon
101 winked closed my eyes

sights. The men are not yet cold under water, nor the bear half dined on the gentleman. He's at it now.

SHEPHERD   Would I had been by, to have helped the old man!

CLOWN   I would you had been by the ship side, to have helped her. There your charity would have lacked footing.   108

SHEPHERD   Heavy matters, heavy matters! But look thee here, boy. Now bless thyself. Thou mett'st with things dying, I with things newborn. Here's a sight for thee; look thee, a bearing cloth for a squire's child! Look   112 thee here; take up, take up, boy. Open 't. So, let's see. It was told me I should be rich by the fairies. This is some changeling. Open 't. What's within, boy?   115

[*The Clown opens the box.*]

CLOWN   You're a made old man. If the sins of your youth are forgiven you, you're well to live. Gold, all   117 gold!

SHEPHERD   This is fairy gold, boy, and 'twill prove so. Up with 't, keep it close. Home, home, the next way.   120 We are lucky, boy, and to be so still requires nothing   121 but secrecy. Let my sheep go. Come, good boy, the   122 next way home.

CLOWN   Go you the next way with our findings. I'll go see if the bear be gone from the gentleman, and how much he hath eaten. They are never curst but when   126 they are hungry. If there be any of him left, I'll bury it.

SHEPHERD   That's a good deed. If thou mayest discern by that which is left of him what he is, fetch me to the sight of him.

CLOWN   Marry, will I; and you shall help to put him i'   131 the ground.

SHEPHERD   'Tis a lucky day, boy, and we'll do good deeds on 't.   *Exeunt.*

❖

108 footing (1) foothold (2) establishment of a charitable foundation, one that would provide *charity* (l. 107)   **112 bearing cloth** rich cloth or mantle in which a child was carried to its baptism   **115 changeling** child left or taken by fairies   **117 well to live** well-to-do   **120 close** secret.   **next** nearest   **121–122 to be . . . secrecy** (To talk about fairy gifts would be to insure bad luck.)   **still** always   **126 curst** mean, fierce   **131 Marry** i.e., indeed. (Originally an oath, "by the Virgin Mary.")

4.1 *Enter Time, the Chorus.*

TIME

I, that please some, try all, both joy and terror   1
Of good and bad, that makes and unfolds error,   2
Now take upon me, in the name of Time,
To use my wings. Impute it not a crime
To me or my swift passage, that I slide
O'er sixteen years and leave the growth untried   6
Of that wide gap, since it is in my power
To o'erthrow law and in one self-born hour   8
To plant and o'erwhelm custom. Let me pass
The same I am ere ancient'st order was   10
Or what is now received. I witness to   11
The times that brought them in; so shall I do   12
To th' freshest things now reigning, and make stale
The glistering of this present, as my tale   14
Now seems to it. Your patience this allowing,   15
I turn my glass and give my scene such growing   16
As you had slept between. Leontes leaving—   17
Th' effects of his fond jealousies so grieving   18
That he shuts up himself—imagine me,
Gentle spectators, that I now may be
In fair Bohemia. And remember well
I mentioned a son o' the King's, which Florizel
I now name to you; and with speed so pace   23
To speak of Perdita, now grown in grace
Equal with wondering. What of her ensues   25

4.1.

1 try test   **2 that . . . error** i.e., I who make error, thus bringing joy to
the bad and terror to the good, and then at last unfold or disclose error,
thus bringing joy to the good and terror to the bad   **6 growth untried**
developments unexplored   **8 law** i.e., the rule of the unity of time in a
dramatic performance, normally limiting the action to twenty-four
hours.   **self-born** selfsame, or born of myself (since hours are the
creations of Time)   **10–11 ere . . . received** i.e., from the beginnings of
time to the present   **12 them** i.e., law and custom   **14 glistering** glisten-
ing freshness   **15 seems to it** seems (stale) when compared with the
present   **16 glass** hourglass   **17 As** as if.   **Leontes leaving** leaving
behind Leontes for the moment   **18 Th' effects . . . grieving** so grieving
at the effects of his foolish jealousies   **23 pace** proceed   **25 Equal with
wondering** as great as the wonder people feel in seeing her

I list not prophesy; but let Time's news   26
Be known when 'tis brought forth. A shepherd's
  daughter,
And what to her adheres, which follows after,   28
Is th' argument of Time. Of this allow,   29
If ever you have spent time worse ere now;
If never, yet that Time himself doth say   31
He wishes earnestly you never may.   *Exit.*

4.2   *Enter Polixenes and Camillo.*

POLIXENES I pray thee, good Camillo, be no more importunate. 'Tis a sickness denying thee anything, a
death to grant this.

CAMILLO It is fifteen years since I saw my country.
Though I have for the most part been aired abroad, I 5
desire to lay my bones there. Besides, the penitent
King, my master, hath sent for me, to whose feeling 7
sorrows I might be some allay—or I o'erween to think 8
so—which is another spur to my departure.

POLIXENES As thou lov'st me, Camillo, wipe not out the
rest of thy services by leaving me now. The need I
have of thee thine own goodness hath made. Better
not to have had thee than thus to want thee. Thou, 13
having made me businesses which none without thee
can sufficiently manage, must either stay to execute
them thyself or take away with thee the very services
thou hast done; which if I have not enough
considered—as too much I cannot—to be more thank- 18
ful to thee shall be my study, and my profit therein the
heaping friendships. Of that fatal country, Sicilia, prith- 20
ee, speak no more, whose very naming punishes me
with the remembrance of that penitent, as thou call'st

26 **list not** do not care to   28 **to her adheres** concerns her
29 **argument** subject of a story   31 **yet that** i.e., yet allow that

4.2. Location: Bohemia. The court of Polixenes.
5 **been aired abroad** lived abroad   7 **feeling** heartfelt   8 **allay** means
of abatement.   **o'erween** am presumptuous enough   13 **want** lack
18 **considered** i.e., rewarded   20 **heaping friendships** heaping up of
(your) kind services and our mutual affection

him, and reconciled king, my brother, whose loss of
his most precious queen and children are even now to
be afresh lamented. Say to me, when sawst thou the
Prince Florizel, my son? Kings are no less unhappy,
their issue not being gracious, than they are in losing 27
them when they have approved their virtues. 28

CAMILLO   Sir, it is three days since I saw the Prince.
What his happier affairs may be are to me unknown;
but I have missingly noted he is of late much retired 31
from court and is less frequent to his princely exer- 32
cises than formerly he hath appeared.

POLIXENES   I have considered so much, Camillo, and 34
with some care, so far that I have eyes under my ser- 35
vice which look upon his removedness; from whom I 36
have this intelligence, that he is seldom from the 37
house of a most homely shepherd—a man, they say, 38
that from very nothing, and beyond the imagination
of his neighbors, is grown into an unspeakable estate. 40

CAMILLO   I have heard, sir, of such a man, who hath a
daughter of most rare note. The report of her is ex- 42
tended more than can be thought to begin from such
a cottage.

POLIXENES   That's likewise part of my intelligence; but,
I fear, the angle that plucks our son thither. Thou shalt 46
accompany us to the place, where we will, not appearing what we are, have some question with the shep- 48
herd; from whose simplicity I think it not uneasy to 49
get the cause of my son's resort thither. Prithee, be my
present partner in this business, and lay aside the
thoughts of Sicilia.

CAMILLO   I willingly obey your command.

POLIXENES   My best Camillo! We must disguise ourselves.   *Exit [with Camillo].*

27 **their . . . gracious** if their children behave ungraciously   **28 approved**
proved   **31 missingly** i.e., regretfully aware of the Prince's absence
32 frequent to devoted to   **34 so much** i.e., all that you say   **35–36 eyes
. . . removedness** spies who keep an eye on him in his absence
37 intelligence news.   **from** away from   **38 homely** simple
40 unspeakable i.e., beyond description   **42 note** distinction   **46 angle**
baited fishhook.   **our** (The royal "we"; also in *us,* l. 47.)   **48 question**
talk   **49 uneasy** difficult

4.3   *Enter Autolycus, singing.*

AUTOLYCUS

> When daffodils begin to peer,   1
> > With heigh, the doxy over the dale!   2
> Why, then comes in the sweet o' the year,
> > For the red blood reigns in the winter's pale.   4

> The white sheet bleaching on the hedge,
> > With heigh, the sweet birds, O, how they sing!
> Doth set my pugging tooth on edge,   7
> > For a quart of ale is a dish for a king.   8

> The lark, that tirralirra chants,
> > With heigh, with heigh, the thrush and the jay!
> Are summer songs for me and my aunts,   11
> > While we lie tumbling in the hay.

I have served Prince Florizel and in my time wore three-pile, but now I am out of service.   14

> But shall I go mourn for that, my dear?   15
> > The pale moon shines by night,
> And when I wander here and there,   17
> > I then do most go right.   18

> If tinkers may have leave to live,   19
> > And bear the sow-skin budget,   20
> Then my account I well may give,   21
> > And in the stocks avouch it.   22

My traffic is sheets; when the kite builds, look to lesser   23

4.3. Location: Bohemia. A road near the Shepherd's cottage.
1 peer peep out   **2 doxy** beggar's wench   **4 pale** (1) paleness (2) domain, region of authority. (The image is of red blood restoring vitality to a pale complexion.)   **7 set ... on edge** i.e., whets the appetite of my thieving tooth, my taste for thieving. (To *pug* is to pull, tug.)   **8 quart of ale** (To be paid for with profits from theft of sheets.)   **11 aunts** i.e., whores   **14 three-pile** velvet having very rich pile or nap   **15 for that** i.e., for being out of service   **17 wander** (i.e., as a thief)   **18 most go right** i.e., live the life that is meant for me   **19 live** i.e., practice their trade   **20 budget** tool bag   **21 my account** my account of myself   **22 in ... avouch it** i.e., affirm that I am a tinker even if I find myself sitting in the stocks, where vagabonds often end up. (Autolycus passes himself off as a tinker to mask his real calling of thief.)   **23 kite** (The kite, a bird of prey, was supposed to carry off small pieces of linen with which to construct its nest, whereas Autolycus makes off with larger linen or sheets hung out to dry.)

linen. My father named me Autolycus, who, being, as   24
I am, littered under Mercury, was likewise a snapper-   25
up of unconsidered trifles. With die and drab I pur-   26
chased this caparison, and my revenue is the silly   27
cheat. Gallows and knock are too powerful on the   28
highway; beating and hanging are terrors to me. For   29
the life to come, I sleep out the thought of it. A prize,   30
a prize!

    Enter Clown.

CLOWN   Let me see: every 'leven wether tods; every tod   32
    yields pound and odd shilling; fifteen hundred shorn,
    what comes the wool to?
AUTOLYCUS *[Aside]* If the springe hold, the cock's mine.   35
CLOWN   I cannot do 't without counters. Let me see;   36
    what am I to buy for our sheepshearing feast? Three
    pound of sugar, five pound of currants, rice—what
    will this sister of mine do with rice? But my father hath
    made her mistress of the feast, and she lays it on. She
    hath made me four-and-twenty nosegays for the shear-   41
    ers—three-man-song men all, and very good ones;   42
    but they are most of them means and basses, but one   43
    Puritan amongst them, and he sings psalms to horn-   44
    pipes. I must have saffron to color the warden pies;   45

---

24 Autolycus (Like his namesake, Ulysses' grandfather, the son of
Mercury, this Autolycus is an expert thief.) **who** i.e., my father
25 littered under Mercury (1) sired by Mercury, the god of
thieves (2) born when the planet Mercury was in the ascendant
26 unconsidered left unattended, not worth thinking about **26–28 With
. . . cheat** i.e., gambling and whoring have brought me to the wearing
of these tattered rags, and my source of income is in cheating simple-
tons **28 Gallows and knock** hanging and being beaten (the hazards of
being a highwayman) **29 For** as for **30 sleep . . . it** i.e., don't give a
thought to punishment in the next world. **prize** booty **32 every . . .
tods** every eleven sheep yield a *tod*, i.e., a bulk of wool weighing twenty-
eight pounds **35 springe** snare. **cock** woodcock. (A proverbially stupid
bird.) **36 counters** metal disks used in reckoning **41 made me** made.
(*Me* is used colloquially.) **42 three-man-song men** singers of songs for
three male voices, bass, tenor, and treble **43 means** tenors **43–45 but
. . . hornpipes** i.e., except for one Puritan, who is a treble but who sings
psalms even to merry dance tunes. (The Puritans were often laughed at
for their pious singing.) **45 warden** made of the warden pear

mace; dates?—none, that's out of my note; nutmegs, 46
seven; a race or two of ginger, but that I may beg; four 47
pound of prunes, and as many of raisins o' the sun. 48

AUTOLYCUS O that ever I was born! [*He grovels on the ground.*]

CLOWN I' the name of me! 50

AUTOLYCUS O, help me, help me! Pluck but off these rags, and then death, death!

CLOWN Alack, poor soul! Thou hast need of more rags to lay on thee, rather than have these off.

AUTOLYCUS O sir, the loathsomeness of them offend me more than the stripes I have received, which are mighty ones and millions.

CLOWN Alas, poor man! A million of beating may come to a great matter.

AUTOLYCUS I am robbed, sir, and beaten; my money and apparel ta'en from me, and these detestable things put upon me.

CLOWN What, by a horseman or a footman? 63

AUTOLYCUS A footman, sweet sir, a footman.

CLOWN Indeed, he should be a footman by the garments he has left with thee. If this be a horseman's coat, it hath seen very hot service. Lend me thy hand; I'll help thee. Come, lend me thy hand. [*He helps him up.*]

AUTOLYCUS O, good sir, tenderly, O!

CLOWN Alas, poor soul!

AUTOLYCUS O, good sir, softly, good sir! I fear, sir, my shoulder blade is out.

CLOWN How now? Canst stand?

AUTOLYCUS [*Picking his pocket*] Softly, dear sir; good sir, softly. You ha' done me a charitable office.

CLOWN Dost lack any money? I have a little money for 76
thee. 77

AUTOLYCUS No, good sweet sir; no, I beseech you, sir.

---

46 out of my note not on my list **47 race** root **48 o' the sun** dried in the sun **50 I' the name of me** (An unusual and perhaps comic oath.) **63 horseman** highwayman. **footman** footpad, robber of pedestrians. (But in l. 65 the Clown uses the word to mean "attendant," who might have poor clothes.) **76–77 I have . . . thee** (The Clown reaches for his money, and might discover the robbery if Autolycus did not quickly beg him not to bother.)

I have a kinsman not past three quarters of a mile
hence, unto whom I was going; I shall there have
money or anything I want. Offer me no money, I pray
you. That kills my heart.

CLOWN   What manner of fellow was he that robbed you?

AUTOLYCUS   A fellow, sir, that I have known to go about
with troll-my-dames. I knew him once a servant of the   85
Prince. I cannot tell, good sir, for which of his virtues
it was, but he was certainly whipped out of the court.

CLOWN   His vices, you would say. There's no virtue
whipped out of the court. They cherish it to make it
stay there; and yet it will no more but abide.   90

AUTOLYCUS   Vices, I would say, sir. I know this man
well. He hath been since an ape bearer, then a pro-   92
cess server, a bailiff. Then he compassed a motion of   93
the Prodigal Son and married a tinker's wife within a
mile where my land and living lies, and, having flown   95
over many knavish professions, he settled only in
rogue. Some call him Autolycus.

CLOWN   Out upon him! Prig, for my life, prig! He   98
haunts wakes, fairs, and bearbaitings.   99

AUTOLYCUS   Very true, sir. He, sir, he. That's the rogue
that put me into this apparel.

CLOWN   Not a more cowardly rogue in all Bohemia. If
you had but looked big and spit at him, he'd have
run.

AUTOLYCUS   I must confess to you, sir, I am no fighter.
I am false of heart that way, and that he knew, I war-   106
rant him.

CLOWN   How do you now?

AUTOLYCUS   Sweet sir, much better than I was. I can
stand and walk. I will even take my leave of you and
pace softly towards my kinsman's.   111

85 troll-my-dames or troll-madams (from the French *trou-madame*), a
game in which the object was to *troll* balls through arches set on a
board. (Autolycus uses the word to suggest women who *troll* or saunter
about.)   **90 no more but abide** make only a temporary stay   **92 ape
bearer** one who carries a monkey about for exhibition   **92–93 process
server** sheriff's officer who serves processes or summonses
93 compassed a motion got possession of or devised a puppet show
95 living property   **98 Prig** thief   **99 wakes** village festivals. (A *wake* is
also a vigil for a dead person or similar ceremony.)   **106 false** cowardly   **111 softly** slowly

CLOWN Shall I bring thee on the way?   112
AUTOLYCUS No, good-faced sir, no, sweet sir.
CLOWN Then fare thee well. I must go buy spices for
our sheepshearing.   *Exit.*
AUTOLYCUS Prosper you, sweet sir! Your purse is not   116
hot enough to purchase your spice. I'll be with you at 117
your sheepshearing too. If I make not this cheat bring 118
out another, and the shearers prove sheep, let me be   119
unrolled and my name put in the book of virtue!   120

> *Song.*
>
> Jog on, jog on, the footpath way,
>   And merrily hent the stile-a;   122
> A merry heart goes all the day,
>   Your sad tires in a mile-a.   *Exit.*

❖

4.4 *Enter Florizel [in shepherd's garb, and] Perdita*
[in holiday attire].

FLORIZEL
  These your unusual weeds to each part of you   1
  Does give a life; no shepherdess, but Flora   2
  Peering in April's front. This your sheepshearing   3
  Is as a meeting of the petty gods,   4
  And you the queen on 't.
PERDITA   Sir, my gracious lord,
  To chide at your extremes it not becomes me.   6
  O, pardon that I name them! Your high self,
  The gracious mark o' the land, you have obscured   8

112 **bring . . . way** go part of the way with you   116 **Prosper . . . sir**
(Said to the departing Clown.)   116–117 **Your . . . spice** i.e., you'll find
but a cold purse to pay for your hot spices; an empty purse is a cold
one. (Said after the Clown's departure.)   118–119 **cheat bring out**
swindle lead to   120 **unrolled** taken off the roll (of rogues and vagabonds)   122 **hent** take hold of (as a means of leaping over)

4.4. Location: Bohemia. The Shepherd's cottage. (See ll. 181–182, 187,
etc.)
1 **unusual weeds** special, holiday attire   2 **Flora** goddess of flowers
3 **Peering . . . front** peeping forth in early April   4 **petty** minor
6 **extremes** extravagant statements   8 **mark o' the land** one who is
noted and used as a model by everyone

With a swain's wearing, and me, poor lowly maid,   9
Most goddesslike pranked up. But that our feasts   10
In every mess have folly, and the feeders   11
Digest it with a custom, I should blush   12
To see you so attired, swoon, I think,
To show myself a glass.

FLORIZEL   I bless the time   14
When my good falcon made her flight across
Thy father's ground.

PERDITA   Now Jove afford you cause!
To me the difference forges dread; your greatness   17
Hath not been used to fear. Even now I tremble
To think your father by some accident
Should pass this way as you did. O, the Fates!
How would he look to see his work, so noble,
Vilely bound up? What would he say? Or how   22
Should I, in these my borrowed flaunts, behold   23
The sternness of his presence?

FLORIZEL   Apprehend
Nothing but jollity. The gods themselves,
Humbling their deities to love, have taken
The shapes of beasts upon them. Jupiter   27
Became a bull and bellowed; the green Neptune,   28
A ram and bleated; and the fire-robed god,   29
Golden Apollo, a poor humble swain,   30
As I seem now. Their transformations
Were never for a piece of beauty rarer,
Nor in a way so chaste, since my desires   33
Run not before mine honor, nor my lusts
Burn hotter than my faith.

PERDITA   O, but, sir,
Your resolution cannot hold when 'tis
Opposed, as it must be, by th' power of the King.

9 **wearing** garb 10 **pranked up** bedecked. **But that** were it not that
11 **In every mess** at every table, in each group or course of dishes
12 **Digest** swallow, i.e., accept. **with a custom** from habit 14 **To show
. . . glass** if I were to see myself in a mirror 17 **difference** i.e., of
rank. **forges** i.e., creates 22 **bound up** i.e., covered in lowly outer
garments. (The metaphor is from bookbinding.) 23 **flaunts** finery
27–30 **Jupiter . . . swain** (Jupiter in the guise of a bull wooed Europa,
Neptune disguised as a ram deceived Bisaltis (Ovid, *Metamorphoses*,
6.117) and Apollo took the guise of a humble shepherd to enable Adme-
tus to woo Alcestis.) 33 **in a way** i.e., pursuing a purpose

One of these two must be necessities,
Which then will speak: that you must change this
    purpose
Or I my life.
FLORIZEL   Thou dearest Perdita,   40
With these forced thoughts, I prithee, darken not   41
The mirth o' the feast. Or I'll be thine, my fair,   42
Or not my father's. For I cannot be
Mine own, not anything to any, if   44
I be not thine. To this I am most constant,
Though destiny say no. Be merry, gentle!   46
Strangle such thoughts as these with anything   47
That you behold the while. Your guests are coming.   48
Lift up your countenance as it were the day   49
Of celebration of that nuptial which
We two have sworn shall come.
PERDITA   O Lady Fortune,
Stand you auspicious!
FLORIZEL   See, your guests approach.
Address yourself to entertain them sprightly,   53
And let's be red with mirth.

    [Enter] Shepherd, Clown; Polixenes, Camillo
    [disguised]; Mopsa, Dorcas; servants.

SHEPHERD
Fie, daughter! When my old wife lived, upon
This day she was both pantler, butler, cook,   56
Both dame and servant; welcomed all, served all;   57
Would sing her song and dance her turn; now here,
At upper end o' the table, now i' the middle;
On his shoulder, and his; her face afire   60
With labor, and the thing she took to quench it   61
She would to each one sip. You are retired,   62
As if you were a feasted one and not

40 Or I my life i.e., or I will be threatened with loss of life (as Polixenes
indeed threatens at ll. 436–443)   41 forced farfetched, unnatural   42 Or
either   44 not anything I will not be anything   46 gentle i.e., my gentle
love   47–48 Strangle . . . while i.e., put down such thoughts by attending to matters at hand   49 as as if   53 Address prepare   56 pantler
pantry servant   57 dame mistress of the household   60 On his . . . his
at one man's . . . another's   61–62 and . . . sip and she would toast each
one with the drink she took to quench the fire of her labor

The hostess of the meeting. Pray you, bid
These unknown friends to 's welcome, for it is   65
A way to make us better friends, more known.   66
Come, quench your blushes and present yourself
That which you are, mistress o' the feast. Come on,
And bid us welcome to your sheepshearing,
As your good flock shall prosper.
PERDITA [*To Polixenes*]   Sir, welcome.
It is my father's will I should take on me
The hostess-ship o' the day. [*To Camillo.*] You're
     welcome, sir.
Give me those flowers there, Dorcas. Reverend sirs,
For you there's rosemary and rue; these keep
Seeming and savor all the winter long.   75
Grace and remembrance be to you both,   76
And welcome to our shearing! [*Giving them flowers.*]
POLIXENES   Shepherdess—
A fair one are you—well you fit our ages
With flowers of winter.
PERDITA   Sir, the year growing ancient,   79
Not yet on summer's death nor on the birth
Of trembling winter, the fairest flow'rs o' the season
Are our carnations and streaked gillyvors,   82
Which some call nature's bastards. Of that kind   83
Our rustic garden's barren, and I care not
To get slips of them.
POLIXENES   Wherefore, gentle maiden,   85
Do you neglect them?
PERDITA   For I have heard it said   86
There is an art which in their piedness shares   87
With great creating nature.
POLIXENES   Say there be;
Yet nature is made better by no mean   89

65 to 's each to his   **66 more known** better acquainted   **75 Seeming**
outward appearance, color   **76 Grace and remembrance** divine grace
and remembrance after death. (Equated respectively with rue and
rosemary.)   **79 the year . . . ancient** i.e., when autumn arrives
82 gillyvors gillyflowers, a kind of carnation or pink   **83 nature's
bastards** i.e., the result of artificial breeding. (See ll. 86–88.)   **85 slips**
cuttings   **86 For** because   **87 art** i.e., of crossbreeding.   **piedness**
particolor appearance. (Perdita disclaims the art of crossbreeding, since
it infringes on what nature itself does so well.)   **89 mean** means

But nature makes that mean. So, over that art   90
Which you say adds to nature is an art
That nature makes. You see, sweet maid, we marry
A gentler scion to the wildest stock,   93
And make conceive a bark of baser kind
By bud of nobler race. This is an art
Which does mend nature—change it, rather—but
The art itself is nature.
PERDITA   So it is.
POLIXENES
Then make your garden rich in gillyvors,
And do not call them bastards.
PERDITA   I'll not put
The dibble in earth to set one slip of them,   100
No more than, were I painted, I would wish   101
This youth should say 'twere well, and only therefore
Desire to breed by me. Here's flowers for you:
                              [*Giving them flowers*]
Hot lavender, mints, savory, marjoram,   104
The marigold, that goes to bed wi' the sun
And with him rises weeping. These are flowers
Of middle summer, and I think they are given   107
To men of middle age. You're very welcome.
CAMILLO
I should leave grazing, were I of your flock,
And only live by gazing.
PERDITA   Out, alas!
You'd be so lean that blasts of January
Would blow you through and through. [*To Florizel.*]
    Now, my fair'st friend,
I would I had some flow'rs o' the spring that might
Become your time of day; [*To the Shepherdesses*] and
    yours, and yours,
That wear upon your virgin branches yet

---

90 But unless. (Polixenes's point is that the art of improving on nature
is itself natural.)   **93 gentler** nobler, more cultivated   **100 dibble** tool
for making holes in which to implant seed   **101 painted** made artificially beautiful by cosmetics   **104 Hot** eager, ardent, aromatic (?)
(Spices were classified as hot or cold.)   **107 middle summer** (Having no
autumn flowers in any case [ll. 79–82], since it is too early in the season,
Perdita flatters her older guests by giving them flowers appropriate to
middle age.)

Your maidenheads growing. O Proserpina,   116
For the flow'rs now that, frighted, thou lett'st fall
From Dis's wagon! Daffodils,
That come before the swallow dares, and take   119
The winds of March with beauty; violets dim,
But sweeter than the lids of Juno's eyes
Or Cytherea's breath; pale primroses,   122
That die unmarried ere they can behold
Bright Phoebus in his strength—a malady   124
Most incident to maids; bold oxlips and   125
The crown imperial; lilies of all kinds,   126
The flower-de-luce being one. O, these I lack   127
To make you garlands of, and my sweet friend,   128
To strew him o'er and o'er!
FLORIZEL   What, like a corpse?
PERDITA
No, like a bank for Love to lie and play on,   130
Not like a corpse; or if, not to be buried,   131
But quick and in mine arms. Come, take your flowers. 132
                              [*Giving flowers.*]
Methinks I play as I have seen them do
In Whitsun pastorals. Sure this robe of mine   134
Does change my disposition.
FLORIZEL   What you do
Still betters what is done. When you speak, sweet,   136
I'd have you do it ever. When you sing,
I'd have you buy and sell so, so give alms,
Pray so; and, for the ordering your affairs,

---

116 Proserpina daughter of Ceres, stolen away by Pluto (*Dis*) and taken
to Hades when, according to Ovid, she was gathering flowers in her
garden   **119 take** charm   **122 Cytherea's** Venus'   **124 Phoebus** the sun
god   **124–125 a malady . . . maids** (Young maids, suffering from greensickness, a kind of anemia, are pale like the primrose.)   **126 crown
imperial** flower from the Levant, cultivated in English gardens
127 flower-de-luce fleur-de-lis.   **I lack** (because the season is too late for
them)   **128 To . . . friend** to make garlands of them for you (Polixenes
and Camillo) and for my sweet friend (Florizel)   **130 Love** i.e., Cupid
131 or if or if for a corpse, that is, a living body   **132 quick** alive
134 Whitsun pastorals plays (including Robin Hood plays) and English
morris dances often performed at Whitsuntide, seven Sundays after
Easter. (The part of Maid Marian strikes Perdita as immodest for her
usual behavior.)   **136 betters what is done** i.e., surpasses anything else

To sing them too. When you do dance, I wish you
A wave o' the sea, that you might ever do
Nothing but that—move still, still so,
And own no other function. Each your doing,   143
So singular in each particular,   144
Crowns what you are doing in the present deeds,
That all your acts are queens.

PERDITA   O Doricles,   146
Your praises are too large. But that your youth   147
And the true blood which peeps fairly through 't
Do plainly give you out an unstained shepherd,   149
With wisdom I might fear, my Doricles,
You wooed me the false way.

FLORIZEL   I think you have
As little skill to fear as I have purpose   152
To put you to 't. But come, our dance, I pray.
Your hand, my Perdita. So turtles pair,   154
That never mean to part.

PERDITA   I'll swear for 'em.   155
                    [*They speak apart.*]

POLIXENES [*To Camillo*]
This is the prettiest lowborn lass that ever
Ran on the greensward. Nothing she does or seems
But smacks of something greater than herself,
Too noble for this place.

CAMILLO   He tells her something
That makes her blood look out. Good sooth, she is   160
The queen of curds and cream.

CLOWN   Come on, strike up!

DORCAS
Mopsa must be your mistress. Marry, garlic,   162
To mend her kissing with!

MOPSA   Now, in good time!   163

---

143 **Each your doing** each thing you do and how you do it   144 **singular**
unique and peerless   146 **Doricles** (Florizel's disguise name.)   147 **large**
lavish.   **But that** were it not that   149 **give you out** proclaim you to
be   152 **skill** reason   154 **turtles** turtledoves, as symbols of faithful
love   155 **I'll swear for 'em** i.e., I'll be sworn they do   160 **makes . . .
out** makes her blush   162 **mistress** i.e., partner in the dance
163 **kissing** i.e., bad breath. (Dorcas jests that even garlic would improve
Mopsa's breath.)   **in good time** (An expression of indignation.)

CLOWN
  Not a word, a word. We stand upon our manners. 164
  Come, strike up! 165
            [*Music.*] *Here a dance of Shepherds and*
                                  Shepherdesses.

POLIXENES
  Pray, good shepherd, what fair swain is this
  Which dances with your daughter?

SHEPHERD
  They call him Doricles, and boasts himself 168
  To have a worthy feeding; but I have it 169
  Upon his own report and I believe it.
  He looks like sooth. He says he loves my daughter. 171
  I think so too, for never gazed the moon
  Upon the water as he'll stand and read,
  As 'twere, my daughter's eyes; and, to be plain,
  I think there is not half a kiss to choose
  Who loves another best.

POLIXENES   She dances featly. 176

SHEPHERD
  So she does anything—though I report it
  That should be silent. If young Doricles
  Do light upon her, she shall bring him that 179
  Which he not dreams of.

    Enter Servant.

SERVANT O master, if you did but hear the peddler at the
  door, you would never dance again after a tabor and 182
  pipe; no, the bagpipe could not move you. He sings
  several tunes faster than you'll tell money. He utters 184
  them as he had eaten ballads and all men's ears grew 185
  to his tunes.

CLOWN He could never come better. He shall come in. 187
  I love a ballad but even too well, if it be doleful matter 188
  merrily set down, or a very pleasant thing indeed and 189
  sung lamentably. 190

164 stand upon set store by **165 s.d. dance** (Probably a morris
dance.) **168** and i.e., and they say he **169 feeding** pasturage, lands
171 like sooth truthful **176 another** the other. **featly** gracefully
179 light upon choose **182 tabor** small drum **184 tell** count **185 as**
as if (also in l. 208) **187 better** at a better time **188 but even too well**
all too well **189 pleasant** merry **190 lamentably** mournfully

SERVANT He hath songs for man or woman, of all sizes. 191
No milliner can so fit his customers with gloves. He 192
has the prettiest love songs for maids, so without
bawdry, which is strange, with such delicate burdens 194
of dildos and fadings, "Jump her and thump her"; and 195
where some stretchmouthed rascal would, as it were, 196
mean mischief and break a foul gap into the matter, 197
he makes the maid to answer, "Whoop, do me no
harm, good man"; puts him off, slights him, with
"Whoop, do me no harm, good man."

POLIXENES This is a brave fellow. 201

CLOWN Believe me, thou talkest of an admirable con- 202
ceited fellow. Has he any unbraided wares? 203

SERVANT He hath ribbons of all the colors i' the rainbow; points more than all the lawyers in Bohemia can 205
learnedly handle, though they come to him by the
gross; inkles, caddisses, cambrics, lawns. Why, he 207
sings 'em over as they were gods or goddesses; you
would think a smock were a she-angel, he so chants to
the sleevehand and the work about the square on 't. 210

CLOWN Prithee, bring him in, and let him approach
singing.

PERDITA Forewarn him that he use no scurrilous words
in 's tunes.   [*The Servant goes to the door.*]

CLOWN You have of these peddlers that have more in 215
them than you'd think, sister.

PERDITA Ay, good brother, or go about to think. 217

Enter Autolycus, singing.

191 sizes sorts **192 milliner** vendor of fancy ware and apparel, including gloves, ribbons, and bonnets **194 burdens** refrains **195 dildos and
fadings** words used as part of the refrains of ballads (but with bawdy
double meaning unperceived by the servant, as also in *jump her, thump
her, do me no harm,* etc.) **196 stretchmouthed** widemouthed, foul-
mouthed **197 break . . . matter** insert some gross obscenity into the
song, or act in a suggestive way **201 brave** excellent
202–203 admirable conceited wonderfully witty and clever
203 unbraided untarnished, undamaged **205 points** (1) laces for fasten-
ing clothes (2) headings in an argument **207 inkles** linen tapes.
caddisses worsted tape used for garters. **cambrics** fine linen fabrics.
lawns fine sheer linens **210 sleevehand** wristband. **square on 't**
embroidered bosom or yoke of the garment **215 You . . . peddlers**
you'll find peddlers **217 go about** intend, wish **s.d. Enter Autolycus**
(Apparently he is wearing a false beard; later in this scene he removes it
to impersonate a courtier to the Clown and Shepherd.)

AUTOLYCUS

    Lawn as white as driven snow,

    Cyprus black as e'er was crow,   219

    Gloves as sweet as damask roses,   220

    Masks for faces and for noses,

    Bugle bracelet, necklace amber,   222

    Perfume for a lady's chamber,

    Golden coifs and stomachers,   224

    For my lads to give their dears,

    Pins and poking-sticks of steel,   226

    What maids lack from head to heel,

    Come buy of me, come. Come buy, come buy.

    Buy, lads, or else your lasses cry.

    Come buy.

CLOWN If I were not in love with Mopsa, thou shouldst
take no money of me, but being enthralled as I am, it 232
will also be the bondage of certain ribbons and gloves. 233

MOPSA I was promised them against the feast, but they 234
come not too late now.

DORCAS He hath promised you more than that, or there 236
be liars. 237

MOPSA He hath paid you all he promised you. Maybe
he has paid you more, which will shame you to give 239
him again. 240

CLOWN Is there no manners left among maids? Will 241
they wear their plackets where they should bear their 242
faces? Is there not milking time, when you are going 243
to bed, or kilnhole, to whistle of these secrets, but 244
you must be tittle-tattling before all our guests? 'Tis
well they are whispering. Clamor your tongues, and 246
not a word more.

219 Cyprus crepe **220 sweet** i.e., perfumed (also in l. 249) **222 Bugle
bracelet** bracelet of black glossy beads **224 coifs** close-fitting caps.
stomachers embroidered fronts for ladies' dresses **226 poking-sticks**
rods used for ironing and stiffening the plaits of ruffs **232–233 it will
. . . bondage** it will mean the taking into custody (by means of purchase
and tying up into a parcel) **234 against** in anticipation of, in time for
236–237 He . . . liars i.e., he promised to marry you too, or else rumor
is a liar **239 paid you more** i.e., made you pregnant **239–240 which
. . . again** i.e., which will shame you by giving birth to his child
241–243 Will . . . faces i.e., will they always be talking and revealing
personal secrets. **plackets** slits in petticoats (with bawdy suggestion of
the pudendum, as at l. 613) **244 kilnhole** fire hole of a baking oven
(where maids might gossip). **whistle** whisper **246 Clamor** i.e., silence

MOPSA I have done. Come, you promised me a tawdry 248
lace and a pair of sweet gloves.   249

CLOWN Have I not told thee how I was cozened by the 250
way and lost all my money?

AUTOLYCUS And indeed, sir, there are cozeners abroad;
therefore it behooves men to be wary.

CLOWN Fear not thou, man, thou shalt lose nothing
here.

AUTOLYCUS I hope so, sir, for I have about me many
parcels of charge.   257

CLOWN What hast here? Ballads?

MOPSA Pray now, buy some. I love a ballad in print
alife, for then we are sure they are true.   260

AUTOLYCUS Here's one to a very doleful tune, how a
usurer's wife was brought to bed of twenty moneybags at a burden, and how she longed to eat adders' 263
heads and toads carbonadoed.   264

MOPSA Is it true, think you?

AUTOLYCUS Very true, and but a month old.

DORCAS Bless me from marrying a usurer!   267

AUTOLYCUS Here's the midwife's name to 't, one Mistress Taleporter, and five or six honest wives that 269
were present. Why should I carry lies abroad?

MOPSA Pray you now, buy it.

CLOWN Come on, lay it by, and let's first see more ballads. We'll buy the other things anon.

AUTOLYCUS Here's another ballad, of a fish that appeared upon the coast on Wednesday the fourscore of 275
April, forty thousand fathom above water, and sung 276
this ballad against the hard hearts of maids. It was
thought she was a woman and was turned into a cold
fish for she would not exchange flesh with one that
loved her. The ballad is very pitiful and as true.

DORCAS Is it true too, think you?

248–249 tawdry lace cheap and showy lace, or neckerchief. (So called
from St. Audrey's Fair.) **250 cozened** cheated **257 parcels of charge**
valuable items **260 alife** dearly **263 at a burden** in one childbirth
264 carbonadoed scored across and grilled **267 Bless** protect, keep
269 Taleporter i.e., talebearer, gossip **275 fourscore** eightieth (!) **276
forty thousand fathom** 240,000 feet

AUTOLYCUS Five justices' hands at it, and witnesses 282
  more than my pack will hold.

CLOWN Lay it by too. Another.

AUTOLYCUS This is a merry ballad, but a very pretty
  one.

MOPSA Let's have some merry ones.

AUTOLYCUS Why, this is a passing merry one and goes 288
  to the tune of "Two Maids Wooing a Man." There's
  scarce a maid westward but she sings it. 'Tis in re- 290
  quest, I can tell you.

MOPSA We can both sing it. If thou'lt bear a part, thou
  shalt hear; 'tis in three parts.

DORCAS We had the tune on 't a month ago. 294

AUTOLYCUS I can bear my part; you must know 'tis my
  occupation. Have at it with you. 296

Song.

AUTOLYCUS

    Get you hence, for I must go
    Where it fits not you to know.

DORCAS

        Whither?

MOPSA   O, whither?

DORCAS   Whither?

MOPSA

    It becomes thy oath full well,
    Thou to me thy secrets tell.

DORCAS

      Me too. Let me go thither.

MOPSA

    Or thou goest to th' grange or mill. 303

DORCAS

    If to either, thou dost ill.

AUTOLYCUS

    Neither.

DORCAS   What, neither?

AUTOLYCUS   Neither.

---

282 hands signatures **288 passing** surpassingly **290 westward** in the
West Country **294 on 't** of it **296 Have at it** i.e., here goes **303 Or**
either. **grange** farm

DORCAS
    Thou hast sworn my love to be.

MOPSA
    Thou hast sworn it more to me.
    Then whither goest? Say, whither?

CLOWN We'll have this song out anon by ourselves. My 309
father and the gentlemen are in sad talk, and we'll not 310
trouble them. Come, bring away thy pack after me.
Wenches, I'll buy for you both. Peddler, let's have the
first choice. Follow me, girls.
                  [*Exit with Dorcas and Mopsa.*]

AUTOLYCUS And you shall pay well for 'em.
                    [*He follows singing.*]

         Song.

    Will you buy any tape,
    Or lace for your cape,
  My dainty duck, my dear-a?
      Any silk, any thread,
      And toys for your head,   319
  Of the new'st and fin'st, fin'st wear-a?
      Come to the peddler;
      Money's a meddler,   322
  That doth utter all men's ware-a.   *Exit.* 323

[*Enter a Servant.*]

SERVANT Master, there is three carters, three shepherds, three neatherds, three swineherds, that have 325
made themselves all men of hair. They call themselves 326
saultiers, and they have a dance which the wenches say 327
is a gallimaufry of gambols, because they are not in 't; 328
but they themselves are o' the mind, if it be not too
rough for some that know little but bowling, it will 330
please plentifully.

SHEPHERD Away! We'll none on 't. Here has been too

309 have this song out finish this song **310 sad** serious **319 toys**
trifles **322 meddler** i.e., go-between in commercial transactions
323 utter put on the market **325 neatherds** cowherds **326 of hair**
dressed in skins **327 saultiers** leapers or vaulters (with perhaps a play
on *Saltiers* as a blunder for "satyrs") **328 gallimaufry** jumble
330 bowling (A more gentle sport than the vigorous satyr dancing.)

much homely foolery already.—I know, sir, we weary 333
you.

POLIXENES   You weary those that refresh us. Pray, let's
see these four threes of herdsmen.

SERVANT   One three of them, by their own report, sir, 337
hath danced before the King, and not the worst of the
three but jumps twelve foot and a half by the square. 339

SHEPHERD   Leave your prating. Since these good men
are pleased, let them come in; but quickly now.

SERVANT   Why, they stay at door, sir.

[He goes to the door.]

Here a dance of twelve Satyrs.

POLIXENES *[To Shepherd]*

O, father, you'll know more of that hereafter.   343
[To Camillo.] Is it not too far gone? 'Tis time to part
them.
He's simple and tells much. *[To Florizel.]* How now,
fair shepherd?   345
Your heart is full of something that does take
Your mind from feasting. Sooth, when I was young
And handed love as you do, I was wont   348
To load my she with knacks. I would have ransacked
The peddler's silken treasury and have poured it
To her acceptance; you have let him go,
And nothing marted with him. If your lass   352
Interpretation should abuse and call this   353
Your lack of love or bounty, you were straited   354
For a reply, at least if you make a care
Of happy holding her.

FLORIZEL   Old sir, I know   356
She prizes not such trifles as these are.
The gifts she looks from me are packed and locked   358
Up in my heart, which I have given already

333 **homely** unpolished   337 **three** threesome   339 **square** foot rule
343 **O . . . hereafter** (Polixenes completes the conversation he has been
having with the old Shepherd during the dance.)   345 **He's simple**
i.e., the old Shepherd is guileless   348 **handed** handled, dealt in
352 **nothing marted with** done no business with   353 **Interpretation
should abuse** should interpret wrongly   354 **were straited** would be
hard-pressed   356 **happy holding her** keeping her happy   358 **looks**
looks for

But not delivered. [*To Perdita.*] O, hear me breathe my
    life   360
Before this ancient sir, who, it should seem,   361
Hath sometime loved! I take thy hand, this hand,
As soft as dove's down and as white as it,
Or Ethiopian's tooth, or the fanned snow that's bolted 364
By th' northern blasts twice o'er.   [*Taking her hand.*]
POLIXENES   What follows this?
How prettily the young swain seems to wash
The hand was fair before! I have put you out.   367
But to your protestation; let me hear   368
What you profess.
FLORIZEL   Do, and be witness to 't.
POLIXENES
And this my neighbor too?
FLORIZEL   And he, and more
Than he, and men—the earth, the heavens, and all:
That, were I crowned the most imperial monarch,
Thereof most worthy, were I the fairest youth   373
That ever made eye swerve, had force and knowledge 374
More than was ever man's, I would not prize them
Without her love; for her employ them all,
Commend them and condemn them to her service   377
Or to their own perdition.
POLIXENES   Fairly offered.   378
CAMILLO
This shows a sound affection.
SHEPHERD   But, my daughter,
Say you the like to him?
PERDITA   I cannot speak
So well, nothing so well; no, nor mean better.

---

360 But not delivered i.e., but I have not confirmed it by a solemn vow
before witnesses, making binding the contract. **breathe my life** i.e.,
pronounce eternal vows **361 this ancient sir** i.e., Polixenes **364 fanned**
blown. **bolted** sifted **367 was** that was. **put you out** interrupted what
you were saying **368 to your protestation** on with your public affirmation **373 Thereof most worthy** the most worthy of monarchs
374 swerve turn in my direction (out of awe and respect)
377–378 Commend . . . perdition either commend them to her service,
or, failing that, condemn them to deserved destruction

By th' pattern of mine own thoughts I cut out   382
The purity of his.
SHEPHERD   Take hands, a bargain!   383
 And, friends unknown, you shall bear witness to 't:
 I give my daughter to him and will make
 Her portion equal his.
FLORIZEL   O, that must be
 I' the virtue of your daughter. One being dead,
 I shall have more than you can dream of yet;
 Enough then for your wonder. But come on: 389
 Contract us 'fore these witnesses.
SHEPHERD   Come, your hand;
 And, daughter, yours.
POLIXENES   Soft, swain, awhile, beseech you.   391
 Have you a father?
FLORIZEL   I have, but what of him?
POLIXENES   Knows he of this?
FLORIZEL   He neither does nor shall.
POLIXENES   Methinks a father
 Is at the nuptial of his son a guest
 That best becomes the table. Pray you, once more,
 Is not your father grown incapable
 Of reasonable affairs? Is he not stupid   400
 With age and altering rheums? Can he speak? Hear?   401
 Know man from man? Dispute his own estate?   402
 Lies he not bedrid, and again does nothing
 But what he did being childish?
FLORIZEL   No, good sir,   404
 He has his health and ampler strength indeed
 Than most have of his age.
POLIXENES   By my white beard,
 You offer him, if this be so, a wrong

382–383 By . . . of his (Perdita uses a metaphor of clothes-making to
express her view that Florizel's pure thoughts must be like her own—
not patterned on hers but rather perceived by her to be a model for her
own.)   389 Enough . . . wonder there will be enough then for you to
wonder at   391 Soft wait a minute   400 reasonable affairs matters
requiring the use of reason   401 altering rheums weakening catarrhs or
other diseases   402 Dispute discuss.   estate affairs, condition
404 being childish when he was a child

Something unfilial. Reason my son   408
Should choose himself a wife, but as good reason
The father, all whose joy is nothing else
But fair posterity, should hold some counsel   411
In such a business.
FLORIZEL   I yield all this;   412
But for some other reasons, my grave sir,
Which 'tis not fit you know, I not acquaint
My father of this business.
POLIXENES   Let him know 't.
FLORIZEL
He shall not.
POLIXENES   Prithee, let him.
FLORIZEL   No, he must not.
SHEPHERD
Let him, my son. He shall not need to grieve
At knowing of thy choice.
FLORIZEL   Come, come, he must not.
Mark our contract.
POLIXENES   Mark your divorce, young sir,
                        [*Discovering himself*]
Whom son I dare not call. Thou art too base
To be acknowledged. Thou a scepter's heir,
That thus affects a sheephook?—Thou old traitor,   422
I am sorry that by hanging thee I can
But shorten thy life one week.—And thou, fresh piece
Of excellent witchcraft, who of force must know   425
The royal fool thou cop'st with—
SHEPHERD   O, my heart!   426
POLIXENES
I'll have thy beauty scratched with briers and made
More homely than thy state.—For thee, fond boy,   428
If I may ever know thou dost but sigh
That thou no more shalt see this knack—as never   430
I mean thou shalt—we'll bar thee from succession,

408 Something somewhat.   **Reason** it is reasonable that.   **my son** (The disguised Polixenes seems to be speaking hypothetically, using himself as an example, but of course the application to Florizel is direct.)
411 hold some counsel be consulted   **412 yield** concede   **422 affects** desires, shows inclination for   **425 of force** of necessity   **426 thou cop'st** you deal   **428 homely** (1) unattractive (2) humble.   **fond** foolish   **430 knack** trifle, schemer

Not hold thee of our blood, no, not our kin,
Far than Deucalion off. Mark thou my words.   433
Follow us to the court.—Thou churl, for this time,   434
Though full of our displeasure, yet we free thee
From the dead blow of it.—And you, enchantment,   436
Worthy enough a herdsman—yea, him too,   437
That makes himself, but for our honor therein,   438
Unworthy thee—if ever henceforth thou   439
These rural latches to his entrance open,
Or hoop his body more with thy embraces,
I will devise a death as cruel for thee
As thou art tender to 't.   *Exit.*

PERDITA   Even here undone!
I was not much afeard; for once or twice
I was about to speak and tell him plainly
The selfsame sun that shines upon his court
Hides not his visage from our cottage, but
Looks on alike. Will 't please you, sir, begone?   448
I told you what would come of this. Beseech you,
Of your own state take care. This dream of mine—
Being now awake, I'll queen it no inch farther,
But milk my ewes and weep.

CAMILLO   Why, how now, father?
Speak ere thou diest.

SHEPHERD   I cannot speak, nor think,   453
Nor dare to know that which I know. [*To Florizel.*] O sir,
You have undone a man of fourscore three,
That thought to fill his grave in quiet, yea,
To die upon the bed my father died,   457
To lie close by his honest bones; but now
Some hangman must put on my shroud and lay me
Where no priest shovels in dust. [*To Perdita.*] O cursed
  wretch,

433 Far . . . off farther off in kinship than Deucalion (the Noah of
classical mythology)   434 churl i.e., the Shepherd   436 dead deadly.
enchantment i.e., Perdita   437–439 him too . . . thee worthy indeed of
him (Florizel) whose behavior renders him unworthy even of you, if we
were to set aside for the moment the question of the dignity of our royal
house   448 alike indifferently   453 ere thou diest before you die of
grief (?) (Although Polixenes has relented of his threat to hang the
Shepherd, the Shepherd is gloomily sure it will come to a hanging,
ll. 459–460.)   457 died i.e., died on

That knew'st this was the Prince, and wouldst adven-
   ture
To mingle faith with him! Undone, undone!   462
If I might die within this hour, I have lived
To die when I desire.   *Exit.*
FLORIZEL [*To Perdita*]   Why look you so upon me?
I am but sorry, not afeard; delayed,
But nothing altered. What I was, I am,
More straining on for plucking back, not following   468
My leash unwillingly.
CAMILLO   Gracious my lord,
You know your father's temper. At this time
He will allow no speech, which I do guess
You do not purpose to him; and as hardly
Will he endure your sight as yet, I fear.
Then, till the fury of his highness settle,   474
Come not before him.
FLORIZEL   I not purpose it.
I think Camillo?
CAMILLO   Even he, my lord.
PERDITA
How often have I told you 'twould be thus!
How often said my dignity would last   478
But till 'twere known!
FLORIZEL   It cannot fail but by
The violation of my faith; and then   480
Let nature crush the sides o' th' earth together
And mar the seeds within! Lift up thy looks.   482
From my succession wipe me, Father; I
Am heir to my affection.
CAMILLO   Be advised.   484
FLORIZEL
I am, and by my fancy. If my reason   485

---

462 mingle faith exchange pledges   **468 More . . . back** i.e., like a hound
on the leash, all the more eager to go forward for having been restrained   **474 his highness** his towering rage (or else *His Highness*, as a
title)   **478 my dignity** i.e., the new status this marriage would have
offered   **480 then** when that happens   **482 mar the seeds within** i.e.,
destroy the very sources of life on earth (since all material life was
thought to be derived from *seeds*)   **484 affection** passionate love.   **Be
advised** think carefully, be receptive to wise advice   **485 fancy** love

Will thereto be obedient, I have reason;   486
If not, my senses, better pleased with madness,
Do bid it welcome.
CAMILLO   This is desperate, sir.
FLORIZEL
So call it, but it does fulfill my vow;
I needs must think it honesty. Camillo,
Not for Bohemia nor the pomp that may
Be thereat gleaned, for all the sun sees or
The close earth wombs or the profound seas hides   493
In unknown fathoms, will I break my oath
To this my fair beloved. Therefore, I pray you,
As you have ever been my father's honored friend,
When he shall miss me—as, in faith, I mean not
To see him any more—cast your good counsels
Upon his passion. Let myself and fortune   499
Tug for the time to come. This you may know   500
And so deliver: I am put to sea   501
With her who here I cannot hold on shore;   502
And most opportune to our need I have
A vessel rides fast by, but not prepared
For this design. What course I mean to hold
Shall nothing benefit your knowledge nor   506
Concern me the reporting.
CAMILLO   O my lord,   507
I would your spirit were easier for advice   508
Or stronger for your need.
FLORIZEL   Hark, Perdita.
[*To Camillo*.] I'll hear you by and by.
                         [*He draws Perdita aside*.]
CAMILLO [*Aside*]   He's irremovable,   510
Resolved for flight. Now were I happy if
His going I could frame to serve my turn,   512
Save him from danger, do him love and honor,
Purchase the sight again of dear Sicilia
And that unhappy king, my master, whom
I so much thirst to see.

486 have reason (1) will be reasonable (2) will be sane   **493 wombs**
encloses, conceals   **499 passion** anger   **500 Tug** contend   **501 deliver**
report   **502 who** whom   **506–507 Shall . . . reporting** would not behoove you to know nor me to report   **508 easier for** more open to
510 irremovable immovable   **512 frame** shape

FLORIZEL   Now, good Camillo,
I am so fraught with curious business that   517
I leave out ceremony.
CAMILLO   Sir, I think   518
You have heard of my poor services i' the love
That I have borne your father?
FLORIZEL   Very nobly
Have you deserved. It is my father's music
To speak your deeds, not little of his care
To have them recompensed as thought on.
CAMILLO   Well, my lord, 523
If you may please to think I love the King
And through him what's nearest to him, which is
Your gracious self, embrace but my direction,
If your more ponderous and settled project   527
May suffer alteration. On mine honor,   528
I'll point you where you shall have such receiving
As shall become your highness, where you may   530
Enjoy your mistress—from the whom I see
There's no disjunction to be made but by,
As heavens forfend, your ruin—marry her,   533
And, with my best endeavors in your absence,   534
Your discontenting father strive to qualify   535
And bring him up to liking.
FLORIZEL   How, Camillo,   536
May this, almost a miracle, be done,
That I may call thee something more than man,
And after that trust to thee?
CAMILLO   Have you thought on   539
A place whereto you'll go?
FLORIZEL   Not any yet.
But as th' unthought-on accident is guilty   541
To what we wildly do, so we profess   542

517 **curious** demanding care   518 **I leave out ceremony** (Florizel apologizes for whispering with Perdita and failing to observe proper ceremony toward Camillo.)   523 **as thought on** as deservingly as in his
opinion of them   527 **ponderous** serious and carefully deliberated
528 **suffer** permit   530 **become your highness** suit your royal rank; or,
suit Your Highness   533 **forfend** forbid   534 **with** together with
535 **discontenting** discontented, displeased.   **qualify** appease, pacify
536 **bring . . . liking** get him to the point of approval   539 **after** ever
after   541–542 **as . . . wildly do** just as the unexpected happening
(e.g., of our being discovered by the King) is responsible for what we
rashly do at this point

Ourselves to be the slaves of chance and flies   543
Of every wind that blows.
CAMILLO   Then list to me.
This follows, if you will not change your purpose
But undergo this flight: make for Sicilia,
And there present yourself and your fair princess—
For so I see she must be—'fore Leontes.
She shall be habited as it becomes   549
The partner of your bed. Methinks I see
Leontes opening his free arms and weeping   551
His welcomes forth; asks thee there "Son, forgiveness!"
As 'twere i' the father's person; kisses the hands
Of your fresh princess; o'er and o'er divides him   554
Twixt his unkindness and his kindness. Th' one   555
He chides to hell, and bids the other grow
Faster than thought or time.
FLORIZEL   Worthy Camillo,   557
What color for my visitation shall I   558
Hold up before him?
CAMILLO   Sent by the King your father 559
To greet him and to give him comforts. Sir,
The manner of your bearing towards him, with
What you, as from your father, shall deliver—   562
Things known betwixt us three—I'll write you down,
The which shall point you forth at every sitting   564
What you must say, that he shall not perceive
But that you have your father's bosom there   566
And speak his very heart.
FLORIZEL   I am bound to you.
There is some sap in this.
CAMILLO   A course more promising
Than a wild dedication of yourselves
To unpathed waters, undreamed shores, most certain
To miseries enough; no hope to help you,

543 **flies** i.e., insignificant insects, blown about by the winds of
chance   549 **habited** (richly) dressed   551 **free** generous, noble
554 **fresh** young and beautiful   554–555 **divides . . . kindness** divides
his speech between his former unkindness (which he condemns) and his
present intention of kindness   557 **Faster** firmer; also, more swiftly
558 **color** excuse, pretext   559 **Hold up before** present to.   **Sent** i.e., say
you are sent   562 **deliver** say   564 **point you forth** indicate to you.
sitting conference   566 **bosom** inmost thoughts

But as you shake off one to take another;   572
Nothing so certain as your anchors, who   573
Do their best office if they can but stay you   574
Where you'll be loath to be. Besides, you know   575
Prosperity's the very bond of love,   576
Whose fresh complexion and whose heart together   577
Affliction alters.

PERDITA   One of these is true: 578
I think affliction may subdue the cheek,   579
But not take in the mind.

CAMILLO   Yea, say you so?   580
There shall not at your father's house these seven years   581
Be born another such.

FLORIZEL   My good Camillo,
She's as forward of her breeding as she is   583
I' the rear 'our birth.

CAMILLO   I cannot say 'tis pity   584
She lacks instructions, for she seems a mistress   585
To most that teach.

PERDITA   Your pardon, sir; for this   586
I'll blush you thanks.

FLORIZEL   My prettiest Perdita!
But O, the thorns we stand upon! Camillo,
Preserver of my father, now of me,
The medicine of our house, how shall we do?
We are not furnished like Bohemia's son,
Nor shall appear in Sicilia.

CAMILLO   My lord,   592
Fear none of this. I think you know my fortunes

---

572 one i.e., one misery, one misfortune. **take** encounter   **573 Nothing**
not at all.   **who** which   **574–575 Do . . . to be** are doing about as well
as can be hoped if they simply hold you in some hateful place (rather
than allowing you to be shipwrecked and perhaps drowned)
576–578 Prosperity's . . . alters i.e., young love flourishes while things
are going well, but loses its fresh complexion and strength of feeling
under the test of adversity   **579 subdue the cheek** make the complexion
look pale and wasted   **580 take in** overcome   **581 your father's** (Said to
Florizel, and meaning Polixenes's palace?)   **these seven years** i.e., for a
long time to come. (Camillo's point is that she is a nonpareil.)
583 forward . . . breeding far in advance of her lowly upbringing   **584 I'**
the rear 'our below me in   **585 instructions** formal schooling
585–586 a mistress To most one who could teach something to most
people   **592 appear** appear as such

Do all lie there. It shall be so my care
To have you royally appointed as if   595
The scene you play were mine. For instance, sir,
That you may know you shall not want, one word.
                                    [*They talk aside.*]

    Enter Autolycus.

AUTOLYCUS Ha, ha, what a fool Honesty is! And Trust,
  his sworn brother, a very simple gentleman! I have
  sold all my trumpery; not a counterfeit stone, not a
  ribbon, glass, pomander, brooch, table book, ballad,   601
  knife, tape, glove, shoe tie, bracelet, horn ring, to
  keep my pack from fasting. They throng who should   603
  buy first, as if my trinkets had been hallowed and   604
  brought a benediction to the buyer; by which means
  I saw whose purse was best in picture, and what I   606
  saw, to my good use I remembered. My clown, who
  wants but something to be a reasonable man, grew so   608
  in love with the wenches' song that he would not stir
  his pettitoes till he had both tune and words, which   610
  so drew the rest of the herd to me that all their other
  senses stuck in ears. You might have pinched a   612
  placket, it was senseless. 'Twas nothing to geld a cod- 613
  piece of a purse. I could have filed keys off that hung 614
  in chains. No hearing, no feeling, but my sir's song,   615
  and admiring the nothing of it. So that in this time of 616
  lethargy I picked and cut most of their festival purses;
  and had not the old man come in with a hubbub
  against his daughter and the King's son and scared my
  choughs from the chaff, I had not left a purse alive in 620
  the whole army.
      [*Camillo, Florizel, and Perdita come forward.*]

595 appointed equipped, outfitted **601 pomander** scent-ball. **table
book** notebook **603 from fasting** i.e., from being empty **604 hallowed**
made sacred, like a relic **606 best in picture** i.e., best to look at, most
promising **608 wants but something** lacks one thing only (i.e., intelligence) **610 pettitoes** pig's toes; here, toes **612 stuck in ears** were
occupied with their ears **613 placket** (Literally, slit in a petticoat; with
bawdy suggestion.) **senseless** insensible **613–614 geld a codpiece of a
purse** cut a purse loose from the pouch worn at the front of a man's
breeches **615 my sir's** i.e., the Clown's **616 nothing** (1) vacuity
(2) noting, tune. (*Nothing* and *noting* sounded alike in Elizabethan
English.) **620 choughs** jackdaws

CAMILLO
  Nay, but my letters, by this means being there
  So soon as you arrive, shall clear that doubt.
FLORIZEL
  And those that you'll procure from King Leontes—
CAMILLO
  Shall satisfy your father.
PERDITA   Happy be you!
  All that you speak shows fair.
CAMILLO [*Seeing Autolycus*]   Who have we here?
  We'll make an instrument of this, omit
  Nothing may give us aid.
AUTOLYCUS [*Aside*]   If they have overheard me now, why,
  hanging.
CAMILLO   How now, good fellow? Why shak'st thou so?
  Fear not, man, here's no harm intended to thee.
AUTOLYCUS   I am a poor fellow, sir.
CAMILLO   Why, be so still. Here's nobody will steal that
  from thee. Yet for the outside of thy poverty we must 635
  make an exchange. Therefore discase thee instantly— 636
  thou must think there's a necessity in 't—and change 637
  garments with this gentleman. Though the penny- 638
  worth on his side be the worst, yet hold thee, there's 639
  some boot.   [*He gives money.*] 640
AUTOLYCUS   I am a poor fellow, sir. [*Aside.*] I know ye
  well enough.
CAMILLO   Nay, prithee, dispatch. The gentleman is half 643
  flayed already.   644
AUTOLYCUS   Are you in earnest, sir? [*Aside.*] I smell the
  trick on 't.
FLORIZEL   Dispatch, I prithee.
AUTOLYCUS   Indeed, I have had earnest, but I cannot 648
  with conscience take it.
CAMILLO   Unbuckle, unbuckle.
      [*Florizel and Autolycus exchange garments.*]

---

635 the outside of thy poverty i.e., your ragged clothing   **636 discase**
undress   **637 think** understand   **638–639 pennyworth** i.e., value of the
bargain   **640 some boot** something in addition   **643 dispatch** hurry
(also in l. 647)   **644 flayed** skinned, i.e., undressed   **648 earnest** advance
payment (playing on *in earnest* in l. 645)

Fortunate mistress—let my prophecy   651
Come home to ye!—you must retire yourself   652
Into some covert. Take your sweetheart's hat   653
And pluck it o'er your brows, muffle your face,
Dismantle you, and, as you can, disliken   655
The truth of your own seeming, that you may—   656
For I do fear eyes over—to shipboard   657
Get undescried.

PERDITA   I see the play so lies
That I must bear a part.

CAMILLO   No remedy.—
Have you done there?

FLORIZEL   Should I now meet my father,
He would not call me son.

CAMILLO   Nay, you shall have no hat. [*He gives it to Perdita.*]
Come, lady, come. Farewell, my friend.

AUTOLYCUS   Adieu, sir.

FLORIZEL
O Perdita, what have we twain forgot?
Pray you, a word.   [*They speak aside.*]

CAMILLO [*Aside*]
What I do next shall be to tell the King
Of this escape and whither they are bound;
Wherein my hope is I shall so prevail
To force him after, in whose company
I shall re-view Sicilia, for whose sight   670
I have a woman's longing.

FLORIZEL   Fortune speed us!
Thus we set on, Camillo, to the seaside.

CAMILLO   The swifter speed the better.
                    Exit [*with Florizel and Perdita*].

AUTOLYCUS   I understand the business; I hear it. To
have an open ear, a quick eye, and a nimble hand is
necessary for a cutpurse; a good nose is requisite also,
to smell out work for th' other senses. I see this is the
time that the unjust man doth thrive. What an ex-

651–652 **let . . . to ye** i.e., let my prophecy that you, Perdita, will be
fortunate be fulfilled for you   653 **covert** secret place   655 **as you can**
as much as you can   655–656 **disliken . . . seeming** disguise your outward appearance   657 **eyes over** spying eyes   670 **re-view** see again

change had this been without boot! What a boot is 679
here with this exchange! Sure the gods do this year
connive at us, and we may do anything extempore. 681
The Prince himself is about a piece of iniquity, stealing
away from his father with his clog at his heels. If I 683
thought it were a piece of honesty to acquaint the King
withal, I would not do 't. I hold it the more knavery to 685
conceal it; and therein am I constant to my profession.

*Enter Clown and Shepherd [carrying a bundle
and a box].*

Aside, aside! Here is more matter for a hot brain.
Every lane's end, every shop, church, session, hang- 688
ing, yields a careful man work.   [*He stands aside.*]

CLOWN   See, see, what a man you are now! There is no
other way but to tell the King she's a changeling and 691
none of your flesh and blood.

SHEPHERD   Nay, but hear me.

CLOWN   Nay, but hear me.

SHEPHERD   Go to, then.   695

CLOWN   She being none of your flesh and blood, your
flesh and blood has not offended the King, and so
your flesh and blood is not to be punished by him.
Show those things you found about her, those secret
things, all but what she has with her. This being done,
let the law go whistle, I warrant you.

SHEPHERD   I will tell the King all, every word, yea, and
his son's pranks too; who, I may say, is no honest
man, neither to his father nor to me, to go about to 704
make me the King's brother-in-law.

CLOWN   Indeed, brother-in-law was the farthest off you
could have been to him, and then your blood had
been the dearer by I know not how much an ounce.

AUTOLYCUS [*Aside*]   Very wisely, puppies!

SHEPHERD   Well, let us to the King. There is that in this
fardel will make him scratch his beard.   711

---

679 without boot i.e., even without added payment.   **What a boot** what a
profit   **681 connive at** look indulgently at   **683 clog** encumbrance (i.e.,
Perdita)   **685 withal** with it   **688 session** court session   **691 changeling**
child left by the fairies   **695 Go to** go ahead. (Or, an expression of impatience.)   **704 go about** make it his object   **711 fardel** bundle

AUTOLYCUS [*Aside*] I know not what impediment this
complaint may be to the flight of my master.   713

CLOWN   Pray heartily he be at' palace.   714

AUTOLYCUS [*Aside*] Though I am not naturally honest,
I am so sometimes by chance. Let me pocket up my
peddler's excrement. [*He takes off his false beard.*] 717
How now, rustics, whither are you bound?

SHEPHERD   To the palace, an it like your worship.   719

AUTOLYCUS   Your affairs there, what, with whom, the
condition of that fardel, the place of your dwelling, 721
your names, your ages, of what having, breeding, and 722
anything that is fitting to be known, discover.   723

CLOWN   We are but plain fellows, sir.   724

AUTOLYCUS   A lie; you are rough and hairy. Let me have
no lying. It becomes none but tradesmen, and they
often give us soldiers the lie, but we pay them for it 727
with stamped coin, not stabbing steel; therefore they
do not give us the lie.   729

CLOWN   Your worship had like to have given us one, if 730
you had not taken yourself with the manner.   731

SHEPHERD   Are you a courtier, an 't like you, sir?

AUTOLYCUS   Whether it like me or no, I am a courtier.
Seest thou not the air of the court in these enfoldings? 734
Hath not my gait in it the measure of the court? Re- 735
ceives not thy nose court odor from me? Reflect I not
on thy baseness court contempt? Think'st thou, for 737
that I insinuate to toze from thee thy business, I am 738
therefore no courtier? I am courtier cap-a-pie, and one 739

---

713 my master i.e., Florizel   **714 at'** at the   **717 excrement** outgrowth
of hair, beard   **719 an it like** if it please   **721 condition** nature
722 having property   **723 discover** reveal   **724 plain** simple. (But
Autolycus plays on the meaning "smooth.")   **727 give . . . lie** i.e., cheat
us. (But *giving the lie* also means to accuse a person to his face of lying,
an affront which a soldier would repay with *stabbing steel*.)   **729 give**
(Autolycus punningly observes that since soldiers pay tradesmen for
their wares, the tradesmen cannot be said to have *given* the lie, and so a
duel is avoided.)   **730 had like** was about   **731 taken . . . manner** i.e.,
caught yourself in the act, stopped short. (The Clown observes that
Autolycus has once again avoided the "giving of the lie" and its consequences in a duel by his clever equivocation. Cf. Touchstone in *As You
Like It*, 5.4.)   **734 enfoldings** clothes   **735 measure** stately tread
737–738 for that because   **738 insinuate** pry.   **to toze** in order to tease,
draw out, comb out   **739 cap-a-pie** from head to foot

that will either push on or pluck back thy business
there. Whereupon I command thee to open thy affair. 741
SHEPHERD   My business, sir, is to the King.
AUTOLYCUS   What advocate hast thou to him?
SHEPHERD   I know not, an 't like you.
CLOWN [*Aside to Shepherd*]   "Advocate" 's the court word
for a pheasant. Say you have none.   746
SHEPHERD   None, sir. I have no pheasant, cock nor hen.
AUTOLYCUS
  How blessed are we that are not simple men!
  Yet nature might have made me as these are;
  Therefore I will not disdain.
CLOWN [*To Shepherd*]   This cannot be but a great court-
ier.
SHEPHERD   His garments are rich, but he wears them
not handsomely.
CLOWN   He seems to be the more noble in being fantas- 755
tical. A great man, I'll warrant. I know by the picking 756
on 's teeth.   757
AUTOLYCUS   The fardel there? What's i' the fardel?
Wherefore that box?
SHEPHERD   Sir, there lies such secrets in this fardel and
box which none must know but the King, and which
he shall know within this hour if I may come to the
speech of him.
AUTOLYCUS   Age, thou hast lost thy labor.   764
SHEPHERD   Why, sir?
AUTOLYCUS   The King is not at the palace. He is gone
aboard a new ship to purge melancholy and air himself; for, if thou be'st capable of things serious, thou 768
must know the King is full of grief.
SHEPHERD   So 'tis said, sir; about his son, that should
have married a shepherd's daughter.
AUTOLYCUS   If that shepherd be not in handfast, let him 772
fly. The curses he shall have, the tortures he shall feel,
will break the back of man, the heart of monster.

---

741 open reveal   **746 pheasant** (The rustics suppose that Autolycus has
asked them what gift they propose to present as a bribe, as one might
do to a judge in a court of law.)   **755–756 fantastical** eccentric
756–757 picking on 's teeth (A stylish affectation in Shakespeare's
time.)   **764 Age** old man   **768 be'st capable of** know anything about
772 handfast custody (with a play on "betrothal")

CLOWN Think you so, sir?

AUTOLYCUS Not he alone shall suffer what wit can make 776
heavy and vengeance bitter; but those that are ger- 777
mane to him, though removed fifty times, shall all 778
come under the hangman—which, though it be great
pity, yet it is necessary. An old sheep-whistling rogue, 780
a ram tender, to offer to have his daughter come into 781
grace? Some say he shall be stoned; but that death is 782
too soft for him, say I. Draw our throne into a sheep-
cote? All deaths are too few, the sharpest too easy.

CLOWN Has the old man e'er a son, sir, do you hear,
an 't like you, sir?

AUTOLYCUS He has a son, who shall be flayed alive; then,
'nointed over with honey, set on the head of a wasp's
nest; then stand till he be three-quarters and a dram 789
dead; then recovered again with aqua vitae or some 790
other hot infusion; then, raw as he is, and in the hot-
test day prognostication proclaims, shall he be set 792
against a brick wall, the sun looking with a southward
eye upon him, where he is to behold him with flies 794
blown to death. But what talk we of these traitorly ras- 795
cals, whose miseries are to be smiled at, their offenses
being so capital? Tell me, for you seem to be honest
plain men, what you have to the King. Being some- 798
thing gently considered, I'll bring you where he is 799
aboard, tender your persons to his presence, whisper 800
him in your behalfs; and if it be in man besides the
King to effect your suits, here is man shall do it.

CLOWN [To Shepherd] He seems to be of great authority. Close with him, give him gold; and though au- 804
thority be a stubborn bear, yet he is oft led by the nose
with gold. Show the inside of your purse to the outside of his hand, and no more ado. Remember—
"stoned," and "flayed alive."

---

776 wit ingenuity **777–778 germane** related **780 sheep-whistling**
tending sheep by whistling after them **781 offer** dare **782 grace**
favor **789 a dram** i.e., a small amount, a fraction **790 aqua vitae**
brandy **792 prognostication** forecasting (in the almanac) **794 he** i.e.,
the sun **795 blown** swollen. **what** i.e., why **798 what you have to**
what business you have with **798–799 Being . . . considered** i.e.,
(1) being a gentleman of some influence (2) if I receive a gentlemanly
consideration, a bribe **800 tender your persons** introduce you
804 Close with him accept his offer

SHEPHERD An 't please you, sir, to undertake the business for us, here is that gold I have. [*He offers money.*] I'll make it as much more and leave this young man in pawn till I bring it you.

AUTOLYCUS After I have done what I promised?

SHEPHERD Ay, sir.

AUTOLYCUS [*Taking the money*] Well, give me the moiety. 815
[*To the Clown.*] Are you a party in this business?

CLOWN In some sort, sir. But, though my case be a piti- 817
ful one, I hope I shall not be flayed out of it.

AUTOLYCUS O, that's the case of the shepherd's son. Hang him, he'll be made an example.

CLOWN [*To Shepherd*] Comfort, good comfort! We must to the King and show our strange sights. He must know 'tis none of your daughter nor my sister; we are gone else.—Sir, I will give you as much as this old man 824
does when the business is performed, and remain, as he says, your pawn till it be brought you.

AUTOLYCUS I will trust you. Walk before toward the seaside; go on the right hand. I will but look upon the 828
hedge and follow you. 829

CLOWN [*To Shepherd*] We are blessed in this man, as I may say, even blessed.

SHEPHERD Let's before, as he bids us. He was provided to do us good.   *Exeunt* [*Shepherd and Clown*].

AUTOLYCUS If I had a mind to be honest, I see Fortune would not suffer me; she drops booties in my mouth. I am courted now with a double occasion: gold, and a 836
means to do the Prince my master good, which who knows how that may turn back to my advancement? I 838
will bring these two moles, these blind ones, aboard 839
him. If he think it fit to shore them again and that the 840
complaint they have to the King concerns him noth- 841
ing, let him call me rogue for being so far officious, for 842
I am proof against that title and what shame else be- 843
longs to 't. To him will I present them. There may be matter in it.   [*Exit.*]

❧

815 **moiety** half 817 **case** (1) cause (2) skin 824 **gone else** undone otherwise 828–829 **look . . . hedge** i.e., relieve myself 836 **occasion** opportunity 838 **turn back** redound 839–840 **aboard him** i.e., to him (Prince Florizel) aboard his ship 840 **shore** put ashore 841–842 **nothing** not at all 843 **proof against** invulnerable to

5.1   *Enter Leontes, Cleomenes, Dion, Paulina, [and]*
servants.

CLEOMENES
Sir, you have done enough, and have performed
A saintlike sorrow. No fault could you make
Which you have not redeemed—indeed, paid down
More penitence than done trespass. At the last,
Do as the heavens have done, forget your evil;
With them forgive yourself.

LEONTES   Whilst I remember
Her and her virtues, I cannot forget
My blemishes in them, and so still think of   8
The wrong I did myself, which was so much
That heirless it hath made my kingdom and
Destroyed the sweet'st companion that e'er man
Bred his hopes out of.

PAULINA   True, too true, my lord.
If one by one you wedded all the world,
Or from the all that are took something good   14
To make a perfect woman, she you killed
Would be unparalleled.

LEONTES   I think so. Killed?
She I killed? I did so, but thou strik'st me
Sorely to say I did. It is as bitter
Upon thy tongue as in my thought. Now, good now,   19
Say so but seldom.

CLEOMENES   Not at all, good lady.
You might have spoken a thousand things that would
Have done the time more benefit and graced
Your kindness better.

PAULINA   You are one of those
Would have him wed again.

DION   If you would not so,
You pity not the state nor the remembrance   25
Of his most sovereign name, consider little

5.1. Location: Sicilia. The royal court.
8 in them in thinking of them, or, in comparison with them   **14 the all
that are** all that there are   **19 good now** i.e., if you please   **25 nor the
remembrance** i.e., nor give consideration to the perpetuation (through
bearing a child and heir)

What dangers by His Highness' fail of issue   27
May drop upon his kingdom and devour
Incertain lookers-on. What were more holy   29
Than to rejoice the former queen is well?   30
What holier than, for royalty's repair,
For present comfort and for future good,
To bless the bed of majesty again
With a sweet fellow to 't?

PAULINA   There is none worthy,
Respecting her that's gone. Besides, the gods   35
Will have fulfilled their secret purposes;   36
For has not the divine Apollo said,
Is 't not the tenor of his oracle,
That King Leontes shall not have an heir
Till his lost child be found? Which that it shall
Is all as monstrous to our human reason
As my Antigonus to break his grave   42
And come again to me, who, on my life,
Did perish with the infant. 'Tis your counsel   44
My lord should to the heavens be contrary,
Oppose against their wills. [*To Leontes.*] Care not for
   issue.   46
The crown will find an heir. Great Alexander
Left his to the worthiest; so his successor   48
Was like to be the best.

LEONTES   Good Paulina,
Who hast the memory of Hermione,
I know, in honor, O, that ever I
Had squared me to thy counsel! Then even now   52
I might have looked upon my queen's full eyes,
Have taken treasure from her lips—

PAULINA   And left them
More rich for what they yielded.

LEONTES   Thou speak'st truth.

27 fail failure   **29 Incertain** not knowing what to think or do (about the
royal succession)   **30 well** happy, at rest (in heaven)   **35 Respecting** in
comparison with   **36 Will . . . purposes** are determined to have their
secret purposes fulfilled   **42 As** as for   **44 'Tis your counsel** it's your
advice that   **46 Oppose** oppose himself.   **Care not for** do not be anxious about   **48 Left . . . worthiest** (When Alexander the Great died in
323 B.C., his son Alexander was yet unborn, necessitating the choice of
an heir.)   **52 squared me** adjusted or regulated myself

No more such wives, therefore no wife. One worse,   56
And better used, would make her sainted spirit   57
Again possess her corpse, and on this stage,   58
Where we're offenders now, appear soul-vexed,
And begin, "Why to me?"

PAULINA   Had she such power,   60
She had just cause.

LEONTES   She had, and would incense me   61
To murder her I married.

PAULINA   I should so.   62
Were I the ghost that walked, I'd bid you mark
Her eye and tell me for what dull part in 't
You chose her. Then I'd shriek, that even your ears
Should rift to hear me, and the words that followed   66
Should be, "Remember mine."

LEONTES   Stars, stars,   67
And all eyes else dead coals! Fear thou no wife;
I'll have no wife, Paulina.

PAULINA   Will you swear
Never to marry but by my free leave?

LEONTES
Never, Paulina, so be blest my spirit!

PAULINA
Then, good my lords, bear witness to his oath.

CLEOMENES
You tempt him overmuch.

PAULINA   Unless another,   73
As like Hermione as is her picture,
Affront his eye.

CLEOMENES   Good madam—

PAULINA   I have done.   75
Yet if my lord will marry—if you will, sir,
No remedy, but you will—give me the office
To choose you a queen. She shall not be so young
As was your former, but she shall be such

56–57 One . . . used i.e., if I took a new wife and treated her better
57 her i.e., Hermione's   **58 possess her corpse** i.e., return to earth (*this stage*) in Hermione's human shape   **60 Why to me** i.e., why this offense to me   **61 had** would have. **incense** stir up, incite   **62 should so** would similarly incite you   **66 rift** rive, split   **67 mine** my eyes. **Stars** i.e., her eyes were stars   **73 tempt** bear down on   **75 Affront** confront

As, walked your first queen's ghost, it should take joy　80
To see her in your arms.

LEONTES　　　　　　　　　　My true Paulina,
We shall not marry till thou bidd'st us.

PAULINA　　　　　　　　　　　That
Shall be when your first queen's again in breath;
Never till then.　　　　　　　　　　　　　84

Enter a Gentleman.

GENTLEMAN
One that gives out himself Prince Florizel,　　85
Son of Polixenes, with his princess—she
The fairest I have yet beheld—desires access
To your high presence.

LEONTES　　　　　　　What with him? He comes not　88
Like to his father's greatness. His approach,　　89
So out of circumstance and sudden, tells us　　90
'Tis not a visitation framed, but forced　　91
By need and accident. What train?

GENTLEMAN　　　　　　　　　　But few,　　92
And those but mean.

LEONTES　　　　　His princess, say you, with him?　93

GENTLEMAN
Ay, the most peerless piece of earth, I think,
That e'er the sun shone bright on.

PAULINA　　　　　　　　　　O Hermione,
As every present time doth boast itself
Above a better gone, so must thy grave
Give way to what's seen now! [*To the Gentleman.*] Sir,
　　you yourself
Have said and writ so, but your writing now
Is colder than that theme. She had not been　　102
Nor was not to be equaled—thus your verse　　103

80 walked . . . ghost if your first queen's ghost were to walk.　**take joy**
be overjoyed　**84 s.d. Enter a Gentleman** (He is called a "Servant" in
the Folio text, but his writing poetry at ll. 100–104 is more consistent
with his being a courtier. Any such person at court is a servant of the
king.)　**85 gives out himself** reports himself to be　**88 What** what
retinue　**89 Like to** in a manner consistent with　**90 out of circumstance** without ceremony　**91 framed** planned　**92 train** retinue
93 mean lowly　**102 that theme** i.e., Hermione, the subject of your
verses　**102–103 She . . . equaled** (Presumably the poet wrote, "She has
not been nor is not to be equaled.")

Flowed with her beauty once. 'Tis shrewdly ebbed   104
To say you have seen a better.
GENTLEMAN   Pardon, madam.
The one I have almost forgot—your pardon!
The other, when she has obtained your eye,
Will have your tongue too. This is a creature,
Would she begin a sect, might quench the zeal
Of all professors else, make proselytes   108
Of who she but bid follow.
PAULINA   How? Not women!
GENTLEMAN
Women will love her that she is a woman
More worth than any man; men, that she is
The rarest of all women.
LEONTES   Go, Cleomenes.
Yourself, assisted with your honored friends,
Bring them to our embracement.
                    Exit [Cleomenes with others].
                              Still, 'tis strange
He thus should steal upon us.
PAULINA   Had our prince,
Jewel of children, seen this hour, he had paired
Well with this lord. There was not full a month
Between their births.
LEONTES   Prithee, no more, cease. Thou know'st
He dies to me again when talked of. Sure,
When I shall see this gentleman, thy speeches
Will bring me to consider that which may
Unfurnish me of reason. They are come.   123

          Enter Florizel, Perdita, Cleomenes, and others.

Your mother was most true to wedlock, Prince,
For she did print your royal father off,
Conceiving you. Were I but twenty-one,
Your father's image is so hit in you,   127
His very air, that I should call you brother,
As I did him, and speak of something wildly

---

104 'Tis shrewdly ebbed i.e., you've egregiously gone back on your word   **108 professors else** believers in other sects or deities   **123 Unfurnish** deprive, divest   **127 hit** exactly reproduced

By us performed before. Most dearly welcome!
And your fair princess—goddess! O! Alas,
I lost a couple that twixt heaven and earth
Might thus have stood begetting wonder as
You, gracious couple, do. And then I lost—
All mine own folly—the society,
Amity too, of your brave father, whom,   136
Though bearing misery, I desire my life   137
Once more to look on him.
FLORIZEL   By his command   138
Have I here touched Sicilia, and from him
Give you all greetings that a king, at friend,   140
Can send his brother; and but infirmity,   141
Which waits upon worn times, hath something seized   142
His wished ability, he had himself   143
The lands and waters twixt your throne and his
Measured to look upon you, whom he loves—   145
He bade me say so—more than all the scepters
And those that bear them living.
LEONTES   O my brother!   147
Good gentleman, the wrongs I have done thee stir
Afresh within me, and these thy offices,   149
So rarely kind, are as interpreters   150
Of my behindhand slackness. Welcome hither,   151
As is the spring to th' earth. And hath he too
Exposed this paragon to th' fearful usage—
At least ungentle—of the dreadful Neptune,
To greet a man not worth her pains, much less
Th' adventure of her person?
FLORIZEL   Good my lord,   156
She came from Libya.
LEONTES   Where the warlike Smalus,
That noble honored lord, is feared and loved?

---

136 brave noble   **137 my life** i.e., to live long enough   **138 him** (Redundant in modern syntax.)   **140 at friend** in friendship   **141 but** were it not that   **142 waits . . . times** attends old age.   **something** to some extent   **142–143 seized . . . ability** taken away his ability (to travel) as he wishes   **145 Measured** traversed   **147 those . . . living** those living kings who bear scepters   **149 offices** messages of good will, courteous attentions   **150 rarely** exceptionally   **150–151 interpreters Of** commentators on   **156 adventure** hazard

FLORIZEL
　Most royal sir, from thence, from him, whose daughter 159
　His tears proclaimed his, parting with her. Thence, 160
　A prosperous south wind friendly, we have crossed,
　To execute the charge my father gave me
　For visiting Your Highness. My best train
　I have from your Sicilian shores dismissed,
　Who for Bohemia bend, to signify
　Not only my success in Libya, sir,
　But my arrival and my wife's in safety
　Here where we are.
LEONTES　　　　　　The blessèd gods
　Purge all infection from our air whilst you
　Do climate here! You have a holy father, 170
　A graceful gentleman, against whose person, 171
　So sacred as it is, I have done sin,
　For which the heavens, taking angry note,
　Have left me issueless; and your father's blest,
　As he from heaven merits it, with you,
　Worthy his goodness. What might I have been,
　Might I a son and daughter now have looked on,
　Such goodly things as you?

　　　Enter a Lord.

LORD　　　　　　　　　Most noble sir,
　That which I shall report will bear no credit
　Were not the proof so nigh. Please you, great sir,
　Bohemia greets you from himself by me;
　Desires you to attach his son, who has— 182
　His dignity and duty both cast off— 183
　Fled from his father, from his hopes, and with
　A shepherd's daughter.
LEONTES　　　　　　Where's Bohemia? Speak.
LORD
　Here in your city. I now came from him.
　I speak amazedly, and it becomes 187
　My marvel and my message. To your court 188

159-160 whose . . . her whose tears, as he parted with her, proclaimed
her to be his daughter　**170 climate** dwell, reside (in this clime)
171 graceful full of grace, gracious　**182 attach** arrest　**183 dignity and
duty** princely dignity and filial duty　**187-188 I . . . message** i.e., I speak
perplexedly as befits my perplexity and my astonishing news

Whiles he was hastening—in the chase, it seems,
Of this fair couple—meets he on the way
The father of this seeming lady and
Her brother, having both their country quitted
With this young prince.

FLORIZEL   Camillo has betrayed me,
Whose honor and whose honesty till now
Endured all weathers.

LORD   Lay 't so to his charge.   195
He's with the King your father.

LEONTES   Who? Camillo?

LORD
Camillo, sir. I spake with him, who now
Has these poor men in question. Never saw I   198
Wretches so quake. They kneel, they kiss the earth,
Forswear themselves as often as they speak.
Bohemia stops his ears and threatens them
With divers deaths in death.

PERDITA   O my poor father!   202
The heaven sets spies upon us, will not have
Our contract celebrated.

LEONTES   You are married?

FLORIZEL
We are not, sir, nor are we like to be.   205
The stars, I see, will kiss the valleys first;
The odds for high and low's alike.

LEONTES   My lord,   207
Is this the daughter of a king?

FLORIZEL   She is,
When once she is my wife.

LEONTES
That "once," I see, by your good father's speed
Will come on very slowly. I am sorry,
Most sorry, you have broken from his liking
Where you were tied in duty, and as sorry

195 Lay . . . charge i.e., confront him with it directly   **198 in question**
under interrogation   **202 deaths** i.e., tortures   **205 like** likely   **207 The
odds . . . alike** i.e., Fortune is the same for the high and low (?) or
perhaps, the odds of a high roll in dice are the same as those of a low
roll—we are at the mercy of chance; or, the odds of a union of high and
low in marriage are about the same as those of the stars kissing the
valleys

Your choice is not so rich in worth as beauty,   214
That you might well enjoy her.

FLORIZEL [*To Perdita*]   Dear, look up.
Though Fortune, visible an enemy,   216
Should chase us with my father, power no jot   217
Hath she to change our loves.—Beseech you, sir,
Remember since you owed no more to time   219
Than I do now. With thought of such affections,   220
Step forth mine advocate. At your request
My father will grant precious things as trifles.

LEONTES
Would he do so, I'd beg your precious mistress,
Which he counts but a trifle.

PAULINA   Sir, my liege,
Your eye hath too much youth in 't. Not a month
'Fore your queen died, she was more worth such gazes
Than what you look on now.

LEONTES   I thought of her
Even in these looks I made. [*To Florizel.*] But your
petition
Is yet unanswered. I will to your father.
Your honor not o'erthrown by your desires,   230
I am friend to them and you. Upon which errand
I now go toward him. Therefore follow me,
And mark what way I make. Come, good my lord.   233
                                              Exeunt.

❖

5.2   *Enter Autolycus and a Gentleman.*

AUTOLYCUS   Beseech you, sir, were you present at this
   relation?   2

---

214 **worth** rank   216–217 **Though . . . father** though Fortune were to
become visible as our enemy and join my father in chasing us
219–220 **since . . . now** when you were no older than I am now
220 **With . . . affections** recalling what it was to be in love at that age
230 **Your . . . desires** i.e., if your chaste honor has not been overcome by
sexual desire; or, if what you want in this match is compatible with
your royal honor   233 **way** progress

5.2. Location: Sicilia. At court.
2 **relation** narrative, account

FIRST GENTLEMAN I was by at the opening of the fardel,
heard the old shepherd deliver the manner how he 4
found it; whereupon, after a little amazedness, we
were all commanded out of the chamber. Only this,
methought, I heard the shepherd say: he found the
child.

AUTOLYCUS I would most gladly know the issue of it.

FIRST GENTLEMAN I make a broken delivery of the busi- 10
ness, but the changes I perceived in the King and Camillo were very notes of admiration. They seemed al- 12
most, with staring on one another, to tear the cases of 13
their eyes. There was speech in their dumbness, lan- 14
guage in their very gesture. They looked as they had 15
heard of a world ransomed, or one destroyed. A notable
passion of wonder appeared in them, but the wisest
beholder, that knew no more but seeing, could not say 18
if th' importance were joy or sorrow; but in the ex- 19
tremity of the one it must needs be.   20

Enter another Gentleman.

Here comes a gentleman that haply knows more.— 21
The news, Rogero?

SECOND GENTLEMAN Nothing but bonfires. The oracle
is fulfilled; the King's daughter is found. Such a deal of
wonder is broken out within this hour that ballad
makers cannot be able to express it.

Enter another Gentleman.

Here comes the Lady Paulina's steward. He can deliver
you more.—How goes it now, sir? This news which is
called true is so like an old tale that the verity of it is in
strong suspicion. Has the King found his heir?

THIRD GENTLEMAN Most true, if ever truth were preg- 31
nant by circumstance. That which you hear you'll 32
swear you see, there is such unity in the proofs. The

---

4 deliver report **10 broken** disjointed, fragmented **12 notes of admiration** (1) marks of wonderment (2) exclamation marks **13–14 cases of
their eyes** eyelids **15 as** as if **18 no . . . seeing** nothing except what he
could see **19 importance** import, meaning **20 of the one** of one or the
other **21 haply** perhaps **31–32 pregnant by circumstance** made
apparent by detailed evidence

mantle of Queen Hermione's, her jewel about the neck
of it, the letters of Antigonus found with it which they
know to be his character, the majesty of the creature in 36
resemblance of the mother, the affection of nobleness 37
which nature shows above her breeding, and many 38
other evidences proclaim her with all certainty to be
the King's daughter. Did you see the meeting of the
two kings?

SECOND GENTLEMAN　No.

THIRD GENTLEMAN　Then have you lost a sight which
was to be seen, cannot be spoken of. There might you
have beheld one joy crown another, so and in such
manner that it seemed Sorrow wept to take leave of
them, for their joy waded in tears. There was casting
up of eyes, holding up of hands, with countenance of 48
such distraction that they were to be known by garment, not by favor. Our king, being ready to leap out 50
of himself for joy of his found daughter, as if that joy 51
were now become a loss, cries, "O, thy mother, thy
mother!" then asks Bohemia forgiveness; then embraces his son-in-law; then again worries he his
daughter with clipping her; now he thanks the old 55
shepherd, which stands by like a weather-bitten con- 56
duit of many kings' reigns. I never heard of such an- 57
other encounter, which lames report to follow it and
undoes description to do it. 59

SECOND GENTLEMAN　What, pray you, became of Antigonus, that carried hence the child?

THIRD GENTLEMAN　Like an old tale still, which will have
matter to rehearse though credit be asleep and not an 63
ear open. He was torn to pieces with a bear. This 64
avouches the shepherd's son, who has not only his 65
innocence, which seems much, to justify him, but a 66
handkerchief and rings of his that Paulina knows. 67

36 character handwriting　**37 affection of** natural disposition to
38 breeding rearing　**48 countenance** bearing, demeanor　**50 favor**
features　**51 if that** if　**55 clipping** embracing　**56–57 conduit** fountain
(weeping tears)　**57 of many** i.e., that has stood there during many
59 undoes . . . it i.e., surpasses the power of language to describe it
63 rehearse relate.　**credit** belief　**64 with** by　**65 avouches** confirms,
corroborates　**66 innocence** simplemindedness (such that he would
seem unable to invent such a story)　**67 his** i.e., Antigonus's

FIRST GENTLEMAN What became of his bark and his followers?

THIRD GENTLEMAN Wrecked the same instant of their
master's death and in the view of the shepherd; so that
all the instruments which aided to expose the child
were even then lost when it was found. But O, the
noble combat that twixt joy and sorrow was fought in
Paulina! She had one eye declined for the loss of her   75
husband, another elevated that the oracle was fulfilled.   76
She lifted the Princess from the earth, and so locks her
in embracing as if she would pin her to her heart, that
she might no more be in danger of losing.   79

FIRST GENTLEMAN The dignity of this act was worth the
audience of kings and princes, for by such was it
acted.

THIRD GENTLEMAN One of the prettiest touches of all,
and that which angled for mine eyes—caught the water,
though not the fish—was when, at the relation of the
Queen's death, with the manner how she came to 't
bravely confessed and lamented by the King, how at-   87
tentiveness wounded his daughter; till, from one sign   88
of dolor to another, she did, with an "Alas!" I would   89
fain say, bleed tears, for I am sure my heart wept
blood. Who was most marble there changed color;   91
some swooned, all sorrowed. If all the world could
have seen 't, the woe had been universal.

FIRST GENTLEMAN Are they returned to the court?

THIRD GENTLEMAN No. The Princess, hearing of her
mother's statue, which is in the keeping of Paulina—
a piece many years in doing and now newly performed   97
by that rare Italian master, Julio Romano, who, had he   98
himself eternity and could put breath into his work,
would beguile Nature of her custom, so perfectly he is   100
her ape; he so near to Hermione hath done Hermione   101
that they say one would speak to her and stand in

75–76 She . . . fulfilled i.e., she wept and laughed at the same time
79 losing being lost 87–88 attentiveness listening to it 89 dolor
grief 91 Who . . . marble even the most hardhearted 97 performed
completed 98 Julio Romano Italian painter and sculptor of the six-
teenth century, better known as a painter (and an anachronism in this
play) 100 beguile deprive, cheat. custom trade 101 ape imitator

hope of answer—thither with all greediness of affec- 103
tion are they gone, and there they intend to sup.   104

SECOND GENTLEMAN   I thought she had some great matter there in hand, for she hath privately twice or thrice
a day, ever since the death of Hermione, visited that
removed house. Shall we thither and with our company piece the rejoicing?   109

FIRST GENTLEMAN   Who would be thence that has the
benefit of access? Every wink of an eye some new
grace will be born. Our absence makes us unthrifty to 112
our knowledge. Let's along.   *Exeunt* [*Gentlemen*].

AUTOLYCUS   Now, had I not the dash of my former life 114
in me, would preferment drop on my head. I brought
the old man and his son aboard the Prince, told him I
heard them talk of a fardel and I know not what. But
he at that time overfond of the shepherd's daughter—
so he then took her to be—who began to be much sea-
sick, and himself little better, extremity of weather
continuing, this mystery remained undiscovered. But
'tis all one to me, for had I been the finder out of this 122
secret, it would not have relished among my other dis- 123
credits.

Enter Shepherd and Clown, [*dressed in finery*].

Here come those I have done good to against my will,
and already appearing in the blossoms of their fortune.

SHEPHERD   Come, boy. I am past more children, but thy
sons and daughters will be all gentlemen born.

CLOWN   You are well met, sir. You denied to fight with
me this other day because I was no gentlemen born. 131
See you these clothes? Say you see them not and think
me still no gentleman born. You were best say these
robes are not gentlemen born. Give me the lie, do, and 134
try whether I am not now a gentleman born.

103–104 greediness of affection eagerness born of love   **104 sup** i.e.,
feed their hungry eyes (?) or perhaps, have a commemorative
banquet (?)   **109 piece** add to, augment   **112 unthrifty to** passing up an
opportunity to increase   **114 dash** touch   **122 'tis all one** it's all the
same   **123 relished** tasted well, suited   **131 this other** the other
134 Give me the lie accuse me to my face of lying (an insult that requires a challenge to a duel)

AUTOLYCUS I know you are now, sir, a gentleman born.

CLOWN Ay, and have been so any time these four hours.

SHEPHERD And so have I, boy.

CLOWN So you have. But I was a gentleman born before my father; for the King's son took me by the hand and called me brother; and then the two Kings called my father brother; and then the Prince my brother and the Princess my sister called my father father; and so we wept, and there was the first gentlemanlike tears that ever we shed.

SHEPHERD We may live, son, to shed many more.

CLOWN Ay, or else 'twere hard luck, being in so pre- 148
posterous estate as we are. 149

AUTOLYCUS I humbly beseech you, sir, to pardon me all the faults I have committed to your worship, and to give me your good report to the Prince my master.

SHEPHERD Prithee, son, do; for we must be gentle, now 153
we are gentlemen.

CLOWN Thou wilt amend thy life?

AUTOLYCUS Ay, an it like your good worship. 156

CLOWN Give me thy hand. I will swear to the Prince thou art as honest a true fellow as any is in Bohemia. 158

SHEPHERD You may say it, but not swear it.

CLOWN Not swear it, now I am a gentleman? Let boors 160
and franklins say it; I'll swear it. 161

SHEPHERD How if it be false, son?

CLOWN If it be ne'er so false, a true gentleman may swear it in the behalf of his friend.—And I'll swear to the Prince thou art a tall fellow of thy hands and that 165
thou wilt not be drunk; but I know thou art no tall fellow of thy hands and that thou wilt be drunk. But I'll swear it, and I would thou wouldst be a tall fellow of thy hands.

AUTOLYCUS I will prove so, sir, to my power. 170

CLOWN Ay, by any means prove a tall fellow. If I do not wonder how thou dar'st venture to be drunk, not

---

148–149 preposterous (Blunder for *prosperous*.) **153 gentle** nobly generous **156 an it like** if it please **158 honest a true** worthy an honest **160 boors** peasants **161 franklins** farmers owning their own small farms **165 tall . . . hands** brave fellow **170 my power** the best of my ability

being a tall fellow, trust me not. Hark, the kings and
the princes, our kindred, are going to see the Queen's
picture. Come, follow us. We'll be thy good masters.   175

Exeunt.

❖

5.3   *Enter Leontes, Polixenes, Florizel, Perdita,
Camillo, Paulina, lords, etc.*

LEONTES
O grave and good Paulina, the great comfort
That I have had of thee!

PAULINA   What, sovereign sir,
I did not well, I meant well. All my services
You have paid home. But that you have vouchsafed,   4
With your crowned brother and these your contracted
Heirs of your kingdoms, my poor house to visit,
It is a surplus of your grace which never
My life may last to answer.

LEONTES   O Paulina,   8
We honor you with trouble. But we came   9
To see the statue of our queen. Your gallery
Have we passed through, not without much content
In many singularities; but we saw not   12
That which my daughter came to look upon,
The statue of her mother.

PAULINA   As she lived peerless,
So her dead likeness, I do well believe,
Excels whatever yet you looked upon
Or hand of man hath done. Therefore I keep it
Lonely, apart. But here it is. Prepare   18
To see the life as lively mocked as ever   19
Still sleep mocked death. Behold, and say 'tis well.
            [*Paulina draws a curtain, and discovers*]
                    Hermione [*standing*] *like a statue.*

---

175 picture i.e., likeness, painted statue

5.3. Location: Sicilia. Paulina's house.
4 home fully   **8 last** last long enough.   **answer** repay adequately   **9 We
. . . trouble** i.e., we trouble you with the demands of hospitality, though
you are kind enough to call it an honor   **12 singularities** rarities, curi-
osities   **18 Lonely** isolated   **19 as lively mocked** as realistically counterfeited

I like your silence; it the more shows off
Your wonder. But yet speak; first, you, my liege.
Comes it not something near?

LEONTES   Her natural posture!   23
Chide me, dear stone, that I may say indeed
Thou art Hermione; or rather, thou art she
In thy not chiding, for she was as tender
As infancy and grace. But yet, Paulina,
Hermione was not so much wrinkled, nothing   28
So agèd as this seems.

POLIXENES   O, not by much.

PAULINA
So much the more our carver's excellence,
Which lets go by some sixteen years and makes her
As she lived now.

LEONTES   As now she might have done,   32
So much to my good comfort as it is
Now piercing to my soul. O, thus she stood,
Even with such life of majesty—warm life,
As now it coldly stands—when first I wooed her!
I am ashamed. Does not the stone rebuke me
For being more stone than it? O royal piece!   38
There's magic in thy majesty, which has
My evils conjured to remembrance and
From thy admiring daughter took the spirits,   41
Standing like stone with thee.

PERDITA   And give me leave,
And do not say 'tis superstition, that
I kneel and then implore her blessing. Lady,

                              [Kneeling]

Dear Queen, that ended when I but began,
Give me that hand of yours to kiss.

PAULINA   O, patience!
The statue is but newly fixed; the color's   47
Not dry.

CAMILLO
My lord, your sorrow was too sore laid on,   49
Which sixteen winters cannot blow away,

---

23 something somewhat   **28 nothing** not at all   **32 As she** as if she
38 piece work of art   **41 admiring** filled with wonder.   **spirits** vital
spirits   **47 fixed** made fast in its color   **49 sore** heavily

So many summers dry. Scarce any joy   51
Did ever so long live; no sorrow
But killed itself much sooner.

POLIXENES   Dear my brother,
Let him that was the cause of this have power   54
To take off so much grief from you as he
Will piece up in himself.

PAULINA   Indeed, my lord,   56
If I had thought the sight of my poor image
Would thus have wrought you—for the stone is mine— 58
I'd not have showed it.

LEONTES   Do not draw the curtain.

PAULINA
No longer shall you gaze on 't, lest your fancy
May think anon it moves.

LEONTES   Let be, let be.
Would I were dead but that methinks already—
What was he that did make it? See, my lord,
Would you not deem it breathed? And that those veins
Did verily bear blood?

POLIXENES   Masterly done.
The very life seems warm upon her lip.

LEONTES
The fixture of her eye has motion in 't,   67
As we are mocked with art.

PAULINA   I'll draw the curtain.   68
My lord's almost so far transported that
He'll think anon it lives.

LEONTES   O sweet Paulina,
Make me to think so twenty years together!
No settled senses of the world can match   72
The pleasure of that madness. Let 't alone.

PAULINA
I am sorry, sir, I have thus far stirred you; but
I could afflict you farther.

---

51 So ... dry i.e., and sixteen summers cannot dry up. (Camillo tells the King that he has imposed too heavy a sorrow on himself if even sixteen years' time cannot end it.)   **54 him** i.e., myself (as an innocent cause, but still a cause)   **56 piece up in himself** take upon himself   **58 wrought** affected   **67 The fixture ... in 't** i.e., her eye, though motionless, gives the appearance of motion   **68 As ... art** in such a way that we are fooled by artistic illusion   **72 No settled ... world** no calm mind in the world

LEONTES   Do, Paulina;
For this affliction has a taste as sweet
As any cordial comfort. Still methinks   77
There is an air comes from her. What fine chisel
Could ever yet cut breath? Let no man mock me,
For I will kiss her.
PAULINA   Good my lord, forbear.
The ruddiness upon her lip is wet;
You'll mar it if you kiss it, stain your own
With oily painting. Shall I draw the curtain?   83
LEONTES
No, not these twenty years.
PERDITA   So long could I
Stand by, a looker on.
PAULINA   Either forbear,   85
Quit presently the chapel, or resolve you   86
For more amazement. If you can behold it,
I'll make the statue move indeed, descend
And take you by the hand. But then you'll think—
Which I protest against—I am assisted
By wicked powers.
LEONTES   What you can make her do
I am content to look on, what to speak
I am content to hear; for 'tis as easy
To make her speak as move.
PAULINA   It is required
You do awake your faith. Then all stand still.
On; those that think it is unlawful business   96
I am about, let them depart.
LEONTES   Proceed.
No foot shall stir.
PAULINA   Music, awake her; strike!   [*Music.*] 98
'Tis time. Descend. Be stone no more. Approach.
Strike all that look upon with marvel. Come,   100
I'll fill your grave up. Stir, nay, come away,
Bequeath to death your numbness, for from him   102
Dear life redeems you.—You perceive she stirs.
                         [*Hermione comes down.*]

---

77 cordial restorative, heartwarming **83 painting** paint **85 forbear**
withdraw **86 presently** immediately **96 On; those** (Often emended to
Or those.) **98 strike** strike up **100 upon** on **102 him** i.e., death

Start not. Her actions shall be holy as
You hear my spell is lawful. Do not shun her   105
Until you see her die again, for then   106
You kill her double. Nay, present your hand.   107
When she was young you wooed her. Now in age
Is she become the suitor?   [*Leontes touches her.*]

LEONTES   O, she's warm!
If this be magic, let it be an art
Lawful as eating.

POLIXENES   She embraces him.

CAMILLO   She hangs about his neck.
If she pertain to life, let her speak too.

POLIXENES
Ay, and make it manifest where she has lived,
Or how stol'n from the dead.

PAULINA   That she is living,
Were it but told you, should be hooted at
Like an old tale; but it appears she lives,
Though yet she speak not. Mark a little while.
[*To Perdita.*] Please you to interpose, fair madam. Kneel,   120
And pray your mother's blessing.—Turn, good lady;
Our Perdita is found.

HERMIONE   You gods, look down
And from your sacred vials pour your graces
Upon my daughter's head!—Tell me, mine own,
Where hast thou been preserved? Where lived? How
    found
Thy father's court? For thou shalt hear that I,
Knowing by Paulina that the oracle
Gave hope thou wast in being, have preserved
Myself to see the issue.

PAULINA   There's time enough for that,
Lest they desire upon this push to trouble   131
Your joys with like relation. Go together,   132
You precious winners all; your exultation
Partake to everyone. I, an old turtle,   134

105–107 Do . . . double i.e., if you shun her now, you will kill her
again.   then in that case   107 double a second time   120 madam
(Addressed to Perdita as Princess and affianced to be married.)
131–132 Lest . . . relation lest they desire, at this stressful time, to
trouble you by demanding like relation of your story   134 Partake to
share with, communicate.   turtle turtledove

Will wing me to some withered bough and there
My mate, that's never to be found again,
Lament till I am lost.

LEONTES   O, peace, Paulina!   137
Thou shouldst a husband take by my consent,
As I by thine a wife. This is a match,
And made between 's by vows. Thou hast found mine,
But how is to be questioned, for I saw her,
As I thought, dead, and have in vain said many
A prayer upon her grave. I'll not seek far—
For him, I partly know his mind—to find thee   144
An honorable husband. Come, Camillo,
And take her by the hand, whose worth and honesty   146
Is richly noted and here justified   147
By us, a pair of kings. Let's from this place.
[To Hermione.] What? Look upon my brother. Both your
    pardons,
That e'er I put between your holy looks
My ill suspicion. This' your son-in-law   151
And son unto the King, whom, heavens directing,
Is trothplight to your daughter. Good Paulina,   153
Lead us from hence, where we may leisurely
Each one demand and answer to his part
Performed in this wide gap of time since first
We were dissevered. Hastily lead away.   *Exeunt.*

137 **till I am lost** i.e., until I die   144 **For** as for   146 **whose** i.e., Camillo's   147 **richly noted** abundantly acknowledged.   **justified** avouched
151 **This'** this is   153 **trothplight** betrothed

Date and Text

The Winter's Tale was first printed in the First Folio of 1623. Its text is a good one, taken evidently from Ralph Crane's transcript of Shakespeare's own well-finished draft. As in most other Crane transcriptions, the stage directions are sparse and the characters' names are grouped at the beginning of each scene. The first recorded performance was on May 15, 1611, when the quack astrologer Simon Forman saw the play at the Globe Theatre and recorded a summary of it in his commonplace book. Another performance that year at court, on November 5, is recorded in the *Revels Account*, and still another during the winter of 1612–1613. Quite possibly the play was new at the time Forman saw it. It apparently contains an allusion to the dance of ten or twelve satyrs in Ben Jonson's *Masque of Oberon*, performed at court on January 1, 1611. A 1623 entry in the *Office book* of Sir Henry Herbert, Master of the Revels, refers to *The Winter's Tale* as "an old play . . . formerly allowed of by Sir George Bucke." Bucke (or Buc) was first appointed Master of the Revels in 1610, but had occasionally licensed plays before that date during his predecessor's illness, so that the backward limit of 1610 cannot be considered absolute. Still, matters of style confirm the likelihood that Forman was seeing a new play in 1611.

Textual Notes

These textual notes are not a historical collation, either of the early folios or of more recent editions; they are simply a record of departures in this edition from the copy text. The reading adopted in this edition appears in boldface, followed by the rejected reading from the copy text, i.e., the First Folio. Only major alterations in punctuation are noted. Changes in lineation are not indicated, nor are some minor and obvious typographical errors.

Abbreviations used:
F the First Folio
s.d. stage direction
s.p. speech prefix

Copy text: the First Folio. Characters' names are grouped at the heads of scenes throughout the play.

The Names of the Actors [printed in F at the end of the play] **Archidamus** [after Autolycus in F]

1.1. 9 us, we vs: we

1.2. 104 And A   137–138 be?— / Affection, thy be / Affection? thy **148 What . . . brother** [assigned in F to Leontes] **151–153 folly, . . . tenderness, . . . bosoms!** folly? . . . tendernesse? . . . bosomes? **158 do** do's **208 you, they** you **253 forth. In . . . lord,** forth in . . . (my Lord.) **275 hobbyhorse** Holy-Horse **386 How? Caught** How caught

2.1. 2 s.p. [and throughout scene] First Lady Lady **91 fedarie** Federarie

2.2. 32–33 me. / If . . . blister me, / If . . . blister.

2.3. 39 What Who

3.2. 10 Silence [printed in F as a s.d.] **s.d. Hermione, as to her trial . . . Ladies** [at start of scene in F, as generally with the s.d. in this play] **33 Who** Whom **99 Starred** Star'd **156 woo** woe

3.3. 64 scared scarr'd **116 made** mad

4.2. 13 thee. Thou thee, thou

4.3. 1 s.p. Autolycus [not in F] **7 on** an **10 With heigh, with heigh** With heigh **38 currants** Currence

4.4. 12 Digest it Digest **83 bastards. Of** bastards) of **98 your** you **160 out on't **218 s.p. Autolycus** [not in F] **244 kilnhole** kill-hole **297 s.p. Autolycus** [in F, appears at l. 298] **299 Whither** Whether [and similarly throughout song] **316 cape** Crpe **355 reply, at least** reply at least, **361 who** whom **421 acknowledged** acknowledge **425 who** whom **430 see** neuer see **441 hoop** hope **470 your** my **485–486 fancy. If . . . obedient, I** fancie, if . . . obedient: I **503 our** her **614 could** would **filled** fill'd **off** of **644 flayed** fled **738 to** at **833 s.d. Exeunt** [at l. 845 in F]

5.1. 12 True [assigned in F to Leontes] **59 Where . . . appear** (Where we Offenders now appeare) **61 just** just such **75 I have done** [assigned in F to

Cleomenes]   84 s.d. Gentleman Seruant   85 s.p. [and through l. 110] Gentleman Ser   114 s.d. Exit [after "us" in l. 115 in F]

5.2. 113 s.d. Exeunt Exit

5.3. 18 Lonely Louely   67 fixture fixure

Shakespeare's Sources

Shakespeare based *The Winter's Tale* on Robert Greene's romantic novel called *Pandosto: The Triumph of Time* (1588), or *The History of Dorastus and Fawnia* in its running title, an abbreviated version of which follows. Shakespeare changes the names, reverses the two kingdoms of Sicilia and Bohemia, compresses the element of time, and alters the unhappy ending that afflicts King Pandosto and Queen Bellaria of Bohemia (Leontes and Hermione of Sicilia). Otherwise, the narrative outline remains intact. The story begins with the state visit of King Egistus of Sicilia (Polixenes of Bohemia) to his boyhood companion, King Pandosto of Bohemia. Queen Bellaria entertains their guest with such warmth, "oftentimes coming herself into his bedchamber to see that nothing should be amiss to mislike him," that Pandosto grows jealous. He commands his cupbearer Franion (Camillo) to murder Egistus, and the latter seems to agree but instead warns his victim to flee with him. Their hasty departure appears to confirm Pandosto's worst suspicions. He sends the guard to arrest Bellaria as she plays with her young son Garinter (Mamillius). When the Queen gives birth to a daughter in prison, the King orders the child destroyed, but relents upon the insistence of his courtiers and causes the infant to be set adrift in a small boat. The Queen nobly defends herself at her trial (in language that Shakespeare has copied in some detail). She herself requests that the oracle at Delphos be consulted. The oracle replies in words that Shakespeare has altered only slightly: "Bellaria is chaste, Egistus blameless, Franion a true subject, Pandosto treacherous, his babe an innocent; and the King shall live without an heir if that which is lost be not found." Unlike Shakespeare's Leontes, however, Pandosto is immediately stricken with remorse; and when Queen Bellaria collapses at the news of her son Garinter's death, she is truly and irrecoverably dead.

A similarly close parallel in the narrative, along with telling changes in a number of details, is characteristic of the story's second half. The babe is conveyed by a tempest to the coast of Sicilia and is discovered by an impoverished shepherd named Porrus. He and his wife Mopsa adopt the child, naming her Fawnia. By the age of sixteen, Fawnia's natural beauty rivals that of the goddess Flora. At a meeting of the farmers' daughters of Sicilia, where she is chosen mistress of the feast, Fawnia is seen by the King's son Dorastus on his way home from hawking. She counters his importunate suit with the argument that she is too lowly a match for him, but he replies that the gods themselves sometimes take earthly lovers. Her foster father, distressed by the Prince's repeated visits (though he comes in shepherd's costume), resolves to carry the jewels he found with Fawnia to the King and reveal her story, thereby escaping blame for the goings-on. Dorastus escapes with Fawnia to a ship, aided by his servant Capnio (cf. Camillo). Capnio also fulfills a role given by Shakespeare to Autolycus, for he manages to trick the shepherd Porrus into thinking he can see the King if he comes aboard Dorastus's ship. A storm drives these voyagers to Bohemia where, because of the ancient enmity between Egistus and Pandosto, they disguise themselves. Pandosto, happening to hear of Fawnia's beauty, orders her and the others to be arrested as spies and summoned to court, whereupon he falls incestuously in love with the disguised Fawnia. He promises to free the young man (who has taken the name of Meleagrus to conceal his identity) only if he will relinquish his claim to Fawnia. King Egistus meanwhile has discovered his son's whereabouts and sends ambassadors to Bohemia demanding the return of Dorastus and the execution of Fawnia, Capnio, and Porrus. Pandosto, his love for Fawnia having turned to hate, is about to comply when Porrus reveals the circumstances of Fawnia's infancy. Overjoyed to rediscover his daughter, Pandosto permits her to marry Dorastus, but then falls into a melancholy fit and commits suicide.

Shakespeare has almost entirely created some characters, such as Paulina, Antigonus, the clownish shepherd's son, and Autolycus, though Capnio does perform one of Autolycus's functions by inveigling the old shepherd aboard ship. Antigonus's journey to the seacoast of Bohemia with the infant Perdita, and his fatal exit "pursued by a bear," are Shakespearean additions. The character of Time is also added, and the shift in tone from tragedy to romance is more pronounced than in Greene. The shepherdesses at

the sheepshearing are Shakespearean. The old Shepherd
has a more substantial and comic role; Camillo is a
stronger person than Capnio. Greene's Mopsa, the shrewish
wife of old Porrus, disappears from the play. Shakespeare
omits the incestuous love of Pandosto for his daughter and
brings Hermione back to life. (For this motif of a statue
made to breathe, he may well have recalled Ovid's account
of Pygmalion in Ovid's *Metamorphoses*, Book 10.) Shakespeare's Leontes is more irrationally jealous than in
Greene's account. Leontes's purgative sorrow is more intense and also more restorative than in the source; he is a
truly noble and tragicomic figure, the center of a play about
forgiveness and renewal.

Shakespeare may also have known Francis Sabie's *The
Fisherman's Tale* (1595) and its continuation, *Flora's Fortune* (1595). From Greene's pamphlets, describing in vividly
colloquial detail the life of London's underworld, Shakespeare probably derived many of Autolycus's tricks.

Pandosto: The Triumph of Time
By Robert Greene

In the country of Bohemia there reigned a king called Pandosto, whose fortunate success in wars against his foes and
bountiful courtesy towards his friends in peace made him
to be greatly feared and loved of all men. This Pandosto had
to wife a lady called Bellaria, by birth royal, learned by education, fair by nature, by virtues famous, so that it was hard
to judge whether her beauty, fortune, or virtue wan[1] the
greatest commendations. These two, linked together in perfect love, led their lives with such fortunate content that
their subjects greatly rejoiced to see their quiet disposition.

They had not been married long, but Fortune, willing to
increase their happiness, lent them a son, so adorned with
the gifts of nature as[2] the perfection of the child greatly augmented the love of the parents and the joy of their commons,
insomuch that the Bohemians, to show their inward joys by
outward actions, made bonfires and triumphs throughout all
the kingdom, appointing jousts and tourneys for the honor of

1 wan won   2 as that

their young prince; whither resorted not only his nobles, but also divers kings and princes which were his neighbors, willing to show their friendship they ought[3] to Pandosto and to win fame and glory by their prowess and valor. Pandosto, whose mind was fraught with princely liberality, entertained the kings, princes, and noblemen with such submiss[4] courtesy and magnifical[5] bounty that they all saw how willing he was to gratify their good wills, making a general feast for his subjects which continued by the space of twenty days, all which time the jousts and tourneys were kept to the great content both of the lords and ladies there present. This solemn triumph being once ended, the assembly, taking their leave of Pandosto and Bellaria, the young son (who was called Garinter) was nursed up in the house to the great joy and content of the parents.

Fortune, envious of such happy success, willing to show some sign of her inconstancy, turned her wheel and darkened their bright sun of prosperity with the misty clouds of mishap and misery. For it so happened that Egistus, King of Sicilia, who in his youth had been brought up with Pandosto, desirous to show that neither tract of time nor distance of place could diminish their former friendship, provided a navy of ships and sailed into Bohemia to visit his old friend and companion, who, hearing of his arrival, went himself in person and his wife Bellaria, accompanied with a great train of lords and ladies, to meet Egistus; and, espying him, alighted from his horse, embraced him very lovingly, protesting that nothing in the world could have happened more acceptable to him than his coming, wishing his wife to welcome his old friend and acquaintance. Who, to show how she liked him whom her husband loved, entertained him with such familiar courtesy as[6] Egistus perceived himself to be very well welcome. After they had thus saluted and embraced each other, they mounted again on horseback and rode toward the city, devising and recounting how being children they had passed their youth in friendly pastimes; where, by the means of the citizens, Egistus was received with triumphs and shows, in such sort that he marveled how on so small a warning they could make such preparation.

3 ought owed   **4 submiss** humble   **5 magnifical** munificent   **6 as** that

Passing the streets thus, with such rare sights, they rode on to the palace, where Pandosto entertained Egistus and his Sicilians with such banqueting and sumptuous cheer, so royally, as they all had cause to commend his princely liberality. Yea, the very basest slave that was known to come from Sicilia was used with such courtesy that Egistus might easily perceive how both he and his were honored for his friend's sake. Bellaria, who in her time was the flower of courtesy, willing to show how unfeignedly she loved her husband by his friend's entertainment,[7] used him likewise so familiarly that her countenance bewrayed[8] how her mind was affected towards him, oftentimes coming herself into his bedchamber to see that nothing should be amiss to mislike[9] him.

This honest familiarity increased daily more and more betwixt them; for Bellaria noting in Egistus a princely and bountiful mind adorned with sundry and excellent qualities, and Egistus finding in her a virtuous and courteous disposition, there grew such a secret uniting of their affections that the one could not well be without the company of the other, insomuch that when Pandosto was busied with such urgent affairs that he could not be present with his friend Egistus, Bellaria would walk with him into the garden, where they two in private and pleasant devices would pass away the time to both their contents.

This custom still continuing betwixt them, a certain melancholy passion entering the mind of Pandosto drave him into sundry and doubtful thoughts. First, he called to mind the beauty of his wife Bellaria, the comeliness and bravery of his friend Egistus, thinking that love was above all laws and therefore to be stayed with no law; that it was hard to put fire and flax together without burning; that their open pleasures might breed his secret displeasures. He considered with himself that Egistus was a man and must needs love, that his wife was a woman and therefore subject unto love, and that where fancy forced,[10] friendship was of no force.

These and suchlike doubtful thoughts, a long time smoth-

7 **by his friend's entertainment** by the hospitality she showed to his friend 8 **bewrayed** revealed 9 **mislike** displease 10 **where fancy forced** where love compelled

ering[11] in his stomach, began at last to kindle in his mind a secret mistrust, which, increased by suspicion, grew at last to a flaming jealousy that so tormented him as he could take no rest. He then began to measure all their actions and to misconstrue of their too private familiarity, judging that it was not for honest affection but for disordinate fancy, so that he began to watch them more narrowly to see if he could get any true or certain proof to confirm his doubtful suspicion. While thus he noted their looks and gestures and suspected their thoughts and meanings, they two silly[12] souls, who doubted[13] nothing of this his treacherous intent, frequented daily each other's company, which drave him into such a frantic passion that he began to bear a secret hate to Egistus and a louring[14] countenance to Bellaria; who, marveling at such unaccustomed frowns, began to cast beyond the moon,[15] and to enter into a thousand sundry thoughts which way she should offend[16] her husband; but, finding in herself a clear conscience, ceased to muse until such time as she might find fit opportunity to demand the cause of his dumps.

In the meantime, Pandosto's mind was so far charged with jealousy that he did no longer doubt, but was assured, as he thought, that his friend Egistus had entered a wrong point in his tables,[17] and so had played him false play. Whereupon, desirous to revenge so great an injury, he thought best to dissemble the grudge with a fair and friendly countenance, and so under the shape of a friend to show him the trick of a foe. Devising with himself a long time how he might best put away Egistus without suspicion of treacherous murder, he concluded at last to poison him, which opinion pleasing his humor he became resolute in his determination. And the better to bring the matter to pass he called unto him his cupbearer, with whom in secret he brake the matter, promising to him for the performance thereof to give him a thousand crowns of yearly revenues.

His cupbearer, either being of a good conscience or willing for fashion's sake to deny such a bloody request, began

11 **smothering** remaining hidden, like smoldering fire   12 **silly** innocent
13 **doubted** suspected   14 **louring** scowling   15 **cast beyond the moon**
i.e., indulge in wild conjecture   16 **which . . . offend** how she might
have offended   17 **tables** (The metaphor is from backgammon.)

with great reasons to persuade Pandosto from his determinate mischief, showing him what an offense murder was to the gods, how such unnatural actions did more displease the heavens than men, and that causeless cruelty did seldom or never escape without revenge. He laid before his face[18] that Egistus was his friend, a king, and one that was come into his kingdom to confirm a league of perpetual amity betwixt them; that he had and did show him a most friendly countenance; how Egistus was not only honored of his own people by obedience but also loved of the Bohemians for his courtesy; and that if now he should without any just or manifest cause poison him, it would not only be a great dishonor to his majesty and a means to sow perpetual enmity between the Sicilians and the Bohemians, but also his own subjects would repine at[19] such treacherous cruelty.

These and suchlike persuasions of Franion—for so was his cupbearer called—could no whit prevail to dissuade him from his devilish enterprise, but, remaining resolute in his determination (his fury so fired with rage as it could not be appeased with reason), he began with bitter taunts to take up[20] his man and to lay before him two baits, preferment and death, saying that if he would poison Egistus he should advance him to high dignities; if he refused to do it of an obstinate mind, no torture should be too great to requite his disobedience. Franion, seeing that to persuade Pandosto any more was but to strive against the stream, consented, as soon as opportunity would give him leave, to dispatch Egistus; wherewith Pandosto remained somewhat satisfied, hoping now he should be fully revenged of such mistrusted injuries, intending also as soon as Egistus was dead to give his wife a sop of the same sauce and so be rid of those which were the cause of his restless sorrow.

[Alone in his chamber, Franion meditates on his hard choice.]

Franion having muttered out these or suchlike words, seeing either he must die with a clear mind or live with a

18 **before his face** before him   19 **repine at** dislike, complain about
20 **take up** rebuke, take up short

spotted conscience, he was so cumbered with divers cogitations that he could take no rest until at last he determined to break the matter to Egistus; but, fearing that the King should either suspect or hear of such matters, he concealed the device till opportunity would permit him to reveal it. Lingering thus in doubtful fear, in an evening he went to Egistus's lodging and, desirous to break with him of[21] certain affairs that touched the King, after all were commanded out of the chamber, Franion made manifest the whole conspiracy which Pandosto had devised against him, desiring Egistus not to account him a traitor for bewraying[22] his master's counsel but to think that he did it for conscience; hoping that although his master, inflamed with rage or incensed by some sinister reports or slanderous speeches, had imagined such causeless mischief, yet when time should pacify his anger and try[23] those talebearers but flattering parasites, then he[24] would count him as a faithful servant that with such care had kept his master's credit.

Egistus had not fully heard Franion tell forth his tale but a quaking fear possessed all his limbs, thinking that there was some treason wrought and that Franion did but shadow his craft with these false colors. Wherefore he began to wax in choler[25] and said that he doubted not Pandosto, sith[26] he was his friend, and there had never as yet been any breach of amity. He had not sought to invade his lands, to conspire with his enemies, to dissuade his subjects from their allegiance, but in word and thought he rested his[27] at all times. He knew not, therefore, any cause that should move Pandosto to seek his death, but suspected it to be a compacted knavery[28] of the Bohemians to bring the King and him at odds.

Franion, staying[29] him in the midst of his talk, told him that to dally with princes was with the swans to sing against their death,[30] and that, if the Bohemians had intended any such secret mischief, it might have been better

21 **break with him of** disclose his mind to Egistus concerning
22 **bewraying** revealing 23 **try** prove 24 **he** i.e., Pandosto 25 **wax in choler** grow angry 26 **sith** since 27 **rested his** remained loyal to him, Pandosto 28 **compacted knavery** conspiratorial villainy 29 **staying** stopping 30 **was with . . . death** i.e., was tantamount to flirting with death, like swans who, according to popular belief, sing in anticipation of (*against*) their death

brought to pass than by revealing the conspiracy; therefore
His Majesty did ill to misconstrue of his good meaning,
sith[31] his intent was to hinder treason, not to become a traitor; and to confirm his promises,* if it pleased* His Majesty
to flee into Sicilia for the safeguard of his life, he would go
with him, and if then he found not such a practice to be
pretended,[32] let his imagined treachery be repaid with most
monstrous torments. Egistus, hearing the solemn protestation of Franion, began to consider that in love and kingdoms neither faith nor law is to be respected, doubting[33]
that Pandosto thought by his death to destroy his men and
with speedy war to invade Sicilia. These and such doubts
throughly weighed, he gave great thanks to Franion, promising, if he might with life return to Syracusa, that he would
create him a duke in Sicilia, craving his counsel how he
might escape out of the country. Franion, who having some
small skill in navigation was well acquainted with the ports
and havens, and knew every danger in the sea, joining in
counsel with the master of Egistus's navy, rigged all their
ships and, setting them afloat, let them lie at anchor to be in
the more readiness when time and wind should serve.

Fortune, although blind, yet by chance favoring this just
cause, sent them within six days a good gale of wind; which
Franion seeing fit for their purpose, to put Pandosto out of
suspicion, the night before they should sail he went to him
and promised that the next day he would put the device in
practice, for he had got such a forcible poison as the very
smell thereof should procure sudden death. Pandosto was
joyful to hear this good news, and thought every hour a day
till he might be glutted with bloody revenge; but his suit
had but ill success. For Egistus, fearing that delay might
breed danger, and willing that the grass should not be cut
from under his feet, taking bag and baggage, with the help
of Franion conveyed himself and his men out of a postern[34]
gate of the city, so secretly and speedily that without any
suspicion they got to the seashore; where, with many a bitter curse taking their leave of Bohemia, they went aboard.
Weighing their anchors and hoisting sail, they passed as
fast as wind and sea would permit towards Sicilia, Egistus

31 **sith** since   32 **pretended** intended   33 **doubting** fearing, suspecting   34 **postern** back

being a joyful man that he had safely passed such treacherous perils.

But as they were quietly floating on the sea, so Pandosto and his citizens were in an uproar; for, seeing that the Sicilians without taking their leave were fled away by night, the Bohemians feared some treason, and the King thought that without question his suspicion was true, seeing his cupbearer had bewrayed the sum of his secret pretense.[34] Whereupon he began to imagine that Franion and his wife Bellaria had conspired with Egistus, and that the fervent affection she bare him was the only means of his secret departure; insomuch that, incensed with rage, he commanded that his wife should be carried to straight prison until they heard further of his pleasure. The guard, unwilling to lay their hands on such a virtuous princess and yet fearing the King's fury, went very sorrowfully to fulfill their charge. Coming to the Queen's lodging they found her playing with her young son Garinter, unto whom with tears doing[35] the message, Bellaria, astonished at such a hard censure and finding her clear conscience a sure advocate to plead in her case, went to the prison most willingly, where with sighs and tears she passed away the time till she might come to her trial.

But Pandosto, whose reason was suppressed with rage and whose unbridled folly was incensed with fury, seeing Franion had bewrayed his secrets and that Egistus might well be railed on but not revenged, determined to wreak all his wrath on poor Bellaria. He therefore caused a general proclamation to be made through all his realm that the Queen and Egistus had, by the help of Franion, not only committed most incestuous adultery but also had conspired the King's death, whereupon the traitor Franion was fled away with Egistus, and Bellaria was most justly imprisoned. This proclamation being once blazed[36] through the country, although the virtuous disposition of the Queen did half discredit the contents, yet the sudden and speedy passage of Egistus and the secret departure of Franion induced them[37]—the circumstances throughly considered—to think that both the proclamation was true and the King

34 **bewrayed . . . pretense** revealed all his secret intent   35 **doing** (the guards) delivering   36 **blazed** proclaimed   37 **them** i.e., the people

greatly injured. Yet they pitied her case, as sorrowful that so good a lady should be crossed with such adverse fortune.

But the King, whose restless rage would admit no pity, thought that although he might sufficiently requite his wife's falsehood with the bitter plague of pinching penury, yet his mind should never be glutted with revenge till he might have fit time and opportunity to repay the treachery of* Egistus with a fatal injury. But a curst[38] cow hath ofttimes short horns, and a willing mind but a weak arm; for Pandosto, although he felt that revenge was a spur to war and that envy[39] always proffereth steel, yet he saw that Egistus was not only of great puissance[40] and prowess to withstand him, but had also many kings of his alliance to aid him if need should serve, for he married to the Emperor's daughter of Russia. These and the like considerations something daunted Pandosto his[41] courage, so that he was content rather to put up a manifest injury with peace than hunt after revenge, dishonor, and loss, determining, since Egistus had escaped scot-free, that Bellaria should pay for all at an unreasonable price.

[Bellaria, in prison and prevented from defending herself against the unjust accusation, laments her high estate, which has exposed her to such infamy, and her untimely pregnancy.]

The jailer, pitying these her heavy passions, thinking that if the King knew she were with child he would somewhat appease his fury and release her from prison, went in all haste and certified Pandosto what the effect of Bellaria's complaint was, who no sooner heard the jailer say she was with child but as one possessed with a frenzy he rose up in a rage, swearing that she and the bastard brat she was big* withal should die if the gods themselves said no, thinking assuredly by computation of time that Egistus and not he was father to the child. This suspicious thought galled afresh this half-healed sore, insomuch as he could take no rest until he might mitigate his choler with a just revenge,

38 curst vicious (and therefore likely to attack and do harm except for its short horns)   **39 envy** malice   **40 puissance** might   **41 Pandosto his** Pandosto's

which happened presently after. For Bellaria was brought to bed of a fair and beautiful daughter, which no sooner Pandosto heard but he determined that both Bellaria and the young infant should be burnt with fire.

His nobles, hearing of the King's cruel sentence, sought by persuasions to divert him from this bloody determination, laying before his face the innocency of the child and the virtuous disposition of his wife, how she had continually loved and honored him so tenderly that without due proof he could not nor ought not to appeach[42] her of that crime. And if she had faulted, yet it were more honorable to pardon with mercy than to punish with extremity, and more kingly to be commended of pity than accused of rigor. And as for the child, if he should punish it for the mother's offense, it were to strive against nature and justice; and that unnatural actions do more offend the gods than men; how causeless cruelty nor innocent blood never scapes without revenge. These and suchlike reasons could not appease his rage, but he rested resolute in this: that Bellaria being an adulteress, the child was a bastard, and he would not suffer that such an infamous brat should call him father.

Yet at last, seeing his noblemen were importunate upon him, he was content to spare the child's life, and yet to put it to a worser death. For he found out this device: that seeing, as he thought, it came by fortune, so he would commit it to the charge of fortune. And therefore he caused a little cockboat[43] to be provided, wherein he meant to put the babe and then send it to the mercy of the seas and the destinies. From this his peers in no wise could persuade him, but that he sent presently two of his guard to fetch the child; who, being come to the prison and with weeping tears recounting their master's message, Bellaria no sooner heard the rigorous resolution of her merciless husband but she fell down in a swoon, so that all thought she had been dead.

[Queen Bellaria, revived at last, beweeps her new misfortune and that of her child.]

Such and so great was her grief that, her vital spirits be-

42 **appeach** accuse   43 **cockboat** small boat, often towed behind a larger vessel

ing suppressed with sorrow, she fell again down in a trance, having her senses so sotted with care that after she was revived yet she lost her memory and lay for a great time without moving as one in a trance. The guard left her in this perplexity, and carried the child to the King, who, quite devoid of pity, commanded that without delay it should be put in the boat, having neither sail nor rudder* to guide it, and so to be carried into the midst of the sea and there left to the wind and wave as the destinies please to appoint. The very shipmen, seeing the sweet countenance of the young babe, began to accuse the King of rigor[44] and to pity the child's hard fortune; but fear constrained them to that which their nature did abhor, so that they placed it in one of the ends of the boat, and with a few green boughs made a homely cabin to shroud it as they could from wind and weather. Having thus trimmed the boat, they tied it to a ship and so haled it into the main sea, and then cut in sunder the cord; which they had no sooner done but there arose a mighty tempest, which tossed the little boat so vehemently in the waves that the shipmen thought it could not continue long without sinking; yea, the storm grew so great that with much labor and peril they got to the shore.

But leaving the child to her fortunes, again to Pandosto, who, not yet glutted with sufficient revenge, devised which way he should best increase his wife's calamity. But first assembling his nobles and counselors, he called her for the more reproach into open court, where it was objected[45] against her that she had committed adultery with Egistus and conspired with Franion to poison Pandosto her husband, but, their pretense[46] being partly spied, she counseled them to fly away by night for their better safety. Bellaria, who, standing like a prisoner at the bar, feeling in herself a clear conscience to withstand her false accusers, seeing that no less than death could pacify her husband's wrath, waxed bold and desired that she might have law and justice, for mercy she neither craved nor hoped for; and that those perjured wretches which had falsely accused her to the King might be brought before her face to give in evidence. But Pandosto, whose rage and jealousy was such as

44 rigor hardness of heart, cruelty   **45 objected** charged   **46 pretense** intent

no reason nor equity could appease, told her that, for[47] her accusers, they were of such credit as their words were sufficient witness, and that the sudden and secret flight of Egistus and Franion confirmed that which they had confessed; and as for her, it was her part to deny such a monstrous crime and to be impudent in forswearing the fact, since she had passed all shame in committing the fault; but her stale countenance should stand for no coin,[48] for, as[49] the bastard which she bare[50] was served, so she should with some cruel death be requited. Bellaria, no whit dismayed with this rough reply, told her husband Pandosto that he spake upon choler[51] and not conscience, for her virtuous life had been ever such as no spot of suspicion could ever stain. And if she had borne a friendly countenance to Egistus, it was in respect he was his friend and not for any lusting affection; therefore, if she were condemned without any further proof it was rigor and not law.

The noblemen which sat in judgment said that Bellaria spake reason and entreated the King that the accusers might be openly examined and sworn, and if then the evidence were such as the jury might find her guilty (for seeing she was a prince she ought to be tried by her peers), then let her have such punishment as the extremity of the law will assign to such malefactors. The King presently made answer that in this case he might and would dispense with the law, and that the jury being once paneled they should take his word for sufficient evidence; otherwise he would make the proudest of them repent it. The noblemen, seeing the King in choler, were all whist.[52] But Bellaria, whose life then hung in the balance, fearing more perpetual infamy than momentary death, told the King if his fury might stand for a law that it were vain to have the jury yield their verdict; and therefore she fell down upon her knees and desired the King that for the love he bare to his young son Garinter, whom she brought into the world, that he would grant her a request, which was this: that it would please His

---

47 **for** as for 48 **her stale countenance . . . coin** i.e., she would certainly not be honored by having her stale countenance reproduced on the royal coinage. (*Stale* suggests old, worn out, no longer attractive, and also whorelike.) 49 **as** just as 50 **bare** bore 51 **upon choler** moved by anger 52 **whist** silent

Majesty to send six of his noblemen whom he best trusted
to the Isle of Delphos, there to inquire of the oracle of
Apollo whether she had committed adultery with Egistus
or conspired to poison him with Franion. And if the god
Apollo, who by his divine essence knew all secrets, gave
answer that she was guilty, she were content to suffer any
torment, were it never so terrible. The request was so reasonable that Pandosto could not for shame deny it unless he
would be counted of all his subjects more willful than wise.
He therefore agreed that with as much speed as might be
there should be certain ambassadors dispatched to the Isle
of Delphos, and in the mean season[53] he commanded that
his wife should be kept in close prison.

Bellaria, having obtained this grant, was now more careful[54] for her little babe that floated on the seas than sorrowful for her own mishap, for of that she doubted;[55] of herself
she was assured, knowing if Apollo should give oracle according to the thoughts of the heart, yet the sentence should
go on* her side, such was the clearness of her mind in this
case. But Pandosto, whose suspicious head still remained
in one song, chose out six of his nobility whom he knew
were scarce indifferent[56] men in the Queen's behalf, and,
providing all things fit for their journey, sent them to
Delphos. They, willing to fulfill the King's command and
desirous to see the situation and custom of the island, dispatched their affairs with as much speed as might be and
embarked themselves to this voyage, which, the wind and
weather serving fit for their purpose, was soon ended. For
within three weeks they arrived at Delphos, where they
were no sooner set on land but with great devotion they
went to the temple of Apollo, and there, offering sacrifice to
the god and gifts to the priest, as the custom was, they humbly craved an answer of their demand.

They had not long kneeled at the altar but Apollo with a
loud voice said: "Bohemians, what you find behind the altar take, and depart." They, forthwith obeying the oracle,
found a scroll of parchment wherein was written these
words in letters of gold:

---

53 mean season meantime   **54 careful** worried   **55 of that she doubted**
i.e., she feared for the safety of her babe   **56 indifferent** impartial

The Oracle

Suspicion is no proof; jealousy is an unequal judge. Bellaria is chaste, Egistus blameless, Franion a true subject, Pandosto treacherous, his babe an innocent; and the King shall live without an heir if that which is lost be not found.

As soon as they had taken out this scroll, the priest of the god commanded them that they should not presume to read it before they came in the presence of Pandosto unless they would incur the displeasure of Apollo. The Bohemian lords, carefully obeying his command, taking their leave of the priest with great reverence, departed out of the temple and went to their ships, and as soon as wind would permit them sailed toward Bohemia, whither in short time they safely arrived and, with great triumph issuing out of their ships, went to the King's palace, whom they found in his chamber accompanied with other noblemen.

Pandosto no sooner saw them but with a merry countenance he welcomed them home, asking what news. They told His Majesty that they had received an answer of the god written in a scroll, but with this charge, that they should not read the contents before they came in the presence of the King, and with that they delivered him the parchment. But his noblemen entreated him that, sith therein was contained either the safety of his wife's life and honesty or her death and perpetual infamy, that he would have his nobles and commons assembled in the judgment hall, where the Queen, brought in as prisoner, should hear the contents. If she were found guilty by the oracle of the god, then all should have cause to think his rigor proceeded of due desert; if Her Grace were found faultless, then she should be cleared before all, sith she had been accused openly. This pleased the King so that he appointed the day, and assembled all his lords and commons, and caused the Queen to be brought in before the judgment seat, commanding that the indictment should be read wherein she was accused of adultery with Egistus and of conspiracy with Franion. Bellaria, hearing the contents,[57] was no whit astonished, but made this cheerful answer:

57 the contents i.e., the King's command

"If the divine powers be privy to human actions—as no
doubt they are—I hope my patience shall make fortune
blush and my unspotted life shall stain spiteful* discredit.[58]
For although lying report hath sought to appeach mine
honor and suspicion hath intended to soil my credit with
infamy, yet where virtue keepeth the fort, report and suspicion may assail but never sack.[59] How I have led my life before Egistus's coming, I appeal, Pandosto, to the gods and
to thy conscience. What hath passed betwixt him and me
the gods only know and I hope will presently reveal. That I
loved Egistus I cannot deny; that I honored him I shame not
to confess; to the one I was forced by his virtues, to the
other for his dignities. But as touching lascivious lust, I say
Egistus is honest, and hope myself to be found without
spot. For Franion, I can neither accuse him nor excuse him,
for I was not privy to his departure; and that this is true
which I have here rehearsed[60] I refer myself to the divine
oracle."

Bellaria had so sooner said but the King commanded that
one of his dukes should read the contents of the scroll,
which after the commons had heard they gave a great shout,
rejoicing and clapping their hands that the Queen was clear
of that false accusation. But the King, whose conscience
was a witness against him of his witless fury and false suspected jealousy, was so ashamed of his rash folly that he
entreated his nobles to persuade Bellaria to forgive and forget these injuries, promising not only to show himself a
loyal and loving husband but also to reconcile himself to
Egistus and Franion, revealing then before them all the
cause of their secret flight and how treacherously he
thought to have practiced his death if the good mind of his
cupbearer had not prevented his purpose.

As thus he was relating the whole matter, there was word
brought him that his young son Garinter was suddenly
dead, which news so soon as Bellaria heard, surcharged before with* extreme joy and now suppressed with heavy sorrow, her vital spirits were so stopped that she fell down
presently dead and could be never revived. This sudden
sight so appalled the King's senses that he sank from his

58 shall stain spiteful discredit will eclipse spiteful slander   **59 sack**
plunder, despoil   **60 rehearsed** recited, declared

seat in a swoon, so as he was fain[61] to be carried by his nobles to his palace, where he lay by the space of three days without speech. His commons were as men in despair, so diversely distressed. There was nothing but mourning and lamentation to be heard throughout all Bohemia—their young prince dead, their virtuous queen bereaved of her life, and their king and sovereign in great hazard. This tragical discourse of fortune so daunted them as[62] they went like shadows, not men; yet somewhat to comfort their heavy hearts, they heard that Pandosto was come to himself and had recovered his speech, who as in a fury brayed out[63] these bitter speeches:

"O miserable Pandosto! What surer witness than conscience! What thoughts more sour than suspicion! What plague more bad than jealousy! Unnatural actions offend the gods more than men, and causeless cruelty never scapes without revenge. I have committed such a bloody fact as repent I may but recall I cannot. Ah, jealousy! A hell to the mind and a horror to the conscience, suppressing reason and inciting rage; a worse passion than frenzy, a greater plague than madness. Are the gods just? Then let them revenge such brutish cruelty. My innocent babe I have drowned in the seas; my loving wife I have slain with slanderous suspicion; my trusty friend I have sought to betray, and yet the gods are slack to plague such offenses. Ah, unjust Apollo! Pandosto is the man that hath committed the fault; why should Garinter, silly[64] child, abide the pain? Well, sith the gods mean to prolong my days to increase my dolor, I will offer my guilty blood a sacrifice to those sackless[65] souls whose lives are lost by my rigorous folly."

And with that he reached at a rapier to have murdered himself, but his peers being present stayed him from such a bloody act, persuading him to think that the commonwealth consisted[66] on his safety and that those sheep could not but perish that wanted a shepherd; wishing that if he would not live for himself, yet he should have care of his subjects, and to put such fancies out of his mind, sith in sores past help salves do not heal but hurt, and in things past cure, care is a corrosive. With these and suchlike per-

61 fain obliged   62 as that   63 brayed out cried out   64 silly innocent
65 sackless innocent   66 consisted depended

suasions the King was overcome,[67] and began somewhat to quiet his mind; so that as soon as he could go abroad[68] he caused his wife to be embalmed and wrapped in lead with her young son Garinter; erecting a rich and famous sepulcher wherein he entombed them both, making such solemn obsequies at her funeral as all Bohemia might perceive he did greatly repent him of his forepassed folly; causing this epitaph to be engraven on her tomb in letters of gold:

The Epitaph

Here lies entombed Bellaria fair,
   Falsely accused to be unchaste,
Cleared by Apollo's sacred doom
   Yet slain by jealousy at last.
Whate'er thou be that passest by,
Curse him that caused this queen to die.

This epitaph being engraven, Pandosto would once a day repair to[69] the tomb and there with watery plaints[70] bewail his misfortune, coveting no other companion but sorrow nor no other harmony but repentance. But leaving him to his dolorous passions, at last let us come to show the tragical discourse of the young infant.

Who, being tossed with wind and wave, floated two whole days without succor, ready at every puff to be drowned in the sea, till at last the tempest ceased and the little boat was driven with the tide into the coast of Sicilia, where, sticking upon the sands, it rested. Fortune, minding to be wanton,[71] willing to show that as she hath wrinkles on her brows so she hath dimples in her cheeks, thought after so many sour looks to lend a feigned smile, and, after a puffing storm to bring a pretty calm, she began thus to dally. It fortuned a poor mercenary[72] shepherd that dwelled in Sicilia, who got his living by other men's flocks, missed one of his sheep, and, thinking it had strayed into the covert[73] that was hard by, sought very diligently to find that which he could not see, fearing either that the wolves or eagles had undone him (for he was so poor as a sheep was half his substance), wandered down toward the sea cliffs to see if perchance the

67 overcome prevailed upon 68 abroad out of doors, freely about
69 repair to visit 70 watery plaints tearful laments 71 minding to be
wanton of a mind to be fickle and playful 72 mercenary working for
wages 73 covert sheltered spot

sheep was browsing on the sea ivy, whereon they greatly do feed; but not finding her there, as he was ready to return to his flock he heard a child cry, but knowing there was no house near, he thought he had mistaken the sound and that it was the bleating of his sheep. Wherefore, looking more narrowly, as he cast his eye to the sea he spied a little boat, from whence, as he attentively listened, he might hear the cry to come. Standing a good while in a maze,[74] at last he went to the shore and, wading to the boat, as he looked in he saw the little babe lying all alone, ready to die for hunger and cold, wrapped in a mantle of scarlet richly embroidered with gold and having a chain about the neck.

The shepherd, who before had never seen so fair a babe nor so rich jewels, thought assuredly that it was some little god, and began with great devotion to knock on his breast. The babe, who writhed with the head to seek for the pap,[75] began again to cry afresh, whereby the poor man knew that it was a child which by some sinister means was driven thither by distress of weather; marveling how such a silly[76] infant, which by the mantle and the chain could not be but born of noble parentage, should be so hardly crossed[77] with deadly mishap. The poor shepherd, perplexed thus with divers thoughts, took pity of the child and determined with himself to carry it to the King, that there it might be brought up according to the worthiness of birth, for his ability could not afford to foster it, though his good mind was willing to further it. Taking therefore the child in his arms, as he folded the mantle together the better to defend it from cold there fell down at his foot a very fair and rich purse wherein he found a great sum of gold, which sight so revived the shepherd's spirits as he was greatly ravished with joy and daunted with fear—joyful to see such a sum in his power, and fearful, if it should be known, that it might breed his further danger. Necessity wished him at the least to retain the gold, though he would not keep the child; the simplicity of* his conscience feared him from [78] such deceitful bribery. Thus was the poor man perplexed with a doubtful dilemma, until at last the covetousness of the coin overcame him; for what will not the greedy desire of gold

74 **maze** state of bewilderment   75 **pap** breast   76 **a silly** an innocent
77 **crossed** thwarted   78 **feared him from** made him frightened of

cause a man to do? So that he was resolved in himself to foster the child and with the sum to relieve his want.

Resting thus resolute in this point, he left seeking of his sheep and, as covertly and secretly as he could, went by a byway to his house, lest any of his neighbors should perceive his carriage.[79] As soon as he was got home, entering in at the door, the child began to cry, which his wife hearing, and seeing her husband with a young babe in his arms, began to be somewhat jealous, yet marveling that her husband should be so wanton abroad sith he was so quiet at home. But, as women are naturally given to believe the worst, so his wife, thinking it was some bastard, began to crow against her goodman,[80] and taking up a cudgel (for the most master went breechless)[81] sware solemnly that she would make clubs trumps[82] if he brought any bastard brat within her doors. The goodman, seeing his wife in her majesty with her mace in her hand, thought it was time to bow for fear of blows, and desired her to be quiet, for there was none such matter; but if she could hold her peace they were made forever. And with that he told her the whole matter, how he had found the child in a little boat without any succor, wrapped in that costly mantle and having that rich chain about the neck. But at last, when he showed her the purse full of gold, she began to simper something sweetly, and, taking her husband about the neck, kissed him after her homely fashion, saying that she hoped God had seen their want and now meant to relieve their poverty, and, seeing they could get no children, had sent them this little babe to be their heir. "Take heed, in any case," quoth the shepherd, "that you be secret and blab it not out when you meet with your gossips, for, if you do, we are like[83] not only to lose the gold and jewels, but our other goods and lives." "Tush," quoth his wife, "profit is a good hatch before the door.[84] Fear not, I have other things to talk of than of this.

---

79 his carriage what he was carrying   **80 goodman** husband   **81 the most master went breechless** i.e., the person holding mastery in this household was not he who nominally wore the breeches   **82 she would make clubs trumps** i.e., she would beat him with a club (playing on the metaphor of a card game)   **83 like** likely   **84 profit . . . door** ("To keep or set a hatch before the door" is proverbial for keeping silent. A *hatch* is a lower half-door that can be closed when the upper half is open.)

But, I pray you, let us lay up the money surely and the jewels, lest by any mishap it be spied."

[The child Fawnia, as she is named, cared for by her foster parents Porrus and Mopsa, becomes in time a beautiful young shepherdess of sixteen, sought after by many a rich farmer's son. Decked in garlands of flowers, she seems "to be the goddess Flora herself for beauty." Meantime, Egistus's only son, Dorastus, a handsome young prince of about twenty, angers his father by showing a reluctance to marry; without directly challenging his father's authority, he makes it plain that he has no taste for a marriage proposed with the daughter of the King of Denmark. When, soon afterward, Dorastus happens to encounter Fawnia, his attitude toward love and marriage is suddenly changed.]

It happened not long after this that there was a meeting of all the farmers' daughters in Sicilia, whither Fawnia was also bidden as the mistress of the feast, who, having attired herself in her best garments, went among the rest of her companions to the merry meeting, there spending the day in such homely pastimes as shepherds use. As the evening grew on and their sports ceased, each taking their leave at other, Fawnia, desiring one of her companions to bear her company, went home by the flock to see if they were well folded.[85] And as they returned it fortuned that Dorastus, who all that day had been hawking and killed store[86] of game, encountered by the way these two maids, and, casting his eye suddenly on Fawnia, he was half afraid, fearing that with Actaeon[87] he had seen Diana, for he thought such exquisite perfection could not be found in any mortal creature. As thus he stood in a maze, one of his pages told him that the maid with the garland on her head was Fawnia, the fair shepherd whose beauty was so much talked of in the court. Dorastus, desirous to see if nature had adorned her mind with any inward qualities, as she had decked her body

85 folded put into their folds or pens   **86 store** a plentiful supply
87 Actaeon a hunter in Greek mythology who, because he affronted Diana, the goddess of the hunt and of virginity, by intruding on her bathing or by boasting of his skill in hunting, was changed into a stag and torn to pieces by his own hounds

with outward shape, began to question with her whose
daughter she was, of what age, and how she had been
trained up. Who answered him with such modest reverence
and sharpness of wit that Dorastus thought her outward
beauty was but a counterfeit to darken her inward qualities,
wondering how so courtly behavior could be found in so
simple a cottage, and cursing fortune that had shadowed
wit and beauty with such hard fortune.

As thus he held her a long while with chat, Beauty, seeing
him at discovert,[88] thought not to lose the vantage, but
struck him so deeply with an envenomed shaft as[89] he
wholly lost his liberty and became a slave to love which[90]
before contemned love, glad now to gaze on a poor shepherd, who before refused the offer of a rich princess. For
the perfection of Fawnia had so fired his fancy as he felt his
mind greatly changed and his affections altered, cursing
Love that had wrought such a change and blaming the baseness of his mind that would make such a choice; but, thinking these were but passionate toys[91] that might be thrust
out at pleasure, to avoid the siren that enchanted him he put
spurs to his horse and bade this fair shepherd farewell.

[Fawnia too perceives the effects of passion in herself and
resolves to resist, though to no effect; she is sleepless and
unable to think of anyone else but him, yet painfully aware
how much Dorastus is above her in social station. Dorastus
for his part is distressed to think that he loves one of such
low degree and so unfit for his princely fortunes, but comes
around to the view that the gods themselves do not disdain
to love mortal women. "Phoebus liked Sibylla, Jupiter Io,
and why not I then Fawnia?" Seeking her out in the fields,
he strikes up a conversation by asking her what pleasures
can possibly be found in the life of a shepherd, to which
Fawnia answers with a defense of humble contentment and
quiet. She sternly refuses his suggestion that she change
her fortune for that of a courtly mistress, and insists that
she can love Dorastus only if he becomes a shepherd.

Driven by his passion, he at length adopts her suggestion
and visits her in shepherd's apparel, wryly smiling to him-

---

88 at discovert in an exposed position. (A hunting term.)   **89 as** that
90 which (he) who   **91 passionate toys** trifling passions

self at his low transformation. She is wary at first of a mere outward show of devotion, but is soon convinced by Dorastus's solemn protestations to accept and reciprocate his love. They plight their troth to each other and resolve to elope into Italy where they can live a contented life "until such time as either he could be reconciled to his father or else by succession come to the kingdom." For the time being, however, he continues to visit her in disguise as she tends her flocks, doing so with such frequency that the neighbors (who see through the disguise) begin to wonder at it and tell old Porrus what they have seen. Porrus, distraught, informs his wife that their daughter is keeping company with the King's son and is sure to lose her virginity as a result. He fears that the King will not be pleased with them if Dorastus gets Fawnia with child, and so resolves on a plan that will neither offend the King nor displease Dorastus.]

"I mean to take the chain and the jewels that I found with Fawnia and carry them to the King, letting him then to understand how she is none of my daughter, but that I found her beaten up with the water,[92] alone in a little boat, wrapped in a rich mantle wherein was enclosed this treasure. By this means, I hope the King will take Fawnia into his service, and we, whatsoever chanceth, shall be blameless." This device pleased the goodwife very well, so that they determined, as soon as they might know the King at leisure, to make him privy to this case.[93]

In the meantime, Dorastus was not slack in his affairs, but applied his matters with such diligence that he provided all things fit for their journey. Treasure and jewels he had gotten great store, thinking there was no better friend than money in a strange country. Rich attire he had provided for Fawnia, and, because he could not bring the matter to pass without the help and advice of someone, he made an old servant of his, called Capnio, who had served him from his childhood, privy to his affairs; who, seeing no persuasions could prevail to divert him from his settled determination, gave his consent, and dealt so secretly in the

---

92 beaten up with the water i.e., driven onto shore by the storm
93 make him . . . case disclose everything of the matter to him

cause that within short space he had gotten a ship ready for
their passage. The mariners, seeing a fit gale of wind for
their purpose, wished Capnio to make no delays, lest, if
they pretermitted[94] this good weather, they might stay long
ere they had such a fair wind. Capnio, fearing that his negligence should hinder the journey, in the nighttime conveyed
the trunks full of treasure into the ship, and by secret
means let Fawnia understand that the next morning they
meant to depart.

She, upon this news, slept very little that night, but got up
very early and went to her sheep, looking every minute
when she should see Dorastus, who tarried not long for fear
delay might breed danger, but came as fast as he could gallop and without any great circumstance[95] took Fawnia up
behind him and rode to the haven where the ship lay, which
was not three quarters of a mile distant from that place. He
no sooner came there but the mariners were ready with
their cockboat to set them aboard, where, being couched[96]
together in a cabin, they passed away the time in recounting
their old loves till their man Capnio should come.

Porrus, who had heard that this morning the King would
go abroad to take the air, called in haste to his wife to bring
him his holiday hose[97] and his best jacket, that he might go,
like an honest substantial man, to tell his tale. His wife, a
good cleanly wench, brought him all things fit, and sponged
him up very handsomely, giving him the chain* and jewels
in a little box, which Porrus, for the more safety, put in his
bosom. Having thus all his trinkets in a readiness, taking
his staff in his hand he bade his wife kiss him for good luck,
and so he went towards the palace. But, as he was going,
fortune, who meant to show him a little false play, prevented his purpose in this wise.

He met by chance in his way Capnio, who, trudging as
fast as he could with a little coffer under his arm to the
ship, and spying Porrus, whom he knew to be Fawnia's
father, going towards the palace, being a wily fellow, began
to doubt the worst, and therefore crossed him by* the way[98]
and asked him whither he was going so early this morning.

---

94 pretermitted failed to make use of   **95 circumstance** ado
96 couched lodged   **97 hose** trousers   **98 crossed him by the way**
intercepted him in his path

Porrus, who knew by his face that he was one of the court, meaning simply,[99] told him that the King's son Dorastus dealt hardly with him, for he had but one daughter who was a little beautiful, and that his neighbors told him the young Prince had allured her to folly. He went therefore now to complain to the King how greatly he was abused.

Capnio, who straightway smelt the whole matter, began to soothe* him in his talk, and said that Dorastus dealt not like a prince to spoil[100] any poor man's daughter in that sort. He therefore would do the best for him he could, because he knew he was an honest man. "But," quoth Capnio, "you lose your labor in going to the palace, for the King means this day to take the air of the sea and to go aboard of a ship that lies in the haven. I am going before, you see, to provide all things in a readiness, and, if you will follow my counsel, turn back with me to the haven, where I will set you in such a fit place as you may speak to the King at your pleasure." Porrus, giving credit to[101] Capnio's smooth tale, gave him a thousand thanks for his friendly advice and went with him to the haven, making all the way his complaints of Dorastus, yet concealing secretly the chain and the jewels. As soon as they were come to the seaside, the mariners, seeing Capnio, came aland with their cockboat, who,[102] still dissembling the matter, demanded of Porrus if he would go see the ship, who, unwilling and fearing the worst, because he was not well acquainted with Capnio, made his excuse that he could not brook the sea, therefore would not trouble him.

Capnio, seeing that by fair means he could not get him aboard, commanded the mariners that by violence they should carry him into the ship; who, like sturdy knaves, hoisted the poor shepherd on their backs and, bearing him to the boat, launched from the land.

Porrus, seeing himself so cunningly betrayed, durst not cry out, for he saw it would not prevail, but began to entreat Capnio and the mariners to be good to him and to pity his estate: he was but a poor man that lived by his labor. They, laughing to see the shepherd so afraid, made as much haste as they could and set him aboard. Porrus was no sooner in

99 meaning simply speaking with innocent intent   **100 spoil** despoil
101 giving credit to believing   **102 who** i.e., Capnio

the ship but he saw Dorastus walking with Fawnia; yet he scarce knew her, for she had attired herself in rich apparel, which so increased her beauty that she resembled rather an angel than a mortal creature.

Dorastus and Fawnia were half astonished to see the old shepherd, marveling greatly what wind had brought him thither, till Capnio told them all the whole discourse—how Porrus was going to make his complaint to the King if by policy he had not prevented him—and therefore now, sith he was aboard, for the avoiding of further danger it were best to carry him into Italy.

Dorastus praised greatly his man's device and allowed of[103] his counsel; but Fawnia, who still feared[104] Porrus as her father, began to blush for shame that by her means he should either incur danger or displeasure.

The old shepherd, hearing this hard sentence, that he should on such a sudden be carried from his wife, his country, and kinsfolk into a foreign land amongst strangers, began with bitter tears to make his complaint, and on his knees to entreat Dorastus that, pardoning his unadvised[105] folly, he would give him leave to go home, swearing that he would keep all things as secret as they could wish. But these protestations could not prevail, although Fawnia entreated Dorastus very earnestly; but the mariners, hoisting their mainsails, weighed anchors and haled[106] into the deep, where we leave them to the favor of the wind and seas, and return to Egistus.

[Egistus discovers that his son is missing and sends out troops to search for him everywhere. They learn from a fisherman that Dorastus and Fawnia have taken ship along with Capnio and old Porrus. Porrus's wife, Mopsa, being sent for, tells of her husband's intention to tell the King of Fawnia's remarkable history because of his worry about Dorastus's overly great familiarity with Fawnia, and of Porrus's subsequent strange disappearance. Egistus falls ill with vexation and worry. Meantime Dorastus's ship weathers a severe storm and reaches the shore of Bohemia.]

---

103 allowed of commended, approved **104 feared** held in reverence and awe **105 unadvised** ill-considered **106 haled** proceeded under sail

Dorastus, hearing that they were arrived at some harbor, sweetly kissed Fawnia and bade her be of good cheer. When they told him that the port belonged unto the chief city of Bohemia, where Pandosto kept his court, Dorastus began to be sad, knowing that his father hated no man so much as Pandosto, and that the King himself had sought secretly to betray Egistus. This considered, he was half afraid to go on land, but that Capnio counseled him to change his name and his country until such time as they could get some other bark to transport them into Italy. Dorastus, liking this device, made his case privy to[107] the mariners, rewarding them bountifully for their pains and charging them to say that he was a gentleman of Trapolonia called Meleagrus. The shipmen, willing to show what friendship they could to Dorastus, promised to be as secret as they could or he might wish; and upon this they landed in a little village a mile distant from the city, where, after they had rested a day, thinking to make provision for their marriage, the fame of Fawnia's beauty was spread throughout all the city, so that it came to the ear of Pandosto who, then being about the age of fifty, had, notwithstanding, young and fresh affections, so that he desired greatly to see Fawnia. And, to bring this matter the better to pass, hearing they had but one man,[108] and how they rested at a very homely house,[109] he caused them to be apprehended as spies, and sent a dozen of his guard to take them. Who,[110] being come to their lodging, told them the King's message. Dorastus, no whit dismayed, accompanied with Fawnia and Capnio, went to the court (for they left Porrus to keep the stuff), who, being admitted to the King's presence, Dorastus and Fawnia with humble obeisance saluted His Majesty.

Pandosto, amazed at the singular perfection of Fawnia, stood half astonished, viewing her beauty, so that he had almost forgot himself what he had to do. At last with stern countenance he demanded their names and of what country they were and what caused them to land in Bohemia. "Sir," quoth Dorastus, "know that my name Meleagrus is, a knight born and brought up in Trapolonia, and this gentle-

---

107 made his case privy to divulged his secret situation to   **108 man** servant   **109 rested . . . house** stayed at a very humble house   **110 Who** i.e., the guard

woman, whom I mean to take to my wife, is an Italian, born in Padua, from whence I have now brought her. The cause I have so small a train with me is for that, her friends unwilling to consent, I intended secretly to convey her into Trapolonia; whither, as I was sailing, by distress of weather I was driven into these coasts. Thus have you heard my name, my country, and the cause of my voyage."

Pandosto, starting from his seat as one in choler,[111] made this rough reply: "Meleagrus, I fear this smooth tale hath but small truth, and that thou coverest a foul skin with fair paintings. No doubt, this lady by her grace and beauty is of her degree more meet for a mighty prince than for a simple knight, and thou, like a perjured traitor, hast bereft her of her parents, to their present grief and her ensuing sorrow. Till, therefore, I hear more of her parentage and of thy calling I will stay[112] you both here in Bohemia."

Dorastus, in whom rested nothing but kingly valor,[113] was not able to suffer the reproaches of Pandosto but that he made him this answer: "It is not meet for a king, without due proof, to appeach[114] any man of ill behavior, nor, upon suspicion, to infer belief.[115] Strangers ought to be entertained with courtesy, not to be entreated with cruelty, lest, being forced by want to put up injuries,[116] the gods revenge their cause with rigor."

Pandosto, hearing Dorastus utter these words, commanded that he should straight be committed to prison until such time as they heard further of his pleasure; but as for Fawnia, he charged that she should be entertained[117] in the court with such courtesy as belonged to a stranger and her calling. The rest of the shipmen he put into the dungeon.

Having thus hardly[118] handled the supposed Trapolonians, Pandosto, contrary to his aged years, began to be somewhat tickled with the beauty of Fawnia, insomuch that he could take no rest, but cast in his old head a thousand new devices.

111 **as one in choler** like one who is angry   112 **stay** keep   113 **in whom . . . valor** i.e., who was nothing if not royally valiant   114 **appeach** accuse   115 **upon . . . belief** upon mere suspicion to believe him guilty   116 **lest . . . injuries** lest, those strangers being forced by their necessity to endure insults and injurious treatment   117 **entertained** welcomed, received   118 **hardly** harshly

[The King is chagrined to find himself the victim of love's passion at his advanced age. He is loath to crave the love of another man's "concubine" and to lust after a woman who is in his custody, but he cannot resist Fawnia's beauty. Encountering her one day in a park adjoining his house, he woos her to forsake Meleagrus and perseveres when she refuses, "seeking with fair words and great promises to scale the fort of her chastity" and offering to free Meleagrus if she consents. Alone, she bewails her misfortune, while Dorastus, confined to his prison, is no less loud in his laments. Pandosto assails Fawnia once more, first with fair speeches and then with unveiled threats of force.]

While thus these two lovers[119] strove, the one to win love, the other to live in hate, Egistus heard certain news by merchants of Bohemia that his son Dorastus was imprisoned by Pandosto, which made him fear greatly that his son should be but hardly entreated.[120] Yet considering that Bellaria and he was cleared by the oracle of Apollo from that crime wherewith Pandosto had unjustly charged them, he thought best to send with all speed to Pandosto that he should set free his son Dorastus and put to death Fawnia and her father Porrus. Finding this by the advice of counsel the speediest remedy to release his son, he caused presently two of his ships to be rigged and thoroughly furnished with provision of men and victuals, and sent divers of his nobles ambassadors into Bohemia; who, willing to obey their king and receive[121] their young prince, made no delays for fear of danger, but with as much speed as might be, sailed towards Bohemia. The wind and seas favored them greatly, which made them hope of some good hap, for within three days they were landed; which Pandosto no sooner heard of their arrival but he in person went to meet them, entreating[122] them with such sumptuous and familiar courtesy that they might well perceive how sorry he was for the former injuries he had offered to their king and how willing, if it might be, to make amends.

As Pandosto made report to them how one Meleagrus, a

119 **two lovers** i.e., Pandosto, in love with Fawnia, and Fawnia, in love with Dorastus   120 **entreated** treated   121 **receive** recover
122 **entreating** treating

knight of Trapolonia, was lately arrived with a lady, called
Fawnia, in his land, coming very suspiciously, accompanied
only with one servant and an old shepherd, the ambassadors perceived by the half what the whole tale meant, and
began to conjecture that it was Dorastus, who, for fear to be
known, had changed his name. But, dissembling the matter,
they shortly arrived at the court, where, after they had been
very solemnly[123] and sumptuously feasted, the noblemen of
Sicilia being gathered together, they made report of their
embassage, where they certified Pandosto that Meleagrus
was son and heir to the King Egistus and that his name was
Dorastus; how, contrary to the King's mind, he had privily
conveyed away that Fawnia, intending to marry her, being
but daughter to that poor shepherd Porrus; whereupon, the
King's request was that Capnio, Fawnia, and Porrus might
be murdered and put to death and that his son Dorastus
might be sent home in safety.

Pandosto, having attentively and with great marvel heard
their embassage, willing to reconcile himself to Egistus
and to show him how greatly he esteemed his favor,* although love and fancy[124] forbade him to hurt Fawnia, yet in
despite of love he determined to execute Egistus's will without mercy. And therefore he presently[125] sent for Dorastus
out of prison, who, marveling at this unlooked-for courtesy,
found at his coming to the King's presence that which he
least doubted of,[126] his father's ambassadors; who no
sooner saw him but with great reverence they honored him,
and Pandosto, embracing Dorastus, set him by him very lovingly in a chair of estate.

Dorastus, ashamed that his folly was bewrayed,[127] sat a
long time as one in a muse, till Pandosto told him the sum of
his father's embassage; which he had no sooner heard but
he was touched at the quick for the cruel sentence that was
pronounced against Fawnia. But neither could his sorrow
nor persuasions prevail, for Pandosto commanded that
Fawnia, Porrus, and Capnio should be brought to his presence; who were no sooner come but Pandosto, having his
former love turned to a disdainful hate, began to rage
against Fawnia in these terms:

123 solemnly ceremoniously   124 fancy amorous passion
125 presently immediately   126 doubted of feared, suspected
127 bewrayed revealed

"Thou disdainful vassal, thou currish kite, assigned by the destinies to base fortune, and yet with an aspiring mind gazing after honor, how durst thou presume, being a beggar, to match with a prince? By thy alluring looks to enchant the son of a king to leave his own country to fulfill thy disordinate lusts? O despiteful mind! A proud heart in a beggar is not unlike to a great fire in a small cottage, which warmeth not the house but burneth it. Assure thyself thou shalt die. And thou, old doting fool, whose folly hath been such as to suffer thy daughter to reach above thy fortune, look for no other meed[128] but the like punishment. But Capnio, thou which hast betrayed the King and hast consented to the unlawful lust of thy lord and master, I know not how justly I may plague thee. Death is too easy a punishment for thy falsehood, and to live, if not in extreme misery, were not to show thee equity. I therefore award that thou shalt* have thine eyes put out, and continually till* thou diest grind in a mill like a brute beast." The fear of death brought a sorrowful silence upon Fawnia and Capnio, but Porrus, seeing no hope of life, burst forth into these speeches:

"Pandosto, and ye noble ambassadors of Sicilia, seeing without cause I am condemned to die, I am yet glad I have opportunity to disburden my conscience before my death. I will tell you as much as I know, and yet no more than is true. Whereas I am accused that I have been a supporter of Fawnia's pride, and she disdained as a vile beggar, so it is that I am neither father unto her nor she daughter unto me. For so it happened that I, being a poor shepherd in Sicilia living by keeping other* men's flocks, one of my sheep straying down to the seaside, as I went to seek her I saw a little boat driven upon the shore wherein I found a babe of six days old, wrapped in a mantle of scarlet, having about the neck this chain. I, pitying the child and desirous of the treasure, carried it home to my wife, who with great care nursed it up and set it to keep sheep. Here is the chain and the jewels, and this Fawnia is the child whom I found in the boat. What she is or of what parentage I know not, but this I am assured, that she is none of mine."

Pandosto would scarce suffer him to tell out his tale but that he inquired the time of the year, the manner of the

128 meed reward

boat, and other circumstances; which when he found agreeing to his count,[129] he suddenly leapt from his seat and kissed Fawnia, wetting her tender cheeks with his tears and crying, "My daughter Fawnia! Ah, sweet Fawnia! I am thy father, Fawnia." This sudden passion of the King drave them all into a maze, especially Fawnia and Dorastus. But when the King had breathed himself awhile in this new joy, he rehearsed[130] before the ambassadors the whole matter, how he had entreated[131] his wife Bellaria for jealousy, and that this was the child whom he sent to float in the seas.

Fawnia was not more joyful that she had found such a father than Dorastus was glad he should get such a wife. The ambassadors rejoiced that their young prince had made such a choice, that those kingdoms, which through enmity had long time been dissevered, should now through perpetual amity be united and reconciled. The citizens and subjects of Bohemia, hearing that the King had found again his daughter which was supposed dead, joyful that there was an heir apparent to his kingdom, made bonfires and shows throughout the city. The courtiers and knights appointed jousts and tourneys to signify their willing minds in gratifying the King's hap.[132]

Eighteen days being passed in these princely sports, Pandosto, willing to recompense old Porrus, of[133] a shepherd made him a knight; which done, providing a sufficient navy to receive[134] him and his retinue, accompanied with Dorastus, Fawnia, and the Sicilian ambassadors, he sailed towards Sicilia, where he was most princely entertained by Egistus, who, hearing this comical[135] event, rejoiced greatly at his son's good hap, and without delay, to the perpetual joy of the two young lovers, celebrated the marriage. Which was no sooner ended but Pandosto, calling to mind how first he betrayed his friend Egistus, how his jealousy was the cause of Bellaria's death, that contrary to the law of nature he had lusted after his own daughter, moved with these desperate thoughts he fell into a melancholy fit and,

---

129 **count** account   130 **rehearsed** recited, told   131 **entreated** treated   132 **hap** (good) fortune   133 **of** from being   134 **receive** hold   135 **comical** ending happily, joyful

to close up the comedy with a tragical stratagem,[136] he slew himself; whose death being many days bewailed of Fawnia, Dorastus, and his dear friend Egistus, Dorastus, taking his leave of his father, went with his wife and the dead corpse into Bohemia, where, after they[137] were sumptuously entombed, Dorastus ended his days in contented quiet.

Robert Greene's *Pandosto: The Triumph of Time* was published in London in 1588 (Q1), printed by Thomas Orwin for Thomas Cadman, with the running title *The History of Dorastus and Fawnia*.

A second quarto (Q2) appeared in 1592 and a third (Q3) in 1595, each a reprint of the previous. The present edition, somewhat abbreviated, is based on the first quarto. Although Shakespeare may have read one of the later quartos, the differences between the 1588 text and those of 1592 and 1595 are minor and appear to be entirely compositorial. Shakespeare appears not to have used the edition of 1607, in which Apollo's oracle reads, "the King shall die without an heir" instead of, as in the earlier texts, "the King shall live without an heir." Gathering B of the 1588 quarto is missing, and for this material the second quarto serves as the copy text; this affects the textual notes below on pp. 472 and 474.

In the following, departures from the original text appear in boldface; original readings are in roman.

p. 472 **promises** premises [Q2, Q3]   **pleased** please [Q2, Q3]   p. 474 **of** [omitted in Q2, Q3]   **big** [omitted in Q2, Q3]   p. 476 **rudder** other   p. 478 **on** one   p. 480 **spiteful** spitefully   **with** which   p. 483 **of** if   p. 488 **chain** chaines   **by** [omitted in Q1–Q3]   p. 489 **soothe** soth   p. 494 **favor** labour   p. 495 **shalt** shall   **till** while   **other** others

---

136 stratagem device   **137 they** i.e., Pandosto's remains

Further Reading

Bartholomeusz, Dennis. *"The Winter's Tale" in Performance in England and America, 1611–1976*. Cambridge and New York: Cambridge Univ. Press, 1982. Focusing on changing standards of stagecraft and fidelity to the text, Bartholomeusz's stage history traces the play in performance from its appearance on the "open stage at Whitehall" in 1611 to a production directed by John Barton and Trevor Nunn at Stratford-upon-Avon in 1976.

Draper, R. P. *"The Winter's Tale": Text and Performance*. London: Macmillan, 1985. Draper's monograph provides both an account of the rhythm and structure of the play and a consideration of four distinctive modern productions: the Royal Shakespeare Company's in 1969, 1976, and 1981, and the BBC television version directed by Jane Howell in 1980.

Egan, Robert. " 'The Art Itself Is Nature': *The Winter's Tale*." *Drama Within Drama: Shakespeare's Sense of His Art*. New York: Columbia Univ. Press, 1975. Exploring the relationship of dramatic art to the reality of experience, Egan argues that in *The Winter's Tale* Shakespeare recognizes the efficacy of drama as an agent of belief. Camillo's staging of Perdita's return and Paulina's staging of Hermione's restoration provide models of Shakespeare's own artistry that similarly work to compel faith.

Erickson, Peter. "The Limitations of Reformed Masculinity in *The Winter's Tale*." *Patriarchal Structures in Shakespeare's Drama*. Berkeley, Calif.: Univ. of California Press, 1985. Erickson sees culturally determined notions of gender shaping the action of a play that traces the replacement of a tyrannical patriarchy with a benign version capable of "including and valuing women." Nonetheless, while the regenerative movement of the play depends upon the mediation of women, their efforts can only repair, not replace, the patriarchal body politic that still insists upon "restrictive definitions of gender."

Ewbank, Inga-Stina. "The Triumph of Time in *The Winter's Tale*." *Review of English Literature* 5.2 (1964): 83–100.

Rpt. in *Shakespeare's Later Comedies: An Anthology of Modern Criticism*, ed. D. J. Palmer, Baltimore.: Penguin, 1971. Ewbank explores the ways in which the action, structure, and poetry of *The Winter's Tale* work to communicate a vital engagement with "the theme of time and change." The Chorus doesn't merely signal time's passage but serves as a "pivotal image of the Triumph of Time" in a play that resists the simplifications of conventional understanding of time "as either Revealer or Destroyer."

Felperin, Howard. " 'Tongue-tied Our Queen?': The Deconstruction of Presence in *The Winter's Tale*." In *Shakespeare and the Question of Theory*, ed. Patricia Parker and Geoffrey Hartman. New York and London: Methuen, 1985. Felperin considers Leontes's charge of Hermione's infidelity and finds that, though we have "oracular proof" to discredit it, the jealous passion is not quite "so flimsy and fanciful" as is often assumed. Felperin's point is not to indict Hermione but to indicate how much in the play depends only upon unverifiable interpretation—by characters, audiences, and actors—of what is not represented. Through the insistent "interpretive uncertainty," the play engages "the fallen and irredeemable nature of language as a medium for defining human reality."

Foakes, R. A. "Shakespeare's Last Plays." *Shakespeare, the Dark Comedies to the Last Plays: From Satire to Celebration*, pp. 118–144. Charlottesville, Va.: Univ. Press of Virginia, 1971. The sudden and unmotivated quality of events in the play leads Foakes to see it as "a series of strange actions under an uncertain providence." He argues that finally the play is "optimistic," testifying to the benevolent purposiveness of the gods, but "it is also clear-sighted," revealing the terrifying fears and devastating losses that afflict human beings.

Frey, Charles. *Shakespeare's Vast Romance: A Study of "The Winter's Tale."* Columbia, Mo.: Univ. of Missouri Press, 1980. Believing the play unusually resistant to analysis, Frey takes a tripartite approach to "the paradoxical amalgam of coherence and vastness" at the heart of *The Winter's Tale:* first he examines theatrical and critical responses to the play, then considers various literary

sources of its technique and vision, and finally he traces
the play's strategies of control that lead an audience from
its own isolated existence to a world of communal faith.

Frye, Northrop. "Recognition in *The Winter's Tale*." In *Essays on Shakespeare and Elizabethan Drama in Honor of Hardin Craig*, ed. Richard Hosley. Columbia, Mo.: Univ. of Missouri Press, 1962. Rpt. in *Shakespeare's Later Comedies: An Anthology of Modern Criticism*, ed. D. J. Palmer. Baltimore: Penguin, 1971. Frye finds in the structure of the play, especially in its "double recognition scene," evidence that art itself is "part of the regenerating power of the play." The art manifested in *The Winter's Tale*, however, is not opposed to nature nor merely imitative of it, but rather belongs to its unfallen aspect and participates in its renewing powers.

Gourlay, Patricia Southard. " 'O My Most Sacred Lady': Female Metaphor in *The Winter's Tale*." *English Literary Renaissance* 5 (1975): 375–395. Examining the roles of Hermione, Paulina, and Perdita, Gourlay traces the anxieties and hostilities that the women arouse in the play and also their creative and consoling actions. She concludes that "the women in the play embody those ambiguities of Leontes's own nature which he has feared and despised, but without which his masculine world is a wasteland."

Hartwig, Joan. "*The Winter's Tale:* 'The Pleasure of that Madness.' " *Shakespeare's Tragicomic Vision*. Baton Rouge, La.: Louisiana State Univ. Press, 1972. Focusing on the contradictions revealed in characterization, tone, and structure, Hartwig considers the "profound dislocation of fixed perceptions which Shakespeare's tragicomedy produces." The play works to suspend logic and rationality in both its characters and audience, permitting their recognition of a world of grace and wonder beyond "the limits of human possibility."

Hunter, R. G. "*The Winter's Tale*." *Shakespeare and the Comedy of Forgiveness*. New York: Columbia Univ. Press, 1965. Hunter sees *The Winter's Tale* as a mature example of Shakespeare's "comedy of forgiveness" in which erring humankind repents, is forgiven its sin, and is permitted to reenter an order of grace. The revelation of

Hermione testifies to Leontes's regeneration, miraculously erasing the consequence of his sin; but Mamillius remains dead, reminding Leontes and the audience that "happiness and misery, 'both joy and terror,' are human possibilities."

Matchett, William H. "Some Dramatic Techniques in *The Winter's Tale*." *Shakespeare Survey* 22 (1969): 93–108. Focusing on the scenes of Leontes's jealousy, Antigonus's death, and the animation of the statue, Matchett examines Shakespeare's mature stagecraft, exploring "the range of Shakespeare's final control over audience response."

McDonald, Russ. "Poetry and Plot in *The Winter's Tale*." *Shakespeare Quarterly* 36 (1985): 315–329. McDonald locates "the sources and functions" of the play's stylistic complexity in a tragicomic vision that generates "both story and style." In the play's characteristically convoluted speeches that become intelligible "only in their final clauses or movements" McDonald finds a parallel to the play world itself that only belatedly "rewards bewildered characters and spectators with understanding and happiness."

Pyle, Fitzroy. *"The Winter's Tale": A Commentary on the Structure*. New York: Barnes and Noble, 1969. Pyle, in a scene-by-scene comparison of the play with its source (Robert Greene's *Pandosto*), is concerned with the "beauty of the plotting" of *The Winter's Tale*. He resists seeing the play as a representation of divine agency, finding, rather, that it attests to the "miraculous power of the human spirit, rightly directed, to achieve the impossible."

Schanzer, Ernest. "The Structural Pattern of *The Winter's Tale*." *Review of English Literature* 5.2 (1964): 72–82. Rpt. in *Shakespeare: A Casebook, "The Winter's Tale,"* ed. Kenneth Muir. London: Macmillan, 1968. Schanzer analyzes the shape of the play, observing that it splits into two carefully paralleled halves. Each begins with a prose scene that focuses on a harmonious relationship about to be disrupted, and each ends with a public scene fixing our attention on Hermione. These repetitions are accentuated by the Chorus, who divides the play and, in the

image of the turning hourglass, "enhances our sense of
the similarity of the shape and structure of the two
halves."

Tayler, Edward William. "Shakespeare's *The Winter's
Tale*." *Nature and Art in Renaissance Literature*. New
York: Columbia Univ. Press, 1964. Tayler focuses on the
conventional division between Nature and Art as it is reflected in the language and structure of the play. The opposition of the two terms, most fully elaborated in the
exchange between Florizel and Perdita in Act 4, provides
Shakespeare with a means of focusing a series of ethical
and social concerns, but in the final scene it "dissolves in
the pageantry of the statue's descent."

Wickham, Glynne. "Romance and Emblem: A Study in the
Dramatic Structure of *The Winter's Tale*." In *The Elizabethan Theatre III*, ed. David Galloway. Hamden, Conn.:
Archon, 1973. Wickham suggests that Shakespeare wrote
The Winter's Tale with a particular event in mind: the in-
vestiture of the Prince of Wales in 1610. In adapting popular romance themes of reunion and renewal to the
specific political aspirations of James's court, Shakespeare succeeds in creating a play that was "as effective
an emblem for his court audience as it was an enjoyable
dramatic romance for his wider public in the city of London."

THE
TEMPEST

Introduction

Shakespeare creates in *The Tempest* an idealized world of
imagination, a place of magical rejuvenation like the forests
of *A Midsummer Night's Dream* and *As You Like It*. The
journey to Shakespeare's island is to a visionary realm,
where everything is controlled by the artist. Yet the journey
is no escape from reality, for the island shows men what
they are and what they ought to be. Even its location juxta-
poses "real" world with idealized landscape: like Plato's
New Atlantis or Thomas More's Utopia, Shakespeare's island is to be found both somewhere and nowhere. On the
narrative level it is located in the Mediterranean Sea. Yet
there are overtones of the New World, the Western Hemisphere, where Thomas More had situated his island of Utopia. Ariel fetches dew at Prospero's command from the
"Bermudas" (1.2.230). Caliban when prostrate reminds Trinculo of a "dead Indian" (2.2.33) who might be displayed before gullible crowds eager to see such a prodigious creature from across the seas; and Caliban's god, Setebos, was,
according to Richard Eden's account of Magellan's circumnavigation of the globe (in *History of Travel*, 1577),
worshiped by South American natives. An inspiration for
Shakespeare's story (for which no direct literary source is
known) may well have been various accounts of the shipwreck in the Bermudas in 1609 of the *Sea Venture*, which
was carrying settlers to the new Virginian colony. Shakespeare borrowed details from Sylvester Jourdain's *A Discovery of the Bermudas, Otherwise Called the Isle of Devils*,
published in 1610, and from William Strachey's *A True
Repertory of the Wreck and Redemption . . . from the Islands
of the Bermudas*, which Shakespeare must have seen in
manuscript since it was not published until after his death.
He wrote the play shortly after reading these works, for *The
Tempest* was acted at court in 1611. He may also have
known or heard of various accounts of Magellan's circumnavigation of the world in 1519–1522 (including Richard
Eden's shortened English version, as part of his *History of
Travel*, of an Italian narrative by Antonio Pigafetta), Francis
Fletcher's journal of Sir Francis Drake's circumnavigation

in 1577–1580, Richard Rich's *News from Virginia* (1610), and still other potential sources of information. Shakespeare's fascination with the Western Hemisphere gave him, not the actual location of his story, which remains Mediterranean, but a state of mind associated with newness and hope. Miranda sees on the island a "new world" in which mankind appears "brave" (5.1.185); and, although her wonder must be tempered by Prospero's rejoinder that "'Tis new to thee" (l. 186) and by Aldous Huxley's still more ironic use of her phrase in the title of his satirical novel *Brave New World*, the island still endures as a restorative vision. Even though we experience it fleetingly, as in a dream, this nonexistent realm assumes a permanence enjoyed by all great works of art.

Prospero rules as the artist-king over this imaginary world, conjuring up trials to test men's intentions and visions to promote their renewed faith in goodness. To the island come an assortment of men who, because they require varied ordeals, are separated by Prospero and Ariel into three groups: King Alonso and those accompanying him; Alonso's son, Ferdinand; and Stephano and Trinculo. Prospero's authority over them, though strong, has limits. As Duke of Milan he was bookishly inattentive to political matters and thus vulnerable to the Machiavellian conniving of his younger brother Antonio. Only in this world apart, the artist's world, do his powers derived from learning find their proper sphere. Because he cannot control the world beyond his isle, he must wait for "strange, bountiful Fortune, / Now my dear lady" (1.2.179–180) to bring his enemies near his shore. He eschews, moreover, the black arts of diabolism. His is a white magic, devoted ultimately to merciful ends: rescuing Ariel from the spell of the witch Sycorax, curbing the appetite of Caliban, spying on Antonio and Sebastian in the role of Conscience. He uses Fortune's gift of delivering his enemies into his hands to forgive and restore them, not to be revenged. Such a use of power imitates the divine, though Prospero is no god. His chief power, learned from books and exercised through Ariel, is to control the elements so as to create illusion—of separation, of death, of the gods' blessing. Yet since he is a man, even this power is an immense burden. Prospero has much to learn, like those whom he controls. He must subdue his anger, his self-pity, his readiness to blame others, his domineering over Miranda. He must overcome the vengeful impulse he experiences toward those who have wronged him, and he must conquer the longing any father feels to hold on to his daughter when she is desired by another man. He does these things through his art, devising games and shows in which his angry self-pity and jealousy are transmuted into playacting scenes of divine warning and forgiveness toward his enemies and watchful parental austereness toward Miranda and Ferdinand. Prospero's responsibilities cause him to behave magisterially and to be resented by the spirits of the isle. Even Ariel longs to be free, and it is with genuine relief as well as melancholy that Prospero finally lays aside his demanding role as creative moral intelligence.

Alonso and his court party variously illustrate the unregenerate world left behind in Naples and Milan. We first see them on shipboard, panicky and desperate, their titles and finery mocked by roaring waves. Futile ambition seems destined for a watery demise. Yet death by water in this play is a transfiguration rather than an end, a mystical rebirth as in the regenerative cycle of the seasons from winter to summer. Ariel suggests as much in his song about a drowned father: "Those are pearls that were his eyes. / Nothing of him that doth fade / But doth suffer a sea change / Into something rich and strange" (1.2.402–405). Still, this miracle is not apparent at first to those who are caught in the illusion of death. As in T. S. Eliot's *The Waste Land*, which repeatedly alludes to *The Tempest*, self-blinded human beings fear a disaster that is ironically the prelude to reawakening.

Prospero creates an illusion of loss to test his enemies and to make them reveal their true selves. Only Gonzalo, no enemy at all but one who long ago aided Prospero and Miranda when they were banished from Milan, responds affirmatively. He alone notices that his garments and those of his shipwrecked companions have miraculously been left unharmed by the salt water. His ideal commonwealth (2.1.150–171), which Shakespeare drew in part from an essay by Montaigne, postulates a natural goodness in man and makes no allowance for the dark propensities of Caliban, but at least Gonzalo's cheerfulness is in refreshing contrast to the jaded sneers of some of his companions. Se-

bastian and Antonio react to the magic isle, as to Gonzalo's
commonwealth, by cynically refusing to believe in miracles.
Confident that they are unobserved, they seize the opportunity afforded by Alonso's being asleep to plot a murder and
political coup. This attempt is not only despicable but
madly ludicrous, for they are all shipwrecked and no longer
have kingdoms over which to quarrel. Even more ironically,
Sebastian and Antonio, despite their insolent belief in their
self-sufficiency, are being observed. The villains must be
taught that an unseen power keeps track of their misdeeds.
They may revert to type when returned to their usual habi-
tat, but even they are at least briefly moved to an awareness
of the unseen (3.3.21–27). Alonso, more worthy than they
though burdened too with sin, responds to his situation
with guilt and despair, for he assumes that his son Ferdinand's death is the just punishment of the gods for Alonso's part in the earlier overthrow of Prospero. Alonso must
be led, by Prospero's curative illusions, through the purgative experience of contrition to the reward he thinks impossible and undeserved: reunion with his lost son.

Alonso is thus, like Posthumus in *Cymbeline* or Leontes
in *The Winter's Tale*, a tragicomic figure—sinful, contrite,
forgiven. Alonso's son, Ferdinand, must also undergo ordeals and visions devised by Prospero to test his worth, but
more on the level of romantic comedy. Ferdinand is young,
innocent, and hopeful, well-matched to Miranda. From the
start Prospero obviously approves of his prospective son-in-
law. Yet even Prospero, needing to prepare himself for a life
in which Miranda will no longer be solely his, is not ready
to lay aside at least the comic fiction of parental opposition.
He invents difficulties, imposes tasks of logbearing (like
those assigned Caliban) and issues stern warnings against
premarital lust. In the comic mode, parents are expected to
cross their children in matters of the heart. As a teacher of
youth, moreover, Prospero is convinced by long experience
that prizes too easily won are too lightly esteemed. Manifold are the temptations urging Ferdinand to surrender to
the natural rhythms of the isle and to fulfill his desire like
Caliban. In place of ceremonies conducted in civilized societies by the church, Prospero must create the illusion of
ceremony by his art. The marriage of Ferdinand and
Miranda accordingly unites the best of both worlds: the nat-

ural innocence of the island, which teaches them to avoid the corruptions of civilization at its worst, and the higher law of nature achieved through moral wisdom at its best. To this marriage, the goddesses Iris, Ceres, and Juno bring promises of bounteous harvest, "refreshing showers," celestial harmony, and a springtime brought back to the earth by Proserpina's return from Hades (4.1.79–117). In Ferdinand and Miranda, "nurture" is wedded to "nature." This bond unites spirit and flesh, legitimizing erotic pleasure by incorporating it within a cosmic moral order.

At the lowest level of this same cosmic and moral framework are Stephano and Trinculo. Their comic scenes juxtapose them with Caliban, for he represents untutored nature whereas they represent the unnatural depths to which persons brought up in civilized society can fall. In this they resemble Sebastian and Antonio, who have learned in supposedly civilized Italy arts of intrigue and political murder. The antics of Stephano and Trinculo burlesque the conduct of their presumed betters, thereby exposing to ridicule the self-deceptions of ambitious humans. The clowns desire to exploit the natural wonders of the isle by taking Caliban back to civilization to be shown in carnivals, or by plying him with strong drink and whetting his resentment against authority. These plottings are in vain, however, for like Sebastian and Antonio the clowns are being watched. The clowns teach Caliban to cry out for "freedom" (2.2.184), by which they mean license to do as one pleases, but are foiled by Ariel as comic nemesis. Because they are degenerate buffoons, their exposure is appropriately humiliating and satirical.

In contrast with them, Caliban is almost a sympathetic character. His sensitivity to natural beauty, as in his descriptions of the "nimble marmoset" or the dreaming music he so often hears (2.2.168; 3.2.137–145), is entirely appropriate to this child of nature. He is, to be sure, the child of a witch, and is called many harsh names such as "Abhorrèd slave" and "a born devil, on whose nature / Nurture can never stick" (1.2.354; 4.1.188–189). Yet he protests with some justification that the island was his in the first place and that Prospero and Miranda are interlopers. His very existence calls radically into question the value of civilization, which has shown itself capable of limitless depravity. What profit has Caliban derived from learning Prospero's language other than, as he puts it, to "know how to curse" (1.2.367)? With instinctive cunning he senses that books are his chief enemy, and plots to destroy them first in his attempt at rebellion. The unspoiled natural world does indeed offer civilization a unique perspective on itself. In this it resembles Gonzalo's ideal commonwealth, which, no matter how laughably implausible from the cynic's point of view, does at least challenge the very assumptions upon which Western civilization is based.

The play's ending is far from perfectly stable. Antonio never repents, and we cannot be sure what the island will be like once Prospero has disappeared from the scene. Since Prospero's occupation of the island replicates in a sense the process by which he himself was overthrown, we cannot know when the cycle of revolution will ever cease. Ultimately, however, Shakespeare's play strives to celebrate humanity's highest achievement in the union of the island with the civilized world. Miranda and Ferdinand have bright hopes for the future, even if they must be qualified by Prospero's melancholic observation that the "brave new world" with "such people in it" is only "new to thee," to those who are young and not yet experienced in the world's vexations. Even Caliban may be at last reconciled to Prospero's insistent idea of a harmony between will and reason, no matter how perilously and delicately achieved. Prospero speaks of Caliban as a "thing of darkness I / Acknowledge mine," and Caliban vows to "be wise hereafter / And seek for grace" (5.1.278–279, 298–299). This synthesis suggests that the natural man within us is more contented, better understood, and more truly free when harmonized with reason.

Caliban is a part of humanity, Ariel is not. Ariel can comprehend what compassion and forgiveness would be like, "were I human" (5.1.20), and can take good-natured part in Prospero's designs to castigate or reform his fellow creature, but Ariel longs to be free in quite another sense from that meant by Caliban. Ariel takes no part in the final integration of human society. This spirit belongs to a magic world of song, music, and illusion that the artist borrows for his use but which exists eternally outside of him. Like the elements of air, earth, fire, and water in which it mysteriously dwells, this spirit is morally neutral but incredibly vital. From it the artist achieves powers of imagination, enabling him to bedim the noontide sun or call forth the dead from their graves. These visions are illusory in the profound sense that all life is illusory, an "insubstantial pageant" melted into thin air (4.1.150–155). Prospero the artist cherishes his own humanity, as a promise of surcease from his labors. Yet the artifact created by the artist endures, existing apart from time and place as does Ariel: "Then to the elements / Be free, and fare thou well!" (5.1.321–322). No doubt it is a romantic fiction to associate the dramatist Shakespeare with Prospero's farewell to his art, but it is an almost irresistible idea because we are so moved by the sense of completion and yet humility, the exultation and yet the calm, contained in this leave-taking.

The Tempest
in Performance

Mark Twain once joked that Shakespeare's plays were not by Shakespeare but by another author of the same name. His joke might, with a slight alteration, be applied to the performance history of *The Tempest*. Something called *The Tempest* has never failed to delight audiences, but from the mid-seventeenth until the late eighteenth century what audiences saw was truly another play of the same name. Adaptation began shortly after Shakespeare's death, if not before. His own play had been acted before King James by Shakespeare's acting company, the King's men, on November 1, 1611, and in the winter of 1612–1613 "before the Princess' Highness the Lady Elizabeth and the Prince Palatine Elector" in honor of their betrothal. Scholars have argued, though without much evidence, that Shakespeare composed the masque in Act 4 especially for this occasion; if he did, the process of musical elaboration began early and with his own imprimatur. More likely, the short play we have, masque and all, was written to be acted in late 1611 and afterward at the Globe Theatre, at the Blackfriars playhouse, and at court when the King so wished. Dr. Simon Forman, who recorded in his journal that he saw *Cymbeline* and *The Winter's Tale* in 1611, does not mention *The Tempest*. In any event, the King's men were soon performing a fanciful reply to Shakespeare's play, by John Fletcher, called *The Sea Voyage* (1622), and in 1667 the theater in Lincoln's Inn Fields, London, staged a production of *The Tempest* as altered by William Davenant and John Dryden.

This version of *The Tempest* was a great success. Diarist Samuel Pepys saw it eight times between 1667 and 1669, more times than any other Shakespeare play he saw except *Macbeth*, and bestowed on it his warmest praise: in January of 1669 he wrote that he "could not be more pleased almost in a comedy," and later that same year he declared it "the most innocent play that ever I saw." The authors' success lay in appealing to the tastes of their age for symmetry. Davenant hit on the idea that Shakespeare's story of a young woman (Miranda) who has never seen a man could be paired with that of a young man who has never seen a woman. "By this means," wrote Davenant afterward, "those two characters of innocence and love might the more illustrate and commend each other."

The added counterplot is thus a mirror of the main plot. Long ago, the story goes, Prospero brought with him to the island the young Duke of Mantua, named Hippolito, and has kept him secluded in a remote cave where, improbably enough, he has never seen Miranda—or her sister Dorinda. When Hippolito does see Dorinda for the first time, in a scene that parallels Miranda's first encounter with Ferdinand, Hippolito's male response is to want her and all beautiful women besides, and so he quarrels with Ferdinand and is seemingly killed by him. For this offense Ferdinand is condemned to death by Prospero, until Hippolito is revived by Ariel's aid and goes on to join the other three lovers in a predictable contretemps of jealousies and misplaced affections. Caliban, meanwhile, has a sister, Sycorax, and Ariel has a fellow-spirit named Milcha. The broadly comic plot of Stephano, Trinculo, and Caliban is enlarged into a quarrel for royal supremacy between Stephano, Mustacho, and Ventoso on the one hand and Trincalo (i.e., Trinculo), Caliban, and Sycorax on the other, with pointed satirical application to the recent factionalism of England's mid-century civil war.

With its many songs, Shakespeare's *The Tempest* was an obvious candidate for operatic treatment. Thomas Shadwell's *The Tempest* (produced in 1673, published the following year) retains the plot symmetries of Davenant and Dryden, including the topical satire directed at civil strife, while adding substantially to the music and spectacle. Shadwell gives an enlarged part to Milcha so that she and Ariel can sing together and dance a saraband. At the dramatic moment when Prospero sets Ariel and then Milcha free, "both fly up and cross in the air." When Ariel sings "Come unto these yellow sands," as in Shakespeare (1.2.378–390), Milcha answers with "Full fathom five" (ll. 400–407). Together they sing an added song, "Dry those tears which are o'erflowing." The musical settings by Pietro Reggio, Matthew Locke, and Pelham Humphrey were of a high order, and the standard remained high when, later in the century, the songs were reset to music by Henry Purcell and others.

Scenic and musical splendor prevail everywhere in Shadwell's opera. It opens with an overture, a rising curtain, and the discovery of a noble arched frontispiece supported by Corinthian columns wreathed in roses. Several Cupids fly about them. The allegorical figure of Fame appears; angels hold the royal arms of England. Behind the arch lies the menacing scene, a sky darkened by storm clouds, a coast strewn with rocks, a troubled sea in continual motion. Frightful spirits fly among the terrorized sailors. When the ship begins to sink, "the whole house is darkened, and a shower of fire falls upon 'em"—presumably the sailors, not the audience. Lightning flashes and thunder sounds. Thereupon, "in the midst of the shower of fire, the scene changes. The cloudy sky, rocks, and sea vanish, and, when the lights return, discover that beautiful part of the island which was the habitation of Prospero. 'Tis composed of three walks of cypress trees. Each sidewalk leads to a cave, in one of which Prospero keeps his daughters, in the other Hippolito. The middle walk is of great depth, and leads to an open part of the island." Possibly the effect of darkness was achieved by the shutting of flats (theatrical scenery), or the removal and then return of hanging candle-fixtures, or both.

Later in the opera, according to the contemporary account of John Downes, the audience sees one of Ariel's spirits "flying away with a table furnished out with fruits, sweetmeats, and all sorts of viands, just when Duke Trinculo and his companions were going to dinner." A masque of Furies, introduced by Dryden in 1667, is much enlarged by Shadwell with allegorical figures such as Pride, Fraud, Rapine, and Murder. A concluding masque of Neptune and Amphitrite shows these sea gods, along with Oceanus and Tethys, arising "in a chariot drawn with sea-horses," while Tritons and Nereides sport at their side. A dance of twelve Tritons is followed by a scene at sunrise in which Ariel, accompanied by other spirits, flies from the sun toward the spectators and hovers in the air while speaking the last lines. In Shadwell's hands *The Tempest* has become the embodiment of the seventeenth-century courtly masque, complete with antimasque in the ludicrous antics of Stephano and Trinculo.

The Davenant-Dryden and Shadwell adaptations, or variations of them, held the stage for much of the eighteenth century. At the Theatre Royal, Drury Lane, there were over one hundred and eighty performances in the first half of the century alone. A revival of *The Tempest*—or *The Enchanted Island*, as the adaptation was also known—in 1706 included a masque composed by "the late Mr. Henry Purcell." A revival in 1712 was again a great success; according to actor-manager Colly Cibber, the production achieved "the greatest profit that in so little a time had yet been known in my memory." In 1715 Drury Lane produced a similar version "with the tempest, with scenes, machines, dances, and all the original decorations proper to the play," in response to a revival of Beaumont and Fletcher's popular *The Island Princess* at the theater in Lincoln's Inn Fields, London. When money could not be found for the Shadwell extravaganza, Davenant and Dryden's adaptation filled in. Although James Lacy claimed to produce the play at Drury Lane in 1746 "as written by Shakespeare, never acted there before," he in fact added Shadwell's elaborate masque of Neptune and Amphitrite in Act 5, and at all events the theater soon returned to Davenant and Dryden. Actor-manager David Garrick produced *The Tempest: An Opera, Taken from Shakespeare* in 1756 at Drury Lane, without Hippolito and Dorinda but with Davenant's added clowns. John Christopher Smith, a protégé of Handel, composed the opera, with some thirty-two songs, duets, and a trio for Trinculo, Stephano, and Ventoso. Sixty children presented a garland dance at the end of Act 2, and subsequently there was a pantomime of Fortunatus, or the Genii. Garrick did revive Shakespeare's play in 1757 with Henry Mossop as Prospero and Hannah Pritchard as Miranda, albeit with some heavy cutting in Act 2, scene 1, and this version enjoyed sixty-one performances before Garrick retired in 1776.

We get a clear impression of costuming and setting during this period from a contemporary engraving seemingly based on De Loutherbourg's designs for a 1777 production at Drury Lane. Ferdinand is in the powdered wig and elegant attire of an eighteenth-century gentleman, Miranda in a sweeping coiffure with outfit to match. Such costuming evidently did not seem out of keeping with the spectacle of the Davenant-Dryden-Shadwell tradition, which continued only somewhat abated. John Philip Kemble, in his 1789 revival at Drury Lane, sought "to admit in a temperate way the additions of Dryden," retaining the Hippolito-Dorinda plot though eliminating Milcha, Sycorax, Ventoso, and Mustacho. Kemble added music in 1789, including a duet for Ferdinand and Miranda, though he cut it back in subsequent years. He cast an actress as Hippolito. In staging effects, Kemble continued the focus on the shipwreck, transferring it to the beginning of Act 2 with the following directions: "The sea. A ship in a tempest. Spirits of the wind dancing. Chorus by spirits of the storm. The ship seems to founder. Ariel and all the other spirits disappear." At the play's end, Prospero waves his wand and the scene vanishes, discovering "a view of a calm sea, and the King's ship riding at anchor . . . Ariel and the spirits re-ascend into the sky." The Haymarket Theatre, not to be outdone, staged a ballet of *The Enchanted Island* in 1804 that went beyond the effects called for by Kemble. In 1806, Kemble, who had by this time moved to the Theatre Royal, Covent Garden, produced the play there, retaining the tradition of spectacular staging but reducing the operatic content. This version of the play became the standard acting version in the first third of the nineteenth century. Kemble's own performance as Prospero was well received, even though he was criticized for his controversial decision to pronounce "aches" in the Elizabethan manner as "aitches."

The Tempest offered many temptations to the theater manager predisposed toward musical and visual elaboration, and nineteenth-century managers, with their growing fondness for scenic *vraisemblance*, made few attempts to resist. Frederic Reynolds and H. R. Bishop brought out an operatic version in 1821 at Covent Garden "as altered and adapted by Dryden and Davenant." The musical score borrowed not only from Purcell but from Haydn, Mozart, Rossini, and others. William Charles Macready played Prospero and John Emery played Caliban, while most other parts were assigned to singers. The scenes included Prospero's cave, the interior of the island, a rocky part of the island, Hippolito's cave, a lake and mountains by moonlight,

a volcanic mountain and lake, and finally a cave that
changes to the last scene. Caliban gave the appearance of "a
hairy man of the woods"; Ariel, portrayed as feminine, had
painted gauze wings. The chorus singers in the finale came
down from the ceiling on wires.

Macready, after playing Prospero in this 1821 production
and also in Alfred Bunn's revival at Drury Lane in 1833 as
"altered by Dryden and Davenant," brought out his own
The Tempest in 1838 at Covent Garden with a restored
Shakespeare text but still with a female Ariel (played by
Priscilla Horton) suspended in the air while she sang and
wearing a diaphanous long gown and fairy wings. Macready took out the dialogue of the first scene to allow
room for a spectacular storm. When Ferdinand drew his
sword on Prospero but was prevented by Prospero's spell
from doing harm with it (1.2), the young man's sword was
made to fly off over his head. Helen Faucit played Miranda.
Macready had at last brought an end to the long reign of
Davenant and Dryden, but the resort to scenic effects was
destined to continue for some time.

A Covent Garden revival of 1842, again by Macready,
opened with a huge sea vessel, fully rigged and manned,
and tossing about on a tempestuous ocean. "The size of the
ship," wrote the reviewer for *John Bull*, "and the ingenuity
with which it was managed, now rising so as to discover the
keel and then dipping to the level of the stage, seeming to
sink into the mimic waters, rendered the effect particularly
real." Samuel Phelps, at the Sadler's Wells Theatre in 1847,
similarly used spectacular effects: a full-scale ship was bat-
tered in the opening storm, its mast struck by a fireball.
Phelps's own performance as Prospero was widely praised,
and the production itself was hailed by the reviewer for *The
Times* as the "best combination of Shakespeare and scenery." Influenced by Phelps's success, the Surrey Theatre
produced *The Tempest* in 1853 with "dioramic and pictorial
illusion of a storm and wreck," masques, dances, and mechanical effects. Even in America the impact of Phelps was
felt. William Burton's production in 1854 in New York followed Macready in restoring Shakespeare's text to the
stage, but its spectacular theatrical effects were largely inspired by Phelps.

Charles Kean's *The Tempest* of 1857 at the Princess's

Theatre may have reached some sort of pinnacle in spectacular staging. The deck actually tossed and pitched during the storm scene and appeared to founder with all on board, whereupon the storm dispersed, allowing the sun to rise on the island where Prospero (Kean), accompanied by Miranda, stood on a rock and supervised the calming of the waters. In Act 3 a scene of desolation changed suddenly into a tropical paradise, with trees rising from the earth, fountains and waterfalls flowing from the rocks, and nymphs and satyrs bearing fruit and flowers. In an allegorical finale, Prospero released the spirits who had aided him in his art and then delivered the epilogue from the deck of a vessel that sailed off into the distance, leaving Ariel alone and suspended in air. A distant chorus of spirits accompanied the fall of the curtain. Throughout, Ariel took the various forms of a ball of fire, a delicate creature arising from a tuft of flowers, a water nymph on the back of a dolphin, or a spirit riding on a bat. Kean, in other words, literalized the words of Shakespeare's song, "Where the bee sucks, there suck I. / In a cowslip's bell I lie; / There I couch when owls do cry. / On the bat's back I do fly" (5.1.88–91). Little could be added in this vein by Frank Benson at the Lyceum Theatre in 1900 or by Herbert Beerbohm Tree at His Majesty's in 1904, though they certainly did their best.

The modern stage thus had a clear mandate for change: to free *The Tempest* from a spectacular tradition that was not only costly and inflexible, requiring cuts and rearrangements of the text to accommodate the scenery, but also was ready to visualize externally and superficially what Shakespeare's own theater leaves to the imagination. A return to a theater in which stage image can suggest conflicts and the characters' states of mind, rather than literalize, was long overdue.

The inevitability of the change can in fact be sensed in the last years of the nineteenth century. In part because of a tight budget, Frank Benson's production at Stratford-upon-Avon in 1891 began the movement away from lavish stage traditions of Phelps and Kean. Benson cut the opening shipwreck and in general simplified the play's staging (though he did add a fanciful entrance for Ferdinand "drawn by a silver thread, held by two tiny Cupids"). Benson's version was regularly revived over the next quarter-century, and his

own performance as Caliban was enormously influential.
Benson based his interpretation of the character on a book
by Daniel Wilson, Professor of History and English Literature at the University of Toronto, who argued that Shakespeare's Caliban is the missing link that Darwinian
evolutionary theory demands. The athletic Benson, dressed
in a costume his wife described "as half-monkey, half
cocoanut," climbed trees, hung upside down, and carried
an actual fish.

The two significant aspects of Benson's production, the
simplified staging and the emphasis upon Caliban, were to
exert a significant impact upon subsequent performances
of the play. William Poel and the Elizabethan Stage Society
performed the play in 1897 on an open stage with limited
scenery and without scene shifts. The elaborate music of
the operatic *Tempest*s gave way to a simple score for pipe
and tabor by Arnold Dolmetsch, leading George Bernard
Shaw to rejoice in Poel's decision to "leave to the poet the
work of conjuring up the isle 'full of noises, sounds, and
sweet airs.'"

In 1904, Herbert Beerbohm Tree tried to recapture the
visual splendor of the lavish nineteenth-century productions. "Of all of Shakespeare's works," wrote Tree,
"*The Tempest* is probably the one which most demands
the aid of modern stagecraft." But if his elaborate lighting
effects and his extensive use of pantomime and ballet
pointed back to—and brought to an end—the tradition of
spectacular staging, his portrayal of Caliban as thoughtful
and sensitive looked forward to the shifting emphasis of
modern productions that would increasingly see Caliban as
less demonic and more tragic than earlier productions allowed and would recognize Prospero's power as more prob-
lematic. Tree's version ended with a final tableau of
Caliban on the shore reaching out "in mute despair" to the
departing ship.

In 1914 Ben Greet brought his production, previously on
tour in England and America, to London's Old Vic. Greet
followed the new tradition of simplified staging, using "no
special scenery" but introducing background music by Arthur Sullivan. Sybil Thorndike, who in America had played
Ceres, now took the role of Ferdinand. Two years later in
New York John Corbin and Louis Calvert produced the play

at the Century Theater "in the manner of the Elizabethan stage." The text was presented "in its full integrity" and every effort was made to reproduce the full range of staging possibilities offered by Shakespeare's theater. Corbin criticized Poel and Greet for an impoverished conception of these possibilities, maintaining that Shakespeare's company inevitably would have dressed its actors in lavish costumes and made use of spectacular "flyings." "There is no reason to suppose," he argued, "that the public theatres would neglect an effect so striking." Though some reviewers criticized the production as merely an "archaeological experiment" devoid of any theatrical ingenuity, others praised Corbin's reconstruction for its quick pacing, which permitted "the fine full text of Shakespeare's play [to] unfold rapidly without long, tedious, disillusioning waits between scenes."

The growing effort to understand the conditions of Shakespeare's theater led William Bridges-Adams in 1919 to produce his revival at Stratford-upon-Avon as the play might have been done at court. He used a gauze drop curtain with the portraits and coats-of-arms of the Princess Elizabeth and the Elector Palatine for whose betrothal *The Tempest* had been performed at court in 1612–1613. Though the production attempted to reproduce the pageantry of the Jacobean masque, it used only a simple set of movable, bare platforms, seeking its stateliness in speech and movement.

At the Old Vic in 1930 Harcourt Williams directed John Gielgud as Prospero, Ralph Richardson as Caliban, and Leslie French as Ariel (the first male to play the role since 1734). Ten years later at the Old Vic, Gielgud again played Prospero, this time in a production by George Devine and Marius Goring. Gielgud's Prospero was anxious and ironic. Goring's Ariel, as Audrey Williamson wrote, was "not cruel, but cool and remote," while Jack Hawkins's Caliban "vividly suggested the slow groping towards humanity." In 1957 Peter Brook directed Gielgud in his third *Tempest*. Increasingly Gielgud's interpretations of Prospero, as they moved from benign serenity to brooding irritability, revealed the price Prospero pays for his power, and Brook's production continued the movement away from the innocent theatrical magic of the stage tradition and toward an exploration of the tensions and ambiguities discovered in the text. The island was dark, overgrown with vegetation, a projection of Prospero's tortured mind, and Gielgud was an embittered anchorite determined on revenge.

Brook returned to the play in 1968 at London's Roundhouse Theatre in an experimental version commissioned by Jean-Louis Barrault using French, Japanese, English, and American actors to explore the very nature of theater. Gielgud returned to *The Tempest* for a fourth time in 1974 at the National Theatre. Directed by Peter Hall, this production, like that of Bridges-Adams in 1919, conceived of the play as a Jacobean masque, but unlike the earlier production it understood the masque not as mere royal pageantry but as an expression of royal authority. Gielgud's Prospero was, in Hall's words, "a man of power, of intelligence, as shrewd and cunning and egocentric as Churchill." Costumed like the Elizabethan astrologer John Dee, Gielgud's Prospero exerted his power over a Caliban (played by Denis Quilley) who was made up to be half monster and half noble savage.

The benign magician of the early stage history of the play has given way to something more interesting and complex. In Jonathan Miller's 1970 production at London's Mermaid Theatre the play's colonial themes were explicitly explored. Basing his conception on Dominique O. Mannoni's account of the 1947 revolution in Madagascar, *La Psychologie de la Colonisation* (published in English as *Prospero and Caliban* in 1953), Miller had two black actors, Norman Beaton and Rudolph Walker, play Ariel and Caliban, clarifying the colonial parable that he found in the play. Beaton's Ariel was a noble African who successfully internalized the skills of his master, while Walker's Caliban was a demoralized and degraded slave. Miller's production ended with Ariel eagerly picking up the staff Prospero has discarded and Caliban shaking his fist in fury at the departing ship.

Derek Jarman's innovative film version, released in 1980, also explored the play's concern with subordination and mastery. Set not on an island but in the dilapidated interior of Stoneleigh Abbey in Warwickshire, the film is more gothic romance than Shakespearean romance. Heathcote Williams's Prospero is a shabby nineteenth-century aristocrat; Jack Birkett's Caliban as his butler is alternatively menacing and petulant; Karl Johnson's punk Ariel, with close-cropped hair and a white jumpsuit, is unnervingly bitter and remote, an unwilling technician for his master's experiments. Prospero's magic, which Jarman invokes with cabalistic signs and symbols and Prospero's library of occult literature, becomes a means of political and psychological domination rather than of moral renewal.

Perhaps the most remarkable modern production of *The Tempest* was one that heroically resisted the disillusionment that has characterized so many recent versions even as it recognized the play as a play of failure—the failure of the dream of perfectibility. Performed first in Milan in 1977, revived in 1982, and brought to America for the Olympic Arts Festival in Los Angeles in 1984, Giorgio Strehler's *La Tempesta* (translated into Italian by Agostino Lombardo) represented an extraordinary triumph of theatrical illusion. Prospero's relationship with Ariel was at the center of Strehler's understanding of the play, a resonant metaphor for the relationship of the director and the actor. Until the end, Ariel, a commedia dell'arte Pierrot, was attached to a wire, soaring in the air, sometimes landing nimbly on Prospero's raised finger, yet always unable to escape Prospero's will. When at last he was released, he stumbled on shaky legs, exiting through the audience. Prospero's epilogue became an apology for the limitations of his magic and for the limitations of the theater itself. As he came before the audience, the simple set suddenly disassembled, revealing the bareness and artifice of the theater's illusions. With the audience's applause, the set reformed and Ariel returned to Prospero's side. Strehler's innovative production achieved the theatrical magic that the play demands, offering thereby a profound and moving investigation of the power of theater itself. "In this *Tempest*," Strehler wrote, "we have felt the fallible, desperate, triumphant grandeur and responsibility of our profession." Strehler's *Tempest* fully allowed its audiences to feel the magic of Shakespeare's art.

THE
TEMPEST

Names of the Actors

ALONSO, *King of Naples*
SEBASTIAN, *his brother*
PROSPERO, *the right Duke of Milan*
ANTONIO, *his brother, the usurping Duke of Milan*
FERDINAND, *son to the King of Naples*
GONZALO, *an honest old councillor*
ADRIAN *and* } *lords*
FRANCISCO,
CALIBAN, *a savage and deformed slave*
TRINCULO, *a jester*
STEPHANO, *a drunken butler*
MASTER *of a ship*
BOATSWAIN
MARINERS

MIRANDA, *daughter to Prospero*

ARIEL, *an airy spirit*
IRIS,
CERES,
JUNO, } *[presented by] spirits*
NYMPHS,
REAPERS,

[Other Spirits attending Prospero]

SCENE: *An uninhabited island*

1.1 *A tempestuous noise of thunder and lightning heard. Enter a Shipmaster and a Boatswain.*

MASTER Boatswain!

BOATSWAIN Here, Master. What cheer?

MASTER Good, speak to the mariners. Fall to 't yarely, 3
or we run ourselves aground. Bestir, bestir!   *Exit.*

Enter Mariners.

BOATSWAIN Heigh, my hearts! Cheerly, cheerly, my 5
hearts! Yare, yare! Take in the topsail. Tend to the Mas- 6
ter's whistle.—Blow till thou burst thy wind, if room 7
enough!   8

*Enter Alonso, Sebastian, Antonio, Ferdinand,
Gonzalo, and others.*

ALONSO Good Boatswain, have care. Where's the Master? Play the men.   10

BOATSWAIN I pray now, keep below.   11

ANTONIO Where is the Master, Boatswain?

BOATSWAIN Do you not hear him? You mar our labor.
Keep your cabins! You do assist the storm.   14

GONZALO Nay, good, be patient.   15

BOATSWAIN When the sea is. Hence! What cares these 16
roarers for the name of king? To cabin! Silence! Trou- 17
ble us not.

GONZALO Good, yet remember whom thou hast
aboard.

BOATSWAIN None that I more love than myself. You are
a councillor; if you can command these elements to
silence and work the peace of the present, we will not 23

1.1. **Location: On board ship, off the island's coast.**
3 **Good** i.e., it's good you've come; or, my good fellow.   **yarely** nimbly
5 **Cheerly** cheerily   6 **Tend** attend   7 **Blow** (Addressed to the wind.)
7–8 **if room enough** as long as we have sea room enough   10 **Play the
men** act like men (?) ply, urge the men to exert themselves (?)   11 **keep**
stay   14 **Keep** remain in   15 **good** good fellow   16 **Hence** get away
17 **roarers** waves or winds, or both; spoken to as though they were
"bullies" or "blusterers"   23 **work . . . present** bring calm to our
present circumstances

hand a rope more. Use your authority. If you cannot, 24
give thanks you have lived so long and make yourself
ready in your cabin for the mischance of the hour, if it 26
so hap.—Cheerly, good hearts!—Out of our way, 27
I say.   *Exit.*

GONZALO I have great comfort from this fellow. Methinks he hath no drowning mark upon him; his com- 30
plexion is perfect gallows. Stand fast, good Fate, to his 31
hanging! Make the rope of his destiny our cable, for
our own doth little advantage. If he be not born to be 33
hanged, our case is miserable.   *Exeunt.* 34

Enter Boatswain.

BOATSWAIN Down with the topmast! Yare! Lower,
lower! Bring her to try wi' the main course. (*A cry* 36
within.) A plague upon this howling! They are louder
than the weather or our office.   38

Enter Sebastian, Antonio, and Gonzalo.

Yet again? What do you here? Shall we give o'er and 39
drown? Have you a mind to sink?

SEBASTIAN A pox o' your throat, you bawling, blasphe-
mous, incharitable dog!

BOATSWAIN Work you, then.

ANTONIO Hang, cur! Hang, you whoreson, insolent
noisemaker! We are less afraid to be drowned than
thou art.

GONZALO I'll warrant him for drowning, though the 47
ship were no stronger than a nutshell and as leaky as
an unstanched wench.   49

24 hand handle **26 mischance** misfortune **27 hap** happen **30–31 complexion . . . gallows** appearance shows he was born to be hanged (and
therefore, according to the proverb, in no danger of drowning) **33 our . . .
advantage** i.e., our own cable is of little benefit **34 case is miserable** circumstances are desperate **36 Bring . . . course** sail her close to the wind
by means of the mainsail **38 our office** i.e., the noise we make at our
work **39 give o'er** give up **47 warrant him for drowning** guarantee that
he will never be drowned **49 unstanched** insatiable, loose, unrestrained

BOATSWAIN   Lay her ahold, ahold! Set her two courses. 50
  Off to sea again! Lay her off!

  Enter Mariners wet.

MARINERS   All lost! To prayers, to prayers! All lost!
                                        [*Exeunt Mariners.*]
BOATSWAIN   What, must our mouths be cold?   53
GONZALO
  The King and Prince at prayers! Let's assist them,
  For our case is as theirs.
SEBASTIAN   I am out of patience.
ANTONIO
  We are merely cheated of our lives by drunkards.   56
  This wide-chapped rascal! Would thou mightst lie
    drowning   57
  The washing of ten tides!
GONZALO   He'll be hanged yet,   58
  Though every drop of water swear against it
  And gape at wid'st to glut him.
  (*A confused noise within:*)   "Mercy on us!"—   60
  "We split, we split!"—"Farewell my wife and
    children!"—   61
  "Farewell, brother!"—"We split, we split, we split!"
                                        [*Exit Boatswain.*]
ANTONIO   Let's all sink wi' the King.
SEBASTIAN   Let's take leave of him. *Exit* [*with Antonio*].
GONZALO   Now would I give a thousand furlongs of sea
  for an acre of barren ground: long heath, brown furze, 66
  anything. The wills above be done! But I would fain   67
  die a dry death.   *Exit.*

                          ❖

50 ahold ahull, close to the wind.   **courses** sails, i.e., foresail as well as
mainsail, set in an attempt to get the ship back out into open water
53 must . . . cold i.e., must we drown in the cold sea; or, let us heat up
our mouths with liquor   **56 merely** utterly   **57 wide-chapped** with
mouth wide open   **57–58 lie . . . tides** (Pirates were hanged on the shore
and left until three tides had come in.)   **60 at wid'st** wide.   **glut** swallow   **61 split** break apart   **66 heath** heather.   **furze** gorse, a weed
growing on wasteland   **67 fain** rather

1.2   *Enter Prospero [in his magic cloak] and*
            Miranda.

MIRANDA
   If by your art, my dearest father, you have   1
   Put the wild waters in this roar, allay them.   2
   The sky, it seems, would pour down stinking pitch,   3
   But that the sea, mounting to th' welkin's cheek,   4
   Dashes the fire out. O, I have suffered
   With those that I saw suffer! A brave vessel,   6
   Who had, no doubt, some noble creature in her,
   Dashed all to pieces. O, the cry did knock
   Against my very heart! Poor souls, they perished.
   Had I been any god of power, I would
   Have sunk the sea within the earth or ere   11
   It should the good ship so have swallowed and
   The freighting souls within her.
PROSPERO   Be collected.   13
   No more amazement. Tell your piteous heart   14
   There's no harm done.
MIRANDA   O, woe the day!
PROSPERO   No harm.
   I have done nothing but in care of thee,   16
   Of thee, my dear one, thee, my daughter, who
   Art ignorant of what thou art, naught knowing
   Of whence I am, nor that I am more better   19
   Than Prospero, master of a full poor cell,   20
   And thy no greater father.
MIRANDA   More to know
   Did never meddle with my thoughts.
PROSPERO   'Tis time   22

1.2. Location: The island. Prospero's cell is visible, and on the Elizabethan stage it presumably remains so throughout the play, although in
some scenes the convention of flexible distance allows us to imagine
characters in other parts of the island.
1 art magic **2 roar** uproar. **allay** pacify **3 pitch** a thick, viscous
substance produced by boiling down tar or turpentine **4 welkin's**
cheek sky's face **6 brave** gallant, splendid **11 or ere** before
13 freighting forming the cargo. **collected** calm, composed **14 amaze-**
ment consternation. **piteous** pitying **16 but** except **19 more better** of
higher rank **20 full** very **22 meddle** mingle

I should inform thee farther. Lend thy hand
And pluck my magic garment from me. So,
          [*Laying down his magic cloak and staff*]
Lie there, my art.—Wipe thou thine eyes. Have comfort.
The direful spectacle of the wreck, which touched   26
The very virtue of compassion in thee,   27
I have with such provision in mine art   28
So safely ordered that there is no soul—
No, not so much perdition as an hair   30
Betid to any creature in the vessel   31
Which thou heardst cry, which thou sawst sink. Sit
     down,   32
For thou must now know farther.
MIRANDA [*Sitting*]   You have often
     Begun to tell me what I am, but stopped
     And left me to a bootless inquisition,   35
     Concluding, "Stay, not yet."
PROSPERO   The hour's now come;
     The very minute bids thee ope thine ear.   37
     Obey, and be attentive. Canst thou remember
     A time before we came unto this cell?
     I do not think thou canst, for then thou wast not
     Out three years old.
MIRANDA   Certainly, sir, I can.   41
PROSPERO
     By what? By any other house or person?
     Of anything the image, tell me, that
     Hath kept with thy remembrance.
MIRANDA   'Tis far off,
     And rather like a dream than an assurance   45
     That my remembrance warrants. Had I not   46
     Four or five women once that tended me?   47
PROSPERO
     Thou hadst, and more, Miranda. But how is it
     That this lives in thy mind? What seest thou else

---

26 wreck shipwreck **27 virtue** essence **28 provision** foresight **30 perdition** loss **31 Betid** happened **32 Which** whom **35 bootless inquisi-
tion** profitless inquiry **37 ope** open **41 Out** fully **45–46 assurance . . .
warrants** certainty that my memory guarantees **47 tended** attended,
waited upon

In the dark backward and abysm of time?   50
If thou rememberest aught ere thou cam'st here,   51
How thou cam'st here thou mayst.
MIRANDA   But that I do not.
PROSPERO
Twelve year since, Miranda, twelve year since,
Thy father was the Duke of Milan and
A prince of power.
MIRANDA   Sir, are not you my father?
PROSPERO
Thy mother was a piece of virtue, and   56
She said thou wast my daughter; and thy father
Was Duke of Milan, and his only heir
And princess no worse issued.
MIRANDA   O the heavens!   59
What foul play had we, that we came from thence?
Or blessèd was 't we did?
PROSPERO   Both, both, my girl.
By foul play, as thou sayst, were we heaved thence,
But blessedly holp hither.
MIRANDA   O, my heart bleeds   63
To think o' the teen that I have turned you to,   64
Which is from my remembrance! Please you, farther.   65
PROSPERO
My brother and thy uncle, called Antonio—
I pray thee, mark me; that a brother should
Be so perfidious!—he whom next thyself   68
Of all the world I loved, and to him put
The manage of my state, as at that time   70
Through all the seigniories it was the first,   71
And Prospero the prime duke, being so reputed   72
In dignity, and for the liberal arts
Without a parallel; those being all my study,
The government I cast upon my brother

---

50 backward . . . time abyss of the past **51 aught** anything **56 piece**
masterpiece, exemplar **59 no worse issued** no less nobly born, descended **63 holp** helped **64 teen . . . to** trouble I've caused you to
remember, or put you to **65 from** out of **68 next** next to **70 manage**
management, administration **71 seigniories** i.e., city-states of northern
Italy **72 prime** of highest rank

And to my state grew stranger, being transported   76
And rapt in secret studies. Thy false uncle—
Dost thou attend me?

MIRANDA   Sir, most heedfully.

PROSPERO
Being once perfected how to grant suits,   79
How to deny them, who t' advance and who
To trash for overtopping, new created   81
The creatures that were mine, I say, or changed 'em,   82
Or else new formed 'em; having both the key   83
Of officer and office, set all hearts i' the state
To what tune pleased his ear, that now he was   85
The ivy which had hid my princely trunk
And sucked my verdure out on 't. Thou attend'st not.   87

MIRANDA
O, good sir, I do.

PROSPERO   I pray thee, mark me.
I, thus neglecting worldly ends, all dedicated
To closeness and the bettering of my mind   90
With that which, but by being so retired,   91
O'erprized all popular rate, in my false brother   92
Awaked an evil nature; and my trust,
Like a good parent, did beget of him   94
A falsehood in its contrary as great
As my trust was, which had indeed no limit,
A confidence sans bound. He being thus lorded   97
Not only with what my revenue yielded
But what my power might else exact, like one   99

76 to . . . stranger i.e., withdrew from my responsibilities as duke.
transported carried away   **79 perfected** grown skillful   **81 trash**
check a hound by tying a cord or weight to its neck. **overtopping**
running too far ahead of the pack; surmounting, exceeding one's
authority   **82 creatures** dependents   **82–83 or changed . . . formed**
'em i.e., either changed their loyalties and duties or else created new
ones   **83 key** (1) key for unlocking (2) tool for tuning stringed instruments   **85 that** so that   **87 verdure** vitality.   **on 't** of it   **90 closeness**
retirement, seclusion   **91–92 but . . . rate** simply because it was
done in such seclusion, had a value not appreciated by popular
opinion   **94 good parent** (Alludes to the proverb that good parents
often bear bad children; see also l. 120.)   **of** in   **97 sans** without.
lorded raised to lordship, with power and wealth   **99 else** otherwise,
additionally

Who, having into truth by telling of it,   100
Made such a sinner of his memory   101
To credit his own lie, he did believe   102
He was indeed the Duke, out o' the substitution   103
And executing th' outward face of royalty   104
With all prerogative. Hence his ambition growing—
Dost thou hear?
MIRANDA   Your tale, sir, would cure deafness.
PROSPERO
To have no screen between this part he played   107
And him he played it for, he needs will be   108
Absolute Milan. Me, poor man, my library   109
Was dukedom large enough. Of temporal royalties   110
He thinks me now incapable; confederates—   111
So dry he was for sway—wi' the King of Naples   112
To give him annual tribute, do him homage,   113
Subject his coronet to his crown, and bend   114
The dukedom yet unbowed—alas, poor Milan!—   115
To most ignoble stooping.
MIRANDA   O the heavens!
PROSPERO
Mark his condition and th' event, then tell me   117
If this might be a brother.
MIRANDA   I should sin
To think but nobly of my grandmother.   119
Good wombs have borne bad sons.
PROSPERO   Now the condition.
This King of Naples, being an enemy
To me inveterate, hearkens my brother's suit,   122

100–102 Who . . . lie i.e., who, by repeatedly telling the lie (that he was
indeed Duke of Milan), made his memory such a confirmed sinner
against truth that he began to believe his own lie. **into** unto, against.
To so as to **103 out o'** as a result of **104 And . . . royalty** and (as a
result of) his carrying out all the ceremonial functions of royalty
107–108 To have . . . it for i.e., to have no separation or barrier between
his role and himself. (Antonio wanted to act in his own person, not as
substitute.) **108 needs** necessarily **109 Absolute Milan** unconditional
Duke of Milan **110 temporal royalties** practical prerogatives and
responsibilities of a sovereign **111 confederates** conspires, allies
himself **112 dry** thirsty. **sway** power **113 him** i.e., the King of Naples **114 his . . . his** Antonio's . . . the King of Naples's. **bend** make
bow down **115 yet** hitherto **117 condition** pact. **event** outcome
119 but other than **122 hearkens** listens to

Which was that he, in lieu o' the premises   123
Of homage and I know not how much tribute,
Should presently extirpate me and mine   125
Out of the dukedom and confer fair Milan,
With all the honors, on my brother. Whereon,
A treacherous army levied, one midnight
Fated to th' purpose did Antonio open
The gates of Milan, and, i' the dead of darkness,
The ministers for the purpose hurried thence   131
Me and thy crying self.
MIRANDA   Alack, for pity!
I, not remembering how I cried out then,
Will cry it o'er again. It is a hint   134
That wrings mine eyes to 't.
PROSPERO   Hear a little further,   135
And then I'll bring thee to the present business
Which now's upon 's, without the which this story
Were most impertinent.
MIRANDA   Wherefore did they not   138
That hour destroy us?
PROSPERO   Well demanded, wench.   139
My tale provokes that question. Dear, they durst not,
So dear the love my people bore me, nor set   141
A mark so bloody on the business, but   142
With colors fairer painted their foul ends.   143
In few, they hurried us aboard a bark,   144
Bore us some leagues to sea, where they prepared
A rotten carcass of a butt, not rigged,   146
Nor tackle, sail, nor mast; the very rats   147
Instinctively have quit it. There they hoist us,   148
To cry to th' sea that roared to us, to sigh

123 in . . . premises in return for the stipulation   125 presently extirpate at once remove   131 ministers . . . purpose agents employed to do
this.   thence from there   134 hint occasion   135 wrings (1) constrains
(2) wrings tears from   138 impertinent irrelevant.   Wherefore why
139 demanded asked.   wench (Here a term of endearment.)   141–142 set
. . . bloody i.e., make obvious their murderous intent. (From the practice
of marking with the blood of the prey those who have participated in
a successful hunt.)   143 fairer apparently more attractive   144 few
few words.   bark ship   146 butt cask, tub   147 Nor tackle neither
rigging (i.e., the pulleys and ropes designed for hoisting sails)   148 quit
abandoned

To th' winds whose pity, sighing back again,
Did us but loving wrong.
MIRANDA   Alack, what trouble   151
Was I then to you!
PROSPERO   O, a cherubin   152
Thou wast that did preserve me. Thou didst smile,
Infusèd with a fortitude from heaven,
When I have decked the sea with drops full salt,   155
Under my burden groaned, which raised in me   156
An undergoing stomach, to bear up   157
Against what should ensue.
MIRANDA   How came we ashore?
PROSPERO   By Providence divine.
Some food we had, and some fresh water, that
A noble Neapolitan, Gonzalo,
Out of his charity, who being then appointed
Master of this design, did give us, with
Rich garments, linens, stuffs, and necessaries,   165
Which since have steaded much. So, of his gentleness,   166
Knowing I loved my books, he furnished me
From mine own library with volumes that
I prize above my dukedom.
MIRANDA   Would I might   169
But ever see that man!
PROSPERO   Now I arise.   170
       [He puts on his magic cloak.]
Sit still and hear the last of our sea sorrow.   171
Here in this island we arrived; and here
Have I, thy schoolmaster, made thee more profit   173
Than other princess' can, that have more time   174
For vainer hours and tutors not so careful.   175
MIRANDA
Heavens thank you for 't! And now, I pray you, sir—

---

151 loving wrong (i.e., the winds pitied Prospero and Miranda though of
necessity they blew them from shore)   **152 cherubin** angel   **155 decked**
covered (with salt tears); adorned   **156 which** i.e., the smile   **157 undergoing stomach** courage to go on   **165 stuffs** supplies   **166 steaded**
much been of much use   **169 Would** I wish   **170 But ever** i.e., someday   **171 sea sorrow** sorrowful adventure at sea   **173 more profit** profit
more   **174 princess'** princesses. (Or the word may be *princes*, referring
to royal children both male and female.)   **175 vainer** more foolishly
spent

For still 'tis beating in my mind—your reason
For raising this sea storm?

PROSPERO   Know thus far forth:
By accident most strange, bountiful Fortune,
Now my dear lady, hath mine enemies
Brought to this shore; and by my prescience
I find my zenith doth depend upon   182
A most auspicious star, whose influence   183
If now I court not, but omit, my fortunes   184
Will ever after droop. Here cease more questions.
Thou art inclined to sleep. 'Tis a good dullness,   186
And give it way. I know thou canst not choose.   187

                              [*Miranda sleeps.*]

Come away, servant, come! I am ready now.   188
Approach, my Ariel, come.

        Enter Ariel.

ARIEL
All hail, great master, grave sir, hail! I come
To answer thy best pleasure; be 't to fly,
To swim, to dive into the fire, to ride
On the curled clouds, to thy strong bidding task   193
Ariel and all his quality.

PROSPERO   Hast thou, spirit,   194
Performed to point the tempest that I bade thee?   195

ARIEL   To every article.
I boarded the King's ship. Now on the beak,   197
Now in the waist, the deck, in every cabin,   198
I flamed amazement. Sometimes I'd divide   199
And burn in many places; on the topmast,
The yards, and bowsprit would I flame distinctly,   201
Then meet and join. Jove's lightning, the precursors
O' the dreadful thunderclaps, more momentary
And sight-outrunning were not. The fire and cracks   204

---

182 zenith height of fortune. (Astrological term.)   **183 influence** astrological power   **184 omit** ignore   **186 dullness** drowsiness   **187 give it
way** let it happen (i.e., don't fight it)   **188 Come away** come   **193 task**
make demands upon   **194 quality** (1) fellow spirits (2) abilities   **195 to
point** to the smallest detail   **197 beak** prow   **198 waist** midships.
deck poop deck at the stern   **199 flamed amazement** struck terror in
the guise of fire, i.e., Saint Elmo's fire   **201 distinctly** in different
places   **204 sight-outrunning** swifter than sight

Of sulfurous roaring the most mighty Neptune   205
Seem to besiege and make his bold waves tremble,
Yea, his dread trident shake.

PROSPERO   My brave spirit!
Who was so firm, so constant, that this coil   208
Would not infect his reason?

ARIEL   Not a soul
But felt a fever of the mad and played   210
Some tricks of desperation. All but mariners
Plunged in the foaming brine and quit the vessel,
Then all afire with me. The King's son, Ferdinand,
With hair up-staring—then like reeds, not hair—   214
Was the first man that leapt; cried, "Hell is empty,
And all the devils are here!"

PROSPERO   Why, that's my spirit!
But was not this nigh shore?

ARIEL   Close by, my master.

PROSPERO
But are they, Ariel, safe?

ARIEL   Not a hair perished.
On their sustaining garments not a blemish,   219
But fresher than before; and, as thou bad'st me,   220
In troops I have dispersed them 'bout the isle.   221
The King's son have I landed by himself,
Whom I left cooling of the air with sighs   223
In an odd angle of the isle, and sitting,   224
His arms in this sad knot.   [*He folds his arms.*]

PROSPERO   Of the King's ship,   225
The mariners, say how thou hast disposed,
And all the rest o' the fleet.

ARIEL   Safely in harbor
Is the King's ship; in the deep nook, where once   228
Thou calledst me up at midnight to fetch dew
From the still-vexed Bermudas, there she's hid;   230

205 Neptune Roman god of the sea   **208 coil** tumult   **210 of the mad**
i.e., such as madmen feel   **214 up-staring** standing on end   **219 sustaining garments** garments that buoyed them up in the sea   **220 bad'st**
ordered   **221 troops** groups   **223 cooling of** cooling   **224 angle** corner   **225 sad knot** (Folded arms are indicative of melancholy.)
228 nook bay   **230 still-vexed Bermudas** ever-stormy Bermudas. (Perhaps refers to the then-recent Bermuda shipwreck; see play Introduction. The Folio text reads "Bermoothes.")

The mariners all under hatches stowed,
Who, with a charm joined to their suffered labor,   232
I have left asleep. And for the rest o' the fleet,
Which I dispersed, they all have met again
And are upon the Mediterranean float   235
Bound sadly home for Naples,
Supposing that they saw the King's ship wrecked
And his great person perish.

PROSPERO   Ariel, thy charge
Exactly is performed. But there's more work.
What is the time o' the day?

ARIEL   Past the mid season.   240

PROSPERO
At least two glasses. The time twixt six and now   241
Must by us both be spent most preciously.

ARIEL
Is there more toil? Since thou dost give me pains,   243
Let me remember thee what thou hast promised,   244
Which is not yet performed me.

PROSPERO   How now? Moody?
What is 't thou canst demand?

ARIEL   My liberty.

PROSPERO
Before the time be out? No more!

ARIEL   I prithee,
Remember I have done thee worthy service,
Told thee no lies, made thee no mistakings, served
Without or grudge or grumblings. Thou did promise
To bate me a full year.

PROSPERO   Dost thou forget   251
From what a torment I did free thee?

ARIEL   No.

PROSPERO
Thou dost, and think'st it much to tread the ooze
Of the salt deep,
To run upon the sharp wind of the north,

232 **with . . . labor** by means of a spell added to all the labor they have
undergone   235 **float** sea   240 **mid season** noon   241 **glasses** i.e.,
hourglasses   243 **pains** labors   244 **remember** remind   251 **bate** remit,
deduct

To do me business in the veins o' the earth   256
When it is baked with frost.

ARIEL   I do not, sir.   257

PROSPERO
Thou liest, malignant thing! Hast thou forgot
The foul witch Sycorax, who with age and envy   259
Was grown into a hoop? Hast thou forgot her?   260

ARIEL   No, sir.

PROSPERO
Thou hast. Where was she born? Speak. Tell me.

ARIEL
Sir, in Algiers.

PROSPERO   O, was she so? I must
Once in a month recount what thou hast been,
Which thou forgett'st. This damned witch Sycorax,
For mischiefs manifold and sorceries terrible
To enter human hearing, from Algiers,
Thou know'st, was banished. For one thing she did   268
They would not take her life. Is not this true?

ARIEL   Ay, sir.

PROSPERO
This blue-eyed hag was hither brought with child   271
And here was left by the sailors. Thou, my slave,
As thou report'st thyself, was then her servant;
And, for thou wast a spirit too delicate   274
To act her earthy and abhorred commands,
Refusing her grand hests, she did confine thee,   276
By help of her more potent ministers
And in her most unmitigable rage,
Into a cloven pine, within which rift
Imprisoned thou didst painfully remain
A dozen years; within which space she died
And left thee there, where thou didst vent thy groans
As fast as mill wheels strike. Then was this island—   283

256 do me do for me. veins veins of minerals, or underground
streams thought to be analogous to the veins of the human body
257 baked hardened   259 envy malice   260 grown into a hoop i.e., so
bent over with age as to resemble a hoop   268 one . . . did (Perhaps a
reference to her pregnancy, for which her life would be spared.)
271 blue-eyed with dark circles under the eyes or with blue eyelids,
implying pregnancy. with child pregnant   274 for because   276 hests
commands   283 as mill wheels strike as the blades of a mill wheel
strike the water

Save for the son that she did litter here,   284
A freckled whelp, hag-born—not honored with   285
A human shape.
ARIEL   Yes, Caliban her son.
PROSPERO
Dull thing, I say so: he, that Caliban   287
Whom now I keep in service. Thou best know'st
What torment I did find thee in. Thy groans
Did make wolves howl, and penetrate the breasts
Of ever-angry bears. It was a torment
To lay upon the damned, which Sycorax
Could not again undo. It was mine art,
When I arrived and heard thee, that made gape   294
The pine and let thee out.
ARIEL   I thank thee, master.
PROSPERO
If thou more murmur'st, I will rend an oak
And peg thee in his knotty entrails till   297
Thou hast howled away twelve winters.
ARIEL   Pardon, master.
I will be correspondent to command   299
And do my spriting gently.   300
PROSPERO   Do so, and after two days
I will discharge thee.
ARIEL   That's my noble master!
What shall I do? Say what? What shall I do?
PROSPERO
Go make thyself like a nymph o' the sea. Be subject
To no sight but thine and mine, invisible
To every eyeball else. Go take this shape
And hither come in 't. Go, hence with diligence!
                                        Exit [Ariel].
Awake, dear heart, awake! Thou hast slept well.
Awake!
MIRANDA   The strangeness of your story put
Heaviness in me.
PROSPERO   Shake it off. Come on,   310

284 Save except. **litter** give birth to   **285 whelp** offspring. (Used of animals.)   **hag-born** born of a female demon   **287 Dull . . . so** i.e., exactly, that's what I said, you dullard   **294 gape** open wide   **297 his** its   **299 correspondent** responsive, submissive   **300 spriting** duties as a spirit.   **gently** willingly, ungrudgingly   **310 Heaviness** drowsiness

We'll visit Caliban, my slave, who never
Yields us kind answer.

MIRANDA   'Tis a villain, sir,
I do not love to look on.

PROSPERO   But, as 'tis,
We cannot miss him. He does make our fire,   314
Fetch in our wood, and serves in offices   315
That profit us.—What ho! Slave! Caliban!
Thou earth, thou! Speak.

CALIBAN (*Within*)   There's wood enough within.

PROSPERO
Come forth, I say! There's other business for thee.
Come, thou tortoise! When?   319

Enter Ariel like a water nymph.

Fine apparition! My quaint Ariel,   320
Hark in thine ear.   [*He whispers.*]

ARIEL   My lord, it shall be done.   *Exit.*

PROSPERO
Thou poisonous slave, got by the devil himself   322
Upon thy wicked dam, come forth!   323

Enter Caliban.

CALIBAN
As wicked dew as e'er my mother brushed   324
With raven's feather from unwholesome fen   325
Drop on you both! A southwest blow on ye   326
And blister you all o'er!

PROSPERO
For this, be sure, tonight thou shalt have cramps,
Side-stitches that shall pen thy breath up. Urchins   329
Shall forth at vast of night that they may work   330
All exercise on thee. Thou shalt be pinched

314 **miss** do without   315 **offices** functions, duties   319 **When** (An
exclamation of impatience.)   320 **quaint** ingenious   322 **got** begotten,
sired   323 **dam** mother. (Used of animals.)   324 **wicked** mischievous,
harmful   325 **fen** marsh, bog   326 **southwest** i.e., wind thought to
bring disease   329 **Urchins** hedgehogs; here, suggesting goblins in the
guise of hedgehogs   330 **vast** lengthy, desolate time. (Malignant spirits
were thought to be restricted to the hours of darkness.)

As thick as honeycomb, each pinch more stinging   332
Than bees that made 'em.

CALIBAN   I must eat my dinner.   333
This island's mine, by Sycorax my mother,
Which thou tak'st from me. When thou cam'st first,
Thou strok'st me and made much of me, wouldst give
      me
Water with berries in 't, and teach me how
To name the bigger light, and how the less,   338
That burn by day and night. And then I loved thee
And showed thee all the qualities o' th' isle,
The fresh springs, brine pits, barren place and fertile.
Cursed be I that did so! All the charms   342
Of Sycorax, toads, beetles, bats, light on you!
For I am all the subjects that you have,
Which first was mine own king; and here you sty me   345
In this hard rock, whiles you do keep from me
The rest o' th' island.

PROSPERO   Thou most lying slave,
Whom stripes may move, not kindness! I have used thee,   348
Filth as thou art, with humane care, and lodged thee   349
In mine own cell, till thou didst seek to violate
The honor of my child.

CALIBAN
Oho, Oho! Would 't had been done!
Thou didst prevent me; I had peopled else   353
This isle with Calibans.

MIRANDA   Abhorrèd slave,   354
Which any print of goodness wilt not take,   355
Being capable of all ill! I pitied thee,
Took pains to make thee speak, taught thee each hour
One thing or other. When thou didst not, savage,
Know thine own meaning, but wouldst gabble like

332 **As thick as honeycomb** i.e., all over, with as many pinches as a
honeycomb has cells   333 **'em** i.e., the honeycomb   338 **the bigger . . .
less** i.e., the sun and the moon. (See Genesis 1:16: "God then made two
great lights: the greater light to rule the day, and the less light to rule
the night.")   342 **charms** spells   345 **sty** confine as in a sty   348 **stripes**
lashes   349 **humane** (Not distinguished as a word from *human*.)
353 **peopled else** otherwise populated   354–365 **Abhorrèd . . . prison** (Sometimes assigned by editors to Prospero.)   355 **print** imprint, impression

A thing most brutish, I endowed thy purposes   360
With words that made them known. But thy vile race, 361
Though thou didst learn, had that in 't which good
    natures
Could not abide to be with; therefore wast thou
Deservedly confined into this rock,
Who hadst deserved more than a prison.

CALIBAN
You taught me language, and my profit on 't
Is I know how to curse. The red plague rid you   367
For learning me your language!

PROSPERO   Hagseed, hence!   368
Fetch us in fuel, and be quick, thou'rt best,   369
To answer other business. Shrugg'st thou, malice?   370
If thou neglect'st or dost unwillingly
What I command, I'll rack thee with old cramps,   372
Fill all thy bones with aches, make thee roar   373
That beasts shall tremble at thy din.

CALIBAN   No, pray thee.
[*Aside.*] I must obey. His art is of such power
It would control my dam's god, Setebos,   376
And make a vassal of him.

PROSPERO   So, slave, hence!   377
                              Exit Caliban.

*Enter Ferdinand; and Ariel, invisible, playing and
singing. [Ferdinand does not see Prospero and
Miranda.]*

                Ariel's Song.

ARIEL
        Come unto these yellow sands,
            And then take hands;

---

360 purposes meanings, desires   **361 race** natural disposition; species,
nature   **367 red plague** plague characterized by red sores and evacua-
tion of blood.   **rid** destroy   **368 learning** teaching.   **Hagseed** offspring
of a female demon   **369 thou'rt best** you'd be well advised   **370 answer
other business** perform other tasks   **372 old** such as old people suffer;
or, plenty of   **373 aches** (Pronounced "aitches.")   **376 Setebos** (A god
of the Patagonians, named in Robert Eden's *History of Travel*, 1577.)
377 s.d. Ariel, invisible (Ariel wears a garment that by convention
indicates he is invisible to the other characters.)

    Curtsied when you have, and kissed   380
        The wild waves whist,   381
Foot it featly here and there,   382
    And, sweet sprites, bear   383
The burden. Hark, hark!   384
        Burden, dispersedly [*within*]. Bow-wow. 385
The watchdogs bark.
        [*Burden, dispersedly within.*] Bow-wow.
Hark, hark! I hear
The strain of strutting chanticleer
    Cry Cock-a-diddle-dow.

FERDINAND
Where should this music be? I' th' air or th' earth?
It sounds no more; and sure it waits upon   392
Some god o' th' island. Sitting on a bank,   393
Weeping again the King my father's wreck,
This music crept by me upon the waters,
Allaying both their fury and my passion   396
With its sweet air. Thence I have followed it,   397
Or it hath drawn me rather. But 'tis gone.
No, it begins again.

Ariel's Song.

ARIEL
    Full fathom five thy father lies.
        Of his bones are coral made.
    Those are pearls that were his eyes.
        Nothing of him that doth fade
    But doth suffer a sea change
    Into something rich and strange.
    Sea nymphs hourly ring his knell.   406
            Burden [*within*]. Ding dong.
Hark, now I hear them, ding dong bell.

FERDINAND
The ditty does remember my drowned father.   409

380 Curtsied . . . have when you have curtsied   **380–381 kissed . . . whist**
kissed the waves into silence, or, kissed while the waves are being hushed
382 Foot it featly dance nimbly   **383 sprites** spirits   **384 burden** refrain,
undersong   **385 s.d. dispersedly** i.e., from all directions, not in unison
392 waits upon serves, attends   **393 bank** sandbank   **396 passion** grief
397 Thence i.e., from the bank on which he sat   **406 knell** announcement of
a death by the tolling of a bell   **409 remember** commemorate

This is no mortal business, nor no sound
That the earth owes. I hear it now above me.   411

PROSPERO [*To Miranda*]
    The fringèd curtains of thine eye advance   412
    And say what thou seest yond.

MIRANDA   What is 't? A spirit?
    Lord, how it looks about! Believe me, sir,
    It carries a brave form. But 'tis a spirit.   415

PROSPERO
    No, wench, it eats and sleeps and hath such senses
    As we have, such. This gallant which thou seest
    Was in the wreck; and, but he's something stained   418
    With grief, that's beauty's canker, thou mightst call him 419
    A goodly person. He hath lost his fellows
    And strays about to find 'em.

MIRANDA   I might call him
    A thing divine, for nothing natural
    I ever saw so noble.

PROSPERO [*Aside*]   It goes on, I see,   423
    As my soul prompts it.—Spirit, fine spirit, I'll free thee
    Within two days for this.

FERDINAND [*Seeing Miranda*] Most sure, the goddess
    On whom these airs attend!—Vouchsafe my prayer   426
    May know if you remain upon this island,   427
    And that you will some good instruction give
    How I may bear me here. My prime request,   429
    Which I do last pronounce, is—O you wonder!—   430
    If you be maid or no?

MIRANDA   No wonder, sir,   431
    But certainly a maid.

FERDINAND   My language? Heavens!
    I am the best of them that speak this speech,   433
    Were I but where 'tis spoken.

---

411 owes owns   **412 advance** raise   **415 brave** excellent   **418 but** except
that.   **something stained** somewhat disfigured   **419 canker** canker-
worm (feeding on buds and leaves)   **423 It goes on** i.e., my plan works
426 airs songs.   **Vouchsafe** grant   **427 May know** i.e., that I may
know.   **remain** dwell   **429 bear me** conduct myself.   **prime** chief
430 wonder (Miranda's name means "to be wondered at.")   **431 maid
or no** i.e., a human maiden as opposed to a goddess or married
woman   **433 best** i.e., in birth

PROSPERO [*Coming forward*]   How? The best?
  What wert thou if the King of Naples heard thee?
FERDINAND
  A single thing, as I am now, that wonders   436
  To hear thee speak of Naples. He does hear me,   437
  And that he does I weep. Myself am Naples,   438
  Who with mine eyes, never since at ebb, beheld   439
  The King my father wrecked.
MIRANDA   Alack, for mercy!
FERDINAND
  Yes, faith, and all his lords, the Duke of Milan
  And his brave son being twain.
PROSPERO [*Aside*]   The Duke of Milan   442
  And his more braver daughter could control thee,   443
  If now 'twere fit to do 't. At the first sight
  They have changed eyes.—Delicate Ariel,   445
  I'll set thee free for this. [*To Ferdinand.*] A word, good sir.
  I fear you have done yourself some wrong. A word!   447
MIRANDA [*Aside*]
  Why speaks my father so ungently? This
  Is the third man that e'er I saw, the first
  That e'er I sighed for. Pity move my father
  To be inclined my way!
FERDINAND   O, if a virgin,
  And your affection not gone forth, I'll make you
  The Queen of Naples.
PROSPERO   Soft, sir! One word more.
  [*Aside.*] They are both in either's powers; but this swift
    business   454
  I must uneasy make, lest too light winning   455
  Make the prize light. [*To Ferdinand.*] One word more: I
    charge thee   456

436 single (1) solitary, being at once King of Naples and myself
(2) feeble   437, 438 Naples the King of Naples   437 He does hear me
i.e., the King of Naples does hear my words, for I am King of Naples
438 And . . . weep i.e., and I weep at this reminder that my father is
seemingly dead, leaving me heir   439 at ebb i.e., dry, not weeping
442 son (The only reference in the play to a son of Antonio.)   443 more
braver more splendid.   control refute   445 changed eyes exchanged
amorous glances   447 done . . . wrong i.e., spoken falsely   454 both in
either's each in the other's   455 uneasy difficult   455–456 light . . .
light easy . . . cheap

That thou attend me. Thou dost here usurp   457
The name thou ow'st not, and hast put thyself   458
Upon this island as a spy, to win it
From me, the lord on 't.

FERDINAND   No, as I am a man.   460

MIRANDA
There's nothing ill can dwell in such a temple.
If the ill spirit have so fair a house,
Good things will strive to dwell with 't.

PROSPERO   Follow me.—   463
Speak not you for him; he's a traitor.—Come,
I'll manacle thy neck and feet together.
Seawater shalt thou drink; thy food shall be
The fresh-brook mussels, withered roots, and husks
Wherein the acorn cradled. Follow.

FERDINAND   No!
I will resist such entertainment till   469
Mine enemy has more power.
                    He draws, and is charmed from moving.

MIRANDA   O dear father,   470
Make not too rash a trial of him, for   471
He's gentle, and not fearful.

PROSPERO   What, I say,   472
My foot my tutor?—Put thy sword up, traitor,   473
Who mak'st a show but dar'st not strike, thy conscience
Is so possessed with guilt. Come from thy ward,   475
For I can here disarm thee with this stick
And make thy weapon drop.
                              [*He brandishes his staff.*]

MIRANDA [*Trying to hinder him*] Beseech you, father!

PROSPERO
Hence! Hang not on my garments.

MIRANDA   Sir, have pity!
I'll be his surety.

PROSPERO   Silence! One word more   479

457 **attend** follow, obey   458 **ow'st** ownest   460 **on 't** of it   463 **strive
. . . with 't** i.e., expel the evil and occupy the *temple*, the body
469 **entertainment** treatment   470 **s.d. charmed** magically prevented
471 **rash** harsh   472 **gentle** wellborn.   **fearful** frightening, dangerous; or,
perhaps, cowardly   473 **foot** subordinate. (Miranda, the foot, presumes to
instruct Prospero, the head.)   475 **ward** defensive posture (in fencing)
479 **surety** guarantee

Shall make me chide thee, if not hate thee. What,
An advocate for an impostor? Hush!
Thou think'st there is no more such shapes as he,
Having seen but him and Caliban. Foolish wench,
To the most of men this is a Caliban,   484
And they to him are angels.

MIRANDA   My affections
Are then most humble; I have no ambition
To see a goodlier man.

PROSPERO [*To Ferdinand*]   Come on, obey.
Thy nerves are in their infancy again   488
And have no vigor in them.

FERDINAND   So they are.
My spirits, as in a dream, are all bound up.   490
My father's loss, the weakness which I feel,
The wreck of all my friends, nor this man's threats
To whom I am subdued, are but light to me,   493
Might I but through my prison once a day
Behold this maid. All corners else o' th' earth   495
Let liberty make use of; space enough
Have I in such a prison.

PROSPERO [*Aside*]   It works. [*To Ferdinand.*] Come on.—
Thou hast done well, fine Ariel! [*To Ferdinand.*] Follow
    me.
[*To Ariel.*] Hark what thou else shalt do me.

MIRANDA [*To Ferdinand*]   Be of comfort. 499
My father's of a better nature, sir,
Than he appears by speech. This is unwonted   501
Which now came from him.

PROSPERO [*To Ariel*]   Thou shalt be as free
As mountain winds; but then exactly do   503
All points of my command.

ARIEL   To th' syllable.

PROSPERO [*To Ferdinand*]
Come, follow. [*To Miranda.*] Speak not for him.
                                        Exeunt.

                            ❧

484 To compared to   **488 nerves** sinews   **490 spirits** vital powers
493 light unimportant   **495 corners else** other corners, regions
499 me for me   **501 unwonted** unusual   **503 then** until then, or, if that
is to be so

2.1 *Enter Alonso, Sebastian, Antonio, Gonzalo,*
Adrian, Francisco, and others.

GONZALO [*To Alonso*]
Beseech you, sir, be merry. You have cause,
So have we all, of joy, for our escape
Is much beyond our loss. Our hint of woe   3
Is common; every day some sailor's wife,
The masters of some merchant, and the merchant   5
Have just our theme of woe. But for the miracle, 6
I mean our preservation, few in millions
Can speak like us. Then wisely, good sir, weigh
Our sorrow with our comfort.

ALONSO   Prithee, peace.   9

SEBASTIAN [*To Antonio*]   He receives comfort like cold
porridge.   11

ANTONIO [*To Sebastian*]   The visitor will not give him 12
o'er so.   13

SEBASTIAN   Look, he's winding up the watch of his wit;
by and by it will strike—

GONZALO [*To Alonso*]   Sir—

SEBASTIAN [*To Antonio*]   One. Tell.   17

GONZALO   When every grief is entertained   18
That's offered, comes to th' entertainer—   19

SEBASTIAN   A dollar.   20

GONZALO   Dolor comes to him, indeed. You have spoken truer than you purposed.

SEBASTIAN   You have taken it wiselier than I meant you
should.

GONZALO [*To Alonso*]   Therefore, my lord—

2.1. Location: Another part of the island.
3 much beyond more remarkable than. **hint of** occasion for **5 masters
. . . the merchant** officers of some merchant vessel and the merchant
himself, the owner (or else the ship itself) **6 just** exactly **9 with**
against **11 porridge** (with a pun on *peace* and *peas* or *pease*, a common
ingredient of porridge) **12 visitor** one taking nourishment and comfort
to the sick, i.e., Gonzalo **12–13 give him o'er** abandon him **17 Tell**
keep count **18–19 When . . . entertainer** when every sorrow that
presents itself is accepted without resistance, there comes to the recipi-
ent **20 dollar** widely circulated coin, the German thaler and the Spanish piece of eight. (Sebastian puns on *entertainer* in the sense of
innkeeper; to Gonzalo, *dollar* suggests *dolor*, grief.)

ANTONIO   Fie, what a spendthrift is he of his tongue!

ALONSO [*To Gonzalo*]   I prithee, spare.   27

GONZALO   Well, I have done. But yet—

SEBASTIAN   He will be talking.

ANTONIO   Which, of he or Adrian, for a good wager,   30
first begins to crow?   31

SEBASTIAN   The old cock.   32

ANTONIO   The cockerel.   33

SEBASTIAN   Done. The wager?

ANTONIO   A laughter.   35

SEBASTIAN   A match!   36

ADRIAN   Though this island seem to be desert—   37

ANTONIO   Ha, ha, ha!

SEBASTIAN   So, you're paid.   39

ADRIAN   Uninhabitable and almost inaccessible—

SEBASTIAN   Yet—

ADRIAN   Yet—

ANTONIO   He could not miss 't.   43

ADRIAN   It must needs be of subtle, tender, and delicate   44
temperance.   45

ANTONIO   Temperance was a delicate wench.   46

SEBASTIAN   Ay, and a subtle, as he most learnedly de-   47
livered.   48

27 spare forbear, cease   **30–31 Which . . . crow** which of the two, Gonzalo or Adrian, do you bet will speak (crow) first   **32 old cock** i.e., Gonzalo   **33 cockerel** i.e., Adrian   **35 laughter** (1) burst of laughter (2) sitting of eggs. (When Adrian, the *cockerel*, begins to speak two lines later, Sebastian loses the bet. The Folio speech prefixes in ll. 38–39 are here reversed so that Antonio enjoys his laugh as the prize for winning, as in the proverb "He who laughs last laughs best" or "He laughs that wins." The Folio assignment can work in the theater, however, if Sebastian pays for losing with a sardonic laugh of concession.)   **36 A match** a bargain; agreed   **37 desert** uninhabited   **39 you're paid** i.e., you've had your laugh   **43 miss 't** (1) avoid saying "Yet" (2) miss the island   **44 must needs be** has to be   **45 temperance** mildness of climate   **46 Temperance** a girl's name.   **delicate** (Here it means "given to pleasure, voluptuous"; in l. 44, "pleasant." Antonio is evidently suggesting that *tender, and delicate temperance* sounds like a Puritan phrase, which Antonio then mocks by applying the words to a woman rather than an island. He began this bawdy comparison with a double entendre on *inaccessible*, l. 40.)   **47 subtle** (Here it means "tricky, crafty"; in l. 44, "delicate.")   **47–48 delivered** uttered. (Sebastian joins Antonio in baiting the Puritans with his use of the pious cant phrase *learnedly delivered*.)

ADRIAN   The air breathes upon us here most sweetly.

SEBASTIAN   As if it had lungs, and rotten ones.

ANTONIO   Or as 'twere perfumed by a fen.

GONZALO   Here is everything advantageous to life.

ANTONIO   True, save means to live.   53

SEBASTIAN   Of that there's none, or little.

GONZALO   How lush and lusty the grass looks! How   55
green!

ANTONIO   The ground indeed is tawny.   57

SEBASTIAN   With an eye of green in 't.   58

ANTONIO   He misses not much.

SEBASTIAN   No. He doth but mistake the truth totally.   60

GONZALO   But the rarity of it is—which is indeed almost beyond credit—

SEBASTIAN   As many vouched rarities are.   63

GONZALO   That our garments, being, as they were,
drenched in the sea, hold notwithstanding their freshness and glosses, being rather new-dyed than stained
with salt water.

ANTONIO   If but one of his pockets could speak, would   68
it not say he lies?

SEBASTIAN   Ay, or very falsely pocket up his report.   70

GONZALO   Methinks our garments are now as fresh as
when we put them on first in Afric, at the marriage of
the King's fair daughter Claribel to the King of Tunis.

SEBASTIAN   'Twas a sweet marriage, and we prosper
well in our return.

ADRIAN   Tunis was never graced before with such a par-
agon to their queen.   77

GONZALO   Not since widow Dido's time.   78

ANTONIO   Widow! A pox o' that! How came that "widow"
in? Widow Dido!

---

53 save except   **55 lusty** healthy   **57 tawny** dull brown, yellowish
58 eye tinge, or spot (perhaps with reference to Gonzalo's eye or judgment)   **60 but** merely   **63 vouched** certified   **68 pockets** i.e., because
they are muddy   **70 pocket up** i.e., conceal, suppress; often used in the
sense of "receive unprotestingly, fail to respond to a challenge."   **his
report** (Sebastian's jest is that the evidence of Gonzalo's soggy and sea-
stained pockets would confute Gonzalo's speech and his reputation for
truth telling.)   **77 to** for   **78 widow Dido** Queen of Carthage, deserted
by Aeneas. (She was in fact a widow when Aeneas, a widower, met her,
but Antonio may be amused at Gonzalo's prudish use of the term
"widow" to describe a woman deserted by her lover.)

SEBASTIAN   What if he had said "widower Aeneas" too?
  Good Lord, how you take it!   82
ADRIAN   "Widow Dido" said you? You make me study   83
  of that. She was of Carthage, not of Tunis.   84
GONZALO   This Tunis, sir, was Carthage.
ADRIAN   Carthage?
GONZALO   I assure you, Carthage.
ANTONIO   His word is more than the miraculous harp.   88
SEBASTIAN   He hath raised the wall, and houses too.
ANTONIO   What impossible matter will he make easy
  next?
SEBASTIAN   I think he will carry this island home in his
  pocket and give it his son for an apple.
ANTONIO   And, sowing the kernels of it in the sea, bring   94
  forth more islands.
GONZALO   Ay.   96
ANTONIO   Why, in good time.   97
GONZALO [To Alonso]   Sir, we were talking that our gar-   98
  ments seem now as fresh as when we were at Tunis at
  the marriage of your daughter, who is now queen.
ANTONIO   And the rarest that e'er came there.   101
SEBASTIAN   Bate, I beseech you, widow Dido.   102
ANTONIO   O, widow Dido? Ay, widow Dido.
GONZALO   Is not, sir, my doublet as fresh as the first day   104
  I wore it? I mean, in a sort.   105
ANTONIO   That "sort" was well fished for.   106
GONZALO   When I wore it at your daughter's marriage.
ALONSO
  You cram these words into mine ears against   108
  The stomach of my sense. Would I had never   109

82 take understand, respond to, interpret   **83–84 study of** think about
88 miraculous harp (Alludes to Amphion's harp with which he raised
the walls of Thebes; Gonzalo has exceeded that deed by creating a
modern Carthage—walls *and houses*—mistakenly on the site of Tunis.)
94 kernels seeds   **96 Ay** (Gonzalo may be reasserting his point about
Carthage, or he may be responding ironically to Antonio who in turn
answers sarcastically.)   **97 in good time** (An expression of ironical
acquiescence or amazement; i.e., "sure, right away.")   **98 talking** saying   **101 rarest** most remarkable, beautiful   **102 Bate** abate, except,
leave out. (Sebastian says, don't forget Dido; or, let's have no more talk
of Dido.)   **104 doublet** close-fitting jacket   **105 in a sort** in a way
106 sort (Antonio plays on the idea of drawing lots.)   **108–109 against
. . . sense** i.e., against my will.   **stomach** appetite

Married my daughter there! For, coming thence,   110
My son is lost and, in my rate, she too,   111
Who is so far from Italy removed
I ne'er again shall see her. O thou mine heir
Of Naples and of Milan, what strange fish
Hath made his meal on thee?
FRANCISCO   Sir, he may live.   115
I saw him beat the surges under him   116
And ride upon their backs. He trod the water,
Whose enmity he flung aside, and breasted
The surge most swoll'n that met him. His bold head
'Bove the contentious waves he kept, and oared
Himself with his good arms in lusty stroke   121
To th' shore, that o'er his wave-worn basis bowed,   122
As stooping to relieve him. I not doubt   123
He came alive to land.
ALONSO   No, no, he's gone.   124
SEBASTIAN [*To Alonso*]
Sir, you may thank yourself for this great loss,
That would not bless our Europe with your daughter,   126
But rather loose her to an African,   127
Where she at least is banished from your eye,   128
Who hath cause to wet the grief on 't.
ALONSO   Prithee, peace.   129
SEBASTIAN
You were kneeled to and importuned otherwise   130
By all of us, and the fair soul herself   131
Weighed between loathness and obedience at   132
Which end o' the beam should bow. We have lost your
  son,   133

110 **Married** given in marriage   111 **rate** estimation, opinion
115 **made his meal** fed himself   116 **surges** waves   121 **lusty** vigorous
122 **that ... bowed** i.e., that projected out over the base of the cliff that
had been eroded by the surf, thus seeming to bend down toward the
sea   123 **As** as if.   **I not** I do not   124 **came ... land** reached land
alive   126 **That** you who   127 **rather** would rather.   **loose** (1) release,
let loose (2) lose   128 **is banished from your eye** is not constantly before
your eye to serve as a reproachful reminder of what you have done
129 **Who ... on 't** i.e., your eye, which has good reason to weep because
of this, or, Claribel, who has good reason to weep for it   130 **importuned** urged, implored   131–133 **the fair ... bow** i.e., Claribel herself
was poised uncertainly between unwillingness to marry and obedience
to her father as to which end of the scale should sink, which should
prevail

I fear, forever. Milan and Naples have
More widows in them of this business' making   135
Than we bring men to comfort them.
The fault's your own.
ALONSO   So is the dear'st o' the loss.   138
GONZALO   My lord Sebastian,
The truth you speak doth lack some gentleness
And time to speak it in. You rub the sore   141
When you should bring the plaster.
SEBASTIAN   Very well.   142
ANTONIO   And most chirurgeonly.   143
GONZALO [*To Alonso*]
It is foul weather in us all, good sir,
When you are cloudy.
SEBASTIAN [*To Antonio*] Fowl weather?
ANTONIO [*To Sebastian*]   Very foul.   145
GONZALO
Had I plantation of this isle, my lord—   146
ANTONIO [*To Sebastian*]
He'd sow 't with nettle seed.
SEBASTIAN   Or docks, or mallows.   147
GONZALO
And were the king on 't, what would I do?
SEBASTIAN   Scape being drunk for want of wine.   149
GONZALO
I' the commonwealth I would by contraries   150
Execute all things; for no kind of traffic   151
Would I admit; no name of magistrate;
Letters should not be known; riches, poverty,   153
And use of service, none; contract, succession,   154

---

135 of . . . making on account of this marriage   **138 dear'st** heaviest,
most costly   **141 time** appropriate time   **142 plaster** (A medical application.)   **143 chirurgeonly** like a skilled surgeon. (Antonio mocks Gonzalo's medical analogy of a *plaster* applied curatively to a wound.)
145 Fowl (with a pun on *foul*, returning to the imagery of ll. 30–35)
146 plantation colonization (with subsequent wordplay on the literal
meaning)   **147 docks, mallows** (Weeds used as antidotes for nettle
stings.)   **149 Scape** escape.   **want** lack. (Sebastian jokes sarcastically
that this hypothetical ruler would be saved from dissipation only by the
barrenness of the island.)   **150 by contraries** by what is directly opposite to usual custom   **151 traffic** trade   **153 Letters** learning   **154 use
of service** custom of employing servants.   **succession** holding of property by right of inheritance

Bourn, bound of land, tilth, vineyard, none;   155
No use of metal, corn, or wine, or oil;   156
No occupation; all men idle, all,
And women too, but innocent and pure;
No sovereignty—

SEBASTIAN   Yet he would be king on 't.

ANTONIO   The latter end of his commonwealth forgets
the beginning.

GONZALO
All things in common nature should produce
Without sweat or endeavor. Treason, felony,
Sword, pike, knife, gun, or need of any engine   164
Would I not have; but nature should bring forth,
Of its own kind, all foison, all abundance,   166
To feed my innocent people.

SEBASTIAN   No marrying 'mong his subjects?

ANTONIO   None, man, all idle—whores and knaves.

GONZALO
I would with such perfection govern, sir,
T' excel the Golden Age.

SEBASTIAN   Save His Majesty!   171

ANTONIO
Long live Gonzalo!

GONZALO   And—do you mark me, sir?

ALONSO
Prithee, no more. Thou dost talk nothing to me.

GONZALO   I do well believe Your Highness, and did it to
minister occasion to these gentlemen, who are of such   175
sensible and nimble lungs that they always use to   176
laugh at nothing.

ANTONIO   'Twas you we laughed at.

GONZALO   Who in this kind of merry fooling am nothing
to you; so you may continue, and laugh at nothing still.

ANTONIO   What a blow was there given!

SEBASTIAN   An it had not fallen flat-long.   182

---

155 Bourn boundaries.   **bound of land** landmarks.   **tilth** tillage of
soil   **156 corn** grain   **164 pike** lance.   **engine** instrument of warfare
166 foison plenty   **171 the Golden Age** the age, according to Hesiod,
when Cronus, or Saturn, ruled the world; an age of innocence and
abundance.   **Save** God save   **175 minister occasion** furnish opportunity   **176 sensible** sensitive.   **use** are accustomed   **182 An** if.   **flat-long**
with the flat of the sword, i.e., ineffectually. (Cf. "fallen flat.")

GONZALO You are gentlemen of brave mettle; you 183
would lift the moon out of her sphere if she would 184
continue in it five weeks without changing.

Enter Ariel [invisible] playing solemn music. .

SEBASTIAN We would so, and then go a-batfowling.   186
ANTONIO Nay, good my lord, be not angry.
GONZALO No, I warrant you, I will not adventure my 188
discretion so weakly. Will you laugh me asleep? For I 189
am very heavy.   190
ANTONIO Go sleep, and hear us.   191
[*All sleep except Alonso, Sebastian, and Antonio.*]
ALONSO
What, all so soon asleep? I wish mine eyes
Would, with themselves, shut up my thoughts. I find 193
They are inclined to do so.
SEBASTIAN   Please you, sir,
Do not omit the heavy offer of it.   195
It seldom visits sorrow; when it doth,
It is a comforter.
ANTONIO   We two, my lord,
Will guard your person while you take your rest,
And watch your safety.
ALONSO   Thank you. Wondrous heavy.
[*Alonso sleeps. Exit Ariel.*]
SEBASTIAN
What a strange drowsiness possesses them!
ANTONIO
It is the quality o' the climate.
SEBASTIAN   Why

---

183 mettle temperament, courage. (The sense of *metal*, indistinguishable
as a form from *mettle*, continues the metaphor of the sword.)
184 sphere orbit. (Literally, one of the concentric zones occupied by
planets in the Ptolemaic astronomy.) **186 a-batfowling** hunting birds at
night with lantern and *bat* or stick; also, gulling a simpleton. (Gonzalo is
the simpleton, or fowl, and Sebastian will use the moon as his lantern.) **188–189 adventure . . . weakly** risk my reputation for discretion
for so trivial a cause (by getting angry at these sarcastic fellows)
190 heavy sleepy **191 Go . . . us** let our laughing send you to sleep, or,
go to sleep and hear us laugh at you **193 Would . . . thoughts** would
shut off my melancholy brooding when they close themselves in
sleep **195 omit** neglect. **heavy** drowsy

Doth it not then our eyelids sink? I find not
Myself disposed to sleep.

ANTONIO   Nor I. My spirits are nimble.
They fell together all, as by consent;   204
They dropped, as by a thunderstroke. What might,
Worthy Sebastian, O, what might—? No more.
And yet methinks I see it in thy face,
What thou shouldst be. Th' occasion speaks thee, and   208
My strong imagination sees a crown
Dropping upon thy head.

SEBASTIAN   What, art thou waking?

ANTONIO
Do you not hear me speak?

SEBASTIAN   I do, and surely
It is a sleepy language, and thou speak'st
Out of thy sleep. What is it thou didst say?
This is a strange repose, to be asleep
With eyes wide open—standing, speaking, moving—
And yet so fast asleep.

ANTONIO   Noble Sebastian,
Thou lett'st thy fortune sleep—die, rather; wink'st   217
Whiles thou art waking.

SEBASTIAN   Thou dost snore distinctly;   218
There's meaning in thy snores.

ANTONIO
I am more serious than my custom. You
Must be so too, if heed me; which to do   221
Trebles thee o'er.

SEBASTIAN   Well, I am standing water.   222

ANTONIO
I'll teach you how to flow.

SEBASTIAN   Do so. To ebb   223
Hereditary sloth instructs me.

ANTONIO   O,   224

---

204 consent common agreement **208 occasion** opportunity of the
moment. **speaks thee** i.e., calls upon you, proclaims you usurper of
Alonso's crown **217 wink'st** (you) shut your eyes **218 distinctly** articu-
lately **221 if heed** if you heed **222 Trebles thee o'er** makes you three
times as great and rich. **standing water** water that neither ebbs nor
flows, at a standstill **223 ebb** recede, decline **224 Hereditary sloth**
natural laziness and the position of younger brother, one who cannot
inherit

If you but knew how you the purpose cherish   225
Whiles thus you mock it! How, in stripping it,   226
You more invest it! Ebbing men, indeed,   227
Most often do so near the bottom run   228
By their own fear or sloth.

SEBASTIAN   Prithee, say on.
The setting of thine eye and cheek proclaim   230
A matter from thee, and a birth indeed   231
Which throes thee much to yield.

ANTONIO   Thus, sir: 232
Although this lord of weak remembrance, this   233
Who shall be of as little memory
When he is earthed, hath here almost persuaded—   235
For he's a spirit of persuasion, only   236
Professes to persuade—the King his son's alive,   237
'Tis as impossible that he's undrowned
As he that sleeps here swims.

SEBASTIAN   I have no hope
That he's undrowned.

ANTONIO   O, out of that "no hope"
What great hope have you! No hope that way is   241
Another way so high a hope that even
Ambition cannot pierce a wink beyond,   243
But doubt discovery there. Will you grant with me   244
That Ferdinand is drowned?

SEBASTIAN   He's gone.

225–226 If . . . mock it i.e., if you only knew how much you really
enhance the value of ambition even while your words mock your purpose   **226–227 How . . . invest it** i.e., how the more you speak flippantly
of ambition, the more you in effect affirm it.   **invest** clothe. (Antonio's
paradox is that by skeptically stripping away illusions Sebastian can see
the essence of a situation and the opportunity it presents, or that by
disclaiming and deriding his purpose Sebastian shows how he values
it.)   **228 the bottom** i.e., on which unadventurous men may go aground
and miss the tide of fortune   **230 setting** set expression (of earnest-
ness)   **231 matter** matter of importance   **232 throes** causes pain, as in
giving birth.   **yield** give forth, speak about   **233 this lord** i.e., Gonzalo.   **remembrance** (1) power of remembering (2) being remembered
after his death   **235 earthed** buried   **236–237 only . . . persuade** i.e.,
whose whole function (as a privy councillor) is to persuade   **241 that
way** i.e., in regard to Ferdinand's being saved   **243–244 Ambition . . .
there** ambition itself cannot see any further than that hope (of the
crown), but is unsure of itself in seeing even so far, is dazzled by daring
to think so high.   **wink** glimpse

ANTONIO   Then tell me,
  Who's the next heir of Naples?
SEBASTIAN   Claribel.
ANTONIO
  She that is Queen of Tunis; she that dwells
  Ten leagues beyond man's life; she that from Naples   248
  Can have no note, unless the sun were post—   249
  The man i' the moon's too slow—till newborn chins
  Be rough and razorable; she that from whom   251
  We all were sea-swallowed, though some cast again,   252
  And by that destiny to perform an act
  Whereof what's past is prologue, what to come
  In yours and my discharge.   255
SEBASTIAN   What stuff is this? How say you?
  'Tis true my brother's daughter's Queen of Tunis,
  So is she heir of Naples, twixt which regions
  There is some space.
ANTONIO   A space whose every cubit   259
  Seems to cry out, "How shall that Claribel
  Measure us back to Naples? Keep in Tunis,   261
  And let Sebastian wake." Say this were death   262
  That now hath seized them, why, they were no worse
  Than now they are. There be that can rule Naples   264
  As well as he that sleeps, lords that can prate   265
  As amply and unnecessarily
  As this Gonzalo. I myself could make   267
  A chough of as deep chat. O, that you bore   268
  The mind that I do! What a sleep were this
  For your advancement! Do you understand me?
SEBASTIAN
  Methinks I do.
ANTONIO   And how does your content   271

---

248 Ten . . . life i.e., it would take more than a lifetime to get there
249 note news, intimation. **post** messenger **251 razorable** ready for
shaving. **from** on our voyage from **252 cast** were disgorged (with a
pun on *casting* of parts for a play) **255 discharge** performance
259 cubit ancient measure of length of about twenty inches
261 Measure us i.e., traverse the cubits, find her way. **Keep** stay.
(Addressed to Claribel.) **262 wake** i.e., to his good fortune **264 There
be** there are those **265 prate** speak foolishly **267–268 I . . . chat** I
could teach a jackdaw to talk as wisely, or, be such a garrulous talker
myself **271 content** desire, inclination

Tender your own good fortune?

SEBASTIAN   I remember   272
You did supplant your brother Prospero.

ANTONIO   True.
And look how well my garments sit upon me,
Much feater than before. My brother's servants   275
Were then my fellows. Now they are my men.

SEBASTIAN   But, for your conscience?

ANTONIO
Ay, sir, where lies that? If 'twere a kibe,   278
'Twould put me to my slipper; but I feel not   279
This deity in my bosom. Twenty consciences
That stand twixt me and Milan, candied be they   281
And melt ere they molest! Here lies your brother, 282
No better than the earth he lies upon,
If he were that which now he's like—that's dead,
Whom I, with this obedient steel, three inches of it,
Can lay to bed forever; whiles you, doing thus,   286
To the perpetual wink for aye might put   287
This ancient morsel, this Sir Prudence, who
Should not upbraid our course. For all the rest,   289
They'll take suggestion as a cat laps milk;   290
They'll tell the clock to any business that   291
We say befits the hour.

SEBASTIAN   Thy case, dear friend,
Shall be my precedent. As thou gott'st Milan,
I'll come by Naples. Draw thy sword. One stroke
Shall free thee from the tribute which thou payest, 295
And I the king shall love thee.

ANTONIO   Draw together;
And when I rear my hand, do you the like
To fall it on Gonzalo.   [*They draw.*]

SEBASTIAN   O, but one word.   298
                              [*They talk apart.*]

---

272 Tender regard, look after   **275 feater** more becomingly, fittingly
278 kibe chilblain, here a sore on the heel   **279 put me to** oblige me to
wear   **281 Milan** the dukedom of Milan.   **candied** frozen, congealed in
crystalline form.   **be they** may they be   **282 molest** interfere   **286 thus**
(The actor makes a stabbing gesture.)   **287 wink** sleep, closing of eyes.
aye ever   **289 Should not** would not then be able to   **290 take suggestion** respond to prompting   **291 tell the clock** i.e., agree, answer appropriately, chime   **295 tribute** (See 1.2.113–124.)   **298 fall it** let it fall

Enter Ariel [invisible], with music and song.

ARIEL
  My master through his art foresees the danger
  That you, his friend, are in, and sends me forth—
  For else his project dies—to keep them living.
                              Sings in Gonzalo's ear.

    While you here do snoring lie,
    Open-eyed conspiracy
        His time doth take.   304
    If of life you keep a care,
    Shake off slumber, and beware.
        Awake, awake!

ANTONIO   Then let us both be sudden.   308
GONZALO [*Waking*]   Now, good angels preserve the King!
                              [*The others wake.*]
ALONSO
  Why, how now, ho, awake? Why are you drawn?
  Wherefore this ghastly looking?
GONZALO   What's the matter?
SEBASTIAN
  Whiles we stood here securing your repose,   312
  Even now, we heard a hollow burst of bellowing
  Like bulls, or rather lions. Did 't not wake you?
  It struck mine ear most terribly.
ALONSO   I heard nothing.
ANTONIO
  O, 'twas a din to fright a monster's ear,
  To make an earthquake! Sure it was the roar
  Of a whole herd of lions.
ALONSO   Heard you this, Gonzalo?
GONZALO
  Upon mine honor, sir, I heard a humming,
  And that a strange one too, which did awake me.
  I shaked you, sir, and cried. As mine eyes opened,   322
  I saw their weapons drawn. There was a noise,
  That's verily. 'Tis best we stand upon our guard,   324
  Or that we quit this place. Let's draw our weapons.

304 time opportunity   **308 sudden** quick   **312 securing** standing guard
over   **322 cried** called out   **324 verily** true

ALONSO
  Lead off this ground, and let's make further search
  For my poor son.
GONZALO   Heavens keep him from these beasts!
  For he is, sure, i' th' island.
ALONSO   Lead away.
ARIEL [*Aside*]
  Prospero my lord shall know what I have done.
  So, King, go safely on to seek thy son.
                         Exeunt [separately].

❧

2.2   *Enter Caliban with a burden of wood. A noise
       of thunder heard.*

CALIBAN
  All the infections that the sun sucks up
  From bogs, fens, flats, on Prosper fall, and make him   2
  By inchmeal a disease! His spirits hear me,   3
  And yet I needs must curse. But they'll nor pinch,   4
  Fright me with urchin shows, pitch me i' the mire,   5
  Nor lead me, like a firebrand, in the dark   6
  Out of my way, unless he bid 'em. But
  For every trifle are they set upon me,
  Sometimes like apes, that mow and chatter at me   9
  And after bite me; then like hedgehogs, which
  Lie tumbling in my barefoot way and mount
  Their pricks at my footfall. Sometimes am I
  All wound with adders, who with cloven tongues   13
  Do hiss me into madness.

    Enter Trinculo.

                 Lo, now, lo!
  Here comes a spirit of his, and to torment me
  For bringing wood in slowly. I'll fall flat.
  Perchance he will not mind me.   [*He lies down.*] 17

2.2. Location: Another part of the island.
2 flats swamps   **3 By inchmeal** inch by inch   **4 needs must** have to.
nor neither   **5 urchin shows** elvish apparitions shaped like hedgehogs
6 like a firebrand in the guise of a will-o'-the-wisp   **9 mow** make
faces   **13 wound with** entwined by   **17 mind** notice

TRINCULO Here's neither bush nor shrub to bear off 18
any weather at all. And another storm brewing; I hear
it sing i' the wind. Yond same black cloud, yond huge
one, looks like a foul bombard that would shed his 21
liquor. If it should thunder as it did before, I know not
where to hide my head. Yond same cloud cannot
choose but fall by pailfuls. [*Seeing Caliban.*] What have
we here, a man or a fish? Dead or alive? A fish, he
smells like a fish; a very ancient and fishlike smell; a
kind of not-of-the-newest Poor John. A strange fish! 27
Were I in England now, as once I was, and had but
this fish painted, not a holiday fool there but would 29
give a piece of silver. There would this monster make 30
a man. Any strange beast there makes a man. When 31
they will not give a doit to relieve a lame beggar, they 32
will lay out ten to see a dead Indian. Legged like a
man, and his fins like arms! Warm, o' my troth! I do 34
now let loose my opinion, hold it no longer: this is no 35
fish, but an islander, that hath lately suffered by a 36
thunderbolt. [*Thunder.*] Alas, the storm is come again!
My best way is to creep under his gaberdine. There is 38
no other shelter hereabout. Misery acquaints a man
with strange bedfellows. I will here shroud till the 40
dregs of the storm be past. 41

        [*He creeps under Caliban's garment.*]

   Enter Stephano, singing, [a bottle in his hand].

STEPHANO
    "I shall no more to sea, to sea,
      Here shall I die ashore—"
This is a very scurvy tune to sing at a man's funeral.
Well, here's my comfort.   *Drinks.*

---

18 bear off keep off **21 foul bombard** dirty leather jug. **his** its
27 Poor John salted fish, type of poor fare **29 painted** i.e., painted on a
sign set up outside a booth or tent at a fair **30–31 make a man**
(1) make one's fortune (2) be indistinguishable from an Englishman
32 doit small coin **34 o' my troth** by my faith **35 hold it** hold it in
36 suffered i.e., died **38 gaberdine** cloak, loose upper garment
40 shroud take shelter **41 dregs** i.e., last remains (as in a *bombard* or
jug, l. 21)

(Sings.)

"The master, the swabber, the boatswain, and I,   46
     The gunner and his mate,
Loved Mall, Meg, and Marian, and Margery,
     But none of us cared for Kate.
       For she had a tongue with a tang,   50
       Would cry to a sailor, 'Go hang!'
She loved not the savor of tar nor of pitch,
Yet a tailor might scratch her where'er she did itch.   53
     Then to sea, boys, and let her go hang!"

This is a scurvy tune too. But here's my comfort.
                                     Drinks.

CALIBAN   Do not torment me! O!   56

STEPHANO   What's the matter? Have we devils here? Do   57
you put tricks upon 's with savages and men of Ind,   58
ha? I have not scaped drowning to be afeard now of
your four legs. For it hath been said, "As proper a man   60
as ever went on four legs cannot make him give   61
ground"; and it shall be said so again while Stephano
breathes at' nostrils.   63

CALIBAN   This spirit torments me! O!

STEPHANO   This is some monster of the isle with four
legs, who hath got, as I take it, an ague. Where the   66
devil should he learn our language? I will give him   67
some relief, if it be but for that. If I can recover him   68
and keep him tame and get to Naples with him, he's
a present for any emperor that ever trod on neat's   70
leather.   71

CALIBAN   Do not torment me, prithee. I'll bring my
wood home faster.

---

46 swabber crew member whose job is to wash the decks   **50 tang**
sting   **53 tailor . . . itch** (A dig at tailors for their supposed effeminacy
and a bawdy suggestion of satisfying a sexual craving.)   **56 Do . . . me**
(Caliban assumes that one of Prospero's spirits has come to punish
him.)   **57 What's the matter** what's going on here   **58 put tricks
upon 's** trick us with conjuring shows.   **Ind** India   **60 proper** handsome   **61 four legs** (The conventional phrase would supply *two legs*.)
63 at' at the   **66 ague** fever. (Probably both Caliban and Trinculo are
quaking; see ll. 56 and 81.)   **67 should he learn** could he have learned
68 for that i.e., for knowing our language.   **recover** restore
70–71 neat's leather cowhide

STEPHANO He's in his fit now and does not talk after   74
the wisest. He shall taste of my bottle. If he have never   75
drunk wine afore, it will go near to remove his fit. If I   76
can recover him and keep him tame, I will not take too   77
much for him. He shall pay for him that hath him, and   78
that soundly.

CALIBAN Thou does me yet but little hurt; thou wilt
anon, I know it by thy trembling. Now Prosper works   81
upon thee.

STEPHANO Come on your ways. Open your mouth. Here
is that which will give language to you, cat. Open your   84
mouth. This will shake your shaking, I can tell you,   85
and that soundly. [*Giving Caliban a drink.*] You cannot
tell who's your friend. Open your chaps again.   87

TRINCULO I should know that voice. It should be—but
he is drowned, and these are devils. O, defend me!

STEPHANO Four legs and two voices—a most delicate   90
monster! His forward voice now is to speak well of his
friend; his backward voice is to utter foul speeches and   92
to detract. If all the wine in my bottle will recover him, 93
I will help his ague. Come. [*Giving a drink.*] Amen! I   94
will pour some in thy other mouth.

TRINCULO Stephano!

STEPHANO Doth thy other mouth call me? Mercy,   97
mercy! This is a devil, and no monster. I will leave
him. I have no long spoon.   99

TRINCULO Stephano! If thou beest Stephano, touch me
and speak to me, for I am Trinculo—be not afeard—
thy good friend Trinculo.

STEPHANO If thou beest Trinculo, come forth. I'll pull

74–75 after the wisest in the wisest fashion **76 afore** before. **go near
to** nearly **77 recover** restore **77–78 I will . . . much** i.e., no sum can be
too much **78 He shall . . . hath him** i.e., anyone who wants him will
have to pay dearly for him. **hath** possesses, receives **81 anon** presently **84–85 cat . . . mouth** (Allusion to the proverb "Good liquor will
make a cat speak.") **87 chaps** jaws **90 delicate** ingenious **92 backward voice** (Trinculo and Caliban are facing in opposite directions.
Stephano supposes the monster to have a rear end that can emit *foul
speeches* or foul-smelling wind at the monster's *other mouth*, l. 95.)
93 If . . . him even if it takes all the wine in my bottle to cure him
94 help cure **97 call me** i.e., call me by name, know supernaturally
who I am **99 long spoon** (Allusion to the proverb "He that sups with
the devil has need of a long spoon.")

thee by the lesser legs. If any be Trinculo's legs, these
are they. [*Pulling him out.*] Thou art very Trinculo indeed! How cam'st thou to be the siege of this moon-   106
calf? Can he vent Trinculos?   107

TRINCULO   I took him to be killed with a thunderstroke.
But art thou not drowned, Stephano? I hope now thou
art not drowned. Is the storm overblown? I hid me un-   110
der the dead mooncalf's gaberdine for fear of the
storm. And art thou living, Stephano? O Stephano,
two Neapolitans scaped!   [*He capers with Stephano.*]

STEPHANO   Prithee, do not turn me about. My stomach
is not constant.   115

CALIBAN
These be fine things, an if they be not spirits.   116
That's a brave god, and bears celestial liquor.   117
I will kneel to him.

STEPHANO   How didst thou scape? How cam'st thou
hither? Swear by this bottle how thou cam'st hither. I
escaped upon a butt of sack which the sailors heaved   121
o'erboard—by this bottle, which I made of the bark of   122
a tree with mine own hands since I was cast ashore.   123

CALIBAN [*Kneeling*]   I'll swear upon that bottle to be thy
true subject, for the liquor is not earthly.

STEPHANO   Here. Swear then how thou escapedst.

TRINCULO   Swum ashore, man, like a duck. I can swim
like a duck, I'll be sworn.

STEPHANO   Here, kiss the book. Though thou canst   129
swim like a duck, thou art made like a goose.
[*Giving him a drink.*]

TRINCULO   O Stephano, hast any more of this?

STEPHANO   The whole butt, man. My cellar is in a rock
by the seaside, where my wine is hid.—How now,
mooncalf? How does thine ague?

CALIBAN   Hast thou not dropped from heaven?

---

106 siege excrement   **106–107 mooncalf** monstrous or misshapen
creature (whose deformity is caused by the malignant influence of the
moon)   **107 vent** excrete, defecate   **110 overblown** blown over   **115 not
constant** unsteady   **116 an if** if   **117 brave** fine, magnificent.   **bears** he
carries   **121 butt of sack** barrel of Canary wine   **122 by this bottle** i.e.,
I swear by this bottle   **123 since** after   **129 book** i.e., bottle (but with
ironic reference to the practice of kissing the Bible in swearing an oath;
see *I'll be sworn* in l. 128)

STEPHANO   Out o' the moon, I do assure thee. I was the
man i' the moon when time was.   137
CALIBAN
I have seen thee in her, and I do adore thee.
My mistress showed me thee, and thy dog, and thy bush 139
STEPHANO   Come, swear to that. Kiss the book. I will
furnish it anon with new contents. Swear.
                              [*Giving him a drink.*]
TRINCULO   By this good light, this is a very shallow   142
monster! I afeard of him? A very weak monster! The
man i' the moon? A most poor credulous monster! Well 144
drawn, monster, in good sooth!   145
CALIBAN [*To Stephano*]
I'll show thee every fertile inch o' th' island,
And I will kiss thy foot. I prithee, be my god.
TRINCULO   By this light, a most perfidious and drunken
monster! When 's god's asleep, he'll rob his bottle.   149
CALIBAN
I'll kiss thy foot. I'll swear myself thy subject.
STEPHANO   Come on then. Down, and swear.
                              [*Caliban kneels.*]
TRINCULO   I shall laugh myself to death at this puppy-
headed monster. A most scurvy monster! I could find
in my heart to beat him—
STEPHANO   Come, kiss.
TRINCULO   But that the poor monster's in drink. An   156
abominable monster!
CALIBAN
I'll show thee the best springs. I'll pluck thee berries.
I'll fish for thee and get thee wood enough.
A plague upon the tyrant that I serve!
I'll bear him no more sticks, but follow thee,
Thou wondrous man.
TRINCULO   A most ridiculous monster, to make a won-
der of a poor drunkard!

---

137 when time was once upon a time   **139 dog . . . bush** (The man in
the moon was popularly imagined to have with him a dog and a bush
of thorn.)   **142 By . . . light** by God's light, by this good light from
heaven   **144–145 Well drawn** well pulled (on the bottle)   **145 in good
sooth** truly, indeed   **149 When . . . bottle** i.e., Caliban wouldn't even
stop at robbing his god of his bottle if he could catch him asleep
156 in drink drunk

CALIBAN

I prithee, let me bring thee where crabs grow;   165
And I with my long nails will dig thee pignuts,   166
Show thee a jay's nest, and instruct thee how
To snare the nimble marmoset. I'll bring thee   168
To clustering filberts, and sometimes I'll get thee
Young scamels from the rock. Wilt thou go with me?   170

STEPHANO   I prithee now, lead the way without any
more talking.—Trinculo, the King and all our company
else being drowned, we will inherit here.—Here, bear   173
my bottle.—Fellow Trinculo, we'll fill him by and by
again.

CALIBAN (*Sings drunkenly*)

Farewell, master, farewell, farewell!

TRINCULO   A howling monster; a drunken monster!

CALIBAN

No more dams I'll make for fish,
    Nor fetch in firing   179
    At requiring,
Nor scrape trenchering, nor wash dish.   181
    'Ban, 'Ban, Ca–Caliban
    Has a new master. Get a new man!   183
Freedom, high-day! High-day, freedom! Freedom,   184
high-day, freedom!

STEPHANO   O brave monster! Lead the way.   *Exeunt.*

❦

165 crabs crab apples, or perhaps crabs   **166 pignuts** earthnuts, edible
tuberous roots   **168 marmoset** small monkey   **170 scamels** (Possibly
seamews, mentioned in Strachey's letter, or shellfish; or perhaps from
squamelle, furnished with little scales. Contemporary French and
Italian travel accounts report that the natives of Patagonia in South
America ate small fish described as *fort scameux* and *squame*.)
173 else in addition, besides ourselves.   **inherit** take possession
179 firing firewood   **181 trenchering** trenchers, wooden plates   **183 Get
a new man** (Addressed to Prospero.)   **184 high-day** holiday

3.1   *Enter Ferdinand, bearing a log.*

FERDINAND
There be some sports are painful, and their labor   1
Delight in them sets off. Some kinds of baseness   2
Are nobly undergone, and most poor matters   3
Point to rich ends. This my mean task   4
Would be as heavy to me as odious, but   5
The mistress which I serve quickens what's dead   6
And makes my labors pleasures. O, she is
Ten times more gentle than her father's crabbèd,
And he's composed of harshness. I must remove
Some thousands of these logs and pile them up,
Upon a sore injunction. My sweet mistress   11
Weeps when she sees me work and says such baseness
Had never like executor. I forget;   13
But these sweet thoughts do even refresh my labors,
Most busy lest when I do it.

> *Enter Miranda; and Prospero [at a distance,
> unseen].*

MIRANDA   Alas now, pray you,   15
Work not so hard. I would the lightning had
Burnt up those logs that you are enjoined to pile!   17
Pray, set it down and rest you. When this burns,   18
'Twill weep for having wearied you. My father   19
Is hard at study. Pray now, rest yourself.
He's safe for these three hours.

FERDINAND   O most dear mistress,   21

3.1. Location: Before Prospero's cell.
1 sports pastimes, activities. **painful** laborious   **1–2 and their . . . sets
off** i.e., but the pleasure we get from those pastimes compensates for
the effort   **2 baseness** menial activity   **3 undergone** undertaken. **most
poor** poorest   **4 mean** lowly   **5 but** were it not that   **6 quickens** gives
life to   **11 sore injunction** severe command   **13 Had . . . executor** i.e.,
was never before undertaken by one of my noble rank.   **I forget** i.e., I
forget that I'm supposed to be working, or, I forget my happiness,
oppressed by my labor   **15 Most . . . it** i.e., least troubled by my labor,
and most active in my thoughts, when I think of her (?) (The line may be
in need of emendation.)   **17 enjoined** commanded   **18 this** i.e., the
log   **19 weep** i.e., exude resin   **21 these** i.e., the next

The sun will set before I shall discharge   22
What I must strive to do.
MIRANDA   If you'll sit down,
I'll bear your logs the while. Pray, give me that.
I'll carry it to the pile.
FERDINAND   No, precious creature,
I had rather crack my sinews, break my back,
Than you should such dishonor undergo
While I sit lazy by.
MIRANDA   It would become me
As well as it does you; and I should do it
With much more ease, for my good will is to it,
And yours it is against.
PROSPERO [*Aside*]   Poor worm, thou art infected!
This visitation shows it.
MIRANDA   You look wearily.   32
FERDINAND
No, noble mistress, 'tis fresh morning with me
When you are by at night. I do beseech you—   34
Chiefly that I might set it in my prayers—
What is your name?
MIRANDA   Miranda.—O my father,
I have broke your hest to say so.
FERDINAND   Admired Miranda!   37
Indeed the top of admiration, worth
What's dearest to the world! Full many a lady   39
I have eyed with best regard, and many a time   40
The harmony of their tongues hath into bondage
Brought my too diligent ear. For several virtues   42
Have I liked several women, never any
With so full soul but some defect in her
Did quarrel with the noblest grace she owed   45
And put it to the foil. But you, O you,   46

22 discharge complete   **32 visitation** (1) visit of the sick (2) visitation of
the plague, i.e., infection of love   **34 by** nearby   **37 hest** command.
Admired Miranda (Her name means "to be admired or wondered at.")
39 dearest most treasured   **40 best regard** thoughtful and approving
attention   **42 diligent** attentive.   **several** various (also in l. 43)   **45 owed**
owned   **46 put . . . foil** (1) overthrew it (as in wrestling) (2) served as a
foil, or contrast, to set it off

So perfect and so peerless, are created
Of every creature's best!

MIRANDA   I do not know   48
One of my sex; no woman's face remember,
Save, from my glass, mine own. Nor have I seen
More that I may call men than you, good friend,
And my dear father. How features are abroad   52
I am skilless of; but, by my modesty,   53
The jewel in my dower, I would not wish
Any companion in the world but you;
Nor can imagination form a shape,
Besides yourself, to like of. But I prattle   57
Something too wildly, and my father's precepts   58
I therein do forget.

FERDINAND   I am in my condition   59
A prince, Miranda; I do think, a king—
I would, not so!—and would no more endure   61
This wooden slavery than to suffer   62
The flesh-fly blow my mouth. Hear my soul speak: 63
The very instant that I saw you did
My heart fly to your service, there resides
To make me slave to it, and for your sake
Am I this patient log-man.

MIRANDA   Do you love me?

FERDINAND
O heaven, O earth, bear witness to this sound,
And crown what I profess with kind event   69
If I speak true! If hollowly, invert   70
What best is boded me to mischief! I   71
Beyond all limit of what else i' the world   72
Do love, prize, honor you.

MIRANDA [*Weeping*]   I am a fool
To weep at what I am glad of.

---

48 Of out of   **52 How . . . abroad** what people look like other places
53 skilless ignorant.   **modesty** virginity   **57 like of** be pleased with, be
fond of   **58 Something** somewhat   **59 condition** rank   **61 would** wish
(it were)   **62 wooden slavery** being compelled to carry wood   **63 flesh-
fly** insect that deposits its eggs in dead flesh.   **blow** befoul with fly
eggs   **69 kind event** favorable outcome   **70 hollowly** insincerely,
falsely.   **invert** turn   **71 boded** destined for.   **mischief** evil   **72 what**
whatever

PROSPERO [*Aside*]   Fair encounter
  Of two most rare affections! Heavens rain grace
  On that which breeds between 'em!
FERDINAND   Wherefore weep you?
MIRANDA
  At mine unworthiness, that dare not offer
  What I desire to give, and much less take
  What I shall die to want. But this is trifling,   79
  And all the more it seeks to hide itself
  The bigger bulk it shows. Hence, bashful cunning,   81
  And prompt me, plain and holy innocence!
  I am your wife, if you will marry me;
  If not, I'll die your maid. To be your fellow   84
  You may deny me, but I'll be your servant
  Whether you will or no.
FERDINAND   My mistress, dearest,   86
  And I thus humble ever.
MIRANDA   My husband, then?
FERDINAND   Ay, with a heart as willing   89
  As bondage e'er of freedom. Here's my hand.
MIRANDA [*Clasping his hand*]
  And mine, with my heart in 't. And now farewell
  Till half an hour hence.
FERDINAND   A thousand thousand!   92
            Exeunt [Ferdinand and Miranda, separately].
PROSPERO
  So glad of this as they I cannot be,
  Who are surprised with all; but my rejoicing   94
  At nothing can be more. I'll to my book,
  For yet ere suppertime must I perform
  Much business appertaining.   *Exit.* 97

✦

79 die (probably with an unconscious sexual meaning that underlies all
of ll. 77–81). **want** lack   **81 bashful cunning** coyness   **84 maid** hand-
maiden, servant.   **fellow** mate, equal   **86 will** desire it.   **My mistress**
i.e., the woman I adore and serve (not an illicit sexual partner)   **89 willing** desirous   **92 A thousand thousand** i.e., a thousand thousand fare-
wells   **94 with all** by everything that has happened; or *withal*, with it
97 appertaining related to this

3.2   *Enter Caliban, Stephano, and Trinculo.*

STEPHANO   Tell not me. When the butt is out, we will ₁
drink water, not a drop before. Therefore bear up and ₂
board 'em. Servant monster, drink to me.   ₃
TRINCULO   Servant monster? The folly of this island! ₄
They say there's but five upon this isle. We are three
of them; if th' other two be brained like us, the state ₆
totters.
STEPHANO   Drink, servant monster, when I bid thee.
Thy eyes are almost set in thy head. [*Giving a drink.*] ₉
TRINCULO   Where should they be set else? He were a ₁₀
brave monster indeed if they were set in his tail. ₁₁
STEPHANO   My man-monster hath drowned his tongue
in sack. For my part, the sea cannot drown me. I
swam, ere I could recover the shore, five and thirty ₁₄
leagues off and on. By this light, thou shalt be my lieu- ₁₅
tenant, monster, or my standard.   ₁₆
TRINCULO   Your lieutenant, if you list. He's no standard. ₁₇
STEPHANO   We'll not run, Monsieur Monster.   ₁₈
TRINCULO   Nor go neither, but you'll lie like dogs and ₁₉
yet say nothing neither.
STEPHANO   Mooncalf, speak once in thy life, if thou
beest a good mooncalf.
CALIBAN
How does thy honor? Let me lick thy shoe.
I'll not serve him. He is not valiant.
TRINCULO   Thou liest, most ignorant monster, I am in ₂₅
case to jostle a constable. Why, thou debauched fish, ₂₆

3.2. Location: Another part of the island.
1 out empty   **2–3 bear . . . 'em** (Stephano uses the terminology of
maneuvering at sea and boarding a vessel under attack as a way of
urging an assault on the liquor supply.)   **4 folly of** i.e., stupidity found
on   **6 be brained** are endowed with intelligence   **9 set** fixed in a
drunken stare; or sunk, like the sun   **10 set** placed   **11 brave** fine,
splendid   **14 recover** gain, reach   **15 leagues** units of distance each
equaling about three miles.   **off and on** intermittently.   **By this light**
(An oath: by the light of the sun.)   **16 standard** standard-bearer, ensign (as
distinguished from *lieutenant*, ll. 15–17)   **17 list** prefer.   **no standard** i.e.,
not able to stand up   **18 run** (1) retreat (2) urinate (taking Trinculo's
standard, l. 17, in the old sense of "conduit")   **19 go** walk.   **lie** (1) tell lies
(2) lie prostrate (3) excrete   **25–26 in case . . . constable** i.e., in fit condition, made valiant by drink, to taunt or challenge the police

thou, was there ever man a coward that hath drunk so
much sack as I today? Wilt thou tell a monstrous lie, 28
being but half a fish and half a monster?

CALIBAN
Lo, how he mocks me! Wilt thou let him, my lord?

TRINCULO "Lord," quoth he? That a monster should be
such a natural!   32

CALIBAN
Lo, lo, again! Bite him to death, I prithee.

STEPHANO Trinculo, keep a good tongue in your head.
If you prove a mutineer—the next tree! The poor 35
monster's my subject, and he shall not suffer indignity.

CALIBAN
I thank my noble lord. Wilt thou be pleased
To hearken once again to the suit I made to thee?

STEPHANO Marry, will I. Kneel and repeat it. I will 39
stand, and so shall Trinculo.   [*Caliban kneels.*] 40

    Enter Ariel, invisible.

CALIBAN
As I told thee before, I am subject to a tyrant,
A sorcerer, that by his cunning hath
Cheated me of the island.

ARIEL   [*Mimicking Trinculo*]
Thou liest.

CALIBAN   Thou liest, thou jesting monkey, thou!
I would my valiant master would destroy thee.
I do not lie.

STEPHANO   Trinculo, if you trouble him any more in 's
tale, by this hand, I will supplant some of your teeth. 48

TRINCULO Why, I said nothing.

STEPHANO Mum, then, and no more.—Proceed.

CALIBAN
I say by sorcery he got this isle;
From me he got it. If thy greatness will
Revenge it on him—for I know thou dar'st,
But this thing dare not—   54

---

28 sack Spanish white wine   **32 natural** (1) idiot (2) natural as opposed
to unnatural, monsterlike   **35 the next tree** i.e., you'll hang   **39 Marry**
i.e., indeed. (Originally an oath: by the Virgin Mary.)   **40 s.d. invisible**
i.e., wearing a garment to connote invisibility, as at 1.2.377   **48 supplant** uproot, displace   **54 this thing** i.e., Trinculo

STEPHANO That's most certain.

CALIBAN
Thou shalt be lord of it, and I'll serve thee.

STEPHANO How now shall this be compassed? Canst 57
thou bring me to the party?

CALIBAN
Yea, yea, my lord. I'll yield him thee asleep,
Where thou mayst knock a nail into his head.

ARIEL Thou liest; thou canst not.

CALIBAN
What a pied ninny's this! Thou scurvy patch!—   62
I do beseech thy greatness, give him blows
And take his bottle from him. When that's gone
He shall drink naught but brine, for I'll not show him
Where the quick freshes are.   66

STEPHANO Trinculo, run into no further danger. Interrupt the monster one word further and, by this hand, 68
I'll turn my mercy out o' doors and make a stockfish 69
of thee.

TRINCULO Why, what did I? I did nothing. I'll go farther
off.   72

STEPHANO Didst thou not say he lied?

ARIEL Thou liest.

STEPHANO Do I so? Take thou that. [He beats Trinculo.] As
you like this, give me the lie another time.   76

TRINCULO I did not give the lie. Out o' your wits and
hearing too? A pox o' your bottle! This can sack and
drinking do. A murrain on your monster, and the 79
devil take your fingers!

CALIBAN Ha, ha, ha!

STEPHANO Now, forward with your tale. [To Trinculo.]
Prithee, stand further off.

CALIBAN
Beat him enough. After a little time
I'll beat him too.

---

57 compassed achieved **62 pied ninny** fool in motley. **patch** fool
66 quick freshes running springs **68 one word further** i.e., one more
time **69 turn . . . doors** i.e., forget about being merciful. **stockfish**
dried cod beaten before cooking **72 off** away **76 give me the lie** call
me a liar to my face **79 murrain** plague. (Literally, a cattle disease.)

STEPHANO   Stand farther.—Come, proceed.

CALIBAN

Why, as I told thee, 'tis a custom with him
I' th' afternoon to sleep. There thou mayst brain him,
Having first seized his books; or with a log
Batter his skull, or paunch him with a stake,   90
Or cut his weasand with thy knife. Remember   91
First to possess his books, for without them
He's but a sot, as I am, nor hath not   93
One spirit to command. They all do hate him
As rootedly as I. Burn but his books.
He has brave utensils—for so he calls them—   96
Which, when he has a house, he'll deck withal.   97
And that most deeply to consider is
The beauty of his daughter. He himself
Calls her a nonpareil. I never saw a woman
But only Sycorax my dam and she;
But she as far surpasseth Sycorax
As great'st does least.

STEPHANO   Is it so brave a lass?   104

CALIBAN

Ay, lord. She will become thy bed, I warrant,   105
And bring thee forth brave brood.

STEPHANO   Monster, I will kill this man. His daughter
and I will be king and queen—save Our Graces!—and
Trinculo and thyself shall be viceroys. Dost thou like
the plot, Trinculo?

TRINCULO   Excellent.

STEPHANO   Give me thy hand. I am sorry I beat thee;
but, while thou liv'st, keep a good tongue in thy head.

CALIBAN

Within this half hour will he be asleep.
Wilt thou destroy him then?

STEPHANO   Ay, on mine honor.

ARIEL [*Aside*]   This will I tell my master.

CALIBAN

Thou mak'st me merry; I am full of pleasure.

---

90 paunch stab in the belly   **91 weasand** windpipe   **93 sot** fool
96 brave utensils fine furnishings   **97 deck withal** furnish it with
104 brave splendid, attractive   **105 become** suit

Let us be jocund. Will you troll the catch   119
You taught me but whilere?   120

STEPHANO At thy request, monster, I will do reason, 121
any reason. Come on, Trinculo, let us sing.   *Sings.* 122
    "Flout 'em and scout 'em   123
        And scout 'em and flout 'em!
            Thought is free."

CALIBAN That's not the tune.   126

Ariel plays the tune on a tabor and pipe.

STEPHANO What is this same?

TRINCULO This is the tune of our catch, played by the
picture of Nobody.   129

STEPHANO If thou beest a man, show thyself in thy likeness. If thou beest a devil, take 't as thou list. 131

TRINCULO O, forgive me my sins!

STEPHANO He that dies pays all debts. I defy thee.
Mercy upon us!

CALIBAN Art thou afeard?

STEPHANO No, monster, not I.

CALIBAN
Be not afeard. The isle is full of noises,
Sounds, and sweet airs, that give delight and hurt not.
Sometimes a thousand twangling instruments
Will hum about mine ears, and sometimes voices
That, if I then had waked after long sleep,
Will make me sleep again; and then, in dreaming,
The clouds methought would open and show riches
Ready to drop upon me, that when I waked
I cried to dream again.   145

STEPHANO This will prove a brave kingdom to me,
where I shall have my music for nothing.

CALIBAN When Prospero is destroyed.

STEPHANO That shall be by and by. I remember the 149
story.

---

119 jocund jovial, merry. **troll the catch** sing the round **120 but
whilere** only a short time ago **121–122 reason, any reason** anything
reasonable **123 Flout** scoff at. **scout** deride **126 s.d. tabor** small
drum **129 picture of Nobody** (Refers to a familiar figure with head,
arms, and legs but no trunk.) **131 take 't . . . list** i.e., take my defiance
as you please, as best you can **145 to dream** desirous of dreaming
149 by and by very soon

TRINCULO   The sound is going away. Let's follow it, and
     after do our work.
STEPHANO   Lead, monster; we'll follow. I would I could
     see this taborer! He lays it on.   154
TRINCULO   Wilt come? I'll follow Stephano.
                         Exeunt [following Ariel's music].

♣

3.3   *Enter Alonso, Sebastian, Antonio, Gonzalo,
          Adrian, Francisco, etc.*

GONZALO
  By 'r lakin, I can go no further, sir.   1
  My old bones aches. Here's a maze trod indeed
  Through forthrights and meanders! By your patience,   3
  I needs must rest me.
ALONSO   Old lord, I cannot blame thee,   4
  Who am myself attached with weariness,   5
  To the dulling of my spirits. Sit down and rest.   6
  Even here I will put off my hope, and keep it
  No longer for my flatterer. He is drowned   8
  Whom thus we stray to find, and the sea mocks
  Our frustrate search on land. Well, let him go.   10
                       [*Alonso and Gonzalo sit.*]
ANTONIO [*Aside to Sebastian*]
  I am right glad that he's so out of hope.   11
  Do not, for one repulse, forgo the purpose   12
  That you resolved t' effect.
SEBASTIAN [*To Antonio*]   The next advantage
  Will we take throughly.
ANTONIO [*To Sebastian*]   Let it be tonight,   14
  For, now they are oppressed with travel, they   15

---

154 lays it on i.e., plays the drum skillfully and energetically

3.3. Location: Another part of the island.
1 By 'r lakin by our Ladykin, by our Lady   **3 forthrights and meanders**
paths straight and crooked   **4 needs must** have to   **5 attached** seized
6 To . . . spirits to the point of being dull-spirited   **8 for** as   **10 frustrate** frustrated   **11 right** very.   **out of hope** despairing, discouraged
12 for because of   **14 throughly** thoroughly   **15 now** now that.   **travel**
(Spelled *trauaile* in the Folio and carrying the sense of labor as well as
traveling.)

Will not, nor cannot, use such vigilance   16
As when they are fresh.
SEBASTIAN [*To Antonio*]   I say tonight. No more.   17
                    Solemn and strange music; and
                        Prospero on the top, invisible.

ALONSO
What harmony is this? My good friends, hark!
GONZALO   Marvelous sweet music!

> *Enter several strange shapes, bringing in a*
> *banquet, and dance about it with gentle actions*
> *of salutations; and, inviting the King, etc., to eat,*
> *they depart.*

ALONSO
Give us kind keepers, heavens! What were these?   20
SEBASTIAN
A living drollery. Now I will believe   21
That there are unicorns; that in Arabia
There is one tree, the phoenix' throne, one phoenix   23
At this hour reigning there.
ANTONIO   I'll believe both;
And what does else want credit, come to me   25
And I'll be sworn 'tis true. Travelers ne'er did lie,
Though fools at home condemn 'em.
GONZALO   If in Naples
I should report this now, would they believe me
If I should say I saw such islanders?
For, certes, these are people of the island,   30
Who, though they are of monstrous shape, yet note,
Their manners are more gentle, kind, than of
Our human generation you shall find
Many, nay, almost any.
PROSPERO [*Aside*]   Honest lord,
Thou hast said well, for some of you there present
Are worse than devils.

---

16 use apply   **17 s.d. on the top** at some high point of the tiring-house
or the theater, on a third level above the gallery   **20 kind keepers**
guardian angels   **21 living** with live actors.   **drollery** comic entertainment, caricature, puppet show   **23 phoenix** mythical bird consumed to
ashes every 500 to 600 years only to be renewed into another cycle
25 want credit lack credence   **30 certes** certainly

ALONSO   I cannot too much muse   36
  Such shapes, such gesture, and such sound,
    expressing—
  Although they want the use of tongue—a kind   38
  Of excellent dumb discourse.
PROSPERO [*Aside*]   Praise in departing.   39
FRANCISCO
  They vanished strangely.
SEBASTIAN   No matter, since
  They have left their viands behind, for we have
    stomachs.   41
  Will 't please you taste of what is here?
ALONSO   Not I.
GONZALO
  Faith, sir, you need not fear. When we were boys,
  Who would believe that there were mountaineers   44
  Dewlapped like bulls, whose throats had hanging at 'em 45
  Wallets of flesh? Or that there were such men   46
  Whose heads stood in their breasts? Which now we find   47
  Each putter-out of five for one will bring us   48
  Good warrant of.
ALONSO   I will stand to and feed,   49
  Although my last—no matter, since I feel   50
  The best is past. Brother, my lord the Duke,   51
  Stand to, and do as we.   [*They approach the table.*] 52

        Thunder and lightning. Enter Ariel, like a harpy,
        claps his wings upon the table, and with a quaint
        device the banquet vanishes.

36 muse wonder at   **38 want** lack   **39 Praise in departing** i.e., save your
praise until the end of the performance. (Proverbial.)   **41 viands** provisions.   **stomachs** appetites   **44 mountaineers** mountain dwellers
45 Dewlapped having a dewlap, or fold of skin hanging from the neck,
like cattle   **46 Wallets** pendent folds of skin, wattles   **47 in their
breasts** (i.e., like the Anthropophagi described in *Othello*, 1.3.146)
48 putter-out . . . one one who invests money, or gambles on the risks of
travel on the condition that, if he returns safely, he is to receive five
times the amount deposited; hence, any traveler   **49 Good warrant**
assurance.   **stand to** fall to; take the risk   **50 Although my last** even if
this were to be my last meal   **51 best** best part of life   **52 s.d. harpy** a
fabulous monster with a woman's face and breasts and a vulture's
body, supposed to be a minister of divine vengeance.   **quaint device**
ingenious stage contrivance.   **the banquet vanishes** i.e., the food vanishes; the table remains until l. 82

ARIEL
You are three men of sin, whom Destiny—
That hath to instrument this lower world   54
And what is in 't—the never-surfeited sea
Hath caused to belch up you, and on this island
Where man doth not inhabit, you 'mongst men
Being most unfit to live. I have made you mad;
And even with suchlike valor men hang and drown   59
Their proper selves.
                    [*Alonso, Sebastian, and Antonio
                         draw their swords.*]
                    You fools! I and my fellows   60
Are ministers of Fate. The elements
Of whom your swords are tempered may as well   62
Wound the loud winds, or with bemocked-at stabs   63
Kill the still-closing waters, as diminish   64
One dowl that's in my plume. My fellow ministers 65
Are like invulnerable. If you could hurt,   66
Your swords are now too massy for your strengths 67
And will not be uplifted. But remember—
For that's my business to you—that you three
From Milan did supplant good Prospero;
Exposed unto the sea, which hath requit it,   71
Him and his innocent child; for which foul deed
The powers, delaying, not forgetting, have
Incensed the seas and shores, yea, all the creatures,
Against your peace. Thee of thy son, Alonso,
They have bereft; and do pronounce by me
Lingering perdition, worse than any death   77
Can be at once, shall step by step attend
You and your ways; whose wraths to guard you from— 79
Which here, in this most desolate isle, else falls 80
Upon your heads—is nothing but heart's sorrow   81

---

54 to i.e., as its   **59 suchlike valor** i.e., the reckless valor derived from
madness   **60 proper** own   **62 whom** which.   **tempered** composed and
hardened   **63 bemocked-at** scorned   **64 still-closing** always closing
again when parted   **65 dowl** soft, fine feather   **66 like** likewise, similarly.   **If** even if   **67 massy** heavy   **71 requit** requited, avenged
77 perdition ruin, destruction   **79 whose** (Refers to the heavenly powers.)
80 else otherwise   **81 is nothing** there is no way

And a clear life ensuing.   82

> *He vanishes in thunder; then, to soft music, enter*
> *the shapes again, and dance, with mocks and*
> *mows, and carrying out the table.*

PROSPERO
Bravely the figure of this harpy hast thou   83
Performed, my Ariel; a grace it had devouring.   84
Of my instruction hast thou nothing bated   85
In what thou hadst to say. So, with good life   86
And observation strange, my meaner ministers   87
Their several kinds have done. My high charms work,   88
And these mine enemies are all knit up
In their distractions. They now are in my power;
And in these fits I leave them, while I visit
Young Ferdinand, whom they suppose is drowned,
And his and mine loved darling.   [*Exit above.*]

GONZALO
I' the name of something holy, sir, why stand you   94
In this strange stare?
ALONSO   O, it is monstrous, monstrous! 95
Methought the billows spoke and told me of it;   96
The winds did sing it to me, and the thunder,
That deep and dreadful organ pipe, pronounced
The name of Prosper; it did bass my trespass.   99
Therefor my son i' th' ooze is bedded; and   100
I'll seek him deeper than e'er plummet sounded,   101

---

82 clear unspotted, innocent   **s.d. mocks and mows** mocking gestures and grimaces   **83 Bravely** finely, dashingly   **84 a grace . . . devouring** i.e., you gracefully caused the banquet to disappear as if you had consumed it (with puns on *grace* meaning "gracefulness" and "a blessing on the meal," and on *devouring* meaning "a literal eating" and "an all-consuming or ravishing grace")   **85 bated** abated, omitted   **86 So** in the same fashion.   **good life** faithful reproduction   **87 observation strange** exceptional attention to detail.   **meaner** i.e., subordinate to Ariel   **88 several kinds** individual parts   **94 why** (Gonzalo was not addressed in Ariel's speech to the *three men of sin*, l. 53, and is not, as they are, in a maddened state; see ll. 105–107.)   **95 it** i.e., my sin (also in l. 96)   **96 billows** waves   **99 bass my trespass** proclaim my trespass like a bass note in music   **100 Therefor** in consequence of that   **101 plummet** a lead weight attached to a line for testing depth.   **sounded** probed, tested the depth of

And with him there lie mudded.   *Exit.*
SEBASTIAN   But one fiend at a time,
  I'll fight their legions o'er.
ANTONIO   I'll be thy second.   104.
                        Exeunt [Sebastian and Antonio].
GONZALO
  All three of them are desperate. Their great guilt,   105
  Like poison given to work a great time after,
  Now 'gins to bite the spirits. I do beseech you   107
  That are of suppler joints, follow them swiftly
  And hinder them from what this ecstasy   109
  May now provoke them to.
ADRIAN   Follow, I pray you.
                              Exeunt omnes.

✢

---

104 o'er one after another   **105 desperate** despairing and reckless
107 bite the spirits sap their vital powers through anguish   **109 ecstasy**
mad frenzy

4.1   *Enter Prospero, Ferdinand, and Miranda.*

PROSPERO
If I have too austerely punished you,   1
Your compensation makes amends, for I
Have given you here a third of mine own life,   3
Or that for which I live; who once again
I tender to thy hand. All thy vexations   5
Were but my trials of thy love, and thou
Hast strangely stood the test. Here, afore Heaven,   7
I ratify this my rich gift. O Ferdinand,
Do not smile at me that I boast her off,   9
For thou shalt find she will outstrip all praise
And make it halt behind her.
FERDINAND   I do believe it   11
Against an oracle.   12
PROSPERO
Then, as my gift and thine own acquisition
Worthily purchased, take my daughter. But
If thou dost break her virgin-knot before
All sanctimonious ceremonies may   16
With full and holy rite be ministered,
No sweet aspersion shall the heavens let fall   18
To make this contract grow; but barren hate,
Sour-eyed disdain, and discord shall bestrew
The union of your bed with weeds so loathly   21
That you shall hate it both. Therefore take heed,
As Hymen's lamps shall light you.
FERDINAND   As I hope   23

4.1. Location: Before Prospero's cell.
1 austerely severely   **3 a third** i.e., Miranda, into whose education
Prospero has put a third of his life (?) or who represents a large part
of what he cares about, along with his dukedom and his learned
study (?)   **5 vexations** torments   **7 strangely** extraordinarily   **9 boast
her off** i.e., praise her so; or perhaps an error for "boast of her"; the
Folio reads "boast her of"   **11 halt** limp   **12 Against an oracle** i.e., even
if an oracle should declare otherwise   **16 sanctimonious** sacred   **18 aspersion** dew, shower   **21 weeds** (in place of the flowers customarily
strewn on the marriage bed)   **23 As . . . you** i.e., as you long for happiness and concord in your marriage. (Hymen was the Greek and Roman
god of marriage; his symbolic torches, the wedding torches, were
supposed to burn brightly for a happy marriage, smokily for a troubled
one.)

For quiet days, fair issue, and long life,   24
With such love as 'tis now, the murkiest den,
The most opportune place, the strong'st suggestion   26
Our worser genius can, shall never melt   27
Mine honor into lust, to take away   28
The edge of that day's celebration   29
When I shall think or Phoebus' steeds are foundered   30
Or Night kept chained below.
PROSPERO   Fairly spoke.
Sit then and talk with her. She is thine own.
      [*Ferdinand and Miranda sit and talk together.*]
What, Ariel! My industrious servant, Ariel!   33

    Enter Ariel.

ARIEL
What would my potent master? Here I am.
PROSPERO
Thou and thy meaner fellows your last service   35
Did worthily perform, and I must use you
In such another trick. Go bring the rabble,   37
O'er whom I give thee power, here to this place.
Incite them to quick motion, for I must
Bestow upon the eyes of this young couple
Some vanity of mine art. It is my promise,   41
And they expect it from me.
ARIEL   Presently?   42
PROSPERO   Ay, with a twink.   43
ARIEL
    Before you can say "Come" and "Go,"
    And breathe twice, and cry "So, so,"
    Each one, tripping on his toe,
    Will be here with mop and mow.   47
    Do you love me, master? No?

24 issue offspring   **26 suggestion** temptation   **27 worser genius** evil
genius, or evil attendant spirit.   **can** is capable of   **28 to** so as to
29 edge keen enjoyment, sexual ardor   **30 or** either.   **foundered** broken
down, made lame. (Ferdinand will wait impatiently for the bridal
night.)   **33 What** now then   **35 meaner fellows** subordinates   **37 trick**
device.   **rabble** band, i.e., the *meaner fellows* of l. 35   **41 vanity**
(1) illusion (2) trifle (3) desire for admiration, conceit   **42 Presently**
immediately   **43 with a twink** in the twinkling of an eye, in an instant   **47 mop and mow** gestures and grimaces

PROSPERO
  Dearly, my delicate Ariel. Do not approach
  Till thou dost hear me call.

ARIEL   Well, I conceive.   *Exit.* 50

PROSPERO
  Look thou be true; do not give dalliance   51
  Too much the rein. The strongest oaths are straw
  To the fire i' the blood. Be more abstemious,
  Or else good night your vow!

FERDINAND   I warrant you, sir,   54
  The white cold virgin snow upon my heart   55
  Abates the ardor of my liver.

PROSPERO   Well.   56
  Now come, my Ariel! Bring a corollary,   57
  Rather than want a spirit. Appear, and pertly!—   58
  No tongue! All eyes! Be silent.   *Soft music.* 59

    Enter Iris.

IRIS
  Ceres, most bounteous lady, thy rich leas   60
  Of wheat, rye, barley, vetches, oats, and peas;   61
  Thy turfy mountains, where live nibbling sheep,
  And flat meads thatched with stover, them to keep;   63
  Thy banks with pionèd and twillèd brims,   64
  Which spongy April at thy hest betrims   65
  To make cold nymphs chaste crowns; and thy broom
    groves,   66
  Whose shadow the dismissèd bachelor loves,   67
  Being lass-lorn; thy poll-clipped vineyard;   68

50 conceive understand   **51 true** true to your promise   **54 good night** i.e., say good-bye to.   **warrant** guarantee   **55 The white . . . heart** i.e., the ideal of chastity and consciousness of Miranda's chaste innocence enshrined in my heart   **56 liver** (as the presumed seat of the passions)   **57 corollary** surplus, extra supply   **58 want** lack.   **pertly** briskly   **59 No tongue** all the beholders are to be silent (lest the spirits vanish)   **s.d. Iris** goddess of the rainbow, and Juno's messenger   **60 Ceres** goddess of the generative power of nature.   **leas** meadows   **61 vetches** plants for forage, fodder   **63 meads** meadows.   **stover** winter fodder for cattle   **64 pionèd and twillèd** undercut by the swift current and protected by roots and branches that tangle to form a barricade   **65 spongy** wet   **66 broom groves** clumps of broom, gorse, yellow-flowered shrub   **67 dismissèd bachelor** rejected male lover   **68 poll-clipped** pruned, lopped at the top, or *pole-clipped,* hedged in with poles

And thy sea marge, sterile and rocky hard,   69
Where thou thyself dost air: the queen o' the sky,   70
Whose watery arch and messenger am I,   71
Bids thee leave these, and with her sovereign grace,   72
        Juno descends [slowly in her car].
Here on this grass plot, in this very place,
To come and sport. Her peacocks fly amain.   74
Approach, rich Ceres, her to entertain.   75

    Enter Ceres.

CERES
Hail, many-colored messenger, that ne'er
Dost disobey the wife of Jupiter,
Who with thy saffron wings upon my flowers   78
Diffusest honeydrops, refreshing showers,
And with each end of thy blue bow dost crown   80
My bosky acres and my unshrubbed down,   81
Rich scarf to my proud earth. Why hath thy queen
Summoned me hither to this short-grassed green?
IRIS
A contract of true love to celebrate,
And some donation freely to estate   85
On the blest lovers.
CERES   Tell me, heavenly bow,
If Venus or her son, as thou dost know,   87
Do now attend the Queen? Since they did plot
The means that dusky Dis my daughter got,   89
Her and her blind boy's scandaled company   90
I have forsworn.
IRIS   Of her society   91
Be not afraid. I met her deity   92
Cutting the clouds towards Paphos, and her son   93

---

69 **sea marge** shore   70 **queen o' the sky** i.e., Juno   71 **watery arch**
rainbow   72 **s.d. Juno descends** i.e., starts her descent from the "heavens"
above the stage (?)   74 **peacocks** birds sacred to Juno, and used to pull
her chariot. **amain** with full speed   75 **entertain** receive   78 **saffron**
yellow   80 **bow** i.e., rainbow   81 **bosky** wooded. **down** upland   85 **estate** bestow   87 **son** i.e., Cupid. **as** as far as   89 **dusky** dark. **Dis . . .
got** (Pluto, or *Dis*, god of the infernal regions, carried off Persephone,
daughter of Ceres, to be his bride in Hades.)   90 **Her** i.e., Venus'.
scandaled scandalous   91 **society** company   92 **her deity** i.e., Her Highness   93 **Paphos** place on the island of Cyprus, sacred to Venus

Dove-drawn with her. Here thought they to have done   94
Some wanton charm upon this man and maid,   95
Whose vows are that no bed-right shall be paid
Till Hymen's torch be lighted; but in vain.
Mars's hot minion is returned again;   98
Her waspish-headed son has broke his arrows,   99
Swears he will shoot no more, but play with sparrows   100
And be a boy right out.

    [Juno alights.]

CERES   Highest Queen of state,   101
  Great Juno, comes; I know her by her gait.   102

JUNO
How does my bounteous sister? Go with me
To bless this twain, that they may prosperous be
And honored in their issue.   *They sing:*   105

JUNO

    Honor, riches, marriage blessing,
    Long continuance, and increasing,
    Hourly joys be still upon you!   108
    Juno sings her blessings on you.

CERES

    Earth's increase, foison plenty,   110
    Barns and garners never empty,   111
    Vines with clustering bunches growing,
    Plants with goodly burden bowing;

    Spring come to you at the farthest
    In the very end of harvest!   115
    Scarcity and want shall shun you;
    Ceres' blessing so is on you.

FERDINAND
  This is a most majestic vision, and

94 Dove-drawn (Venus' chariot was drawn by doves.) **done** placed
95 wanton charm lustful spell **98 Mars's hot minion** i.e., Venus, the
beloved of Mars. **returned** i.e., returned to Paphos **99 waspish-headed**
fiery, hotheaded, peevish **100 sparrows** (Supposed lustful, and sacred
to Venus.) **101 right out** outright. **Highest . . . state** most majestic
Queen **102 gait** i.e., majestic bearing **105 issue** offspring **108 still**
always **110 foison plenty** plentiful harvest **111 garners** granaries
115 In . . . harvest i.e., with no winter in between

Harmonious charmingly. May I be bold   119
To think these spirits?
PROSPERO   Spirits, which by mine art
I have from their confines called to enact
My present fancies.
FERDINAND   Let me live here ever!
So rare a wondered father and a wife   123
Makes this place Paradise.

> *Juno and Ceres whisper, and send*
> *Iris on employment.*

PROSPERO   Sweet now, silence!
Juno and Ceres whisper seriously;
There's something else to do. Hush and be mute,
Or else our spell is marred.

IRIS
You nymphs, called naiads, of the windring brooks,   128
With your sedged crowns and ever-harmless looks,   129
Leave your crisp channels, and on this green land   130
Answer your summons; Juno does command.
Come, temperate nymphs, and help to celebrate   132
A contract of true love. Be not too late.

> *Enter certain nymphs.*

You sunburnt sicklemen, of August weary,   134
Come hither from the furrow and be merry.   135
Make holiday; your rye-straw hats put on,
And these fresh nymphs encounter every one   137
In country footing.   138

> *Enter certain reapers, properly habited. They join*
> *with the nymphs in a graceful dance, towards the*
> *end whereof Prospero starts suddenly, and*
> *speaks; after which, to a strange, hollow, and*
> *confused noise, they heavily vanish.*

---

119 charmingly enchantingly   **123 wondered** wonder-performing,
wondrous   **128 naiads** nymphs of springs, rivers, or lakes.   **windring**
wandering, winding (?)   **129 sedged** made of reeds.   **ever-harmless** ever-
innocent   **130 crisp** curled, rippled   **132 temperate** chaste   **134 sicklemen** harvesters, field workers who cut down grain and grass.   **weary**
i.e., weary of the hard work of the harvest   **135 furrow** i.e., plowed
fields   **137 encounter** join   **138 country footing** country dancing
s.d. properly suitably.   **heavily** slowly, dejectedly

PROSPERO [*Aside*]
　I had forgot that foul conspiracy
　Of the beast Caliban and his confederates
　Against my life. The minute of their plot
　Is almost come. [*To the Spirits.*] Well done! Avoid; no
　　more!   142
FERDINAND [*To Miranda*]
　This is strange. Your father's in some passion
　That works him strongly.
MIRANDA   Never till this day   144
　Saw I him touched with anger so distempered.
PROSPERO
　You do look, my son, in a moved sort,   146
　As if you were dismayed. Be cheerful, sir.
　Our revels now are ended. These our actors,   148
　As I foretold you, were all spirits and
　Are melted into air, into thin air;
　And, like the baseless fabric of this vision,   151
　The cloud-capped towers, the gorgeous palaces,
　The solemn temples, the great globe itself,   153
　Yea, all which it inherit, shall dissolve,   154
　And, like this insubstantial pageant faded,
　Leave not a rack behind. We are such stuff   156
　As dreams are made on, and our little life   157
　Is rounded with a sleep. Sir, I am vexed.   158
　Bear with my weakness. My old brain is troubled.
　Be not disturbed with my infirmity.   160
　If you be pleased, retire into my cell   161
　And there repose. A turn or two I'll walk
　To still my beating mind.
FERDINAND, MIRANDA   We wish your peace.   163
　　　　　　　　　　Exeunt [*Ferdinand and Miranda*].

PROSPERO
　Come with a thought! I thank thee, Ariel. Come.   164

---

142 Avoid depart, withdraw   **144 works** affects, agitates   **146 moved
sort** troubled state, condition   **148 revels** entertainment, pageant
151 baseless without substance   **153 great globe** (with a glance at the
Globe Theatre)   **154 which it inherit** who subsequently occupy it
156 rack wisp of cloud   **157 on** of   **158 rounded** surrounded, or
crowned, rounded off   **160 with** by   **161 retire** withdraw, go   **163 beating** agitated   **164 with a thought** i.e., on the instant, or summoned by
my thought, no sooner thought of than here

Enter Ariel.

ARIEL
Thy thoughts I cleave to. What's thy pleasure?
PROSPERO   Spirit,   165
We must prepare to meet with Caliban.
ARIEL
Ay, my commander. When I presented Ceres,   167
I thought to have told thee of it, but I feared
Lest I might anger thee.
PROSPERO
Say again, where didst thou leave these varlets?
ARIEL
I told you, sir, they were red-hot with drinking,
So full of valor that they smote the air
For breathing in their faces, beat the ground
For kissing of their feet, yet always bending   174
Towards their project. Then I beat my tabor,
At which, like unbacked colts, they pricked their ears,   176
Advanced their eyelids, lifted up their noses   177
As they smelt music. So I charmed their ears   178
That calflike they my lowing followed through   179
Toothed briers, sharp furzes, pricking gorse, and
    thorns,   180
Which entered their frail shins. At last I left them
I' the filthy-mantled pool beyond your cell,   182
There dancing up to the chins, that the foul lake
O'erstunk their feet.
PROSPERO   This was well done, my bird.   184
Thy shape invisible retain thou still.
The trumpery in my house, go bring it hither,   186
For stale to catch these thieves.
ARIEL   I go, I go.   *Exit.*   187

165 **cleave** cling, adhere   167 **presented** acted the part of, or introduced   174 **bending** aiming   176 **unbacked** unbroken, unridden 177 **Advanced** lifted up   178 **As** as if   179 **lowing** mooing   180 **furzes, gorse** prickly shrubs   182 **filthy-mantled** covered with a slimy coating 184 **O'erstunk** smelled worse than, or, caused to stink terribly 186 **trumpery** cheap goods, the *glistering apparel* mentioned in the following stage direction   187 **stale** (1) decoy (2) out-of-fashion garments (with possible further suggestions of *fit for a stale* or prostitute, *stale* meaning "horse piss," l. 199, and *steal*, pronounced like *stale*)

PROSPERO
A devil, a born devil, on whose nature
Nurture can never stick; on whom my pains,
Humanely taken, all, all lost, quite lost!
And as with age his body uglier grows,
So his mind cankers. I will plague them all,   192
Even to roaring.

    Enter Ariel, loaden with glistering apparel, etc.

          Come, hang them on this line.   193

    [Ariel hangs up the showy finery; Prospero and
    Ariel remain, invisible.] Enter Caliban, Stephano,
    and Trinculo, all wet.

CALIBAN
Pray you, tread softly, that the blind mole may
Not hear a footfall. We now are near his cell.
STEPHANO Monster, your fairy, which you say is a
harmless fairy, has done little better than played the
jack with us.   198
TRINCULO Monster, I do smell all horse piss, at which
my nose is in great indignation.
STEPHANO So is mine. Do you hear, monster? If I
should take a displeasure against you, look you—
TRINCULO Thou wert but a lost monster.
CALIBAN
Good my lord, give me thy favor still.
Be patient, for the prize I'll bring thee to
Shall hoodwink this mischance. Therefore speak softly. 206
All's hushed as midnight yet.
TRINCULO Ay, but to lose our bottles in the pool—
STEPHANO There is not only disgrace and dishonor in
that, monster, but an infinite loss.
TRINCULO That's more to me than my wetting. Yet this
is your harmless fairy, monster!
STEPHANO I will fetch off my bottle, though I be o'er 213
ears for my labor.   214

192 cankers festers, grows malignant   **193 line** lime tree or linden
s.d. Prospero and Ariel remain (The staging is uncertain. They may
instead exit here and return with the spirits at l. 256.)   **198 jack**
(1) knave (2) will-o'-the wisp   **206 hoodwink** cover up, make you not see.
(A hawking term.)   **mischance** mishap, misfortune   **213–214 o'er ears**
i.e., totally submerged and perhaps drowned

CALIBAN

Prithee, my king, be quiet. Seest thou here,
This is the mouth o' the cell. No noise, and enter.
Do that good mischief which may make this island
Thine own forever, and I thy Caliban
For aye thy footlicker.

STEPHANO   Give me thy hand. I do begin to have bloody
thoughts.

TRINCULO [*Seeing the finery*]   O King Stephano! O peer!   222
O worthy Stephano! Look what a wardrobe here is for
thee!

CALIBAN

Let it alone, thou fool, it is but trash.

TRINCULO   Oho, monster! We know what belongs to a
frippery. O King Stephano!   [*He takes a gown.*]   227

STEPHANO   Put off that gown, Trinculo. By this hand, I'll   228
have that gown.

TRINCULO   Thy Grace shall have it.

CALIBAN

The dropsy drown this fool! What do you mean   231
To dote thus on such luggage? Let 't alone   232
And do the murder first. If he awake,
From toe to crown he'll fill our skins with pinches,   234
Make us strange stuff.

STEPHANO   Be you quiet, monster.—Mistress line, is not   236
this my jerkin? [*He takes it down.*] Now is the jerkin un-   237
der the line. Now, jerkin, you are like to lose your hair   238
and prove a bald jerkin.   239

---

222 King . . . peer (Alludes to the old ballad beginning, "King
Stephen was a worthy peer.")   **227 frippery** place where cast-off
clothes are sold   **228 Put off** put down, or take off   **231 dropsy**
disease characterized by the accumulation of fluid in the connective
tissue of the body   **232 luggage** cumbersome trash   **234 crown**
head   **236 Mistress line** (Addressed to the linden or lime tree upon
which, at l. 193, Ariel hung the *glistering apparel*.)   **237 jerkin** jacket
made of leather   **237–238 under the line** under the lime tree (with
punning sense of being south of the equinoctial line or equator;
sailors on long voyages to the southern regions were popularly
supposed to lose their hair from scurvy or other diseases. Stephano
also quibbles bawdily on losing hair through syphilis, and in *Mistress* and *jerkin*.)   **238 like** likely   **239 bald** (1) hairless, napless
(2) meager

TRINCULO Do, do! We steal by line and level, an 't like 240
Your Grace.

STEPHANO I thank thee for that jest. Here's a garment
for 't. [*He gives a garment.*] Wit shall not go unrewarded
while I am king of this country. "Steal by line and
level" is an excellent pass of pate. There's another gar- 245
ment for 't.

TRINCULO Monster, come, put some lime upon your 247
fingers, and away with the rest.

CALIBAN
I will have none on 't. We shall lose our time,
And all be turned to barnacles, or to apes   250
With foreheads villainous low.   251

STEPHANO Monster, lay to your fingers. Help to bear 252
this away where my hogshead of wine is, or I'll turn 253
you out of my kingdom. Go to, carry this.   254

TRINCULO And this.

STEPHANO Ay, and this.
                    [*They load Caliban with more and
                              more garments.*]

*A noise of hunters heard. Enter divers spirits, in
shape of dogs and hounds, hunting them about,
Prospero and Ariel setting them on.*

PROSPERO Hey, Mountain, hey!

ARIEL Silver! There it goes, Silver!

PROSPERO Fury, Fury! There, Tyrant, there! Hark! Hark!
          [*Caliban, Stephano, and Trinculo are driven out.*]
Go, charge my goblins that they grind their joints

---

240 **Do, do** i.e., bravo. (Said in response to the jesting or to the taking of
the jerkin, or both.) **by line and level** i.e., by means of plumb line and
carpenter's level, methodically (with pun on *line*, "lime tree," l. 238,
and *steal*, pronounced like *stale*, i.e., prostitute, continuing Stephano's
bawdy quibble). **an 't like** if it please 245 **pass of pate** sally of wit.
(The metaphor is from fencing.) 247 **lime** birdlime, sticky substance (to
give Caliban sticky fingers) 250 **barnacles** barnacle geese, formerly
supposed to be hatched from seashells attached to trees and to fall
thence into the water; here evidently used, like *apes*, as types of simple-
tons 251 **villainous** miserably 252 **lay to** start using 253 **this** i.e., the
glistering apparel. **hogshead** large cask 254 **Go to** (An expression of
exhortation or remonstrance.)

With dry convulsions, shorten up their sinews   261
With agèd cramps, and more pinch-spotted make them   262
Than pard or cat o' mountain.

ARIEL   Hark, they roar!   263

PROSPERO
Let them be hunted soundly. At this hour   264
Lies at my mercy all mine enemies.
Shortly shall all my labors end, and thou
Shalt have the air at freedom. For a little   267
Follow, and do me service.   *Exeunt.*

❖

---

261 dry associated with age, arthritic (?) **convulsions** cramps
262 agèd characteristic of old age **263 pard** panther or leopard. **cat o'
mountain** wildcat **264 soundly** thoroughly **267 little** little while
longer

5.1   *Enter Prospero in his magic robes, [with his staff,] and Ariel.*

PROSPERO
  Now does my project gather to a head.
  My charms crack not, my spirits obey, and Time   2
  Goes upright with his carriage. How's the day?   3
ARIEL
  On the sixth hour, at which time, my lord,   4
  You said our work should cease.
PROSPERO   I did say so,
  When first I raised the tempest. Say, my spirit,
  How fares the King and 's followers?
ARIEL   Confined together
  In the same fashion as you gave in charge,
  Just as you left them; all prisoners, sir,
  In the line grove which weather-fends your cell.   10
  They cannot budge till your release. The King,   11
  His brother, and yours abide all three distracted,   12
  And the remainder mourning over them,
  Brim full of sorrow and dismay; but chiefly
  Him that you termed, sir, the good old lord, Gonzalo.
  His tears runs down his beard like winter's drops
  From eaves of reeds. Your charm so strongly works 'em   17
  That if you now beheld them your affections   18
  Would become tender.
PROSPERO   Dost thou think so, spirit?
ARIEL
  Mine would, sir, were I human.
PROSPERO   And mine shall.
  Hast thou, which art but air, a touch, a feeling   21
  Of their afflictions, and shall not myself,

5.1. Location: Before Prospero's cell.
2 crack collapse, fail. (The metaphor is probably alchemical, as in
project and *gather to a head*, l. 1.)   **3 his carriage** its burden. (Time is no
longer heavily burdened and so can go *upright*, standing straight and
unimpeded.)   **4 On** approaching   **10 line grove** grove of lime trees.
weather-fends protects from the weather   **11 your release** you release
them   **12 distracted** out of their wits   **17 eaves of reeds** thatched
roofs   **18 affections** feelings   **21 touch** sense, feeling

One of their kind, that relish all as sharply   23
Passion as they, be kindlier moved than thou art?   24
Though with their high wrongs I am struck to the quick,
Yet with my nobler reason 'gainst my fury
Do I take part. The rarer action is   27
In virtue than in vengeance. They being penitent,
The sole drift of my purpose doth extend
Not a frown further. Go release them, Ariel.
My charms I'll break, their senses I'll restore,
And they shall be themselves.

ARIEL   I'll fetch them, sir.

                                        Exit.
                              [*Prospero traces a charmed
                                    circle with his staff.*]

PROSPERO
Ye elves of hills, brooks, standing lakes, and groves,   33
And ye that on the sands with printless foot
Do chase the ebbing Neptune, and do fly him
When he comes back; you demi-puppets that   36
By moonshine do the green sour ringlets make,   37
Whereof the ewe not bites; and you whose pastime
Is to make midnight mushrooms, that rejoice   39
To hear the solemn curfew; by whose aid,   40
Weak masters though ye be, I have bedimmed
The noontide sun, called forth the mutinous winds,
And twixt the green sea and the azured vault   43
Set roaring war; to the dread rattling thunder   44
Have I given fire, and rifted Jove's stout oak   45
With his own bolt; the strong-based promontory   46
Have I made shake, and by the spurs plucked up   47
The pine and cedar; graves at my command

23–24 that . . . they i.e., I who am just as sensitive to suffering as they
24 kindlier (1) more sympathetically (2) more naturally, humanly
27 rarer nobler   **33–50 Ye . . . art** (This famous passage is an embellished paraphrase of Golding's translation of Ovid's *Metamorphoses*, 7.197–219.)   **36 demi-puppets** puppets of half size, i.e., elves and fairies   **37 green sour ringlets** fairy rings, circles in grass (actually produced by mushrooms)   **39 midnight mushrooms** mushrooms appearing overnight   **40 curfew** evening bell, usually rung at nine o'clock, ushering in the time when spirits are abroad   **43 the azured vault** i.e., the sky   **44–45 to . . . fire** I have discharged the dread rattling thunderbolt   **45 rifted** riven, split   **46 bolt** lightning bolt   **47 spurs** roots

Have waked their sleepers, oped, and let 'em forth
By my so potent art. But this rough magic   50
I here abjure, and when I have required   51
Some heavenly music—which even now I do—
To work mine end upon their senses that   53
This airy charm is for, I'll break my staff,   54
Bury it certain fathoms in the earth,
And deeper than did ever plummet sound
I'll drown my book.   *Solemn music.*

> *Here enters Ariel before; then Alonso, with a
> frantic gesture, attended by Gonzalo; Sebastian
> and Antonio in like manner, attended by Adrian
> and Francisco. They all enter the circle which
> Prospero had made, and there stand charmed;
> which Prospero observing, speaks:*

[*To Alonso.*] A solemn air, and the best comforter   58
To an unsettled fancy, cure thy brains,   59
Now useless, boiled within thy skull! [*To Sebastian and
    Antonio.*] There stand,
For you are spell-stopped.—
Holy Gonzalo, honorable man,
Mine eyes, e'en sociable to the show of thine,   63
Fall fellowly drops. [*Aside.*] The charm dissolves apace, 64
And as the morning steals upon the night,
Melting the darkness, so their rising senses
Begin to chase the ignorant fumes that mantle   67
Their clearer reason.—O good Gonzalo,   68
My true preserver, and a loyal sir
To him thou follow'st! I will pay thy graces   70
Home both in word and deed.—Most cruelly   71
Didst thou, Alonso, use me and my daughter.
Thy brother was a furtherer in the act.—   73
Thou art pinched for 't now, Sebastian. [*To Antonio.*]
    Flesh and blood,   74

---

50 rough violent **51 required** requested **53 their senses that** the
senses of those whom **54 airy charm** i.e., music **58 air** song. **and** i.e.,
which is **59 fancy** imagination **63 sociable** sympathetic. **show**
appearance **64 Fall** let fall **67 ignorant fumes** fumes that render them
incapable of comprehension. **mantle** envelop **68 clearer** growing
clearer **70 pay thy graces** reward your favors **71 Home** fully **73 furtherer** accomplice **74 pinched** punished, afflicted

You, brother mine, that entertained ambition,
Expelled remorse and nature, whom, with Sebastian,   76
Whose inward pinches therefore are most strong,
Would here have killed your king, I do forgive thee,
Unnatural though thou art.—Their understanding
Begins to swell, and the approaching tide
Will shortly fill the reasonable shore   81
That now lies foul and muddy. Not one of them
That yet looks on me, or would know me.—Ariel,
Fetch me the hat and rapier in my cell.

> [*Ariel goes to the cell*
> *and returns immediately.*]

I will discase me and myself present   85
As I was sometime Milan. Quickly, spirit!   86
Thou shalt ere long be free.

> *Ariel sings and helps to attire him.*

ARIEL

> Where the bee sucks, there suck I.
> In a cowslip's bell I lie;
> There I couch when owls do cry.   90
> On the bat's back I do fly
> After summer merrily.   92
> Merrily, merrily shall I live now
> Under the blossom that hangs on the bough.

PROSPERO

Why, that's my dainty Ariel! I shall miss thee,
But yet thou shalt have freedom. So, so, so.   96
To the King's ship, invisible as thou art!
There shalt thou find the mariners asleep
Under the hatches. The Master and the Boatswain
Being awake, enforce them to this place,
And presently, I prithee.   101

ARIEL

I drink the air before me and return
Or ere your pulse twice beat.   *Exit.*   103

76 remorse pity. **nature** natural feeling. **whom** i.e., who **81 reasonable shore** shores of reason, i.e., minds. (Their reason returns, like the incoming tide.) **85 discase** disrobe **86 As . . . Milan** in my former appearance as Duke of Milan **90 couch** lie **92 After** i.e., pursuing **96 So, so, so** (Expresses approval of Ariel's help as valet.) **101 presently** immediately **103 Or ere** before

GONZALO
All torment, trouble, wonder, and amazement
Inhabits here. Some heavenly power guide us
Out of this fearful country!

PROSPERO   Behold, sir King,   106
The wrongèd Duke of Milan, Prospero.
For more assurance that a living prince
Does now speak to thee, I embrace thy body;
And to thee and thy company I bid
A hearty welcome.   [*Embracing him.*]

ALONSO   Whe'er thou be'st he or no,
Or some enchanted trifle to abuse me,   112
As late I have been, I not know. Thy pulse   113
Beats as of flesh and blood; and, since I saw thee,
Th' affliction of my mind amends, with which
I fear a madness held me. This must crave—   116
An if this be at all—a most strange story.   117
Thy dukedom I resign, and do entreat   118
Thou pardon me my wrongs. But how should Prospero   119
Be living, and be here?

PROSPERO [*To Gonzalo*]   First, noble friend,
Let me embrace thine age, whose honor cannot   121
Be measured or confined.   [*Embracing him.*]

GONZALO   Whether this be
Or be not, I'll not swear.

PROSPERO   You do yet taste
Some subtleties o' th' isle, that will not let you   124
Believe things certain. Welcome, my friends all!
[*Aside to Sebastian and Antonio.*] But you, my brace of
    lords, were I so minded,   126
I here could pluck His Highness' frown upon you
And justify you traitors. At this time   128
I will tell no tales.

SEBASTIAN   The devil speaks in him.

---

106 fearful frightening   **112 trifle** trick of magic.   **abuse** deceive
113 late lately   **116 crave** require   **117 An . . . all** if this is actually
happening.   **story** i.e., explanation   **118 Thy . . . resign** (Alonso made
arrangement with Antonio at the time of Prospero's banishment for
Milan to pay tribute to Naples; see 1.2.113–127.)   **119 wrongs** wrong-
doings   **121 thine age** your venerable self   **124 subtleties** illusions,
magical powers   **126 brace** pair   **128 justify you** prove you to be

PROSPERO   No.
   [*To Antonio.*] For you, most wicked sir, whom to call
     brother
   Would even infect my mouth, I do forgive
   Thy rankest fault—all of them; and require
   My dukedom of thee, which perforce I know   133
   Thou must restore.
ALONSO   If thou be'st Prospero,
   Give us particulars of thy preservation,
   How thou hast met us here, whom three hours since   136
   Were wrecked upon this shore; where I have lost—
   How sharp the point of this remembrance is!—
   My dear son Ferdinand.
PROSPERO   I am woe for 't, sir.   139
ALONSO
   Irreparable is the loss, and Patience
   Says it is past her cure.
PROSPERO   I rather think
   You have not sought her help, of whose soft grace   142
   For the like loss I have her sovereign aid   143
   And rest myself content.
ALONSO   You the like loss?
PROSPERO
   As great to me as late, and supportable   145
   To make the dear loss, have I means much weaker   146
   Than you may call to comfort you; for I
   Have lost my daughter.
ALONSO   A daughter?
   O heavens, that they were living both in Naples,
   The king and queen there! That they were, I wish   151
   Myself were mudded in that oozy bed   152
   Where my son lies. When did you lose your daughter?
PROSPERO
   In this last tempest. I perceive these lords
   At this encounter do so much admire   155

---

133 perforce necessarily   **136 whom** i.e., who   **139 woe** sorry   **142 of
. . . grace** by whose mercy   **143 sovereign** efficacious   **145 late** recent
145–146 supportable . . . have I to make the deeply felt loss bearable, I
have   **151 That** so that   **152 mudded** buried in the mud   **155 admire**
wonder

That they devour their reason and scarce think   156
Their eyes do offices of truth, their words   157
Are natural breath. But, howsoever you have   158
Been jostled from your senses, know for certain
That I am Prospero and that very duke
Which was thrust forth of Milan, who most strangely   161
Upon this shore, where you were wrecked, was landed
To be the lord on 't. No more yet of this,
For 'tis a chronicle of day by day,   164
Not a relation for a breakfast nor
Befitting this first meeting. Welcome, sir.
This cell's my court. Here have I few attendants,
And subjects none abroad. Pray you, look in.   168
My dukedom since you have given me again,
I will requite you with as good a thing,   170
At least bring forth a wonder to content ye
As much as me my dukedom.   172

*Here Prospero discovers Ferdinand and Miranda
playing at chess.*

MIRANDA   Sweet lord, you play me false.
FERDINAND   No, my dearest love,
I would not for the world.
MIRANDA
Yes, for a score of kingdoms you should wrangle,   176
And I would call it fair play.
ALONSO   If this prove   177
A vision of the island, one dear son   178
Shall I twice lose.

156 devour their reason i.e., are dumbfounded   **156–158 scarce . . .
breath** scarcely believe that their eyes inform them accurately what
they see or that their words are naturally spoken   **161 of** from   **164 of
day by day** requiring days to tell   **168 abroad** away from here, anywhere else   **170 requite** repay   **172 s.d. discovers** i.e., by opening a
curtain, presumably rear stage   **176–177 Yes . . . play** i.e., yes, even if
we were playing for twenty kingdoms, something less than the whole
world, you would still contend mightily against me and play me false,
and I would let you do it as though it were fair play; or, if you were to
play not just for stakes but literally for kingdoms, my accusation of
false play would be out of order in that your "wrangling" would be
proper   **178 vision** illusion

SEBASTIAN   A most high miracle!
FERDINAND [*Approaching his father*]
  Though the seas threaten, they are merciful;
  I have cursed them without cause.   [*He kneels.*]
ALONSO   Now all the blessings
  Of a glad father compass thee about!   182
  Arise, and say how thou cam'st here.

                              [*Ferdinand rises.*]
MIRANDA   O, wonder!
  How many goodly creatures are there here!
  How beauteous mankind is! O, brave new world,   185
  That has such people in 't!
PROSPERO   'Tis new to thee.
ALONSO
  What is this maid with whom thou wast at play?
  Your eld'st acquaintance cannot be three hours.   188
  Is she the goddess that hath severed us
  And brought us thus together?
FERDINAND   Sir, she is mortal;
  But by immortal Providence she's mine.
  I chose her when I could not ask my father
  For his advice, nor thought I had one. She
  Is daughter to this famous Duke of Milan,
  Of whom so often I have heard renown
  But never saw before, of whom I have
  Received a second life; and second father
  This lady makes him to me.
ALONSO   I am hers.
  But O, how oddly will it sound that I
  Must ask my child forgiveness!
PROSPERO   There, sir, stop.
  Let us not burden our remembrances with
  A heaviness that's gone.
GONZALO   I have inly wept,   202
  Or should have spoke ere this. Look down, you gods,
  And on this couple drop a blessèd crown!

---

182 compass encompass, embrace **185 brave** splendid, gorgeously
appareled, handsome **188 eld'st** longest **202 heaviness** sadness. **inly**
inwardly

For it is you that have chalked forth the way   205
Which brought us hither.

ALONSO   I say amen, Gonzalo!

GONZALO
Was Milan thrust from Milan that his issue   207
Should become kings of Naples? O, rejoice
Beyond a common joy, and set it down
With gold on lasting pillars: In one voyage
Did Claribel her husband find at Tunis,
And Ferdinand, her brother, found a wife
Where he himself was lost; Prospero his dukedom
In a poor isle; and all of us ourselves   214
When no man was his own.

ALONSO [*To Ferdinand and Miranda*]   Give me your hands.   215
Let grief and sorrow still embrace his heart   216
That doth not wish you joy!

GONZALO   Be it so! Amen!   217

Enter Ariel, with the Master and Boatswain
amazedly following.

O, look, sir, look, sir! Here is more of us.
I prophesied, if a gallows were on land,
This fellow could not drown.—Now, blasphemy,   220
That swear'st grace o'erboard, not an oath on shore?   221
Hast thou no mouth by land? What is the news?

BOATSWAIN
The best news is that we have safely found
Our King and company; the next, our ship—
Which, but three glasses since, we gave out split—   225
Is tight and yare and bravely rigged as when   226
We first put out to sea.

ARIEL [*Aside to Prospero*] Sir, all this service
Have I done since I went.

---

205 chalked . . . way marked as with a piece of chalk the pathway
207 Was Milan was the Duke of Milan   **214–215 all . . . own** all of us
have found ourselves and our sanity when we all had lost our senses
216 still always.   **his** that person's   **217 That** who   **220 blasphemy** i.e.,
blasphemer   **221 That swear'st grace o'erboard** i.e., you who banish
heavenly grace from the ship by your blasphemies.   **not an oath** aren't
you going to swear an oath   **225 glasses** i.e., hours.   **gave out** reported,
professed to be   **226 yare** ready.   **bravely** splendidly

PROSPERO [*Aside to Ariel*]   My tricksy spirit!   228
ALONSO
  These are not natural events; they strengthen   229
  From strange to stranger. Say, how came you hither?
BOATSWAIN
  If I did think, sir, I were well awake,
  I'd strive to tell you. We were dead of sleep,   232
  And—how we know not—all clapped under hatches,
  Where but even now, with strange and several noises   234
  Of roaring, shrieking, howling, jingling chains,
  And more diversity of sounds, all horrible,
  We were awaked; straightway at liberty;
  Where we, in all her trim, freshly beheld
  Our royal, good, and gallant ship, our Master
  Cap'ring to eye her. On a trice, so please you,   240
  Even in a dream, were we divided from them   241
  And were brought moping hither.
ARIEL [*Aside to Prospero*]   Was 't well done?   242
PROSPERO [*Aside to Ariel*]
  Bravely, my diligence. Thou shalt be free.
ALONSO
  This is as strange a maze as e'er men trod,
  And there is in this business more than nature
  Was ever conduct of. Some oracle   246
  Must rectify our knowledge.
PROSPERO   Sir, my liege,
  Do not infest your mind with beating on   248
  The strangeness of this business. At picked leisure,   249
  Which shall be shortly, single I'll resolve you,   250
  Which to you shall seem probable, of every   251
  These happened accidents; till when, be cheerful   252
  And think of each thing well. [*Aside to Ariel.*] Come
    hither, spirit.   253

---

228 tricksy ingenious, sportive **229 strengthen** increase **232 dead of
sleep** deep in sleep **234 several** different, diverse **240 Cap'ring to eye**
dancing for joy to see. **On a trice** in an instant **241 them** i.e., the
other crew members **242 moping** in a daze **246 conduct** guide,
leader **248 infest** harass, disturb. **beating on** worrying about
249 picked chosen, convenient **250 single** i.e., by my own human
powers. **resolve** satisfy, explain to **251 probable** explicable, plausible **251–252 of every These** about every one of these **252 accidents**
occurrences **253 well** favorably

Set Caliban and his companions free.
Untie the spell. [*Exit Ariel.*] How fares my gracious sir?
There are yet missing of your company
Some few odd lads that you remember not.   257

    Enter Ariel, driving in Caliban, Stephano, and
    Trinculo in their stolen apparel.

STEPHANO   Every man shift for all the rest, and let no   258
man take care for himself; for all is but fortune. Corag-   259
gio, bully monster, coraggio!   260

TRINCULO   If these be true spies which I wear in my   261
head, here's a goodly sight.

CALIBAN
O Setebos, these be brave spirits indeed!   263
How fine my master is! I am afraid   264
He will chastise me.

SEBASTIAN   Ha, ha!
What things are these, my lord Antonio?
Will money buy 'em?

ANTONIO   Very like. One of them
Is a plain fish, and no doubt marketable.

PROSPERO
Mark but the badges of these men, my lords,   270
Then say if they be true. This misshapen knave,   271
His mother was a witch, and one so strong
That could control the moon, make flows and ebbs,
And deal in her command without her power.   274
These three have robbed me, and this demidevil—
For he's a bastard one—had plotted with them   276
To take my life. Two of these fellows you
Must know and own. This thing of darkness I   278
Acknowledge mine.

---

257 odd unaccounted for   **258 shift** provide.   **for all the rest** (Stephano drunkenly gets wrong the saying "Every man for himself.") **259–260 Coraggio** courage   **260 bully monster** gallant monster. (Ironical.)   **261 true spies** accurate observers (i.e., sharp eyes)   **263 brave** handsome   **264 fine** splendidly attired   **270 badges** emblems of cloth or silver worn on the arms of retainers. (Prospero refers here to the stolen clothes as emblems of their villainy.)   **271 true** honest   **274 deal . . power** wield the moon's power, either without her authority or beyond her influence   **276 bastard** counterfeit   **278 own** recognize, admit as belonging to you

CALIBAN   I shall be pinched to death.
ALONSO
  Is not this Stephano, my drunken butler?
SEBASTIAN   He is drunk now. Where had he wine?
ALONSO
  And Trinculo is reeling ripe. Where should they   282
  Find this grand liquor that hath gilded 'em?   283
  [*To Trinculo.*] How cam'st thou in this pickle?   284
TRINCULO   I have been in such a pickle since I saw you
  last that, I fear me, will never out of my bones. I shall
  not fear flyblowing.   287
SEBASTIAN   Why, how now, Stephano?
STEPHANO   O, touch me not! I am not Stephano, but a
  cramp.
PROSPERO   You'd be king o' the isle, sirrah?   291
STEPHANO   I should have been a sore one, then.   292
ALONSO [*Pointing to Caliban*]
  This is a strange thing as e'er I looked on.
PROSPERO
  He is as disproportioned in his manners
  As in his shape.—Go, sirrah, to my cell.
  Take with you your companions. As you look
  To have my pardon, trim it handsomely.   297
CALIBAN
  Ay, that I will; and I'll be wise hereafter
  And seek for grace. What a thrice-double ass
  Was I to take this drunkard for a god
  And worship this dull fool!
PROSPERO   Go to. Away!
ALONSO
  Hence, and bestow your luggage where you found it.
SEBASTIAN   Or stole it, rather.
                [*Exeunt Caliban, Stephano, and Trinculo.*]
PROSPERO
  Sir, I invite Your Highness and your train

282 reeling ripe stumblingly drunk **283 gilded** (1) flushed, made drunk
(2) covered with gilt (suggesting the horse urine) **284 pickle** (1) fix,
predicament (2) pickling brine (in this case, horse urine) **287 flyblowing** i.e., being fouled by fly eggs (from which he is saved by being pick-
led) **291 sirrah** (Standard form of address to an inferior, here expressing reprimand.) **292 sore** (1) tyrannical (2) sorry, inept (3) wracked by
pain **297 trim** prepare, decorate

To my poor cell, where you shall take your rest
For this one night; which, part of it, I'll waste   306
With such discourse as, I not doubt, shall make it
Go quick away: the story of my life,
And the particular accidents gone by   309
Since I came to this isle. And in the morn
I'll bring you to your ship, and so to Naples,
Where I have hope to see the nuptial
Of these our dear-belovèd solemnized;
And thence retire me to my Milan, where   314
Every third thought shall be my grave.
ALONSO   I long
To hear the story of your life, which must
Take the ear strangely.
PROSPERO   I'll deliver all;   317
And promise you calm seas, auspicious gales,
And sail so expeditious that shall catch
Your royal fleet far off. [*Aside to Ariel.*] My Ariel, chick,
That is thy charge. Then to the elements
Be free, and fare thou well!—Please you, draw near.   322
                              Exeunt omnes.

❖

306 **waste** spend   309 **accidents** occurrences   314 **retire me** return
317 **Take** take effect upon, enchant.   **deliver** declare, relate   322 **draw
near** i.e., enter my cell

Epilogue   *Spoken by* PROSPERO.

Now my charms are all o'erthrown,
And what strength I have 's mine own,
Which is most faint. Now, 'tis true,
I must be here confined by you
Or sent to Naples. Let me not,
Since I have my dukedom got
And pardoned the deceiver, dwell
In this bare island by your spell,
But release me from my bands   9
With the help of your good hands.   10
Gentle breath of yours my sails   11
Must fill, or else my project fails,
Which was to please. Now I want   13
Spirits to enforce, art to enchant,   14
And my ending is despair
Unless I be relieved by prayer,   16
Which pierces so that it assaults   17
Mercy itself, and frees all faults.   18
As you from crimes would pardoned be,   19
Let your indulgence set me free.   *Exit.*   20

Epilogue.
9 bands bonds   **10 hands** i.e., applause (the noise of which would break
the spell of silence)   **11 Gentle breath** favorable breeze (produced by
hands clapping or favorable comment)   **13 want** lack   **14 enforce**
control   **16 prayer** i.e., Prospero's petition to the audience   **17 assaults**
rightfully gains the attention of   **18 frees** obtains forgiveness for
19 crimes sins   **20 indulgence** (1) humoring, lenient approval (2) re-
mission of punishment for sin

Date and Text

The Tempest was first printed in the First Folio of 1623. It occupies first place in the volume and is a scrupulously prepared text from a transcript by Ralph Crane of a theater promptbook or of Shakespeare's draft after it had been annotated for production; or Crane may have provided some of the elaboration of stage directions. Shakespeare's colleagues may have placed *The Tempest* first in the Folio because they considered it his most recent complete play. The first recorded performance was at court on November 1, 1611: "Hallomas nyght was presented att Whithall before ye kinges Maiestie a play Called the Tempest." The actors were "the Kings players" (*Revels Account*). The play was again presented at court during the winter of 1612–1613, this time "before the Princes Highnes the Lady Elizabeth and the Prince Pallatyne Elector." The festivities for this important betrothal and wedding were sumptuous, and included at least thirteen other plays. Various arguments have been put forward that Shakespeare composed parts of *The Tempest*, especially the masque, for this occasion, but there is absolutely no evidence that the play was singled out for special prominence among the many plays presented, and the masque is integral to the play as it stands. Probably the 1611 production was of a fairly new play. Simon Forman, who saw *Cymbeline* and *The Winter's Tale* in 1611, does not mention *The Tempest*. He died in September of 1611. According to every stylistic test, such as run-on and hypermetric lines, the play is very late. Shakespeare probably knew Sylvester Jourdain's *A Discovery of the Bermudas*, published in 1610, and William Strachey's *A True Repertory of the Wreck and Redemption*, dated July 1610 although not published until 1625.

Textual Notes

These textual notes are not a historical collation, either of the early folios or of more recent editions; they are simply a record of departures in this edition from the copy text. The reading adopted in this edition appears in boldface, followed by the rejected reading from the copy text, i.e., the First Folio. Only major alterations in punctuation are noted. Changes in lineation are not indicated, nor are some minor and obvious typographical errors.

Abbreviations used:
F the First Folio
s.d. stage direction
s.p. speech prefix

Copy text: the First Folio. Characters' names are grouped at the heads of scenes throughout.

Names of the Actors [printed in F at the end of the play]

1.1. 8 s.d. Ferdinand Ferdinando   **34 s.d. Exeunt** Exit   **36 [and elsewhere] wi' the** with   **38 s.d.** [at l. 37 in F]

1.2. 99 exact, like exact. Like   **166 steaded much.** steeded much,
201 bowsprit Bore-spritt   **213 me. The** me the   **263, 267 Algiers** Argier
284 she he   **288 service. Thou** service, thou   **330 forth at** for that
377, 399 s.d. Ariel's Ariel (or Ariell)   **400 s.p. Ariel** [not in F]   **385 s.d. Burden, dispersedly** [before "Hark, hark!" l. 384 in F]   **387** [F provides a speech prefix, *Ar.*]

2.1. 38 s.p. Antonio Seb   **39 s.p. Sebastian** Ant   **232 throes** throwes

2.2. 9 mow moe   **116 spirits** sprights

3.1. 2 sets set

3.2. 123 scout cout

3.3. 17 s.d. Solemn . . . invisible [after "they are fresh" in F, and followed by the s.d. at l. 19, *Enter . . . depart*]   **28 me** me?   **29 islanders?** Islands;
33 human humaine   **65 plume** plumbe

4.1. 9 off of   **13 gift** guest   **68 poll-clipped** pole-clipt   **74 Her** here
110 s.p. Ceres [not in F]   **123 wife** wise   **124 s.d.** [at l. 127 in F]
163 s.d. Exeunt Exit   **193 s.d. Enter . . . etc.** [after "on this line" in F]
193 them on on them   **232 Let 't** let's

5.1. 60 boiled boile   **72 Didst** Did   **75 entertained** entertaine
82 lies ly   **88 s.p. Ariel** [not in F]   **236 horrible,** horrible.   **238 her** our
249 business. At businesse, at   **250 Which . . . single** (Which shall be shortly single)   **259–260 Coraggio** Corasio

Shakespeare's Sources

No direct literary source for the whole of *The Tempest* has been found. Shakespeare does seem to have drawn material from various accounts of the shipwreck of the *Sea Venture* in the Bermudas, in 1609, although the importance of these materials should not be overstated. Several of the survivors wrote narratives of the shipwreck itself and of their life on the islands for some nine months. Sylvester Jourdain, in *A Discovery of the Bermudas*, published 1610 (see the selection that follows), speaks of miraculous preservation despite the island's reputation for being "a most prodigious and enchanted place." William Strachey's letter, written in July of 1610 and published much later (1625) as *A True Repertory of the Wreck and Redemption . . . from the Islands of the Bermudas*, describes (as can be seen in the selection that follows) the panic among the passengers and crew, the much-feared reputation of the island as the habitation of devils and wicked spirits, the actual beauty and fertility of the place with its abundance of wild life (cf. Caliban's descriptions), and the treachery of the Indians they later encounter in Virginia. Shakespeare seems to have read Strachey's letter in manuscript and may have been acquainted with him. The storm scene in Chapter 4 of Laurence Twine's *The Pattern of Painful Adventures*, a major source for *Pericles*, may also have given Shakespeare material for the first scene of *The Tempest;* see the source materials in the Bantam edition of that play. Shakespeare also kept up with travel accounts of Sir Walter Ralegh and Thomas Harriot, and knew various classical evocations of a New World. The name "Setebos" came from Richard Eden's *History of Travel* (1577), translated from Peter Martyr's *De Novo Orbe* and from other travel accounts of the period. (See the Introduction to the play for the potential relevance of various journals of the circumnavigation of the globe.) All these hints are indeed suggestive, but they are scattered and relate more to the setting and general circumstance of Shakespeare's play than to the plot.

Shakespeare certainly consulted Michel de Montaigne's essay "Of the Cannibals," as translated by John Florio in

1603. Gonzalo's reverie on an ideal commonwealth
(2.1.150–171) contains many verbal echoes of the essay, as
can be seen in the selection that follows. Montaigne's point
is that supposedly civilized persons who condemn as barbarous any society not conforming with their own are simply refusing to examine their own shortcomings. A
supposedly primitive society may well embody perfect religion, justice, and harmony; civilized art can never rival the
achievements of nature. The ideal commonwealth has no
need of magistrates, riches, poverty, and contracts, all of
which breed dissimulation and covetousness. The significance of these ideas for *The Tempest* extends well beyond
the particular passage in which they are found. And Caliban himself, whose name is an anagram of "cannibal," illustrates (even though he is not an eater of human flesh) the
truth of Montaigne's observation apropos of the intense
and wanton cruelty he finds so widespread in so-called
Western civilization: "I think there is more barbarism in
eating men alive than to feed upon them being dead."

Prospero's famous valedictory speech to "Ye elves of
hills, brooks, standing lakes, and groves" (5.1.33–57) owes
its origin to Medea's similar invocation in Ovid's *Metamorphoses* (Book 7), which Shakespeare knew both in the Latin
original and in Golding's translation: "Ye airs and winds,
ye elves of hills, of brooks, of woods alone, / Of standing
lakes . . ." Medea also anticipates Shakespeare's Sycorax.
Medea thus provides material for the representation of
both black and white magic in *The Tempest*, so carefully
differentiated by Shakespeare. Ariel is part English fairy,
like Puck, and part daemon. The pastoral situation in *The
Tempest* is perhaps derived from Edmund Spenser's *The
Faerie Queene*, Book 6 (with its distinctions between savage
lust and true courtesy, between nature and art). Italian pastoral drama as practiced by Guarini and (in England) by
John Fletcher may also have been an influence. The masque
element in *The Tempest*, prominent as in much late Shakespeare, bears the imprint of the courtly masque tradition of
Ben Jonson, Francis Beaumont, and John Fletcher. Virgil's
Aeneid may have provided Shakespeare with a more indi-
rect source, with its story of wandering in the Mediterranean and storm at sea, love in Carthage, the intervention of
the gods, and the fulfillment of destiny in Italy.

A German play, *Die Schöne Sidea* by Jacob Ayrer, written before 1605, was once thought to have been based on an earlier version of *The Tempest* as performed by English players traveling in Germany. Today the similarities between the two plays are generally attributed to conventions found everywhere in romance.

A Discovery of the Bermudas
By Sylvester Jourdain

Being in ship called the *Sea Venture,* with Sir Thomas
Gates, our governor, Sir George Somers, and Captain Newport, three most worthy honored gentlemen, whose valor
and fortitude the world must needs take notice of, and that
in most honorable designs bound for Virginia, in the height
of thirty degrees of northerly latitude or thereabouts, we
were taken with a most sharp and cruel storm upon the five
and twentieth day of July, Anno 1609. Which did not only
separate us from the residue of our fleet, which were eight
in number, but, with the violent working of the seas, our
ship became so shaken, torn, and leaked that she received
so much water as covered two tier of hogsheads[1] above the
ballast, that our men stood up to the middles with buckets,
barricos,[2] and kettles to bail out the water and continually
pumped for three days and three nights together without
any intermission, and yet the water seemed rather to increase than to diminish. Insomuch that all our men, being
utterly spent, tired, and disabled for longer labor, were even
resolved, without any hope of their lives, to shut up the
hatches and to have committed themselves to the mercy of
the sea (which is said to be merciless) or rather to the mercy
of their mighty God and redeemer (whose mercies exceed
all his works), seeing no help nor hope in the apprehension
of man's reason that any mother's child could escape that
inevitable danger which every man had proposed and digested[3] to himself of present[4] sinking.

So that some of them, having some good and comfortable
waters[5] in the ship, fetched them and drunk one to the
other, taking their last leave one of the other until their
more joyful and happy meeting in a more blessed world.
When it pleased God, out of his most gracious and merciful
providence, so to direct and guide our ship, being left to the
mercy of the sea for her most advantage, that Sir George
Somers, sitting upon the poop of the ship, where he sat

---

1 hogsheads large barrels or casks   **2 barricos** kegs   **3 digested** pon-
dered   **4 present** immediate   **5 waters** distilled alcohol

three days and three nights together without meals' meat[6] and little or no sleep, conning[7] the ship to keep her as upright as he could (for otherwise she must needs instantly have foundered),[8] most wishedly happily descried land.

Whereupon he most comfortably encouraged the company to follow[9] their pumping and by no means to cease bailing out of the water with their buckets, barricos, and kettles, whereby they were so over-wearied, and their spirits so spent with long fasting and continuance of their labor, that for the most part they were fallen asleep in corners and wheresoever they chanced first to sit or lie. But hearing news of land, wherewith they grew to be somewhat revived, being carried with will and desire beyond their strength, every man bustled up and gathered his strength and feeble spirits together to perform as much as their weak force would permit him.

Through which weak means it pleased God to work so strongly as[10] the water was stayed[11] for that little time, which, as we all much feared, was the last period of our breathing,[12] and the ship kept from present sinking, when it pleased God to send her within half an English mile of that land Sir George Somers had not long before descried— which were the islands of the Bermudas. And there neither did our ship sink, but, more fortunately in so great a misfortune, fell in[13] between two rocks, where she was fast lodged and locked for further budging. Whereby we gained not only sufficient time, with the present help of our boat and skiff, safely to set and convey our men ashore (which were one hundred and fifty in number), but afterwards had time and leisure to save some good part of our goods and provision which the water had not spoiled, with all the tackling[14] of the ship and much of the iron about her, which were necessaries not a little available for the building and furnishing of a new ship and pinnace,[15]* which we made there for the transporting and carrying of us to Virginia.

But our delivery was not more strange in falling so oppor-

---

6 meals' meat food   7 conning steering, navigating   8 foundered be engulfed, sent to the bottom   9 follow keep up   10 as that   11 stayed held back   12 the last . . . breathing i.e., our last gasp   13 fell in i.e., steered her way   14 tackling ropes and pulleys   15 pinnace a light sailing vessel used as a tender for a larger ship

tunely and happily upon the land as our feeding and preservation was beyond our hopes and all men's expectations most admirable. For the islands of the Bermudas, as every man knoweth that hath heard or read of them, were never inhabited by any Christian or heathen people, but ever esteemed and reputed a most prodigious and enchanted place, affording nothing but gusts, storms, and foul weather, which made every navigator and mariner to avoid them as Scylla and Charybdis,[16] or as they would shun the devil himself; and no man was ever heard to make for[17] the place but as[18] against their wills they have, by storms and dangerousness of the rocks lying seven leagues into the sea, suffered shipwreck. Yet did we find there the air so temperate and the country so abundantly fruitful of all fit necessaries for the sustenation and preservation of man's life, that most in a manner of all[19] our provisions of bread, beer, and victual being quite spoiled in lying long drowned in salt water, notwithstanding we were there for the space of nine months (few days over or under) not only well refreshed, comforted, and with good satiety contented but, out of the abundance thereof, provided us some reasonable quantity and proportion[20] of provision to carry us for Virginia and to maintain ourselves and that company we found there, to the great relief of them, as it fell out in their so great extremities and in respect of the shortness of time, until it pleased God that, by my lord's[21] coming thither, their store was better supplied. And greater and better provisions we might have had if we had had better means for the storing and transportation thereof. Wherefore my opinion sincerely of this island is that whereas it hath been and is still accounted the most dangerous, infortunate, and most forlorn place of the world, it is in truth the richest, healthfulest, and pleasing land (the quantity and bigness thereof considered) and merely[22] natural as ever man set foot upon.

---

16 Scylla and Charybdis monster and whirlpool facing each other across a narrow strait in *The Odyssey*, Book 12   **17 make for** head for **18 as** that   **19 most in a manner of all** i.e., even though nearly all **20 proportion** share   **21 my lord's** i.e., Sir Thomas Gates's   **22 merely** utterly

[Most of the remainder of *A Discovery of the Bermudas* is taken up with a description of the island, its flora and fauna, etc., much as in William Strachey's account.]

Text based on *A Discovery of the Bermudas* [spelled *Barmudas* in the original], *Otherwise Called the Isle of Devils*, by Sir Thomas Gates, Sir George Somers, and Captain Newport, with Divers Others. . . . London, Printed by John Windet . . . 1610.

In the following, the departure from the original text appears in boldface; the original reading is in roman.

p. 617 *pinnace pinms

A True Repertory of the Wreck and Redemption of Sir Thomas Gates, Knight, upon and from the Islands of the Bermudas

By William Strachey

[Strachey's account is in the form of a letter, beginning as the fleet of seven ships and two pinnaces—i.e., light sailing vessels used as tenders for the larger ships—is within seven or eight days sailing of Cape Henry, Virginia, in late July of 1609.]

When on Saint James his day, July 24, being Monday, preparing for no less all the black night before, the clouds gathering thick upon us and the winds singing and whistling most unusually, which made us to cast off our pinnace, towing the same until then astern, a dreadful storm and hideous began to blow from out the northeast, which, swelling and roaring as it were by fits, some hours with more violence than others, at length did beat all light from heaven; which like an hell of darkness turned black upon us, so much the more fuller of horror as in such cases horror and fear use to¹ overrun the troubled and overmastered senses of all, which, taken up with amazement, the ears lay so sensible to the terrible cries and murmurs of the winds and distraction of our company as who was most armed² and best prepared was not a little shaken. . . .

For four and twenty hours the storm in a restless tumult had blown so exceedingly as we could not apprehend in our imaginations any possibility of greater violence. Yet did we still find it not only more terrible but more constant, fury added to fury and one storm urging a second more outrageous than the former, whether it so wrought upon our fears or indeed met with new forces. Sometimes shrieks³* in our ship amongst women and passengers not used to such hurly and discomforts made us look one upon the other with troubled hearts and panting bosoms. Our clamors drowned in the winds, and the winds in thunder.

1 use to habitually, characteristically   **2 as who was most armed** that even that person who was most ready to protect himself   **3 shrieks** (The original *strikes* is probably an error for *shrieks*.)

Prayers might well be in the heart and lips, but drowned in the outcries of the officers. Nothing heard that could give comfort, nothing seen that might encourage hope.

It is impossible for me, had I the voice of Stentor[4] and expression of as many tongues as his throat of voices, to express the outcries and miseries. . . . In which the sea swelled above the clouds and gave battle unto heaven. It could not be said to rain; the waters like whole rivers did flood in the air. And this I did still observe: that whereas upon the land, when a storm hath poured itself forth once in drifts of rain, the wind, as beaten down and vanquished therewith not long after endureth; here the glut of water, as if throttling the wind erewhile,[5] was no sooner a little emptied and qualified but instantly the winds, as having gotten their mouths now free and at liberty, spake more loud and grew more tumultuous and malignant.

What shall I say? Winds and seas were as mad as fury and rage could make them. For mine own part, I had been in some storms before. . . . Yet all that I had ever suffered gathered together might not hold comparison with this. There was not a moment in which the sudden splitting or instant oversetting of the ship was not expected.

Howbeit, this was not all. It pleased God to bring a greater affliction yet upon us, for in the beginning of the storm we had received likewise a mighty leak. And the ship . . . was grown five foot suddenly deep with water above her ballast, and we almost drowned within whilst we sat looking when to perish from above. This, imparting no less terror than danger, ran through the whole ship with much fright and amazement, startled and turned the blood and took down the braves[6] of the most hardy mariner of them all, insomuch as he that before happily felt not the sorrow of others now began to sorrow for himself when he saw such a pond of water so suddenly broken in, and which he knew could not, without present avoiding, but instantly sink him. . . .

Once, so huge a sea brake upon the poop and quarter upon us, as it covered our ship from stern to stem like a garment or a vast cloud; it filled her brim full for a while within, from the hatches up to the spar deck. This source,

---

4 Stentor a Greek with a voice as loud as fifty men   **5 erewhile** formerly   **6 braves** courage

or confluence, of water was so violent as[7] it rushed and carried the helmsman from the helm and wrested the whipstaff[8] out of his hand, which so flew from side to side that, when he would have seized[9] the same again, it so tossed him from starboard to larboard as it was God's mercy it had not split him. It so beat him from his hold and so bruised him as[10] a fresh man, hazarding in by chance, fell fair with it and, by main strength bearing somewhat up, made good his place,[11] and with much clamor encouraged and called upon others, who gave her now up, rent in pieces and absolutely lost. . . .

During all this time, the heavens looked so black upon us that it was not possible the elevation of the pole might be observed,[12] nor a star by night nor sunbeam by day was to be seen. Only upon the Thursday night, Sir George Somers, being upon the watch, had an apparition of a little round light, like a faint star, trembling and streaming along with a sparkling blaze half the height upon the mainmast and shooting sometimes from shroud to shroud, tempting[13] to settle as it were upon any of the four shrouds. And for three or four hours together, or rather more, half the night it kept with us, running sometimes along the mainyard to the very end and then returning. At which Sir George Somers called divers about him and showed them the same, who observed it with much wonder and carefulness. But upon a sudden, towards the morning watch, they lost the sight of it and knew not what way it made. The superstitious seamen make many constructions of this sea fire, which nevertheless is usual in storms—the same, it may be, which the Grecians were wont in the Mediterranean to call Castor and Pollux, of which, if one only appeared without the other, they took it for an evil sign of great tempest.[14] The Italians

---

7 as that   8 whipstaff handle attached to the tiller   9 seized i.e., secured, stopped its uncontrolled whipping about   10 as that   11 made good his place (Another seaman, coming on the scene by chance, manages by brute strength to secure the tiller and its handle.)   made good supplied   12 the elevation . . . observed to measure the elevation of the polestar above the horizon (and thereby determine latitude)
13 tempting attempting. (The phenomenon observed is St. Elmo's fire, as in *The Tempest*, 1.2.197–202.)   14 Castor and Pollux . . . tempest (This name, taken from the twin sons of Tyndarus and Leda, was applied to St. Elmo's fire because, when the phenomenon appeared in pairs simultaneously, it was thought to signal the cessation of a storm.)

and such, who lie open to the Adriatic and Tyrrhene Sea,[15] call it a sacred body, *Corpo sancto*. The Spaniards call it Saint Elmo, and have an authentic and miraculous legend for it. Be it what it will, we laid other foundations of safety or ruin than in the rising or falling of it. Could it have served us now miraculously to have taken our height by,[16] it might have strucken amazement and a reverence in our devotions, according to the due of a miracle. But it did not light us any whit the more to our known way, who ran now (as do hoodwinked men) at all adventures,[17] sometimes north and northeast, then north and by west . . . and sometimes half the compass. . . .

It being now Friday, the fourth morning, it wanted little but that there had been[18] a general determination to have shut up hatches, and, commending our sinful souls to God, committed the ship to the mercy of the sea. Surely that night we must have done it, and that night had we then perished. But see the goodness and sweet introduction of better hope by our merciful God given unto us! Sir George Somers, when no man dreamed of such happiness, had discovered and cried[19] land. . . . But having no hope to save her by coming to an anchor in the same [some smooth water under the southeast point of the land], we were enforced to run her ashore as near the land as we could, which brought us within three quarters of a mile of shore; and, by the mercy of God unto us, making out our boats,[20] we had ere night brought all our men, women, and children—about the number of one hundred and fifty—safe into the island.

We found it to be the dangerous and dreaded island, or rather islands, of the Bermuda, whereof let me give Your Ladyship[21] a brief description before I proceed to my narration. And that the rather,[22] because they be so terrible to all that ever touched on them, and such tempests, thunders, and other fearful objects are seen and heard about them, that they be called commonly the Devil's Islands, and are feared and avoided of all sea travelers alive above any other

---

15 Tyrrhene Sea Tyrrhenian Sea, lying between Italy, Sicily, and Sardinia   **16 to have . . . by** to have measured our latitude by. (See note 12 above.)   **17 at all adventures** totally at random   **18 it wanted . . . been** i.e., we were very close to.   **it wanted** there lacked   **19 cried** announced, called out   **20 making out our boats** setting out our small ship's boats   **21 Your Ladyship** the noble lady to whom the letter is written   **22 rather** sooner

place in the world. Yet it pleased our merciful God to make even this hideous and hated place both the place of our safety and means of our deliverance.

And hereby also I hope to deliver the world from a foul and general error, it being counted[23] of most that they can be no habitation for men, but rather given over to devils and wicked spirits. Whereas indeed we find them now by experience to be as habitable and commodious as most countries of the same climate and situation, insomuch as, if the entrance into them were as easy as the place itself is contenting, it had long ere this been inhabited as well as other islands. Thus shall we make it appear that Truth is the daughter of Time, and that men ought not to deny everything which is not subject to their own sense.

[Strachey proceeds with a description of the islands—their climate, topography, flora and fauna, etc.]

Sure it is that there are no rivers nor running springs of fresh water to be found upon any of them. When we came first, we digged and found certain gushings and soft bubblings which, being either in bottoms or on the side of hanging ground, were only fed with rain water which nevertheless soon sinketh into the earth and vanisheth away, or emptieth itself out of sight into the sea without any channel above or upon the superficies[24] of the earth. For according as their rains fell, we had wells and pits which we digged either half full or absolute exhausted and dry; howbeit some low bottoms, which the continual descent from the hills filled full, and in those flats could have no passage away, we found to continue as fishing ponds or standing pools, continually summer and winter full of fresh water.

The shore and bays round about when we landed first afforded great store of fish, and that of divers kinds, and good. . . . We have taken also from under the broken rocks crevices[25] oftentimes greater than any of our best English lobsters, and likewise abundance of crabs, oyster, and whelks. True it is, for fish in every cove and creek we found snaules and skulles[26] in that abundance as I think no island in the world may have greater store or better fish. . . .

23 counted reckoned, supposed   **24 superficies** surface   **25 crevices** crayfish. (French *écrevisse*.)   **26 snaules and skulles** (Identity uncertain: snails or snailfish and schools or skullfish?)

Fowl there is great store. . . . A kind of webfooted fowl there is, of the bigness of an English green plover or seamew,[27] which all the summer we saw not, and in the darkest nights of November and December (for in the night they only feed) they would come forth but not fly far from home and, hovering in the air and over the sea, made a strange hollow and harsh howling. . . . Our men found a pretty way to take them, which was by standing on the rocks or sands by the seaside and halooing, laughing, and making the strangest outcry that possibly they could. With the noise whereof the birds would come flocking to that place and settle upon the very arms and head of him that so cried, and still creep nearer and nearer, answering the noise themselves; by which our men would weigh them with their hand, and which weighed heaviest they took for the best and let the others alone, and so our men would take twenty dozen in two hours of the chiefest of them; and they were a good and well-relished fowl, fat and full as a partridge.

[Among the other adventures reported by Strachey is a conspiracy or mutiny aimed at the life of their governor, but the leaders are apprehended. Later, when they reach Virginia and find the colony of Jamestown in a perilous state, the voyagers encounter some native Indians and are surprised to discover "how little a fair and noble entreaty works upon a barbarous disposition."]

Strachey's letter, written in 1610, was published as *A True Repertory of the Wreck and Redemption of Sir Thomas Gates, Knight, upon and from the Islands of the Bermudas, His Coming to Virginia, and the Estate of the Colony Then and After under the Government of the Lord La Warre. July, 15, 1610, written by William Strachey, Esquire.* In Samuel Purchas, *Purchas His Pilgrims* (1625), Part 4, Book 9, Chapter 6, pp. 1734 ff.

In the following, the departure from the original text appears in boldface; the original reading is in roman.

p. 620 *shrieks strikes

---

27 seamew sea gull (perhaps to be identified with the *scamels* mentioned by Caliban in *The Tempest*, 2.2.170)

The Essays of Michael, Lord of Montaigne
Translated by John Florio

BOOK 1, CHAPTER 30: OF THE CANNIBALS

[Montaigne begins by citing approvingly the opinion of King Pyrrhus of Greece that the so-called barbarians are often far from barbarous. "Lo, how a man ought to take heed lest he overweeningly follow vulgar opinions, which should be measured by the rule of reason and not by the common report." Montaigne cites various examples and then turns to the American Indians.]

Now, to return to my purpose, I find (as far as I have been informed) there is nothing in that nation that is either barbarous or savage, unless men call that barbarism which is not common to them. As indeed we have no other aim of truth and reason than the example and idea of the opinions and customs of the country we live in. There is ever perfect religion, perfect policy,[1] perfect and complete use of all things. They[2] are even "savage" as we call those fruits wild which nature of herself and of her ordinary progress[3] hath produced, whereas indeed they are those which ourselves have altered by our artificial devices and diverted from their common order we should rather term "savage."[4] In those[5] are the true and most profitable virtues and natural properties most lively and vigorous, which in these[6] we have bastardized, applying them to the pleasure of our corrupted taste. And if, notwithstanding, in divers fruits of those countries that were never tilled we shall find that, in respect of[7] ours, they are most excellent and as delicate unto our taste, there is no reason art should gain the point

1 **There ... policy** i.e., there, in our own society as we complacently view it, is always perfect religion, perfect government 2. **They** i.e., those "savage" people 3 **progress** course, way 4 **they are those ... "savage"** we should instead term "savage" those things we ourselves have artificially diverted from their natural function 5 **those** i.e., things made by nature 6 **these** i.e., things diverted by us from their natural function 7 **in respect of** in comparison with

of honor of[8] our great and puissant mother Nature. We have
so much by our inventions surcharged[9] the beauties and
riches of her works that we have altogether overchoked her;
yet wherever her purity shineth, she makes our vain and
frivolous enterprises wonderfully ashamed.

> *Et veniunt hederae sponte sua melius,*
> *Surgit et in solis formosior arbutu antris,*
> *Et volucres nulla dulcius arte canunt.*
>   [Propertius]

> Ivies spring better of their own accord;
> Unhaunted[10] plots much fairer trees afford;
> Birds by no art much sweeter notes record.

All our endeavors or wit cannot so much as reach to represent the nest of the least birdlet, its contexture, beauty,
profit, and use, no, nor the web of a silly[11] spider. "All
things," saith Plato, "are produced either by nature, by fortune, or by art. The greatest and fairest by one or other of
the two first, the least and imperfect by the last."

Those nations seem therefore so barbarous unto me because they have received very little fashion from human
wit[12] and are yet near their original naturality. The laws of
nature do yet command them, which are but little bastardized[13] by ours, and that with such purity as I am sometimes
grieved the knowledge of it came no sooner to light at what
time[14] there were men that better than we could have judged
of it. I am sorry Lycurgus[15] and Plato had it not, for me-
seemeth that, what in those nations we see by experience
doth not only exceed all the pictures wherewith licentious[16]
poesy hath proudly embellished the golden age and all her

---

8 should . . . honor of should be awarded the prize over   **9 by our
inventions surcharged** by means of our artificial contrivances overwhelmed   **10 Unhaunted** unfrequented   **11 silly** innocent, simple, tiny
12 Those . . . wit i.e., those so-called savage nations seem therefore
"barbarous" to me only in the sense that they have received little
fashioning from civilized intellect   **13 but little bastardized** scarcely
diverted from their natural function   **14 at what time** when
15 Lycurgus legendary Spartan legislator whose name was applied to
important social and legal reforms c. 600 B.C.   **16 licentious** taking free
poetic license, playing fast and loose with the truth

quaint inventions to feign[17] a happy condition of man, but
also the conception and desire of philosophy. They[18] could
not imagine a genuity[19] so pure and simple as we see it by
experience,[20] nor ever believe[21] our society might be maintained with so little art and humane combination. It is a
nation, would I answer Plato, that hath no kind of traffic,[22]
no knowledge of letters,[23] no intelligence[24] of numbers, no
name of magistrate,[25] nor of politic superiority,[26] no use of
service,[27] of riches, or of poverty, no contracts, no succes-
sions, no dividances, no occupation but idle,[28] no respect of
kindred but common,[29] no apparel but natural, no manur-
ing of lands, no use of wine, corn,[30] or metal. The very
words that import lying, falsehood, treason, dissimula-
tions, covetousness, envy, detraction,[31] and pardon, were
never heard of amongst them. How dissonant would he
find[32] his imaginary commonwealth from this perfection!

Hos natura modos primum dedit.

Nature at first uprise[33]
These manners did devise.
[Virgil]

Furthermore, they live in a country of so exceeding pleasant and temperate situation that, as my testimonies[34] have
told me, it is very rare to see a sick body amongst them; and
they have further assured me they never saw any man there
either shaking with the palsy, toothless, with eyes dropping,[35] or crooked and stooping through age.

---

17 all her . . . feign all of poesy's ingenious fabrications used to imagine
or pretend   **18 They** i.e., poesy and philosophy   **19 genuity** ingenuous-
ness, simplicity   **20 by experience** i.e., by looking at the ways of so-
called "savage" peoples   **21 believe** believe that   **22 traffic** trade
23 letters writing   **24 intelligence** knowledge, science   **25 of magistrate**
for a magistrate   **26 politic superiority** political hierarchy   **27 service**
servitude   **28 but idle** except leisure ones   **29 no respect . . . common**
no kinship ties except those held in common   **30 corn** wheat. (Grains
grow naturally, not by agriculture.)   **31 detraction** belittling   **32 How
dissonant would he find** i.e., how far (from this ideal state of affairs)
would he, Plato, find   **33 at first uprise** at her very beginnings
34 testimonies witnesses   **35 with eyes dropping** i.e., bleary-eyed or
discharging fluid

[Montaigne continues with a description of their abundance. Later in the essay he examines cannibalism in the same relativistic terms:]

I am not sorry we note the barbarous horror of such an action, but grieved that, prying so narrowly into their faults, we are so blinded in ours. I think there is more barbarism in eating men alive than to feed upon them being dead—to mangle by tortures and torments a body full of lively sense,[36] to roast him in pieces, to make dogs and swine to gnaw and tear him in mammocks[37] (as we have not only read but seen very lately, yea, and in our own memory, not amongst ancient enemies but our neighbors and fellow citizens, and, which is worse, under pretense of piety and religion) than to roast and tear him after he is dead.

———————

Text based on *The Essays, or Moral, Politic, and Military Discourses of Lord Michael de Montaigne.... First written by him in French. And now done into English by ... John Florio. Printed at London by Val. Sims for Edward Blount ... 1603.*

36 lively sense acute feeling   **37 mammocks** shreds

Metamorphoses
By Ovid
Translated by Arthur Golding

BOOK 7

[Medea, preparing to use her magical powers to prolong the life of Jason's father, Aeson, invokes the spirits of the unseen world.]

> Ye airs and winds, ye elves of hills, of brooks, of
>   woods alone,
> Of standing lakes, and of the night, approach ye
>   everychone!   266
> Through help of whom, the crooked banks much
>   wondering at the thing,
> I have compellèd streams to run clean backward to
>   their spring.
> By charms I make the calm seas rough and make the
>   rough seas plain,
> And cover all the sky with clouds and chase them
>   thence again.
> By charms I raise and lay the winds, and burst the
>   viper's jaw,   271
> And from the bowels of the earth both stones and
>   trees do draw.
> Whole woods and forests I remove; I make the
>   mountains shake,
> And even the earth itself to groan and fearfully to
>   quake.
> I call up dead men from their graves; and thee, O
>   lightsome Moon,   275
> I darken oft, though beaten brass abate thy peril
>   soon.   276

---

266 everychone everyone   **271 lay** allay, cause to subside   **275 lightsome** light-giving   **276 though . . . soon** (Alludes to the belief that a loud noise such as that produced by beating on metal would frighten away the malign influence of an eclipse.)

Our sorcery dims the morning fair and darks the sun
  at noon.

———————————

Text based on *The XV Books of P. Ovidius Naso, Entitled Metamorphoses.
Translated out of Latin into English meter by Arthur Golding, Gentleman. A
work very pleasant and delectable. . . . Imprinted at London by William Seres.
1567.*

Further Reading

Auden, W. H. "The Sea and the Mirror: A Commentary on Shakespeare's *The Tempest*." *For the Time Being*. New York: Random House, 1944. Rpt. in *The Collected Poetry of W. H. Auden*. New York: Random House, 1945. Auden's "The Sea and the Mirror" is a poetic meditation on *The Tempest*, a sequence of imagined speeches taking up where Shakespeare's play ends. Characters declare their new knowledge of what they are: Antonio still recalcitrant, Prospero poignantly aware of his own limitations, and Caliban voicing the disturbing reality that he represents for both Prospero and the audience.

Berger, Harry, Jr. "Miraculous Harp: A Reading of Shakespeare's *Tempest*." *Shakespeare Studies* 5 (1969): 253–283. Berger offers a complex refutation of the familiar romantic readings of the play. Focusing on Prospero's efforts at mastery in the recurring scenes in which he attempts to evoke fear, guilt, or sympathy, Berger argues that the play dramatizes the limitations of Prospero's power as well as his deep reluctance to abandon it.

Brockbank, J. Philip. "*The Tempest*: Conventions of Art and Empire." In *Later Shakespeare*, ed. John Russell Brown and Bernard Harris. Stratford-upon-Avon Studies 8. London: Edward Arnold; New York: St. Martin's, 1966. In the accounts of the wreck of the *Sea Venture* and the miraculous survival of its crew, Brockbank finds the origins of *The Tempest*'s emphasis upon providential control and moral change. For him the play celebrates the process of conversion and repentance, not in the organic metaphors of seasonal growth as in Shakespeare's pastoral plays, but in images of the mysterious, renewing action of the sea.

Coleridge, Samuel Taylor. "*The Tempest*." *Coleridge's Writings on Shakespeare*, ed. Terence Hawkes. New York: G. P. Putnam's Sons, 1959. In a series of lectures, Coleridge discusses the "astonishing and intuitive knowledge" of character that Shakespeare reveals in "this, almost miraculous, drama." Ariel is a spirit of the air, necessarily resenting that "he is bound to obey Prospero."

Caliban "is all earth," but Shakespeare "has raised him far above contempt." Of Prospero and Miranda Coleridge says: "I have often thought of Shakespeare as the mighty wizard himself introducing as the first and fairest pledge of his so potent art, the female character in all its charms."

Felperin, Howard. "Undream'd Shores: *The Tempest*." *Shakespearean Romance*. Princeton, N.J.: Princeton Univ. Press, 1972. Romance, according to Felperin, is both the subject and the genre of *The Tempest*. The play tests the ability of the imagination to perfect reality, and if Prospero's magic is ultimately found unable to reconcile the idealizing impulses of romance and the resistances of history, Shakespeare's art can—in the play's ingenious combination of a fictional political action and a romantic account of a shipwreck based on historical sources.

Fiedler, Leslie A. "The New World Savage as Stranger; or, 'Tis New to Thee.' " *The Stranger in Shakespeare*. New York: Stein and Day, 1972. In a provocative reading of the play focusing on its relation to the colonizing enterprise of Renaissance Europe, Fiedler argues that Caliban's role as "a savage and deformed slave" reveals the inadequacy of the play's twin utopian hopes: Gonzalo's vision of an idealized political existence and Prospero's fantasy of innocent love.

Frey, Charles. "*The Tempest* and the New World." *Shakespeare Quarterly* 30 (1979): 29–41. Believing the play to be neither "an autonomous imaginative construct" nor "an historical document," Frey suggestively examines accounts of Sir Francis Drake's circumnavigation of the globe and records of the Jamestown settlement to explore *The Tempest*'s "peculiar merger of history and romance."

Frye, Northrop. *A Natural Perspective: The Development of Shakespeare's Comedy and Romance*, passim. New York: Columbia Univ. Press, 1965. Frye treats the late romances as a return to and culmination of the logic of the earlier romantic comedies. In *The Tempest* Frye discovers the comic movement from confusion to identity and from sterility to renewed life, lifting us out of the world of ordinary experience into a world perfected by the human imagination.

James, D. G. *The Dream of Prospero*. Oxford: Clarendon Press, 1967. James locates the play in the context of Shakespeare's own achievement in *Hamlet* and *King Lear* as well as in the intellectual and political currents of the early seventeenth century. He explores the play's complex play of tone as it reveals a world in which love and hope cannot deny the possibility of tragedy but do make it possible to bear the burden of tragic knowledge.

James, Henry. "Introduction to *The Tempest*." In *Complete Works of Shakespeare*, 1907, ed. Sydney Lazarus Lee. Rpt. in *Henry James: Selected Literary Criticism*, ed. Morris Shapira. London: Heineman, 1963; New York: Horizon, 1964. In his introduction to *The Tempest*—one of "the supreme works of all literature"—James reflects upon the contradiction between the man who, having written the play, retires to Stratford, and the artist at the peak of his powers of expression, aware of his mastery of style and characterization.

Kermode, Frank. *"The Tempest." William Shakespeare: The Final Plays*. London: Longmans, Green, 1963. While *The Tempest*, like Shakespeare's other late plays, develops the familiar themes of repentance and renewal, its handling of this romantic material differs from the others in the neoclassic design of the plot and the philosophical and spectacular elements drawn from the masque. Above all, for Kermode, the play is strange and elusive, lacking the other romances' sustained notes of joy and rising above the ingenuities of criticism that would contain its mystery.

Kernan, Alvin B. " 'The Great Globe Itself': The Public Playhouse and the Ideal Theater of *The Tempest*." *The Playwright as Magician: Shakespeare's Image of the Poet in the English Public Theater*. New Haven, Conn.: Yale Univ. Press, 1979. Kernan finds that in the creation and control of Prospero's island kingdom through art lie Shakespeare's strongest claims for the power of the theatrical imagination: the play is both visionary and moral, recreating in Prospero's suffering and exile the central pattern of existence.

Kott, Jan. "Prospero's Staff." *Shakespeare Our Contemporary*, trans. Boleslaw Taborski. Garden City, N.Y.: Doubleday, 1964. In Kott's dark vision of *The Tempest*, the island is not a utopian landscape but a stage on which the history of the world with its endless struggles for power is elementally enacted. Prospero's rule over Caliban's island mirrors Antonio's usurpation of Prospero's throne; Sebastian's hope to murder Alonso repeats Antonio's fratricidal desires; and the plot of Stephano, Trinculo, and Caliban to depose and murder Prospero farcically reenacts all of the grim human history that Kott sees centrally reflected in the play.

Marx, Leo. "Shakespeare's American Fable." *The Machine in the Garden: Technology and the Pastoral Ideal in America.* London and New York: Oxford Univ. Press, 1964. Marx argues that the early European travel narratives envisioning the New World either as an earthly paradise or a hideous wilderness generate the poles of *The Tempest*'s dialectical treatment of nature and civilization. The final affirmations of the play, he argues, rest on the successful mediation of this opposition, as Prospero learns both the necessity of his art to control and shape fallen nature and the limitations of his art to perfect it.

Orgel, Stephen. "New Uses of Adversity: Tragic Experience in *The Tempest*." In *In Defense of Reading: A Reader's Approach to Literary Criticism*, ed. Reuben A. Brower and Richard Poirier. New York: E .P. Dutton, 1962; rpt. in *Essays in Shakespearean Criticism*, ed. James L. Calderwood and Harold E. Toliver. Englewood Cliffs, N.J.: Prentice-Hall, 1970. Examining the play's movement toward harmony, Orgel discovers the power and authority of the redemptive action in the experience of tragedy. Prospero leads the characters through suffering to reconciliation, not denying but transforming tragedy in the shifts of perspective achieved by his art. Even in the happy end, however, the tragic implications of human nature are not evaded as Prospero leaves the island and his magic for the imperfect world of human society.

Palmer, D. J., ed. *Shakespeare, "The Tempest": A Casebook.* London: Macmillan, 1968. Palmer's useful casebook provides extracts from William Davenant and John Dryden's Restoration adaptation of the play, comments by early critics and editors such as Nicholas Rowe, Samuel Johnson, and William Hazlitt, and modern essays, including studies by Kermode and Kott (cited above).

Peterson, Douglas L. "*The Tempest:* 'Remember, for That's My Business with You.'" *Time, Tide and Tempest: A Study of Shakespeare's Romances.* San Marino, Calif.: Huntington Library, 1973. Informed by a benign conception of time that presents Prospero with the opportunity to correct the mistakes of the past, *The Tempest,* according to Peterson, celebrates the renewing power of love. Prospero succeeds in redeeming the past and insuring the future by using the present moment to forgive rather than revenge old wrongs.

Summers, Joseph H. "The Anger of Prospero." *Dreams of Love and Power.* Oxford: Clarendon Press, 1984. Examining the various scenes in which Prospero appears irritated or angry, Summers discovers the cause in Prospero's anxiety about both his own responsibility for the past and his ability to shape the future to the happy end he desires. Only when the play's complex harmonies have been achieved and Prospero is without power is he also without anger.

Sundelson, David. "So Rare a Wonder'd Father: Prospero's *Tempest.*" In *Representing Shakespeare: New Psychoanalytic Essays,* ed. Murray M. Schwartz and Coppélia Kahn. Baltimore: Johns Hopkins Univ. Press, 1980. Rev. and rpt. in *Shakespeare's Restorations of the Father.* New Brunswick, N.J.: Rutgers Univ. Press, 1983. Sundelson brings the vocabulary and concerns of psychoanalytic criticism to *The Tempest,* locating the play's central concerns in its complex representation of fatherhood. He traces the articulated anxieties about power and sexuality and examines the process by which Prospero masters these, making possible the play's final harmony in his altruistic surrender to the desires of others.

William, David. "*The Tempest* on the Stage." In *Jacobean Theatre,* ed. John Russell Brown and Bernard Harris. Stratford-upon-Avon Studies 1. London: Edward Arnold; New York: St. Martin's Press, 1960. Sensitively attending to the play's theatrical qualities, William argues that the play in performance must resist the tendency toward visual display and sentimentality that has often obscured its strength. He charts how effective control of the play's tone, rhythm, and characterization might reveal the play's power and poignancy as its sense of triumph is tempered by an awareness of the intractable aspects of human nature that refuse to be shaped by Prospero's art.

Memorable Lines

Pericles

See where she comes, appareled like the spring.

(PERICLES 1.1.13)

Few love to hear the sins they love to act. (PERICLES 1.1.93)

The sad companion, dull-eyed melancholy.

(PERICLES 1.2.2)

I'll show you those in trouble's reign,
Losing a mite, a mountain gain. (GOWER 2.0.7–8)

Till fortune, tired with doing bad,
Threw him ashore, to give him glad. (GOWER 2.0.37–38)

THIRD FISHERMAN Master, I marvel how the fishes live in the
sea.
FIRST FISHERMAN Why, as men do aland: the great ones eat
up the little ones. (2.1.27–29)

Whereby I see that Time's the king of men;
He's both their parent and he is their grave,
And gives them what he will, not what they crave.

(PERICLES 2.3.47–49)

Yet thou dost look
Like Patience gazing on kings' graves and smiling
Extremity out of act. (PERICLES 5.1.140–142)

This is the rarest dream that e'er dull sleep
Did mock sad fools withal. (PERICLES 5.1.166–167)

O, come hither,
Thou that begett'st him that did thee beget.

(PERICLES 5.1.199–200)

This, this! No more, you gods! Your present kindness
Makes my past miseries sports. (PERICLES 5.3.41–42)

Memorable Lines

Cymbeline

... hath his bellyful of fighting ... (CLOTEN 2.1.21)

[*Song*] Hark, hark, the lark at heaven's gate sings.
(MUSICIAN 2.3.20)

Is there no way for men to be, but women
Must be half-workers? We are all bastards.
(POSTHUMUS 2.5.1–2)

As chaste as unsunned snow. (POSTHUMUS 2.5.13)

Could I find out
The woman's part in me! (POSTHUMUS 2.5.19–20)

O, for a horse with wings! (IMOGEN 3.2.48)

O, this life
Is nobler than attending for a check,
Richer than doing nothing for a bauble,
Prouder than rustling in unpaid-for silk.
(BELARIUS 3.3.21–24)

The game is up. (BELARIUS 3.3.107)

I have not slept one wink. (PISANIO 3.4.101)

The breach of custom
Is breach of all. (IMOGEN 4.2.10–11)

Society is no comfort
To one not sociable. (IMOGEN 4.2.12–13)

[*Song*] Fear no more the heat o' the sun,
   Nor the furious winter's rages;
Thou thy worldly task hast done,
   Home art gone, and ta'en thy wages.

Golden lads and girls all must,
As chimney sweepers, come to dust.

(GUIDERIUS   4.2.261–266)

Some falls are means the happier to arise.   (LUCIUS   4.2.406)

Fortune brings in some boats that are not steered.

(PISANIO   4.3.46)

Whom best I love I cross, to make my gift,
    The more delayed, delighted.   (JUPITER   5.4.101–102)

Memorable Lines

The Winter's Tale

You pay a great deal too dear for what's given freely.
(CAMILLO   1.1.17–18)

           We were, fair Queen,
Two lads that thought there was no more behind
But such a day tomorrow as today,
And to be boy eternal.   (POLIXENES   1.2.62–65)

We were as twinned lambs that did frisk i' the sun
And bleat the one at th' other. What we changed
Was innocence for innocence.   (POLIXENES   1.2.67–69)

Affection, thy intention stabs the center.
Thou dost make possible things not so held,
Communicat'st with dreams.   (LEONTES   1.2.138–140)

          Should all despair
That have revolted wives, the tenth of mankind
Would hang themselves.   (LEONTES   1.2.198–200)

A sad tale's best for winter. I have one
Of sprites and goblins.   (MAMILLIUS   2.1.25–26)

The silence often of pure innocence
Persuades when speaking fails.   (PAULINA   2.2.41–42)

          What's gone and what's past help
Should be past grief.   (PAULINA   3.2.222–223)

Exit, pursued by a bear.   (*Stage direction*   3.3.57)

[*Song*]   Why, then comes in the sweet o' the year.
(AUTOLYCUS   4.3.3)

[*Song*]   Jog on, jog on, the footpath way,
   And merrily hent the stile-a;
A merry heart goes all the day,
   Your sad tires in a mile-a.   (AUTOLYCUS   4.3.121–124)

Daffodils,
That come before the swallow dares, and take
The winds of March with beauty.   (PERDITA 4.4.118–120)

When you do dance, I wish you
A wave o' the sea, that you might ever do
Nothing but that.   (FLORIZEL 4.4.140–142)

Good sooth, she is
The queen of curds and cream.   (CAMILLO 4.4.160–161)

Lawn as white as driven snow.   (AUTOLYCUS 4.4.218)

Let me have no lying. It becomes none but tradesmen.
                     (AUTOLYCUS 4.4.725–726)

If I had a mind to be honest, I see Fortune would not suffer
me.   (AUTOLYCUS 4.4.834–835)

There was speech in their dumbness, language in their very
gesture.   (FIRST GENTLEMAN 5.2.14–15)

Then have you lost a sight which was to be seen, cannot be
spoken of.   (THIRD GENTLEMAN 5.2.43–44)

I never heard of such another encounter, which lames report to follow it and undoes description to do it.
                  (THIRD GENTLEMAN 5.2.57–59)

Like an old tale still.   (THIRD GENTLEMAN 5.2.62)

I like your silence; it the more shows off
Your wonder.   (PAULINA 5.3.21–22)

It is required
You do awake your faith.   (PAULINA 5.3.94–95)

That she is living,
Were it but told you, should be hooted at
Like an old tale; but it appears she lives . . .
                     (PAULINA 5.3.116–118)

Memorable Lines

The Tempest

Methinks he hath no drowning mark upon him; his complexion is perfect gallows. (GONZALO   1.1.30–31)

> What seest thou else
> In the dark backward and abysm of time?
> (PROSPERO   1.2.49–50)

Your tale, sir, would cure deafness. (MIRANDA   1.2.106)

> My library
> Was dukedom large enough. (PROSPERO   1.2.109–110)

From the still-vexed Bermudas . . . (ARIEL   1.2.230)

You taught me language, and my profit on 't
Is I know how to curse. The red plague rid you
For learning me your language! (CALIBAN   1.2.366–368)

This music crept by me upon the waters,
Allaying both their fury and my passion
With its sweet air. (FERDINAND   1.2.395–397)

[*Song*]   Full fathom five thy father lies.
    Of his bones are coral made.
Those are pearls that were his eyes.
    Nothing of him that doth fade
But doth suffer a sea change
Into something rich and strange. (ARIEL   1.2.400–405)

. . . lest too light winning
Make the prize light. (PROSPERO   1.2.455–456)

There's nothing ill can dwell in such a temple.
If the ill spirit have so fair a house,
Good things will strive to dwell with 't.
(MIRANDA   1.2.461–463)

He receives comfort like cold porridge.

(SEBASTIAN   2.1.10–11)

I' the commonwealth I would by contraries
Execute all things; for no kind of traffic
Would I admit; no name of magistrate . . .

(GONZALO   2.1.150–152)

. . . nature should bring forth,
Of its own kind, all foison, all abundance,
To feed my innocent people.   (GONZALO   2.1.165–167)

What's past is prologue.   (ANTONIO   2.1.254)

Misery acquaints a man with strange bedfellows.

(TRINCULO   2.2.39–40)

I prithee, let me bring thee where crabs grow;
And I with my long nails will dig thee pignuts.

(CALIBAN   2.2.165–166)

[Song]   'Ban, 'Ban, Ca—Caliban
Has a new master. Get a new man!   (CALIBAN   2.2.182–183)

Be not afeared. The isle is full of noises,
Sounds, and sweet airs, that give delight and hurt not.

(CALIBAN   3.2.137–138)

Do not give dalliance
Too much the rein.   (PROSPERO   4.1.51–52)

Our revels now are ended. These our actors,
As I foretold you, were all spirits and
Are melted into air, into thin air.   (PROSPERO   4.1.148–150)

We are such stuff
As dreams are made on, and our little life
Is rounded with a sleep.   (PROSPERO   4.1.156–158)

A devil, a born devil, on whose nature
Nurture can never stick.   (PROSPERO   4.1.188–189)

> I have bedimmed
> The noontide sun, called forth the mutinous winds,
> And twist the green sea and the azured vault
> Set roaring war.   (PROSPERO   5.1.41–44)

> Graves at my command
> Have waked their sleepers, oped, and let 'em forth
> By my so potent art.   (PROSPERO   5.1.48–50)

> [*Song*]   Where the bee sucks, there suck I.
> In a cowslip's bell I lie;
> There I couch when owls do cry.
> On the bat's back I do fly.   (ARIEL   5.1.88–91)

> O, brave new world,
> That has such people in 't!   (MIRANDA   5.1.185–186)

> This thing of darkness I
> Acknowledge mine.   (PROSPERO   5.1.278–279)

> Then to the elements
> Be free, and fare thou well!   (PROSPERO   5.1.321–322)

Contributors

DAVID BEVINGTON, Phyllis Fay Horton Professor of Humanities at the University of Chicago, is editor of *The Complete Works of Shakespeare* (Scott, Foresman, 1980) and of *Medieval Drama* (Houghton Mifflin, 1975). His latest critical study is *Action Is Eloquence: Shakespeare's Language of Gesture* (Harvard University Press, 1984).

DAVID SCOTT KASTAN, Professor of English and Comparative Literature at Columbia University, is the author of *Shakespeare and the Shapes of Time* (University Press of New England, 1982).

JAMES HAMMERSMITH, Associate Professor of English at Auburn University, has published essays on various facets of Renaissance drama, including literary criticism, textual criticism, and printing history.

ROBERT KEAN TURNER, Professor of English at the University of Wisconsin–Milwaukee, is a general editor of the New Variorum Shakespeare (Modern Language Association of America) and a contributing editor to *The Dramatic Works in the Beaumont and Fletcher Canon* (Cambridge University Press, 1966–).

JAMES SHAPIRO, who coedited the bibliographies with David Scott Kastan, is Assistant Professor of English at Columbia University.

✦

JOSEPH PAPP, one of the most important forces in theater today, is the founder and producer of the New York Shakespeare Festival, America's largest and most prolific theatrical institution. Since 1954 Mr. Papp has produced or directed all but one of Shakespeare's plays—in Central Park, in schools, off and on Broadway, and at the Festival's permanent home, The Public Theater. He has also produced such award-winning plays and musical works as *Hair, A Chorus Line, Plenty,* and *The Mystery of Edwin Drood,* among many others.